EXPERT SYSTEMS FOR HUMAN, MATERIALS AND AUTOMATION

Edited by **Petrică Vizureanu**

INTECHOPEN.COM

Expert Systems for Human, Materials and Automation
Edited by Petrică Vizureanu

Published by InTech
Janeza Trdine 9, 51000 Rijeka, Croatia

Publishing Process Manager Sandra Bakic

Technical Editor Teodora Smiljanic

Cover Designer InTech Design Team

Additional hard copies can be obtained from orders@intechopen.com

Expert Systems for Human, Materials and Automation, Edited by Petrică Vizureanu
p. cm.
ISBN 978-953-307-334-7

For EU product safety concerns:
IN TECH d.o.o., Prolaz Marije Krucifikse Kozulić 3, 51000 Rijeka, Croatia,
info@intechopen.com or visit our website at intechopen.com.

Meet the editor

Dr. Petrică Vizureanu was born on the 17th of October 1967, in Barlad, Romania. He received the following degrees: M.Sc. in Heating Equipment, from „Gh. Asachi" Technical University of Iasi (1992), and Ph.D. at „Gh. Asachi" Technical University of Iasi (1999). Vizureanu's past and present positions include Assistant (1993-1999), Lecturer (1999-2002), Ass. Professor (2002-2009), Professor (2009-today) in „Gh. Asachi" Technical University of Iasi – Romania. His research activity is in Expert System for Heating System Programming, Computer Assisted Design for Heating Equipment, Heating Equipment for Materials Processing, Heat Transfer. Vizureanu's publications consist of 36 papers in international journals and conferences (proceedings) and 14 books.

Contents

Preface

The ability to create intelligent machines has intrigued humans since ancient times, and today with the advent of the computer and 50 years of research into AI programming techniques, the dream of smart machines is becoming a reality. Researchers are creating systems, which can mimic human beings. Accurate mathematical models neither always exist nor can they be derived for all complex environments because the domain may not be thoroughly understood. The solution consists of constructing rules that apply when input values lie within certain designer-defined categories.

The concept of human-computer interfaces (HCI) has been undergoing changes over the years. Currently the demand is for user interfaces for ubiquitous computing. In this context, one of the basic requirements is the development of interfaces with high usability that meet different modes of interaction depending on users, environments and tasks to be performed.

In carrying out the most important tasks is the lack of formalized application methods, mathematical models and advanced computer support. Decisions and adopted solutions are often based on knowledge resulting from experience and intuition of designers. Use of information on previously executed projects of similar ships allow expert systems using the Case Based Reasoning method (CBR), which is a relatively new way of solving problems related to databases and knowledge bases.

The evolution of biological systems to adapt to their environment has fascinated and challenged scientists to increase their level of understanding of the functional characteristics of such systems. Such understanding has already benefited our society though increased life expectancy and quality, improved and cost effective health care and prevention. Engineers have looked for inspiration from such biological systems functionalities to enhance our society's communication, economic and transportation infrastructure.

This book has 19 chapters and explain that the expert systems are products of the artificial intelligence, branch of computer science that seeks to develop intelligent programs for human, materials and automation.

Petrică Vizureanu
„Gh. Asachi" Technical University of Iasi,
Romania

Part 1

Human

1

Expert System for Identification of Sport Talents: Idea, Implementation and Results

Vladan Papić, Nenad Rogulj and Vladimir Pleština
University of Split,
Croatia

1. Introduction

Selecting children for appropriate sport is the most demanding and the most responsible task for sport experts and kinesiology in general. Sport activities have significant differences regarding structural and substance features. Different sports are determined by authentic kinesiological structures and specific anthropological characteristics of an individual (Chapman, 2008; Abernethy, 2005). Success of an individual in particular sport activity is predominantly determined by the compatibility of his/her anthropological characteristics with the anthropologic model of top athletes in that sport (Morrow & James, 2005). Extensive research that has been done in order to test, analyze and compare athletes of various sports (MacDougall et al, 1991; Stergiou, 2004) brings precious information and knowledge that can be used for the sport talents identification, also.

Unfortunately, there is usually no systematic selection in sport. The selection is based on a subjective and non-scientific judgment with a low technological and methodological support. However, fast development of new information technologies as well as the introduction of new methods and knowledge provide a novel, systematic and scientifically based approach in selecting the appropriate sport for an individual.

In sports talent recognition process, two main problems were detected. First, task of finding an expert in this field is quite difficult due to the fact that domain of specific knowledge is separated into various sports. Also, usually experts have in-depth knowledge of the relevant factors for a specific sport and more superficial for other sports. The second problem is in fact similar with the first one and it relates to the availability of the knowledge (expert) even if we have the right person. In order to avoid this problems, the decision of developing a computer based expert system was brought (Rogulj et al., 2006).

Generally, knowledge acquisition techniques that are most frequently used today, require an enormous amount of time and effort on the part of both the knowledge engineer and the domain expert. They also require the knowledge engineer to have an unusually wide variety of interviewing and knowledge representation skills in order to be successful (Wagner et al., 2003). As a result, inclusion of the experts with the knowledge from both worlds, in the development of the expert system is a pre-request that should be satisfied if possible. Due to previously mentioned problem with availability of the knowledge, expert system accessibility through Internet was also required. Also, in the second version of the expert system, fuzzy logic was introduced because of detected specific issues in the evaluation process of a children or student (Papić et al., 2009). This approach is even intuitive because

of the vagueness of expert knowledge, grades and some other data. Our approach can, in some aspects of fuzzy logic implementation, be compared to the solution proposed by Weon and Kim (2001) or the system developed for the evaluation of students' learning achievement (Bai & Chen, 2008).
The World Wide Web is reducing technological barriers and make it easier for users in different geographical locations to access the decision support models and tools (Shim et al., 2002; Bhargava et al., 2007). Internet based expert systems can have different architectures, such as centralized, replicated or distributed. This categorization is done according to the place where the code is executed (Šimić & Devedžić, 2003). Another, similar categorization (Kim, et al., 2005) of the existing methodologies is into two categories, the server-side and the client-side, depending on the location of the inference engine of a Web-enabled, rule-based system. Less burden to Web servers is present when the ASP as the server-side script approach (Wang, 2005) is used.
Review of the uses of artificial intelligence in the area of sport science and applications with focusing on introduction of expert systems as diagnostic tools for evaluating faults in sports movements has been presented in (Bartlett, 2006). The use of the expert systems for the assessment of sports talent in children have been reported in the past (Rajković et al., 1991; Leskošek et al., 1992). Some results obtained by this research were used for the development of a more specific expert system for the basketball performance prediction and assessment (Dežman et al, 2001a, 2001b). Neither of these systems have used web technologies nor implementation of fuzzy logic.
An expert system should be adaptive to constant changes of new standard values and measures as well as open to insertion of new knowledge. As already stated, first version of the expert system developed by the authors was presented in (Rogulj et al., 2006) but further development and evaluation of the system showed that there are many questions left unanswered. Improvements regarding methodology, technology and a scope of the application were done and preliminary results were presented by Papić et al. (2009). Current version of developed software based solution has the following characteristics: ability of forming a referent measurement database with the records of all potential and active sportsmen, diagnostics of their anthropological characteristics, sports talent recognition, advising and guiding amateurs into the sports activities suitable for their potential. Also, a comparison of the test results for the same person and for overall achievement monitoring through a longer time period is possible. Evaluation and tests of the presented fuzzy-based approach with some other approaches used for the evaluation of the morphology models suggest that it is capable of successful recognition of the sport compatible for the tested individual based on his/her morphological characteristics (Rogulj et al., 2009). In this chapter, detailed description of the complete system will be given along with some new results and discoveries obtained during passed time.

2. Idea and knowledge acquisition

Basic idea and development steps of the expert system are presented in figure 1. It should be noted that thorough testing has to be done after each development phase. In the case of detected bugs and deficiency, previous steps should be repeated. As it can be seen from the figure 1, first four steps are relating to knowledge base forming and knowledge engineering. Basic assumptions used for this stage will be explained in the following text.
In Croatia, there is already defined set of functional, motorical and morphological tests that are mandatory for all children age 6-18 during every school year. These tests are used for the

evaluation of each children/student capabilities. Thus, in order to make proposed system widely applied without any additional demands on new tests and equipment, these tests were chosen as the measurement instrument for input data to our expert system.
Also, normative values for chosen tests are available from the literature (Findak et al., 1996) and updated according to Norton and Olds (2001).

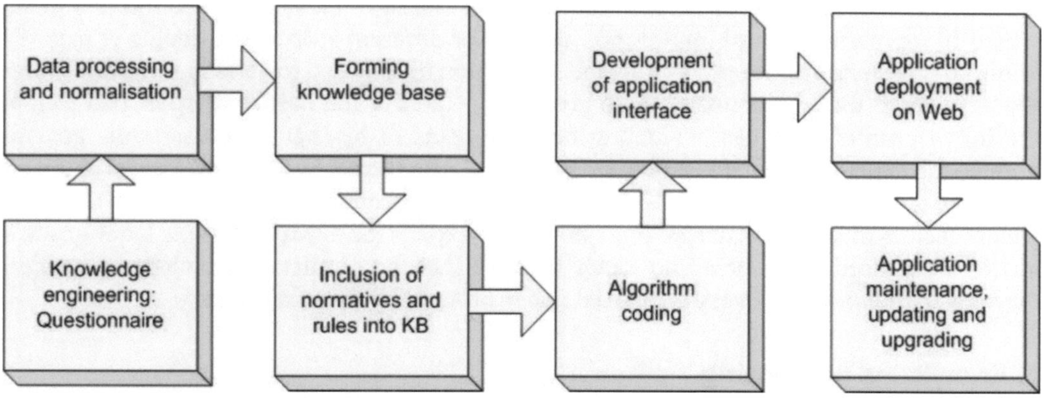

Fig. 1. Idea and development of the expert system.

As a first step, importance of each test for every sport has to be determined and stored in the knowledge base of the expert system. At this point, we have limited number of sports to 14 although using the approach that will be presented here, modular knowledge for other

Sport	Morphology				Motorical						Funct-ional
	MO 1	MO 2	M0 3	MO 4	MT 1	MT 2	MT 3	MT 4	MT 5	MT 6	FU1
Gymnastics											
Swimming											
Athletics: sprint/jump											
Athletics: throwing											
Athletics: long dist. running											
Handball											
Football											
Basketball											
Volleyball											
Water polo											
Rowing											
Tennis											
Martial arts: pinning											
Martial arts: kicking											

Table 1. Example of a blank questionnaire handed to the kinesiology experts. Importance of each test has to be entered (0 - no importance, 10 - max. importance). Tests: MO1 – height; MO2 – weight; MO3 - Forearm girth; M04 - upper arm skin fold; MT1 - hand tapping; MT2 - long jump from a spot; MT3 - astride touch-toe; MT4 - backward polygon; MT5 - trunk lifting; MT6 - hanging endurance; FU1 - 3/6-minute running.

sports can easily be added to the knowledge base. Determination of the tests importance was based on the expert knowledge obtained from 97 kinesiology experts. A questionnaire presented by Table 1 was prepared and handed out to two groups of experts: general knowledge experts (kinesiology teachers in high and elementary schools) and experts in a particular sport (trainers and university professors).

Each expert had to fill the table with an integer importance factor from the interval [0,10] where 10 represents highest importance. Because of different scopes and depths of expert's knowledge, extensive data processing and adaptation of acquired knowledge was done after the answers to the questionnaire were given. An expert in the particular sport had to rate the importance of each test evaluating only the sport of his/her expertise while general knowledge experts evaluated test importance for all the sports. Test weight factors obtained by experts for particular sport (47 experts) have significantly more importance than test weight factors obtained by the general knowledge experts (52 experts), but the latter group's results were used as a correction factor because their accumulated knowledge provided more clear "big picture" than only partial image brought by the first group.

3. Knowledge processing

In this section calculation procedure for the person's adequacy for fourteen chosen sports will be explained in detail. Although in first implementation attempts fuzzy logic wasn't used, preliminary results have shown that fuzzy reasoning should be introduced for some specific tests.

3.1 Calculation of body fitness using fuzzy logic

Sport activities differ to a large extent in structure and content. Different sports are characterized by authentic kinesiological structures and specific anthropological features. The success of an individual in a certain sport activity depends mostly on the compatibility of his anthropological features, or the so-called anthropological model for the given sport (Katić et al., 2005). Therefore, in evaluation process, it is crucial to detect persons whose anthropological features match specific qualities of a certain kinesiological activity.

Measurements obtained by height and weight tests are used together in order to obtain body fitness for the particular sport. In kinesiology, this is an issue known as athletic body and this feature has its own membership grade instead of two separate ones for body weight and height. Importance factor of the indirect test equals sum of their individual weights. Evaluation of the tested person's body fitness for the particular sport is calculated using the rules with implemented fuzzy logic. In fact, athletic body of a person is represented by person's height and body mass index (BMI), so BMI, has to be calculated from height and weight of a person using the following equation:

$$BMI = \frac{w}{h^2} \tag{1}$$

where w is weight and h is height of a person.

After the analysis of the results from the filled and returned questionnaires and also with the comparison of the available national teams' anthropometric data, models of the ideal height and BMI were included into the expert system database.

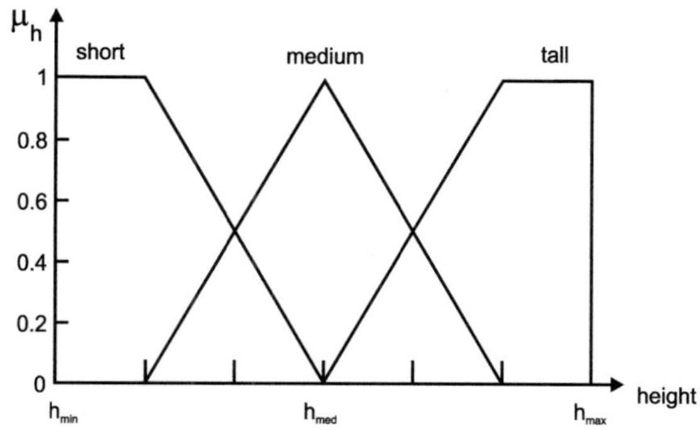

Fig. 2. Membership functions of the fuzzy sets "short", "medium" and "tall" used for the calculation of fuzzy membership grade for height.

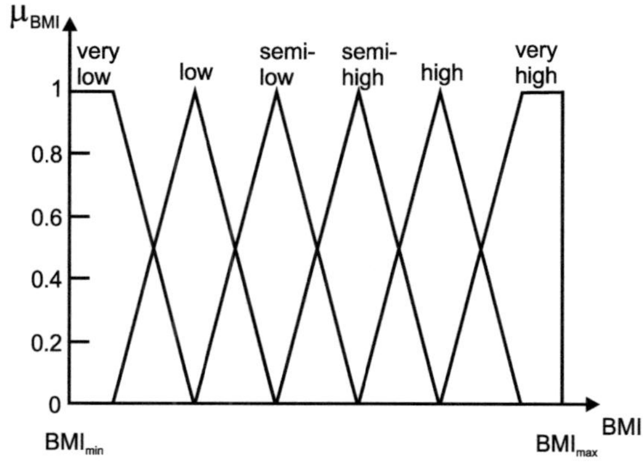

Fig. 3. Membership functions of the fuzzy sets "very low", "low", "semi-low", "semi-high", "high" and "very high" used for the calculation of fuzzy membership grade for BMI.

Fuzzification of the measured height and calculated BMI has been done according to the fuzzy sets presented in Figs. 2 and 3. Fuzzy grade vector for height (*FH*) can be presented as follows:

$$FH = \begin{bmatrix} FH_1 & FH_2 & FH_3 \\ \mu_{h1} & \mu_{h2} & \mu_{h3} \end{bmatrix}$$

where FH_1, FH_2, FH_3 denote the fuzzy terms "short", "medium" and "tall", respectively, whereas μ_{hi} denote the membership value of the height belonging to the linguistic term FH_i, $\mu_{hi} \in [0,1], \quad 1 \le i \le 3$.
Fuzzy grade vector for BMI (FB) can be presented as follows:

$$FB = \begin{bmatrix} FB_1 & FB_2 & FB_3 & FB_4 & FB_5 & FB_6 \\ \mu_{BMI1} & \mu_{BMI2} & \mu_{BMI3} & \mu_{BMI4} & \mu_{BMI5} & \mu_{BMI6} \end{bmatrix}$$

where FB_1, FB_2, FB_3 FB_4, FB_5 and FB_6 denote the fuzzy terms "very low", "low", "semi-low", "semi-high", "high" and "very high", respectively, whereas μ_{BMIi} denote the membership value of the BMI belonging to the linguistic term FB_i, $\mu_{BMIi} \in [0,1], \quad 1 \le i \le 6$.

An example of a fuzzy rule matrix to infer the body model adequacy is presented in Table 1. Each sport has different rule matrix.
Based on the fuzzy grade vectors *FH, FB* and fuzzy rules which are partially shown in Table 2, fuzzy reasoning is performed in order to evaluate the athletic body adequacy for each sport.

Height	Body mass index (BMI)					
	Very low	Low	Semi-low	Semi-high	High	Very high
Short	$a_{1,1}(S_k)$	$a_{2,1}(S_k)$	$a_{3,1}(S_k)$	$a_{4,1}(S_k)$	$a_{5,1}(S_k)$	$a_{6,1}(S_k)$
Medium	$a_{1,2}(S_k)$	$a_{2,2}(S_k)$	$a_{3,2}(S_k)$	$a_{4,2}(S_k)$	$a_{5,2}(S_k)$	$a_{6,2}(S_k)$
Tall	$a_{1,3}(S_k)$	$a_{2,3}(S_k)$	$a_{3,3}(S_k)$	$a_{4,3}(S_k)$	$a_{5,3}(S_k)$	$a_{6,3}(S_k)$

Table 2. Fuzzy rule matrix for sport S_k. Possible linguistic values for $a_{i,j}(S_k)$ are: unmatched, semi-matched, matched.

Generally, we can write a fuzzy rule as follows:

IF the sport is S_k and the height is FH_i and BMI is FB_j THEN model is Ml

where Ml can have three linguistic values: M1 = "unmatched", M2 = "semi-matched" and M3 = "matched".
The triggering of each rule as a result gives the model membership grade. Linguistic value (Ml) in the consequent part of the rule determines which linguistic variable the membership grade relates to. Result of each rule is calculated as follows:

$$\mu''_M(M_l) = w_H(S_k) \times \mu_{Hi} + w_{BMI}(S_k) \times \mu_{BMIj} \tag{2}$$

where $w_H(S_K)$ and $w_{BMI}(S_K)$ denotes weight factor of the height and BMI test for a particular sport *Sk*, and Ml is the linguistic value in the consequent part of the rule. Other linguistic variables $M_j, j \neq l$ are not affected on the rule and their membership grades are zero.
Because of the simplicity, in the equation (2), sport verification is left out from the antecedent part of the rule. In fact, in the expert system database, rules are grouped by sports and only rules related to the particular sport will be fired. Model matrix (M) used for calculation of body model membership μ_M for each sport (S_1, ..., S_P) is obtained after the triggering of all the fuzzy rules and the aggregation of their output for each linguistic value M1, M2 and M3 by using the Max() function.
Matrix elements $\mu'_{11},...,\mu'_{p3}$ are fuzzy values obtained by evaluation of fuzzy rules.

$$M = \begin{matrix} & M_1 & M_2 & M_3 \\ S_1 \\ S_2 \\ \vdots \\ S_p \end{matrix} \begin{bmatrix} \mu'_{11} & \mu'_{12} & \mu'_{13} \\ \mu'_{21} & \mu'_{22} & \mu'_{23} \\ \vdots & \vdots & \vdots \\ \mu'_{p1} & \mu'_{p2} & \mu'_{p3} \end{bmatrix}$$

Each element μ'_{ij} is calculated according to fuzzy rules as follows:

$$\mu_{ij}^{'} = Max\left\{\mu_{M,1}^{''}\left(M_j\right), \mu_{M,2}^{''}\left(M_j\right), \ldots \mu_{M,N}^{''}\left(M_j\right)\right\} \quad (3)$$

where N is a total number of rules that as an output have membership grade of the linguistic value M_j. Finally, the athletic body membership grade of the observed individual for particular sport is calculated as follows:

$$\mu_M\left(S_k\right) = Max\left(0.5 \times \mu_{k2}^{'}, \mu_{k3}^{'}\right). \quad (4)$$

3.2 Calculation of the total fitness for particular sport

Now, complete procedure for calculation of person's fitness for particular sport will be explained in details.

Assume that there is a series of sports $S_1, S_2, \ldots, S_p$ in sports domain S,

$$S = S_1, S_2, \ldots, S_p \quad (5)$$

where S_K denotes the k-th sport in S and $1 \le K \le p$. Now, let's assume that there is a series of test groups $G_1, G_2, \ldots, G_n$ in test group domain G,

$$G = G_1, G_2, \ldots, G_n \quad (6)$$

where G_i denotes the i-th test group in G and $1 \le i \le n$. Assume that test group G_i consists of m tests $T_{i1}, T_{i2}, \ldots, T_{im}$. We can define the input vector with the elements representing the measurement result R_{ij} for each conducted test T_{ij} of the observed individual:

$$R = \begin{bmatrix} R_{11} & R_{12} & \cdots & R_{1n} & R_{21} & \cdots & R_{2n} & \cdots & R_{mn} \end{bmatrix}^T$$

Next, the contribution of the test group G_i for the evaluation of a person's fitness for a particular sport (S_K) is defined as:

$$C_{S_K}\left(G_i\right) = \sum_{j=1}^{m} C_{S_K}\left(T_{ij}\right) = \sum_{j=1}^{m}\left(\mu_{ij}^{*} \times w_{ij}\left(S_K\right)\right) \quad (7)$$

where μ_{ij}^{*} denotes the membership grade of the test T_{ij}, $w_{ij}\left(S_K\right)$ denotes weight factor of the test T_{ij} for a particular sport S_K, $\sum$ denotes the algebraic sum and $\times$ denotes the algebraic product. Note: membership grades for height and weight tests are substituted with the athletic body membership grade calculated according to equation (4).

If the value of the membership grade is 0 ($\mu_{ij}^{*} = 0$), then the test T_{ij} result was poor, and maximal membership grade value ($\mu_{ij}^{*} = 1$) means that the test T_{ij} result was excellent. Total fitness index (TFI) for sport S_K is calculated as the algebraic sum of test group contributions:

$$TFI\left(S_K\right) = \sum_{i=1}^{n} C_{S_K}\left(G_i\right) \quad (8)$$

As it can be noticed, in order to compare TFI for different sports, normalization of weight factors has to be done. Normalization assumes that the maximum fitness index (MFI) that can be obtained for each sport is equal which means that the following condition must be satisfied

$$MFI(S_K) = \sum_{i=1}^{n} M_{S_K}(G_i) = 1, \qquad \forall S_K \in S \tag{9}$$

where maximum possible contribution of i-th test group for sport S_K is given by equation:

$$M_{S_K}(G_i) = \sum_{j=1}^{m} w_{ij}(S_K) \tag{10}$$

Membership grade μ_{ij}^{*} of the test T_{ij} needed for the equation (7) is calculated using the available test normative data for a particular gender and age. Each normative class (c_l) is defined by its minimal (n_1) and maximal value (n_2) and it can be expressed with the rule in the following form:

$$\textbf{IF}\left(\text{test } = T_{ij},\ \text{gender } = X,\ \text{age } = k\right)\textbf{THEN}\left(c_{l,min} = n_1; c_{l,max} = n_2\right)$$

where $c_{l,min}$ and $c_{l,max}$ are the lower and upper boundary of the normative class l, respectively. Normative classes boundaries are directly associated with discrete membership grade values (Fig. 4).

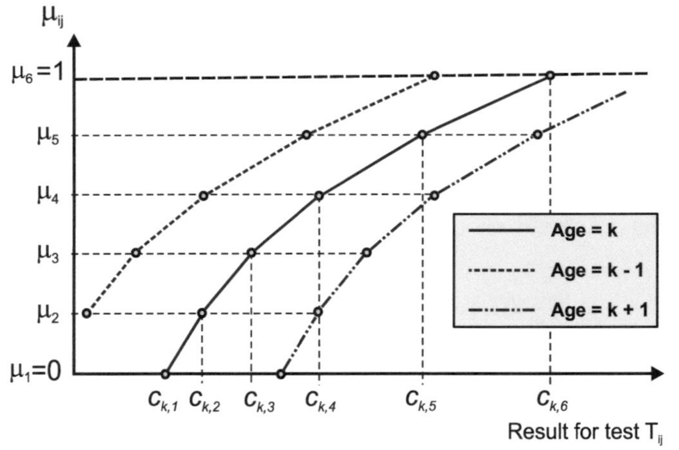

Fig. 4. Membership grade μ_{ij} of the test T_{ij} as a function of test normative classes for particular age (and gender).

For the measured or induced (in the case of height and BMI measurements) result (R_{ij}) of the test (T_{ij}), membership grade can be calculated using the equation

$$\mu_k = \frac{\mu_{k,l+1} - \mu_{k,l}}{c_{k,l+1} - c_{k,l}} \cdot \left(R_{ij} - c_{k,l}\right) + \mu_{k,l} \qquad ; R_{ij} \in \left(c_{k,l}, c_{k,l+1}\right] \tag{11}$$

where k is age of the tested person (integer value), $c_{k,l}$ is the lower boundary of the normative class which includes measured value, and $\mu_{k,l}$ is a membership grade for the

normative class lower boundary value; $c_{k,l+1}$ is the upper boundary of normative class which includes measured value, and $\mu_{k,l+1}$ is membership grade for the normative class upper boundary value.
Because the age of the tested person (κ) is generally not an integer number (in years), an interpolation of normative classes and corresponding grades is done. In fact, two rules are fired - one with the nearest lower age in the antecedent part of the rule and another with the nearest upper age in the antecedent part of the rule. Final membership grade value can be calculated using the following equations:

$$\begin{aligned} c_l^* &= c_{k,l} + (\kappa - k)\cdot\left(c_{k+1,l} - c_{k,l}\right) \\ c_{l+1}^* &= c_{k,l+1} + (\kappa - k)\cdot\left(c_{k+1,l+1} - c_{k,l+1}\right) \end{aligned} \tag{12}$$

Membership grade indexes for particular age value can be simplified:

$$\mu_{k,l} = \mu_{k+1,l} = \mu_l ; \mu_{k,l+1} = \mu_{k+1,l+1} = \mu_{l+1} .$$

Finally,

$$\mu_{ij}^* = \frac{\mu_{l+1} - \mu_l}{c_{l+1}^* - c_l^*}\cdot\left(R_{ij} - c_l^*\right) + \mu_l \tag{13}$$

4. Implementation and development

Although entity names presented in Fig. 5 are descriptive and may differ to the table names in the database, structure that is presented gives the main relations between them.

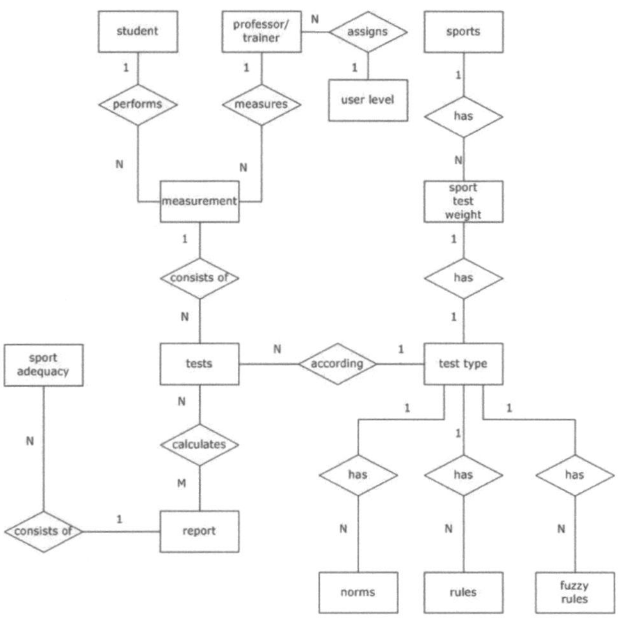

Fig. 5. Expert system structure. Expert knowledge is stored as rules, norms and test weights for each sport.

Knowledge engineering, forming of the knowledge base and coding of the stand-alone application lasted for about 12 months. After testing phase that lasted for about 3 months, fuzzy logic was introduced into the measurement evaluation and the migration of the code to the web application was done.
Web version of Sport Talent is built on a Microsoft asp.net platform with Borland Delphi 2005 as asp.net application. Application database is Microsoft SQL server 2000 which is connected with Sport Talent application using SQLConnection component (Fig. 6).
The application consists of files with aspx extension made available via http using the Internet Information Service as web server. These files are containing both HTML and server-side code which is written in object pascal. HTML and server-side code is combined in order to create the final output of the page consisting of HTML markup that is sent to the client browser. User controls i.e. fully programmable objects (both code and presentation layer) of the asp.net (.ascx) web page were also done to provide full functionality of the application.

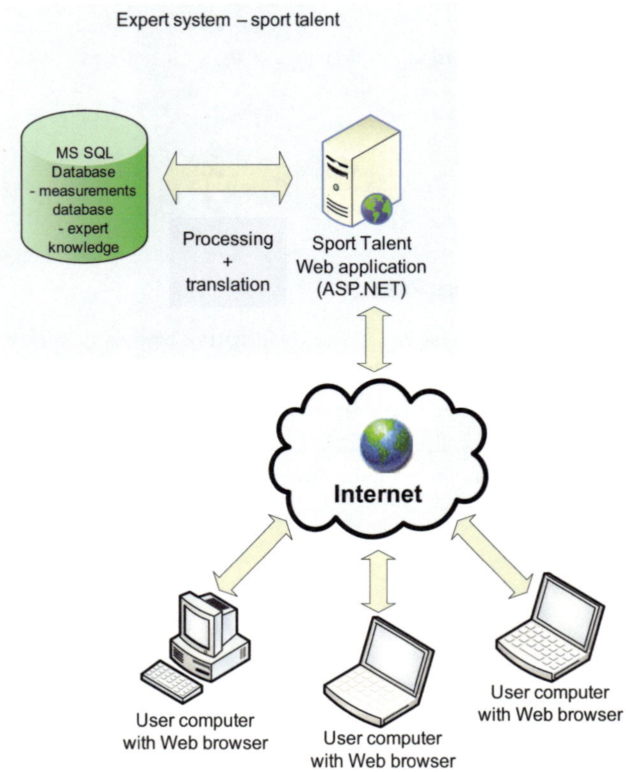

Fig. 6. Web server with application and user connection.

Since beginning of 2008, web version of the system along with the fuzzy module has been mounted on the web server. Chosen group of experts and school teachers has used the application since then and the database is growing daily.
Output generated by the expert system was compared with answers obtained by the human users and, in second test, prediction of the system based on the measurements of the successful athletes that are collected several years before they achieved elite level in sport. System evaluation results showed high reliability and high correlation with top experts in the field and the results for the second test also showed good match (Papić et al., 2009).

Within last year, quantitative contributions of certain motor abilities to the potential dance efficiency through expert knowledge were determined. Good metrical characteristics of the expert knowledge were determined, and after the experimental implementation of the results of research into the system, fine prognostic efficiency in recognising individuals engaged in dance activities was established (Srhoj, Lj. Et al., 2010).

5. Results and analysis

Typical output of the presented system consists of calculated percentages that are corresponding to the adequacy of the examinee for each sport that has needed data (norms, test weights) stored in the knowledge base (Fig. 7).

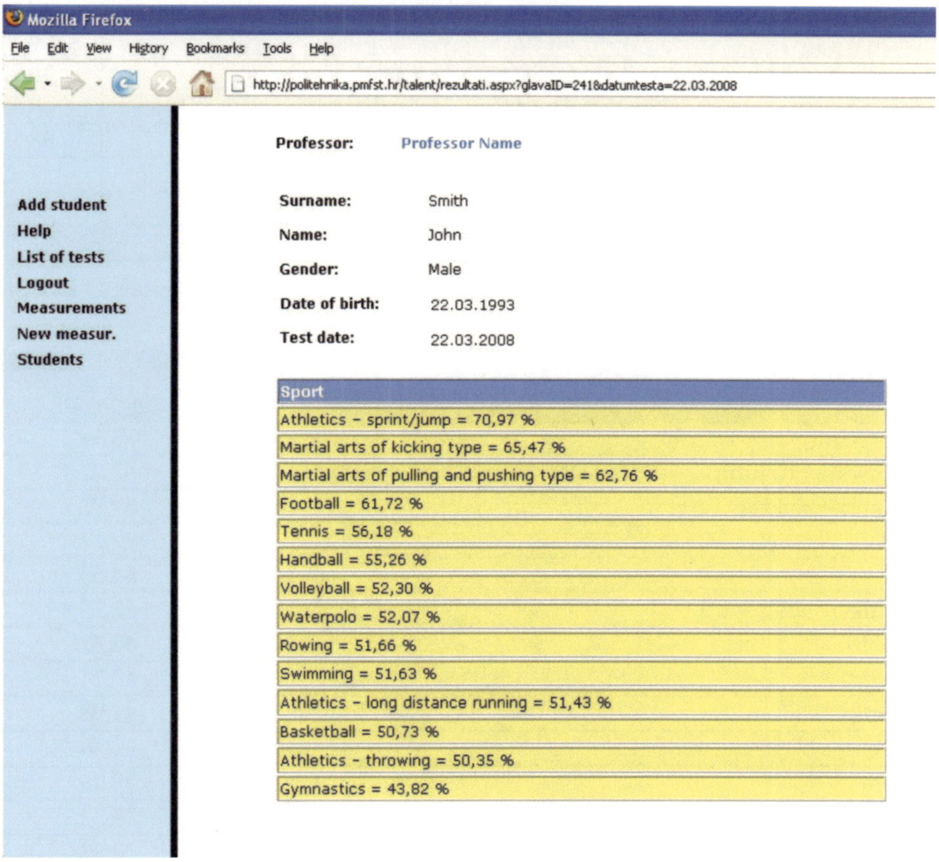

Fig. 7. Typical output of the expert system

In order to evaluate objectivity of the normative values and test weights stored in the knowledge base, average results for group of 106 examinees (45 female, 61 male) of various ages were analysed (Table 3). Combined results for both groups (female and male) are presented in Table 4.

Differences obtained between sports are generally small except maybe athletics - long distance running. This is indicating to unbalanced tests for this sport. In fact, this could be expected because of only one functional test in the tests battery. Also, almost 4% average differences between males and females indicate possible deviations of the present normative values.

Gender: Female, N = 46		Gender: Male, N = 61	
Sport	Average result (%)	Sport	Average result (%)
Athletics – long dist. running	60,50	Athletics – long dist. running	52,57
Martial arts – kicking	55,44	Athletics – sprint/jump	49,90
Athletics – sprint/jump	55,11	Martial arts – kicking	49,08
Football	49,94	Football	45,75
Tennis	46,44	Tennis	42,85
Martial arts – push/pull	45,33	Martial arts – push/pull	40,82
Gymnastics	44,99	Swimming	40,55
Water polo	44,20	Gymnastics	40,51
Handball	43,50	Water polo	40,51
Swimming	43,20	Handball	40,12
Rowing	41,29	Volleyball	38,69
Volleyball	39,73	Rowing	38,19
Basketball	39,15	Basketball	37,43
Athletics - throwing	38,61	Athletics - throwing	35,69
Total average:	46,25	Total average:	42,33

Table 3. Average output results for 106 examinees, female and male separately.

N = 106, Min: 3,54 ; Max: 95,01 ; STD: 15,85	
Sport	Average result (%)
Athletics – long dist. running	55,59
Athletics – sprint/jump	52,02
Martial arts – kicking	51,78
Football	47,42
Tennis	44,53
Martial arts – push/pull	42,75
Water polo	42,31
Gymnastics	42,14
Swimming	41,95
Handball	41,68
Rowing	39,75
Volleyball	39,32
Basketball	38,42
Athletics - throwing	37,07
Total average:	44,05

Table 4. Average output results for all examinees.

6. Conclusion and discussion

In this chapter we have presented an expert system for the selection and identification of an optimal sport for a child. This is the first expert system developed for this purpose that uses fuzzy logic and has wide Internet accessibility. Expert knowledge stored in the knowledge base is the result of the knowledge acquired from 97 kinesiology experts. System evaluation results that were conducted during testing phase of the system showed high reliability and correlation with top experts in the field.

At present, measurements database has several hundreds measured children of various ages (primary and secondary schools) so updating of the normative data for the currently active tests is possible. Authors expect that it would further improve prediction reliability. It should be accented that presented system allows real time insight into the current anthropometric measures of the examinees.

As the consequence of using this system, the possibility of wrong selection and losing several years in training of an inappropriate sport should be significantly reduced. Other benefits are: proper use of the anthropometric potential of a sportsman, fewer frustrations due to poor performance, achievement of the top results in sport and improved efficiency of spending finances.

At the moment, the system stores normative data and weight factors information on fourteen sports. Recent research includes adding other sports into the domain of the presented expert system. First sport that is expected to be added is dance. Also, some sports such as basketball and athletics should be separated into new entities according to player's position (basketball) or specialization (athletics). Generation of output reports for the users are also part of the current work. Our intention is to make the reports more users friendly and to avoid output results in the terms of percentages. Automatic generation of linguistically rich and visually attractive report is expected to be more adequate for the users. Perhaps the most important issue that we are currently dealing with is the establishing new set of standard tests that are expected to have better metric characteristics than present one.

Present configuration is modular and that makes implementation of various modifications quite simple i.e. without the need to make some structural changes that could take time and would make the expert system unavailable for a longer period. As the authors see it, the main goal of this research is to make using this system mandatory to all school teachers and to allow trainers of various sports to have access to the measurement results as well. Only then, benefits of this expert system could be used up to its full potential.

7. Acknowledgment

This work was supported by the Ministry of Science and Technology of the Republic Croatia under projects: 177-0232006-1662 and 177-0000000-1811.

8. References

Abernethy, B. (2005). *Biophysical Foundations of Human Movement*. 2nd Edition, Human Kinetics, Champaign.

Bai, S. M.; & Chen, S. M. (2008). Evaluating students' learning achievement using fuzzy membership functions and fuzzy rules. *Expert Systems with Applications*, 34, 399–410.

Bartlett, R. (2006). Artificial intelligence in sports biomechanics: New dawn or false hope? *Journal of Sports Science and Medicine*, 5, 474-479.

Bhargava, H. K.; Power, D. J. & Sun, D. (2007). Progress in Web-based decision support technologies. *Decision Support Systems*, 43, 1083–1095.

Chapman, A. (2008). *Biomechanical Analysis of Fundamental Human Movements*. Human Kinetics, Champaign.

Dežman, B.; Trninić, S. & Dizdar, D. (2001a). Models of expert system and decision-making systems for efficient assessment of potential and actual quality of basketball players, *Kinesiology*, 33(2), 207-215.

Dežman, B, Trninić, S, Dizdar, D. (2001b). Expert model of decision-making system for efficient orientation of basketball players to positions and roles in the game - empirical verification. *Collegium antropologicum*, 25(1), 141-152.

Findak, V.; Metikoš, D.; Mraković, M., & Neljak, B. (1996). *Primjenjena kineziologija u školstvu - norme*. Hrvatski pedagoško-književni zbor, Zagreb.

Katić, R.; Miletić, Đ.; Maleš, B.; Grgantov, Z. & Krstulović, S. (2005). *Anthropological systems in athletes: selection models and training models*, University of Split, Faculty of mathematics, natural sciences and kinesiology, Split (in Croatian).

Kim, W.; Song, Y. U. & Hong, J. S. (2005). Web enabled expert systems using hyperlink-based inference. *Expert Systems with Applications*, Issue 28, 79-91.

Leskošek, B.; Bohanec, M.; Rajkovič, V. & Šturm, J. (1992). Expert system for the assessment of sports talent in children. *Proceedings of the International conference of computer applications in sport and physical education*, Wingate institute for physical education and sport and the Zinman college of physical education, 45-52.

MacDougall, J. D.; Wenger, H. A., & Green, H. J. (1991). *Physiological testing of the high-performance athlete*. Champaign, IL: Human Kinetics.

Morrow, J. & James, R. (2005). *Measurement and evaluation in human performance*. Human Kinetics, Champaign.

Norton, K., & Olds, T. (2001). Morphological Evolution of Athletes Over the 20th Century – Causes and Consequences. *Sports Med, 31*(11), 763-783.

Papić, V.; Rogulj, N. & Pleština, V. (2009). Identification of sport talents using a web-oriented expert system with a fuzzy module, *Expert Systems with Applications*. 36(5), 8830-8838.

Rogulj, N.; Papić, V.; & Pleština, V. (2006). Development of the Expert System for Sport Talents Detection. *WSEAS Transactions on Information Science & Applications* , Issue 3, Volume 9, 1752-1755.

Rogulj, N.; Papić, V. & Čavala, M. (2009). Evaluation Models of Some Morphological Characteristics for Talent Scouting in Sport, *Collegium Antropologicum*, 33(1), 105-110.

Shim, J. P.; Warkentin, M.; Courtney, J.F.; Power, D. J., Sharda, R. & Carlsson, C. (2002). Past, present, and future of decision support technology. *Decision Support Systems*, Volume 33 (2), 111-126(16).

Srhoj, Lj.; Mihaljević, D. & Čavala, M. (2010). Application of expert-system for talent scouting in dancing. *Acta Kinesiologica* 4(1), 109-113.

Stergiou, N. (2004). *Innovative Analysis of Human Movement*. Champaign, IL: Human Kinetics.

Šimić, G. & Devedžić, V. (2003). Building an intelligent system using modern Internet technologies. *Expert Systems with Applications*, Issue 25, 231-246.

Rajković, V.; Bohanec, M.; Šturm, J.; Leskošek, B. (1991). An expert system for advising children in choosing sports. *Proceedings of I. International Symposium "Sport of Young"*, Faculty of Sport, Ljubljana, 641-646.

Wagner, W. P.; Chung, Q. B. & Najdawi, M. K. (2003). The impact of problem domains and knowledge acquisition techniques: a content analysis of P/OM expert system case studies. *Expert Systems with Applications*, 24, 79–86.

2

SeDeM Diagram: A New Expert System for the Formulation of Drugs in Solid Form

Josep M. Suñé Negre, et al*
Service of Development of Medicines (SDM), Pharmaceutical Technology Unit, Pharmacy and Pharmaceutical Technology Department, University of Barcelona, Spain

1. Introduction

The SeDeM expert system is a methodology which is applied in preformulation and formulation studies of medicines specifically in solid dosage forms. This system informs on the physical profile of powdered substances (APIs and excipients) used to formulate drugs (Suñé et al, 2005; García et al, 2010; Aguilar et al, 2009). By determining whether powders (API or excipient) are suitable for direct compression, the SeDeM profile will inform about the advantages and gaps of those powdered substance to be used in direct compression, so the system informs on whether the direct compression method is appropriate (e.g.. wet granulation should be applied before compression).
The characterization of powdered substances by SeDeM facilitates the identification of the characteristics that require amendment in order to obtain tablets by direct compression. This system thus provides information that will ensure the robust design of the formulation in the final product.
This new method is based on the selection and application of several parameters that the formulation must fulfill to ensure a successful tablet elaborated by direct compression. The following criteria are applied:

a. The formulation must be representative and appropriate for the requirements of compression technology.
b. The execution of the experimental methodology and calculus must be readily applicable.

2. Parameters examined by the SeDeM method

SeDeM uses 12 tests (Suñé et al, 2005; García et al, 2010; Aguilar et al, 2009) to examine whether a powder is suitable for direct compression.

- Bulk density (Da)
- Tapped density (Dc)
- Inter-particle porosity (Ie)
- Carr index (IC)

---

* Encarna García Montoya, Pilar Pérez Lozano, Johnny E. Aguilar Díaz, Manel Roig Carreras, Roser Fuster García, Montserrat Miñarro Carmona, Josep R. Ticó Grau

- Cohesion index (Icd)
- Hausner ratio (IH)
- Angle of repose (α)
- Flowability (t")
- Loss on drying (%HR)
- Hygroscopicity (%H)
- Particle size (%Pf)
- Homogeneity index (Iθ)

These tests are grouped into five factors on the basis of the physical characteristics of the powder and the functionality of the drug:

Dimensional Parameter. Bulk density (Da) and Tapped density (Dc). These affect the size of the tablet and its capacity to pile up. In addition, these tests are used in the calculus of other mathematical indexes for the determination of the compression parameter.

Compressibility Parameter. Inter-particle porosity (Ie), Carr index (IC) and Cohesion index (Icd). These affect the compressibility of the powder.

Flowability/Powder Flow Parameter. Hausner ratio (IH), Angle of repose (α) and Flowability (t"). These influence the flowability of the powdered substance when compressed.

Lubricity/Stability Parameter. Loss on drying (%HR) and Hygroscopicity (%H). These affect the lubricity and future stability of the tablets.

Lubricity/Dosage parameter. % Particles < 50 µm and Homogeneity Index. These influence the lubricity and dosage of the tablets.

Table 1 shows the 5 parameters, with the abbreviations, units, formulas and incidence on compression.

Incidence factor	Parameter	Symbol	Unit	Equation
Dimension	Bulk Density	Da	g/ml	Da = P/Va
	Tapped Density	Dc	g/ml	Dc = P/Vc
Compressibility	Inter-particle Porosity	Ie	-	Ie = Dc − Da/Dc × Da
	Carr Index	IC	%	IC = (Dc − Da/Dc) 100
	Cohesion Index	Icd	N	Experimental
Flowability/Powder Flow	Hausner Ratio	IH	-	IH = Dc/Da
	Angle of Repose	(α)	°	tg α = h/r
	Powder Flow	t"	s	Experimental
Lubricity/Stability	Loss on Drying	%HR	%	Experimental
	Hygroscopicity	%H	%	Experimental
Lubricity/Dosage	Particles < 50 µm	%Pf	%	Experimental
	Homogeneity Index	(Iθ)	-	* Iθ = Fm / 100 + Δ Fmn

Table 1. Parameters and tests used by the SeDeM method.

2.1 Experimental procedure used to study a powdered substance with parameters considered by the SeDeM method

Pharmacopoeia methodologies are used to calculate these parameters. When this is impossible, a common strategy used in pharmaceutical technology development is applied. The methods used for each test are described below (Pérez et al, 2006):

- Bulk density (Da): The method is described in Section 2.9.34 of Eur. Ph. (Ph Eur, 2011)
- Tapped density (Dc): The method is described in Section 2.9.34 of Eur. Ph. (Ph Eur, 2011) The volume taken is the value obtained after 2500 strokes using a settling apparatus with a graduated cylinder (voluminometer).
- Inter-particle porosity (Ie) of the powder mixture (Font, 1962) is calculated from the following equation: Ie=Dc-Da/Dc×Da
- Carr index (IC%) (Córdoba et al, 1996; Rubinstein, 1993; Torres & Camacho, 1991; Wong, 1990). The method is described in Section 2.9.34 of Eur. Ph. (Ph Eur, 2011) This is calculated from Da and Dc as: IC=(Dc-Da/Dc)100
- Cohesion index (Icd): This index is determined by compressing the powder, preferably in an eccentric press. The mean hardness (N) of the tablets is calculated. First, the raw powder is tested, but if it cannot be compressed, 3.5% of the following mixture is added to the mix: talc 2.36%, Aerosil® 200 0.14% and magnesium stearate 1.00%.
- Hausner ratio (IH) (Ph Eur, 2011; Rubinstein, 1993). The method is described in Section 2.9.34 of Eur Ph (Ph Eur, 2011). This is calculated from Da and Dc as: IH=Dc/Da
- Angle of repose (α) (Rubinstein, 1993, Muñoz, 1993). The method is described in Section 2.9.36 of Eur Ph (Ph Eur, 2011). This is the angle of the cone formed when the product is passed through a funnel with the following dimensions: height 9.5 cm, upper diameter of spout 7.2 cm, internal diameter at the bottom, narrow end of spout 1.8 cm. The funnel is placed on a support 20 cm above the table surface, centred over a millimetre-grid sheet on which two intersecting lines are drawn, crossing at the centre. The spout is plugged and the funnel is filled with the product until it is flush with the top end of the spout when smoothed with a spatula. Remove the plug and allow the powder to fall onto the millimetre sheet. Measure the four radii of the cone base with a slide calliper and calculate the mean value (r). Measure the cone height (h). Deduce α from tan(α)=h/r.
- Flowability (t"): The method is described in Section 2.9.16 of Eur. Ph (Ph Eur, 2011). It is expressed in seconds and tenths of a second per 100 grams of sample, with a mean value of three measurements.
- Loss on drying (%HR): This is measured by the method described in 2.2.32 in Eur. Ph (Ph Eur, 2011). The sample is dried in an oven at 105 °C ± 2 °C, until a constant weight is obtained.
- Hygroscopicity (%H): Determination of the percentage increase in sample weight after being kept in a humidifier at a relative humidity of 76% (±2%) and a temperature of 22°C± 2°C for 24 h.
- Percentage of particles measuring <50 μm (%Pf): Particle size is determined by means of the sieve test following the General method 2.9.12 of Eur. Ph. (Ph Eur, 2011). The value returned is the % of particles that pass through a 0.05-mm sieve when vibrated for 10 min at speed 10 (CISA vibrator).
- Homogeneity index (Iθ): This is calculated according to the General method 2.9.12 of Eur. Ph (Ph Eur, 2011).To determine particle size by means of the sieve test, the grain size of a 100g sample is measured by subjecting a sieve stack to vibration for 10 min at speed 10 (CISA vibrator). The sieve sizes used are 0.355 mm, 0.212 mm, 0.100 mm and 0.05 mm. The percentage of product retained in each sieve is calculated and the amount that passes through the 0.05mm sieve is measured. The percentage of fine particles (<50 μm) (%Pf) was calculated as described above. Note that if this percentage is higher than that calculated in the complete sieve test, it is because some of the particles become

adhered to the product retained in the sieves during the grain-size test, and the percentage of <50 μm particles found may be lower than the true figure. The following equation is then applied to the data obtained.

$$*I\theta = \frac{Fm}{100 + (dm - dm\text{-}1)Fm\text{-}1 + (dm\text{+}1 - dm)Fm\text{+}1 + (dm - dm\text{-}2)Fm\text{-}2 + (dm\text{+}2 - dm)Fm\text{+}2 + ... + (dm - dm\text{-}n)Fm\text{-}n + (dm\text{+}n - dm)Fm\text{+}n} \quad (1)$$

Where:

- Iθ, Relative homogeneity index. Particle-size homogeneity in the range of the fractions studied;
- Fm, percentage of particles in the majority range;
- Fm−1, percentage of particles in the range immediately below the majority range;
- Fm+1, percentage of particles in the range immediately above the majority range;
- n, order number of the fraction studied under a series, with respect to the major fraction;
- dm, mean diameter of the particles in the major fraction;
- dm−1, mean diameter of the particles in the fraction of the range immediately below the majority range;
- dm+1, mean diameter of the particles in the fraction of the range immediately above the majority range.

2.2 Determination of acceptable limit values for each parameter included by the SeDeM method

Having obtained the values as described above, certain limits are set (Table 2) on the basis of the parameters chosen and the values described in the Handbook of Pharmaceutical Excipients (Kibbe, 2006), or alternatively on the basis of experimental tests.

Incidence	Parameter	Acceptable range
Dimension	Bulk density	0–1 g/ml
	Tapped density	0-1 g/ml
Compressibility	Inter-particle porosity	0–1.2
	Carr index	0–50 (%)
	Cohesion index	0–200 (N)
Flowability/powder flow	Hausner ratio	3–1
	Angle of repose	50–0 (°)
	Powder flow	20–0 (s)
Lubricity/stability	Loss on drying	0-10 (%)
	Higroscopicity	20–0 (%)
Lubricity/dosage	Particles < 50 μ	50–0 (%)
	Homogeneity index	0–2 × 10−2

Table 2. Limit values accepted for the SeDeM Diagram parameters.

The rationale to establish the limits for each parameter is:

- Da, Dc, Ie e IC are calculated from the extreme values (excluding the most extreme values) described in "Handbook of Pharmaceutical Excipients" (Kibbe, 2006). For the

Carr Index, limits are based on references in "Tecnologia Farmaceutica" by S. Casadio (Casadio, 1972) and on monograph 2.9.36 of Ph Eur (Ph Eur, 2011).

- Icd. The limit is determined empirically from compression tests on many powdered substances, based on the maximum hardness obtained without producing capped or broken tablets. This hardness is then established as the maximum limit. The minimum value is "0". This value implies that no tablets are obtained when the powders are compressed.
- IH, Powder flow, repose angle. The limits are set on the basis of the monographs described in "Handbook of Pharmaceutical Excipients" (Kibbe, 2006), and monograph 2.9.36 of Ph Eur (Ph Eur, 2011) or other references in "Tecnologia Farmaceutica" by S. Casadio (Casadio, 1972).
- %HR. The limits are established on the basis of the references cited elsewhere, such as "Farmacotecnia teórica y práctica" by José Helman (Helman, 1981). The optimum humidity is between 1% to 3%.
- Hygroscopicity is based on the "Handbook of Pharmaceutical Excipients" (Kibbe, 2006): based on manitol (not hygroscopic) and sorbitol (highly hygroscopic).
- Particle size. The limits are based on the literature. These sources (Kibbe, 2006) report that rheological and compression problems occur when the percentage of fine particles in the formulation exceeds 25%.

The limits for the Homogeneity Index (Iθ) are based on the distribution of the particles of the powder (see Table 3, indicating the size of the sieve (in mm), average particle size in each fraction and the difference in average particle size in the fraction between 0.100 and 0.212 and the others). A value of 5 on a scale from 0 to 10 was defined as the minimum acceptable value (MAV), as follows:

Sieve (mm)	Corresponding fraction	Average of the diameter of the fraction	Corresponding diameter (dm ... dm ± n)	Dif dm with the mayor component
0,355 - 0,500	Fm+2	427	dm+2	271
0,212 - 0,355	Fm+1	283	dm+1	127
0,100 - 0,212	Fm	156	dm	0
0,050 -0,100	Fm-1	75	dm-1	81
< 0,050	Fm-2	25	dm-2	131

Table 3. Distribution of particles in the determination of Iθ.

The major fraction (Fm) corresponds to the interval from 0.100 to 0.212 mm, because it falls in the middle of the other fractions of the table. This interval is calculated as the proportion in which the powder particles are found in each fraction considered in the table (as described above). Those particles located in the major fraction (Fm) in a proportion of 60% are considered to represent the MAV of 5. The distributions of the other particles are considered to be Gaussian. The limits for the Homogeneity Index are set between 0 and 0.02.

2.3 Conversion of the limits considered in each parameter of the SeDeM method into the radius (r) of the SeDeM Diagram

The numerical values of the parameters of the powder, which are obtained experimentally (v) as described above, are placed on a scale from 0 to 10, considering 5 as the MAV.

Incidence	Parameter	Limit value (v)	Radius (r)	Factor applied to v
Dimensions	Bulk density	0–1	0–10	10v
	Tapped density	0–1	0–10	10v
Compressibility	Inter-particle porosity	0–1.2	0–10	10v/1.2
	Carr index	0–50	0–10	v/5
	Cohesion index	0–200	0–10	v/20
Flowability/powder flow	Hausner ratio (a)	3–1	0–10	(30-10v)/2
	Angle of repose	50–0	0–10	10 – (v/5)
	Powder flow	20–0	0–10	10 – (v/2)
Lubricity/estability	Loss on drying (b)	10-0	0-10	10-v
	Higroscopicity	20–0	0–10	10 – (v/2)
Lubricity/dosage	Particles < 50 μ	50–0	0–10	10 – (v/5)
	Homogeneity index	0–2 × 10–2	0–10	500v

Table 4. Conversion of limits for each parameter into radius values (r).
(a) The values that exceptionally appear below 1 are considered values corresponding to non-sliding products.
(b) Initially, relative humidity was calculated based on the establishment of three intervals because the percentage relation obtained from the measurement of the humidity of the substance does not follow a linear relation with respect to the correct behaviour of the dust. Humidity below 1% makes the powder too dry, and electrostatic charge is induced, which affects the rheology. Furthermore, low humidity percentages do not allow compression of the substance (moisture is necessary for compacting powders). Moreover, more than 3% moisture causes caking, in addition to favouring the adhesion to punches and dyes. Consequently, it was considered that this parameter should present optimal experimental values from 1% to 3% (Braidotti, 1974). Nevertheless, experience using the SeDeM Diagram has demonstrated no significant variations in the results, so the previous three intervals of relative humidity can be simplified to the calculation of the parameter, thus finally the linear criterion of treatment of results is adopted (Suñé et al, 2011).

The correspondence of the value of the parameters with this scale takes into account the limit values (see 2.2), using the factors indicated in Table 4. When all radius values are 10, the SeDeM Diagram takes the form of a circumscribed regular polygon, drawn by connecting all the radius values of the parameters with linear segments. Table 4 shows the factors used for calculating the numerical value of each parameter required for the SeDeM method.

2.4 Graphical representation of the SeDeM Diagram

When all radius values are 10, the SeDeM Diagram takes the form of a circumscribed regular polygon, drawn by connecting the radius values with linear segments. The results obtained from the earlier parameter calculations and conversions are represented by the radius. The figure formed indicates the characteristics of the product and of each parameter that determines whether the product is suitable for direct compression. In this case, the SeDeM Diagram is made up of 12 parameters, thus forming an irregular 12-sided polygon (Figure 1).

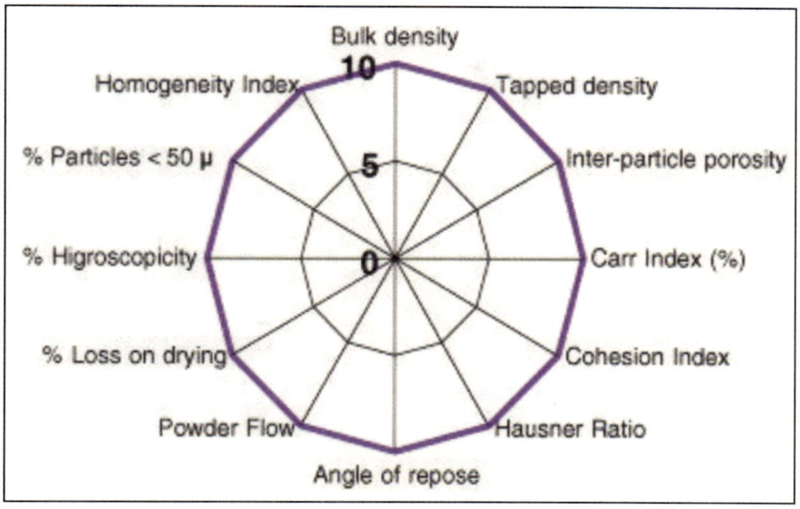

Fig. 1. The SeDeM Diagram with 12 parameters.

2.5 Acceptable limits for Indexes

To determine whether the product is suitable for direct compression using a numerical method, the following indexes are calculated based on the SeDeM Diagram as follows:

$$\text{– Parameter index} \quad IP = \frac{n^{\circ}P \geq 5}{n^{\circ}Pt} \tag{2}$$

Where:

No. p ≥ 5: Indicates the number of parameters whose value is equal to or higher than 5

No. Pt: Indicates the total number of parameters studied

The acceptability limit would correspond to:

$$IP = \frac{n^{o}P \geq 5}{n^{o}Pt} = 0{,}5 \tag{3}$$

$$\text{– Parameter profile Index} \quad IPP = \text{Average of}(r) \text{ all parameters} \tag{4}$$

Average (r) = mean value of the parameters calculated.

The acceptability limit would correspond to: IPP = media (r) = 5

$$\text{– Good Compressibility Index} \quad IGC = IPP \times f \tag{5}$$

$$f = \quad \text{Reliability factor} = \frac{\text{Polygon area}}{\text{Circle area}} \tag{6}$$

The acceptability limit would correspond to: ICG = IPP x f = 5.

The reliability factor indicates that the inclusion of more parameters increases the reliability of the method (Figure 2).

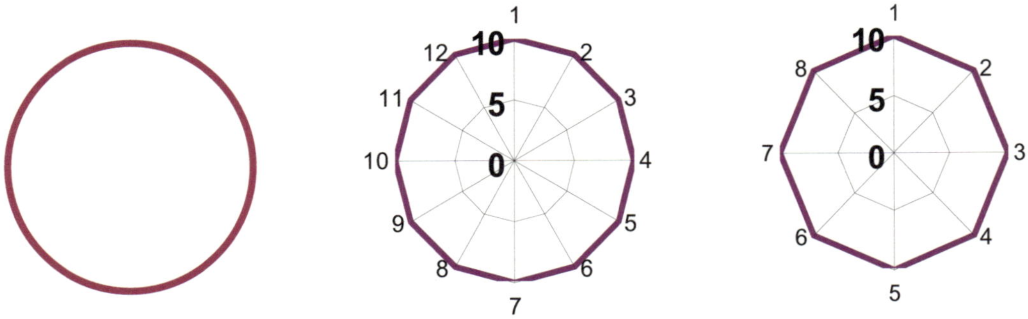

Fig. 2. On the left graph with ∞ parameters (maximum reliability), f = 1. In the center, graph with 12 parameters (nº of parameters in this study), f = 0.952. On the right, graph with 8 parameters (minimum reliability), f = 0.900.

3. Practical applications of SeDeM

3.1 Determination of the suitability of an API to be subjected to direct compression technology

Here we used the SeDeM method to characterize an active product ingredient in powder form (API SX-325) and to determine whether it is suitable for direct compression, applying the profile to the SeDeM Diagram.

We measured the 12 parameters proposed in the SeDeM method following the procedures indicated. Thus we obtained the values on which the factors set out in Table 5 are applied to obtain the numerical values corresponding to the radius of the diagram and the values of the mean incidence. All the values in Table 5 correspond to the average of two determinations. The radius values are represented in the diagram shown in Figure 3.

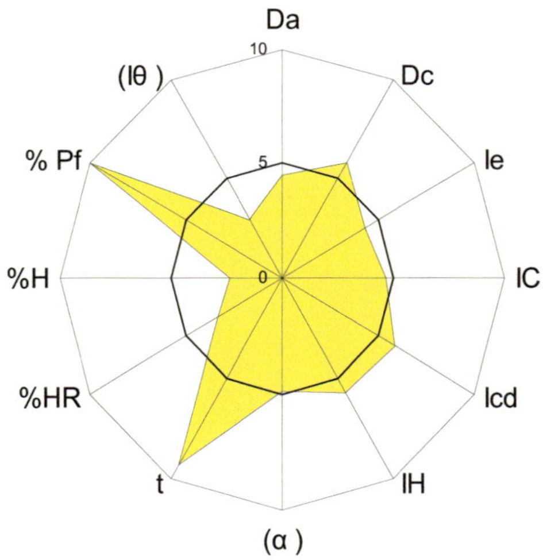

Fig. 3. SeDeM Diagram for API SX-325.

To obtain the indices of acceptance or qualification for formulation by direct compression, the formulas corresponding to the parametric index were applied from the numerical results of the radius shown in Table 5. The results of the acceptance indices are shown in Table 6.

Incidence factor	Parameter	Symbol	Unit	Value (v)	(r)	Mean incidence
Dimension	Bulk Density	Da	g/ml	0.448	4.48	5.16
	Tapped Density	Dc	g/ml	0.583	5.83	
Compressibility	Inter-particle Porosity	Ie	–	0.517	4.31	4.95
	Carr Index	IC	%	23.156	4.63	
	Cohesion Index	Icd	N	118.00	5.90	
Flowability/Powder Flow	Hausner Ratio	IH	–	1.868	5.66	6.59
	Angle of Repose	(α)	°	25.770	4.85	
	Powder Flow	t	s	1.500	9.25	
Lubricity/Stability	Loss on Drying	%HR	%	5.650	4.35	3.37
	Hygroscopicity	%H	%	15.210	2.40	
Lubricity/Dosage	Particles < 50 μm	%Pf	%	0.000	10.0	6.45
	Homogeneity Index	(Iθ)	–	0.0058	2.90	

Table 5. Application of the SeDeM method to API in powder form (API SX-325), and calculation of radii.

Parameter index		0.42	
Parametric profile index (mean r of all parameters)		5.38	
Good compression index (IGC)		5.12	

Table 6. SeDeM acceptance index for API SX-325

On the basis of the results of the radius corresponding to the SeDeM Diagram, the parametric profile was > 5. This value implies that API SX-325 is suitable for direct compression. However, in order to discern the appropriateness of this substance for this formulation technology, we analyzed the 5 groups of individual factors classified by the type of incidence in this compression.

In the case study above, only the parameters involved in the general factor of denominated incidence lubrication/stability presented values below 5 (median = 3.37). This finding implies deficient rheological qualities and poor stability, expressed by a high intrinsic humidity of balance and high hygroscopicity. The product tended to capture humidity, thus worsening the rheological profile (compression, lack of flow) and consequently impairing its stability. These deficiencies are reflected graphically in the SeDeM Diagram, which shows that a large shaded area (activity area) (the greater the shaded area, the more suitable the characteristics for direct compression) is present for most of the parameters. However, some parameters show a small shaded area, thus indicating that the powder is not suitable for direct compression.

In this regard, the SeDeM method informed (table 5) on the following for API SX-325: it is a dusty substance with correct dimensional characteristics (Da and Dc); it shows moderately acceptable compressibility (IE, IC, Icd), which can be improved with the addition of excipients of direct compression (DC); it shows very good fluidity/flowability (IH, α, t") and correct lubrication/dosage (%Pf, Iθ). Given these characteristics API SX-325 is suitable for compression with the addition of standardized formula of lubricant. The group of factors with deficient incidence corresponds to lubricity/stability and, considering the parameters HR and H, corrective measures can be taken to prevent its negative influence on direct compression. These measures include drying the material and preparing the tablet in rooms with controlled relative humidity below 25%.

The results given by the SeDeM method in this example demonstrate that it is reliable in establishing whether powdered substances have suitable profiles to be subjected to direct compression. Consequently, SeDeM is a tool that will contribute to preformulation studies of medicines and help to define the manufacturing technology required. Indeed, the application of the SeDeM Diagram allows the determination of the direct compression behaviour of a powdered substance from the index of parametric profile (IPP) and the index of good compression (IGC), in such a way that an IPP and an IGC equal or over 5 indicates that the powder displays characteristics that make it suitable for direct compression, adding only a small amount of lubricant (3.5% of the magnesium stearate, talc and Aerosil® 200). Also, with IPP and IGC values between 3 and 5, the substance will require a DC diluent excipient suitable for direct compression. In addition, it is deduced that techniques other than direct compression (wet granulation or dry granulation) will be required for APIs with IPP and IGC values below 3.
The SeDeM Diagram is not restricted to active products since it can also be used with new or known excipients to assess their suitability for application as adjuvants in direct compression. Thus, knowledge of excipient profiles, with their corresponding parameters, will allow identification of the most suitable excipient to correct the characteristics of APIs registering values under 5.
Of note, the greater the number of parameters selected, the greater the reliability of the method, in such a way that to obtain a reliability of the 100%, the number of parameters applied would have to be infinite (reliability factor = 1). The number of parameters could be extended using additional complementary ones, such as the true density, the index of porosity, the electrostatic charge, the specific surface, the adsorption power, % of lubrication, % friability, and the index of elasticity. However, while improving the reliability of the method, the inclusion of further parameters would be to the detriment of its simplicity and rapidity, since complementary parameters are difficult to apply.

3.2 Application of the SeDeM method to determine the amount of excipient required for the compression of an API that is not apt for direct compression

Experimental determination of the parameters of the SeDeM method for a range of APIs and excipients allows definition of their corresponding compressibility profiles and their subsequent mathematical treatment and graphical expression (SeDeM Diagram). Various excipient diluents can be analyzed to determine whether a substance is appropriate for direct compression and the optimal proportion of excipient required to design a suitable formulation for direct compression based on the SeDeM characteristics of the API (Suñé et al, 2008a). In this regard, the SeDeM method is a valid tool with which to design the formulation of tablets by direct compression.
The mathematical equation can be applied to the 5 parameters (dimension, compressibility, flowability/powder flow, lubricity/stability lubricity/dosage) considered deficient by the SeDeM system. The mathematical equation is applied to correct a deficient parameter of the API. The equation proposed (Equation 7) allows calculation of the amount of excipient required to compress the API on the basis of the SeDeM radius considered minimum (5) for each parameter of incidence that allows correct compression.

$$CP = 100 - \left(\frac{RE - R}{RE - RP} \times 100 \right) \tag{7}$$

Where:
CP = % of corrective excipient

RE = mean-incidence radius value (compressibility) of the corrective excipient
R = mean-incidence radius value to be obtained in the blend
RP = mean-incidence radius value (compressibility) of the API to be corrected
The unknown values are replaced by the calculated ones required for each substance in order to obtain R = 5 (5 is the minimum value considered necessary to achieve satisfactory compression). For example, if a deficient compressibility parameter for an API requires correction, Equation 7 is applied by replacing the terms RE and RP with the values calculated for each substance with the purpose to obtain a R=5, thus obtaining the optimal excipient to design a first drug formulation and the maximum amount required for a comprehensive understanding of the proposed formula. From this first formulation, research can get underway for the final optimization of the formulation, taking into consideration the biopharmaceutical characteristics required in the final tablet (disintegration, dissolution, etc). We thus present a method to establish the details of the formulation of a given drug by direct compression.

3.2.1 Practical application of the mathematical equation to calculate the amount of excipient required for a deficient API to be subjected to direct compression technology

When an API requires an appropriate formula for the direct compression, it must be characterized following the SeDeM Diagram. Furthermore, a series of excipients used for DC are also characterized using the diagram. If the API has deficient compressibility parameters (<5), it is mixed with an excipient with a satisfactory compressibility parameter (>5), thereby correcting the deficiency. The excipient that shows the smallest amount to correct this parameter should be used. The amount of excipient is determined by the mathematical equation of the SeDeM system (Equation 7).
Here we describe an example using an API 842SD and 6 diluents used for DC. The corresponding parameters and the radius mean values obtained with samples of this substance are shown in Table 7 and the parameters and the radius mean values of six excipient diluents used in DC are shown in Table 8 (Suñé et al, 2008a).

Incidence factor	Parameter	Symbol	Unit	Value (v)	(r)	Mean incidence
Dimension	Bulk Density	Da	g/ml	0.775	7.75	8.88
	Tapped Density	Dc	g/ml	1.140	10.00	
Compressibility	Inter-particle Porosity	Ie	–	0.413	3.44	3.40
	Carr Index	IC	%	32.018	6.40	
	Cohesion Index	Icd	N	7.330	0.37	
Flowability/Powder Flow	Hausner Ratio	IH	–	1.98	5.10	4.15
	Angle of Repose	(α)	°	37.450	2.51	
	Powder Flow	t	s	10.330	4.84	
Lubricity/Stability	Loss on Drying	%HR	%	9.865	0.68	5.34
	Hygroscopicity	%H	%	0.007	10.0	
Lubricity/Dosage	Particles < 50 μm	%Pf	%	12.000	7.60	4.40
	Homogeneity Index	(Iθ)		0.0024	1.20	
Parameter index				0.50		
Parametric profile index (mean r of all parameters)				4.99		
Good compression index (IGC)				4.75		

Table 7. Parameters, mean incidence and parametric index for API 842SD

	PARAMETERS (radius)												FACTOR					INDEX		
Excipient	Da	Dc	Ie	IC	Icd	IH	α	t"	%HR	%H	%pf	(Iθ)	Dimension.	Compressibility	Flowability/ Powder Flow	Lubricity/ Stability.	Lubricity/ Dosage	IP	PP	IGC
Avicel PH 101 Batch 6410C	3.47	4.63	6.02	5.01	10.00	5.55	3.46	0.00	3.84	8.17	3.38	10.00	4.05	7.01	3.01	6.01	6.69	0.50	5.29	5.04
Isomalt® Batch LRE 539	4.40	5.60	4.06	4.29	10.00	5.76	6.24	6.85	4.01	9.89	9.00	2.00	5.00	6.11	6.28	6.95	5.50	0.58	6.01	5.72
Kleptose® Batch 774639	5.58	8.46	5.08	6.81	10.00	4.95	3.51	6.50	0.00	8.12	3.60	1.90	7.02	7.30	4.98	4.06	2.75	0.58	5.38	5.12
Kollindon® VA64 Batch 28-2921	2.53	3.43	8.64	5.25	6.91	5.48	6.04	5.25	3.19	2.85	8.40	5.50	2.98	6.93	5.59	3.02	6.95	0.67	5.29	5.03
Plasdone ®S630 Batch 6272473	2.48	3.73	10.00	6.70	10.00	4.99	4.13	0.00	3.46	3.17	3.60	5.70	3.11	8.90	3.04	3.32	4.65	0.33	4.83	4.60
Prosolv® HD90 Batch K950044	4.86	5.96	3.17	3.69	10.00	5.91	5.99	6.75	3.44	8.86	6.24	10.00	5.41	5.62	6.22	6.15	8.12	0.67	6.24	5.94

Table 8. Radius parameters, mean incidence and parametric index for excipients DC

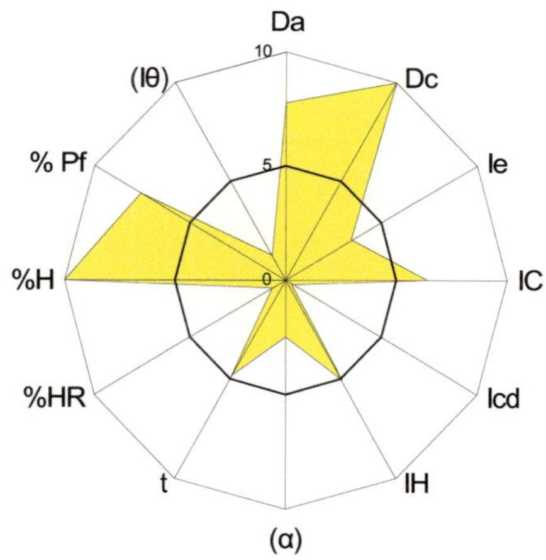

Fig. 4. SeDeM Diagram for API 842SD

The SeDeM Diagram for API 842SD (Figure 4, Table 7) indicates that this substance has deficient compressibility (r=3.40), limited rheological characteristics (r=4.15) and low lubricity/dosage (r=4.40). Consequently, to apply direct compression to API 842SD, it requires formulation with an excipient that enhances the compressibility factor. This excipient is identified by the SeDeM system.

In order to select the excipient and the concentration used to correct the deficiencies and, in particular, the compressibility, we applied the mathematical equation of the SeDeM Expert system (Equation 7): replacing the unknowns (RE and RP) with the values calculated for each substance (RE for excipients and RP for API) with aim to obtain R=5. The results obtained are shown in Table 9.

EXCIPIENT	Avicel® PH101	Kleptose®	Koll VA®	Plasdone® S630	Prosolv® HD90	Isolmalt® 721
RE	7.01	7.30	6.93	8.90	5.62	6.11
RP (API)	3.40	3.40	3.40	3.40	3.40	3.40
R	5.00	5.00	5.00	5.00	5.00	5.00
% excipient	44.32	41.03	45.33	29.09	72.07	59.04

Table 9. Amount of excipient required to be mixed with the API to obtain a compressibility factor equal to 5.

Plasdone S630 was the most suitable excipient to correct the deficit (compressibility) of API 842SD with the lowest concentration (29.09 %). (Table 9)

To better understand the SeDeM system, the graphical representations of the profiles of the API and the excipient can be superposed. Figure 5 shows how the deficiencies of an API would be compensated when formulated. The green line corresponds to the excipient that theoretically provides the final mixture the characteristics to be compressed. In this way, the information provided by the SeDeM system allows the formulator to start working with excipients that have a high probability to provide suitable formulations, thus reducing the lead time of formulation.

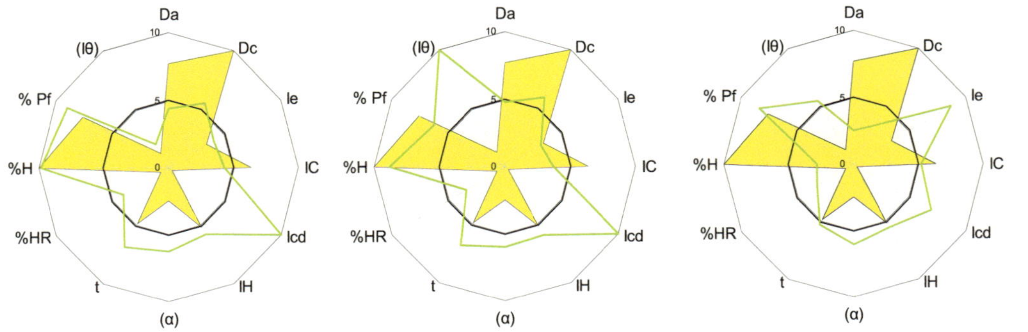

Fig. 5. Green indicates the part that corresponds to the excipient that provides suitable compressibility to the final mixture with the API (in yellow). Three excipients are shown, all of them covering the deficiencies of the API.

3.3 Application of the SeDeM system to the quality control of batches of a single API or excipient used for direct compression

The SeDeM system is also apt for verification of the reproducibility of manufacturing standards between batches of the same powdered raw material (API or excipient). Indeed, superposing the SeDeM Diagrams of each batch, the degree of similarity or difference between the same API on the basis of the established parameters can determine its appropriateness for compression.

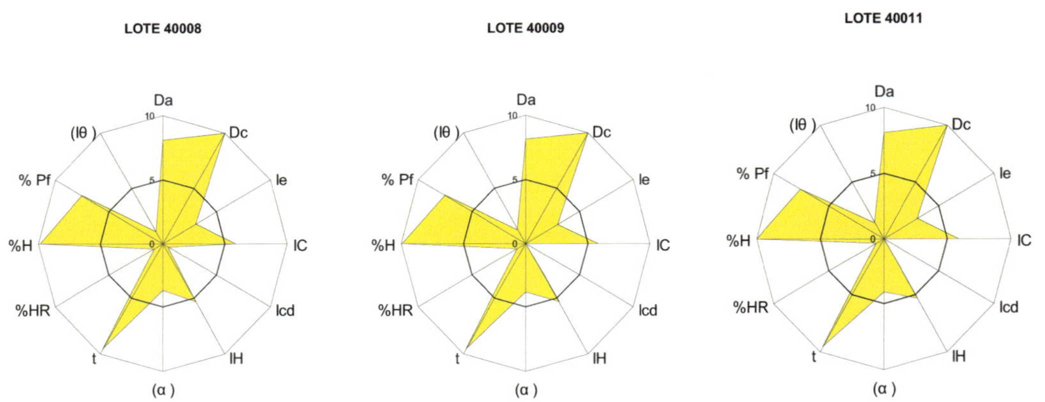

Fig. 6. SeDeM Diagram of 3 batches of API FO130.

The SeDeM method is also a useful tool for the study of the reproducibility of a manufacturing method used for a powdered substance and, thus of the validation of systematic variation during elaboration. A manufacturing process gives rise to variations in the final product and these variations must fall within limits or established specifications. By applying the SeDeM method to study reproducibility between batches of the same API or excipient, specifications in the different parameters can be established to ensure the same quality of the product regardless of the batch analyzed. In addition, these specifications must be used for the establishment of particular limits for quality control applications. To achieve this goal it is necessary to study the parameters of the SeDeM Diagram, applying the same statistic analyses required to establish the pharmacotechnical equivalence between batches. Correct reproducibility between batches will ensure the reproducibility and the quality of the tablets formulated with this API or excipient, regardless of the batch used.

Figure 6 shows the SeDeM Diagrams of three batches from the same API (Perez et al, 2006). In this case the mark and the indices were very similar. This control has the advantage that the method has the capacity to detect variations in particle size between batches of the product. This capacity thus contributes to the formulation of the pharmaceutical forms and their correct dissolution.

3.4 Application of the SeDeM method to differentiate the excipient in the same chemical family

The SeDeM system also allows differentiation between excipients of the same chemical family but that differ in physical characteristics. These characteristics will determine their use in a formulation for direct compression of a given API. In a previous study (Suñé et al, 2008b) several lactoses were characterized, and in figure 7 can be observed the clear differentiation that makes the SeDeM methodology between the same chemical substances (but different functionally).

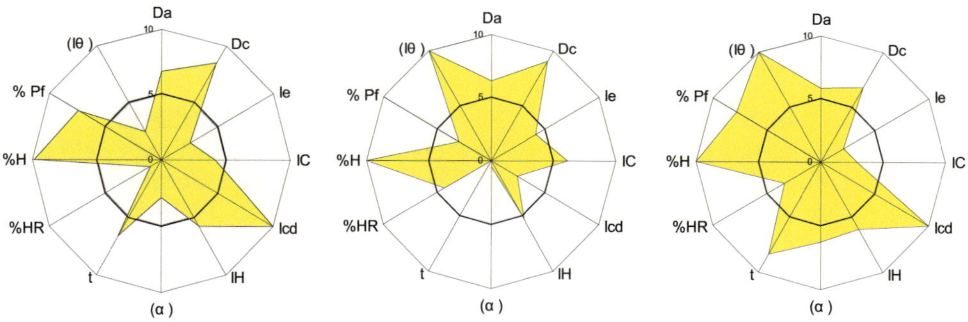

Fig. 7. SeDeM Diagram for three kinds of lactose. On the left: Lactose anhydre IGC: 5.39. In the center: Lactose monohydrate IGC: 4.83. On the right: Lactose fast-flow IGC: 6.30.

3.5 Application of the SeDeM Diagram to differentiate excipients of the same functional type

Also, the SeDeM Expert system allows differentiation between excipients from the same functional type, for example disintegrants or diluents. In the former, the SeDeM characterization provides the information required to predict the difficulties encountered for compression.

By quantifying the 12 tests provided by the system, the deficient values for their compression can be defined; on the basis of these values, an adequate (applying the same SeDeM Diagram) substance can be selected to improve the compressibility in the final mixture of the disintegrants and the API. Figure 8 shows the characterization of several disintegrants using the SeDeM technique, where the differences between each one in relation to their major or minor compression capacity are shown, although all are used because of their disintegrant function (Aguilar et al, 2009).

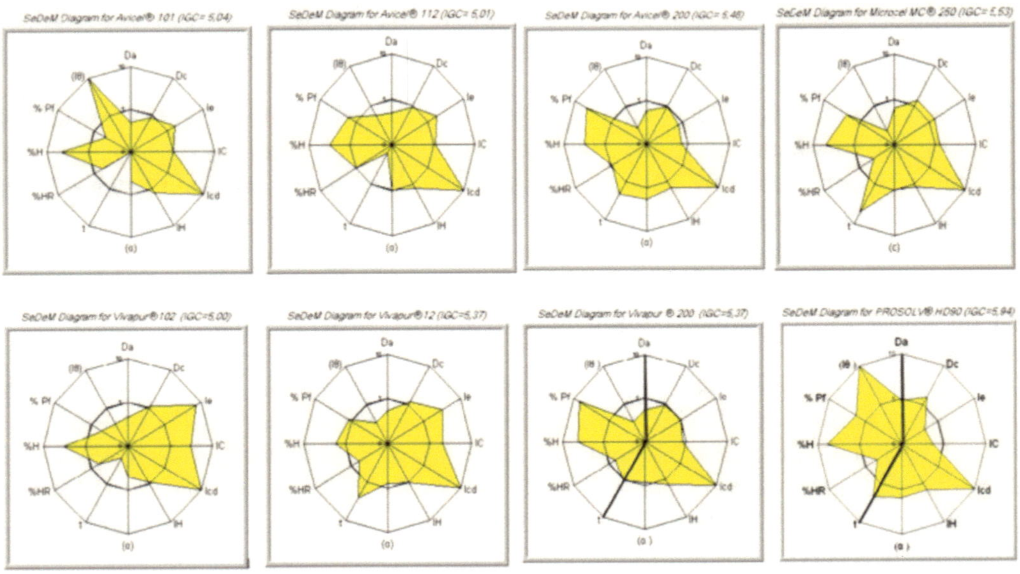

Fig. 8. SeDeM diagram for several disintegrant excipients.

3.6 The new model SeDeM-ODT to develop orally disintegrating tablets by direct compression

This innovative tool is the new SeDeM-ODT model which provides the Index of Good Compressibility & Bucodispersibility (IGCB index) obtained from the previous SeDeM method (Aguilar et al, 2011). The IGCB index is composed by 6 factors that indicate whether a mixture of powder lends itself to be subjected to direct compression. Moreover, the index simultaneously indicates whether these tablets are suitable as bucodispersible tablet (disintegration in less than 3 minutes). The new factor, disgregability (Table 10), has three parameters that influence this parameter. The graph now comprises 15 parameters (Figure 9).

Factor	Parameter	Limit value (v)	Radius
Disgregability	Effervescence	0-5 (minutes)	10-0
	Disintegration Time with disc (DCD)	0-3(minutes)	10-0
	Disintegration Time without disc (DSD)	0-3 (minutes)	10-0

Table 10. The new factor disgregability is added to the SeDeM expert system to achieve the SeDeM-ODT expert system.

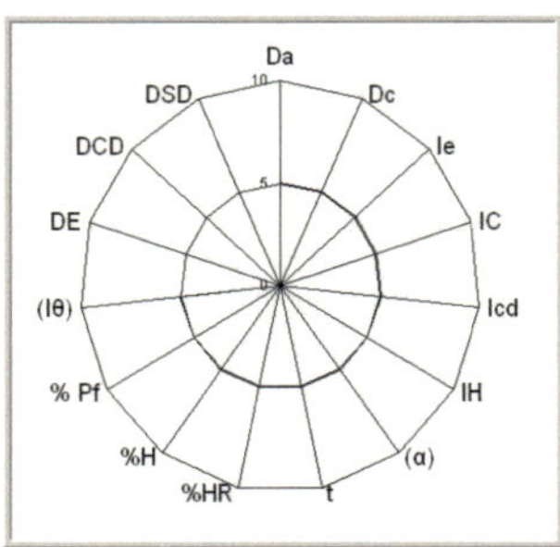

Fig. 9. SeDeM-ODT Diagram

4. Conclusions

Here we developed an original methodology for the preformulation and powder substance characterization. This method facilitates studies on the design and development of formulations for the production of tablets by direct compression. The SeDeM expert system is a useful tool because, in addition to considering the type of components, it also provides recommendations on intrinsic properties, such as the characteristics and morphology of the particles. We propose that given the accuracy of the information provided by this system, formulations will have a higher probability of being successfully compressed.

This method characterizes the individual components of a formulation and applies a mathematical analysis to determine the exact amount of each in the final formulation.

The formulation provided will be valid for direct compression. This manufacturing procedure offers many advantages from a production perspective. In addition to being faster than other techniques, it is straightforward as it reduces the number of steps during the manufacturing process.

In addition SeDeM has the advantage of providing formulation with the lowest amount of excipients as it combines the API with only one excipient and the standard formula of lubricants, thus avoiding the used of unnecessary excipients, such as diluents, binders and agglutinants.

The information given by the SeDeM system contributes to a Quality by Design Development. Consequently, this innovative tool is consistent with the current requirements of regulatory health authorities such as the FDA and ICH.

5. References

Aguilar_Díaz, J.E.; García-Montoya, E.; Pérez-Lozano, P.; Suñé-Negre, J.M.; Miñarro, M. & Ticó, J.R. (2009). The use of the SeDeM Diagram expert system to determine the suitability of diluents-disintegrants for direct compression and their use in formulation of ODT. *Eur J Pharm & Biopharm*, 73, pp. 414-423, ISSN: 0939-6411

Aguilar_Díaz, J.E.; García_Montoya, E.; Pérez_Lozano, P.; Suñé_Negre, J.M.; Miñarro, M. & Ticó, J.R. (2011). Contribution to development of ODT using an innovator tool: SeDeM-ODT. *Proceedings of X Congreso de la Sociedad Española de Farmacia Industrial y Galénica,* Madrid, 2-4 febrero 2011.

Braidotti, L. & Bulgarelli, D. (1974) *Tecnica Farmaceutica.* (1ª ed), Lleditrice Scientifica LG Guadagni, Milan

Brittain, H.G. (1997). On the Physical Characterization of Pharmaceutical Solids. *Pharm Techn*, 1, pp. 100-106, ISSN: 1543-2521

Casadio, S. (1972). *Tecnologia Farmaceutica.* (2ª ed), Cisalpino-Goliardica Ed., Milan

Córdoba Borrego, M.; Moreno Cerezo, J.M.; Córdoba Díaz, M. & Córdoba Díaz, D. (1996). Preformulación y desarrollo galénico de nuevas formulaciones por compresión directa con agentes hidrotrópicos. *Inf Farm*, 4, pp. 65-70, ISSN: 0213-5574

European Pharmacopeia. (2011) (7th ed), Council of Europe, ISBN: 978-92-871-6053-9, Strasbourgh

Font Quer, P. *Medicamenta: guía teórico práctica para farmacéuticos y médicos.* (1962) (6th ed), Labor Ed., Barcelona (1): 340 - 341.

García Montoya, E.; Suñé Negre, J.M.; Pérez Lozano, P.; Miñarro Carmona, M. & Ticó Grau, J.R. (2010). Metodología de preformulación galénica para la caracterización de sustancias en relación a su viabilidad para la compresión: Diagrama SeDeM. *Farmespaña Industrial*, enero/febrero, pp.58-62, ISSN: 1699-4205.

Helman, J. *Farmacotecnia teórica y práctica*. (1981), Compañía Internacional Continental. ISBN: 950-06-5081-9, Méjico 6: 1721.

Kibbe, A.H. *Handbook of Pharmaceutical Excipients*. (2006) (5th ed), American Pharmaceutical Association. Pharmaceutical Press, ISBN: 0-85369-381-1, London

Muñoz Ruíz, A.; Muñoz Muñoz, N.; Monedero Perales, M.C.; Velasco Antequera, M.V. & Jiménez Castellanos Ballesteros, M.R. (1993). Determinación de la fluidez de sólidos a granel. Métodos (I). *Ind Farm*, 1, pp. 49-55, ISSN: 0213-5574

Pérez Lozano, P.; Suñé Negre, J.M.; Miñarro, M.; Roig, M.; Fuster, R.; García Montoya, E.; Hernández, C.; Ruhí, R. & Ticó, J.R. (2006). A new expert system (SeDeM Diagram) for control batch powder formulation and preformulation drug products. *Eur J Pharm & Biopharm*, 64, pp. 351-359, ISSN:0939-6411

Suñé Negre, Pérez Lozano, P.; J.M.; Miñarro, M.; Roig, M.; Fuster, R.; García Montoya, E.; Hernández, C.; Ruhí, R. & Ticó, J.R. Optimization of parameters of the SeDeM Diagram Expert System: Hausner index (HI) and Relative Humidity (%HR). (2011). Approved April 2011 *Eur J Pharm & Biopharm*. ISSN: 0939-6411. DOI: 10.1016/J.EJPB.2011.04.002

Rubinstein, M.H. *Pharmaceutical Technology (Tabletting Technology)*. (1993), (1st Ed), SA de Ediciones, ISBN:978-0136629580, Madrid

Suñé Negre, J.M.; Pérez Lozano, P.; Miñarro, M.; Roig, M.; Fuster, R.; García Montoya, E.; Hernández, C.; Ruhí, R. & Ticó, J.R. Nueva metodología de preformulación galénica para la caracterización de sustancias en relación a su viabilidad para la compresión: Método SeDeM. (2005). *Cienc Tecnol Pharm*, 15, 3, pp. 125-136, ISSN:1575-3409

Suñé Negre JM, Pérez Lozano, P.; J.M.; Miñarro, M.; Roig, M.; Fuster, R.; García Montoya, E.; Hernández, C.; Ruhí, R. & Ticó, J.R. (2008). Application of the SeDeM Diagram and a new mathematical equation in the design of direct compression tablet formulation. *Eur J Pharm & Biopharm*, 69, pp.1029-1039, ISSN: 0939-6411.

Suñé Negre, J.M.; Pérez Lozano, P.; Miñarro, M.; Roig, M.; Fuster, R.; García Montoya, E. & Ticó, J.R. (2008). Characterization of powders to preformulation studies with a new expert system (sedem diagram). *Proceedings of 6th World Meeting on Pharmaceutics, Biopharmaceutics and Pharmaceutical Technology*, Barcelona, April 2008.

Torres Suárez, A.I. & Camacho Sánchez MA. (1991). Planteamiento de un programa de preformulación y formulación de comprimidos. *Ind Farm*, 2, pp. 85-92, ISSN: 0213-5574

Wong, L.W & Pilpel N. (1990). The effect of particle shape on the mechanical properties of powders. *Int J Pharm*, 59, pp.145-154, ISSN: 0378-5173

3

Parametric Modeling and Prognosis of Result Based Career Selection Based on Fuzzy Expert System and Decision Trees

Avneet Dhawan
Lovely Faculty of Technology and Sciences,
Lovely Professional University, Punjab,
India

1. Introduction

1.1 Expert system and its applications

An Expert System is a set of programs that manipulate encoded knowledge to solve problems in a specialized domain that normally requires human expertise. The expert's knowledge is obtained from the specialists or other sources of expertise, such as texts, journal articles and databases

Year	# of expert systems developed
1985	50
1986	86
1987	1100
1988	2200
1992	12000

Table 1. Increase in number of expert systems developed yearly (based on Durkin, 1998)

Area systems	% of Expert
Engineering & manufacturing	35
Business	29
Medicine	11
Environment & Energy	9
Agriculture	5
Telecommunications	4
Government	4
Law	3
Transportation	1

Table 2. Applications of expert systems in various fields.

Human computer interaction and web-based intelligent tutoring concepts come into play while implementing an online educational tool whose target is mostly unskilled or novice users. The users (the students in this context) have to be provided with tools that will be helpful in improving their skills in the targeted area. A successful web based education system should have intelligence to tackle the variation in student skills and backgrounds and it should also be able to adapt its contents according to that variation. These mentioned issues are the main concerns for web-based intelligent tutoring research area. For a robot supported laboratory the skill building is both to learn and to gain experience about the control of the robot involved in the experiment setup and to be successful in carrying out the experimentation that is required for the student in order to gain practical knowledge in the targeted area. In order to adapt the context of the experimentation to the variation in student behaviors, students should be modeled according to their skills and knowledge backgrounds. User modelling is an important aspect of both human computer interaction and web-based intelligent tutoring research areas. AI techniques can be applied to the user modelling for implementation of online experimentation framework to get useful information about the student skill and knowledge level for providing help when necessary and assessing his/her performance.

Examples of the early and famous expert systems

- DENDRAL - Stanford Univ. (1965)
  - Analysis of chemical compunds
  - Rule-based system
- CADACEUS - Univ. of Pittsburgh (1970)
  - Diagnosis of human internal diseases
- MYCYSMA - MIT (1971)
  - Symbolic mathematical analysis

ES are appropriate in domains when/where:

- there are no established theories
- human expertise is scarce or in high demand, but recognized experts exist
- the information is fuzzy, inexact or incomplete
- the domain is highly specific

Human computer interaction field deals with enhancing the ways in which users interact with one or more computational machines through design, evaluation and implementation of interactive computing systems. From the perspective of telerobotics or more specifically online robotic experimentation, human computer interaction field deals with providing interfaces for remote users which enable them to do the necessary manipulation successfully. There is a strong need for an intelligent interface for a framework for remote access of robot supported laboratories through the Internet. The two main reasons for that are:

1. The need for intelligently coaching the student to achieve the goals of the experimentation successfully.
2. The need for evaluating student's performance while carrying out the experiment.

Student evaluation, the first main issue mentioned above, is one of the key issues for a remote experimentation framework. Students who are carrying out the experimentation, online without a human assistant or a teacher, should all be evaluated according to their varying success levels. The interface should possess suitable intelligence to categorize the student according to his or her performance during the course of the experiment and possibly to evaluate whether an increase or decrease in performance is present according to the past performance of the users. Necessary grades can then be given to those students according to the performance category in which they tend to fall.

Students, while doing the experiments online by themselves should be coached just as in the case for a traditional laboratory work where the coach is a human assistant or a teacher. They can be given useful directions and recommendations in the form of messages on the interface. Another aspect of coaching is to adapt the level of the complexity of the experiment to the level of the student. Skilled students can be excluded from some parts of the experiment, where unskilled students or students showing a poor performance can be directed to finish the fundamental parts or repeat the unsuccessful parts of the experiment. This idea coincides with the aim of using adaptive hypermedia for intelligent web-based tutoring tools, where the content of the tutor is changed adaptively to suit the student's individual needs and interests.

There are also other key aspects for a successful interface, which are:

- Having a layout that provides the student with all the necessary information about the objectives and the states of the experiment, and visual displays for aiding the users to see the state of the robot and the experimental setup.
- Providing a security mechanism that prevents unwanted and unauthorized access to protect the system from possible malicious use. Another issue for the robot-supported online experimentation is providing a scenario for the experiment. The experiment should involve a useful scenario that is relevant to the educational context that it is applied to and which must have tasks that have different levels of complexity to be accomplished.

By this way, using an intelligent interface for an online robot-supported experimentation will be justified. The educational contexts to benefit from remote experimentation can be range from mechatronics laboratories to chemistry laboratories. According to the scenario, the students can be directed to complete the levels of the experiment according to their skill level and be coached without the actual presence of a human assistant or a teacher.

In accordance with the issues and the needs stated, the aim of the work given in this thesis is to build a user assessment and coaching framework for an intelligent interface in use during remote access of labs through the Internet involving telerobotics or teleoperation. The lab setup can be assisted by either a robot or any device that is connected to the Internet.

The specific goals of the approach are that:

1. The interface should provide the student with "hands on" experimentation by using visual feedback and give the user as much freedom as possible to control the experiment;\
2. The system should evaluate the user performance, adapt the context to the level of acquired knowledge and skill of the user, and thus intelligently coach him/her to successfully do the experiment and get the most out of the experimentation.

The concepts and tools borrowed from fields such as web-based intelligent tutoring, human-computer interaction, user-adapted interaction and Internet telerobotics are necessary for the successful accomplishment of our goals in the education oriented lab access through the Internet.

The main objective of this study is, thus, to develop an intelligent interface that can be used for the Internet access of robot supported laboratory. The main differences from the previously surveyed works that are already present in the literature are that the proposed system learns how to assess based on the user behavior while providing online robotics-enhanced experimentation, and coaches him/her towards the successful achievement of the tasks while evaluating user performances. Thus, the proposed approach is behavior-based task planning of online users by being a combination of concepts borrowed from intelligent tutoring, student modeling and Internet robotics. Some important properties of the system can be stated briefly as follows:

- From the nature of the Internet, the system serves to a diverse number of students each having different knowledge and skill levels. The system is adaptive to these different levels and provides each student with enough assistance for accomplishing the desired experiment and getting the necessary knowledge and experience.
- Assistance provided to the student is in the form of generated messages or mandatory commands such as the repetition of a previously failed step of the experiment.
- Students are assigned experiments having different complexity levels according to their past and present performances.
- The system grades students according to their performances, and stores grades and student profiles in a database.
- The system has an authentication module to ensure security and to recall a previous user from the database.

Fuzzy approach is most suitable for modelling user behaviours from a pattern matching point of view because of its abilities of generalization over the training data set to deal with the fuzzy nature of the user behaviour data. A rule-based system only on its own would require every combination of possible user behaviour data should be explicitly encoded within. Therefore employing a neural network is a feasible solution to the problem of modelling students while doing an online experimentation by using previously defined behaviour stereotypes.

2. Fuzzy expert systems

A fuzzy expert system is an expert system that uses fuzzy logic instead of Boolean logic. In other words, a fuzzy expert system is a collection of membership functions and rules that are used to reason about data. Unlike conventional expert systems, which are mainly symbolic reasoning engines, fuzzy expert systems are oriented toward numerical processing. The rules in a fuzzy expert system are usually of a form similar to the following:

if x is low and y is high then z = medium

Where x and y are input variables (names for know data values), z is an output variable (a name for a data value to be computed), low is a membership function (fuzzy subset) defined on x, high is a membership function defined on y, and medium is a membership function defined on z. The part of the rule between the "if" and "then" is the rule's premise or antecedent. This is a fuzzy logic expression that describes to what degree the rule is applicable. The part of the rule following the "then" is the rule's conclusion or consequent. This part of the rule assigns a membership function to each of one or more output variables. Most tools for working with fuzzy expert systems allow more than one conclusion per rule. A typical fuzzy expert system has more than one rule. The entire group of rules is collectively known as a rule base or knowledge base.

2.1 The inference process

With the definition of the rules and membership functions in hand, we now need to know how to apply this knowledge to specific values of the input variables to compute the values of the output variables. This process is referred to as inferencing. In a fuzzy expert system, the inference process is a combination of four subprocesses: fuzzification, inference, composition, and defuzzification. The defuzzification subprocess is optional. For the sake of example in the following discussion, assume that the variables x, y, and z all take on values in the interval [0, 10], and that we have the following membership functions and rules defined.

$$\text{Low}(t) = 1 - t / 10$$
$$\text{High}(t) = t / 10$$

Rule 1 : if x is low and y is low then z is high
Rule 2 : if x is low and y is high then z is low
Rule 3 : if x is high and y is low then z is low
Rule 4 : if x is high and y is high then z is high

Notice that instead of assigning a single value to the output variable z, each rule assigns an entire fuzzy subset (low or high). In this example, low (t)+high (t)=1.0 for all t. This is not required, but it is fairly common. The value of t at which low (t) is maximum is the same as the value of t at which high (t) is minimum, and vice-versa. This is also not required, but fairly common. The same membership functions are used for all variables.
A fuzzy rule based expert system contains fuzzy rules in its knowledge base and derives conclusions from the user inputs and fuzzy reasoning process. A fuzzy controller is a knowledge based control scheme in which scaling functions of physical variables are used to cope with uncertainty in process dynamics or the control environment. They must usually predefined membership function and fuzzy inference rules to map numeric data into linguistic variable terms (e.g. very high, young,) and to make fuzzy reasoning work. The linguistic variables are usually defined as fuzzy sets with appropriate membership functions. Recently, many fuzzy systems that automatically derive fuzzy if-then rules from numeric data have been developed. In these systems, prototypes of fuzzy rule bases can then be built quickly without the help of human experts, thus avoiding a development bottleneck. Membership functions still need to be predefined, however, and thus are usually built by human experts or experienced users. The same problem as before then arises: if the experts are not available, then the membership functions cannot be accurately defined, or the fuzzy systems developed may not perform well. A recent methodology was developed to automatically generate membership functions by Hong. et al. this methodology can be applied to a set of data used for a speaker independent voice recognition application.
The conventional practice of student performance practices used globally is based on the marks obtained in the courses opted. The marks are averaged for an overall estimation of the show of the students. In an advanced system the cumulative assessment is done in a group for awarding the grades based on the cumulative performance index (CPI) evaluated on the statistical model, agreed upon by the Academic Council of the University.
The attendance is taken as variable A_1 to A_N (Fig. 1.0) in the respective subjects, the overall attendance A_O is calculated on simple averaging function. The evaluated A_O is then taken into account for deciding whether the student will be allowed to appear in the examination or the student will be detained. This is based on simple comparison operator of less than or equal to the specified attendance. Once the student satisfies this condition of minimum attendance required, the student is made to appear in the examination. On the basis of evaluation of the answer sheets individualistic marks B_1 to B_N are derived for subjects 1,2, 3 … N respectively. As in case of attendance, the marks of individual subjects are also averaged to fetch overall

marks B_O. On the basis of this B_O the result of the student is formulated and a division based on characterization of marks range is done. Mathematically on the basis of overall attendance the students qualify to appear in the examination based on a crisp rule as

$$x : X \to \{0, 1\}, \text{ where } f_A(x) = \begin{cases} 1, \text{if } x \in A \\ 0, \text{if } x \notin A \end{cases}$$

Fig. 1.

Where X is the eligibility percentage of overall attendance, if the overall attendance is > 65%, $f_A(x)$ is 1, then the student is allowed to appear in the exam.
In an advanced conventional system a grading system is eviscerated which is based on the cumulative indexing of the students. This is also a linear method reporting the output of performance on the basis of comparative grading in a group.
The conventional system adopted by the academic institutions is well endeavored and is time tested. The intelligence or the cognitive performance derivation is lacking. Moreover the logical weaving of attendance and the marks obtained in a subject is not done, the outcome of this results in a standalone performance rating and is also not amicable for the parents to assimilate.

2.2 Architecture of a fuzzy expert system

Fig. 2 shows the basic architecture of a fuzzy expert system. Individual components are illustrated as follows.

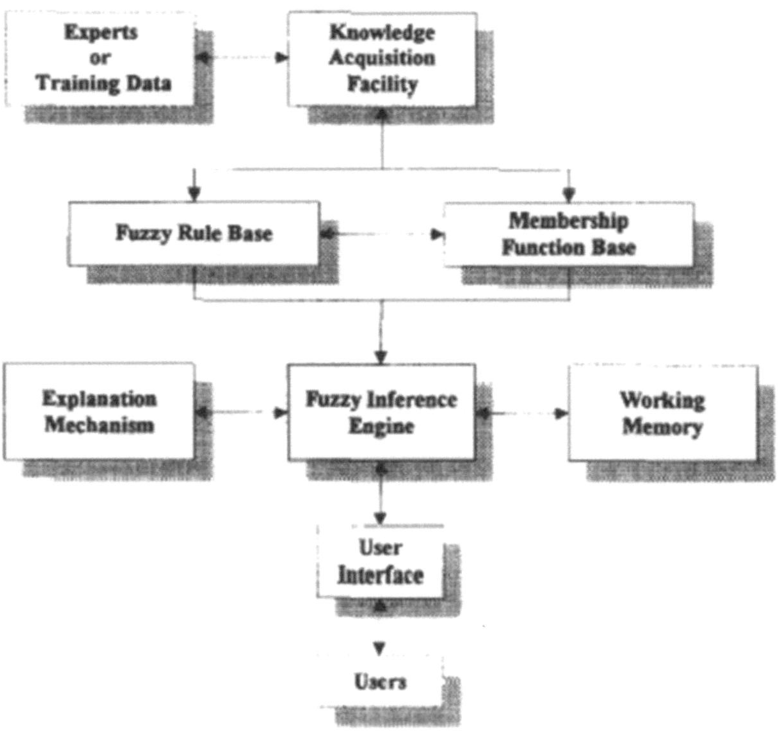

Fig. 2. Architecture of a fuzzy expert system

User interface: For communication between users and the fuzzy expert system. The interface should be as friendly as possible.
Membership function base: A mechanism that presents the membership functions of different linguistic terms.
Fuzzy rule base: A mechanism for storing fuzzy rules as expert knowledge.
Fuzzy inference engine: A program that executes the inference cycle of fuzzy matching, fuzzy conflict resolution, and fuzzy rule firing according to given facts.
Explanation mechanism: A mechanism that explains the inference process to users.
Working memory: A storage facility that saves user inputs and temporary results.
Knowledge-acquisition facility: An effective knowledge-acquisition tool for conventional interviewing or automatically acquiring the expert's knowledge, or an effective machine-learning approach to deriving rules and membership functions automatically from training instances, or both. Here the membership functions are stored in a knowledge base (instead of being put in the interface) since by our method, decision rules and membership functions are acquired by a learning method. When users input, facts through the user interface, the fuzzy inference engine automatically reasons using the fuzzy rules and the membership functions, and sends fuzzy or crisp results through the user interface to the users as outputs. In the next section, we propose a general learning method as a knowledge-acquisition facility for automatically deriving membership functions and fuzzy rules from a given set of training instances. Based on the membership functions and the fuzzy rules derived, a corresponding fuzzy inference procedure to process user inputs is developed.

2.3 Data-driven fuzzy rule based approach

Reasoning based on fuzzy approaches has been successfully applied for the inference of multiple attributes containing imprecise data; in particular, fuzzy rule-based systems (FRBS) which provide intuitive methods of reasoning have enjoyed much success in solving real-world problems. Recent developments in this area also show the availability of FRBS which allow interpretation of the inference in the form of linguistic statements whilst having high accuracy rates. The use of linguistic rule models such as "If assignment is very poor and exam is average then the final result is poor" helps capturing the natural way in which humans make judgements and decisions. Furthermore, historical data that is readily available in certain application domains can be used to build fuzzy models which integrate information from data with expert opinions. It is also important that the designed fuzzy models are interpretable by, and explainable to, the user . This section describes a newly proposed data-driven fuzzy rule induction method that achieves such objectives, and shows how the method can be applied to the classification of student performance. Description of Neuro-Fuzzy Classification (NEFCLASS) algorithm, which will be used later for comparison, is also given briefly in this section.

2.4 Inducting primitive machine intelligence in performance analysis and reporting by linear logic

The present scenario of performance evaluation is on the basis of a linear model where the result of the process is in terms of the division or the grades obtained by the student. The system is not capable of deriving cognitive inherence based on the attendance and the marks obtained. It is left to the student, parent and the employer to derive the performance on the division or the grades.

3. The logical engine

Several approaches using fuzzy techniques have been proposed to provide a practical method for evaluating student academic performance. However, these approaches are largely based on expert opinions and are difficult to explore and utilize valuable information embedded in collected data. This paper proposes a new method for evaluating student academic performance based on data-driven fuzzy rule induction. A suitable fuzzy inference mechanism and associated Rule Induction Algorithm is given. The new method has been applied to perform *Criterion-Referenced Evaluation (CRE)* and comparisons are made with typical existing methods, revealing significant advantages of the present work. The new method has also been applied to perform *Norm- Referenced Evaluation (NRE)*, demonstrating its potential as an extended method of evaluation that can produce new and informative scores based on information gathered from data. The need of the hour is to device a proposition where, an intelligent system sits inside the conventional system and deduce decisions based on the attendance and the marks obtained. Two sets are formulated Set A is for attendance and Set B is for marks obtained in the examination by the student.

$\mu_A(x)$: X $\rightarrow \{0, 1\}$, where

$$\mu_A(x) = 1 \text{ if x is totally in A; (Eligible)}$$

$$\mu_A(x) = 0 \text{ if x is not in A; (Not Eligible)}$$

$0 < \mu_A(x) < 1$ if x is partly in A.

3.1 The knowledge acquisition facility

A new learning method for automatically deriving fuzzy rules and membership functions from a given set of training instances is proposed here as the knowledge acquisition facility.

3.1.1 Notation and definitions

In a training instance, both input and desired output are known. For a m-dimensional input space, the ith training example can then be described as

$$(x_{i1}, x_{i2,} \dots, x_{im}; y_i),$$

where x_{ir} $(1 < r < m)$ is the rth attribute value of the ith training example and y_i is the output value of the ith training example.

For example, assume an insurance company decides *insurance fees* according to two attributes: *age* and *property*. If the insurance company evaluates and decides the insurance fee for a person of age 20 possessing property worth $30000 should be $1000, then the example is represented as (age = 20, property = $30 000, insurance fee = $1000).

3.1.2 The algorithm

The learning activity is shown in Fig. 3

A set of training instances is collected from the environment. Our task here is to generate automatically reasonable membership functions and appropriate decision rules from these training data, so that they can represent important features of the data set. The proposed learning algorithm can be divided into five main steps:

Step 1. cluster and fuzzify the output data;

Step 2. construct initial membership functions for input attributes;
Step 3. construct the initial decision table;
Step 4. simplify the initial decision table;
Step 5. rebuild membership functions in the simplification process;
Step 6. derive decision rules from the decision table.

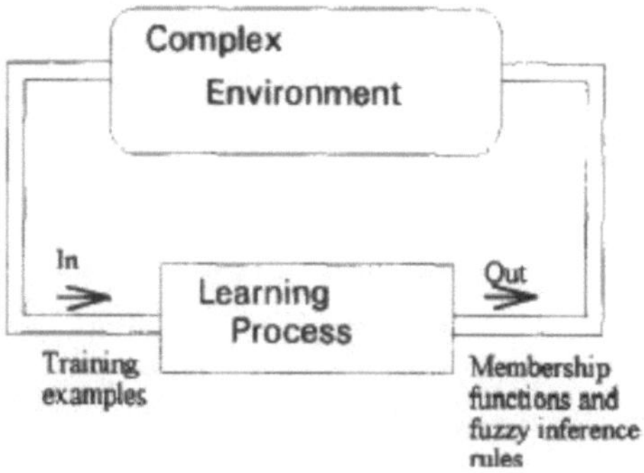

Fig. 3. Learning activity.

3.2 Weighted Subset Hood-Based Algorithm (WSBA)

Simplicity in generating fuzzy rules and the ability to produce high classification accuracy are the main objectives in the development of WSBA. To achieve these objectives, fuzzy subset hood measures and weighted linguistic fuzzy modelling are employed.

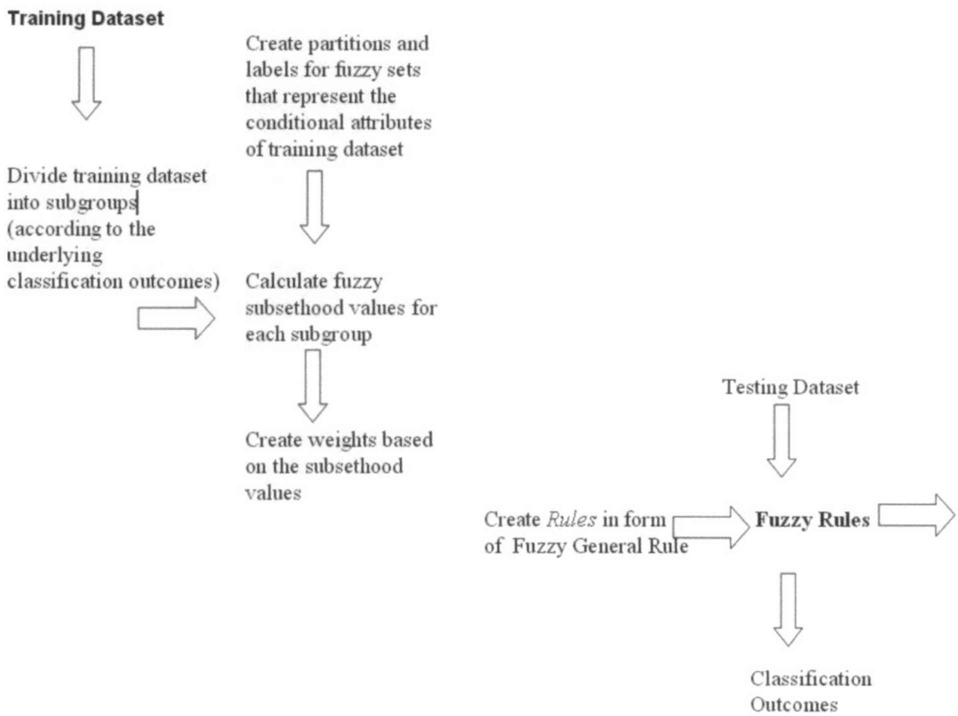

Fig. 4. Structure of WSBA Approach

This method does not require any threshold value and generates a fixed number of rules according to the number of classes of interest (i.e. one rule will be created for each class). In the process of generating fuzzy rules, linguistic terms that have a weight greater than zero will automatically be promoted to become part of the antecedents of the resulting fuzzy rules. Any linguistic term that has a weight equal to 0 will of course be removed from the fuzzy rule. This will make the rules simpler than the original default rules. In running WSBA for classification tasks, the concluding classification will be that of the rule whose overall weight is the highest amongst all. The structure of WSBA approach is shown in Figure 4. Example applications of WSBA can be found in.

3.3 Neuro-Fuzzy Classification (NEFCLASS)

Neuro-Fuzzy Classification (NEFCLASS) is an FRBS which combines a neural network learning approach with a fuzzy rule-based inference method . NEFCLASS can be encoded as a three-layer feedforward neural network. The first layer represents the fuzzy input variables, the second layer represents the fuzzy rulesets and the third layer represents the output variables. The functional units in this network implement t-norms and t-conorms, replacing the activation functions that are commonly used in conventional neural networks. NEFCLASS is a data-driven FRBS that has the ability to create fuzzy membership functions and fuzzy rules automatically from training instances. Prior knowledge in the form of fuzzy rules can also be added to the rule base and used alongside new rules created using the training dataset.

Fuzzy rules are generated based on overlapping rectangular clusters that are created by the grid representing fuzzy sets for the conditional attributes. Clusters that cover areas where training data is located are added to the emerging rule-base. The system allows the user to choose the maximum number of rules, otherwise the number of rules are restricted to that of just the best performing ones. The firing strength of each rule is used to reach the conclusion on the decision class of new observations.

The number of partitions and the shape of membership functions of the conditional attributes are user-defined. The rule learning process can be started, for example, using a fixed number of equally distributed triangular membership functions. A simple heuristic method is used for the optimization of membership functions. The optimization process results in changes to the membership function's shape by making the supports of the fuzzy set larger or smaller. Constraints can be employed in the optimization process to make sure that the fuzzy sets overlap each other.

NEFCLASS has undergone through several refinements over the years. For example, to enhance the interpretability of the induced fuzzy rules, NEFCLASS offers additional features such as rule pruning and variable pruning. The system has also been tested not only for classification of benchmark datasets but also for real world problems such as presented in.

3.4 Experimental results

The experiments presented in this section served as examples to illustrate the potential of WSBA for the evaluation of student performance. Note that a wide range of assessment methods are available and have been used (see for example), depending on the purpose to conduct the assessment. In this paper, only CRE and NRE are considered for the implementation. The objective of the experiment involving CRE is to provide evidence that the proposed algorithm will produce results similar to the original grades obtained using statistical methods, if an ideal and representative training data is available.

The objective of the experiment involving NRE is to show that WSBA is able to produce grades that can be used to provide additional information on the achievement of the students. In conducting these experiments, the following aspects have been taken into account:

In data-driven rule based systems, decision classes of the training instances are typically those given by experts. In students' performance evaluation, such decisions are normally given by experts based on an aggregation of numerical crisp scores. This method is used to obtain the decision class for the training data.

The small training data (SAP50A and SAP50B) is used as an example and in the form of numerical crisp scores, which is the most popular way to measure student performance. Note that the fuzzy approach allows the possibility of utilizing data in the form of fuzzy values such as those proposed in or in terms of linguistic labels that represent the fuzzy sets. In such cases, the decision class for the training data is determined by fuzzy values (see for example).

To avoid confusion, 'original score/grade' in this section will refer to the score and grade obtained from the use of the standard statistical mean and 'new score/grade' will refer to the score or grade obtained from existing fuzzy approaches, including WSBA and NEFCLASS. Note that both datasets used include only numerical scores, to facilitate comparison with other approaches. This need not be the case in general, the scores of individual assessment components may be given in fuzzy terms (as often the case for coursework grading for instances).

3.5 Criterion Referenced Evaluation (CRE)

NEFCLASS is used for further comparison, employing a fuzzy rule-based approach. The dataset used for the purpose of training WSBA and NEFCLASS models is a set of student performance records (labeled SAP50A). It consists of 50 instances, involving three conditional attributes: assignment, test and final exam, and five possible classification outcomes: Unsatisfactory (E), Satisfactory (D), Average (C), Good (B) and Excellent (A). Note that the term 'Average' describing students' performance used in this paper is not referring to the statistical average. For the sake of simplicity, only five linguistic labels similar to the classification outcomes are used to represent student achievements. The fuzzy partitions and labels are based on expert opinions representing the students' performance. The primary assumption is that the partitions chosen by experts are those best possible to represent the training data (SAP50A).

Clearly, better fuzzification, if available will help improve the experimental results reported below. Note that the given definition of the fuzzy sets is obtained solely on the basis of the normal distribution of the crisp marks given. This ensures their comparison with other approaches.

The classification of the grades in this experiment is based on an interval that refers to the level of performance given by experts. To facilitate a fair comparison, the same dataset consisting of 15 instances and having the same features as the training dataset is used for all of the methods. For instance:

Marks	Grade	Level of achievement
0-25	E	Unsatisfactory
26-45	D	Satisfactory
46-55	C	Average
56-75	B	Good
76-100	A	Excellent

It can be seen that the conventional fuzzy approaches produce different scores from the original (that is obtained by statistical mean). Thus, it is expected that when the new scores are translated into new grades, some of them may be different from the original grades. In particular, the results returned by the method of Biswas (1995), give rise to unexpected new scores such as case 10 where the original score of 61.67 (grade B) was downgraded to 35 (grade D). This is due to the approximation that is used in creating mid-grade points, and partly due to the use of fuzzy input values. Note that the use of mid-grade points has also resulted in a minimum score of 12.5 and a maximum score of 87.5, narrower than the original range.

Using Chen and Lee's method, all of the new scores are higher than the original. This is due to the use of maximum values of the degree of satisfaction created for each level of achievement. As for the results produced by Law's method, it is expected that the new scores will be different because the expected value for each grade has been predefined in advance according to the percentage of students who will receive a certain grade. Thus, results produced by this method may not reflect the students' true performance and they will be different if the expert evaluator changes the setting for the percentage.

By using the data-driven fuzzy rule-based approaches, fuzzy membership values obtained from fuzzy rules can be used to determine the new grade. Thus, it can be observed that the use of membership values in describing a student result has several advantages.

First, these membership values can be interpreted as how strong the student's performance belongs to a specific grade. This can be very useful in differentiating smoothly student performances over boundary cases, giving a second opinion in deciding on borderline performances.

Second, with the use of fuzzy values, further analysis of estimated performance can be carried out directly, without the need for fuzzification.

Third, the success of those methods in performing CRE will allow them to be used for NRE. This also provides the possibility that student performance evaluation can be carried out properly using fuzzy values and linguistic terms (Good, Excellent, etc.) rather than the traditional numerical crisp values.

4. Design of non-linear decision vector

The innovation in the present work is to create a logical mechanism which binds the attendance in the class room and the marks obtained in the examination by the student and to infer the decisions weaved on the sets A and B. This juxtapose will endeavor the performance of the student at the said instance and will also delineate the seed for prognostic modeling of futuristic performance of the students.

Mathematically, lowest memberships will be figured out by the intersection of two sets as

$$\mu A \cap B(x) = min\,[\mu A(x), \mu B(x)] = \mu A(x) \cap \mu B(x),$$

where x∈X
The highest memberships will be drawn out by the union of two sets as

$$\mu A \cup B(x) = max\,[\mu A(x), \mu B(x)] = \mu A(x) \cup \mu B(x),$$

where x∈X
Graphically it can be represented as

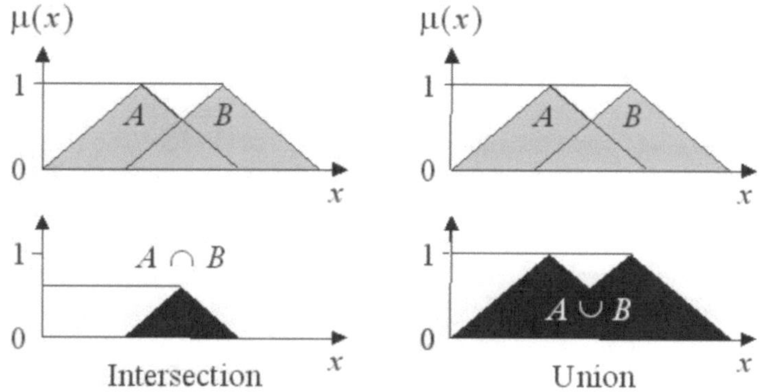

Fig. 5. Non-linear membership degree

The decisions DES41 and DES42 are derivative of the non-linear vector running simultaneously on the set A and set B for attendance and marks respectively. These high end decisions DES4x are being used for the suggestions to be included in the report of the student. These not only make this Communiqué system absolutely unique but also enthrall direction for probabilistic performance modeling of the student.
Mathematically the non-linear (dependent) vector is designed on the Sugeno Fuzzy inference and is as

$$\begin{array}{ll} IF & x \text{ is } A \\ AND & y \text{ is } B \\ THEN & z \text{ is } f(x,y) \end{array}$$

where *x*, *y* and *z* are linguistic variables; *A* and *B* are fuzzy sets on universe of discourses X and *Y*, respectively; and *f*(*x*, *y*) is a mathematical function. The zero order fuzzy model is applied where z is made constant as k.

5. Variables deduction

In the decision support system, the linear and non linear decisions are inferred through the decision vectors devised on the marks obtained and attendance of the student. So the different linguistic variables have been undertaken for the performance analysis and are deduced as follows:

1. The linguistic variables undertaken for the performance reporting of a student at the initial stage are DES1 and DES11 derived from the logical decision agent. These two variables are used for the Gender Confirmation of the student. If the sex of the student

in the student_master table is found to be "M" then the DES1 is set to "son" and the corresponding linguistic variable DES11 is set to "him". In the similar manner if the entry corresponding sex comes out to be false then DES1 is set to "daughter" and the variable DES11 set to "her". Both of these variables are embedded in the report while giving suggestions to the parents regarding their ward.

2. The degree of membership to attendance set A will formulate the linguistic variables DES21 and DES22. The DES21 is derived from the nested block of logical decision agent based on the membership in the set. The attendance of the student can be excellent, good, moderate or non-confirming depending on the regularity of the student. DES22 is the extended decision for suggesting the actions/ modifications to be undertaken by the student and the parent with respect to the overall attendance. While formulating the suggestion regarding attendance the decision variables DES1 and DES11 are also embedded wherever required.
3. On the basis of degree of membership to the marks obtained set B, DES31 and DES32 are formulated. Depending upon the marks obtained by the student, the membership assigns PASS or FAIL status to the student. Set B constitutes the pass students. DES31 determines whether the performance of the student is excellent, good, fair or non confirming. Variable DES32 is used for the suggestion based on the academic performance. It comprises of the individualistic decision based on the linear logical decision agents for attendance and marks obtained. While formulating the suggestion regarding marks DES1, DES11, SUBSHORT, DES21 and DES22 are embedded as per the prerequisite.
4. DES41 and DES42 are the decisions derived from the non linear vector running simultaneously on the set A and set B for attendance and marks respectively. These decisions are embedded for the suggestions regarding career selection given to the parents and are implanted at the end of the student's report.

6. Conclusion

This paper has presented examples of how a fuzzy rule-based approach can be used for aggregation of student academic performance and helps him in his career selection. It has been shown that the proposed approach has several advantages compared to existing fuzzy techniques for the evaluation of student academic performance.

In CRE, the use of fuzzy membership values to determine the decision is very helpful for the user to understand why the new grade was awarded. In CRE, the proposed method has the potential to be developed further for use as an extended method of evaluation by providing new grades that refer to achievements of other groups. The membership values produced by this method are also more meaningful compared to the values produced by statistical standardized-score.

However, it is worth noting that the newly proposed fuzzy approach is not to replace the traditional method of evaluation; instead it is meant to help strengthen the system that is commonly in use, by providing additional information for decision making by the user.

In this paper, WSBA is proposed to be employed for this purpose because of the simplicity of the method. It has been shown that although WSBA employs a simple approach, the proposed method is able to provide classification similar to that produced by more sophisticated algorithm such as NEFCLASS. Of course, more complex fuzzy rule-based methods such as those based on Evolutionary Computation, Fuzzy Clustering and Neural Networks may also be used. However, the simpler approach has an advantage in terms of transparency and understandability of the methods and its results. The proposed method also provides room for other improvements.

In particular, interpretability of learned fuzzy rules has always been regarded as a very important factor in FRBS but has not been sufficiently addressed in this paper. Thus, further research should include this very important issue. As an approximate modellling approach, WSBA has the advantage in producing fuzzy systems of high classification accuracy, but the use of crisp weights to modify fuzzy terms is rather unnatural and may lead to confusion regarding the semantics of the resulting systems. However, the structure of WSBA rulesets enables the system model to be adapted with fuzzy quantifiers , making the model more interpretable whilst maintaining its accuracy.
Also, the creation of fuzzy partitions to be used for WSBA are currently based on expert opinion and partly from statistical information on the training data. The fuzzification is not in any way optimized. Further research should include the use of methods that generate better fuzzy partition automatically from data.The proposed method also provides room for other improvements. In particular, interpretability of learned fuzzy rules has always been regarded as a very important factor in FRBS but has not been sufficiently addressed in this paper.
Thus, further research should include this very important issue. As an approximate modellling approach, WSBA has the advantage in producing fuzzy systems of high classification accuracy, but the use of crisp weights to modify fuzzy terms is rather unnatural and may lead to confusion regarding the semantics of the resulting systems.
However, the structure of WSBA rulesets enables the system model to be adapted with fuzzy quantifiers , making the model more interpretable whilst maintaining its accuracy.
Also, the creation of fuzzy partitions to be used for WSBA are currently based on expert opinion and partly from statistical information on the training data. The fuzzification is not in any way optimized. Further research should include the use of methods that generate better fuzzy partition automatically from data.
Thus, The proposed approach can significantly reduce the time and effort needed for the performance evaluation of large number of students and help build intelligent communiqué system. Based on membership functions and fuzzy rules derived, a corresponding fuzzy inference procedure to process the inputs is developed. Embedding the decision support system fuzzy logic and decision trees , we found that our model gives a rational result, few rules and high performance.

7. References

Y. Caballero, R. Bello, A. Taboada, A. Nowe, M. Garcia, and G. Casas, "A new measure based in the rough set theory to estimate the training set quality", *Proc.8th Int. Symp. Symbolic and Numeric Algorithms for Scientific Computing*, pp.133-140, 2006.

B. Chapman and B. Hall, *Learning Content Management System.* Brandonhall.com, New York, 2005.

Z. Chen, *Computational Intelligence for Decision Support*, CRC Press, 2000.

K. Cios, W. Pedrycz, and R. Swiniarski, *Data Mining Methods forKnowledge Discovery*, Kluwer Academic Publishers, 1998.

C.W. Holsapple and A.B. Whinston, *Decision Support Systems: AKnowledge-Based Approach*, West Publishing Company, 1996.

X. Hu, "Using rough sets theory and database operations to construct a good ensemble of classifiers for data mining application", *Proc.IEEE ICDM*, pp.233-240, 2001.

J. Komorowski, L. Polkowski, and A. Skowron, "Rough sets: A tutorial", In S.K. Pal and A. Skowron (eds.), *Rough Fuzzy Hybridization: A New Trend in Decision-Making*, Springer, pp.3-98, 1999.

A. Lenarcik and Z. Piasta, "Probabilistic rough classifiers with mixture of discrete and continuous variables", In T.Y. Lin and N. Cercone (eds.), *Rough Sets and Data Mining: Analysis for Imprecise Data*, Kluwer Academic Publishers, pp.373-383, 1997.

D. Miao and L. Hou, "A comparison of rough set methods and representative inductive learning algorithms", *Fundamenta Informaticae*, vol.59, pp.203-218, 2004.

P. Pattaraintakorn, N. Cercone, and K. Naruedomkul, "Hybrid intelligent systems: Selecting attributes for soft computing analysis", *Proc.29th Int.Conf. Computer Software and Applications*, pp.319-325, 2006.

S. Pal and P. Mitra, "Case generation using rough sets with fuzzy representation", *IEEE Trans. Knowledge and Data Engineering*, vol.16, no.3, pp.292-300, 2004.

Z. Pawlak, "Rough sets", *Int. Journal of Information and Computer Science*, vol.11, no.5, pp.341-356, 1982.

Dhawan, A. K. and Kaur,K. (2009). Artificial Intelligence and Fuzzy Expert Systems. *International Conference on Artificial Intelligence and Computational Intelligence (AICI'09)*. Shanghai, China: IEEE-CS.

Z. Pawlak, J. Grzymala-Busse, R. Slowinski, and W. Ziarko, "Rough sets", *Communications of the ACM*, vol.38, no.11, pp.88-95, 1995.

J. Peters, D. Lockery, and S. Ramanna, "Monte Carlo off-policy reinforcement learning; A rough set approach", *Proc. 5th Int. Conf. Hybrid Intelligent Systems*, pp.187-192, 2005.

F. Radermacher, "Decision support systems: Scope and potential", *Decision Support Systems*, vol.12, pp.257-265, 1994.

A. Skowron and C. Rauszer, "The discernibility matrices and functions in information systems", In R. Slowinski (ed.), *Intelligent Decision Support, Handbook of Applications and advances of the Rough Set Theory*, Kluwer Academic Publishers, pp.331-362, 1992.

R. Swiniarski, "Rough sets and principal component analysis and their applications in feature extraction and selection, data model building and classification", In S. Pal and A. Skowron (eds.), *Fuzzy Sets, Rough Sets and Decision Making Processes*, Springer, 1998.

L. Yang and L. Yang, "Study of a cluster algorithm based on rough sets theory", *Proc. 6th Int. Conf. Intelligent Systems Design and Applications*, pp.492-496, 2006.

W. Ziarko, "The discovery, analysis, and representation of data dependencies in databases", In G. Piatetsky-Shapiro and W.J. Frawley (eds.), *Knowledge Discovery in Databases*, AAAI Press, pp.195-209, 1991.

Shapiro, Stuart C. (1992), "Artificial Intelligence", in Shapiro, Stuart C., Encyclopedia of Artificial Intelligence (2nd ed.), New York: John Wiley, pp. 54–57, http://www.cse.buffalo.edu/~shapiro/Papers/ai.ps .

Simon, H. A. (1965), The Shape of Automation for Men and Management, New York: Harper & Row

H.R. Berenji, Fuzzy logic controller, in: R.R. Yager and L.A. Zadeh, Eds. An Prognostic modeling. Introduction to Fuzzy Logic Applications in Intelligent Systems (Kluwer Academic Publishers, Dordrecht, 1992)

D.G. Burkhardt and P.P. Bonissone, Automated fuzzy knowledge base generation and tuning, IEEE Internut.Conf: on Fuzzy Systems (San Diego, 1992) 179-1 88.

Graham and P.L. Jones, Expert Systems Knowledge, Uncertainty and Decision (Chapman and Computing, Boston. 1988) I 17-1 58.

K. Hattori and Y. Tor, Effective algorithms for the nearest neighbor method in the clustering problem. Pattern Recognition 26 (1993) 741-746.

4

Question-Answer Shell for Personal Expert Systems

Petr Sosnin
Ulyanovsk State Technical University, Russia

1. Introduction

In the near future a ubiquitous computerization of all spheres of the modern human activity, including various forms of the collective activity, will lead to conditions of a life when all population of the Earth will be involved in interactions with computers. Therefore, in usages of computers by the person it is necessary to aspire to a naturalness of such attitudes. The naturalness should be achieved in that sense that any usage of a computer should be embedded in the activity in accordance with its essence.

Any activity is a naturally-artificial process created on the base of a definite set of precedents the samples of which are extracted from the appropriate experience and its models. Such role of precedents is explained with the help of the following definition: "précédents are actions or decisions that have already happened in the past and which can be referred to and justified as an example that can be followed when the similar situation arises" (Precedent, 2011).

Accessible samples of precedents are necessary means for the activity but in a general case such means can be insufficiently. If absent means will be found and the necessary activity will be created then the new sample of precedent can be built for the reuse of this activity. Hence, told above entitles to assert that "the creation and reuse of precedents defines the essence of the human activity."

Each unit of the fulfilled activity must be modeled by the useful way, be investigated and be coded for its reuse as the precedent. In the life all these actions are similar to creating the programs for the building of which a natural language in its algorithmic usage is applied. Moreover such programs as behavioral schemes are built for tasks which have been solved for already created units of the activity. So, any sample of the precedent can be understood as a program which is coded previously at the natural language (in its algorithmic usage) for the task aimed at the creation of the definite activity unit.

Such understanding of precedents samples allows assert, that any person is solving continuously tasks, programming them in a natural language because the human life is based on precedents. Any person has an experience of programming in a natural language in its algorithmic usage. Let's name such possibility of programming as "a natural programming of a human" (N-programming). Any human has a personal ability of the N-programming the experience of which depends on a set of precedents which have been mastered by the person in the own life.

One can count any human as an expert who owns the valuable information about personal precedents. Such information can be extracted from the human by the same human and can be used for creating the knowledge base of an expert system built by the human for the own usage. In the described case one can speak about the definite type of expert systems which will be named below as personal expert systems (or shortly be denoted as ES^P).

The definite ES^P should be created by the person who fulfills roles of the expert, developer and user of such computer assistant. Such type of expert systems should have the knowledge base containing the accumulated personal experience based on precedents. To create the own personal expert system the human should be provided simple, effective and powerful instrumental means. The Question-Answer shell (QA-shell) which is described in this chapter is a system of such means. QA-shell is built on the base of the instrumental system WIQA (Working In Questions and Answers) previously developed for conceptual designing of software intensive systems.

A very important specificity of QA-shell and ES^P is a pseudo-programming (P-programming) which is used for the creation of precedents samples and also for the work with them in the real time. The language L^{PP} of the P-programming is similar to the natural language in its algorithmic usage. Therefore the P-programming is similar to the N-programming and such similarity essentially simplifies its application in the creation of precedents samples and their use. This specificity takes into account the ordinary human who have decided to use the computer for solving own tasks based on precedents.

The next important specificity is connected with executors of P-programs. There was a time when computers have not been existed and when N-programs of precedents were being executed by certain persons (by intellectual processors or shortly by I-processors). Computer programs (or shortly K-programs) are being executed by computer processors (or shortly K-processors). Any P-program in the ES^P is being executed by I-processor and K-processor collaboratively.

The last important specificity is the "material" which is used by the human for writing data and operators of the P-programs on its "surface". This "material" consists of visualized forms for data originally intended for modeling questions and answers in processes of problem-solving. The initial orientation and features of such type of data are being inherited by data and operators of P-programs and for this reason they are declared as P-programs of the QA-type. In further text the abbreviation of QA will use frequently to emphasize the importance of question(s) and answer(s) for the construction(s) labeled by QA.

2. Question-answering and programming in subject area of expert systems

2.1 Logical framework for precedent model

The use of the precedent as a basic unit of the human interaction with own surrounding demands to choose or build adequate patterns for precedents representations. Appropriate patterns should provide the intellectual mastering of precedents and their natural using by the ordinary person.

In accordance with the author opinion the necessary model for the definite precedent can be created on the base of the following logical framework:

Name of precedent P_i:

choice

while [logical formulae (LF) for motives **M ={M_k}**]

as [LF for aims C = **{C_l}**]

if [LF for precondition U'= {U'_n}],

then [plan of reaction (program) $\mathbf{r_q}$],

end so [LF for postconditions **U" = {U''_m}**]

----

there are alternatives **{$P_j(r_p)$}**.

This framework is a human-oriented scheme the human interaction with which activates the internal logical process on the level of the second signal system in human brains. Such logical processes have a dialog nature and for keeping the naturalness the interaction processes outside brains should keep the dialog form also.

The logical framework is used in ES^P for creating the precedents models and keeping them in the knowledge base. This fact can be used for indicating the difference between the suggested ES^P and known types of ES. It also distinguishes ES^P from systems which use case based reasoning (CBR). Measured similarity between cases and the access to them in the form of "cases recognition" are the other differences between CBR-systems and ES^P.

Let's notice that any ES is a kind of rules-based systems any of which are "software systems that applies the rules and knowledge defined by experts in a particular field to a user's data to solve a problem". Any precedent model can be understood as a rule for its owner and it opens the possibility to define the class of personal expert systems. The shell which is described below helps humans in the creation of expert systems belonged to this class.

2.2 Question-answering in creation and usage of precedents samples

There are three ways for the appearance of the precedent sample. The first way is connected with the intellectual processing of the definite behavior which was happened in the past but was estimated by the human as a potential precedent for its reuse in the future. The second way is the creation of the precedent sample in parallel with the its first performance and the third way is an extraction of the precedent model from another's experience and its models. In any of these cases if the precedent sample is being created as fitting the logical framework and filling it by the appropriate content then the human should solve the retrieval and extraction tasks of the necessary information from useful sources.

Named tasks of the retrieval and extraction should be solved in conditions of the chosen framework and the usage of diverse informational sources including different kinds of texts and reasoning. In the solving of this task the important role is intended for the mental reasoning. Taken into account all told above the question-answering has been chosen by author for retrieval and extraction of informational elements needed in the creation of precedents samples. Question-Answering (or shortly QA) is a type of "an information retrieval in which a direct answer is expected in response to a submitted query, rather than a set of references that may contain the answers"(Question, 2011) .

There were many different QA-methods and QA-systems which have been suggested, investigated and developed in practice of the informational retrieval and extraction (Hirschman, 2001). Possible ways in the evolution of this subject area were marked in the

Roadmap Research (Burger, 2001) which is actual in nowadays. This research has defined the system of concepts, classifications and basic tasks of this subject area.
Applying concepts of the Roadmap Research we can assert that QA-means which are necessary for working with precedents samples should provide the use of "interactive QA" and "advanced reasoning for QA" (Question, 2011). In interactive QA "the questioner might want not only to reformulate the question, but (s)he might want to have a dialogue with the system". The advanced reasoning is used by questioner who „expects answers which are outside the scope of written texts or structured databases" (Question, 2011). Let's remind, that one of informational sources for the creation of precedents samples is mental reasoning in dialog forms.
QA-means are effective and handy instruments not only for the creation of the precedents samples but for their use also. Sequences of questions and answers which had been used in the creation stage of the precedent can be used for the choice of the necessary precedent sample.

2.3 Programming in the work with precedents samples

The important component of logical framework is a reaction plan of the human behavior which should be coded in the precedent sample for the future reuse. Before the appearance of computers and frequently nowadays the ordinary human used and uses the textual forms for registering plans of reactions. If the plan includes conditions and-or cycles then, its text is better to write in pseudo-code language similar to the natural language in its algorithmic use. In this case the reaction plan will have the form of P-program.
The reaction plan in the form of P-program is being created as a technique for solving the major task of the corresponding precedent. The other important task is connected with the search of the suitable sample including its choice in a set of alternatives.
In ES^P both of these tasks should be solved and P-programmed by the human for their reuse in the future with the help of computer by the same human. Hence, a set of effective and handy means should be included to ES^P for writing and fulfilling QA-programs supporting the work of the human with precedents samples.
There is a feature of P-programs oriented on the work of the human with precedents and their samples. As told above any P-program in ES^P is being executed by I-processor and K-processor collaboratively where the role of I-processor is fulfilled by the human. The idea of the human model as I-processor is inherited by the author from a set of publications (Card, 1983; Crystal, 2004) where described the model human processor (MH-processor) as an engineering model of the human performance in solving the different tasks in real time.
The known application of the MH-processor is Executive Process-Interactive Control (EPIC) described detailly in (Kieras, 1997). Means of EPIC support the programming of the human interaction with the computerized system in the specialized pseudo-language Keystrok Level Model (KLM). A set of basic KLM actions includes the following operators: **K -** key press and release (keyboard),**P -** Point the mouse to an object on screen, **B -** button press or release (mouse), **H -** hand from keyboard to mouse or vice versa and others commands. Means of I-processor should support QA-interactions of the human with the precedent reuse process. The major part of such interactions consists of the execution of P-programs embedded to the current precedent sample. The main executor of P-programs is the human who fulfills the role of I-processor.

2.4 Co-ordination of I-processor and K-processor

MH-processor is defined (Card, 1983) as a system of specialized processors which solve the common task collaboratively. One of these processors is a cognitive processor providing mental reasoning the basic form of which is an implicit dialog (question-answer reasoning, QA-reasoning). Let's count that I-processor is similar to MH-processor and includes the cognitive component with its named natural functions.

It is easy to agree that for saving the naturalness the implicit QA-reasoning as a natural form of the cognitive processes inside I-processor should "be translated" and transferred to K-processor as an obvious QA-reasoning. Hence, K-processor should include the embedded QA-processor supporting the work with obvious QA-reasoning (or the work with question and answers). Such combining of processors provide their natural coordination in the collaborative work managed by the human reasoning.

Combining of processors is schematically presented in Fig. 1 which is inherited and adapted from Fig. 1 of the ACM SIGCHI Circulium for Human-Computer Interaction (Hewett, 2002).

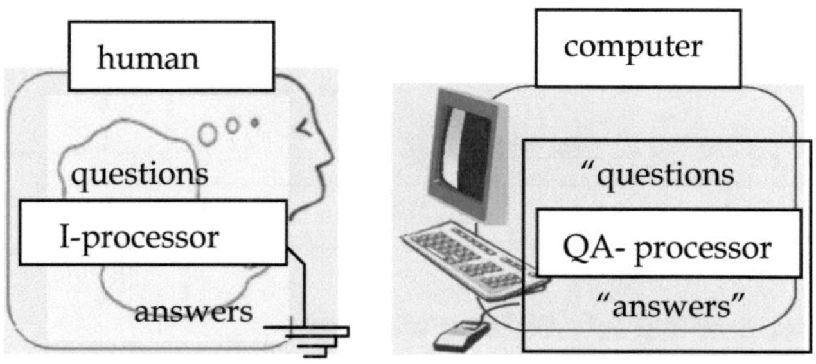

Fig. 1. General question-answer scheme of CHI

In scheme the question is understood by the author as the natural phenomenon which appears at the definite situation when the human interacts with the own experience (own precedents). In this case the „question" is a symbolic (sign) model of the appropriate question. Used understanding helps to explain the necessity of fitting the „question" in QA-processes. Implicit questions and answers exist in reality while „questions" and „answers" present them as sign models.

3. QA-processor and its applications

3.1 Conceptual solution of project tasks

The system named WIQA has been developed previously as QA-processor for the conceptual designing of the Software Intensive System (SIS) by the method of conceptual solving the project tasks.

In most general case the application of a method begins with the first step of QA-analyzing the initial statement of a development task $Z^*(t_0)$. In special cases of its application the initial statement of a task is included in a task tree corresponded to the design technology with which it will be used. The dynamics of the method is presented schematically in Fig.2.

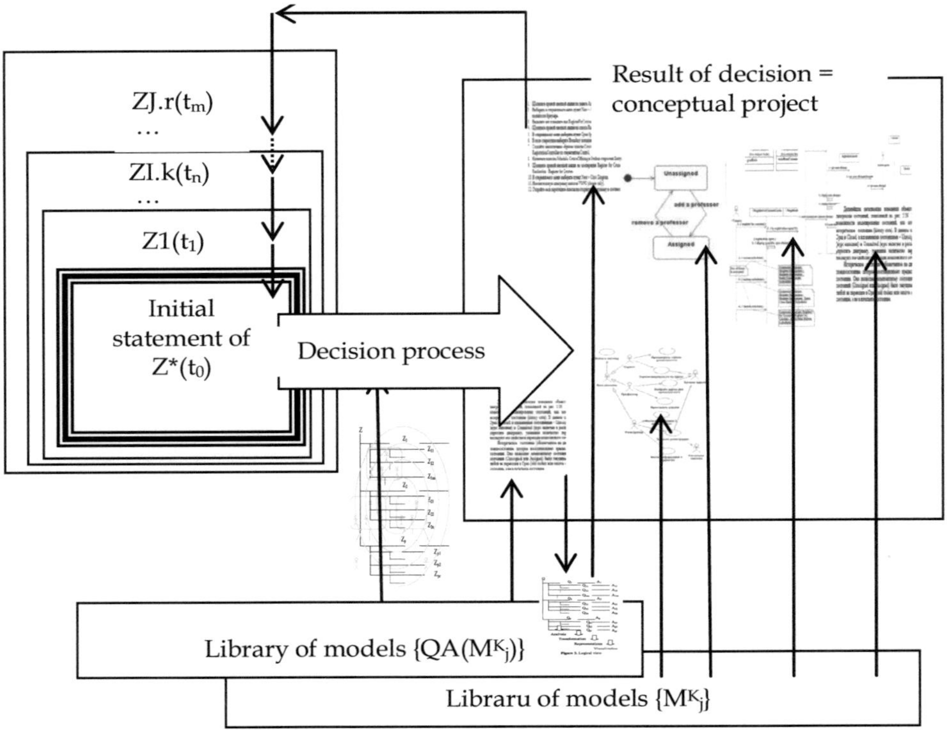

Fig. 2. Dynamics of conceptual solving the project task

The system of tasks of conceptual designing the SIS is being formed and solved according to a method of the stepwise refinement. The initial state of the stepwise refinement is defined by the system of normative tasks of the life cycle of SIS which includes the main project task $Z^*(t_0)$. The base version of normative tasks corresponds to standard ISO/IEC 12207.

The realization of the method begins with the formulation of the main task statement in the form which allows starting the creation of the prime conceptual models. The initial statement of the main task formulates as the text $Z^*(t_0)$ which reflects the essence of the created SIS without details. Details of SIS are being formed with the help of QA-analysis of $Z^*(t_0)$ which evolves the informational content of the designing and includes subordinated project tasks ($Z1(t_1)$, …, $ZI,k(t_n)$, …, $ZJ,r(t_m)$) in the decision of the main task.

The detailed elaboration of SIS forms the system of tasks which includes not only the project tasks connected with the specificity of SIS, but also service tasks, each of which is aimed at the creation of the corresponding conceptual diagram or document. The solutions of project and service tasks are chosen from libraries of normative conceptual models $\{M^k\}$ and service QA-techniques $\{QA(M^k_i)\}$.

During conceptual decision of any task (included in a tasks tree of the SIS project) additional tasks can be discovered and included to the system of tasks as it shown in Fig. 3. The tasks tree is a dynamic system which is evolved iteratively by the group of designers. The step-wise refinement is used by any designer who fulfils QA-analysis and QA-modeling of the each solved task. General conceptual decision integrates all conceptual decision of all tasks included in a tasks tree of the project.

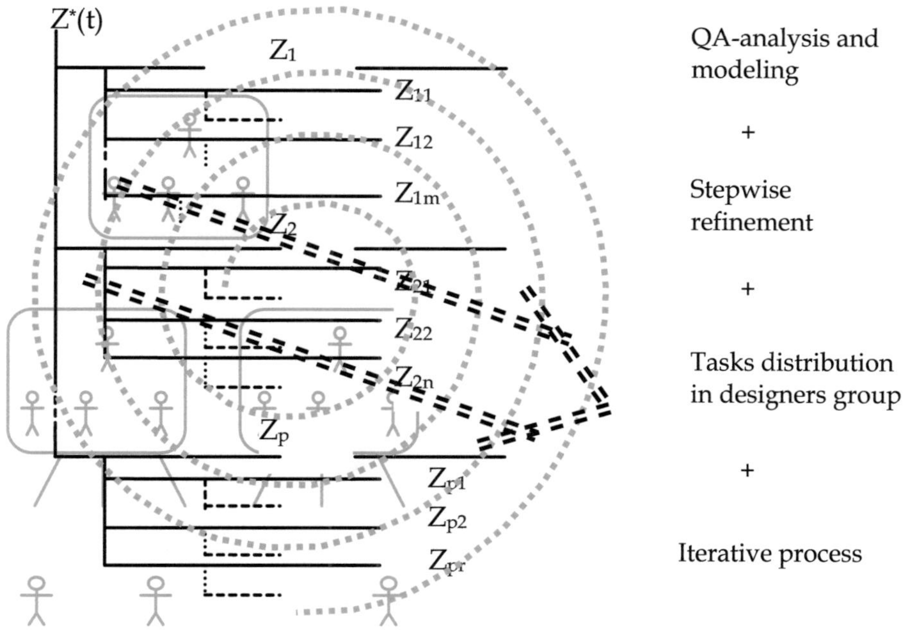

Fig. 3. Task tree of development process

The conceptual solution is estimated as the completed decision if its state is sufficient for the successful work at the subsequent development stages of SIS. The degree of the sufficiency is obviously and implicitly checked. Useful changes are being added for achieving the more adequate conceptual representation of SIS.

Thus, the conceptual solution of the main project task is defined as a system of conceptual diagrams with their accompanied descriptions at the concept language the content of which are sufficient for successful coding of the task solution. Which conceptual diagrams are included to the solution depends on the technology used for developing the SIS.

As a related works which are touched QA-reasoning, we can mention the reasoning in the "inquiry cycle" (Potts, 1994) for working with requirements, "inquiry wheel" (Reiff, 2002) for scientific decisions and "inquiry map" (Rosen, 2008) used for the education aims. Similar ideas are used in the special question-answer system which supports the development of SIS (Henninger, 2003). The typical schemes of reasoning for SIS development are presented in (Bass, 2005), in (Yang, 2003) reasoning is presented on seven levels of its application together with the used knowledge and in (Lee, 2000) model-based reasoning is presented as useful means for the software engineering.

3.2 Question-answering in WIQA

The conceptual solution of any project task is based on QA-analysis and QA-modeling. QA-analysis provides the extraction of questions from the task statement and searching and formulating the answers on them. QA-modeling helps to combine questions and answers in QA-model of the task and its parts and for checking them on the correctness and conformity.

Named QA-actions are fulfilled by designer who translates internal QA-reasoning and registers them in QA-database of WIQA. All these works are implemented with using the visual forms presented in Fig. 4. This form fulfils the role of an inter-mediator between I-processor and QA-processor. The language of WIQA is Russian therefore fields of the screenshot are marked by labels.

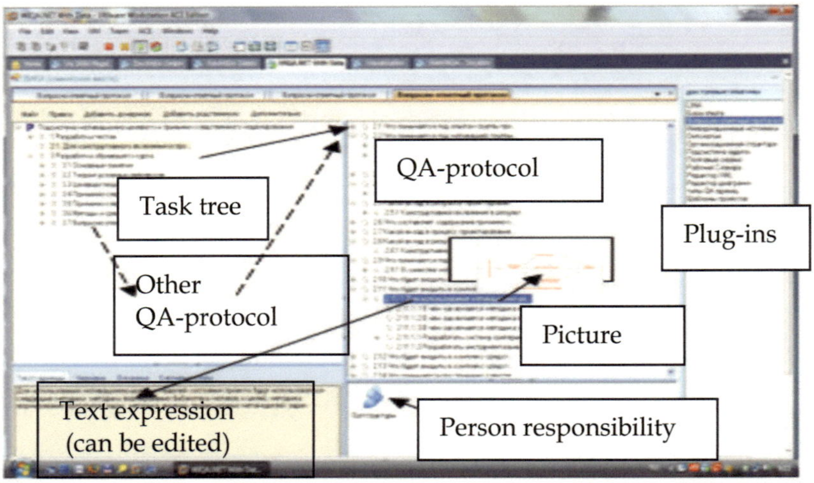

Fig. 4. The main form of QA-processor.

The responsibility for evolving the tasks tree, defining tasks statements and building for them adequate QA-models is laid on designers. For this work they use any informational sources not only mental reasoning. One of these sources is a current content of tasks tree and the current state of QA-model for each task. Therefore a set of commands are accessible to designers for interactions with tasks, questions and answers which are visualized in the main form. The additional commands are accessible via plug-ins of WIQA.

The usage of QA-model of task is a specificity of WIQA as a Question-Answering system. Any QA-model is being formed as an example of QA-sample which is defined as a set of architectural views on the materialization of the model. This set includes, for example, the task view, logical-linguistic view, ontological view and views of other types each of which is being opened for designers with the help of specialized plug-ins.

Question-answer models, as well as any other models, are created "for extraction of answers to the questions enclosed in the model". Moreover, the model is a very important form of representation of questions, answers on which are generated during the interaction with the model. Any designer can get any programmed positive effect with the help of the access to the "answer" on the chosen question actually or potentially included in the appropriate view of QA-model (Fig. 5).

The definite set of questions and answers are available to the designer via visual "side" of QA-model named as QA-protocol the structure of which is presented in Fig. 6.

The field of QA-protocol is marked in the screenshot presented above. The designer can use any visual task for the access to the corresponding QA-protocol. Further the designer can use any question Q_i or answer A_j for the access to the content of the corresponding QA-model. One can interprets labels of Z-, Q- and A-elements at the main interface form as visual addresses of corresponding Z-, Q- and A-objects.

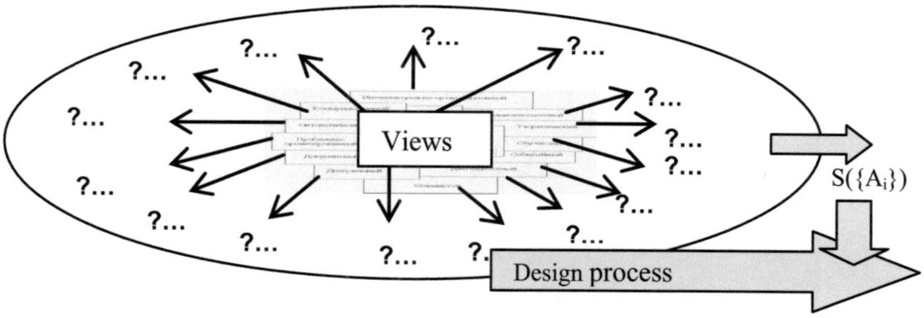

Fig. 5. QA-model of the task

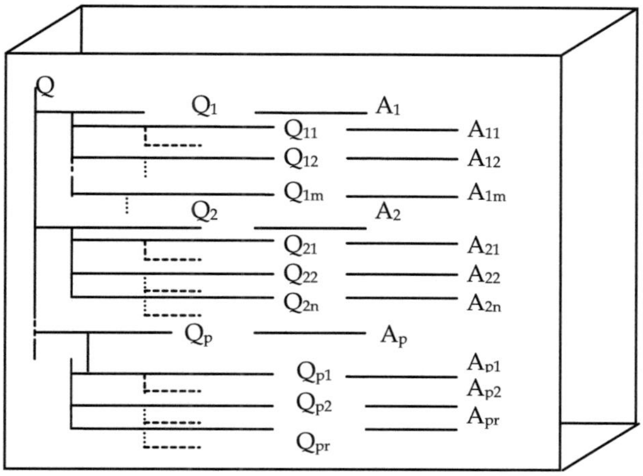

Fig. 6. QA-protocol of QA-model

Any label has a unique code which includes a capital letter (Z, Q, A, or other) and its index appointed automatically. Any capital letter is presented by the icon and indicates the type or subtype of the visualized object. In WIQA there are means for creating the new icons.

The content of such interactive objects are not limited only their textual and graphical expressions which are accessible to the designer via the main interface form. Other "sides" of any QA-model and any interactive object of Z- or Q- or A-type are accessible via plug-ins of WIQA.

3.3 Applications of WIQA

QA processor WIQA has been implemented in several versions. Elaborations of two last versions were based on architectural views of QA-model and the usage of repository, MVC, client-server and interpreter architectural styles. Moreover in created versions have been used object-oriented, component-oriented and service-oriented architectural paradigms. One of the last versions named as NetWIQA has been programmed on Delphi 6.0 and the second version (named as WIQA.Net) has been created on C# at the platform of Microsoft.Net 3.5.

The structure of WIQA, its functional possibilities and positive effects are described in a set of publications of the author. The features of WIQA are reflected by its general components structure presented in Fig 7 on the background of QA-model to emphasize that components are working with the common QA-database.

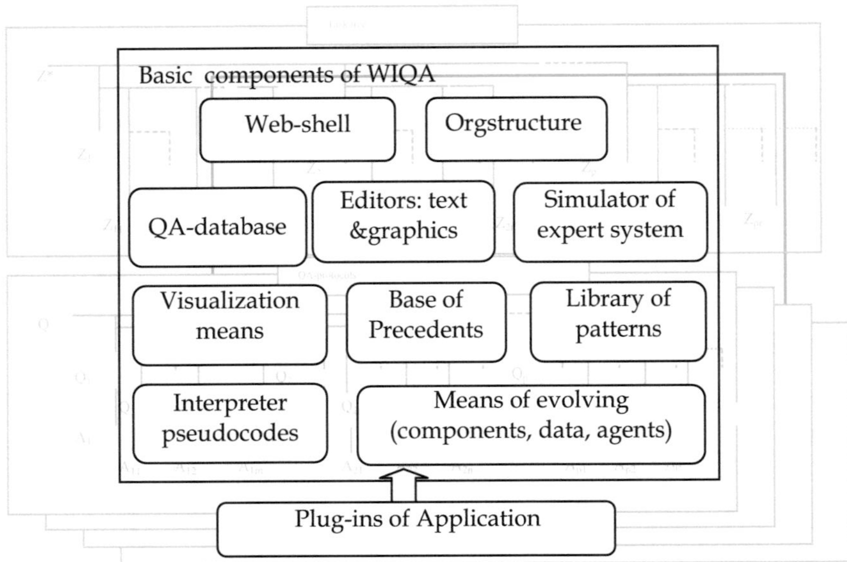

Fig. 7. Components structure of WIQA

As told above WIQA has been created for designing the SIS. The practice of this activity has shown that WIQA can be used as a shell for the creation of some applications. By present time on the basis of this shell, for example, the following applications have been elaborated: DocWIQA for the creation and manage of *living documents,* EduWIQA for the automated teaching, TechWIQA for technological preparation for production and EmWIQA for the expert monitorng of the sea vessel surrounding.
The last application of WIQA is QA-shell for personal expert systems which is being described in this chapter. This QA-shell inherits basic means of WIQA and evolves them by necessary plug-ins supporting the activity based on precedents. Some inheritances were described above and consequently some features of ES^P are already presented.

4. Elaboration of expert system on the base of WIQA

4.1 Question-answer modeling the basic tasks of expert system

The description of ES^P will be continued in the form of its elaboration in WIQA with the inheritance basic means of WIQA, and also their necessary modifying and evolving. First question is about QA-modeling the typical tasks of ES without their orientation to ES^P. The answer this question is connected with immersing the ES into WIQA which is schematically presented in Fig. 8.
The "Block and line" view in Fig 8 is chosen specially, so that it corresponds to the typical scheme of the ES. The structure of the ES is presented on the background of QA-model and also as early for emphasizing the functional style of immersing the ES to its model of QA-type.
The corresponding task should be defined and programmed for each block of ES in its chosen immersing. The tasks structure and the definition of each necessary task can be presented in WIQA in the form of the tasks tree. Each task of this tree can be solved conceptually by the step-wise refinement method. After that each built solution should be distributed between I-processor and QA-processor and necessary computer components should be programmed. In such approach to the elaboration of ES one can assert that possibilities of WIQA means are used for the emulation of ES in WIQA as into the instrumental shell.

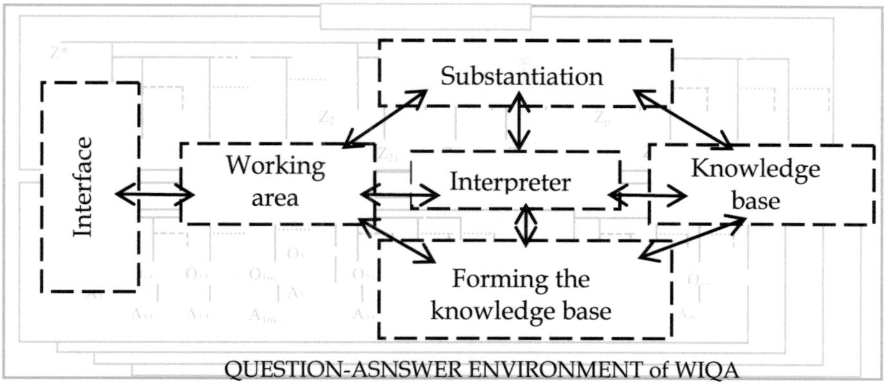

Fig. 8. Emulation of ES in WIQA

First all works named above have been fulfilled for the specialized ES with knowledge base oriented on its filling by samples of precedents extracted from international rules for collision avoidance at sea (COLREG-72) (Cockcroft, 2003). After that the work was repeated creatively and QA-shell for ES^P has been elaborated. Thus the elaboration of the own ES^P is implemented as creating the SIS of the ES^P type.

The usage of Question-Answering is the main specificity of both elaborations which opens for the human the right QA-access not only to the knowledge base (precedents base). The human has the direct access to any task of the tasks tree of ES or ES^P and therefore to any QA-protocol or QA-model in any its state. The human can use such uniform access for the analysis of solution processes in any interval of time and for modeling the evolving the events in ES or ES^P.

4.2 Composite structure of precedent samples

The creation of the new precedent sample P_i is a specially important for the human who elaborates and uses the own ES^P. Such creation is being implemented technologically as the elaboration of SIS also but SIS of the precedent type. This point of view opens the possibility for registering a set of elaboration states in life cycle of precedent (Fig. 9)

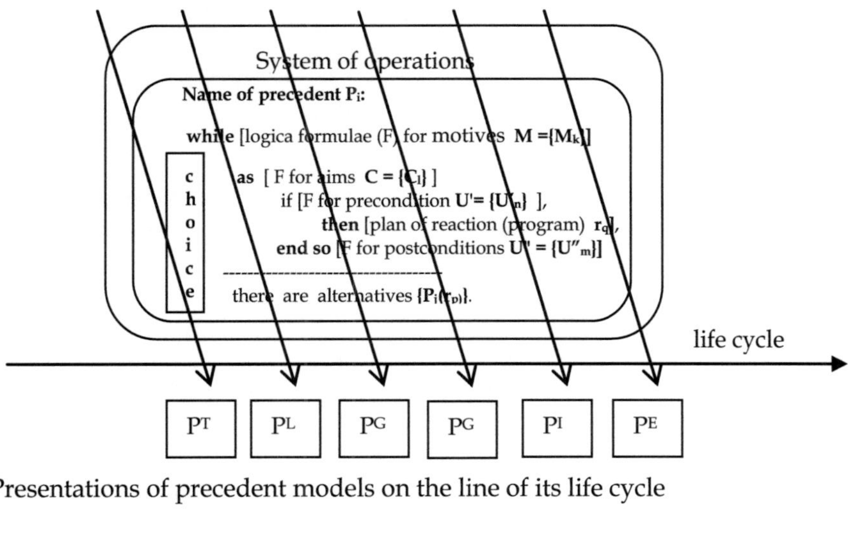

Fig. 9. Presentations of precedent models on the line of its life cycle

This set includes the following useful precedent models: P^T - textual precedent description, P^L - logical (predicate) model, P^G - graphical (diagrammatic) model, P^{QA} - question-answer model, P^I - source program code and P^E - executed code. All of these models are included to the typical materialization of the precedent sample in the knowledge base (precedets base).
The composite structure of the precedent sample and the specificity of its production units were chosen for their usage by I-processor firstly and for the usage by K-processor secondly. The first version of the typical precedent sample which was used for coding the rules of COLREG'72 is presented in Fig. 10. This version is included to QA-shell of ES^P

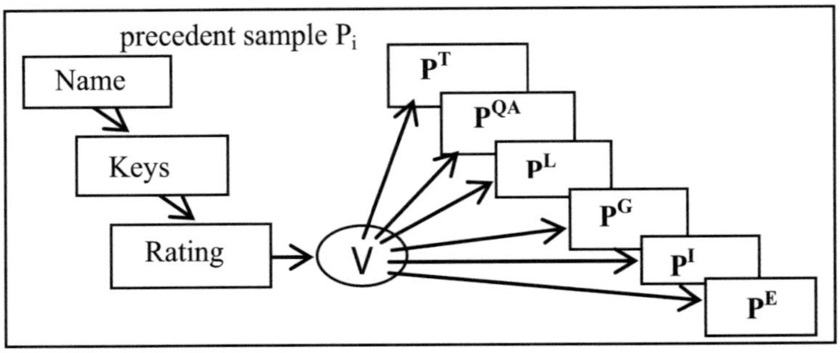

Fig. 10. Structure of the typical precedent sample in the knowledge base of EmWIQA

Precedents used in EmWIQA are accessible as for the user (sailor on duty) so for software agents which are presenting the vessels in the definite sea area. The usage of the automatic access of the vessel agent to the precedents sample in EmWIQA has led the author to the second version of precedents samples which uses P-programming for the work with conditions and reactions in samples of precedents in the form of software agents (Fig. 11).

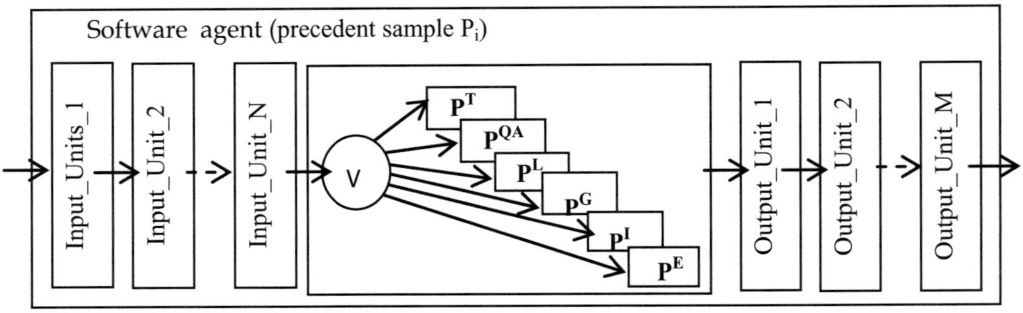

Fig. 11. Precedent sample as a sotware agent

In the second version any precedent sample is presented as an autonomous software unit the access to which is being processed in accordance with conditions of the precedent usage. It is supposed that conditions are defined and described by the person (human) in text form in the natural language (from this point of text we will use the word „person" instead the word „human" to emphasize the context of the personal expert system).
The input text is being processed step by step by a set of input units (morfologic analyzer, ontological filter,key words filter, compiler of condition). If the precedent sample has been chosen and the corresponding precedent has been fulfilled then a set of output units can be activate automated by the person and automatically for registering post-conditions (events on blackboard, output data). The second version is included to QA-shell of ES^P partially.

5. Pseudo-programming in WIQA

5.1 QA-approach to P-programming

The ordinary person in own ES^P should have the possibility for programming the behavior embedded to the precedent sample. As told above the best way for fulfilling such work is the use of P-programming which is supported by handy automated means included to WIQA.

Any P-program is better for understanding as the code of interactions of the person with the corresponding precedent. In WIQA the normative way for interactions is QA-reasoning. Hence is better to adapt the means of QA-reasoning for their use in P-programming. For such adaptation it is necessary to find the ways for emulations (wuith the help of QA-reasoning) data and operators of the appropriate language of P-programming.

Expressions of data and operators of P-programs by means of QA-reasoning is only one part of QA-approach to P-programming. This part should be expanded by the interpreter which transforms any written P-programs in collaborative actions of the person and computer.

Both named parts of QA-approach to P-programming are defined and implemented with their orientation on the ordinary person. To distinguish P-programs of such type from other P-programs they have been named QA-programs.

The type of QA-data has been defined for expressions of data and operators by means of QA- reasoning. Features of this type D will be opened on the example of its simple subtype which consists of a "question" Q_i and appropriate "answer" A_i which haven't the subordinated "questions" and "answers". In this case the "name" and "value" of the definite data D_i are written in attributes of Q_i and A_i which are intended for the textual expression of Q_i and A_i in QA-database. All other attributes Q_i and A_i are inherited by D_i.

The attributes structure of D_i is presented in Fig.12 where not only attributes of QA-database are indicated but additional attributes which are defined by the user also. In general case QA-data are an association of simple data each of which is based on the corresponding pair of Q_i and A_i.

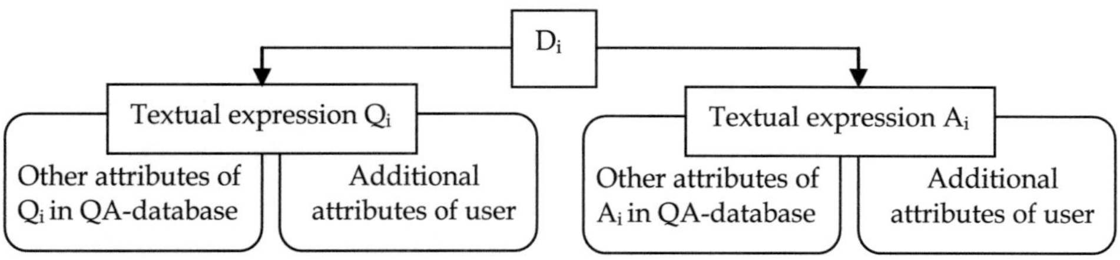

Fig. 12. Attributes stricture of the simple QA-data

Means of additional attributes (AA) are embedded to WIQA for simplifying the elaboration of new plug-ins. The mechanism of AA implements the function of the object-relational mapping of QA-data to programs objects with planned characteristics. One version of such objects is classes in C#. The other version is fitted for pseudo-code programming. The scheme which is used in WIQA for the object-relational mapping is presented in Fig. 13.

The usage of the AA is supported by the specialized plug-ins embedded in WIQA. This plug-ins helps the user to declare the necessary attribute or a group of attributes for definite Z-, Q- and A-elements. In any time the user can view declared attributes for the chosen element. Other actions with the AA must be programmed in C# or in the pseudo-code language supported by WIQA.

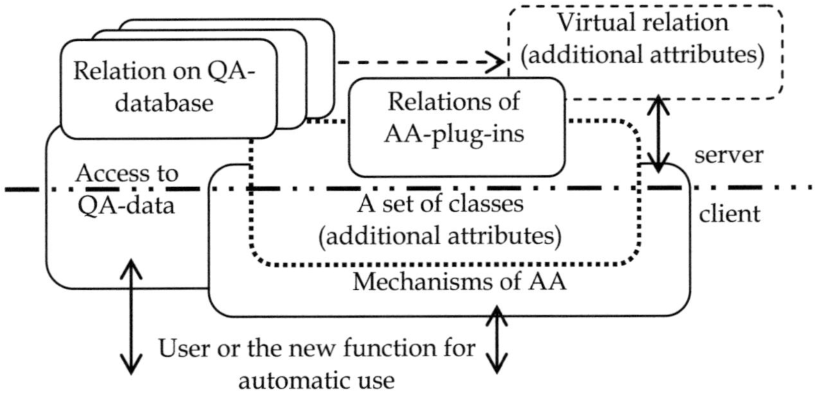

Fig. 13. Creation of additional attributes

Thus in D_i the field for the textual expression of Q_i can be used for writing the declaration of the necessary element of data or operator of P-program. In this case the corresponding field for the textual expression of Ai will be used for coding the "value" of data or the result of the operator execution.

Hence, any line of any P-program is possible to write on the "surface" of the corresponding Q-element which can be interpreted as a "material for writing" with useful properties. This "material" consists of visualized forms for writing the string of symbols. The initial orientation and features of such type of strings are being inherited by data and operators of P-programs and for this reason they are declared as P-programs of QA-type. In order to separate this type of P-programs from P-programs of the others types, they will be named as QA-programs. Such name of P-programs is rightful as the pseudo-code text of any line can be qualified as a "question" on which the interpreter of QA-program builds the corresponding "answer".

5.2 Emulation of pseudo-code data

There are two types of lines of the source pseudo-code one of which intends for the data emulation and another for the operator emulation. Let's begin to describe the emulation of QA-data.

First of all the AA-mechanism was used for the creation a subset of objects imitated the typical data (such as scalars of traditional types, array, record, set and list) in the forms of packed classes (Fig. 14).

For the declaration of variables the constructor of QA-data has been developed. This constructor gives the possibilities to name QA-variable, to choose its type and to appoint the initial value of the variable. The constructor can be used as the self-dependent utility or can be embedded to the translator of pseudo-programs which is implemented as a compiler and an interpreter (in two versions).

Let's remember that any unit of QA-data is created for its use by I-processor firstly and for the computer processor secondly. The visualized declaration of QA-data of the necessary type and the touchable appointment of the necessary visual value take into account the interactions possibilities of I-processor. But any declared QA-variable is accessible automatically for the appropriate programs executed by the computer processor also.

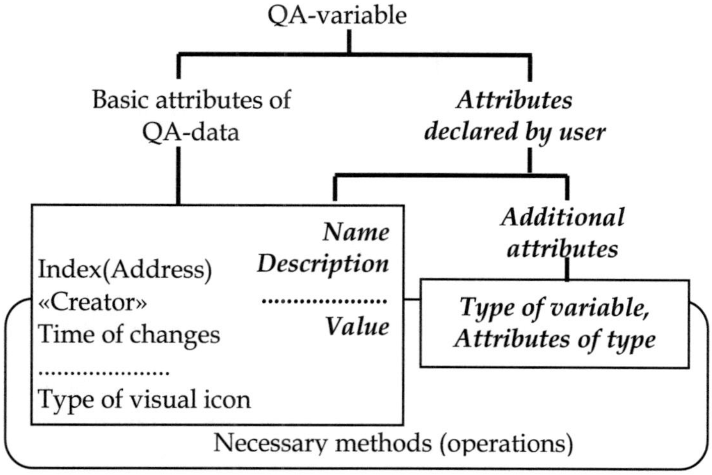

Fig. 14. Imitation of variable

As told above there is a pssibility to create and use the icon for the necessary types or subtypes for Z-, Q- and A-objects. QA-variables can be qualified as a definite type of Q- and A-objects. For this type the icons for letters D and V instead of icons for letters Q and A are created and used.
An example of keeping the array with elements of the integer type is presented in Fig. 8 where a set of additional attributes are used for translating the array declaration to computer codes.

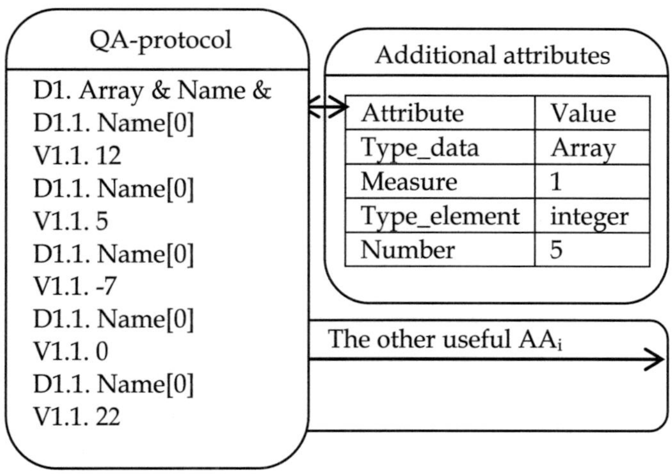

Fig. 15. Declaration of array

Attributes which are assigned for the array are visually accessible for the person at any time and can be used not only for translating. The person can add useful attributes to the set of array attributes for example for describing its semantic features which will be checked in creating and executing QA-program.
Let's open some features of additional attributes for data declarations. For the chosen Q-element the person can appoint not only the definite attribute AA_m but the type T_k of AA_m with characteristics of type T_k and also a set of subordinated attributes $\{AA_{mn}\}$ with the

appropriate type T_n for each of which. All these attributes and types with their values can be used by the person in the creation of QA-programs. Such possibilities help the person in P-programming the work with semantics of QA-variables. The named effects can be used in P-programming the planned or real time work with pseudo-code operators also.

5.3 Emulation of pseudo-code operators

The second type of pseudo-code lines are intended for writing the operators. As it was for QA-data we can define for operators the next interpretations:

- "question" is " a symbolic presentation of an operator";
- "answer" indicates by the special marker about "the fact that the operator was fulfilled".

In other words, the string of symbols for the "question" can be used for writing (in this place) the operator in the pseudo-code form. The fact or the result of the operator execution will be marked or registered in the string of the symbol for the "answer". Such version of emulating the operator has been named as QA-operator. The expression of any QA-operator can be understood as the „question" about the action which is coded. The execution af QA-operator builds the „answer" this „question".

The next step in the emulation of operators is connected with taking into account types of operators. For simulating the basic pseudo-program operators the next constructions were chosen:

- **Appoint**: "question" → "name of variable" and "answer" → "appoint the value;
- **Goto:**"question" → "condition" and "answer" → "go to the definite operator of QA-program;
- **If:** «question» → «condition» **Then** «answer» → **«Execute** the definite operator»;
- **Command**: "question" →" the command of QA-processor" and "answer" → "execute the command";
- **Function**: "question" → "definition of function" and "answer" → "compute the value";
- **Procedure**: "question" → "definition of procedure" and "answer" → "execute the procedure".
- **End**: "question" → "end of program" and "answer" → "finish the work with QA-program".

In named operators the following definitions of functions and procedures are used:

- any function is defined as the expression written in the P-language;
- any procedure is a typical sequence of actions which are accessible in QA-processor for the execution by the person.

The set of basic operators includes traditional pseudo-code operators but each of which inherits the feature of the appropriate QA-unit also. Hence, the basic attributes of QA-unit and necessary additional attributes can be taken into account in processing the operator and not only in its translation. In order to underline the specificity of operators emulation they will be indicated as QA-operators.

In pseudo-programming languages a set of basic operators is being expanded usually. In the described case the expansion includes cycle-operators such as «**for**», "**while-do**" and «**do-until**». Emulations of QA-data and QA-operators are implemented in WIQA and provide the creation of pseudo-code programs for different tasks.

As for QA-variables the special icons for letters „O" (for operator) and „E" (is executed) have been created and used instead icons for letters „Q" and „A". The person can defined and labeled subtypes of QA-operators. The person can appoint additional attributes for any QA-operator and such attributes can be used obviously in the text of QA-program, for example, for operations with comments included to QA-program lines.

6. Specimens of QA-programs

6.1 Types of QA-programs

Any QA-program creates for the division of the problem-solving process among the person an computer. In this case the division is presented in the form of the source pseudo-code the interactions with which are used as the person so the computer. The definite task of human-computer interactions can be solved with the help of its QA-programming.

But interactions on the base of QA-programs have the additional features. These features are implemented in interactions of persons with Z-, Q- and A-objects which are used for registering the lines of pseudo-code source of QA-programs. As told above such interactive objects open very useful positive effects for persons.

Both named features define the essence of QA-programming for I-processors firstly and for computer processors secondly. The basic aim of the interaction is the access to the person experience in the precedents forms for its inclusion to the problem-solving processes.

The structure of any precedent includes a condition part and a part of a reaction each of which should be QA-programmed. The value "truth" in the estimation of the conditional part opens the access to the execution of the appropriate reaction. Therefore QA-programs for estimating the conditions of precedents and QA-programs for executing the reaction part of precedents are two basic types of QA-programs.

But as told above, some QA-programs can be written for their translating and executing as computer programs. Some of such QA-programs can be created for supporting the work with "precedents" in the definite application. The system of QA-programs was created by author for the collision avoidance expert system of the sea vessel.

QA-programs, which are oriented on the computer execution, are useful in cases when the direct access to the visualized data is profitable for example for developers of SISs or for their users (documenting, decision-making, expert estimating and other tasks). Such programs are suitable when the library of QA-templates (not precedents samples) can be created for a set of typical tasks solving in SISs. The possibility of working with QA-templates and the library of templates are included to WIQA.

For the real time working of I-processor with precedents the following QA-program scheme is useful:

```
QA-PROGRAM_1(condition for the access to the precedent):
D1. Variable V_1 / Comment_1?
V1.Value of V_1.
D2. Variable V_2 / Comment_2?
V2. Value of V_2.
..............................................
DN. Variable V_M / Comment_M?
VN. Value of V_M.
OJ. F = Logical expression (V_1, V_2, …, V_M)?
AJ. Value of Expression.
End.
```

It is necessary to notice that the person can build or to modify or to fulfill (step by step) the definite example of this program in the real time work with the corresponding precedent which, it may be, the person creates. In presented typical scheme the logical expression is defined for the function F.

The next typical scheme reflects the work with techniques programmed as QA-procedures:

QA-PROGRAM_2 (technique for the typical task):
P1.K_i, K_j, …, PL_k ?
E1. *
P2. K_m, QA-P_n, …, K_q?
E2.*
………………………………
PN. K_s, Pl_t, …, QA-P_v?
EN. #
End.

The program text includes the symbolic names K_x and Pl-y for the Command and Plug-ins of WIQA and QA-P_z for QA-program written by means of WIQA. It is necessary to notice that all names of the types K_x, Pl-y and QA-P_z are indicated positions on the monitor screen for initiating the actions by touch of the person. In this typical scheme the symbols "*" and "#" (as "yes" and "no") indicate the facts of the execution for operators.

The following fragment of the Outlook reset actions demonstrates (without E-units) one type of QA-procedures:

P1. Quit all programs.
P2. **Start** On the menu **Run**, click.
P3. **Open** In the box **regedit**, type, and then **OK** the click.
P4. Move to and select the following key:
HKEY_CURRENT_USER/Software/Microsoft/Office/9.0/Outlook/
P5. In the Name list, **FirstRunDialog** select.
P6. If you want to enable only the **Welcome to Microsoft Outlook** greeting, on the Edit menu **Modify**, click the type **True** in the Value Data box, and then **OK** the click.
P7. If you also want to re-create all sample welcome items, move to and select the following key:
HKEY_CURRENT_USER/Software/Microsoft/Office/9.0/Outlook/Setup
P8. In the **Name** list, select and delete the following keys: **CreateWelcome First-Run**
P9. In the **Confirm Value Delete** dialog box click **Yes** , for each entry.
P.10. On the **Registry** menu, click **Exit**,.
P11. End.

This type provides the work of the person with service techniquea of the definite application. WIQA and QA-shell are examples of such application. About three hundred typical techniques are implemented as QA-programs for designing the SISs with instruments of WIQA. A half of these QA-programs are the guide type. To remember such (or more) quantity of QA-programs are impossile. Therefore all typical QA-programs are kept in the special library. Any QA-program of this library is kept in the special area of QA-database and registered in its catalog which is visually accessible to the person. Let's notice that the greater part of WIQA techniques are being inherited by QA-shell for ES^P.

If the person needs to use the typical QA-program (needs to solve the typical task with QA-model implemented as QA-program) the person extracts the typical QA-program from the library, creates the new task, includes the task to the tasks tree and after such actions the person can start to solve the task (to execute the corresponding QA-program).

The reality of the person activity is a parallel work with many tasks at the same time. Therefore the special interpreter for executing QA-procedures and the system of interruption are included into WIQA. It gives the possibility to interrupt any QA-procedure (if it is necessary) for working with other QA-programs. The interruption system supports the return to any interrupted QA-program to its point of the interruption.

6.2 Example of QA-functions

As told above WIQA was used for elaboration the application EmWIQA provided the expert monitoring of the sea vessel surrounding. This application uses the base of precedents and means of QA-programming. The behavior of users in EmWIQA can be qualified as the potential behaviour of the person in ES^P. Therefore QA-programs in EmWIQA can be used as examples of QA-programs in ES^P.

One of such QA-programs is QA-function supports the access to the precedent sample which presents the 15th rule of the International Rules for Preventing Collisions at Sea (Cockcroft, 2003):

QA-PROGRAM_3 (conditional access to the precedent).
D1. Velocity V_1 of the power driven vessel V_1?
V1.Value of V_1.
D2. Bear_B_1 of the vessel V_1?
V2.Value of B_1.
D3. Place of the vessel V_1?
V3. Coordinates of the place_1.
D4. Velocity V_2 of the power driven vessel V_2?
V4.Value of V_2.
D5. Bear_B_2 of the vessel V_2?
V5.Value of B_2.
D6. Place of the vessel V_2?
V6. Coordinates of the place_2.
O7.CPA = expression for computing the Closest Point of Approach (CPA)?
E7. Value of CPA.
O8. Cond = (V_1, "keep out of the way")&
& (| Bear_1 - Bear_2 | > 11, 5°) &
& ($CPA\text{-}D^{DA}\text{-} \Delta D_1 \leq 0$)?
E8. Manoeuvre_M_i / Call of the appropriate QA-procedure.
O9. End.

This QA-function is shown with demonstrated aims only and therefore without explaining the variables and expressions. This function is kept in the knowledge base (with embedded precedents) into the EmWIQA and function is accessible for program agents (automatically) and for the sailor on duty (in the automated regime). The knowledge base of the EmWIQA consists of 155 units each of which includes QA-function for choosing the precedent and QA-procedure for its executing.

7. Means for development and usage of personal expert systems

7.1 Additional means of WIQA

As told above AS-shell of ES^P inherits the basic means of WIQA presented in Fig. 7. These means include the simulator of expert system elaborated previously for EmWIQA, base of precedents with their coding in the first version and the interpreter which uses the means of the dynamic compilation of Microsoft.Net 3.5. After estimation all of these means from the point of view of ES^P the WIQA has been evolved with the orientation on the ordinary person.

The additional technological QA-programs have been added to the specialized system of QA-programs simulating the expert system. The first version of coding the precedent sample is modified by the inclusion to it the possibility of QA-programming the conditional access to the sample (morphologic analysis of key words and compilation of QA-functions). The language of P-programming has been modified by the inclusion to its grammar the description of additional attributes.

Following components have been developed and included in the ES-shell additionally:

- a set of translators (compilers and interpreters) of QA-programs;
- a specialized generator of interface units for helping the person to combine QA-programs and executed codes of other types;
- a set of means for simplifying the work of the person aimed at the creation of precedent samples, their inclusion to the precedents base, access to the necessary sample and its use.

7.2 Translators of QA-programs

Translation means for the pseudo-programming are evolved step by step from one kind of QA-programs to the other kind. Two compilers and two interpreters are embedded in QA-shell for ES^P.

The first compiler provides the processing of QA-programs which describe the conditional parts of precedents. Copies of such compiler can be embedded by the person to the precedent samples implemented as agents. The second compiler supports the translation of QA-programs in the executed codes (.dll-forms).

Both interpreters are intended for I-processors. There are the following differences between interpreters - the first interpreter can work with cycle operators and the second interpreter uses the mechanism of the dynamic compilation for the current line of QA-program which is being executed.

Let's present some details for the first interpreter. As other translators embedded in WIQA this interpreter is worked with the L^P-language. The lexicon of the created QA-program can be chosen by the programmer (by the person). For the declaration of QA-data the specialized utility program is developed. This utility program supports the work with data of traditional algorithmic types. The main window of the interpreter is presented in Fig. 16 with commentary labels.

Interfaces of the main form help to control as executing QA-program so its debugging. The person who is fulfilling the role of I-processor can interrupt I-process on any operator of QA-program with the possibility of returning to the point of the interruption.
In the set of named translators for indicating the types of operators the following variants has been used and checked:

- inclusion the key words into the symbolic presentation of operators;
- selection the type of the operator from the emerging menu;
- appointment the type with the help of additional attributes (as for QA-data).

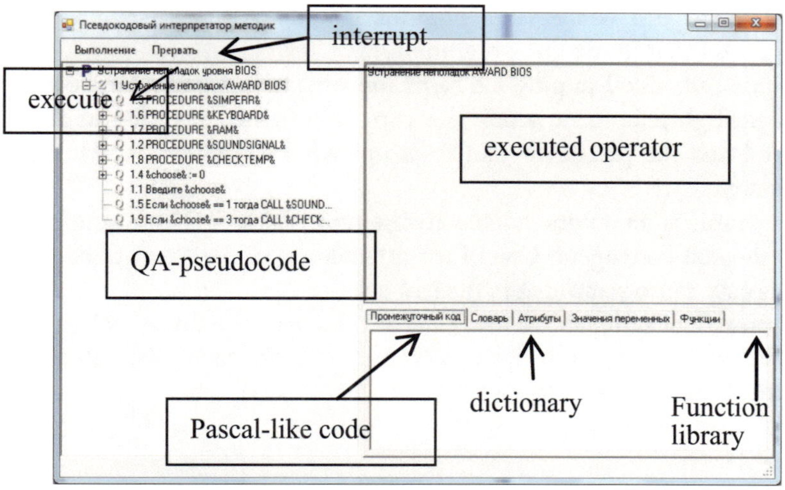

Fig. 16. Screenshot of interpreter

In accordance with told above, the usage of the potential of Z-, Q- and A-objects for emulating the typical data and simulating the basic program operators opens the possibility to create QA-programs which can be translated for their executing by computer processors also.
Pseudo-code texts of QA-programs can be written and executed (in the real time) by the person working in the corporate network. The person interacts with QA-programs as with inter-mediators between the person and computers and it gives the arguments to qualify their as new type of means for human-computer interactions. Moreover, such inter-mediators can be translated (in WIQA) firstly to the C# source code and then to the executed code.

7.3 Generator of interface units

The practice of QA-programming has shown that visual forms of WIQA presented in Fig. 4 are unsufficient for the usability of QA-programs created by the person in ES^P. Therefore the plug-ins „Generator of interface units" has been created and embedded to QA-shell.
The necessary interface unit is being generated from the drawn interface diagram which is being translated to the scheme of the corresponding QA-program. After that the scheme of QA-program is filling by the chosen interfaces precedents.

Any interface precedent is coded the corresponding metrics of usability. A set of usability metrics includes a subset of metrics which are defined in the standard ISO/ MEK-9126. Other metrics were chosen from other useful sources. Any metrics included to the library are defined as an appropriate task which is solved in QA-shell.

7.4 Creation and usage of precedent sample

Any precedent sample is coded as a composite QA-program the integrity of which is provided by its interface shell. The special plug-ins of WIQA which was named „Elaboration of precedent sample" has been created for writing the codes of sample parts and assembling them as a whole. This plug-ins is similar to the elaboration means of traditional programs but it fits on QA-programming.

The graphic editor embedded to plug-ins helps the person to assemble the current sample by filling its typical graphic form which is a copy of scheme presented in Fig. 11. When assembling is finished the precedent sample is uploaded to the corresponding section of QA-program library.

Any precedent sample is an autonomous software unit which is QA-programmed and can be qualified as the software agent. One of the advantages of the agent of such type is the possibility for its easy reprogramming in the real time.

If a number of precedent samples are necessary for the person who are solving the current task they should be extracted from the precedent base (with using the techniques of ES^P) and uploaded into the active tasks tree.

8. Conclusion

Told above contains sufficient arguments to assert that the described QA-shell helps to create the Expert Systems of the new type. This type of ES is intended for the ordinary person who has decided to create the ES which will be filled by the valuable information about personal precedents. In creation of own ES^P the person fulfills roles of the expert, developer and user of such computer assistant.

The main specificity of the elaborated QA-shell for ES^P defines Question Answering which is fitted to pseudo-programming of precedents samples. Accessible means of Question Answering are coordinated with the dialogue nature of consciousness that simplifies transition from internal reasoning of the person to their models in the computer environment. Therefore the owner of ES^P can apply real time P-programming of I-processor and K-processor for solving own tasks on the base of precedents the samples of which are kept in ES^P.

Accessible means of P-programming is similar to N-programming and their power (types of data, additional attributes and system of P-programming) open the possibility for the ordinary person to write non-trivial programs of the own activity. QA-programs manage accustomed (habitual) semi-automatic actions when QA-programs (as techniques of the guide type) show to the person the sequence of actions which the person must execute. Moreover, QA-programs can be translated in the form which can be executed by the computer processors.

QA-shell is elaborated on the base of the sufficient experince of Question Answering applied to the development of SIS and other applications including applied systems with ES subsystem based on precedents. For example, QA-samples of precedents were embedded in system for Expert Monitoring of Environment of the Sea Vessel. QA-samples of precedents also have been used in the solution of following tasks: Creation of Interface Prototypes in context of ISO standard 9126; Information Safety of SIS in the context of ISO standard 15408; Predicative Ontological Testing of Project Solutions.

9. References

Bass, L.; Ivers J. & Klein, M. & Merson, P. (2005). *Reasoning Frameworks*, Software Engineering Institute, Carnegie Mellon University, Pittsburgh, PA, Tech. Rep. CMU/SEI-2005-TR-007.

Burger, J. et al. (2001). *Issues, Tasks and Program Structures to Roadmap Research in Question & Answering (Q&A)*, Tech. Rep. NIST.

Card S.K.; Thomas, T.P. & Newell, A. (1983). *The Psychology of Human-Computer Interaction*, London: Lawrence Erbaum Associates.

Cockcroft, A.N. (2003). *Guide to the Collision Avoidance Rules: International Regulations for Preventing Collisions at Sea*, Butterworth-Heinemann, 2003.

Crystal, A. & Ellington, B. (2004). *Task analysis and human-computer interaction: approaches, techniques, and levels of analysis.* In proceedings of the Tenth Americas Conference on Information Systems, New York, New York, pp 1-9.

Henninger, S. (2003). *Tool Support for Experience-Based Software Development Methodologies*, Advances in Computers, vol. 59, pp. 29-82.

Hewett, T.; Baecker , R., Card , St., Carey , T., Gasen , J., Mantei, M., Perlman , G., Strong, G., & Verplank, W. (2002). *ACM SIGCHI Curricula for Human-Computer Interaction.* ACM Technical Report. P. 162.

Hirschman, L. & Gaizauskas, R. (2001). *Natural Language Question Answering: The View from Here.* Natural Language Engineering, vol. 7, pp. 67-87.

Karray, F.; Alemzadeh, M., Saleh, J. A. & Arab, M. N. (2008). *Human-Computer Interaction: Overview on State of the Art* Smart sensing and intelligent systems, vol. 1, No. 1(Mar), pp 138-159, 2008.

Kieras, D. & Meyer , D.E. (1997). *An overview of the EPIC architecture for cognition and performance with application to human-computer interaction.* Human-Computer Interaction, 12, 1997, 391-438.

Lee, M.H. (2000). *Model-Based Reasoning: A Principled Approach for Software Engineering*, Software - Concepts and Tools, vol.19, #4, pp. 179-189.

Potts, C.; Takahashi, A. & Anton, K. (1994) *Inquiry-based Requirements Analysis*, IEEE Software, vol.11, #2, pp. 21-32.

Precedent. Available from http://dictionary.reference.com/browse/precedent.

Question-Answering. Available from http://www.wordiq.com/definition/Question_ answering.

Reiff, R.; Harwood, W. & Phillipson, T. *A (2002) Scientific Method Based Upon Research Scientists' Conceptions of Scientific Inquiry*, In Proc.2002 Annual International Conference of the Association for the Education of Teachers in Science, pp 546–556.

Rich, C. & Feldman, Y. (1992). *Seven Layers of Knowledge Representation and Reasoning in Support of Software Development,* IEEE Transactions on Software Engineering, vol, 8, # 6, pp.451-469.

Rosen, D. J.; (2008) *How to Make Inquiry Maps.* Available from: http://alri.org/pubs/im3.html.

Yang, F.; Shen, R. & Han, P. (2003). *Adaptive Question and Answering Engine Base on Case Based and Reasoning Technology,* Journal of Computer Engineering, vol.29, #11, pp. 27-28.

5

AI Applications in Psychology

Zaharia Mihai Horia
"Gheorge Asachi" Technical University of Iaşi, România

1. Introduction

The AI role in psychology is still underestimated by the European psychology experts. Sometimes psychologists reject the use of expert systems in their fields of activity because they fear that the computer will replace them. Sometimes they do not perceive the full potential of using IT. The same reactions have been encountered among medicine doctors when the first automatic diagnose system was tested. The AI has not reached yet that level of performance capable of emulating simultaneously all pieces of human behaviour, but researchers are on the right track of getting there (Klein, 1999). Anyhow, there are many intersection points between these two domains.

One intersection is related to the cognitivist approach in psychology. Within this domain, various programs have been developed for environment simulation, automatic emotion recognition, the simulations of social interaction within groups, phobias therapies, computer aided treatment in psychiatry, electronic inquires and automatic results generation, and the list may continue. In the UK, studies related to the efficiency in applying IT in cognitive behaviour therapy have already been conducted (NICE, 2008) and the results are promising. The importance of IT in psychology was recognised by the researchers' community by developing a new area of research - cyberpsychology.

Two distinct levels of IT use in psychotherapy have already been identified (Hovell & Muller, 2010), especially from the patient treatment point of view. Within the first layer, we encounter the common tools developed to increase the efficiency and performance of the therapist. Within the second level, we have the complex systems that help both the patient and the therapist during the treatment. There is a strong possibility that in the future low and medium complexity problems will be handled by the expert systems. Although there are some applications that sustain these assumptions, some controversies on the subject still exist (Marks et al., 2007). In the second part of this chapter, a new approach in information retrieval and testing will be presented.

For the researcher, two information flows are critical. One refers the new discoveries regarding the global research within his area of interest. The other consists of the experimental data needed for his research. Because psychologists measure the thoughts, feelings and behaviour of one or more people at a time, they have a problem in acquiring research data, especially when large numbers of subjects are needed. At a corporate level, this problem is solved by using the electronic version of classical inquires. Though, this solution is limited to a medium where there are strong rules that guide employee behaviour. On the other hand, young people are more and more adapted to the information society. As

a result, the use of cooperative layers provided by the IT permit them to interact in various spaces - more or less virtual.
The psychologists need new tools in order to gather data not only from the point of view of social psychology, where the information about human behaviour can be retrieved without direct interviewing, but also from the point of view of other fields of psychology. As a result, we need a combination between an expert system, an information retrieval system and an intelligent interface to mediate user interaction in order to fulfill these needs. The human computer interface will also have its role in agent interface design.

2. Information technology and psychology

The computer begins to be more and more used in the psychology and psychiatry research or treatment. Not all the experts consider that level of implication as being positive. (Seong-in et al., 2006). In the following section we will analyse their opinions and try to see if there are any alternative ways of solving the controversies.
The classical approach of the domain considers as acceptable only the direct human to human interaction during the treatment. Nowadays, with the informational society becoming more and more part of our life, the idea of human interaction is being altered by the IT tools. For example, personalized wide area communications like telepresence reach the stage of holographic representation of the person on remote (Musion, 2011). Other impersonal or partial personalized methods of communication are the continuously growing as social networks and virtual spaces for collaborative work or relaxing. As a result, the acceptance level of human computer interaction will continuously increase year after year, until this rule will slightly dissipate by itself.
The use of computers can lead, on long term, to significant decreases in the financial flows of this class of experts. This it is possible to happen at the beginning of the process. A free market will quickly adapt in one or two decades and a new equilibrium point will be found.
Because it will be a long time or even so until a computer will have the flexibility and dynamism of a human mind, it is clear that in computer patient relationship a loss of rigor and quality may appear. Yet, this can be avoided by readapting the treatment schemas in order to maximize the advantages offered by the computerized system and to minimize the undesired effects. Anyhow, the current stage in this domain shows that the computer-assisted or computer-replaced therapy cannot be used in any field psychology or psychiatry because it cannot give the minimal required level of quality of treatment.
In terms of organizational resistance, this represents a minor problem on long term. The organization must adapt to the economic and social changes of the society; otherwise it will perish.
Regarding the patient resistance, the same arguments as previously fit very well. The evolution of information society and of the cyberspace will enter in people's life from birth. As a consequence, many things related to human computer interaction will became natural.
Similar rejection reactions have been encountered among medicine doctors when the first automatic diagnostic system was tested like Micyn (Hance, 1976). Unfortunately the Micyn use was prohibited because they do not accept possible liabilities that can appear in case of wrong diagnose, Caduceus (Banks, 1986), or ONCOCIN (Wiederhold et al., 2001). An expert system can reach up to 99% of diagnostic correctness but in the same condition as the medic itself because also need a full and detailed anamnesis. As a result, they remain as help, not as replacement.

Anyhow, nowadays the problem is so important that a new field in social science was created: the cyberpsychology or the psychology of cyberspace. The definition given by Suller (Suller, 2011) is :

"the psychological aspects of environments created by computers and online networks. It presents an evolving conceptual framework for understanding how people react to and behave within cyberspace"

The research of the cyberpsychology is oriented on two main directions:

- How can the IT applications improve the treatment of various psychological problems?
- What are the typical psychological and psychiatric problems that appear when people interact with various tool of the cyberspace?

The new concept emerged naturally when the information society began to be so involved in each aspect of everyday life, and the psychologists began to increase the number and the diversity of the studies related to the use of IT applications.

If we look at the complexity and purposed of the typical IT applications used in real world or into the research laboratories, we see that they usually try to solve only one type or class of problems, and that their complexity is variable. In most cases, the systems used have medium or low complexity. As a result, when the first design of the hardware and software system was emerged, some questions appeared:

- It is rational to make the investments needed to implement a complex system like that?
- The system will really meet the psychology expert needs?
- The user (the psychologist) can adapt to the complexity of this system?

To solve the first question some tests about the system efficiency conducted using a minimal prototype are needed. As for the rest of the mentioned problems of user rejection, they can be easily handled by the use of some feature specific for human computer interface - HCI. Unfortunately, those features will remain at the gadget level without the existence of a good information system based also on an expert system. This means that a simple electronic documentation also called "Help" cannot solve the problem. A more interactive approach will be the use of Intelligent Tutoring Systems - ITS. The ITS is based on an expert system and it requires a "touch" from the combination between authoring event and psychology in order to increase the abilities in handling the customized help offered to the teacher to develop new materials and also how to use them in the context of an ITS (Major et al., 1997).

Haynes proves widely in his PhD thesis the necessity of using the expert systems in information system instead of a simple indexed help file, so that each application that passes over a certain degree of complexity should provide to the user the needed help on each moment of interaction with the system (Hayes, 2003). The approach was improved using so called "situation awareness". Here the concept of smart monitor is used having in mind usually military applications. They represent, in fact, the use of a smart information system in order to change the definition/perception of the display. The transformation is from a simple report that it made from the system's point of view to one that reflects the user's point of view (Guastello, 2007).

The main applications of computer in psychology refer especially to psychotherapy. Here there are a broad band of applications that can be classified as follows (Newman, 2004):

- self - help Internet sites;
- computer administered therapy;
- screening and assessment using web applications over the Internet;
- adjunctive palmtop computer therapy;

- on-line consultation;
- advocacy;
- virtual reality therapy;
- interactive voice messaging systems;
- biofeedback via ambulatory physiological monitoring;
- virtual spaces for support groups (can be based on social networks instruments or by a custom solution).

The main advantages offered by the use of IT in psychotherapy are:

- supplementary time for supervised treatment gained by the patient;
- decrease the time append in direct interaction with the practitioner;
- decrease de cost of the treatment ;
- some help in taking treatment decisions;

The idea of using the computer to help the expert is not new. This was needed especially because of the time consuming tasks like taking interviews. At this level, the computer has more advantages than a human in the same position (Erdman et al., 1985). Yet the roots of artificial intelligence in cognitivism have made the psychiatrists to try to use the computer as help during the treatment process.

The use of computer in psychotherapy has not only some advantages, but also some disadvantages. Some of them are of ethical nature. This refers to the bond created between the expert and the patient. As a result, one big question refers the correctness of leaving a human being into this type of relationship (Rialle et al., 1994). The other problem appears because the software can be bought and used by the patient on free will. This situation is similar to the case of drugs that can be used only under continuous medical supervision because of their extreme danger. There is also the possibility to decrease the adaptability and ability of the human expert because the computer models sometimes need to simplify things too much. As a consequence, in time there is a possibility that the expert will not be able to think "outside the computer box". Yet, there are a lot of advantages of the computer use at any level in psychology, but with the proper caution.

The assisted cognitive psychotherapy has been tested since the 90', and the result seem to be encouraging (Wood et al., 1998). The Computer aided Cognitive Behavioural Therapy – CCBT - is used in conjunction with the psychotherapist and, based on patient input, it can suggest some general directions in patient treatment and even handle some portion of it (Marks et al., 2007). As in other applications, the use of these systems during the therapeutic process can decrease the time spent by the specialist with the patient, but dramatically increase the time of treatment appliance due to electronic supervision. Because in most cases the key of success is increasing as much as possible the time allocated by the patient to the supervised treatment, than there are many expectations from this approach. Yet the system has its limitations. For example, until now it cannot offer solutions to problems like compulsive gambling, nightmares, enuresis and tics. This is expected due to gravity and complexity of mentioned problems. So we may argue that these systems are useful and that they will be continuously developed, but there is no way that they entirely replace the specialist yet.

The hypnotherapy may be conducted in a classic manner, but good effects are also obtained by the use of various partially or totally electronic techniques. Because the computer can fully control the audio/video flow in whatever manner is necessary, the IT involvement in this field is higher. In Table 1, the techniques and methods mostly used in conjunction with a computer are presented (Frost. 2008).

Nowadays, the use of virtual reality has become accepted in the health care services in order to help the psychotherapist. The specialists begin to consider that the VR role will continuously increase in the future within the field of clinical psychology (Riva, 2005).

Problem	Recommended techniques	Used Methods
Stress	Self hypnosis	Interactive web applications
Anxiety	Hypnotherapy	Interactive web applications
Depression	Relaxation therapy	Stand alone applications
Phobias on various forms	Meditation	Multimedia support
Cognitive issues (e.g. positive thinking)	Stress management	Mini mixing desks

Table 1. Computer based hypnotherapy usage

In panic and phobia disorders treatment, the results of using computer application were not so impressive; though from an economic efficiency point of view there was a real success (McCrone et al., 2009).

The games are already used in education of children of different ages, so this potential has reach the psychiatrist expert attention. So, the concept of using games in education at various levels of complexity appears. The games are, in most of cases, based on complex expert systems or on other forms of advanced artificial intelligence. The psychologists have not neglected this approach. As a result, studies about using 3D games as focused therapy instruments have been conducted (Coyle et al., 2005). The first results appear to be promising, but it is difficult to find a general treatment solution. Therefore, the therapeutic games need behaviour rules modification from time to time, under the psychiatrist supervision.

3. Expert systems in psychology

Simon presents the idea that a machine can think. But there are two distinct ways in doing that. Of course this "thinking process" will be also programmed - at least in the early stages; than the machine can evolve. He observes that the programming of the machine can be done taking into account the human way of solving problems or not (Simon 1990). But this raises an interesting question regarding the use of expert systems in psychology. Most of the common applications in psychology take the expert system as it is and try to adapt it to their particular or sometimes more general needs. Cognitive simulations are computer programs for modelling human cognitive activities. Traditionally used to develop expert and learner models for intelligent tutoring systems, building simulations is also an effective learning activity in psychology-related courses. Using inexpensive and easy-to-use expert system shells, students can develop simulations of cognitive processes. This will give them the ability to better understand the rational process of human mind and also will improve their communication ability with the IT experts.

Jonassen presents a case study where expert systems were used as formalism for modelling metacognitive processes in a seminar (Jonassen & Wang, 2003). Building cognitive simulations engages intensive introspection, ownership, and meaning making in learners who build them.

The relation between psychology and expert systems is closer that seems at a first glance. In fact, the bases of artificial intelligence - AI - rely on the cognitive approach in psychology. The AI dynamics was higher than the evolution of psychology due to its strong mathematic support and the important industrial applications AI provided. The production systems, and then the expert systems emerged around the 80's as a market asset (Shaw & Gaines, 2005). The links with the origin are not loosed yet. The expert systems need the help of the psychology. After the first wave of enthusiasm, the IT experts have understood that there is a need for development of some techniques to make an efficient rule extraction from people. Here the repertory grid elicitation was recognized as being useful and integrated into the local "know how". From the point of view of psychology, the expert systems can be used in conjunction with personal construct psychology. Unfortunately, the psychologist approach is not economically feasible. But a compromise can be reached if an expert system with generic rules about human behaviour and thinking is developed, and then, in time, a form of self acquiring new rules from direct dialog with the patient will be used.

The expert systems are complex applications that have as their main concern to capture a particular set of rules regarding the experience of a human expert in some particular field. There are some limits in their implementation, but usually applied to dimension of rules set and eventually to clarity of this set. From the computing power point of view, nowadays there are new approaches in high performance computing like GRID or CLOUD computing that can assure all the needed scalability. Probably the complexity of human thinking, of natural language and also its imperfections as a communication channel, may limit the knowledge transfer. The application of these systems is almost unlimited from a theoretical point of view, because at the origin of artificial intelligence – AI – laid the idea of trying to replicate human thinking. But this cannot be one as a whole yet. As a result, various branches of AI try to replicate pieces of life behaviour at any level, beginning with genetic algorithms and neural networks and finishing with artificial life, fuzzy and game theory. Any expert system must have three key components: the knowledge base, the inference engine, and the interface.

The knowledge base can be composed of structured data like tables of numbers, facts, if-then rules, various relationships, critical values, sometime equations or sets of qualitative descriptors.

In order to process this database, a special logic interpreter is used for the inference machine. Inference engines can have different complexity levels. The good news is that the engine can be parallelized (Urbani et al., 2010), so that, into a scalable computing medium, we can solve problems on any level of complexity we need. On top of the inference engines we find the rule based system. Of course those are parallelizable too (Petcu, 2006). These systems are based on complex groups of rules – metarules - used to handle the execution of other rules.

The fact the systems are parallelizable opens the possibility of creating another form of distributed artificial intelligence. The term usually refers to a complex system of intelligent agents deployed onto a distributed system. It is not clear why the generic term artificial intelligence that nowadays covers all the specific branches was selected to define only the intelligent agents application in distributed computing. Usually the accepted term is distributed expert systems.

A first possible application probably will be the universal translator. Actual level of knowledge offer as a possible solution a combination between an immense database like e.g.

Google and a very powerful expert system. The speech therapy has also benefitted from using expert systems. There are researches that prove the efficiency of a Fuzzy Expert System in handling home treatment of the patient (Schipor et al., 2008). Various techniques from AI are used in psychiatry. For example, in diagnosis of dyslexia a combination of fuzzy and genetic algorithms proves to correctly manage a diagnostic using low quality input data (Palacios et al., 2010).

The system can use the patient voice itself as supplementary information in making a good anamnesis. Important results have already been obtained in making some assumptions about voice pathology, results such as the Massachusetts Eye & Ear Infirmary (MEEI) Voice Disorders Database (Saenz-Lechon et al., 2006). The results of these studies cannot be used separately because there are too many different causes that can drive to the same behaviour to a patient voice (Paulraj et al., 2009). Yet, its use in conjunction with other measurements can provide valuable information about the patient.

4. Social Information retrieval system

The researchers in social sciences or psychology need to readapt to the cyberspace realities. As a result, new ways of gathering data about people or communities must be developed. There are possibilities of handling information retrieval from Internet. There are many stages in extracting knowledge from digital documents, or from social networks. In the beginning, a search engine needs to be implemented because the expert will set some temporary or long term areas of interest, usually referred by the use of a keyword set. One possibility is to fully develop the search engine from scratch. This approach is very costly in terms of project resources, but it has the advantage of having a fine tune around the problem specification. This approach is recommended especially when the search is made in well defined large databases with controlled access; otherwise, the use of available global search engines dynamic libraries can easily handle the problem. The most important search engines are Google, Yahoo or Bing. The commercial approach of Google prohibits the use of their libraries in that scope, but the Microsoft Bing alternative can be used without any problems.

In human to human communication, there are a lot of difficulties regarding the typical ambiguities of natural language or cultural differences. As a result, the main problem of searching involves the minimization of informational redundancy. Worst than that, usually a search process involves a set of words from the user knowledge and there are good chances that his dictionary has only a partial match to the ones of other authors who have written some information that is really needed by that user. In the case of psychology, we have a big problem because many schools have the same universe of discourse (over 50% match), but unfortunately they use different discourse universes, and sometimes even different standard notations. This makes it very difficult to apply an information retrieval system to efficient filter the news appear in the domain. As a result, an efficient dedicated retrieval system for a psychologist will need to be continuously tuned with the researcher in order to quickly adapt. This approach can drive maybe, in time, the system to gather enough rules to decrease gradually the supplementary input demands from the expert. In order to process all the problems regarding different representations of the same knowledge, an expert system can be used. The Internet has more information about an individual than one can expect. That is due to the continuous increasing dependence of the human to the IT related tools.

There are parts of the social life that begin to be partially or fully virtualized. Within this process, a lot of information about a person is given. The information can be classified in two categories:

- Explicit: required by the social network so the user is aware about the content and can judge the implication of making them partially or fully public;
- Implicit: in that case the information is given also by interaction with all the friends from his local social network? In many situations the user is not aware about the nature and some time the confidentiality of the information provided because (s)he makes no difference between virtual world and direct contact with the group members.

So the social networks can provide a lot of information about a person or a group of people. The information is stored in virtual space so an interface with the social network must be developed. There is not problem of accessing private information about the people without their consent because in this system the information can be shared only if the person involved gives his explicit permission to do that. The proposed system will have two components: one is the HCI based interface created using intelligent agents, and the other is the system for information retrieval.

4.1 System HCI

There are various approaches that use HCI techniques and expert systems that try to make the computer appear more "friendly" to the user. The increased emotional intelligence abilities of some humans give them many direct or indirect advantages over others without making too many investments. Therefore, the experts begin to study ways of making computers capable of emulating this kind of abilities.

Klein proposes to make computers emulate emotional intelligence. In fact, he studies the ways of giving the system the possibility to handle the user frustration which is sometimes justified, and sometimes not. Moreover, he proves that the computer can handle the negative emotions of the user in order to partially or totally dissipate them (Klein, 1999). This is a very important result because the user productivity is heavily affected by strong negative emotions and the future of the society involves more and more the use of the computer in every domain of activity.

It may be usefully for the proposed system if we use the research results regarding facial expression classification and interpretation (Cohn & Sayette, 2010). There are similar researches in terms of multimodal emotion recognition. The results seem to be promising and already the cultural differences in emotion handling are being analyzed (Banziger, 2009).

The natural language analysis is very complicated from IT point of view. Even the psychologist has many discussions regarding informational redundancy that may increase even at the level of same culture with large geographical coverage. As result both parts begin to make interdisciplinary researches in the field of text analysis. The psychologists begin to investigate how the text content should be analyzed from their point of view. As result the chances of extracting the original idea of the speaker are increased. For example, some researchers try to identify a subset of Freudian drives in patient and therapist discourse text analysis of a classic interview (Saggion et al., 2010).

As we have seen until now, there is a constant and high interest from both the psychologists and IT specialists in developing more and more complex, but effective, ways to deal with the user in a more natural manner. Until now, we have analyzed separate experiments that try to solve different aspects of the complex relation that appears when two people interact, and to replicate it at the computer system level as good as possible. Because of so many differences between the relevant aspects, a more natural way in handling all of them into a single software system will be to use intelligent agents. Intelligent agents represent static or mobile pieces of programs with various levels of complexity.

Intelligent agents also have some specific AI algorithms integrated. Their development seems to be in close relationship with distributed systems. The agents usually need a special framework to be loaded on each involved machine. The development of industrial applications is slow because of security related problems. No one can guaranty yet that a piece of code executed into the framework cannot be harmful for the host. That's why service oriented architecture begins to gain interest. Anyhow, the intelligent agents have an immense potential both from the theory and the practice point of view. There are various classifications of intelligent agents, but from the implementation point of view, the distinction between week and strong agents seems to be more useful (Wooldrige et al., 1995). The weak agents have the following properties:

- Proactive - when agents can initiate behaviours and courses of action in order to reach their objectives.
- Reactive: agents can answer to external events.
- Autonomous: agents don't need human interaction.
- Social: agents can communicate with other agents using an agreed Agent Communication Language (ACL) and ontology (e.g. KQML for intelligent agents).

Strong agents will inherit the characteristics of weak agents, but enrich them with the following characteristics:

- Rationality: an agent will take no action in such a way that would contradict its objectives.
- Benevolence: agents should not act in such as way that would compromise other agent or its host environment.
- Veracity: agents are truthful.

For our HCI we need to use strong agents. We propose to use the Bickmore approach as a starting base in designing HCI interface. He developed a system based on a combination between intelligent agents and advanced HCI techniques in order to acquire the best possible personal relationship between the human and the computer (Bickmore, 2003). From all types presented, we choose to use the following type of agents:

- Social agents are defined as those artefacts, primarily computational, that are intentionally designed to display social cues or otherwise to produce a social response in the person using them (Bickmore, 2003). Their introduction is based on various studies that prove that people change their behaviour and evaluation of the relation with an animated virtual reality character which can emulate some social interaction abilities.
- Affective agents are those intentionally designed to display affect, recognize affect in users, or manipulate the user's affective state (Bickmore, 2003). They have abilities in the emotional intelligence field. They most control various levels of verbal and nonverbal communication normally used by a person. Here we can mention the facial expression, the body posture, the colour of skin response, the use of grips, the use of natural voice and synchronized the emulated mood with the voice tone. One of the problems is the detection of user mood. This can be done using various pattern recognition tools (for speech, face recognition, voice recognition and analysis, posture and skin colour) and then to use the same knowledge database as the emulated person.

- Embodied Conversational Agents are animated humanoid software agents that use speech, gaze, gesture, intonation and other nonverbal modalities to emulate the experience of human face-to-face conversation with their users (Bickmore, 2003). They are also constructed on top of the affective agents and create a 3D virtual humanoid to increase the efficiency of user interaction.

The following type of agents are also required to assure a proper functionality:

- GUI agents that represent the classical GUI used to communicate with any desired type of application. This approach can be used due to the use of Model View Controller approach in application design.
- The Information retrieval client agent. This will assure the direct communication with the second component of the application.

Regarding the high precision control of the expression for the HCI agent, the research results of MIT (Bickmore, 2003) can be improved if a hierarchical composition model is used. The agent can be seen as an independent service world wide available if an approach based on human to markup language will be used. This approach is based on fuzzy markup language and is used to construct ambient intelligence architecture (Acampora et al., 2007).

If we analyze the existing comparison matrix from various agent frameworks (WIKI, 2011), we see that is a small number fully compatible with FIPA (Foundation for Intelligent Physical Agents):

- ADK (Tryllian Agent Development Kit) was designed for large scale distributed applications; Mobile (distributed) agents.
- JADE was designed for distributed applications composed of autonomous entities.
- SeSAm (Shell for Simulated Agent Systems) (fully integrated graphical simulation environment) was designed for General purpose multi domain (agent based); research, teaching, resources, graph theory that poses a plug-in for FIPA.
- ZEUS was designed for distributed multi-agent simulations.

The last two offer only simulation possibilities, so they are unfeasible for implementation. From ADK and Jade we will choose JADE because they offer support not only on Java, but also for Microsoft .Net and that gives us the liberty of choosing the best fitted technology to develop the system.

4.2 Information retrieval system

An Information Retrieval System - IRS is usually composed from four layers (Kowalski, 2011):

- Data gathering - here the information is retrieved from Internet or local networks in accord with the rules set by the user. Sometimes it is used the solution of distributed search using autonomous entities that will push the filtered information to the central data base. The data normalization process and some pre-indexing algorithms are also executed in this case.
- Indexing - here the creation of quick searchable database is the main concern. There are different approaches to create an indexing system (based by Boolean, by weight and by statistic) but the differences between them begin to be relevant only for a very large collection of data. As a result, a classical database management system (DBMS) is mostly used to store data.
- Searching - the methods used can vary from using the implicit DBMS operators to use custom set of operations sometime based on AI.

- Presentation - here the graphical user interface used in data graphical representation is designed. The methods like clustering if so are also elected.

In the figure 1, the structure of proposed IRS is presented.

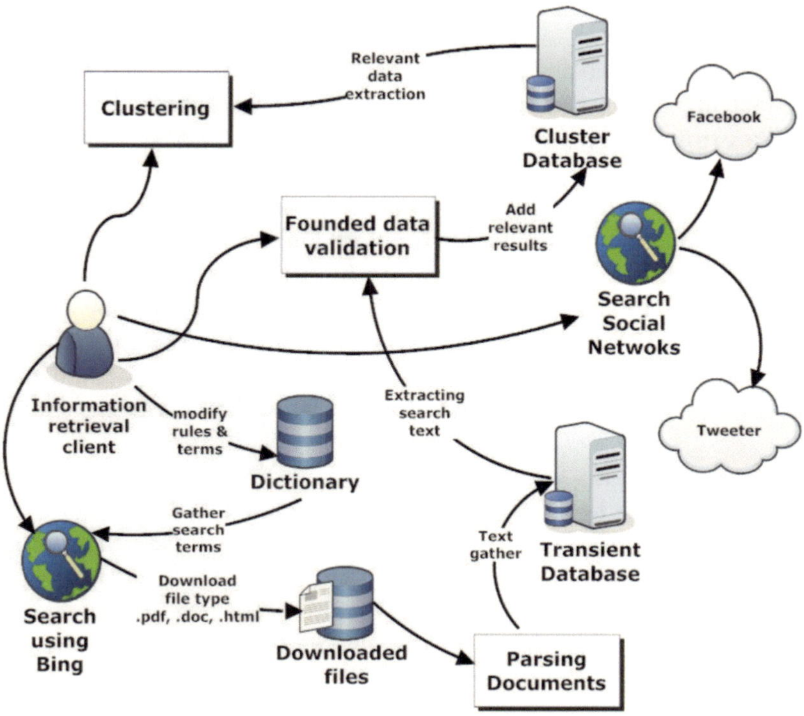

Fig. 1. The proposed IRS system structure

The IRS will have the ability not only to retrieve documents from the Internet, but also to make text analyses in order to find exactly the needed pieces of the information. Supported type of files are portable document format, word and html files. To do that the expert will give the rules, than those rules will be executed by an expert system.

The use of the expert system in the context is similar to the one used in DIRT (Lin & Pantel, 2001), but with supervised control of the rules in conjunction with the ideas specific to the RUBIC system (Mc Cune et al., 1985). So, the expert system is used to make a better selection from an already gathered set of documents, or paragraphs from documents. The rules are established by the IT expert together with the psychology expert.

The IRS can also retrieve information from social networks. The only requirement needed to do that is that all the people involved must have added as a friend the expert.

API Bing can be accessed using various protocols like JSON, SOAP and XML in order to have access to search results.

JSON is ideal to interface with AJAX applications and it is specific in the designing of web applications. SOAP and XML can exchange data with desktop, server or even WEB related applications. The SOAP is specific to the high level layer, where the ability of parsing the request and the answers is required. XML is more general because the request is http type and the answer is in XML format. As a result, the XML was selected to be used in establishing making connection with Bing API.

In order to assure social network access, a connector for Facebook and Twitter was developed (Czeran, 2011). The connection to Facebook social network implies the ability of automatic logging in the network.

In order to solve the problem, the protocol OAuth 2.0 was analyzed. This is an open standard that allows the user to share their private resources stored on the site without needing to provide their credentials (like user and password). Instead of that, the protocol gives the possibility that a user provide tokens. Each token will give access only to a resource or area from the site. As a result, an automatic connector must be created as a Facebook application that will be deployed on the Facebook developers site. This application will provide a pair (AppID, AppSecret) used in OAuth authentication phase. Because the access tokens have limited life time and limited access to resources, analyzing a social graph with large number of nodes (on the higher levels of the associated tree) is not possible yet. Anyhow, the information retrieval begins after the logging into the network and uses the Graph API service. The answer given by this service is serialized JSON (JavaScript Object Notation) objects. This is a standard used for human readable data exchange and it is language independent. To deserialise the answer the JSON .NET was used.

The api.twitter.com was used to access the micro-blog service Twitter data collection. The full history for a user can be retrieved if it is not protected and does not overcame 3200 recordings. The information is given in ATOM - that is a XML based format used in web dataflow.

To create a connector with the Facebook and Twitter a dedicated library named collection factory was used. Its main components are class package FacebookUtil and a separate class oAuthFacebook.

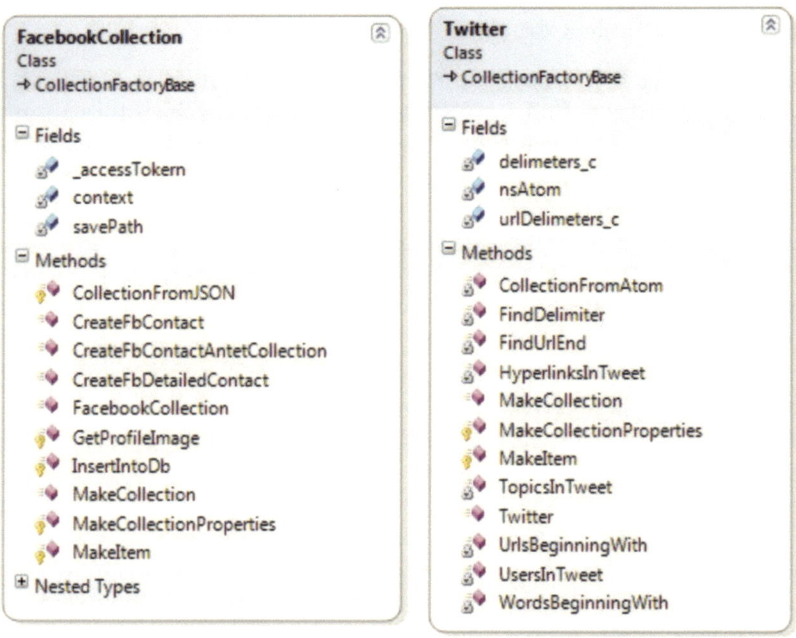

Fig. 2. The main classes used for connection with Facebook and Twitter

The FacebookUtil has utility classes that deserialise the JSON flows coming from Graph API service, and generate the object with relevant information. The base needed for oAuth protocol is also created in this case. The oAuthFacebook works at a higher level.
It takes the parameters given by Facebook type application registration (AppId, AppSecret) and then receives the authorization token to begin data retrieval.
The FacebookCollection (see figure 2) class encapsulate the methods used to retrieve data from Graph API service and MakeCollection method that will generate the data object from retrieved data. The data persistence is assured by the use of InsertIntoDb that writes it into a temporary database. The same approach was used in the design of the Twitter class where the methods used to access the service Twitter API, to parse the retrieved information in the ATOM format are encompassed.

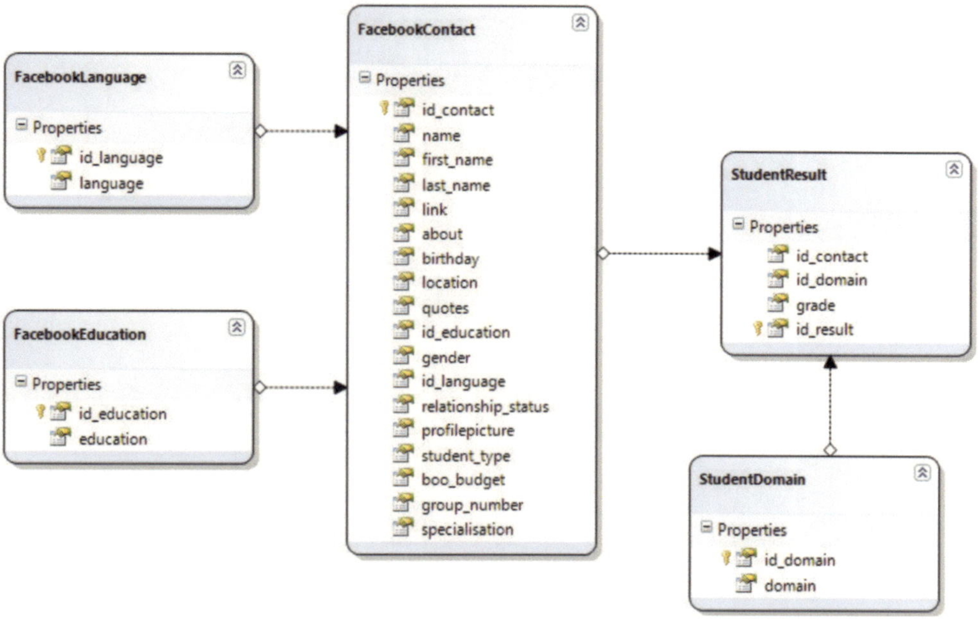

Fig. 3. Data base structure for retrieved social network information persistence

As a supplementary feature, there is the possibility of processing any information posted separately on Twitter. This facilitates the process of information classification by obtaining quantifying characteristics that can be translated into categories using Facet objects. The method TopicsInTweet will count the number of themes from the current post and the UsersInTweet method counts the number of references to a specific user in all posting collection.
In figure 3 we present the part of temporary database that stores some information gathered form the social network. In this case, the gathered information was about a group of students using the social network.
The interface agent has access on the main functions of the IRS. Those are search term control and modification using if necessary supplementary keys and rules, automatic validation of results and clustering module. The action of interface agent is presented in figure 4 as a case diagram.

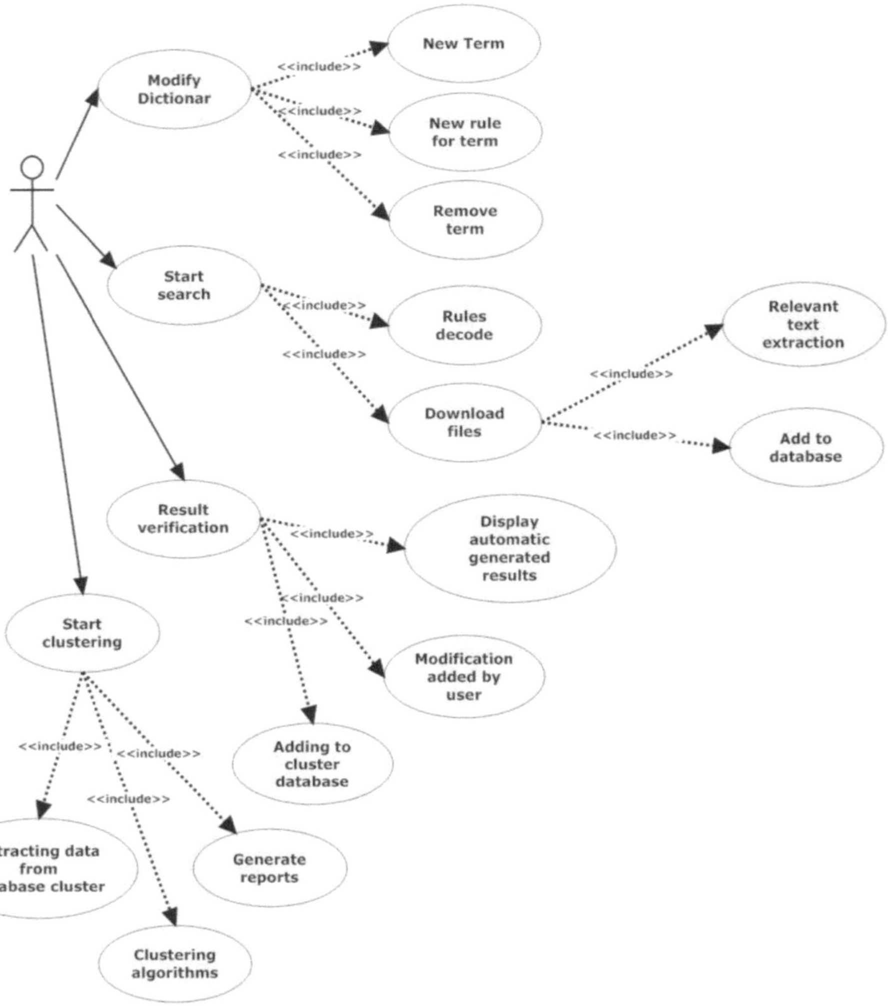

Fig. 4. IRS user use case diagram

The IRS has some separate modules: for interfacing with interface agent, for downloading selected files, for analyzing files content, the module for creating dictionary and rule execution, a database with two parts: one for files, and one for relevant part of text extraction, and finally the clustering module.

In figure 5, an activities diagram presents the way in which each module will interact with each other. The term dictionary module will process the files that contain search terms and use a sub-module used to generate new types of rules. These rules are parsed further to generate the ranking for search terms.

The file used to store dictionary data is XML type and has the following minimal information: search term, works or key notations associated with the search terms, rules and expressions. Also here the document is parsed using rules, terms and afferent keys.

The file downloader or reader module uses the Bing, Facebook and Twitter connectors to search and download the needed files.

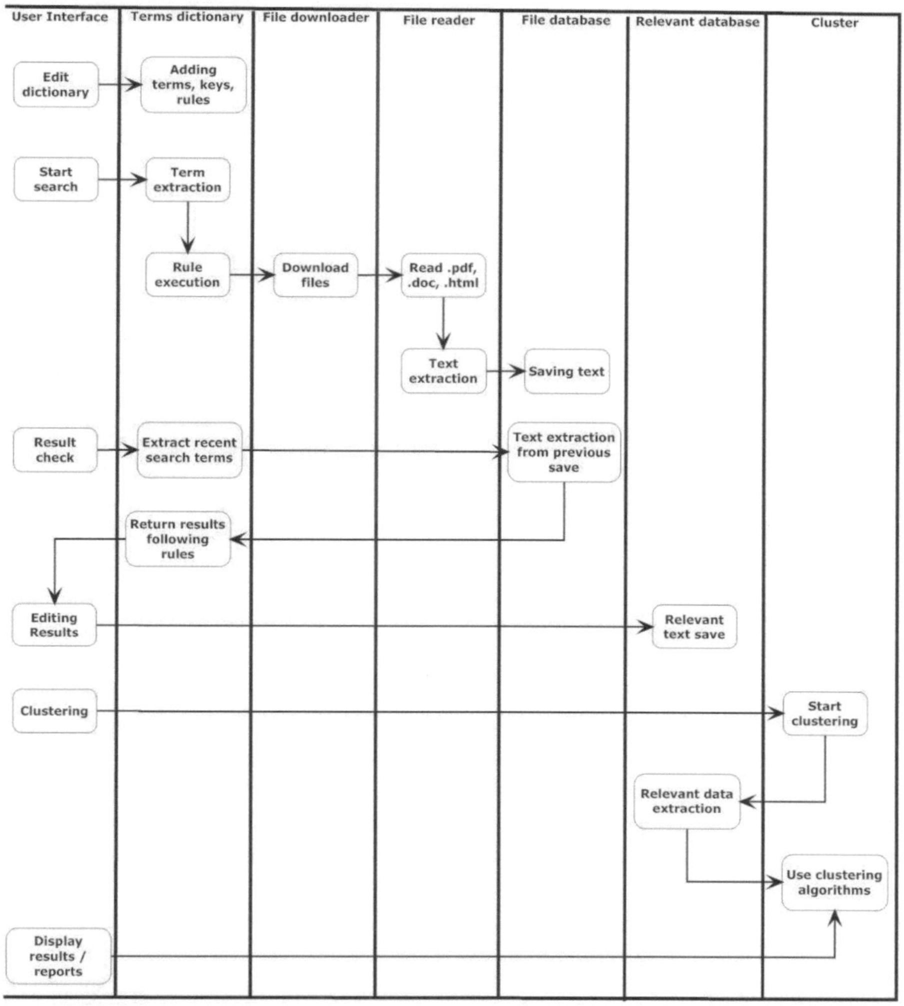

Fig. 5. IRS activities diagram

To download .NET WebRequest methods are used and than they are saved on the temporary data base. After that, the files are sent to text extraction using specific parser for each supported type. When the text is extracted, the structure of initial document is kept as a set of relations from figures, tables and text.

5. Conclusions

In this chapter a short surveillance of IT applications in psychology and psychiatry has been presented. The use of IT in psychology and psychiatry is common nowadays. As a result, more and more interdisciplinary research is conducted. The concept of cyberpsychology is yet vague because it tries to cover this interdisciplinary research, but the potential is unlimited due to the speed of technology development.
The proposed system is intended to increase the abilities of the expert by improving the possibility of finding information about their area of interest and research on the net. Also

this solution gives the possibility to gather some data about social groups using new unconventional methods.
The use of AI will also improve the communication methods in conjunction with HCI specific techniques.
There is a lot research to be done in order to finish the full implementation of the system, but the first results are encouraging.

6. References

Acampora G., Loia V., Nappi M., Ricciardi S. (2007). *Human-Based Models for Ambient Intelligence Environments* published in Xuan F. Zha (Ed.), Artificial Intelligence and Integrated Intelligent Information Systems: Emerging Technologies and Applications IdEA Group publishing, Singapore, pp. 1-18.

Banks, G. (1986). *Artificial intelligence in medical diagnosis: the INTERNIST/CADUCEUS approach.* Critical reviews in medical informatics 1 (1): 23–54. PMID 3331578.

Banziger T., Grandjean D., and Scherer K. R. (2009). *Emotion Recognition From Expressions in Face, Voice, and Body: The Multimodal Emotion Recognition Test (MERT)*, Emotion, Vol. 9, No. 5, 691-704, American Psychological Association.

Bickmore T. W. (2003). *Relational Agents: Effecting Change through Human-Computer Relationships*, Doctor of Philosophy thesis at the Massachusetts Institute of Technology. Available from http://dspace.mit.edu/bitstream/handle/1721.1/36109/52717187.pdf?sequence=1

Cohn J. F. and Sayette M. A. (2010). *Spontaneous facial expression in a small group can be automatically measured: An initial demonstration.* Available from http://www.cs.cmu.edu/~jeffcohn/pubs/Cohn&Sayette%202010.pdf

Coyle D., Matthews M., Sharry J, Nisbet A. and Doherty G. (2005). *Personal Investigator: A therapeutic 3D, game for adolecscent psychotherapy*, Journal of Interactive Technology & Smart Education 2(2): 73–88

Czeran E. (2011), *Regăsirea informatiilor din retele de socializare* – M.Sc. thesis, «Gheorghe Asachi « Technical University of Iasi, Romania

Erdman H.P., Klein M. H., and Greist J. H. (1985). *Direct Patient Computer Interviewing*, Journal of Consulting and Clinical Psychology, Vol. 53, No. 6, pp. 760-773

Frost B. (2008), *Computer and Technology Enhanced Hypnotherapy and Psychotherapy. A review of current and emerging technologies.* Available from www.neuroinnovations.com/ctep/technology_and_computer_enhanced _psychotherapy.pdf

Guastello S. J. (2007), *Coping with Complexity and Uncertainty, knowledge management, organizational intelligence and learning, and complexity.* Available from http://www.eolss.net/ebooks/Sample%20Chapters/C15/E1-29-03-10.pdf

Hance E. (1976). *Computer-Based Medical Consultations. MYCIN.* NewYork: Elsevier.

Haynes R.H. (2002). *Explanation in Information Systems.* Available from http://www.lse.ac.uk/collections/informationSystems//pdf/theses/haynes.pdf

Howell S.R., Muller R., *Computers in Psychotherapy: A New Prescription*, McMaster University Hamilton, Ontario Available from http://www.steverhowell.com/ComputerTherapy.PDF

Jonassen D. H. And Wang S. (2003). Using *expert systems to build cognitive simulations*, Journal of Educational Computing Research, Volume 28, Number 1, pp. 1-13.

Klein J.T. (1999). *Computer Response to User Frustration,* MIT Media, Laboratory Vision and Modeling Group Technical Report TR#480. Available from http://hd.media.mit.edu/tech-reports/TR-480.pdf

Kowalski, G., (2011). *Information Retrieval Architecture and Algorithms,* Ashburn, VA, USA, Springer Science+Business Media

Lin D, Pantel P. (2001), DIRT - Discovery of Inference Rules from Text, *Proceedings of the seventh ACM SIGKDD international conference on knowledge discovery and data mining,* pp. 323-328, ACM, New York.

Major N., Ainsworth S. and Wood D., (1997). *REDEEM: Exploiting Symbiosis Between Psychology and Authoring Environments,* International Journal of Artificial Intelligence in Education, 8, 317-340

Marks M., Cavanagh K. and Gega L. I. (2007). *Computer-aided psychotherapy: revolution or bubble?,* British Journal Of Psychiatry, 191, pp. 471-473.

McCrone, Paul , Marks, Isaac M. , Mataix-Cols, David , Kenwright, Mark and McDonough, Michael (2009). *Computer-Aided Self-Exposure Therapy for Phobia/Panic Disorder: A Pilot Economic Evaluation,* Cognitive Behaviour Therapy, 38: 2, pp. 91 — 99

Mc Cune B., Tong R. M., Dean J. S. and Shapiro D. G., Rubric (1985). *A System For Rule-Based Information Retrieval,* Ieee Transactions On Software engineering, Vol. Se-11, No. 9, pp. 939-945.

Musion Systems, (2011). *Cisco TelePresence - On-Stage Holographic Video Conferencing.* Available from http://www.musion.co.uk/Cisco_TelePresence.html

Newman M. G. (2004). *Technology in Psychotherapy: An Introduction,* Wiley Periodicals, Inc. J Clin Psychol/In Session 60: pp. 141–145.

NICE (2008), Computerised cognitive behaviour therapy for depression and anxiety. Available from http://www.nice.org.uk/nicemedia/pdf/TA097guidance.pdf

Palacios A. M., Sánchez L., Couso I., (2010). *Diagnosis of dyslexia with low quality data with genetic fuzzy systems,* International Journal of Approximate Reasoning 51 pp. 993–1009

Paulraj M P, Sazali Yaacob, and M. Hariharan (2009). *Diagnosis of Voice Disorders using Mel Scaled WPT and Functional Link Neural Network,* Biomedical Soft Computing and Human Sciences, Vol.14, No.2, pp. 55-60.

Petcu D. (2006). *A Parallel Rule-based System and Its Experimental Usage* in Membrane Computing Scalable Computing: Practice and Experience, Vol. 7, No. 3, pp. 39-49.

Rialle V., Stip E., O'connor K., (1994). *Computer mediated psychotherapy ethical issues and difficulties in implementation* Humane medicine 10, 3, pp. 185-192

Riva G., (2005)i *Virtual Reality in Psychotherapy: Review,* Cyberpsychology & Behavior, Volume 8, Number 3, 2005, pp. 220-230 , Mary Ann Liebert, Inc.

Saggion H., Stein-Sparvieri E. , Maldavsky D., Szasz S. (2010). NLP Resources for the Analysis of Patient/Therapist Interviews, LREC 2010 *conference proceedings.* Available from http://www.lrec-conf.org/proceedings/lrec2010/pdf/341_Paper.pdf

Saenz-Lechon N. et al. (2006). *Methodological issues in the development of automatic systems for voice pathology detection,* Biomedical Signal Processing and Control 1 pp. 120–128.

Schipor O. A., Pentiuc St. Gh., Schipor D. M. (2008), A Fuzzy Rules Base for Computer Based Speech Therapy, *proceedings of 9th International Conference on Development And Application Systems,* Suceava, Romania, May 22-24, pp. 305-308

Seong-in K., Hyun-Jung R., Jun-Oh H., M. Seong-Hak K. (2006). *An expert system approach to art psychotherapy*, The Arts in Psychotherapy 33 x, 59–75

Shaw M. L. G. and Gaines B. R. (2005). *Expertise and expert systems: emulating psychological processes*, Knowledge Science Institute, University of Calgary. Available from http://pages.cpsc.ucalgary.ca/~gaines/reports/PSYCH/Expertise/Expertise.pdf

Simon H. A (1990). *Machine as mind*. Available from http://octopus.library.cmu.edu/cgibin/tiff2pdf/simon/box00057/fld04313/bdl0009/doc0002/simon.pdf

Suller J. (20110. The psychology of cyberspace. available at <http://users.rider.edu/~suler/psycyber/psycyber.html>

Urbani J., Kotoulas, S., Maaseen J., Drost N., Seinstra F., van Harmelen, F. & Bal, H. (2010), *WebPIE: a Web-scale Parallel Inference Engine*, Submission to the SCALE competition at CCGrid '10.

Wiederhold, G., Shortliffe, E.H., Fagan, L.M., Perreault L.E. *Medical Informatics: Computer Applications in Health Care and Biomedicine*. New York: Springer, 2001.

WIKI (2011), Comparison of agent-based modeling software. Availble from http://en.wikipedia.org/wiki/Comparison_of_agent-based_modeling_software

Wood S. D., Belar C. D. and Snibbe J. (1998). *A Comparison of Computer-Assisted Psychotherapy and Cognitive-Behavioral Therapy in Groups*, Journal of Clinical Psychology in Medical Settings, Volume 5, Number 1, 103-115.

Wooldridge, M., Jennings, N.R. (1995). *Intelligent agents: Theory and practice*. The Knowledge Engineering Review 10(2)

Xu, Hong Chen, Song-Chun Zhu, and Jiebo Luo Zijian (2008) A Hierarchical Compositional Model for Face Representation and Sketching, IEEE Transactions On Pattern Analysis And Machine Intelligence, VOL. 30, NO. 6, JUNE 2008, pp.955-969

Zuell C., Harkness J., Hoffmeyer-Zlotnik J.H.P. (Eds.) (1996), Contributions to the Text Analysis and Computers Conference, September 18-21, 1995, Publisher: Zentrum für Umfragen, Methoden und Analysen (ZUMA), Druck & Kopie Hanel, Germany

6

An Expert System to Support the Design of Human-Computer Interfaces

Cecilia Sosa Arias Peixoto and Tiago Cinto
Methodist University of Piracicaba - UNIMEP, Brazil

1. Introduction

The concept of human-computer interfaces (HCI) has been undergoing changes over the years. Currently the demand is for user interfaces for ubiquitous computing. In this context, one of the basic requirements is the development of interfaces with high usability that meet different modes of interaction depending on users, environments and tasks to be performed. In this context it was developed an expert system (GuideExpert) to help design human-computer interfaces. The expert system embeds HCI design knowledge of several authors in this field.

As the quantities of recommendations are huge, GuideExpert allows searching the guidelines in a much more friendly and fast manner. It also allows eliciting a series of guidelines for evaluating already implemented interfaces.

GuideExpert was evaluated in three Brazilian universities. Due to professors and students engagement, it was possible to correct issues found, both in the implementation and in the guidelines, and to identify the need to develop a more detailed process of HCI requirements elicitation in order for the expert system results become more accurate.

The expert system was also used in the development of intelligent adaptive interfaces for a data mining tool, aiming to provide friendly and appropriate user interfaces to the person using the tool. To meet this goal, the interfaces are able to evaluate and change their decisions at runtime. In this context some models of interaction are modeled in order to fit the profile of those who use them. One of them (for novice users) is finalized and is presented in this chapter; the other two are under development.

2. Ubiquitous computing

Computing has assumed different forms over the years. Nowadays, focus has been given to the term "ubiquitous". It comes from Latin and it's used to describe something which can be found everywhere, meaning that computer omnipresence in everyday life has begun.

The concept of ubiquitous computing proposed by (Weiser, 1991) is increasingly present in our life. Along with his definition, Weiser envisions people being continuously supported by all kinds of computers in their daily jobs. From small devices such as mobile phones to medium sized devices such as tablets, computing has been focused on entertainment and fun. Cooperative work and enriched virtual reality are also highlights in recent years.

According to (Weiser, 1991), all these devices would be connected together by means of radio frequency or infrared.

There are three research groups for ubiquitous applications in Weiser's opinion:

1. *Knowledge* – it has to do with a user being allowed to register anywhere its knowledge, experiences, or memories by means of traditional documents, video files, or audio recordings. This record may be made throughout multimodal interfaces since they have different ways of doing it. Personal agents may also make this record. Since it is possible to perform this action, there is a need of providing ubiquitous access (MacLaverty & Defee, 1997).
2. *Environment* – it has to do with obtaining computer and physical environment information and dealing with it. Applications are expected to gather data from the place where they are and dynamically build computational models in order to adapt themselves to users' needs. The environment may also be able to identify devices that may be part of it. Due to this interaction there is a need for computers to act in an intelligent way when they are in an environment full of computational services.
3. *Interaction* – it has to do with producing an interaction closer to humans, providing multiple ways of interacting, such as voice and handwriting recognition, gestures, and facial expression. The goal of natural interfaces is to provide ordinary means of human expression the way humans do with environment.

Nevertheless, the wish of Ubiquitous Computing relates to human-computer interfaces whereby systems must adapt themselves to users and not the opposite. It is necessary to identify their real needs when they perform tasks. By means of its interface metaphor, a computer is the user "assistant", and "agent". From the perspective of trying to make interaction as natural as possible, this area is becoming more and more multidisciplinary.

However, in order to achieve these goals, HCI (Human-Computer Interface) techniques must be integrated with AI (Artificial Intelligence).The challenge of making a more natural interaction comes from both areas. Nowadays, computer cannot be seen as a "passive" tool controlled by users. With the emergence of "software agents", capable of interpreting orders and reasoning, and electronic devices that can realize and react to stimulus; the computer has become an "active" tool which tries to communicate with the user, explaining its needs (Jokinen & Raike, 2003).

In this context we can mention some aspects that compose this area development:

- *Multimodal Interfaces* – these are able to provide lots of "interaction modalities" as well as voice, gestures, and handwriting and synchronize them with multimedia output (Oviatt & Cohen, 2000). These modes are mapped to sensory signals captured by different brain areas. It represents a new perspective enhancing users' productivity and grant greater expressiveness.
- *Intelligent user interfaces* – these are able to adapt themselves to different users and usage situations. They may also learn with user by providing help and explanations (Ehlert, 2003). According to Ehlert, Intelligent User Interfaces (IUI) use any type of smart technology to achieve the man-machine dialogue.

A common feature on both sides is the ability of adaptability. Concerning multi-modal interfaces, it is desirable to be able to move from one form of interaction to another more appropriate if we consider who is using it.

By means of an IUI we can improve interface performance and provide more "smartness" while tasks are delegated and the search of solutions is allowed. Adaptability and problem solving are hot topics researched by Artificial Intelligence (Russel & Norvig, 2003), so it is important to incorporate these techniques within this area.

3. Multi-modal interfaces

A multi-modal interactive system is a system that relies on the use of multiple human communication channels. Each different channel for the user is referred to as a modality of interaction. Not all systems are multi-modal, however. Genuine multi-modal systems rely to a greater extent on simultaneous use of multiple communication channels for both input and output (Dix et. al, 1998).

Currently, since there is great user diversity, it is rather important to provide different ways of interacting with the machine. A user who has color-blindness, for example, may consider voice interaction something more exciting. In a crowded place the same user may prefer pen interaction instead. Multi-modal interfaces provide different input options and enhance the interaction whether they are used together.

Since our daily interaction with the world around us is multi-modal, interaction channels that use more than one sensory channel also provide a richer interactive experience. The use of multiple sensory channels increases the bandwidth of the interaction between human and computer and also makes the interaction look more like a natural human-human interaction (Dix et. al., 1998).

We may quote some multimodal applications from systems based on virtual reality to automotive embedded ones. In the 80's there was "Put That There" from Bolt (1980). The work described involves the user commanding simple shapes over a large-screen graphics display surface. Because voice can be augmented with simultaneous pointing, the free usage of pronouns becomes possible, with a corresponding gain in naturalness and economy of expression. Conversely, gesture aided by voice gains precision in its power to reference (Bolt, 1980).

Presented by (Cohen et al, 1998), QuickSet was one multi-modal application whose main characteristic was to provide interaction with distributed systems. It used to occur by means of voice or gestures recognition. Image and voice processing were made by software agents used in its architecture (Cohen et al., 1998). Its usage did not stuck to only one field in particular since it was used to perform different tasks as well as military activities simulation and the search for medical information. Concerning the second case, in order to obtain information related to doctors' offices in certain location the user would have to draw the desired area in the map and then the application would retrieve it.

Another medical system involving different ways of interaction is the Field Medic Information developed by NCR and Trauma Care Information Management System Consortium (Holzman, 1999). This solution involved electronic patient records that could be updated through spoken responses for synthesized speech. To ensure rapid and accurate interpretation of spoken inputs, the system incorporated a grammar and a restricted vocabulary spontaneously used by doctors to describe medical incidents and patient records (Holzman, 2001). This information is then electronically sent to the hospital for patient arrival preparation. Hardware used for the Field Medic system consists of a small wearable computer and attached headset with microphone and earphones called the Field Medic Assistant (FMA), and a handheld tablet computer called the Field Medic Coordinator (FMC). An example of such flexibility is evident in the Field Medic system as it allows a doctor to alternate between using voice, pen, or both as necessary. This provides the doctor with a hands-free interface whilst he or she cares for the patient and the ability to later switch to a pen and tablet based interface for recording more detailed information at a later time (Robbins, 2004).

In this area of multi-modal interfaces we can highlight systems that incorporate "intelligence" in addition to various modes of interaction. In this class of systems we can cite the following systems: CUBRICON, XTRA, and AIMI.

The CUBRICON project (Neal & Shapiro, 1991) developed an intelligent multi-modal interface between a human user and an air mission planning system. The computer displays, which comprised the environment shared between the user and the agent, consisted of one screen containing various windows showing maps, and one screen containing textual forms. User input was in the form of typed text, speech, and one mouse button for pointing.

In the CUBRICON architecture, natural language input is acquired via speech recognition and keyboard input. Location coordinates are specified via a conventional mouse pointing device. An input coordinator processes these multiple input streams and combines them into a single stream which is passed on to the multimedia parser and interpreter. Building upon information from the system's knowledge sources, the parser interprets the compound stream and passed the result on to the executor/communicator. The CUBRICON system's knowledge sources are comprised of: Lexicon, Grammar, Discourse Model that dynamically maintains knowledge pertinent to the current dialog, User Model that aids in interpretation based on user goals and Knowledge Base which contains information related to the task space (Robbins, 2004).

XTRA (eXpert TRAnslator) is an intelligent interface that combines natural language, graphics, and pointing (Wahlster, 1991). According to the author, XTRA is viewed as an intelligent agent, namely a translator that acts as an intermediary between the user and the expert system. XTRA's task is to translate from the high-bandwidth communication with the user into the narrow input/output channel of the interfaces provided by most of the current expert systems. XTRA provides natural language access to an expert system, which assists the user in filling out a tax form. During the dialog, the relevant page of the tax form is displayed on one window of the screen, so that the user can refer to regions of the form by tactile gestures. The TACTILUS subcomponent of XTRA system uses various other knowledge sources of XTRA (e.g., the semantics of the accompanying verbal description, case frame information, the dialog memory) for the disambiguation of the pointing gesture (Wahlster, 1991).

The XTRA system is a multi-modal interface system which accepts and generates NL with accompanying point gestures for input and output, respectively. In contrast to the XTRA system, however, CUBRICON supports a greater number of different types of pointing gestures and does not restrict the user to pointing at form slots alone, but enables the user to point at a variety of objects such as windows, table entries, icons on maps, and geometric points. In added contrast to XTRA, CUBRICON provides for multiple point gestures per NL phrase and multiple point-accompanied phrases per sentence during both user input and system-generated output. CUBRICON also includes graphic gestures (i.e., certain types of simple drawing) as part of its multi-modal language, in addition to pointing gestures. Furthermore, CUBRICON addresses the problem of coordinating NL (speech) and graphic gestures during both input and output (Neal & Shapiro, 1991).

AIMI (*An Intelligent Multimedia Interface*) is aimed to help the user to devise cargo transportation schedules and routes. To fulfil this task the user is provided with maps, tables, charts and text, which are sensitive to further interaction through pointing gestures and other modalities. AIMI uses non-speech audio to convey the speed and duration of processes which are not visible to the user (Burger & Marshall, 1998). The AIMI system utilized design rules which preferred cartographic displays to flat lists to text based on the semantic nature of the query and response. Considerations of query and response included the dimensionality of the answer, if it contained qualitative vs. quantitative information, if it contained cartographic information. For example, a natural language query about airbuses might result in the design of a cartographic presentation, one about planes that have certain qualitative characteristics, a list of ones that have certain quantitative characteristics, a bar chart. AIMI has a focus space segmented by the intentional structure of the discourse (i.e., a model of the domain tasks to be completed).

4. Intelligent user interfaces

Intelligent user interfaces (IUIs) is a subfield of Human-Computer Interaction. The goal of intelligent user interfaces is to improve human-computer interaction by using smart and new technology. This interaction is not limited to a computer (although we will focus on computers in this chapter), but can also be applied to improve the interface of other computerized machines, for example the television, refrigerator, or mobile phone (Ehlert, 2003). The IUI tries to determine the needs of an individual user and attempts to maximize the efficiency of the communication with the user to create personalized systems, providing help on using new and complex programs, taking over tasks from the user and reduce the information overflow associated with finding information in large databases or complex systems. By filtering out irrelevant information, the interface can reduce the cognitive load on the user. In addition, the IUI can propose new and useful information sources not known to the user (Ehlert, 2003).

Intelligent interfaces should assist in tasks, be context sensitive, adapt appropriately (when, where, how) and may:

- Analyze imprecise, ambiguous, and/or partial multimedia/modal input;
- Generate (design, realize) coordinated, cohesive, and coherent multimedia/modal presentations;
- Manage the interaction (e.g., training, error recovery, task completion, tailoring interaction styles) by representing, reasoning, and exploiting models of the domain, task, user, media/mode, and context (discourse, environment).

As an example of a system that has intelligent interfaces we can cite Integrated Interfaces Systems (Arens et. al., 1998). It uses natural language, graphics, menus, and forms. The system can create maps containing icons with string tags and natural language descriptions attached to them. It can further combine such maps with forms and tables presenting additional related information. In addition, the system is capable of dynamically creating menus for choosing among alternative actions, and more complicated forms for specifying desired information. Information to be displayed can be recognized and classified, and display creation can then be performed based on the categories to which information to be presented belongs. Decisions can be made based on given rules. This approach to developing and operating a user interface allows the interfaces to be more quickly created and more easily modified. The system has rules that enable the creation of different types of integrated multi-modal output displays based on the Navy's current manual practices. The rules for presentation enable the system to generate on demand displays appropriate for given needs. The systems is able to present retrieved information using a combination of output modes - natural language text, maps, tables, menus, and forms. It can also handle input through several modes - menus, forms, and pointing.

Both the use of multi-modal interfaces such as intelligent interfaces has shown its wide applicability in various systems. In the following sections, we will present an expert system (GuideExpert) that was used to specify an intelligent interface for a data mining tool.

5. GuideExpert: An expert system to support the design of human-computer interfaces

The interfaces have become easier to learn and difficult to specify. As a result, disagreements related to the implementation of the user interface interaction component become common and are taken to the final stages of development, resulting in a drop in product quality and increase in user dissatisfaction with the system.
Research involving human-computer interfaces makes several recommendations for the pre-design, design and post-design for the development of a well designed interface (Nielsen, 1993). In the design phase it is of fundamental importance to implement guidelines for interface design, which are, according to (Nielsen, 1993), recommendations for interface design used in heuristic evaluations during the development of an interface. A heuristic evaluation of a HCI is a group of people observing and analyzing the interface in order to identify usability problems and verify the implementation of guidelines in order to solve them. (Shneiderman, 2009) places the guidelines as one of the pillars supporting a successful HCI design, along with usability testing, design tools and good requirements gathering.
There are extensive collections dedicated to elicit and propose guidelines for interface design. Two of these collections were put together by (Brown, 1988), with a total of three hundred and two guidelines, and by (Mayhew, 1992), with a total of two hundred eighty eight guidelines. Having too much guidelines to evaluate and apply, one can easily conclude that working with guidelines is not trivial. Working with such a large number of recommendations is the biggest problem faced by the HCI designers.
With the aim of helping HCI designers to handle all this knowledge, our team built an expert system to support designers in making decisions related to HCI development. It was designed to suggest and propose guidelines for interface design, as well as perform heuristic evaluations. Three hundred and twenty six guidelines were cataloged, organized and used to build the expert system knowledge base. This work was based on (Nielsen, 1993), (Brown, 1988), (Schneiderman, 1998), (Galitz, 2002), (Cybis et al., 2007).
The GuideExpert, as seen in Fig.1, is comprised of: user interface, the expert system (inference engine and working memory), and the information repositories (knowledge base and database).
When the system starts, the expert system module (4) accesses the knowledge base contained in Layer 3 to load knowledge rules and build its working memory. The user interface layer gathers some information with the designer through modules (1) to (3). Gathered information is analyzed by the expert system in order to select appropriate meta-guidelines. Finally, as result of this analysis, the system accesses the database at Layer 3 to retrieve guidelines according to meta-guidelines previously selected.
The user interface performs three types of analysis with the designer:

1. *Users role description* - it aims at identifying majority characteristics in the user community such as computer experience (Netto, 2004), personal characteristics (Shneiderman, 2009), domain knowledge (Netto, 2004) and features gathered at requirements phase. The questions the designer has to answer are shown in Fig. 2.
2. *Task description* - it aims to identify what are the tasks performed by each user role that will interact with the system. For each task are asked what kind of information

(alphanumeric, numeric or text) is contained in the HCI, in addition to the graphical interface elements used in its composition. An example of an elicitation screen is given in Fig. 3.

3. *User environment description* - it verifies the existence of an internationalized system, having extensive documentation and the level of experience of the HCI designer. The question the designer has to answer is shown in Fig. 4.

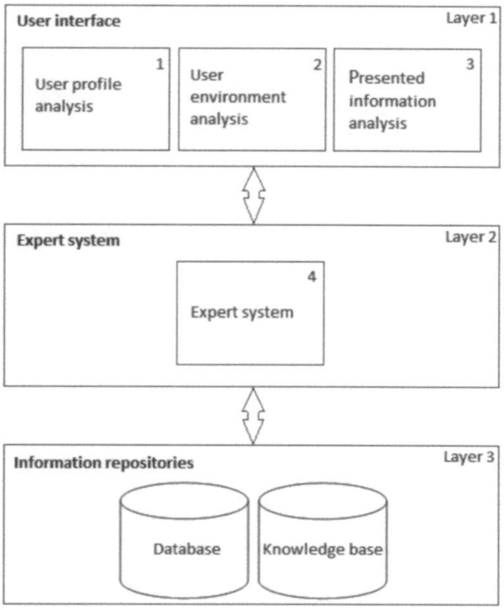

Fig. 1. GuideExpert architecture.

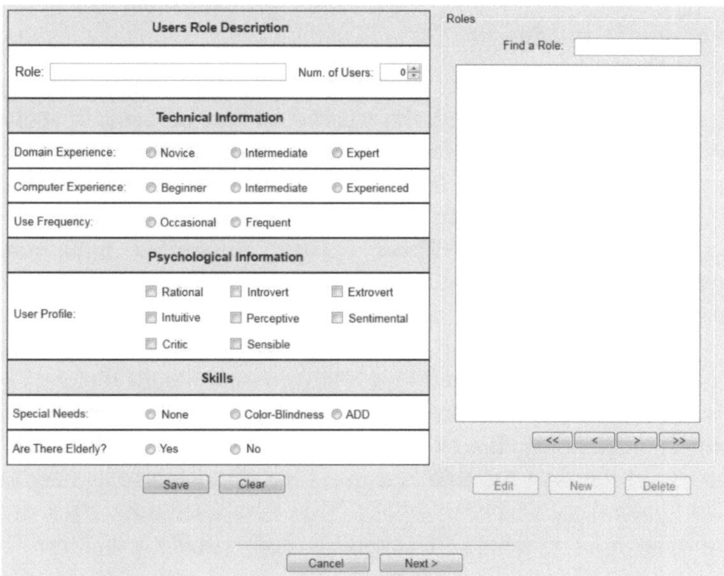

Fig. 2. Users' role description.

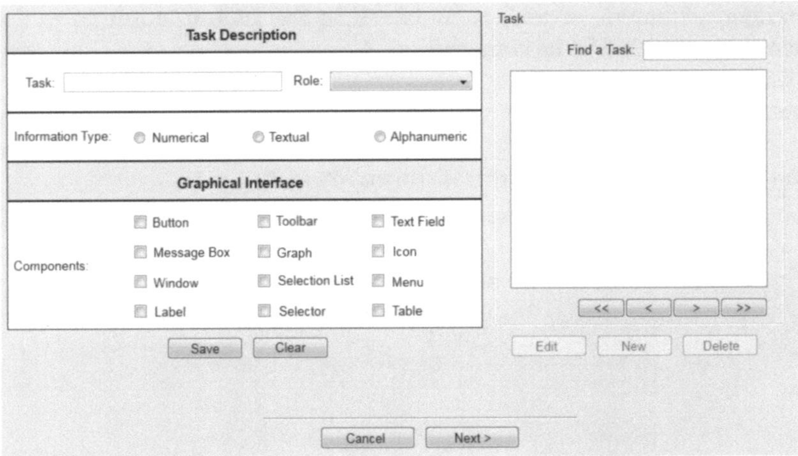

Fig. 3. Task description.

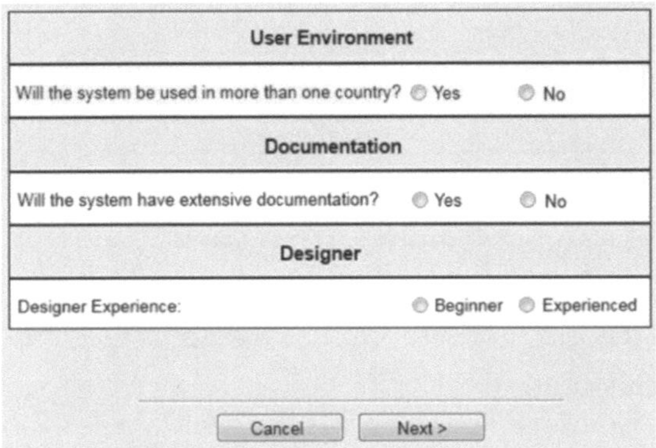

Fig. 4. User environment description.

The expert system inference engine uses the forward chaining strategy to analyze knowledge rules. Through this strategy, the antecedent part of a rule is analyzed and then, in case of a rule that matches the described situation, the consequent part is executed.

To allow the search and selection for the guidelines that best fit a particular design we've established a taxonomy by grouping guidelines according to the characteristics and objectives they have in common. These groups are called meta-guidelines. Their nomenclature was defined by the common goal to which each guideline group had. For example, some guidelines suggested how to provide elements for the protection of user data. So, the meta-guideline generated by these guidelines was named "data protection". The grouping of the guidelines resulted in a total of twenty-eight distinct meta-guidelines that can be further expanded in the future. This taxonomy is new in the literature.

To search within this taxonomy, the expert system gathers the user interface requirements list, focusing on descriptions of the role that users have and the tasks they perform, rather than focusing on general aspects of the HCI. This new elicitation does not consider the usability of the system as a whole. It considers task-specific usability. Thus, beginner, intermediate or even experienced IT users need not be faced with considerations that are not suited to their profiles.

The expert system identifies profiles of cognitive styles of the HCI users based on some recommendations found in the literature, mainly by (Shneiderman, 2009) and (Cybis et al., 2007), in order to meet usage expectations in a satisfactory manner.

(Cybis et al., 2007), describes general recommendations for three types of user personality profiles. Authors such as Norman Warren cited in (Gleitman et al., 2007), Eysenck cited in (Peck & Whitlow, 1975), and Hans Eysenck and Sybil Eysenck cited in (Myers, 1999) are being studied in order to determine other personality profiles and user guidelines to elicit interface requirements.

In our ongoing research, we intend to perform experiments that help develop better guidelines, such as the one mentioned by (Shneiderman, 2009): "For extroverts and introverts users, it can be said that the first prefer external stimuli and variety on actions, while the introverts are characterized by cling to familiar patterns and own ideas."

The system output is composed by a set of guidelines presented to the designer. It allows the designer to perform heuristic evaluations or to design a new HCI. A set of guidelines is suitable for design inspiration, as a checklist in heuristic evaluation or can serve as a reference for answering specific design questions. Fig. 5 shows an example of some guidelines selected by the expert system.

Guidelines

1. Guideline: The button labels should be formatted using system fonts and have the same size.
[1]Pg.408

2. Guideline: Provide a descriptive label to identify the type of information to be typed into a text box.
[1]Pg.422

3. Guideline: Limit the use of fonts for text (up to two types).
[2]Pg.95

4. Guideline: Do not use fonts smaller than 12 points for screens and smaller than 10 points for printed material.
[2]Pg.95

References

[1] Galitz WO. The Essential Guide to User Interface Design: An Introduction to GUI Design Principle and Techniques. New York: John Wiley & Sons, Inc.; 2002
[2] Cybis W, Betiol AH, Faust R. Ergonomia e Usabilidade: Conhecimentos, Métodos e Aplicações. São Paulo: Novatec; 2007.

Fig. 5. Some guidelines selected by the expert system.

Besides suggesting guidelines for an HCI under construction as previously described, the system can also be used as a means of providing guidelines for an expert review. In this context, it was developed a module that provides on-demand guidelines to the designer. Through a single interface, the designer selects items or aspects of HCI to be evaluated, as shown in Fig. 6, and GuideExpert selects the corresponding guidelines.

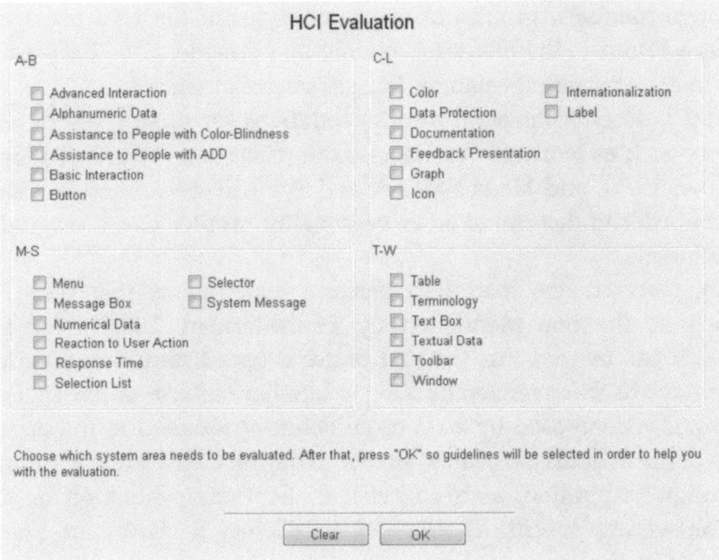

Fig. 6. HCI evaluation.

GuideExpert was used in the development of an intelligent interface for the KIRA tool. It will be presented in the next sections.

6. Data Mining teaching tool

Over the years, information amount stored in companies' databases has been growing exponentially. Besides traditional usage, it is possible to extract knowledge from what is stored by means of a process called Data Mining.

This knowledge may be used with a wide range of possibilities, which makes the interested to find it the responsible to decide what to do. There are several tools to automate Data Mining and maximize its results; however, they need the user to know the entire process, along with its techniques (Mendes & Vieira, 2009).

In this context, Kira tool (Mendes & Vieira, 2009) has been built. Its purpose is to teach user all the knowledge involved with Data Mining while results are showed.

According to (Mendes & Vieira, 2009) and to (Cazzolato & Vieira, 2009), Kira is efficient in fulfilling its proposed goal; however, its user interface has been built without considering usability, something that positively contributes with increasing user satisfaction regarding a product.

Regarding the current user interface, despite focusing on aiding Data Mining learning, its usability has not been evaluated during the development. In order to verify its effectiveness, user evaluations have been performed to obtain feedback from those who have used it.

The capture of post-use feedback occurred by means of an adapted version of PSSUQ (Post-Study System Usability Questionnaire) (Lewis, 1993). The original questionnaire remained the same in its essence, with few modifications added in order to better understand participants and their opinions regarding the occurred interaction.

In order to accomplish evaluations it was necessary to build usage scenarios. These scenarios refer to ordered descriptions of actions performed by application users. Concerning Kira, a scenario of Data Mining as a whole has been developed with the help of staff working on the area.

The usage scenario has been performed by a mixed public: they all had high levels of expertise with computers; however, their domain experiences were very different. There were those who had not kept contact with Kira and Data Mining, those who had already kept contact with Data Mining but not with Kira, and those who had already kept contact with both, tool and domain.

Those who knew both tool and domain were able to perform the usage scenario without major problems and their interaction time was much lower than the others.

The public that knew Data Mining but not Kira was also able to perform the usage scenario without problems; however, their interaction time was higher than those previously described. One of the criticisms had to do with user interface navigation which seemed to be sometimes confusing and not free of errors.

For those who had not kept contact with Kira and Data Mining we can say their interaction time was the highest. Although they had not had domain knowledge, some general concepts were well-known, such as data source, and did not have to be relearned. Their main criticisms related to information excess in interfaces and the lack of information regarding some concepts or even tasks involved.

7. An adaptive interface for data mining

Once identified problems with Kira current user interface, an adaptive interface was proposed. The construction of an intelligent user interface is not something trivial, even ad hoc (relying on informal methods and with dubious effectiveness). There is need for tools and techniques that help proper development and production of satisfactory results. Architecture, for example, is a fundamental item to be adopted. Over the years several proposals have been made by different authors, each one with its own characteristics. To use with Kira, a proposal by (Benyon & Murray, 1993) was adapted and used. Overall, there are three components which can be seen in Fig.7.

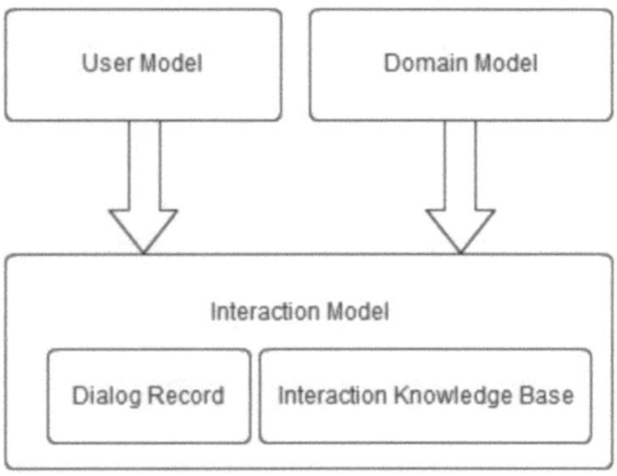

Fig. 7. Adaptive architecture.

The domain model is responsible for representing the interface in its form, the context in which it operates and its logical functioning. User interaction aspects which are able to be changed can only be altered whether they are described in this model. Runtime data collected by the dialog record are represented here (Benyon & Murray, 1993).

The user model is responsible for representing user regarding their profile, knowledge, and cognitive characteristics. For example, attributes that denote user experience with computers or even its frequency of use may be present. According to (Benyon & Murray, 1993), it inherits all attributes from domain model.

The interaction model is composed by another two elements: dialog record, which aims at gathering information during system execution, and interaction knowledge base, which aims at reasoning.

Dialog record, for example, may be composed by the number of occurred errors and successful tasks (Benyon, 1993).

There are in the interaction knowledge base components of a traditional expert system as well as inference engine, working memory, and knowledge base (Russel & Norvig, 2003). Therefore, it has the ability of reasoning, since there are production rules within its knowledge base. These rules refer to characteristics described by user and domain model.

The proposed adaptive system aims at presenting a suitable interface to whoever is interacting with Kira user interface. It is able to change and evaluate its decisions while the interface is being used. Basically, there are three types of users that may use Kira whether we consider the experience with application domain, Data Mining, according to Nielsen (Nielsen, 1993):

1. *Novice*: the person who has less or any experience with application domain. He or she will learn as the interface is used. Hence, there is a strong need of intensive learning support by means of a self-explaining user interface;
2. *Intermediate*: this person refers to an occasional user. They are those who use applications sporadically, or in an infrequent manner. There is no need to provide some specific feature to support learning or even enhance productivity; however, presenting means to make them to remind the user interface every time they use it without having to relearn is necessary;
3. *Specialist*: a user who has high level of expertise with application domain. It does not need learning support as novice does and prefer to have control under interaction flux. We can say it is able to perform tasks rather well without computers or assistive technologies.

Overall, there are three types of user interfaces which may suit profiles described before, one for each case.

1. *Novice user interface*: it must support and teach user Data Mining process along with its main concepts and relationships existent among them. This interface was developed by means of a concept map, later described with further details;
2. *Intermediate user interface*: it must support user in using Kira without imposing unnecessary and excessive learning which may turn interaction into something unpleasant. This interface will still be studied and developed;
3. *Specialist user interface*: it must provide means for experienced users to use Kira and enhance results since they know domain quite well and do not need to relearn it, as occurs with an intermediate user. Their expertise level only tends to increase. This interface will still be studied and developed.

Regarding its functioning, the adaptive system needs user and domain data in order to manipulate them and provide its conclusions. Therefore, data gathering may occur by two different manners: explicit and implicit (Benyon & Murray, 1993).

Gathering data explicitly simply refers to asking user what is necessary to feed user domain. That may be considered easier than implicitly; however, more inconvenient for those who are questioned. In order to minimize this inconvenience survey may be kept short and direct.

Gathering data implicitly refers to inferences made by interaction knowledge base. Whether the system verifies two different characteristics previously described in the knowledge base it can infer about them. For example, let's suppose three attributes present in the domain model: `errors`, `average_completion_time`, and `interface`. The first refers to amount of errors made, while the second is the average completion time of the tasks. The third denotes which interface is being used. In the knowledge base there might be the following production rule: `IF errors > 15 AND average_completion_time >= 20 THEN interface = novice_interface`. Along with this information, inference engine can change interface presented to the user when it makes lots of errors or even takes a long time to perform a task.

7.1 Concept maps

Concept maps are graphical tools used with learning or knowledge representation. It consists of related concepts linked through connections in order to represent a domain in particular (Novak & Cañas, 2008). Overall, we may say they are similar to a graph since it has nodes, equivalent to concepts, and edges, equivalent to connections.

The foundation theory of concept maps is called meaningful learning from (Ausubel et. al., 1980). It is correct to say that concept maps must show a familiar content to learners. According to (Ausubel et. al., 1980): "the most important factor influencing learning is what a learner already knows. Find out what he knows and base upon that your teaching."

Regarding use of concept maps to teach a knowledge domain, we can say a human being learn more efficiently whether it is presented a more general map instead of one with lots of specific issues (Ausubel et. al., 1980).

Despite being simple, concept maps have proven to be a valuable instrument since its use implies attribution of new meanings to concepts and techniques of traditional learning.

Regarding Kira's novice user interface, it was developed by means of a concept map representing all concepts and connections fundamental to understand Data Mining process.

Due to its similarity with a graph, an adjacency list has been used to represent it with when coding took place. Its logic consists of maintaining a linked list containing all graph nodes, which also store those which they relate to.

Fig. 8 shows the initial map presented to a novice user. Respectively, numbers 1 and 2 from it indicate a concept and a connection. Number 3 indicates an area reserved to aid map navigation. Through it, concept explanations and tips about what should be done are given. In order to see them, user only needs to move mouse cursor to a desired concept.

Aiming at reducing complexity regarding presentation of many concepts at the same time (up to 22 depending on the data mining task); we choose to present the map in two parts. What is initially shown is a map which is common to all data mining tasks (Fig. 8). After Kira recognize the task which will be used, map expands itself and presents the rest of process.

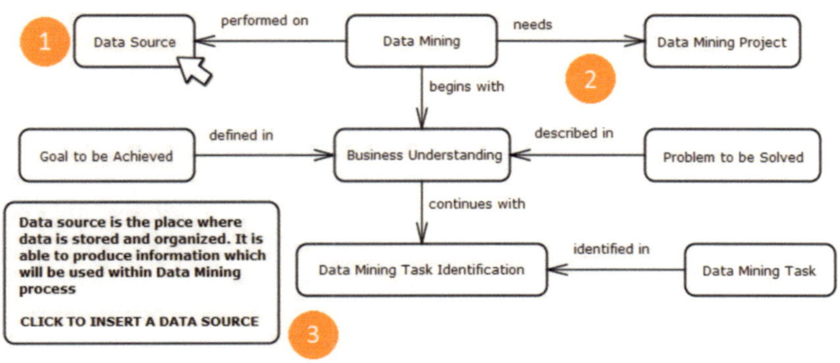

Fig. 8. Initial concept map.

Regarding concepts amount, twenty-four capable of representing the tasks of association rules and classification were identified. Grouping tasks is not coded yet and its concept map was not developed. The two concept maps were built assisted by specialized staff.
Interaction with Kira concept map is not restricted to navigation and obtaining explanations of concepts. Data Mining process requires data to be defined in order to present its results. Therefore, JFrames (adaptive system was coded in Java and so did Kira) internal to the map were developed to perform such function. Each of them performs a specific and well defined task. For example, since it is true that Data Mining needs a data source, there is need to have it inserted. In this context, there is a JFrame triggered by a simple mouse click on concept "Data Source" at the conceptual map of Fig. 8, which allows users to execute this task.
JFrames have also been developed using the recommendations of GuideExpert system as shown in Fig. 9.

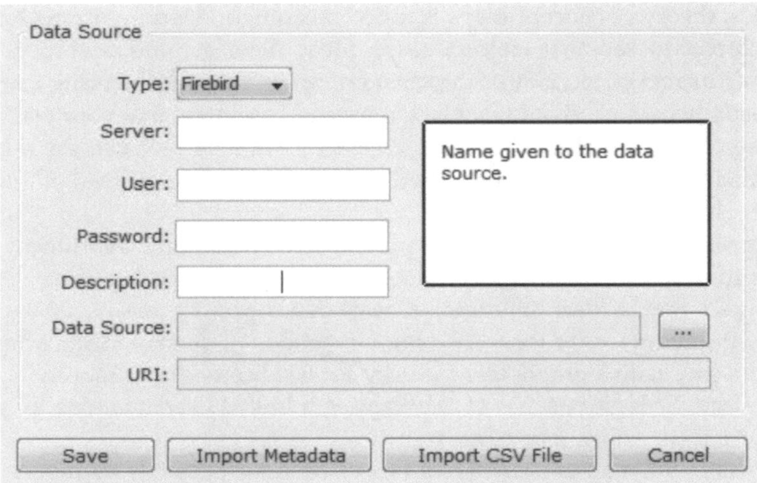

Fig. 9. Frame data source.

The intelligent interface of Kira now fits two types of users: novice through the use of conceptual mappings and monitoring of the user through the stages of data mining; and the old interface of the tool for experienced users. Was elicited in this category that users find it easier if the interface itself controls the dialogue and also allows the use of gestures.
Results of the advantages of adaptive interface for novice users of the KIRA tool are being collected. The incorporation of concept maps to the data mining teaching process and monitoring of the tool has been found positive.

8. Conclusion

This chapter has presented the state of the art regarding the human-computer interfaces and how they are increasingly focusing on tasks and helping users. This meets the tendency of "ubiquitous" systems and natural way to interact with them. Certainly there is much to research and the help of artificial intelligence area is significant. It was also presented two systems that contribute to the area: the expert system for Human-Computer Interface Design Guidelines (GuideExpert) and an intelligent interface for a data mining tool (KIRA). GuideExpert was used in the development of KIRA user interfaces. Certainly, when finalizing the design of KIRA adaptive interfaces, recommendations on intelligent interfaces can be added to GuideExpert thus providing the acquisition of more specialized knowledge.

9. References

Arens, Y., Hovy, E. & Vossers, M. (1998). On the Knowledge Underlying Multimedia Presentations, In: *Intelligent User Interfaces*, M. Maybury & W. Wahlster (eds), pp.157-169, Morgan Kaufmann Publishers, ISBN: 1-55860-444-8, San Francisco

Ausubel, D., Novak, J. & Hanesian, H. (1980). *Psicologia Educacional*, Editora Interamericana, ISBN: 8520100848, Rio de Janeiro

Benyon, D. (1993). Adaptive Systems: A Solution to Usability Problems, *Journal of User Modeling and User-Adapted Interaction*, Vol.3, No.1, pp.65-87, ISSN 0924-1868, DOI: 10.1007/BF01099425

Benyon, D. & Murray, D. (1993). Adaptive Systems: From Intelligent Tutoring to Autonomous Agents, Knowledge-Based Systems, Vol.6, No.4, (December 1993), pp.197-219, ISSN: 0950-7051, DOI: 10.1016/0950-7051(93)90012-I

Bolt, R. (1980). Put-That-There: Voice and Gesture at the Graphics Interface, *Computer Graphics, SIGGRAPH 80 Conference Proceedings*, Vol.14, No.3, (July 1980), pp.262-270, ISBN 0-89791-1021-4.

Brown, C. (1988). *Human-Computer Interface Design Guidelines*, Ablex Publishing Corp, ISBN 0-89391-332-4, Norwood, NJ

Burger, J. & Marshall, R. (1998). The Application of Natural Language Models to Intelligent Multimedia, In: *Intelligent User Interfaces*, M. Maybury & W. Wahlster (eds), pp.429-440, Morgan Kaufmann Publishers, ISBN: 1-55860-444-8, San Francisco

Cazzolato, M. & Vieira, M. (2009). Avaliação da Ferramenta KIRA como Aplicação do Processo de KDD e de técnicas de Mineração de dados, *Anais da XVII Mostra Acadêmica UNIMEP*, Available from: http://www.unimep.br/phpg/mostraacademica/anais/7mostra/1/195.pdf

Cohen, P., Johnston, M., McGree, D., Oviatt, S., Pittman, J., Smith, I., Chen, L. & Clow, J. (1998). Multimodal Interaction for Distributed Interative Simulation, In: *Intelligent User Interfaces*, M. Maybury & W. Wahlster (eds), pp.562-569, Morgan Kaufmann Publishers, ISBN: 1-55860-444-8, San Francisco

Cybis, W., Betiol, A. & Faust, R. (2007). *Ergonomia e Usabilidade: Conhecimentos, Métodos e Aplicações*, Novatec Editora Ltda, ISBN 978-85-7522-138-9, São Paulo

Dix, A.; Finlay, J.; Abowd, G. & Beale, R. (1998). *Human-Computer Interaction*, (2nd edition), Prentice Hall. ISBN 0-13-239864-8, New York

Ehlert, P. (2003). Intelligent User Interfaces, In: *Techical Report DKS03-01/ICE01, Data and Knowledge Systems Group, Department of Information Technology and Systems, The Netherlands: Delft University of Technolog*, 07.11.2010, Available from: http://www.kbs.twi.tudelft.nl/docs/report/DKS03-01.pdf

Galitz, W. (2002). *The Essential Guide to User Interface Design: An Introduction to GUI Design Principles and Techniques*, John Wiley & Sons, ISBN 978-0-471-27139-0, New York

Gleitman, H., Fridlund, A. & Reisberg, D. (2007). *Psicologia*, (7. Edition). Fundação Calouste Gulbenkian, ISBN. 978-9-72311059-3, Lisboa

Holzman, T. (1999). Computer human Interface Solutions for Emergency Medical Care, *Interactions*, Vol.6, No.3, (May 1999), pp.13-24, ISSN: 1072-5520

Holzman, T. (2001). Speech-Audio Interface for Medical Information Management in Field Environments, *International Journal of Speech Technology*, Vol.4, No.3-4, (July-Oct 2001), pp.209-226, DOI 10.1023/A:1011304506915

Jokinen, K. & Raike, A. (2003). Multimodality - Technology, Visions and Demands for the Future, *Proceeding of the First Nordic Symposium on Multimodal Communication*, Paggio P. Jokinen K. Jönsson A. (eds), ISSN: 1600-339X, Copenhagen, (September 2003), pp. 25-26

Lewis, J. (1993). IBM Computer Usability Satisfaction Questionnaires: Psychometric Evaluation and Instructions for Use,In: *Technical Report 54786*, 05.01.2011, Available from: http://drjim.0catch.com/usabqtr.pdf

MacLaverty, R. & Defee, I. (1997). Multimodal Interaction in Multimedia Applications, *Proceeding of First Signal Processing Society Workshop on Multimedia Signal Processing*, ISBN: 0-7803-3780-8, Princeton, (June 1997), pp. 25-30

Mayhew, D. (1992). *Principles and Guidelines in Software User Interface Design*, Prentice Hall, ISBN 0-13-721929-6, New Jersey

Mendes, E. & Vieira, M. (2009). Um Ferramenta instrucional para Apoiar a Aplicação do Processo de Mineração de Dados, Dissertação de Mestrado em Ciência da Computação, Methodist University of Piracicaba, Piracicaba. Brazil

Myers, D. (1999). Introdução à Psicologia Geral, LTC, ISBN 978-8-52161186-8, Rio de Janeiro

Neal, J. & Shapiro, S. (1991). Intelligent Multi-Media Interface Technology, *Intelligent User Interface*, Sullivan, J. W. and Tyler, S. W. (eds.), pp.11-43, Addison-Wesley, ISBN 0-201-50305-0, New York

Netto, A. (2004). *IHC: Modelagem e Gerência de Interfaces com o Usuário*, Visual Books, ISBN: 85-7502-138-9, Florianópolis

Nielsen, J. (1993). *Usability Engineering*, Academic Press, ISBN 0-12-518405-0, Boston

Novak, J. & Cañas, A. (01.2008). The Theory Underlying Concept Maps and How to Construct and Use Them,In: *Technical Report IHMC CmapTools*, Institute for Human and Machine Cognition, 4.11.2010, Available from: http://cmap.ihmc.us /Publications/ResearchPapers/TheoryUnderlyingConceptMaps.pdf

Oviatt , S. & Cohen, P. (2000). Multimodal Interfaces that Process what comes naturally, *Communications of the ACM*,Vol.43, No.3, (March 2000), pp.45-53, ISSN: 0001-0782

Peck, D & Whitlow, D. (1975). *Designing Approaches to Personality Theory (Essential Psychology)*, Methuen Young Books, ISBN 978-0-41682800-9, New Delhi

Robbins, C. (2004). Speech and Gesture Based Multimodal Interface Design, In: *Computer Science Department, New York University*, 07.10.2010, Available from: http://mrl.nyu.edu/~robbins/Papers/MultimodalResearchSurvey.pdf

Russel, S. & Norvig, P. (2003). *Artificial Intelligence*, (2nd edition), Prentice Hall Series, ISBN 0-13-790395-2, New Jersey

Shneiderman, B. (1998). *Designing the User Interface: Strategies for Effective Human-computer Interaction*, (3rd edition), Addison Wesley Longman, ISBN: 0-201-69497-2, Boston

Shneiderman, B. & Plaisant, C. (2009). *Designing the User Interface: Strategies for Effective Human-Computer Interaction*, (5th edition), Addison-Wesley Publishing Co, ISBN 0-321-53735-1, Reading, MA

Wahlster, W. (1991). User and Discourse Models for Multimodal Communication, *Intelligent User Interfaces*, Sullivan, J. W. and Tyler, S. W. (eds.), pp. 45-67, Addison-Wesley, ISBN 0-201-50305-0, New York

Weiser, M. (1991), The Computer for the Twenty-First Century. In: *Scientific American*, Vol.265, No.3, (September 1991), pp.94-104, ISSN 0036-8733

7

Advances in Health Monitoring and Management

Nezih Mrad*[1] and Rim Lejmi-Mrad[2]
[1]*Air Vehicles Research Section (AVRS), Defence R&D Canada (DRDC), Department of National Defence (DND), National Defence Headquarters Ottawa, Ontario,*
[2]*Apoptosis Research Center (ARC), Children's Hospital Eastern Ontario (CHEO), Department of Cellular & Molecular Medicine, Faculty of Medicine University of Ottawa, Ontario, Canada*

1. Introduction

Scientists in engineering, physical and health sciences continue to explore biological systems functions and behaviors to develop bio-inspired human and engineering complex systems, subsystems and components. In the natural sciences, it is demonstrated that such acquisition of knowledge is leading to tangible outcomes in the form of organs growth and implants [1]. Critical human organs have been cultured in the lab from the cell level to a fully functional body parts (e.g. ear, kidney, heart). The advantages of this development are numerous and include increased quality of life and performance, increased life expectancy (life cycle), reduced health care costs and infrastructure (maintenance costs). It has also been demonstrated that an effective man-machine interface [2] has led not only to providing the disabled with a second chance at a higher quality of life, but at times of having even superior life quality, longevity and performance (e.g. artificial limps). Such accomplishments in science and technology are rendered possible by the exploitation of innovation and creative conceptualization, integration of advanced sensor technology, control systems and hybrid material systems. In the last decades and since the decoding of human deoxyribonucleic acid (DNA), significant effort has been expanded on the development of selective biological systems that are expected to be maintenance and disease free or possess some desired biological or functional characteristics (e.g. specific body or esthetic features). For instance, before fertilization, human eggs are screened for potential diseases and genes related to particular diseases are extracted and replaced by healthy ones [3], this is also known as gene therapy. It is well established that the human body is the most complex system that science has encountered. The exploration of this system, which is in its infancy, only now is providing clues and knowledge on how this system functions and how external parameters affect its performance and health. This knowledge has so far contributed to the society advancement in several sectors including health care, education, space exploration, economic and earth resources conservation. Additionally, acquired knowledge has contributed to new age efficient infrastructure development that includes infrastructure for communication, transportation, water, energy, and finance.

As a result of advances in natural and biological sciences, current engineering systems, subsystems, components and platforms have increased and continue to increase in complexity. With advances in multifunctional materials, micro- and nano-fabrication, advanced integrated electronics, flexible circuitry and electronics, innovative power generation and optimal power consumption, artificial intelligence and creative data extraction, fusion, and interpretation, these complex systems are increasingly gaining autonomy and functionality. Several systems are now able to detect and adapt to anomalies (e.g. self-healing materials [4]). Current systems are continuously being designed for efficient manufacturing and materials usage, reduced reliance on human intervention, increased reliance on advanced and intelligent decision making capabilities and functionalities at reduced manufacturing, acquisition, and maintenance costs.

This document introduces the subject of health monitoring and management and its associated terminology. It also introduces the role of nature and biological systems in the design and development of complex multifunctional engineering systems. Finally, it presents some advances in engineering systems and systems components, particularly as they relate to the aerospace sector. It is not the intent of this document to provide detailed accounts for technology development, implementation and integration, but its objective is to highlight technological advances as well as technological and implementation challenges of health monitoring and management systems within different sectors of the industry, particularly the aerospace sector.

2. Terminology and definitions

2.1 Systems

The general definition of a system is a collection of pieces whose collective function is greater than the function of the individual pieces. Depending on the domain of interest, this definition could evolve to a more complex one. It is the opinion of the authors that the definition of a biological system constitutes the foundation for any evolving system. Hence, we define in the following only biological and engineering systems.

2.1.1 Biological system

A biological system (or organ system) is a group of organs that work together to perform a certain task, referred to as a functional task. Common systems, such as those present in mammals and other animals, seen also in human anatomy, are the circulatory system, the respiratory system, the nervous system, etc. Typically, the phrase referring to a "living system" or system containing biological entities is contained by a boundary, across which energy, matter, or work may pass. A typical example of a biological system is the cell, encased by a cell membrane. The term "biological system" is also referred to a system consisting essentially of biological processes [5-6]. In human anatomy, a human body system is a group of organs that work together to accomplish a bodily function. In the human body, cells combine to form tissues (e.g. skin tissues, muscle tissues, bone tissues), tissues combine and form organs, organs combine to form organ systems, and organ systems combine to form the human body. Examples of such human body systems, their functions and their corresponding organs include: digestion system (mouth, esophagus, stomach, large and small intestines), circulatory system (heart, veins, and arteries), muscular system (muscles), skeletal system (bones), nervous system (brain and nerve pathways), respiratory system (lungs), etc.

2.1.2 Engineering system

An engineering system is a system that is technologically enabled, has significant socio-technical interactions and has substantial complexity. Moses [7] presents some types and foundational issues with engineering systems. Engineering systems are interdisciplinary in nature and are devoted to addressing large-scale, complex engineering challenges within their socio-political context. These can further be defined as systems with diverse, complex, physical designs that may include components from several engineering disciplines, as well as economics, public policy, and other sciences. Some of the easiest systems to understand are mechanical systems. Simple systems are often constructed for a single purpose and generally have few parts or subsystems. For instance the cooling system in a car may consist of a radiator, a fan, a water pump, a thermostat, a cooling jacket, and several hoses and clamps. Together they function to keep the engine from overheating, but separately they are useless. Similar to biological systems, all system components must be present and they must be arranged in the proper way. Removing, misplacing or damaging one component puts the whole system out of commission.

2.1.3 Biological-engineering system

Biological-engineering systems also referred to as bioengineering systems, consist of interrelated and interdependent biological and engineering systems or objects. From the medical perspective, bioengineering integrates physical, chemical, or mathematical sciences and engineering principles for the study of biology, medicine, behavior, or health. It advances fundamental concepts, creates knowledge from the molecular to the organ systems levels, and develops innovative biologics, materials, processes, implants, and devices for the prevention, diagnosis, and treatment of disease, for patient rehabilitation, and for improving health. It is clear that bioengineering is concerned with applying an engineering approach (systematic, quantitative, and integrative) and an engineering focus (the solutions of problems) to biological problems, it is also concerned with applying biological knowledge and processes to engineering problems. From an engineering perspective, bioengineering systems are those that are built specifically to work in conjunction with the human body, often to amplify its capability and improve its performance. One of the most basic examples is the operation of a baseball bat or similar tools. The mechanical subsystem does nothing until it is combined with the human component of the system. While the biological component can do a whole lot without the tool, it would be hard pressed for the tool to perform its intended function. Cardiac pacemakers provide another, more complex, bioengineering example of the interrelated and interdependent biological and engineering systems.

Figure 1, represents a simplified perspective of a selected biological system [8-9]. Figure 2 [10] illustrates the human levels of organization from cellular to tissue, organ and organ system (human body). Within each cell is a biological and metabolic system that creates and uses energy that is necessary for the cell's life and function. There are many types of cells in the body, such as bone cells, muscle cells (myocytes), liver cells (hepatocytes), heart cells (cardiocytes), nerve cells, skin cells, and kidney cells. The latter are a large collection permitting the development of tissues hence the development of muscle tissues, connective, epithelial, and nervous tissues. Figure 3 [11-12] represent engineering and bioengineering systems, respectively.

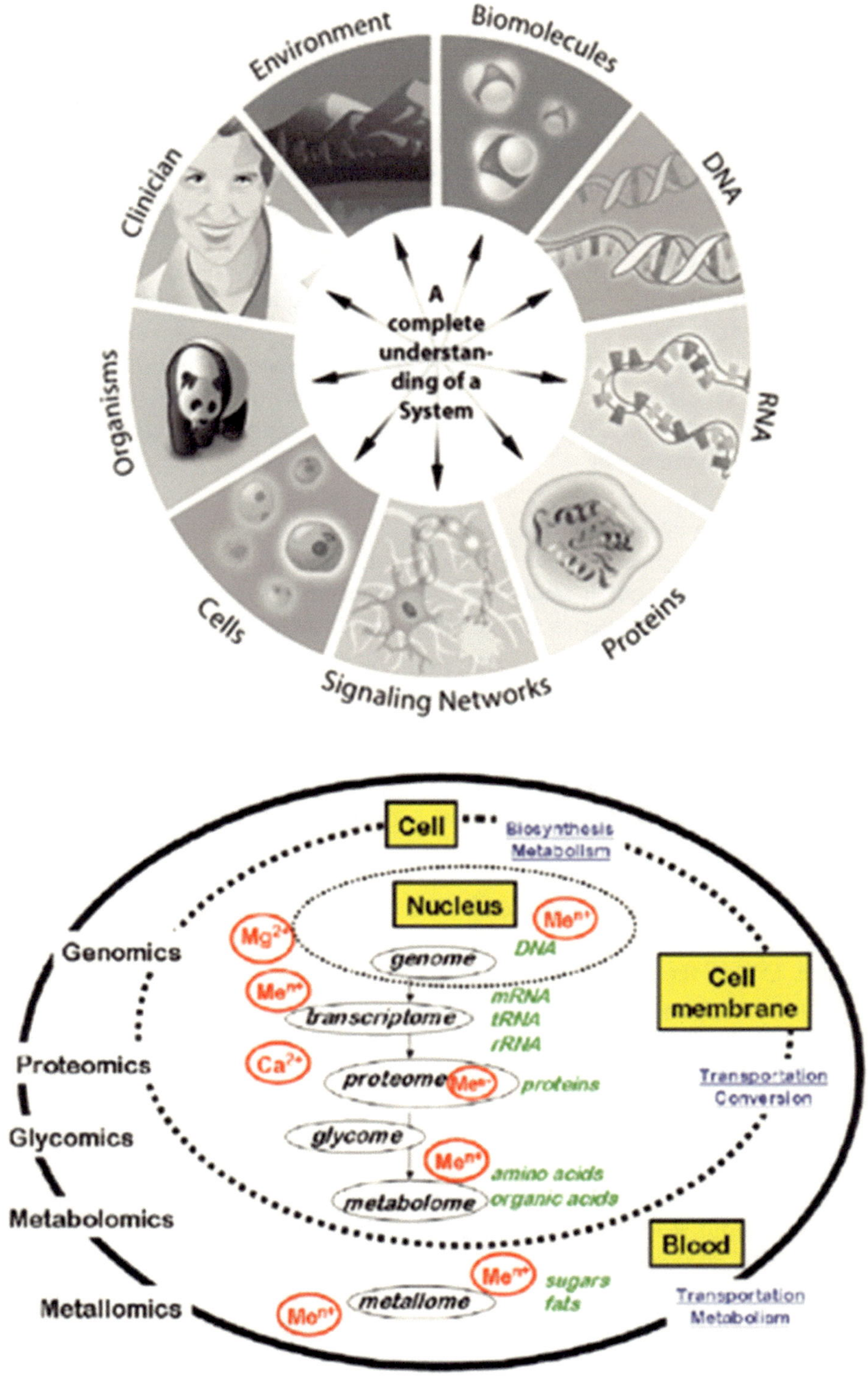

Fig. 1. Perspective and simplified model of a biological system.

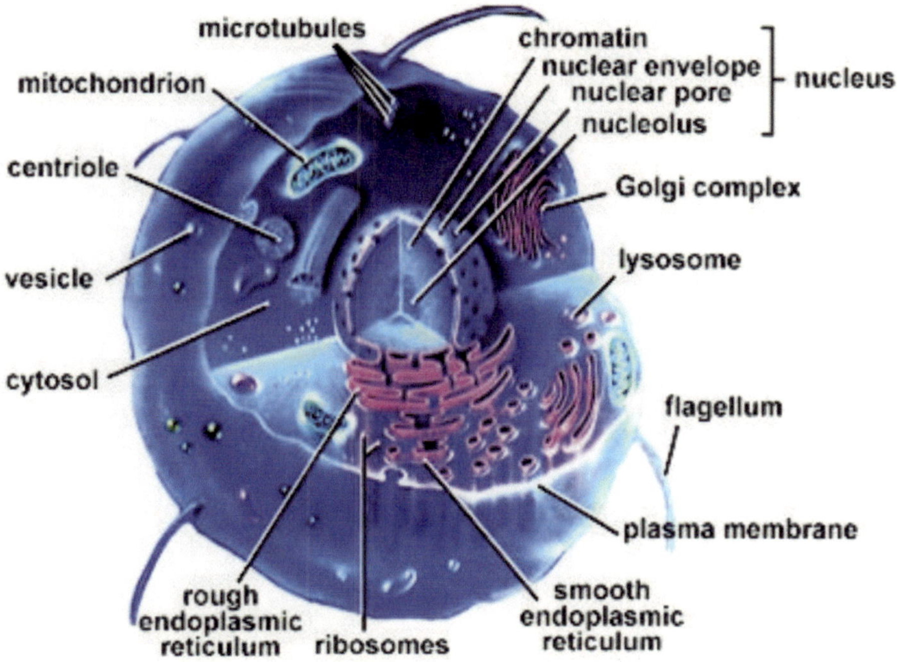

(a)

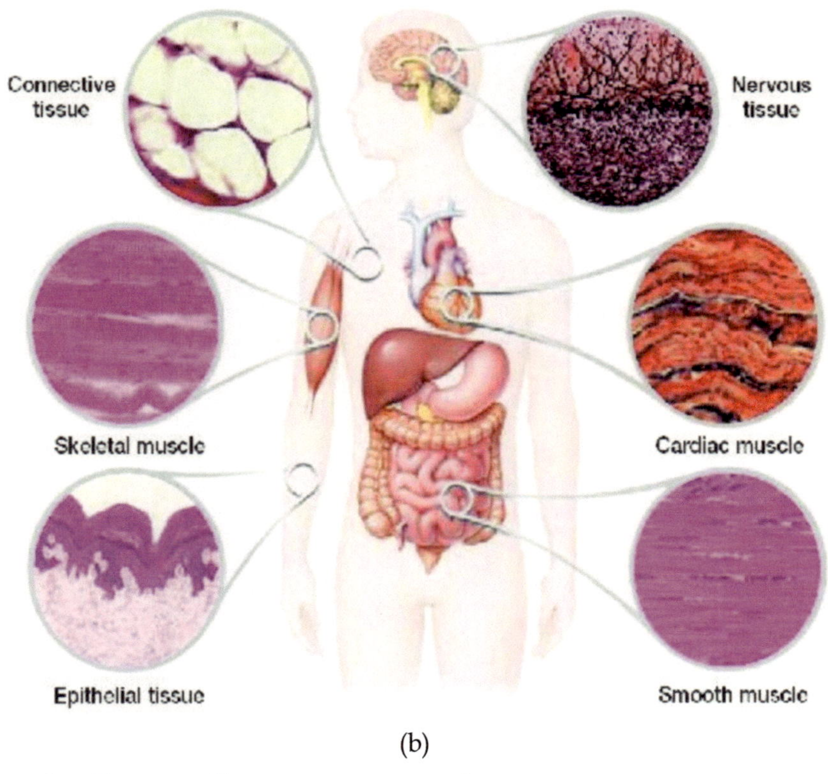

(b)

Fig. 2. Example of human cells, tissues, organs, and organ systems.

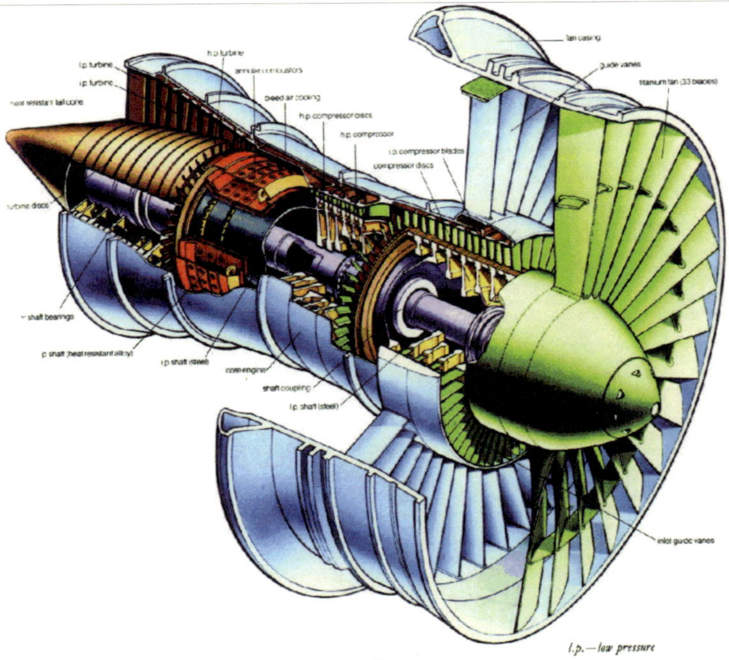

(a)

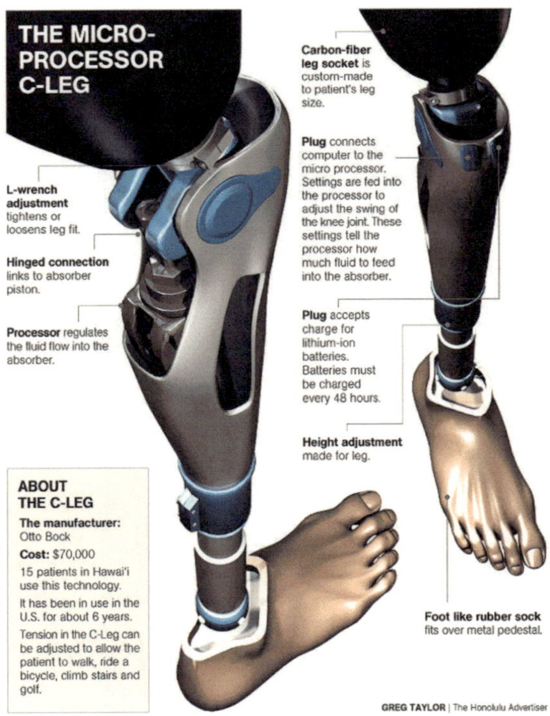

(b)

Fig. 3. Systems – (a) Engineering system (gas turbine engine) (b) Biological-Engineering system (artificial leg).

2.2 Health monitoring, diagnostics and prognostics (HMDP)

2.2.1 Health monitoring (HM)

A health monitoring system is a framework that enables the monitoring and reporting on the state or events of a particular system. Events are detected through a network of sensors. Detected events are logged or registered within the system in an event logger. These events could either be evaluated in the event logger or transmitted for evaluation. Outcome of the evaluation is transmitted through a notification process to systems with decision making capability for action and intervention. Figure 4 illustrates a framework for remote patient and structural health monitoring. This framework goes beyond the monitoring and reporting function and presents the full cycle of health monitoring and prevention process for any system including biological, engineering or bio-engineering systems. Health monitoring is further defined as an approach to evaluating errors in or collecting general information about a system. In general, the approach presented in Figure 4 uses event classification that identifies events to a provider in order to intervene with appropriate actions.

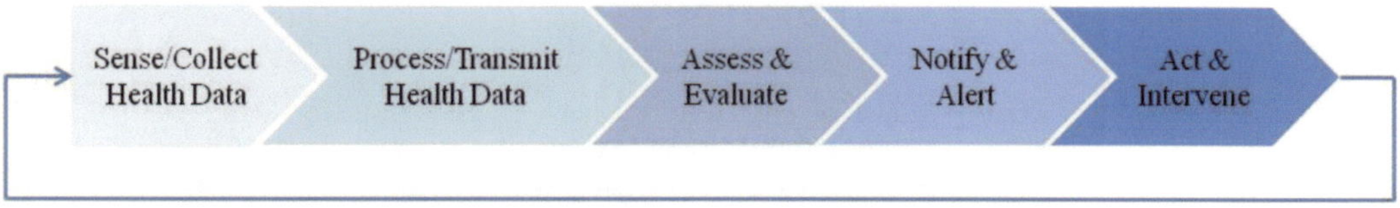

Fig. 4. A framework for remote patient and structural health monitoring.

2.2.2 Health diagnostics (HD)

Diagnostics is the branch of medical science that deals with diagnosis [13]. Diagnosis can be defined as the nature of a disease [14]; the identification of an illness or a conclusion or decision reached by diagnosis. To the Greeks, a diagnosis meant specifically a "discrimination, a distinguishing, or a discerning between two possibilities." Today, in medicine, that corresponds more closely to a differential diagnosis. The latter is defined as the process of weighing the probability of one disease versus that of other diseases possibly accounting for a patient's illnesses. In structural engineering, diagnostics can be defined as the nature of a structural damage (e.g. impact, corrosion, fatigue); the identification of the degree of damage or a conclusion or decision reached by the diagnosis for future action. Figure 5, illustrates a diagnosis system framework applicable to all systems including biological, engineering or bio-engineering systems.

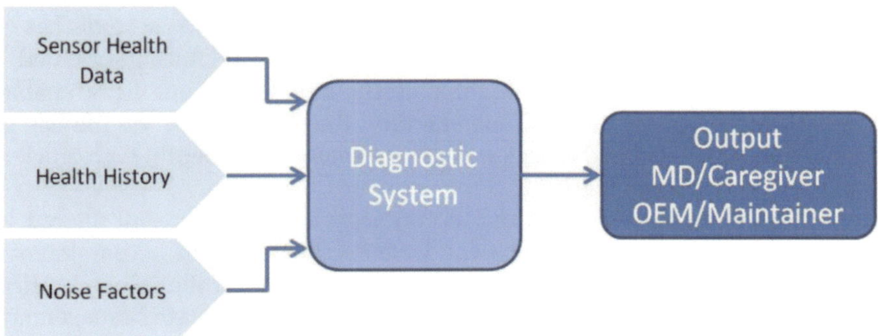

Fig. 5. A framework of a diagnostic system.

2.2.3 Health prognostics (HP)

The word prognostic is taken from the Greek *Prognostikos* (of knowledge beforehand). It combines pro (before) and gnosis (a knowing). The word is used today to mean a foretelling of the course of a disease [14]. Prognostic is also defined as relating to prediction [15]. It is also referred to as a sign of a future happening or a sign or symptom indicating the future course of an event. In medicine as well as in engineering, it refers to any symptom or sign used in making a prognosis. Figure 6 [16] illustrates the relationship between the health monitoring, health diagnostics and prognostics, where the outcome (Remaining Useful Life (RUL)) of the prognostics module is based on the exploitation of modeling tools and sensor data.

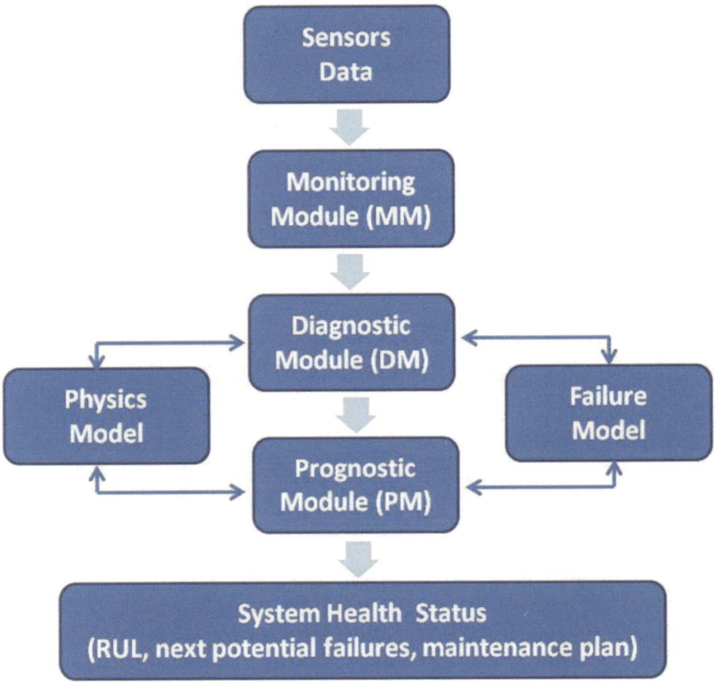

Fig. 6. A framework of a prognostics system.

At this juncture it is important to observe that the referred to terminology employed human systems and medical references as illustration platforms. It is well known that biological systems are the most complex, intelligent, expert and adaptive systems that science has encountered. It is without doubt that the evolution of our engineering systems has exploited these systems to enable the development of our current technologically-oriented, modern society. Lessons learned from bird's flight patterns and techniques have enabled more efficient, reliable and safe air travel. Understanding the evolution of sea life has provided key framework and concepts in the design of unobservable, high depth, high efficiency, self-powered and autonomous submarines.

For bio-inspired engineering systems the terminology is to some extent altered to reflect specific systems, applications, domains, and fields; however, in recent years, several perspectives and terminology have emerged, in the engineering discipline, particularly in the field of Structural Health Monitoring (SHM) and Prognostics Heath Management (PHM) communities. The following provides the evolution on the usage of the introduced terminology.

2.3 Diagnostics, prognostics health management (DPHM or PHM)

In recent years, the discipline of Diagnostics, Prognostics and Health Management (DPHM) has been formalized to address the information management and prediction requirements of operators of complex systems (e.g. aircraft, power plants, and networks) including their need for on-line health monitoring. Generally, PHM systems incorporate functions of condition monitoring, state assessment, fault or failure diagnostics, failure progression analysis, predictive diagnostics (i.e., prognostics), and maintenance or operational decision support. Ultimately, the purpose of any DPHM or PHM system is to maximize the operational efficiency, availability and safety of the target system.

As defined by Industry Canada (IC) [17], diagnostics refers to the process of determining the state of a component to perform its function(s) based on observed parameters; prognostics refers to predictive diagnostics which includes determining the remaining life or time span of proper operation of a component; and health management is the capability to make appropriate decisions about maintenance actions based on diagnostics/prognostics information, available resources, and operational demand. Figures 7 [18] provides a framework for health assessment and prognostics of electronic products as an alternative to traditional reliability prediction methods.

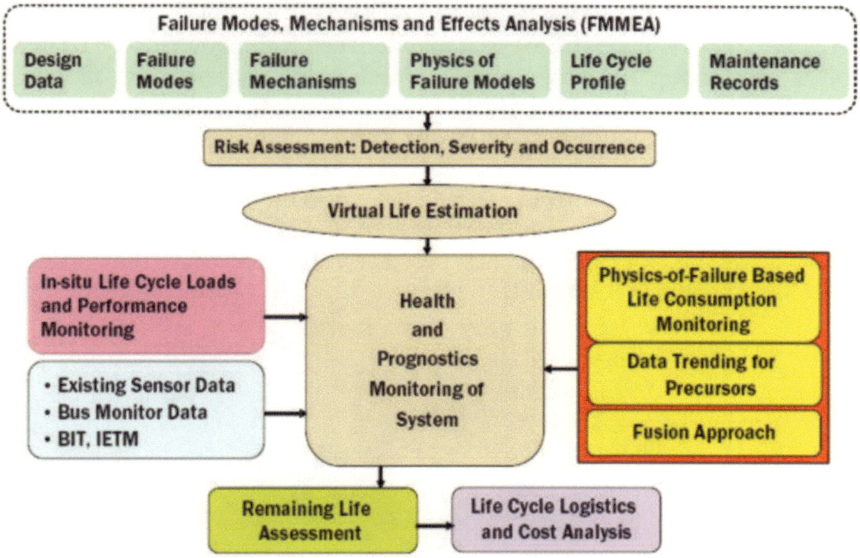

Fig. 7. A framework for health assessment and prognostics of electronic products.

2.4 Structural health monitoring (SHM)

SHM stands principally for structural health monitoring. It also stands for structural health management, systems health monitoring and systems health management. It must not be confused with Vehicle Health Monitoring or Management (VHM) which includes propulsion and avionics systems. Moreover, Structural Damage Sensing (SDS) is also referred to as SHM.

Structural Health Monitoring (SHM) capability is a life cycle management capability that aims at providing, at every moment during the life cycle of a structure, the health state of the structure and its constituent materials. In the aerospace industry, for the structure to be airworthy, its health state must remain in the domain specified in the design, even though the structure may experience some structural degradation due to normal usage, environmental exposure, and accidental events.

As described by Farrar and Worden [19], the SHM process involves the observation of a system over time using periodically sampled dynamic response measurements from an array of sensors, the extraction of damage-sensitive features from these measurements, and the statistical analysis of these features to determine the current state of a system's health. For long term SHM, the output of this process is periodically updated information regarding the ability of the structure to perform its intended function in light of the inevitable aging and degradation resulting from normal usage and operational environments. In the event of excessive loading, SHM is used for rapid condition screening and aims to provide, in near-real-time, reliable information regarding the structural integrity of the structure.
Farrar and Wordon [19] defined SHM as the process of implementing a damage detection and characterization strategy for engineering structures. In this definition, damage is identified as changes to the material and/or geometric properties of a structural system, including changes to the boundary conditions and system connectivity, which adversely affect the system's performance. Figure 8 [20] represent the link between diagnostics, prognostics and structural health monitoring and the process of implementing that framework. Such framework is an extension of the framework presented in Figure 6.

2.5 Condition based maintenance (CBM and CBM+)

Condition Based Maintenance (CBM) is a maintenance technique closely related to PHM that involves monitoring machine condition and predicting machine failure; whereas, Condition Based Maintenance Plus (CBM+) is built upon the concept of CBM, but is enhanced by reliability analysis. The US Air Force (USAF) defined CBM as a set of maintenance processes and capabilities derived from real-time assessment of weapon systems' condition obtained from embedded sensors and/or external tests and measurements using portable equipment. Whereas, CBM+ expands upon these basic concepts, encompassing other technologies, processes, and procedures that enable improved maintenance and logistics practices [21].

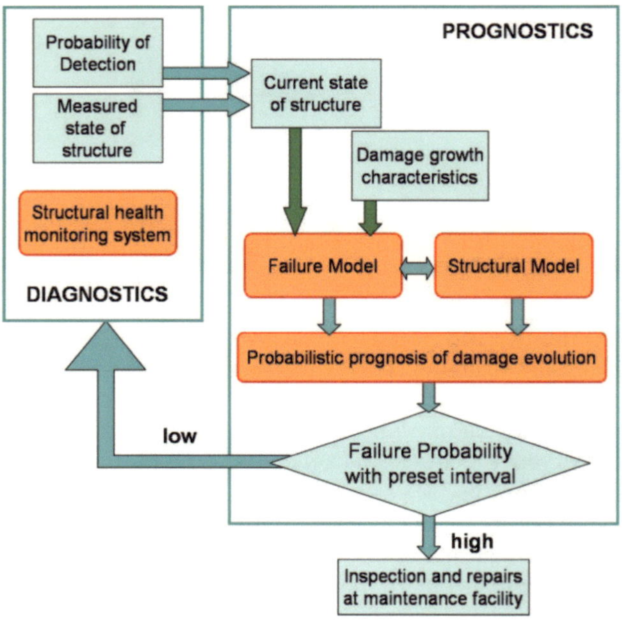

Fig. 8. A framework for diagnostics, prognostics and health monitoring.

2.6 Health and usage monitoring (HUMS)

Health and Usage Monitoring Systems (HUMS) were developed over 30 years ago in reaction to a concern over the airworthiness of helicopters. The purpose of HUMS is to increase safety and reliability, as well as to reduce operating costs, by providing critical component diagnosis and prognosis. Unlike Structural Health Monitoring (SHM) systems or Integrated Vehicles Health Management (IVHM) that have been developed for fixed-wing aircraft, HUMS effort focused on rotorcraft, which benefit from a system's ability to record engine and gearbox performance and provide rotor track and balance. HUMS could also be configured to monitor auxiliary power unit usage and exceedances, and include built-in test and Flight Data Recording (FDR) functions.

Overall, a full HUMS is expected to acquire, analyze, communicate and store data gathered from sensors and accelerometers that monitor the essential components for safe flight. The analyzed data allows operators to target pilot training, establish a Flight Operations and Quality Assurance (FOQA) program, in which they can determine trends in aircraft operations and component usage and provide valuable date for new engine design and certification. Figure 9 [22] shows a systematic process used to successfully identify the crack length during a test of a helicopter transmission with the crack in the planetary carrier plate using vibration signals.

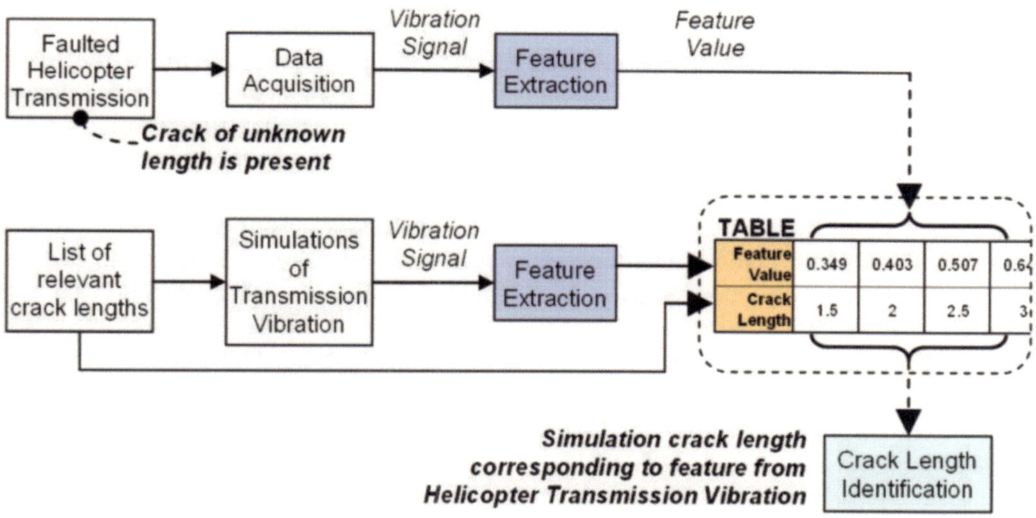

Fig. 9. A process for the identification crack length on a helicopter transmission using vibration measurements.

The terminology provided in both sections 1 and 2, is adhered to by professionals and experts in the corresponding fields; however, within the research communities this terminology is loosely used to reflect the same concept or framework. For instance, when a new vibration sensor is employed to merely provide vibration readings, it is often referred to as a PHM vibration sensor, by engine researchers, and as an SHM vibration sensor, by the structural researchers.

3. Systems development and implementation

Critical infrastructure, such as dams, bridges, nuclear power plants, are currently being monitored and managed using more reliable and advanced sensors networks, diagnostics tools, and advanced predictive/prognostics capabilities, presented in the terminology section. Infrastructure managers and maintainers are now able to obtain the health state of the infrastructure remotely and in a timely fashion through the deployment of wireless capability. Such advanced information, facilitates reliable and efficient maintenance planning and infrastructure upgrades and acquisition and even contribute to future systems design. Additionally, and in recent years, the aerospace sector has significantly intensified its efforts in the development, exploration, qualification and certification of some autonomous systems. Current emerging platforms, such as the Joint Strike Fighter (JSF), possesses integrated autonomic logistic capability that is based on a PHM system, for increased platform safety, reliability, availability, reduced life cycle cost, and enhanced logistics. The deployment of an autonomic logistic capability is expected to reduce the platform life cycle cost by as much as 20%. It has also been reported that even though the platform employs the latest technology and concepts several components of the PHM system employ traditional sensors. However, the next generation fighter could benefit from the continuous evolvement of SHM and PHM concepts, frameworks, and technologies.

Independent of the simplicity or complexity of the system architecture, four building blocks are required to constitute the core of DPHM systems' architecture and structure. These blocks are: sensor networks, usage and damage monitoring (diagnostics), life management (predictive and prognostics), and decision making and asset management. A possible approach to describing the functioning of such a system is that usage and damage parameters, acquired via wired and wireless sensors network, are transmitted to an on-board data acquisition and signal processing system. The acquired data is developed into information related to damage, environmental and operational histories as well as system usage employing information processing algorithms embedded into the usage and damage monitoring block. This information, when provided to the life management block and through the use of predictive diagnostic and prognostics models, is converted into knowledge about the state of operation and health of the system. This knowledge is then disseminated and transmitted to the crew, operations and maintenance services, regulatory agencies, and or Original Equipment Manufacturers (OEM) for decision making and assets management.

Analogous to a biological system, and as shown in Figure 10, the nervous system constitutes the critical and perhaps the most significant and limiting factor in the development and implementation of DPHM systems. Sensors and sensor networks must be accurate, reliable, robust, small size, lightweight, immune to radio frequency and electromagnetic interferences, easily networked to on-board processing capabilities, able of withstanding operational and environmental conditions, requiring no or low power for both passive and active technologies and possess self-monitoring and self-calibrating capabilities. In the engineering community, this "nervous system" is referred to as advanced or smart sensors network. It has the potential to perform several functions delivered by Nondestructive Evaluation (NDE) techniques in a real-time on-line environment with added integrated capabilities, such as signal acquisition, processing, analysis and transmission. These highly networked sensors (passive or active) are suitable for large and complex platforms and wide area monitoring and exploit recent development in micro and nano technologies. These sensors include Microelectromechanical systems (MEMS) sensors [23], fiber optic sensors

[24], piezoelectric sensors [25], piezoelectric wafer active sensor [26], triboluminescent sensors [27], Stanford Multi-Actuator-Receiver Transduction (SMART) layer sensor networks [28], nitinol fiber sensors [29], carbon nanotube sensors [30], and comparative vacuum sensors [31]. In the following sections only selected emerging sensors and sensor concepts, with potential for advancing aircraft DPHM, are presented.

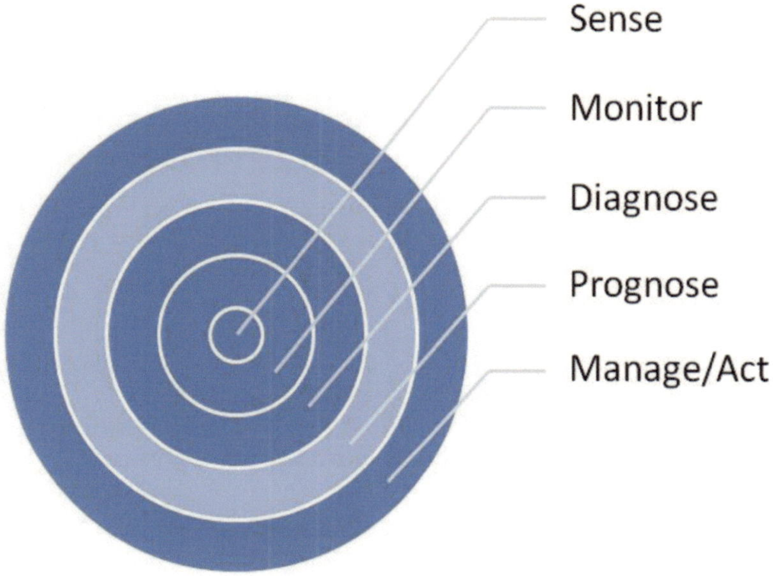

Fig. 10. Core functions of a DPHM or a Biological System (the Prognosis function does not exist for a biological system)

3.1 CNT-based sensors

Carbon nanotubes (CNT) are piezoresistive in nature, i.e. these materials exhibit a change in electrical resistance as a result of change in mechanical strain or deformation. Such characteristics are now used to develop CNT-based strain sensors for potential integration into a DPHM system. Four types of CNT-based films, fibers and structures have successfully been evaluated for this purpose including CNT film ("buckypaper"), CNT-modified polymers, Layer-By-Layer (LBL) assembly of CNT and CNT-fibers.

3.1.1 CNT-based film strain sensor (Buckypaper sensor)

Dharap *et al.* [32] were the first to use buckypaper films as strain sensors. Figure 11 illustrates the linear response of a buckypaper film attached to a brass tensile sample. Vemuru *et al.* [33] have improved the buckypaper strain sensor range (500 με) by using Multi-Walled CNT (MWCNT). They have observed a sensitivity of 0.4 and a linear sensor response up to a strain of 1000 με. In their work they highlighted that the piezoresistive behavior of the CNT-network is not only dependant on the change of the film dimension under strain but about 75% of the change in resistance is due to the characteristics of the CNT network itself. In another related work, a carbon nanotube/polycarbonate thin film was used as a strain sensor, resulting in measurement sensitivity of 3.5 times higher than that of a traditional strain gauge [34].

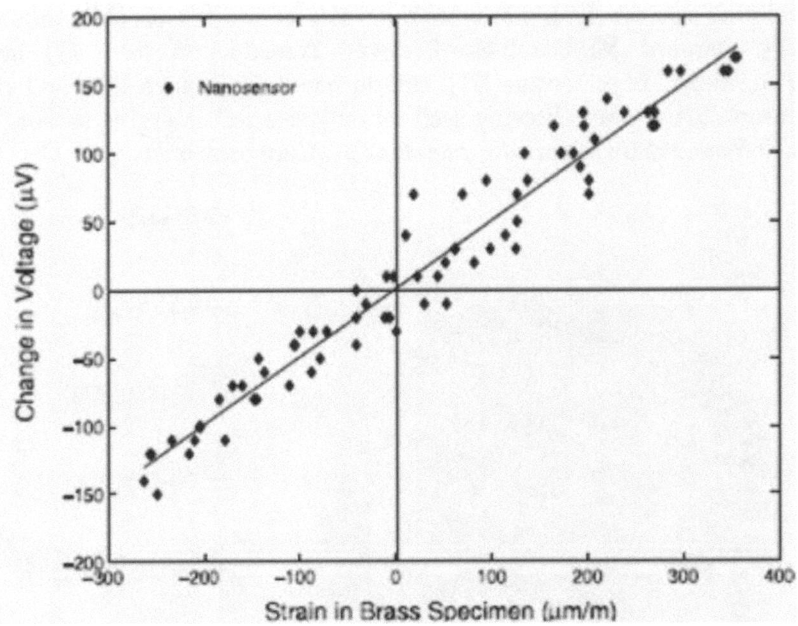

Fig. 11. Linear response of a buckypaper attached to a brass tensile sample.

3.1.2 CNT-based film strain sensor (CNT-modified polymer (SWCNT-PMMA))

Kang *et al.* [35] have used Single Walled CNT (SWCNT) modified PMMA (polymethyl methacrylate) to manufacture CNT-based strain sensors. Using different weight fraction of SWCNT, they were able to tune the guage factor and resistivity of the strain sensor, as shown in Figure 12. It has been observed that some of the benefits provided by this sensor type include increased dynamic range performance and increased linear strain range. For instance the SWCNT-PMMA sensors can withstand strains of up to 1500 µε; whereas buckypaper can withstand strains of up to 500 µε.

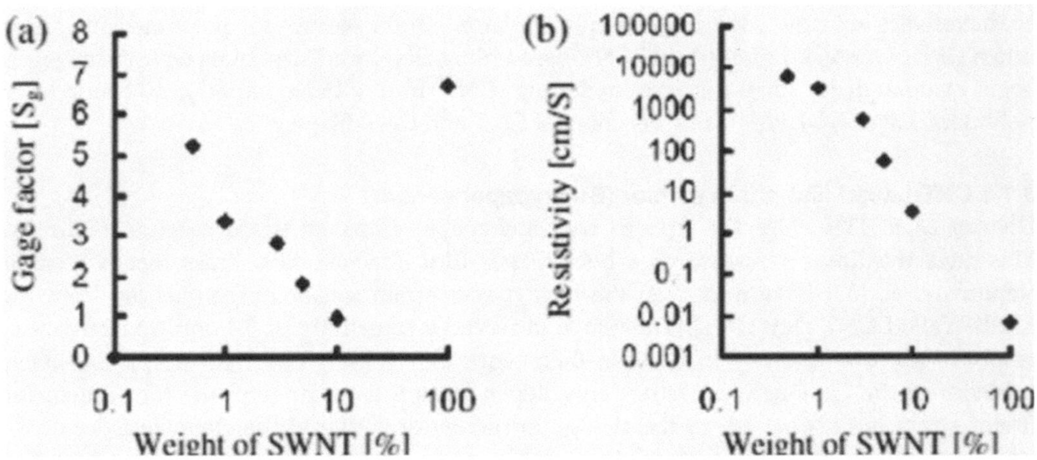

Fig. 12. Gage factor (a) and resistivity of PMMA nanocomposite with different weight fraction of SWCNT.

3.1.3 CNT-based film strain sensor (CNT-modified polymer (LBL assembly, CNT-PDMS))

Unlike Buckypaper sensors and SWCNT-PMMA sensors, composite Layer-By-Layer (LBL) assembly strain sensors, demonstrated lower sensitivity (e.g. one-seventh that of Buckypaper sensor sensitivity [35]) and increased linear strain range of up to 10000 με; as opposed to the aforementioned (e.g. SWCNT-PMMA sensors (1500 με), Buckypaper (500 με). To further improve the sensor performance, increase the mechanical robustness, and enhance the linear strain range (45000 με), Song et al. [36] used a polymer thin film based on polydimethylsiloxane (PDMS). Figure 13 illustrates the linear behavior (up to 0.45% of strain) of the hybrid CNT-PDMS films manufactured through LBL assembly with different concentrations of CNT.

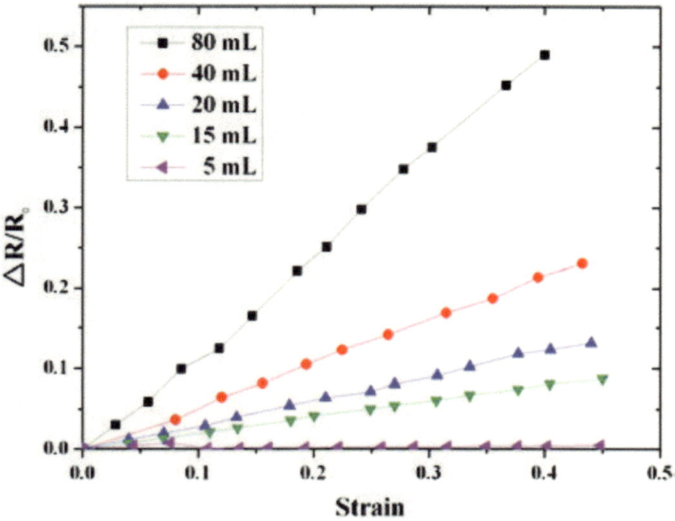

Fig. 13. Sensitivity of CNT-based polymer thin film sensor based on polydimethylsiloxane with different content of CNT.

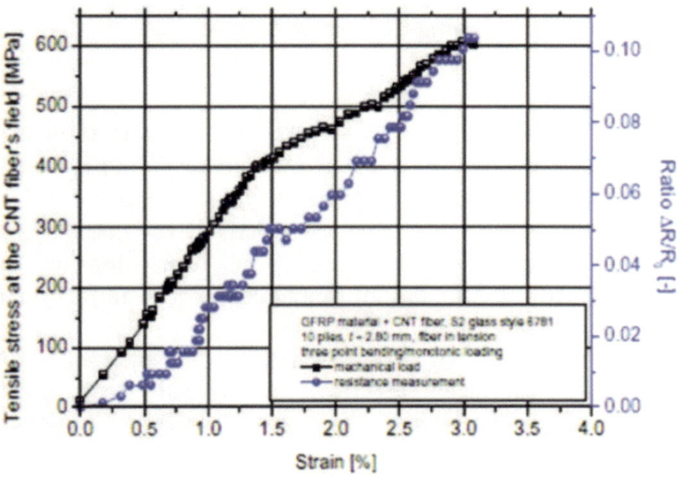

Fig. 14. Correlation between tensile stress of a glass fiber laminate composites and resistance change within an embedded CNT fiber.

3.1.4 CNT-based fiber strain sensor

In their communications, Thostenson and Chou [37], Alexopoulos *et al.* [36] used embedded CNT fibers for strain sensing as well as damage monitoring of glass fiber composites. Their correlation of the resistance change of the embedded fiber and tensile stress (equivalently the tensile strain) of the laminate composite is illustrated in Figure 14.

It is clear that CNT-based sensors provide selectivity, flexibility, and tailored sensor sensitivity and strain range. The latter, is provided by changing of manufacturing process or approach, varying CNT content, and host polymer matrix. Even though these sensor types suffer from lower technology readiness levels, they offer the potential of multifunctional capability and flexibility of instrumentation. Our current efforts and contributions to the development of such sensor capability for DPHM can be seen in [38]. Figure 15 [39], illustrates the results of our current CNT-based crack detection sensor design, where it is illustrated that CNT current output changes in function of number of loading cycle and crack growth.

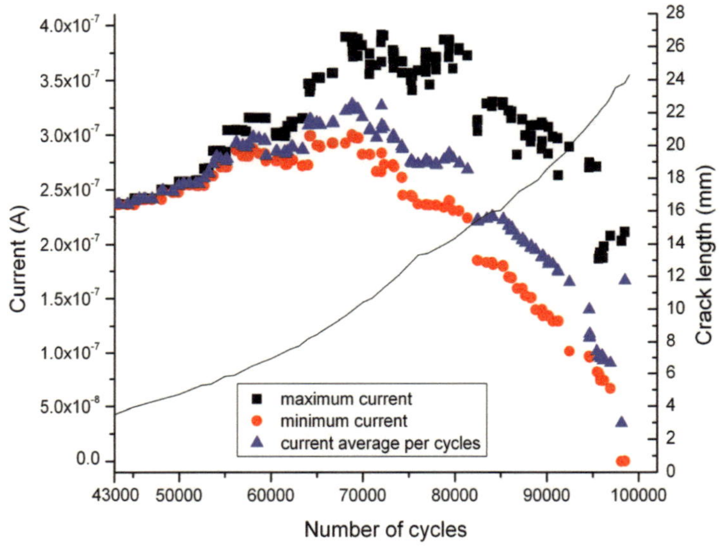

Fig. 15. Crack growth monitoring using CNT-based sensor.

3.2 MEMS-based sensors

Microelectromechanical systems or devices (MEMS) are referred to as smart or advanced devices. A smart device is defined as one that operates using computers [40] (e.g. smart cards); whereas, an advanced device is said to be "highly developed or difficult." According to the IEEE 1451 standard [41], a smart sensor is defined as "one chip, without external components, including the sensing, interfacing, signal processing and intelligence (self-testing, self-identification or self-adaptation) functions". Figure 16 [41] illustrates the smart sensor concept as defined by IEEE 1451.

Sensors based on this smart concept generally exploit development in MEMS and nano technologies along with advanced wireless devices with radio frequency communications. Figure 17 [42] depicts such a smart sensor, known as a sensor node, for multi-parameters sensing, where Figure 17a reflects the original prototype and Figure 17b represents the commercial final node. In this case, the sensor node contains four major components: 3M's MicroflexTM tape carrier, thinned MEMS strain sensors, Linear Polarization Resistor (LPR) sensors to detect wetness and corrosion and electronics module. The electronics module is composed of a Micro Controller Unit (MCU), a signal conditioning unit, a wireless Integrated Circuit (IC) unit, a battery and an antenna. Employing this node design, Niblock et al. [43] developed an Arrayed Multiple Sensor Networks (AMSN) for materials and structural prognostics.

Some of the observed benefits employing smart sensors systems include the wealth of information that can be gathered from the process leading to reduced downtime and improved quality; increased distributed intelligence leading to complete knowledge of a system, subsystem, or component's state of awareness and health for 'optimal' decision making. Additionally, due to their significant small size and integrated structure, these sensors can potentially be embedded into composites structures or sandwiched between metallic components for remote wireless and internet based monitoring. Intelligent signal processing and decision making protocols can also be implemented within the node structure to provide ready to use decisions for reduced downtime and increased maintenance efficiency.

Due to significant potential of MEMS-based sensors and driven by the requirement for the development of advanced SHM and engine PHM capability, our current efforts focused on the development, characterization and demonstration of MEMS-based humidity sensors in anticipation of further development of engine condition monitoring sensors, including sensors that monitor the state of combustion and level of pollution, such as monitoring Nitric Oxide (NO), Carbon Monoxide (CO), Carbon Dioxide (CO_2) and Oxygen (O_2).

Figure 18 [44] presents measurement results for a MEMS-based humidity sensor, which is comprised of the sensor, the integrated circuit (IC) interface and the printed circuit board (PCB). This sensor is based on a capacitor with a moisture sensitive dielectric material. Results show how the capacitance of the sensor varies with relative humidity over the range of 11% to 97% and illustrates how this development allows for accurate measurements without extensive (and costly) calibration schemes.

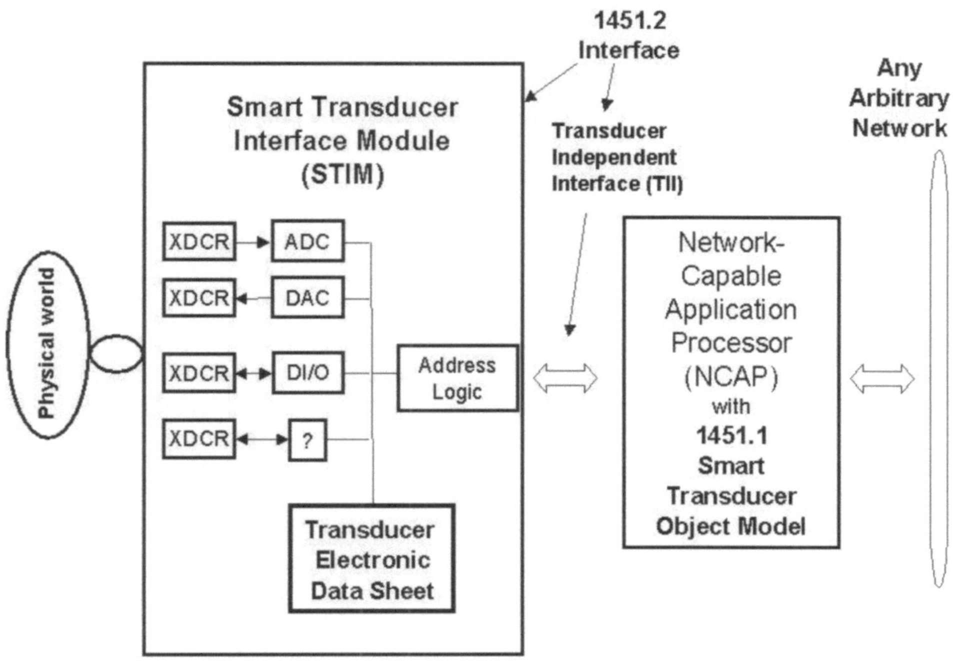

Fig. 16. Smart sensor concept defined by IEEE 1451.

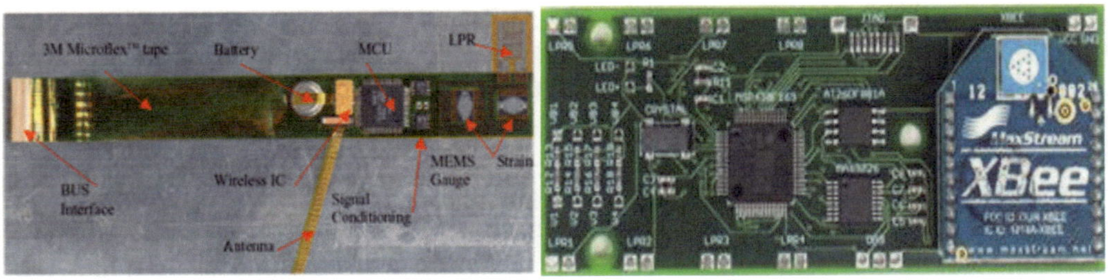

(a) (b)

Fig. 17. Smart MEMS based smart sensor node.

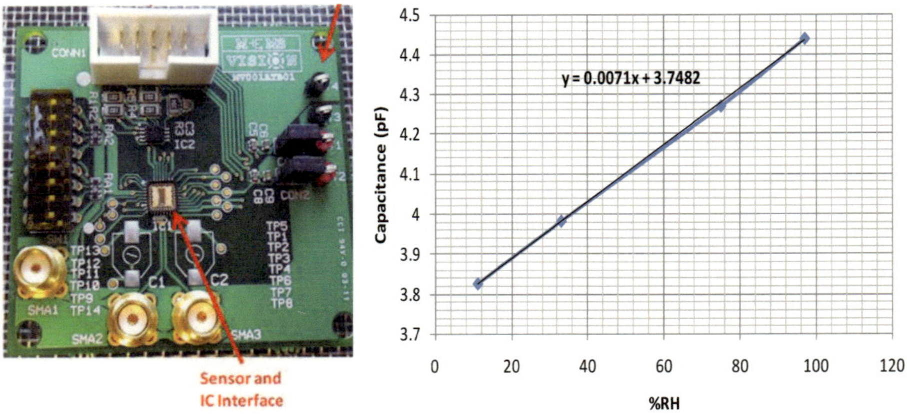

Fig. 18. MEMS based relative humidity sensor node.

3.3 RFID-based sensors

The use of Radiofrequency Identification (RFID) technology dates back to World War II. This technology has and continues to revolutionize the supply chain and assets management. Wal-Mart, FedEx and UPS are examples of the early adopters of the technology [45]. This technology is posed to continue to benefit both military and commercial sectors particularly in the field of focused logistics. The emergence of the DPHM concept and the requirement for autonomous wireless sensor networks has intensified efforts in integrating sensor capability within these identification devices. Current RFID-based sensors can be used for the monitoring of temperatures, chemicals, strains and humidity. Ong *et. al.* [46] demonstrated the use of inductive-based coupling RFID technology, at a frequency of 22.5 MHz, to detect temperature and humidity. Figure 19 illustrates the frequency-temperature relationship for temperatures ranging from 0°C to 110°C. A sensitivity of 6.4 kHz/ °C was demonstrated.

Our current research effort mainly focused on the development of reliable autonomous, power-free RFID-based sensors for integration within a DPHM system in an aircraft environment. Figure 20, illustrates an experimental configuration for the detection of crack initiation in a metallic structure under static loading within an MTS load frame. A handheld multi-purpose MC-9000G RFID reader was used to detect the tag that constituted a component of the closed loop crack detection sensor system. The crack detection sensor was developed in house and its particulars can be found in [47]. Additionally, using backscattering-based RFID technology, at frequency of 915 MHz, we demonstrated temperature and humidity measurements, using RFID tag characteristic variation, such as changes in resonant frequency (phase and magnitude) and impedance. Figure 21, illustrates the frequency-temperature and humidity relationship for temperatures up 100°C. An average temperature sensitivity of 71.3 kHz/ °C and 0.725 MHz/%RH were demonstrated, respectively for temperature and humidity.

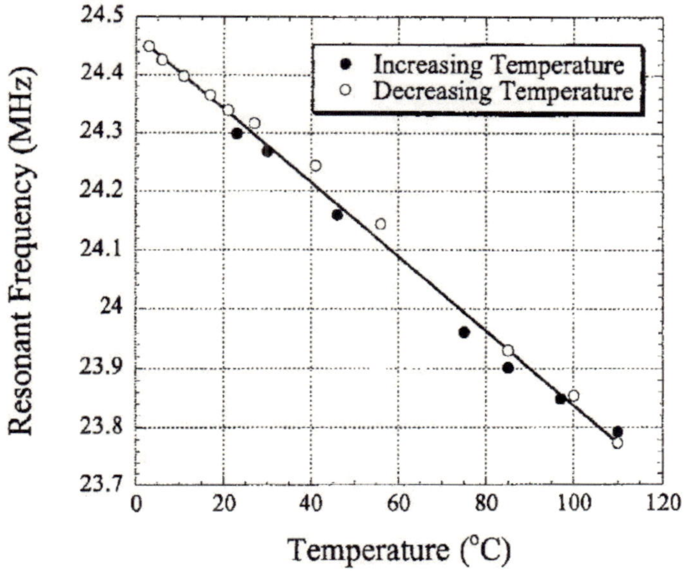

Fig. 19. Frequency-temperature relationship for 22.5 MHz resonant frequency.

Fig. 20. Illustration of an RFID-based crack detection approach.

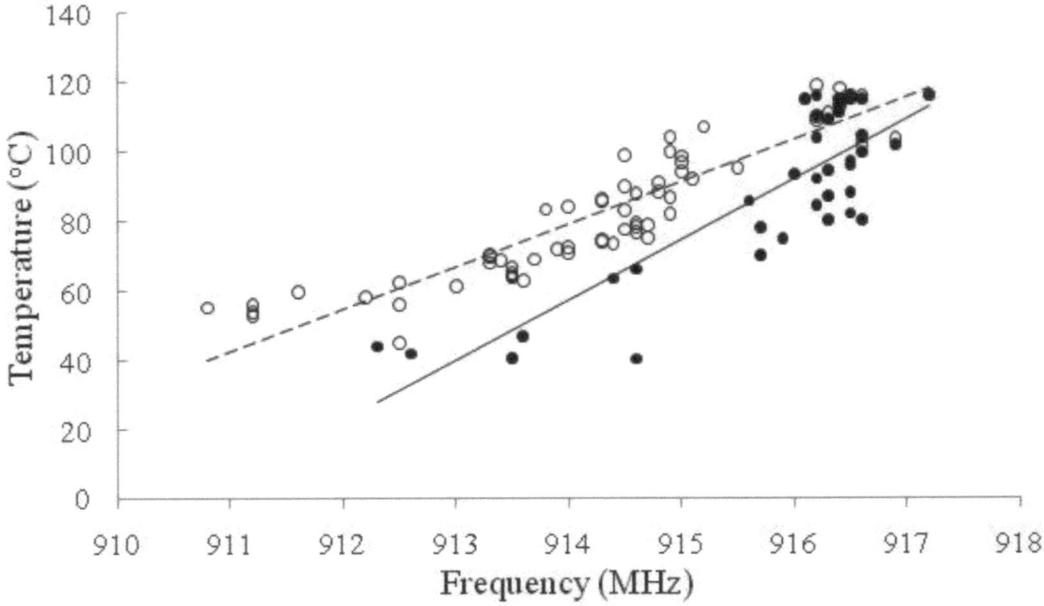

(a)

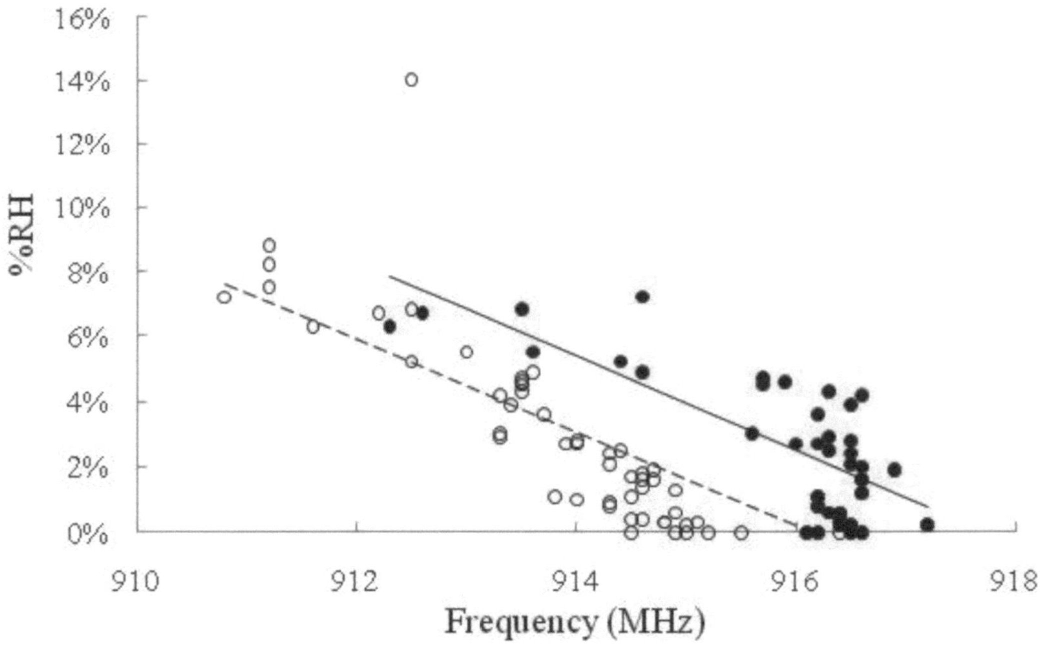

(b)

Fig. 21. Frequency-temperature (a) and Humidity (b) relationship for 915 MHz resonant frequency.

It is noted through our research (not shown here) that High Frequency (HF) inductive-based coupling RFID possesses good immunity to environmental effects and provide limited detection range. Whereas, Ultra High Frequency (UHF) backscattering based RFID possesses an increased detection range with reduced signal-to-noise ratio (SNR). Both HF and UHF provided similar performance for the parameters under consideration (e.g. humidity and temperature).

3.4 Emerging health monitoring sensor systems

This document has so far provided a perspective on the role of biological functions and characteristics in engineering innovation and the development of DPHM related concepts and frameworks. The above briefly presented sensors and sensor concepts have mainly focused on the concept of advancing autonomous sensor networks for potential integration into a health monitoring and management capability. In the following sub-sections a very brief introduction to the main two SHM capabilities (Piezo- and fiber optic-based) that has seen significant development and demonstration within the aerospace sector. It is noted that even though these systems have a high Technology Readiness Level (TRL), their implementation within the commercial or military sectors continue to be limited due to several challenges including size, weight, power requirements and excessive cabling; hence the discussion of Section 3. The reader is encouraged to consult [48] for more details on these systems and other ones.

3.4.1 Piezoelectric (PZT)- based sensor networks

Piezoelectric material can be used both for active and passive defect detection employing a network of sensors. As illustrated in Figure 22 [49], in the active mode, an electric pulse is sent to a piezoelectric actuator that produces Lamb waves within the structure under evaluation. The array of piezoelectric sensors will pick up the resultant Lamb waves for processing and analysis. If defects, such as cracks, delamination, disbond or corrosion, exist within the range of sensors array, a change in the reference "healthy" signal results. These systems rely on a reference signal in the structure before they are placed in service. The location and the size of the defect can generally be determined from the degree of signal change. In the passive mode, sensors are used continuously as "listening" devices for any possible damage initiation or propagation. Sensors within the network can detect impact and defect events, including crack formation, delamination, disbond, and possibly non-visible impact damage.

Systems based on this dual concept of passive and active monitoring have been developed [50-51] (e.g. Stanford Multi-Actuator-Receiver Transduction (SMART) Layer based system) and demonstrated. Such systems are designed and built around a set of piezoelectric sensors/actuators networks, diagnostics software, analysis tools and graphics user interface. Figure 23 depicts a schematic of sensors/actuators network layout. Additionally, Figure 24 illustrates the ability to detect defects using this piezo-based approach. Such Figure clearly illustrates the waves-damage interaction.

This sensor-based approach provides significant SHM potential due to its high multiplexing flexibility and suitability for harsh environment; however it suffers from excessive wiring and reduced imaging software effectiveness. Even though tremendous progress was reported in this area, significant research is still needed to bring this technology to practical deployment and to facilitate its qualification and certification.

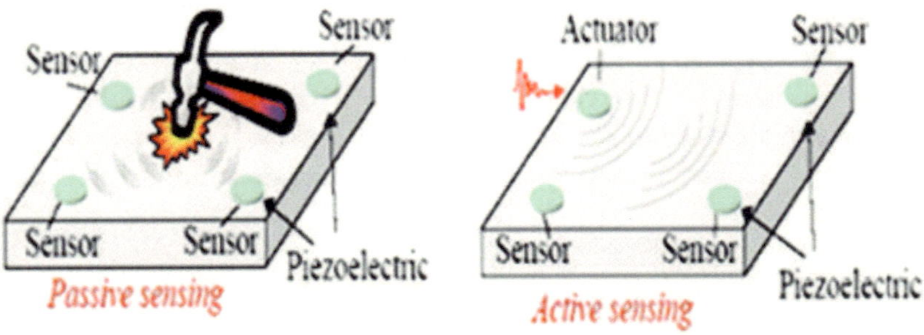

Fig. 22. Passive and active sensing mode using piezoelectric materials.

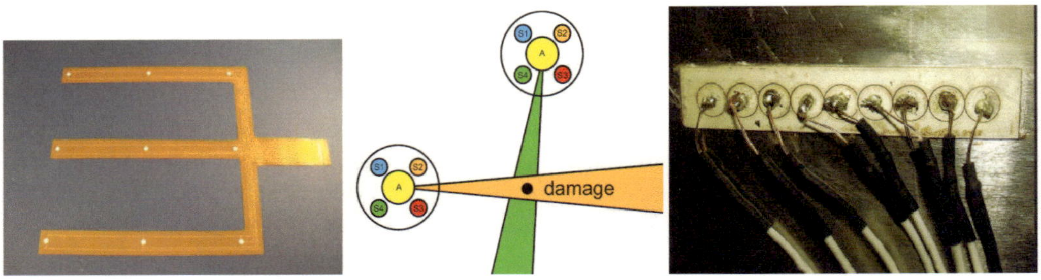

Fig. 23. Schematic of sensors/actuators network Layout (Acellent SMART layer, Metis Design Intelliconnector & Vector locator, and university of Sherbrooke's micro-machined PZT array).

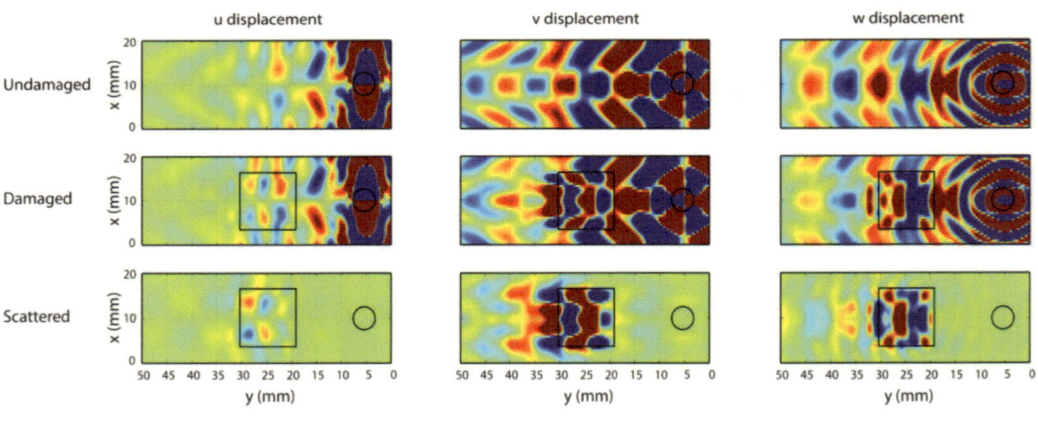

Fig. 24. Simulation results for longitudinal (u,v) and transverse (w) displacement components on the surface of a metallic structure (undamaged case (top), damaged area (middle) and scattered field (bottom)).

3.4.2 Fiber optic based sensor networks

Because of their very low weight, small size, high bandwidth and immunity to electromagnetic and radio frequency interferences, fiber optic sensors have significant performance advantages over traditional sensors. Fiber optic sensors offer unique capability, such as monitoring the manufacturing process of composite and metallic parts, performing non-destructive testing once fabrication is complete, enabling structural and component health monitoring for prognostics health management, and structural control for component life extension. Such capability exploits optical characteristics and makes use of a variety of novel phenomena inherent in the structure of the fiber itself. Some of these phenomena are extensively discussed in the literature [52-53].

In general fiber optic sensors are classified as discrete or distributed. The distributed class of sensors includes Michelson and Mach-Zhender interferometer as well as sensors based on Brillouin scattering. These are generally seen in infrastructure applications where spatial resolution, system's weight and size are not as critical and long range sensing is desired [54]. The discrete class of sensors include cavity-based and grating-based designs. Cavity-based designs utilize an interferometric cavity in the fiber to create the sensor and define its gauge length. Extrinsic and Intrinsic Fabry-Perot interferometers (EFPI, IFPI), along with In-Line Fiber Etalon (ILFE) are the most known ones. Grating-based designs utilize a photo-induced periodicity in the fiber core refractive index to create a sensor whose reflected or transmitted wavelength is a function of the periodicity that is indicative of the parameter being measured. Any shift in the reflected wavelength indicates a change in the monitored parameter. This principle of operation of Bragg gratings based sensors is shown in Figure 25 [52].

Due to their high sensitivity, small size (40-125 μm), high multiplexing capability forming highly effective sensor networks and ease of integration into structural materials, Fiber Bragg Gratings (FBG) are the most commonly used sensors for SHM applications. As shown in Figure 26 [55], these sensors can be used to monitor bondline integrity in bonded joints, acoustic emission resulting from structural damage and corrosion monitoring.

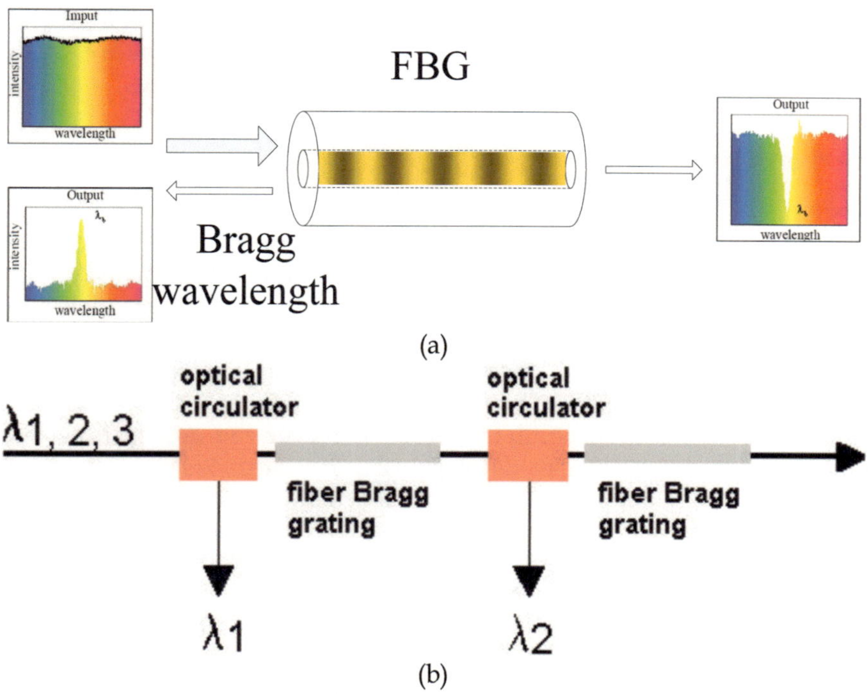

Fig. 25. Fiber Bragg gratings principle of operation for single and serially placed gratings.

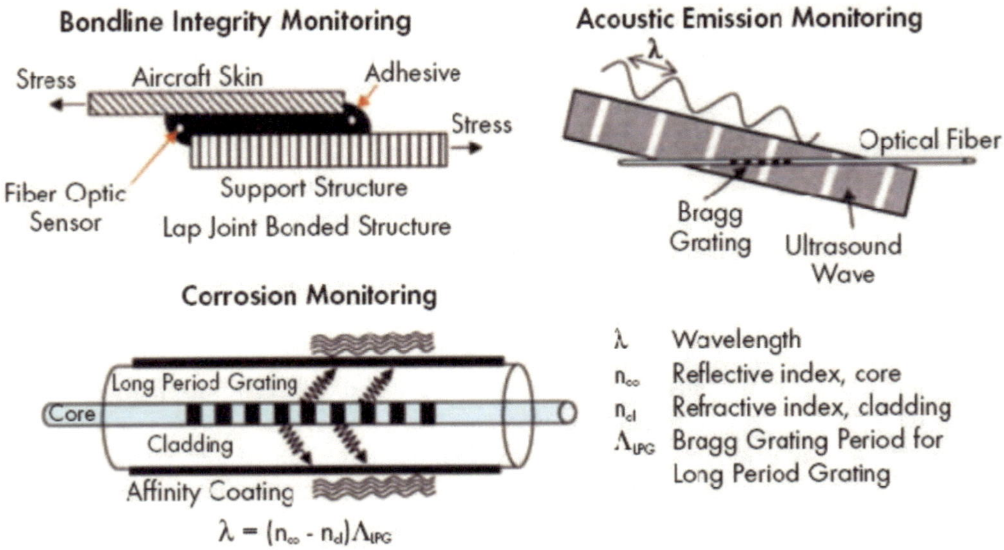

Fig. 26. Fiber Bragg Gratings-based sensing.

Despite the extensive and successful outcomes of several investigations supporting aerospace platform DPHM requirements, research efforts continue to address the critical issues for practical implementation that include adhesive selection, bonding procedures, and quality control for surface mounted fiber optic sensors; optimum selection of sensor configuration, sensor material and host structure for embedded configurations; characterization of embedded fiber optic sensors at elevated and cryogenic temperatures; resolution optimization for desired parameters from multi-gratings as well as sensitivity to transverse and temperature effects; development of an integrity assurance procedure for embedded sensors, particularly sensor protection at egress/ingress points.

4. Conclusion

Understanding the functionality and characteristics of biological systems has significantly contributed to innovation in the engineering and medical disciplines. Engineering systems, such as systems for structural health monitoring, prognostics health management, condition based maintenance, health and usage monitoring, and life cycle management, have exploited such knowledge to develop bio-inspired system functionalities. This document provided a perspective on the role of biological functions and characteristics in engineering innovation. It introduced systems terminology and provided relevant terminology within the scientific and engineering streams, focusing on health monitoring and management. The document further presented a perspective on technology development as it related to aircraft health monitoring and management. The latter is driven by the requirement for increased aircraft safety, reliability, enhanced performance and platform availability at reduced cost. Sensors and sensor concepts that have the potential of advancing autonomous sensor networks within a health monitoring and management capability have also been introduced and discussed. Such sensors included low (Nano, MEMS, RFID) and high technical readiness level (piezo and fiber optic sensors). Implementation of such presented concepts, technologies, and systems within the commercial or military sectors, continues to be limited due to several challenges including size, weight, power requirements, qualification and certification.

5. References

[1] Alice Park, "The Science of Growing Body Parts," Health & Science, TIME, 1 November 2007, (http://www.time.com/time/health/article/0,8599,1679115,00.html), Retrieved on 26 April 2011.

[2] Joshua Topolsky, "Prosthetic-Limbed Runner Disqualified from Olympics," ENGADGET, 17 January 2008, (http://www.engadget.com/2008/01/17/prosthetic-limbed-runner-disqualified-from-olympics/), Retrieved on 26 April 2011.

[3] W. French Anderson, "Human Gene Therapy," Science, Vol. 256, No. 5058, pp. 808-813, May 1992.

[4] Richard P. Wool, "Self-Healing Materials: A Review," Soft Matter, Vol. 4, pp. 400-418, 2008.

[5] "Biological system", (en.wikipedia.org/wiki/Biological_system), Retrieved on 26 April 2011.

[6] Christopher K. Mathews, K.E.Van Holde and Kevin G. Ahern, Biochemistry, pg. 63, Addison Wesley Longman, Inc., 2000.

[7] Joel Moses, "Foundational Issues in Engineering Systems: A Framing Paper," MIT Engineering Systems Symposium, MIT, Cambridge, Mass. USA, March 29-31, 2004.

[8] Joanne fox, "what is bioinformatics," The science Creative Quarterly, Issue 6, 2011(http://www.scq.ubc.ca/what-is-bioinformatics/), Retrieved on 26 April 2011.

[9] Ryszard Lobinski, et al., "Metallomics: Guidelines for Terminology and Critical Evaluation of Analytical Chemistry Approaches (IUPAC Technical Report), Chemistry international: The New Magazine of the International Union of Pure and Applied Chemistry (IUPAC), *Pure and Applied Chemistry*, Vol. 82, No. 2, pp. 493–504, 2010.

[10] Simon R. Downes, "Learning the basic sciences," Basic Science Study Log, September 9, 2010, (http://myroadtomedicalschool.blogspot.com/2010_09_01_archive.html), Retrieved on 26 April 2011.

[11] Paul Fitzgerald, "Borescope Inspection of Aircraft Turbines," The Science of Remote Visual Inspection, Remote Visual Inspection - The Leading Remote Visual Inspection Resource, 3 August 2009, (http://www.remotevisualinspection.org/2009/08/03/borescope-inspection/), Retrieved on 26 April 2011.

[12] Bitter and Sour, "Living a normal life as a cyborg," SBB Visual impact, May 2010. (http://stupidbigblog.blogspot.com/2010/05/living-normal-life-as-cyborg.html), Retrieved on 26 April 2011.

[13] "Definition of Diagnostics", (http://www.thefreedictionary.com/diagnostics), Retrieved on 29 April 2011.

[14] Definition of Diagnosis, Medicine Net.com, (http://www.medterms.com/script/main/), Retrieved on 29 April 2011.

[15] "Definition of Prognostic," (http://www.thefreedictionary.com/Prognostics), Retrieved on 29 April 2011.

[16] Dave Korsmeyer, "Actuator Prognostics," NASA Ames Research Center

(http://ti.arc.nasa.gov/tech/dash/pcoe/actuator-prognostics/research/), Retrieved on 29 April 2011.
[17] Industry Canada, "Aircraft Systems Diagnostics, Prognostics and Health Management Technology Insight Document," Industry Canada Contract 5011101, Vol. 2, 16 December 2004.
[18] Michael Pecht and Jie Gu, "Health Assessment and Prognostics of Electronic Products: An Alternative to Traditional Reliability Prediction Methods," Electronics Cooling (Dedicated to Thermal Management in the Electronics Industry), pp. 1-7, 9 May 2009.
[19] Farrar, Charles R. and Keith Worden, "An Introduction to Structural Health Monitoring," Philosophical Transactions of the Royal Society A (London: Royal Society Publishing) Vol. 365, pp. 303–315, 1851.
[20] "Structural Reliability and Nondestructive Characterization," McCormick - Theoretical and Applied Mechanics, Northwestern University, (http://www.tam.northwestern.edu/wmaster/research/nde.html), Retrieved on 29 April 2011.
[21] Expeditionary Logistics, eLOG 21, "Conditioned-Based Maintenance Plus (CBM+)," Joint Vision 2020, Fact Sheet, (https://acc.dau.mil/), Retrieved on 20 July 2010.
[22] Romano Patrick-Aldaco, "A Model Based Framework for Fault Diagnosis and Prognosis of Dynamical Systems with an Application to Helicopter Transmissions," Doctor of Philosophy Dissertation, Electrical and Computer Engineering, Georgia Institute of Technology, August 2007.
[23] S. Beeby, G. Ensell, M. Kraft and N. White, MEMS Mechanical Sensors, Microelectromechanical systems series, Artech House Inc. 2004, ISBN 1-58053-536-4.
[24] E. Udd, "An Overview of Fiber-Optic Sensors," Review of Scientific Instruments, Vol. 66 Issue 8, pp. 4015-5030, August 1995.
[25] J.F. Tressler, S. Alkoy, R.E. Newnham, "Piezoelectric sensors and sensor materials," Journal of Electroceramics, Vol, 2, Issue 4, pp. 257-272, 1998.
[26] V. Giurgiutiu, "Tuned lamb wave excitation and detection with piezoelectric wafer active sensors for structural health monitoring," Journal of Intelligent Material Systems and Structures, Vol. 16, No. 4, pp. 291–305, 2005.
[27] I. Sage, L Humberstone, I Oswald, P Lloyd and G Bourhill, "Getting light through black composites: embedded triboluminescent structural damage sensors," Smart Mater. Struct. Vol. 10, pp. 332–337, 2001.
[28] S. Beard, X. Q. Peter, M. Hamilton and D. C. Zhang, Acellent Technologies, Inc. (2005).
[29] Kazuhiro Otsuka, Xiaobing Ren, "Recent developments in the research of shape memory alloys," Intermetallics, Vol. 7, pp. 511-528, 1999.
[30] Chang, Neng-Kai Su, Chi-Chung Chang, Shuo-Hung, "Fabrication of single-walled carbon nanotube flexible strain sensors with high sensitivity," Applied Physics Letters, Vol. 92, Issue 6, pp. 063501 - 063501-3, 2008, ISSN: 0003-695.
[31] Sharp, P. K., Rowlands, D. E. and Clark, G., "Evaluation of Innovative NDI Methods for Detection of Service Simulation Cracking", Defence Science and Technology Organization, Report DSTO-TR-0366., August 1996.
[32] Dharap, P., Li, Z., Nagarajaiah, S., and Barrera, E. "Nanotube film based on SWNT for macrostrain sensing," Nanotechnology Journal, Vol. 15 Issue 3, pp. 379-382, 2004.

[33] Vemuru, S. M., Wahi, R., Nagarajaiah, S. and Ajayan, P.M. "Strain sensing using a multiwalled carbon nanotube film," The Journal of Strain Analysis for Engineering Design, Vol. 44, Issue 7, DOI 10.1243/03093247JSA535, 555-562, 2009.
[34] W. Zhang, J. Suhr and N. Koratkar, "Carbon nanotube/polycarbonate composites as multifunctional strain sensors," Journal of Nanoscience and Nanotechnology, Vol. 6, Issue 4, pp. 960-964, 2006.
[35] Inpil Kang, Mark J Schulz, Jay H. Kim, Vesselin Shanov and Donglu Shi, "A carbon nanotube strain sensor for structural health monitoring," Smart Mater. Struct. Vol. 15, pp. 737–748, 2006.
[36] Alexopoulos N.D., Bartholome C., Poulin P., Marioli-Riga Z., Composites Science and Technology Vol. 70, pp. 260-71, 2010.
[37] Erik T Thostenson and Tsu-Wei Chou1, "Real-time in situ sensing of damage evolution in advanced fiber composites using carbon nanotube networks," Nanotechnology, Vol. 19, 215713, 2008.
[38] B. Ashrafi, Nezih Mrad and A. Johnston, "Evaluation of Nanotechnology for Structural Health Monitoring of Airframe Structures," National Research Council Publication, Number LTR-SMPL-2010-0086. April 2010.
[39] B. Ashrafi, L. Johnson, Y. Martinez-Rubi, M. Martinez, N. Mrad, "CNT-modified Epoxy Thin Films for Continuous Crack Monitoring of Metallic Structures," In progress, 2011.
[40] "Definition of Smart", Cambridge Advanced Learner's Dictionary, (http://dictionary.cambridge.org/results.asp?searchword=smart), Retrieved on 29 April 2011.
[41] National Institute of Standards and Technology," IEEE 1451 Smart Transducer Interface Standard," IEEE 1451 Website (http://ieee1451.nist.gov/) , Retrieved on 29 April 2011.
[42] T Niblock, B. C. Laskowski, H. Surangalikar, J. Moreno, "STape (Smart Tape)," proc 6th International Aircraft Corrosion Workshop, 24 - 27 August 2004, Solomons, Maryland, USA, 2004.
[43] Trevor Niblock, Harshal S. Surangalikar, Jeffrey Morse, Bernard C Laskowski, Jose Moreno, "AMSN (Arrayed Multiple Sensor Networks) for Material and Structural Prognostics", Materials Science & Technology 2004, New Orleans, Louisiana, September 2004
[44] Mourad El-Gamal, "MEMS in Aircraft Engine Monitoring - A Humidity Sensor," Defence R&D Canada - Atlantic, Contract Report, DRDC Atlantic CR 2011-069, April 2011.
[45] Do-Yun Kim, Byung-Jun Jang, Hyun-Goo Yoon, Jun-Seok Park and Jong-Gwan Yook , "Effects of Reader Interference on the RFID Interrogation Range", Microwave Conference, pp. 728 - 731, 2007.
[46] K. G. Ong, C. A. Grimes, C. L. Robbins and R. S. Singh, "Design and application of a wireless, passive, resonant-circuit environmental monitoring sensor," Sensors and Actuators A: Physical, Vol. 93, Issue 1, pp. 33-43 25 August 2001.
[47] A. Marincak, T. Benak, M. Fischer, K. Kraemer, "Application of the Surface Mountable Crack Sensor (SMCS) System for the Canadian Forces CP140 Aurora Aircraft Aft Pressure Bulkhead (FS1117)," LM - CP140 FS1117 SMCS Rev 1, 14 February 2008.

[48] Nezih Mrad, "State of Development of Advanced Sensory Systems for Structural Health Monitoring Applications," Proceedings of the NATO RTO AVT-144 Workshop on Enhanced Aircraft Platform Availability Through Advanced Maintenance Concepts and Technologies, Vilnius, Lithuania, 3-5 October 2006 (DRDC Atlantic SL-2008-260).

[49] S.J. Beard, A. Kumar, P.X. Qing, H.L. Chan, C. Zhang and T.K. Ooi, "Practical Issues in Real-World Implementation of Structural Health Monitoring Systems," Proceedings of SPIE on Smart Structures and Material Systems, March 2005.

[50] A. Kumar, S.J. Beard, P.X. Qing, H.L. Chan, T. Ooi, Stephen A. Marotta and F.K. Chang, "A Self-Diagnostic Structural Health Monitoring System for Composite Structures," SEM X International Conference, California, June 2004.

[51] Xinlin P. Qing, Shawn J. Beard, Roy Ikegami, Fu-Kuo Chang, Christian Boller, "Aerospace Applications of SMART Layer Technology," Encyclopedia of Structural Health Monitoring, Wiley Publications, 2009

[52] Mrad N. "Optical sensor technology: introduction and evaluation and application," In: Schwartz M, editor, Encyclopedia of smart materials, Vol. 2. New York: John Wiley & Sons, Inc., p. 715–37, 2002.

[53] E. Udd, "Fiber Optic Sensors - An Introduction for Engineers and Scientists," John Wiley & Sons, 2006.

[54] Lufan Zou, Xiaoyi Bao, Fabien Ravet, and Liang Chen, "Distributed Brillouin fiber sensor for detecting pipeline buckling in an energy pipe under internal pressure," Applied Optics, Vol. 45, Issue 14, pp. 3372-3377, 2006.

[55] I. Perez, "Fiber Sensors for Aircraft Monitoring," Naval Air Warfare Center Aircraft Division, DTIC Doc: AD-A375814, 1999.

Part 2

Materials Processing

8

Expert System for Simulation of Metal Sheet Stamping: How Automation Can Help Improving Models and Manufacturing Techniques

Alejandro Quesada, Antonio Gauchía,
Carolina Álvarez-Caldas and José-Luis San- Román
Department of Mechanical Engineering, University Carlos III of Madrid, Spain

1. Introduction

Nowadays, competitiveness is one of the major determining factors in global markets, forcing product developers to improve their products quality and to reduce development times. Automotive industry is a clear example of this trend and sheet metal forming, as one of the most important manufacturing processes in car manufacturing industry (Samuel, 2004), is very affected by this situation.

Stamping of automotive components is a critical activity characterized by short lead times and constant technological modifications in order to improve quality and reduce manufacturing costs. The sheet metal forming process, in theory, can be viewed as relatively straightforward operation where a sheet of material is plastically deformed into a desired shape. In practice, however, variations in blank dimensions, material properties and environmental conditions make the predictability and reproducibility of a sheet metal forming process difficult (Narasimhan & Lovell, 1999). Because of this, sheet metal forming results on a process that is heavily experience based and involves trial-and error loops.

The less the experience on the part geometry and material is, the more these loops are repeated. In the innovative process design procedure, however, the trial-and error loops are reduced by means of computer simulations.

Virtual manufacturing of automotive stamped components by means of finite element computer analysis is a powerful tool that is capable of helping engineers to solve different technological tasks (Makinouchi, 1996, Silva, et al., 2004). The forming analyses of sheet metals are performed repeatedly in the design feasibility studies of production tooling and stamping dies (Taylor, et al., 1995). With these analyses, the formability of the sheet material part can be calculated, but it is also possible to estimate the deformed geometry of stamped parts.

However, FEA (Finite Element Analysis) procedure is very time-consuming and relies much on the users' experience. So, under the needs of reduction on design time, reduction on development cost, and reduction on parts weight (so called '3-reduction strategy'), there is an urgent need for more efficient and accurate method in order to improve the current design situation (Wei & Yuying, 2008).

One of the main problems in simulation of sheet metal stamping is to quantify accurately the sheet metal springback, which can be defined as the change in the shape of a sheet metal part upon the removal of stamping tooling (Gau, 1999).
The problem of springback deformations in sheet metal parts makes that most of the produced parts do not conform to the design geometry within the required dimensional tolerances right at the first time (Firat, 2007c), and this dimensional accuracy becomes a crucial factor in determining the overall quality of the part as part components get smaller and tolerances get tighter. (Ling, et al., 2005)
It is also well known that the forming limits vary from material to material. Because of these considerations, knowledge of the behaviour of sheet metal is critical for the success of the sheet forming operation (Chen, et al., 2007).
The latest trend in vehicle structure engineering is to reduce weight of vehicle body- in-white structure in order to reduce fuel consumption, forcing the automotive industry to test new materials not used before. This leads to the following problem: behaviour of new materials is not as well known as behaviour of traditional ones. Constitutive modelling for classical steels can be considered as satisfactory, whereas for new high-strength steels as well as for aluminium alloys available models are still unsatisfactory (Tekkaya, 2000). Furthermore, the use of these materials makes the springback problem more important (Morestin, et al., 1996).
Taking into account previous exposition, it is clear that a good material model is essential when trying to simulate a stamping process by FE (Finite Elements) tools. These material models usually involve a lot of parameters, and it is quite difficult for engineers to consider all of them. The selection of a proper finite element plasticity model and the efficient utilization of the material formability data are main factors controlling the accuracy of the sheet metal deformation response prediction using a computer simulation code (Song, et al., 2007)
In this work, several aspects of metal stamping FEM (Finite Elements Method) simulation are analyzed. For each aspect, the most suitable option to automate the process has been chosen. All these decisions have been included in an interface windows application that allows analyzing the process automatically. By using the application developed in this work, the user does not need to have a great knowledge about the FEM tool.
Once the stamping process is automated, a procedure to create an accurate material model is also proposed.
An initial analysis has been done to determine which material model fits better the real material behaviour. A sensitivity analysis has also been done to find the material parameters that influence more simulation results.
These parameters are optimized through a procedure that combines real test results, FEM simulations and optimization tools. This procedure allows the user to find accurate parameters for not well known materials, obtaining good simulation results for new stamping processes.
Finally, since stamping processes usually involve several steps, one of the problems found in previous studies is that a very refined mesh is needed since the first simulation to achieve good results. In fact, this mesh made of small elements is only necessary in certain areas at the lasts steps of simulation.
It seems to be a good idea to introduce adaptive meshing since the beginning, in order to reduce simulation times (Ortiz & Quigley, 1991, Quigley & Monaghan, 2002). However, this kind of mesh forces to make several changes in original procedure.
These changes are studied in this chapter and a comparison between both possibilities (adaptive and not adaptive meshing) is deeply described.

2. Simulating a stamping process by FEM

2.1 Choosing the software

Not any finite elements software is appropriate for the purposes of this work. Manufacturing processes involve intense plastic behavior of the material with deep cupping operations leading to very large deformations. Furthermore, the application of the dies is intermittent and abrupt, resulting in significant strain rates that require the consideration of the dynamic nature of the problem.

Moreover, deformation processes are carried out in several steps. Because of this, simulation must be divided into steps also and for each of them the geometry obtained after springback must be calculated, as well as the stress distribution of the material. This information is fundamental to feed the following steps.

According to previous exposition, it is necessary to take into account dynamic effects, especially those related to:

- Inertia loads produced in the material.
- Stiffening that metals present when the strain rates are important (the σ-ε curve is modified at high strain rates).

Not every software can tackle with such material models, and so the number of possibilities decreases drastically. This work adopts LS-DYNA (LSTC, 2006), specifically the integrated tool ANSYS + LS- DYNA, that allows to use the powerful LS- DYNA processor and the more friendly environment of ANSYS during pre-processor and post-processor stages. LS-DYNA is one of the softwares that passed all the NUMISHEET°93 benchmark tests (Makinouchi, 1996), so it is proved to be suitable for the purposes of this work.

Even using ANSYS pre-processor, creating a finite element model of a stamping process is not a trivial task. Furthermore, in order to design an application that allows to optimize the main parameters of the materials used in the simulation it is absolutely necessary to automate the creation of the model. This implies that several assumptions must be done. These aspects are discussed in the following sections.

2.2 Explicit and implicit simulations

A general stamping process can be divided into two stages:

- Firstly, the blank is deformed by the contact of the dies.
- Secondly, the dies retire and the springback phenomenon appears.

This springback can be defined as the change in the shape of a sheet metal part upon the removal of stamping tooling (Gau, 1999). This deformation is an essential parameter that significantly complicates the design of forming dies, especially with the increasing use of high strength steels, which are not as well known as typical steels. This forces the construction of multiple prototypes (Narasimhan & Lovell, 1999) to find the dies that produces the right deformation in the black to obtain a final component with the desired shape. Because of this, to perform an accurate sheet metal forming simulation, springback effects must be taken into account.

Mathematically, the resolution of the set of equations generated to solve the finite element problem can be tackled through explicit or implicit methods. Explicit codes are usually adopted over implicit codes in industrial sheet metal applications as seen in Buranathiti and Cao (Buranathiti & Cao, 2005a, b), but implicit codes are sometimes used to simulate springback (Narasimhan & Lovell, 1999).

Explicit codes produce simulation results as accurate as the implicit FEM solvers (Belytschko, et al., 2000, Firat, 2007a) and use less computer resources, since the

computational time grows linearly with the problem size instead of the quadratic growth in the implicit codes. On the other hand, using only explicit codes forces to simulate both application and withdrawal of dies, so several iterations must be solved, resulting in much greater computational costs.
According to this, the first proposal of this work is to use explicit codes for application of dies and implicit codes for springback simulation. However, it will be seen in following sections that implict codes have several limitations that can be avoided by using explicit simulations.

2.3 Material model

One of the main points in the simulation of a stamping process by means of finite elements is the choice of the material model of the blank. For a given process and deformation geometry, the forming limits vary from material to material, so knowledge of the formability of sheet metal is critical (Chen, Gao, Zuo & Wang, 2007). The selection of a proper finite element plasticity model and the efficient utilization of the material formability data are main factors controlling the accuracy of the sheet metal deformation response prediction using a computer simulation code (Firat, 2007b).
Nowadays, the isotropic hardening plasticity models are widely accepted in the industry for sheet metal simulation, and it is assumed to be accurate enough for classical steels (Firat, 2007b). But the increasing introduction of high strength metals is showing that this model must be reevaluated. Because of this, several possible models have been taken into account in this work.
When trying to select a material model for the blank (between the more than 100 models implemented in LS-DYNA), several aspects must be considered:

- The model has to be applicable to metals.
- It has to work with shell elements (that are generally used the standard for meshing the blank (Tekkaya, 2000)).
- It must include strain- rate sensitivity.
- It has to deal with plasticity.
- It has to be able to study failure.

According to these statements, three material models have been selected for this study:

1. Kinematic / Isotropic elastic plastic.
2. Strain rate dependent isotropic plasticity.
3. Piecewise linear isotropic plasticity.

2.3.1 Selected material model

A real stamping process has been selected to compare simulation results obtained by using each of previous material models. This process (see Figure 1) is the first of the five stages needed to manufacture a part that belongs to the fix system of the spare tire of a commercial vehicle. Deformed blank obtained by this process is shown in Figure 2.

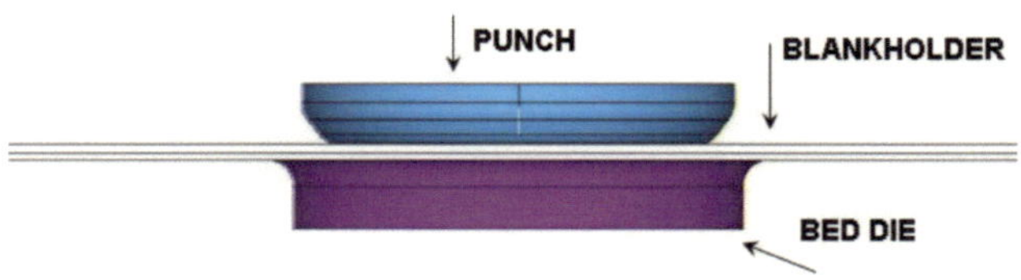

Fig. 1. Starting situation of the dies

Fig. 2. Deformed blank

The comparison between simulation results and the real deformed blank has been carried out by means of a coordinate measuring machine. The dimension used to be compared with simulation results is the stamping depth shown in Figure 3, and its real value is 15,88 mm.

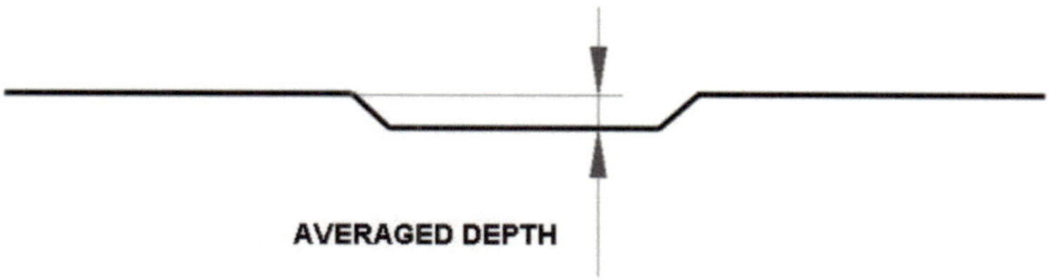

Fig. 3. Stamping depth used to compare experimental and simulation results

Table 1 shows a comparison between results obtained by using the three material models. For each model, several values of the main parameters have been tested. The maximum and minimum value obtained as well as the averaged depth are displayed.

Model	Minimum depth	Averaged depth	Maximum depth
Kinematic / Isotropic elastic plastic model	15,82 mm	15,87 mm	15,92 mm
Strain rate dependent isotropic plasticity model	15,68 mm	15,76 mm	15,85 mm
Piecewise linear isotropic plasticity model	15,85 mm	15,90 mm	15,98 mm

Table 1. Comparison between material models

According to these results, and taking into account the real obtained depth (15,88 mm) it can be concluded that any material model that has been considered in this study is accurate enough to simulate the stamping process and the behavior of the involved material.
However, the kinematic/isotropic elastic plastic model is the simplest one and the most appropriate when the material behavior is not well known. Because of this, this model has been adopted in the present work and is explained in the following section.

2.3.2 Kinematic / Isotropic elastic plastic model

This material model is described by the expresion Eq.(1) (Hallquist, 1998), based on the Cowper- Symonds model (Cowper & Symonds, 1958, Dietenberger, et al., 2005, Jones, 1983), which scales the yield stress by a strain rate dependent factor:

$$\sigma_y = \left[1 + \left(\frac{\dot{\varepsilon}}{C}\right)^{\frac{1}{p}}\right]\left(\sigma_0 + \beta E_p \varepsilon_{eff}^p\right) \tag{1}$$

Where:

σ_0 : Initial yield stress.

σ_y : Yield stress.

$\dot{\varepsilon}$: Strain rate.

β: Varying this parameter, isotropic ($\beta = 1$) or kinematic ($\beta = 0$) hardening can be obtained. In this work, isotropic hardening is supposed, so $\beta = 1$.

E_p : Plastic hardening modulus, defined by Eq.(2), where E_t is the tangent modulus and E is the elastic modulus:

$$E_p = \frac{E_t E}{E - E_t} \tag{2}$$

ε_{eff}^p : Effective plastic strain.

C and p: Strain rate parameters.

The following parameters have to be specified by the user in order to define properly this material when using LS-DYNA. Those parameters are:

- Density.
- Young's module.
- Poisson ratio.
- Initial yield stress.
- Tangent modulus.
- Hardening and strain rate parameters β, C and p.

2.4 Geometry of the dies and the blank

Finally, it is necessary to decide how to generate the geometry of the dies and the blank.

The forming tools are usually intended to impose the forming loads to the sheet metal through the forming interface. In order to reduce computation time, only the surface of the tooling has been included in the FEM model, rather than the complete geometry.

This is a common decision in sheet metal forming analysis (Firat, 2007a, c, Narasimhan & Lovell, 1999), because of the fact that the forming tools should be, theoretically, designed to be rigid and their deformation (that should be elastic with minimal shape changes) is neglected.

The fact of defining dies as rigid bodies allows applying displacement restrictions in the material definition.

The thickness defined for all the dies is 0.001mm, in order to distort the real geometry of the contact faces as less as possible.

Regarding the sheet metal blank, because of its thin geometry, it is usually meshed with shell elements (Darendeliler & Kaftanoglu, 1991, Firat, 2007a, c, Mattiasson, et al., 1995, Narasimhan & Lovell, 1999, Taylor, Cao, Karafillis & Boyce, 1995, Tekkaya, 2000).

In this work, the reduced integration Belitschko-Tsay shell element (Belytschko, Liu & Moran, 2000, Hallquist, 1998) has been used (included in the SHELL163 element implemented in LS-DYNA). Five integration points have been defined through the thickness in order to properly represent plasticity effects (Narasimhan & Lovell, 1999).

The Belitschko-Tsay shell element has proved to produce results that are similar to those obtained with more complex elements and this element is the least expensive element formulation of its kind (Firat, 2007a).

Contacts between the blank and the dies have been defined using an automatic surface-to-surface contact algorithm and a static friction coefficient and a dynamic one are considered during the simulation. With these two coefficients, the finite element simulation carries out a thorough analysis of friction.

3. Developed application

3.1 Automation procedure

Every decision discussed above is aimed at achieving an application that automatically generates the finite element model of a stamping process minimizing the user intervention.

The main steps of a FEM analysis can be resumed as follows (Álvarez- Caldas, 2009):

1. Definition of analysis parameters (materials, loads…).
2. Geometry creation.
3. Analysis.
4. Results post processing.

A different solution has been adopted to automate each one of them.

1. Definition of analysis parameters: This is the hardest step for the user, and the one that needs more automation. The designed application offers the user a window friendly environment where all the parameters needed to define the simulation can be introduced: blank thickness, material properties of the blank and the dies, loads, restrictions, displacements, contact coefficients, simulation time… This windows environment is programmed with Matlab Guide and generates a text file that can be imported to LS-DYNA.
2. Geometry creation: The user can generate the geometry entities for the blank and the dies in any CAD program, exporting them to any graphic format that can be read by LS-DYNA (as IGES).
3. Analysis: All the parameters that have been introduced through the windows environment, as well as the CAD geometries, have to be linked by the appropriate ANSYS commands. The actions that must be done can be resumed as follows:
   - Import CAD geometry of the stamping tooling and the blank.
   - Creation and assignment of material models and real constants sets.
   - Definition of frictional contact conditions.
   - Description of forming process via the prescribed displacements or forces on the tooling surfaces.
   - Meshing of the blank and the dies.
   - Resolution of the finite element model.
   - Since there are two kinds of potential users for this application (the ones that are used to employ finite elements applications, and the ones that are not), two options have been implemented:

- Blind analysis: All previous actions have been implemented in a generic subroutine that is launched by the windows environment, so that all the previous described process does not need user intervention.
- Expert analysis: The automatic process ends before the solution step, allowing the user to make any changes.

4. Results post processing: this step cannot be automated because the user must be the one to carry out the critical reviews of the results.

The proposed procedure is depicted in Figure 4, where stages that require user intervention are drawn with solid line and those that can run "blindly" are drawn with broken line.

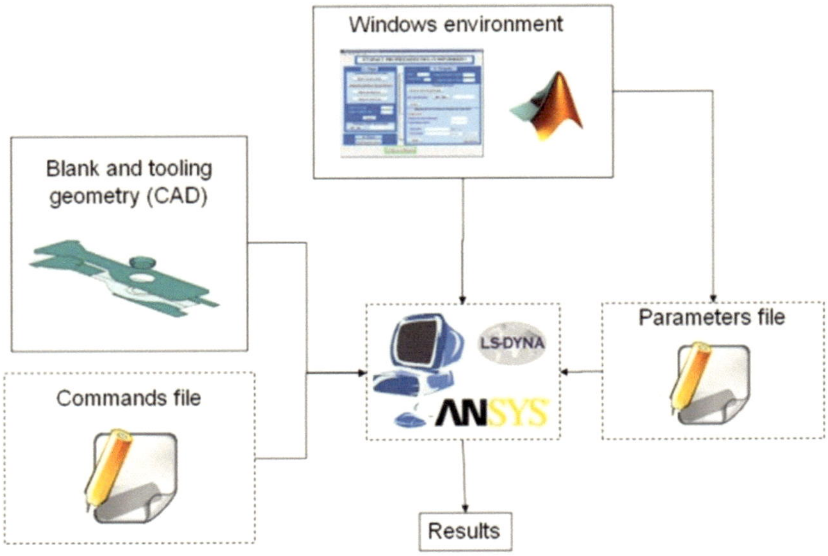

Fig. 4. Automation procedure

Once the proposed procedure is clear and taking into account that the automation may not be done by someone non specialist in ANSYS LS-DYNA it is desirable to operate within a friendly windows environment. In addition, the toolboxes available in some software such as MATLAB are of great help. Therefore, a friendly windows environment has been programmed in MATLAB by means of the GUI (Graphical User Interface) which is deeply described in the following section.

3.2 Windows environment

By means of MATLAB's GUI a friendly window environment has been designed in order to provide the user a step by step procedure that ensures the correct operations that must be done in the finite element model which simulates the stamping process. The proposed environment generates a set of files which is afterwards forwarded automatically by the software to ANSYS LS-DYNA so that it runs in batch mode, that is, under system without having to involve the user in the modelling of the stamping process. In addition, the proposed environment carries out an estimation loop so as to predict the values of the material parameters that best fit the model with experimental test results. Therefore, the software which has been developed allows the user either to simulate a stamping process or to find the material parameters that best suit the stamping process. In Figure 5 the window that allows simulating a stamping process is depicted.

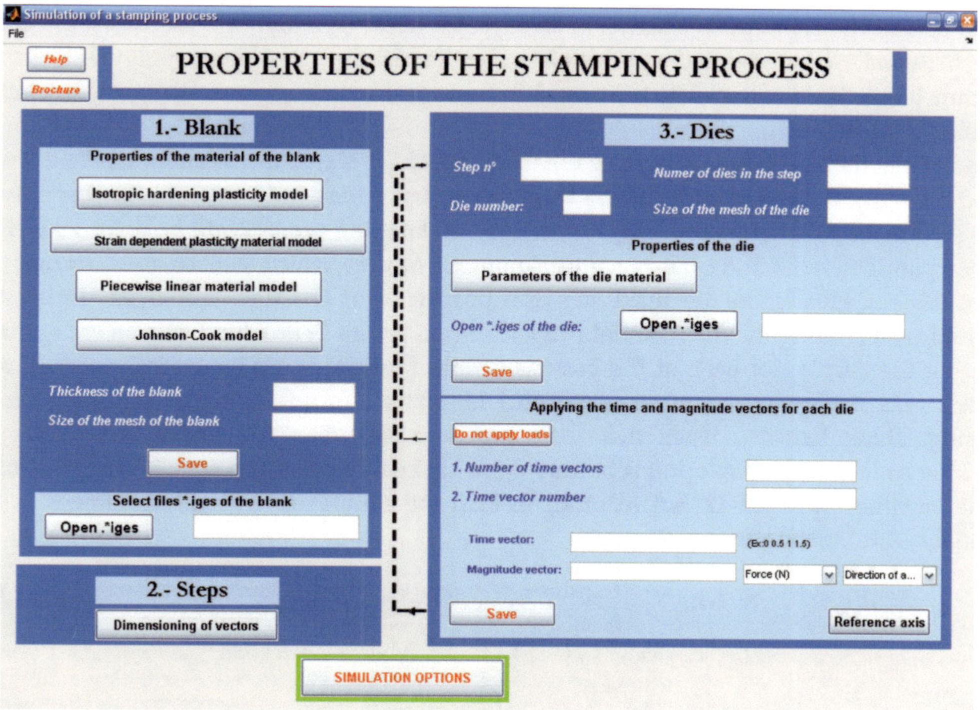

Fig. 5. Window environment of the developed software

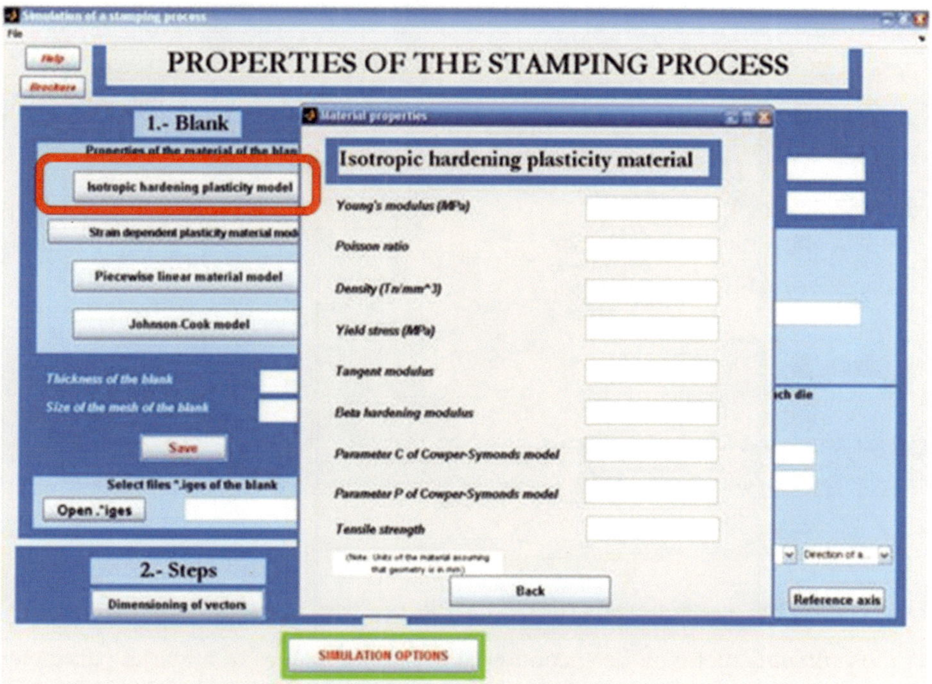

Fig. 6. Specifying the material properties of the blank

This part of the software is divided in three steps. In the first step the user must select the plasticity material model that best describes the material used as a blank. Figure 6 shows the parameters to be introduced by the user if an isotropic hardening plasticity model is selected to model the blank.

In addition, the user has to introduce the thickness of the blank, the meshing size and has to load the "*.iges" file that contains the blank geometry. Afterwards, the user must specify in the second step the number of steps in which the stamping process will be done, as well as other parameters such as the maximum number of dies which will be used during the process, etc. Finally, in the third step the properties of the dies employed during the stamping, including the die material properties (see Figure 7) and load vectors are applied. During the clicking of each of the buttons certain files are being generated automatically which will finally be the input to ANSYS LS-DYNA. In addition, the software allows distinguishing between users that have previous experience in ANSYS LS-DYNA by clicking in the simulation options button. Once clicked, the user can specify the simulation time or either open LS-DYNA in order to load the simulation and allow changes in the model before running the solution.

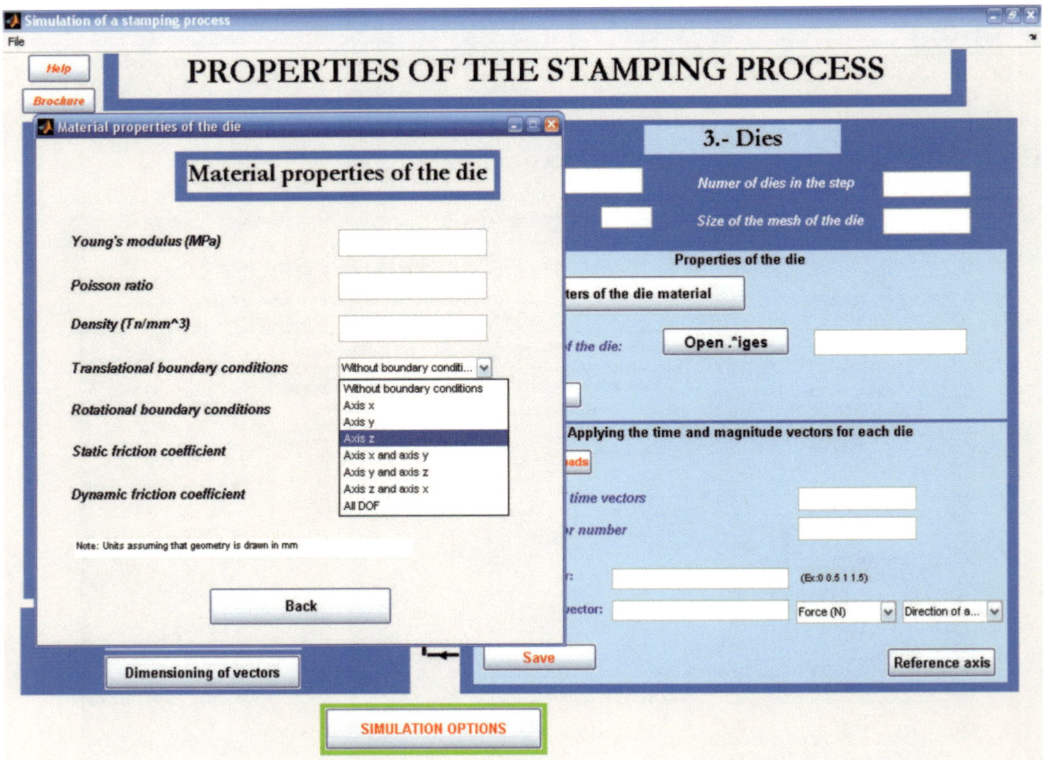

Fig. 7. Specifying the material properties of the die

One of the problems that may be encountered is that the values of material parameters are not known and therefore have to be adjusted before simulating the complete stamping process. To solve this problem the following steps are proposed:

- In the first place the user must select a certain manufacturing process to be simulated.
- Afterwards, this process will be carried out in an industry using the available dies and devices. This test will be defined as a pattern test.
- Thirdly, the pattern test will be done in the material whose parameters want to be computed. Due to the fact that the selected process is well known and defined, all the changes that take place in the final shape will be due to changes in material properties.
- Finally, once the material parameters have been clearly found other processes may be simulated once the optimum material parameters are known. This information may be used for designing new dies for new upcoming processes saving money and time as the number of experimentally tested dies has decreased a lot.

3.3 Estimation of material parameters

In order to adjust the material parameters the designed software provides a specific tool that compares the results of the finite element simulation with the results of a real experimental test (Gauchía, 2009). The user must specify at least two sets of simulations where the values of the material parameters are different. The software will create the files needed to carry out the finite element model and return a solution which will be compared with the experimental test results given by the user. From two simulations, the software provides by means of a linear interpolation an estimation of the material parameters. Because the provided values are the result of a linear interpolation the proposed material parameters may not be the most appropriate. Therefore, the user can modify the proposed values and carry out a third simulation. Once the results of this third simulation are provided the software shows different graphs that show the results obtained in the previous simulations for each of the material parameters. If for example, the depth is considered as the result to be compared with the experimental tests the prediction plots display graphs where each of the material properties is represented in the vertical axis and the depth in the horizontal axis. In addition, the user may modify the polynomial degree (linear, quadratic, etc.) for the simulated results. These graphs, represented inFigure 8, display the polynomial function and confidence bounds. Each of the results are plotted in the polynomial fit estimation and represented as a cross ("+").

The proposed software allows carrying out more than three simulations. If the user does more simulations the confidence bounds will narrow, however, the user will have to find the proper balance between computation time and exactness. It must also by noted that only some of the most sensitive material parameters can be changed by the user, as depicted in Figure 9. The material parameters the user is allowed to change are the yield stress, parameter C and parameter p of the plasticity model. The yield stress is without doubt one of the most important parameters that characterize the plasticity material model. Previous simulations (Quesada, et al., 2009) have shown that variations of approximately 14% in the depth may be encountered. However, it was found that parameters C and p do not have a great influence in the results. Previous simulations revealed that varying parameter C a 900%, produces a variation of less than 0.5% in the result and varying parameter p a 133% produces a variation of 0.4% in the final result. Therefore, the influence of other parameters can be neglected and will not be considered during the material parameter estimation.

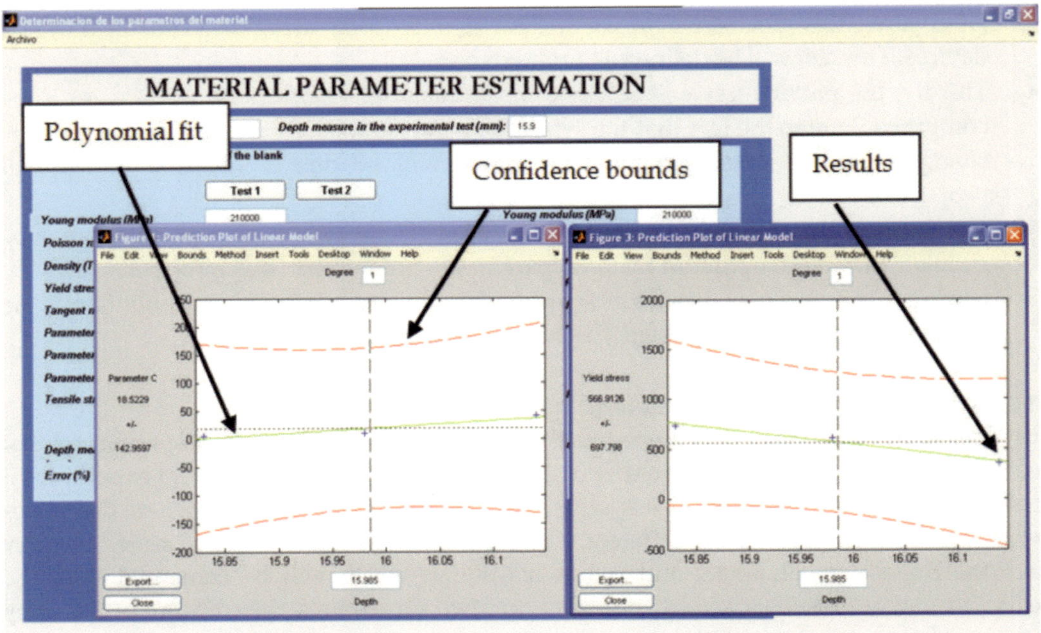

Fig. 8. Polynomial fit estimation and confidence bounds of material parameters

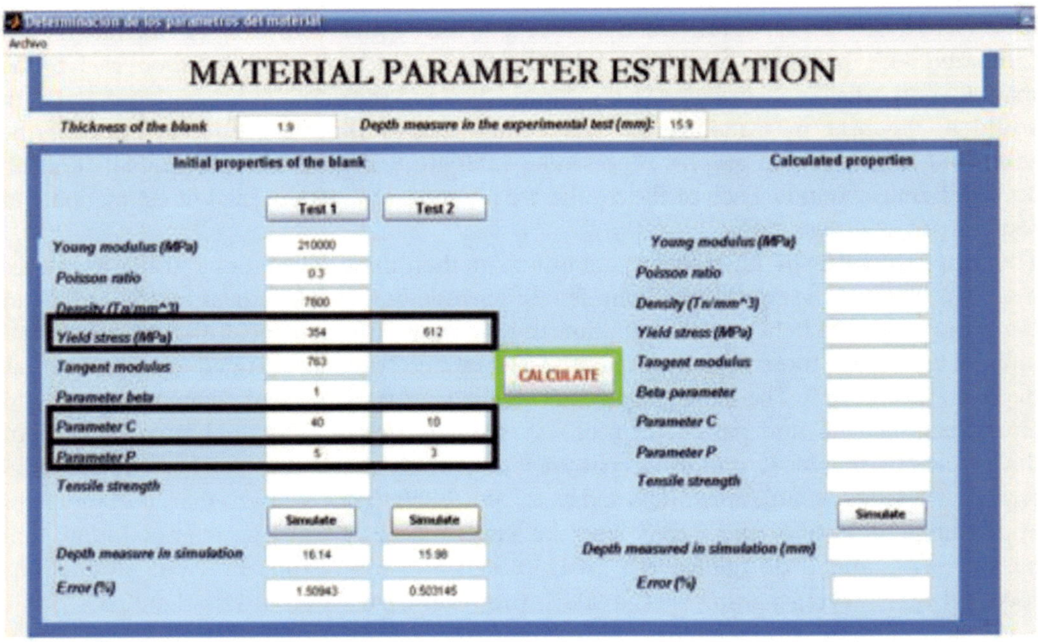

Fig. 9. Material parameters that can be modified by the user

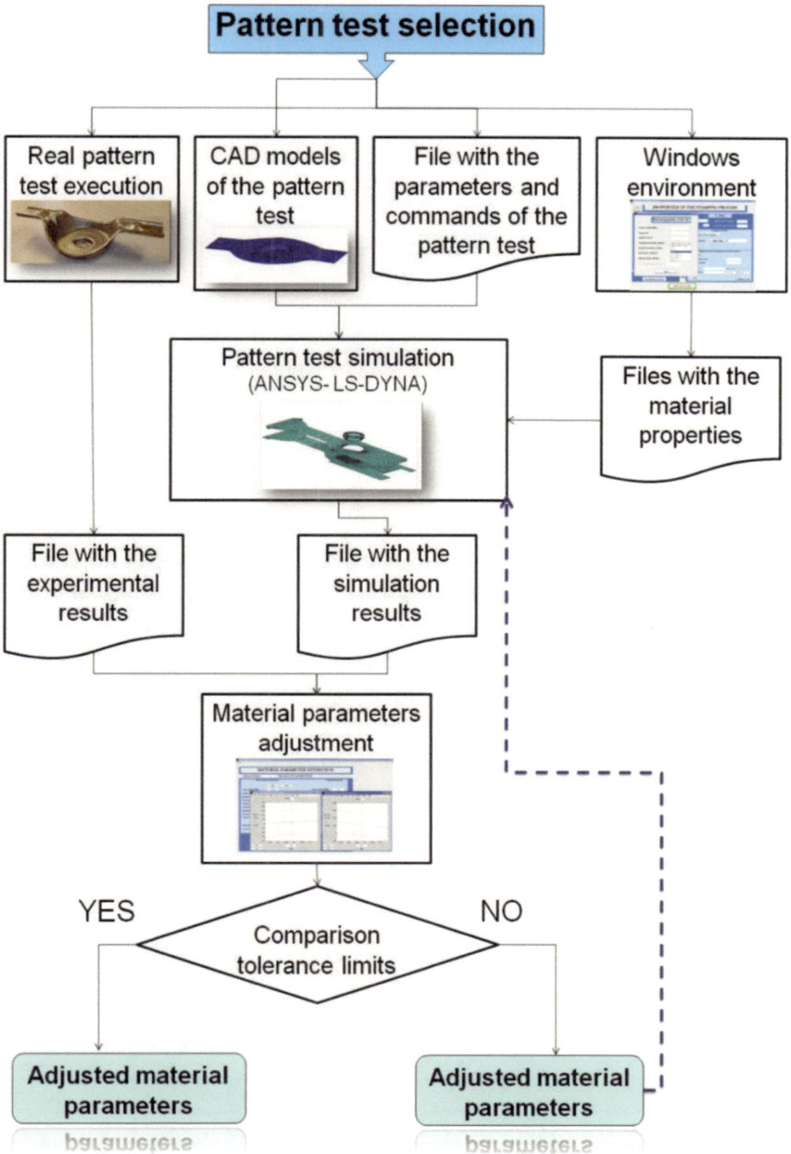

Fig. 10. Material parameters estimation procedure

4. Application example

4.1 Choosing and simulating the pattern test

The first step is choosing the pattern test. For a stamping process, the example explained in 2.3.4 has been chosen. As stated before, this test is the first of the five stages needed to manufacture a part which belongs to the fix system of the spare tire of an real vehicle. The parts involved in this step are shown in Figure 11:

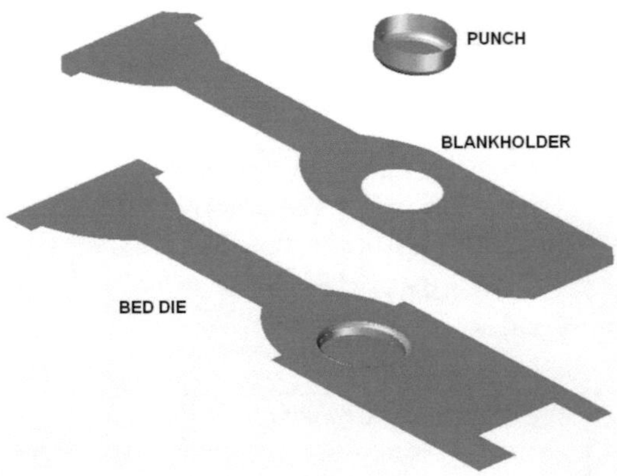

Fig. 11. First step dies

The blank is leaned on the bed die and the process starts with the movement of the blankholder, which applies a load to hold the blank once contact is established between them. After that, punch begins to go down, deforming the blank to obtain the part shown in Figure 2. Deformed blank was measured with a coordinate measuring machine, and the dimension used to be compared with simulation results is shown in Figure 3. Simulation displacements are compared with real ones because displacement measurement assures a controlled final shape of the sheet blank. Other variables such as stress or strains are not useful from a practical point of view for this purpose.
Every parameter involved in this simulation has to be adjusted according to the designer experience and taking into account the conditions of the experimental stamping process (loads, times, boundary conditions...). Boundary and loading conditions have been specified by fixing degrees of freedom of the dies or by aplying displacements and loads to them to simulate the real process (Table 2).

Time [s]	Punch displacement [mm]	Blankholder displacement [mm]	Blankholder load [N]
0	0	0	0
0,5	-38	-25	-90000
1	-78,5	-49,998	-90000
1,5	-116,498	-49,998	-90000
2	-78,5	-49,998	-90000
2,5	-38	-25	-90000
3	0	0	0

Table 2. Loads and displacements used in the pattern test simulation

Those parameters are introduced in the friendly windows environment exposed in chapter 3.2, and the stamping process is automatically simulated by ANSYS LS-DYNA according to the procedure shown in Figure 4.
As long as the patters test is well known and the real experiment can be carried out for any desired material, simulation results can always be compared with experimental values and simulation parameters can be adjusted in order to obtain a validated model.

4.2 Adjusting material parameters for a high strength steel

Once the pattern test can be simulated with great confidence, it is time to use it to adjust parameters of an unknown material in order to optimize results, predict springback and define new dies before carrying out the experimental test.

The material parameter estimation procedure needs two sets of material parameters to start. The program simulates the pattern test with these two sets and the difference between experimental and simulation results is calculated. If this difference is over the tolerance limit specified by the user, the application founds new material parameters by applying linear interpolation to previous ones and launches a new simulation with these new material parameters. The process is repeated until results fit tolerance requirements.

In the experimental test, the displacement of the punch is 16.5 mm. For this value, the final depth of the manufactured part, measured by the MMC machine, is 15.9 mm.

Initial values for the material parameters and the depths obtained for each combination can be seen in Table 3 (1st and 2nd simulations). The last column shows the parameters values obtained after optimization, considering a tolerance limit for the relative error of 0.4%.

Parameter	Number of simulation		
	1st	2nd	**Last**
Density (kg/m^3)	7800	7800	7800
Young's module (MPa)	210000	210000	210000
Poisson ratio	0.3	0.3	0.3
Yield stress (MPa)	354	425	664
Tangent modulus (MPa)	763	763	763
β	1	1	1
C (s^{-1})	40	100	10.99
p	5	5	2.5
Obtained depth (mm)	16.14	16.14	15.96
Relative error	1.5%	1.5%	0.38%

Table 3. Employed parameters

4.3 Results validation

To validate these results, obtained parameters have been used in a new deep stamping process. The selected test covers steps 1, 2 and 3 of the manufacture process of the part shown in Figure 12.

Fig. 12. Manufactured part

This process involves not only geometrical difficulty but also difficulties due to progressive stamping processes. The first step is the pattern test explained in 4.1. Dies used in steps 2 and 3 are shown in Figure 13.

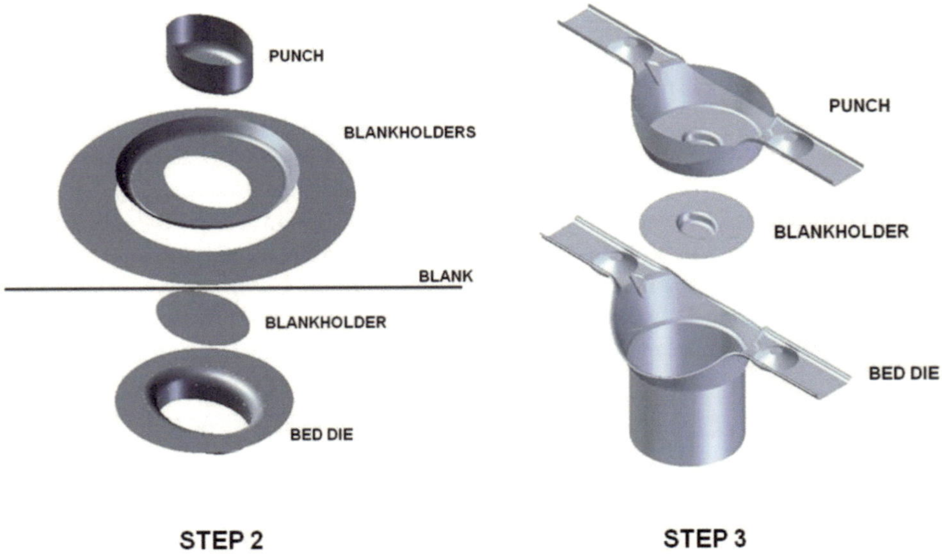

Fig. 13. Second and third steps dies

In this case, the dimension used to validate de model is the one shown in Figure 14. This dimension achieved a value of 77.21 mm in the experimental test after springback. Simulation result was 74.58 mm, representing a 3.4% error.

Fig. 14. Final dimension used for validation

5. Adaptive meshing

It has been mentioned before that computing time becomes an important aspect in this kind of simulations. To solve the developed models, a PC can take from several hours to a week, depending mainly on the mesh size and on the amount of plastic strain reached. Mesh size is critical not only for the results quality but for taking into account properly contact between parts. High relative speed between dies characteristic of stamping processes makes necessary to use fine mesh sizes and high contact stiffness, both of them leading to increase computational load.

In addition, to repeat many times the early steps of a multistep process is needed to adjust properly the mesh size in order to get an acceptable going of the latest steps. It multiplies at the same time programming and computing times. In this context, Numeric Calculation Adaptive Meshing (AM) technique is of paramount importance.

Using the AM tool will allow the stress analyst to save because:

- It is not needed to carry out meshing tests. An initial gross mesh can be provided, and in the first calculation it will be automatically refined in those areas in which strains grow higher. It won't be necessary to have a prediction about the areas that are going to need remeshing neither the remeshing level. Resources are disposed at the time they are required.

- It won't be necessary to provide, for the early steps of the process, a refined mesh in the areas that are going to experiment high strain levels in the last steps. It avoids the calculation in these early steps to be unnecessarily heavy.

5.1 Adaptive meshing tool in LS-DYNA

LS-DYNA (LSTC, 1998) includes an h-adaptive method for the shell elements (Belytschko, et al., 1989). In an h-adaptive method, the elements are subdivided into smaller elements wherever an error indicator shows that subdivision of the elements will provide improved accuracy. The beginning objective of the adaptive process used in LS-DYNA is to obtain the greatest accuracy for a given set of computational resources. The user sets the initial mesh and the maximum level of adaptivity, and the program subdivides those elements in which the error indicator is the largest. Although this does not provide control on the error of the solution, it makes it possible to obtain a solution of comparable accuracy with fewer elements, and, hence, less computational resources, than with a fixed mesh.

The original mesh provided by the user is known as the parent mesh, the elements of this mesh are called the parent elements, and the nodes are called parent nodes. Any elements that are generated by the adaptive process are called descendant elements, and any nodes that are generated by the adaptive process are called descendant nodes. Elements generated by the second level of adaptivity are called first-generation elements, those generated by third level of adaptivity are called second-generation elements, etc. The coordinates of the descendant nodes are generated by using linear interpolation.

Refinement indicators are used to decide the locations of mesh refinement. One deformation based approach checks for a change in angles between contiguous elements.

5.2 Adaptive meshing programming in LS-DYNA

EDADAPT command activates AM for a part of the simulation. It should be applied to blank parts, since dies are modeled as rigid and no strains or stresses are calculated into dies. The mesh size of rigid dies can be as fine as desired because it does not imply additional calculations. For example, to activate AM for PART #1 the following command must be written:

EDADAPT, 1, ON

AM activation command is placed just before SOLVE command, and does not modify any other programming structure, which makes possible an easy incorporation to the automation scheme described in previous sections.

5.3 Adaptive meshing controls

Adaptive Meshing control parameters have to be defined by means of EDCADAPT command. These parameters are defined just below (ANSYS, 2005):

- **FREQ-** Time interval between adaptive mesh refinements.
  - **TOL-** Adaptive angle tolerance (in degrees) for which adaptive meshing will occur. If the relative angle change between elements exceeds the specified tolerance value, the elements will be refined.
  - **OPT-** Adaptivity option:

- 1. Angle change (in degrees) of elements is based on original mesh configuration.
- 2. Angle change (in degrees) of elements is incrementally based on previously refined mesh.
- **MAXLVL-** Maximum number of mesh refinement levels. This parameter controls the number of times an element can be remeshed. Values of 1, 2, 3, 4, etc. allow a maximum of 1, 4, 16, 64, etc. elements, respectively, to be created for each original element.
- **BTIME/DTIME-** Birth/Death time to begin/end adaptive meshing. It controls when AM is activated/deactivated
- **LCID-** Data curve number identifying the interval of remeshing. The abscissa of the data curve is time, and the ordinate is the varied adaptive time interval. If LCID is nonzero, the adaptive frequency (*FREQ*) is replaced by this load curve. Note that a nonzero *FREQ* value is still required to initiate the first adaptive loop.
- **ADPSIZE-** Minimum element size to be adapted based on element edge length.
- **ADPASS-** One or two pass adaptivity option:
- 0. Two pass adaptivity. Results are recalculated after remeshing.
- 1. One pass adaptivity. Results are not recalculated after remeshing.

- **IREFLG-** Uniform refinement level flag. Values of 1, 2, 3, etc. allow 4, 16, 64, etc. elements, respectively, to be created uniformly for each original element.
- **ADPENE-** Adaptive mesh flag for starting adaptivity when approaching (positive *ADPENE* value) or penetrating (negative *ADPENE* value) the tooling surface. Adaptive tool refinement is based on the tool curvature.
- **ADPTH-** Absolute shell thickness level below which adaptivity should begin. This option works only if the adaptive angle tolerance (*TOL*) is nonzero. If thickness based adaptive remeshing is desired without angle change, set *TOL* to a large angle.
- **MAXEL-** Maximum number of elements at which adaptivity will be terminated. Adaptivity is stopped if this number of elements is exceeded.

Adaptive Meshing used to simulate stamping processes has shown to work properly with the combination of control parameters revealed below:

EDCADAPT,0.1,0.5,2,3,0,1 , ,0,0,0,0,0,0,

Which means:

FREQ=0.1; TOL=0.5; OPT=2; MAXLVL=3; BTIME=0; DTIME=1.

These values can vary from one simulation to another.

5.4 Computing time saving

The 2-step stamping process analyzed in section 4 has been carried out with and without AM option, in the same computer, reaching very similar results in both cases.

In the case fine mesh is programmed from the beginning of the calculation, first step took 50 hours and second step 70 hours; 120 hours to complete the entire calculation.

In the case AM is programmed (Figure 15) over a gross initial mesh, 10 hours have been taken to complete calculation.

Additionally, these times does not take account of the efforts made by the stress analyst to find the appropriate mesh density for each blank area as a function of the final plastic strain.

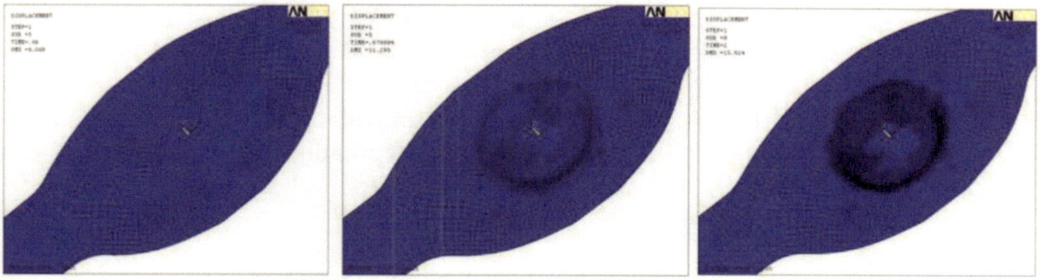

Fig. 15. Evolution of the adaptive mesh in step one simulation

5.5 Problems encountered during adaptive meshing implementation

As has been shown in section 2.2, combined "Explicit to Implicit" simulations have resulted to be the most appropriate way to simulate the complete stamping process, using Full Restart option to concatenate different stamping steps. However, ANSYS Release 10.0 Documentation says textually:

"Adaptive meshing: Adaptive meshing (EDADAPT and EDCADAPT) is not supported in a full restart. In addition, a full restart is not possible if adaptive meshing was used in the previous analysis. "(ANSYS, 2005)

So it can be concluded that using LS-DYNA AM tool to simulate a multistep stamping process forces the stress analyst to develop a unique Explicit procedure, programming different dies approximation and retiring in the same calculation.

6. Conclusions

According with previous expositions and results, it can be concluded:

- A procedure to simulate real sheet metal forming processes by means of finite elements has been established.
- To define this procedure, several options have been analyzed for each step of the process, choosing the one more suitable between the possibilities offered by finite elements software.
- Such a procedure has been automated and allows performing simulations with no user intervention, avoiding the difficulty of using a high-level program as LS-DYNA.
- By means of this automated procedure a methodology to adjust material parameters has been developed.
- Parameters involved in each material model have been identified and their influence in final results has been quantified. This is very useful to fit material properties in other simulations.
- This methodology is based in real experimental and simulation results and in a material parameter fit estimation procedure.
- Real industry experimental tests to validate the simulation results, instead of benchmark theoretical tests, have been carried out. This allows to use previous knowledge of the designer, to particularize material characterization for each kind of process and avoids building specific tooling.
- Simulation model has been validated by comparing its results with those obtained in experimental tests. An example of a real application of the industry has been presented.

- LS-DYNA adaptive meshing has been also tested. Results obtained by using it are virtually the same as those validated before and time is greatly reduced. So, it can be conclude that using adaptive meshing highly recommended.
- Using adaptive meshing forces to avoid implicit simulations in springback estimation. Therefore, a complete explicit simulation of the application and withdrawal of dies must be carried out.

7. Acknowledgment

The authors want to thank ARRAN Automoción Group for its great interest and collaboration in this work and the Government of Spain for the support given through the project 370100-103 of the PROFIT program.

8. References

Álvarez- Caldas, C., et al. (2009). Expert System for Simulation of Metal Sheet Stamping. *Engineering with computers*, Vol. 25, No. 4, pp. 405- 410. ISSN 0177-0667.

ANSYS (2005). *ANSYS LS- DYNA User's Guide. ANSYS release 10.0.* ANSYS Inc. Canonsburg, USA.

Belytschko, T., et al. (1989). Fission - Fusion Adaptivity in Finite Elements for Nonlinear Dynamics of Shells. *Computers and Structures*, Vol. 33, No. pp. 1307- 1323, ISSN

Buranathiti, T.&Cao, J. (2005a). Numisheet2005 Benchmark Analysis on Forming of an Automotive Deck Lid Inner Panel: Benchmark 1, *NUMISHEET 2005: Proceedings of the 6th International Conference and Workshop on Numerical Simulation of 3D Sheet Metal Forming Process. AIP Conference Proceedings*, Detroit, Michigan, USA, 15-19/08/2005.

Buranathiti, T.&Cao, J. (2005b). Numisheet2005 Benchmark Analysis on Forming of an Automotive Underbody Cross Member: Benchmark 2, *NUMISHEET 2005: Proceedings of the 6th International Conference and Workshop on Numerical Simulation of 3D Sheet Metal Forming Process. AIP Conference Proceedings*, Detroit, Michigan, USA, 15-19/08/2005.

Cowper, G. R.&Symonds, P. S. (1958). *Strain Hardening and Strain Rate Effects in the Impact Loading of Cantilever Beams*. Brown University. Providence, Rhode Isl, USA.

Chen, M. H., et al. (2007). Application of the forming limit stress diagram to forming limit prediction for the multi-step forming of auto panels. *Journal of Materials Processing Technology*, Vol. 187-188, No. pp. 173-177, ISSN 0924-0136

Darendeliler, H.&Kaftanoglu, B. (1991). Deformation Analysis of Deep-Drawing by a Finite Element Method. *CIRP Annals - Manufacturing Technology*, Vol. 40, No. 1, pp. 281-284, ISSN 0007-8506

Dietenberger, M., et al. (2005). Development of a High Strain-Rate Dependent Vehicle Model, *4th LS-DYNA Forum*, Bamberg, Germany 20th - 21st of October 2005.

Firat, M. (2007a). Computer aided analysis and design of sheet metal forming processes: Part I - The finite element modeling concepts. *Materials & Design*, Vol. 28, No. 4, pp. 1298-1303, ISSN 0261-3069

Firat, M. (2007b). Computer aided analysis and design of sheet metal forming processes: Part II - Deformation response modeling. *Materials & Design*, Vol. 28, No. 4, pp. 1304-1310, ISSN 0261-3069

Firat, M. (2007c). U-channel forming analysis with an emphasis on springback deformation. *Materials & Design*, Vol. 28, No. 1, pp. 147-154, ISSN 0261-3069

Gau, J.-T. (1999). *A Study of the Influence of the Bauschinger Effect on Springback in Two-Dimensional Sheet Metal Forming*. Ph.D. Degree. The Ohio State University. Ohio.

Gauchía, A. et al. (2009). Material parameters in a simulation of metal sheet stamping. *Proceedings of the Institution of Mechanical Engineers Part D-Journal of Automobile Engineering*. Vol. 223. No. 6, pp. 783- 791. ISSN 0954-4070.

Hallquist, J. O. (1998). *LS-DYNA Theoretical Manual*. LSTC. Livermore, California, USA.

Ling, Y. E., et al. (2005). Finite element analysis of springback in L-bending of sheet metal. *Journal of Materials Processing Technology*, Vol. 168, No. 2, pp. 296-302, ISSN 0924-0136

LSTC (1998). *LS-DYNA Theoretical Manual*. Livermore Software Technology Corporation. Livermore, California, USA.

LSTC (2006). *LS-DYNA: User's Manual Version 971*. Livermore Software Technology Corporation. Livermore, California, USA.

Makinouchi, A. (1996). Sheet metal forming simulation in industry. *Journal of Materials Processing Technology*, Vol. 60, No. 1-4, pp. 19-26, ISSN 0924-0136

Mattiasson, K., et al. (1995). Simulation of springback in sheet metal forming, *Proceedings of the NUMIFORM'95 Simulation of Materials Processing: Theory, Methods and Applications*, Cornell University, Ithaca, NY, USA,

Morestin, F., et al. (1996). Elasto plastic formulation using a kinematic hardening model for springback analysis in sheet metal forming. *Journal of Materials Processing Technology*, Vol. 56, No. 1-4, pp. 619-630, ISSN 0924-0136

Narasimhan, N.&Lovell, M. (1999). Predicting springback in sheet metal forming: an explicit to implicit sequential solution procedure. *Finite Elements in Analysis and Design*, Vol. 33, No. 1, pp. 29-42, ISSN 0168-874X

Ortiz, M.&Quigley, J. J. (1991). Adaptive mesh refinement in strain localization problems. *Computer Methods in Applied Mechanics and Engineering*, Vol. 90, No. 1-3, pp. 781-804, ISSN 0045-7825

Quesada, A., et al. (2009). Influence of the parameters of the material model in finite element simulation of sheet metal stamping, *7th EUROMECH Solid Mechanics Conference*, Lisbon (Portugal), September, 7th- 11th, 2009.

Quigley, E.&Monaghan, J. (2002). Enhanced finite element models of metal spinning. *Journal of Materials Processing Technology*, Vol. 121, No. 1, pp. 43-49, ISSN 0924-0136

Samuel, M. (2004). Numerical and experimental investigations of forming limit diagrams in metal sheets. *Journal of Materials Processing Technology*, Vol. 153-154, No. pp. 424-431, ISSN 0924-0136

Silva, M. B., et al. (2004). Stamping of automotive components: a numerical and experimental investigation. *Journal of Materials Processing Technology*, Vol. 155-156, No. pp. 1489-1496, ISSN 0924-0136

Song, J.-H., et al. (2007). A simulation-based design parameter study in the stamping process of an automotive member. *Journal of Materials Processing Technology*, Vol. 189, No. 1-3, pp. 450-458, ISSN 0924-0136

Taylor, L., et al. (1995). Numerical simulations of sheet-metal forming. *Journal of Materials Processing Technology*, Vol. 50, No. 1-4, pp. 168-179, ISSN 0924-0136

Tekkaya, A. E. (2000). State-of-the-art of simulation of sheet metal forming. *Journal of Materials Processing Technology*, Vol. 103, No. 1, pp. 14-22, ISSN 0924-0136

Wei, L.&Yuying, Y. (2008). Multi-objective optimization of sheet metal forming process using Pareto-based genetic algorithm. *Journal of Materials Processing Technology*, Vol. 208, No. 1-3, pp. 499-506, ISSN 0924-0136

9

Expert System Used on Materials Processing

Vizureanu Petrică
"Gheorghe Asachi" Technical University Iasi, Romania

1. Introduction

Conventional computing programs characterize through an *algorithm* approach as the specialists called it. This approach allows solving a problem by using a preset computing scheme which applies to some structures well-known for input information and produces a result that keep to program operations sequence made within computing scheme. Yet, there is another category of problems whose solving has nothing to do with classic algorithms but supposes a higher volume of specialty knowledge for very strait domains. Such specialty knowledge does not represent the usual "luggage" of a certain human subject, they being on view only for *experts* within the interest domain of the problem. Such problems can treat subjects as automat diagnosis, monitoring, planning, design or technical scientific analysis. Computing programs that solves such problems are known as *expert systems* (ES) and the first development attempts of such programs dates from mid of 1960 - 1970's. Unlike conventional programs, ES are conceived to use, mainly, symbolic sentence, developed through interference. As a branch of *artificial intelligence* (AI), expert systems developed pursuing the study of knowledge processing.
An *expert system* is a program that uses knowledge and interference procedures for solving quite difficult problems, which normally needs the intervention of a human expert to find the solution. Shortly, expert systems are programs that store specialty knowledge inserted by experts.

2. Characteristics of ES

These systems are often used under situations without a clear algorithmic solution. Their main characteristic is the presence of a knowledge base along with a search algorithm proper to the reasoning type. Knowledge base is very large most times, so the way of representing knowledge is very important. Knowledge base of the system must separate from the program, which must be as stable as possible. The most used way of representing knowledge is a multitude of production rules. Operations of these systems are further controlled by a simple procedure whose nature depends on knowledge nature. As in other artificial intelligence programs, when other techniques are not available, search has recourse to. Expert systems built up to date differs from this point of view. The question arises whether there can be written rules as strict as in any situation there is only an applicable solution? And, also, finding all solutions is necessary or it is sufficient only one?

An expert system must have compulsory three main modules that form the so-called *essential system*:

- Knowledge base formed by the assembly of specialized knowledge introduced by human expert. The knowledge stored here is mainly objective descriptions and the relations between them; knowledge base takes part from the cognitive system, knowledge being memorized into a specially organized space; storage form must assure the search of knowledge pieces specified directly through identifying symbols or indirect through associated properties or interferences that start from other knowledge pieces.
- Interference engine represents the novelty of expert system and takes over from knowledge base the fact used for building reasoning. Interference engine pursues a series of major objectives such as control strategy election based on current problem, elaboration of the plan that solves the problem after necessities, switching from a control strategy to another one, execution of the actions preset in solving plan. Although interference mechanism is built from a procedures assembly in the usual meaning of the term, the way in which knowledge are used is not estimated by program but depends on the knowledge it has at command.
- Facts base represents an auxiliary memory that contains all users' data (initial facts that describe the source of the solving problems) and the intermediary results made during reasoning. The content of the facts base is stored generally in volatile memory (RAM) but to user request; it can be stored on hard disk.

2.1 The modules of an ES

Communication module assures specific interfaces for users and for knowledge acquisition. User interface allows the dialogue between user and quasi natural language system. It transmits to interference mechanism user's requests and his results. It facilitates equally the acquisition of the initial problem and result communication.

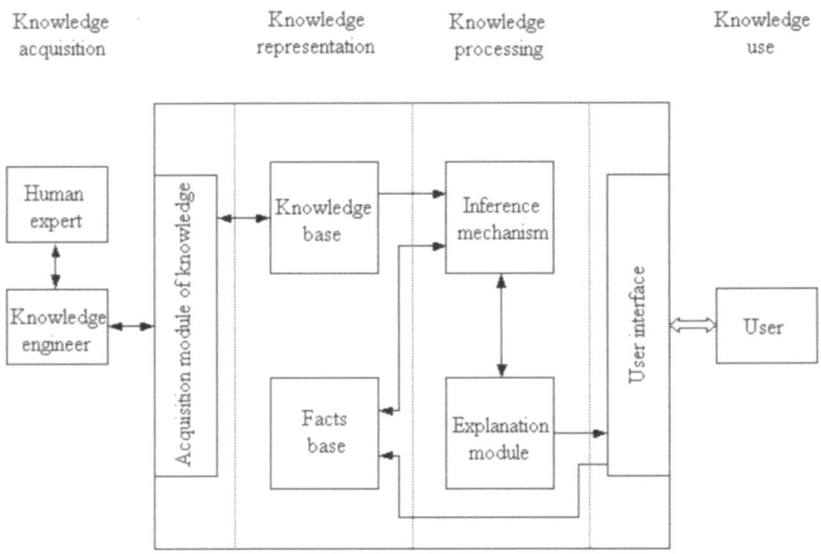

Fig. 1. ES modules

Acquisition module of knowledge takes specialized knowledge given by human expert through the engineer, into a not specific form to intern representation. A series of knowledge can arise as files specific to databases or to other external programs. This module receives the knowledge, verifies their validity and finally generates a coherent knowledge base.

Explaining module allows path tracing followed in reasoning process by resolvent system and explanation issuance for the achieved solution by emphasizing the causes of eventual mistakes or the reason of a failure. It helps the expert to verify the consistency of the knowledge base.

Explanation and updating. In terms of the application that it is built for, the effective structure of an expert system can differ towards the standard structure.

For example, initial data can be acquired from the user and from automatic control equipment

Nevertheless, it is important for expert systems to have two characteristics:

- To explain the reasoning and if it is not possible, human users could not accept it. For this, it must be enough meta-knowledge for explanations and the program must go in intelligible steps.
- To attain new knowledge and to modify the old ones, and usually the only way of introducing knowledge into an expert system is by human expert interaction.

2.2 Development of an ES

The development of an expert system represents design process of the system going from users' demands of implementing testing and finally launching the product onto market for the effective use. Many times, there are distinctions in design stage between physical design and logical one because these stages need different activities and resources both technological nature and human one.

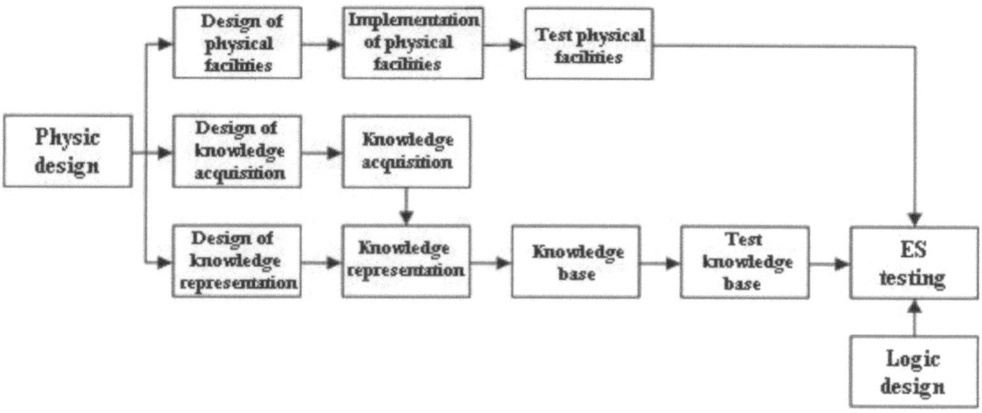

Fig. 2. Physical design.

Physical design includes the design of hardware resources and knowledge base, which includes acquisition components of the knowledge and representation way. When physical part is design sub-systems are appropriate implemented and tested. Only afterwards, they can be tested together with logical part.

Logic design refers to software design and realizes parallel to physical one. First, assembly decisions take such as those linked to the election of a programming language or a shell or a toolkit. Both integration problems of the system and security ones must solve. Then interference engine and interfaces are designed. To program interference engine declarative languages are chosen several times. The design of this part of the system can be seen as an activity of software development, as programming engineering says. The particularity of ES is the importance and development of the knowledge base.
In addition, the exclusive accent is not put on developing interference engine program but on developing the other component such as interfaces.
Each subsystem could need different resources (other programming languages or even other hardware resources) and distinct development techniques.

2.3 ES advantages

- They are valuable collections of information
- They are indispensable without human expertise
- In some situation, they can be cheaper and more effective than human experts can
- They can be faster than human experts can
- If flexible, they can be easily up-dated
- They can be used to instruct new human experts
- At request, they can explain the premises and reasoning line.
- They treat the uncertainty into an explicit manner, which, unlike human experts, can be verified.

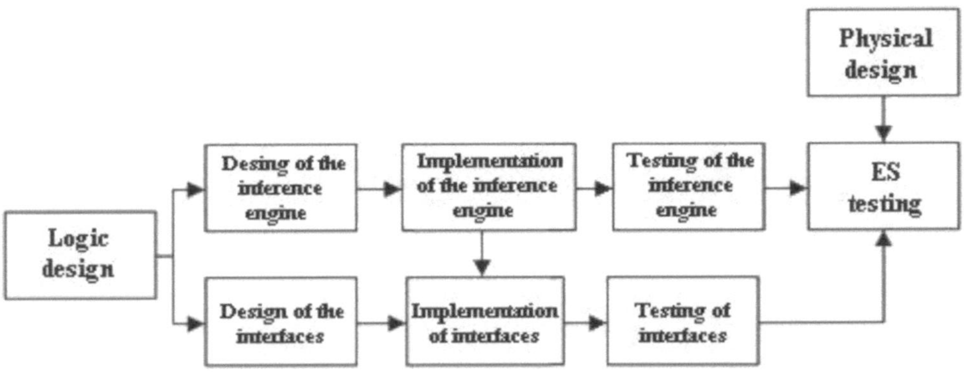

Fig. 3. Logic design.

3. Stages in the design and implementation of an ES

Expert systems are, in fact, particular cases of the *production systems*, which address to some domains with a very strait specialization. In fact, the larger the number of knowledge within a system is the efficient it acts. As human expert, ES has a sphere of competences limited only to a certain domain, usually, very strait, its functionality lying on the human reasoning pattern: starting from certain knowledge or facts, ES develops a series of interferences and reaches to a certain conclusion. Under the context, a synthetic definition of ES would be as follows *programs dedicated usually to a specific domain that try to emulate human experts' behavior.*

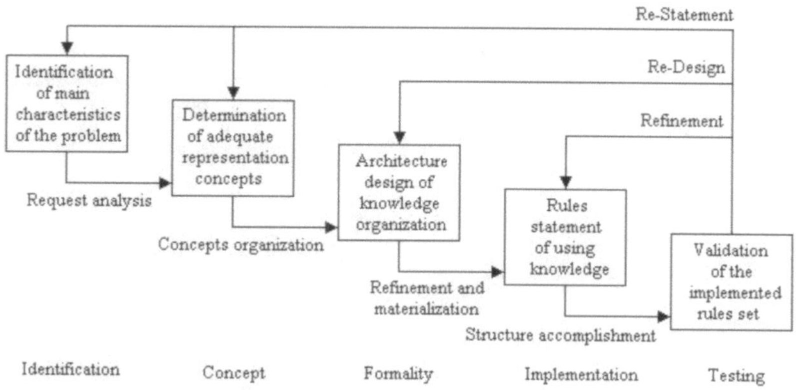

Fig. 4. ES implementation.

- They cannot reason based on intuition or common sense because they cannot be easily representable
- They are limited to a restrained domain; knowledge from other domains cannot be easily integrated nor cannot generalize convincingly
- Learning process is not automate; in order to up-date knowledge it is needed human intervention
- Nowadays, they cannot reason based on theories and analyses
- The knowledge stored in knowledge base depend very much on the human expert that express and articulate them

As a component of *production systems*, ES is one of the most used patterns for representing and control of knowledge. Within this terminology, the word *production* must not be confounded with which happens in factories and plants. Its significance can be translated according to the definition as the *production* of new facts added into knowledge base due to the appliance of these rules. A possible definition of the production system including ES referring to their structure could comprise the following elements:

- A set of rules, each rule has two components such as component *condition* that determines when the rule applies and component *consequence* that describes the action, which results by applying the rule. This set of rules form *rules base*.
- One or many databases contain the information describing the analyzed problem. This database contains initial information where new facts add resulted by applying the rules. This set of information forms *facts base*.
- A control mechanism or rules interpreter frequently named interference engine, which assures the stability of rules appliance order for the existent database. The selection of the rule that applies and solve the appeared conflicts when many rules can be applied simultaneously.
- Communication between operator and ES accomplishes by a specialized interface that assures the efficient exploitation and development of the ES. This interface allows the achievement of two important functions such as:
    a. On one hand, at human operator demand ES can explain the reasoning it achieved. This is necessary because as complex and "praised" ES is, human operator cannot always accept "blindly" the solution proposed by ES but he wants to pursue and analyze the reasoning machine made.
    b. On the other hand, in order ES develop by gathering experience it is necessary the modification of the old knowledge and addition of new ones into knowledge base.

The first two components form the so-called *knowledge base*. Representation and organization of knowledge base are two essential aspects for the correct functioning of ES. If it is desired for a ES to develop it is absolutely necessary that knowledge base is completely separated by the rest of the program that uses it (communication interface with the operator and interference engine). The interaction between human operator and ES is synthetic described in figure 5.

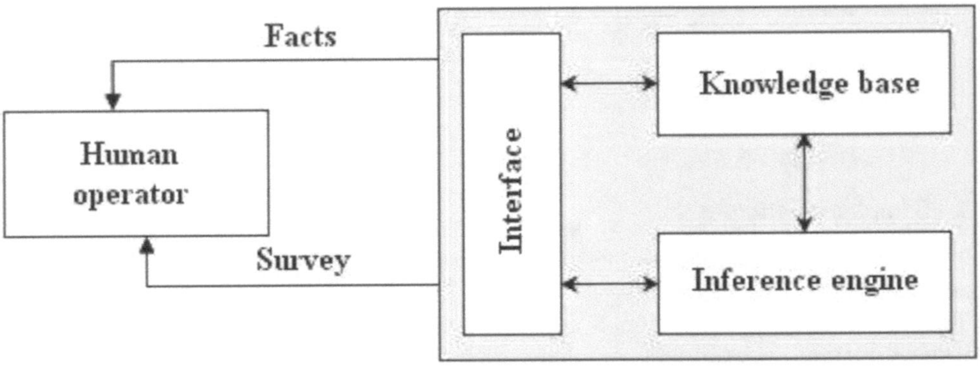

Fig. 5. Communication between human operator and expert system

Under the context of considering ES as formalism of the AI, this organization presents two big advantages such as:

a. On one hand it represents a really inspired simulation of the intelligent processes with a dominant nature on information processing,
b. On the other hand, it assures the possibility of adding new rules without disturbing the system in assembly, property that responds very well to the statement according to which no intelligent system is definitive.

Summarizing the above definition, ES characterizes by the following attributes:

- Necessary knowledge refers to a relative strait domain and they are well specified.
- ES are underlying less on algorithm techniques and more on an important volume of knowledge from a specific domain.
- An ES can be built only with the help of a human expert open to spend an appreciable time to transfer its own expertise to the program. This knowledge transfer makes gradually by frequent interactions between human expert and program.
- The volume of necessary knowledge depends on problem. There can be situations when several dozens of rules and other situations are necessary to establish thousands of rules.
- The selection of the control structure for a particular ES depends on the specific of the problem.
- Knowledge is represented under declarative form by using usually a structure type IF…THEN… As a result, the majority of expert systems use *rules bases*.
- Knowledge base is clearly separated by the control mechanism of knowledge handling (inference engine).
- Communication with human operator makes through a relative complex interface, which assures the integration, communication, explanation and delivery of knowledge.
- In most cases, the interface consists in a specialized module meant for the modification of the existent knowledge and the acquisition of new knowledge for ES development.

The general structure of an ES that reflects these attributes is described in figure 6.

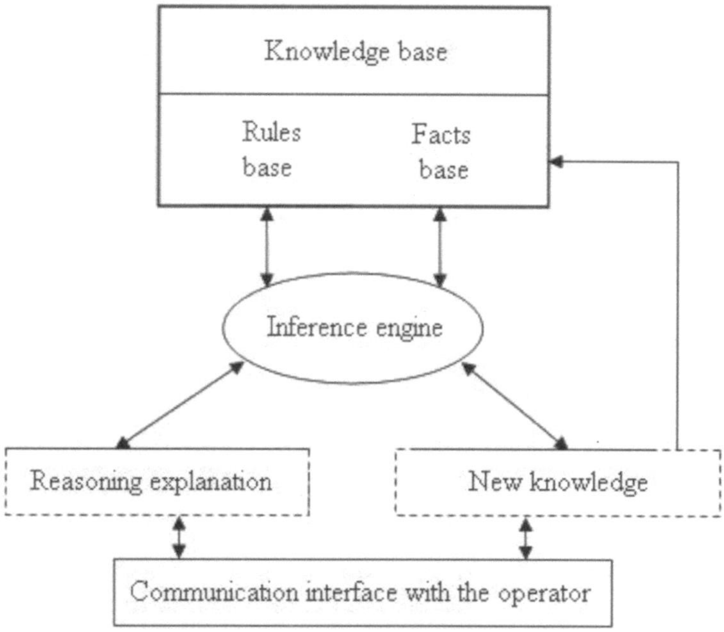

Fig. 6. General structure of an ES.

As for the proper functioning of an ES, the specific mechanism that underlies reasoning realized by program is inference. According to DEX definition, inference is a logic operation that passes from a statement to another one and where the last statement is deduces from the first one. Yet, many times ES are used in parallel with the interface and search techniques, where, at every turn, from the multitude of the rules defined at system level apply only one and once in a while two or most three rules.

Thus, the inference is equivalent to a deduction process that starts from the initial or final conditions, and, by the sequential appliance of some rules, it gets into desired state. Fortunately, in many situations building a set of rules that allow the appliance of pure inference is not possible and, as a result, reasoning row used by ES transforms into a search process. In consequence, intelligent search techniques represent all-important elements in ES functioning.

Inferences development parallel to search processes is controlled by inference engine that assures information handling from knowledge base by realizing four types of actions as follows

a. Overlying of the rules base over facts base to identify the applicable rules;
b. Selection of the applied rules;
c. Rules appliance;
d. Verification of stop criterion.

Inference engines can use two types of inference such as *foreword chaining* (from initial state towards final state) or *backward chaining* (from final state towards initial state). In case of foreword chaining, inference engine controls the production/adding of new facts into facts base and in case of back ward chaining - it verifies certain hypothetical information established during the process of backward chaining.

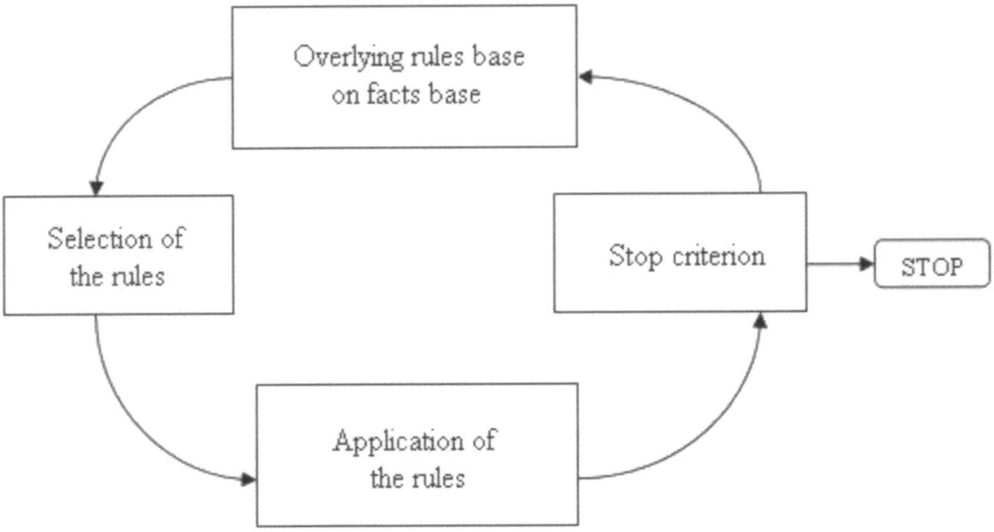

Fig. 7. Functioning of inference engine.

Between the processes controlled by inference engine one of the most important and sensitive is the selection of rules that will be applied. Difficulty of this process lies in the fact that, at a certain moment, the database can contain facts that simultaneously satisfy the conditions of multiple rules; the decision to take is which rules will be applied. Inference engine functioning according to those four actions that it controls is described in figure 7.

4. Neural networks (NN)

Artificial neural networks (ANN) called sometimes simply neural networks (NN) are formed from groups of artificial neurons, interconnected between them, which based on an algorithm process the received information.

Practically networks are work instruments that make a regression analysis on the data from a database.

Neurons, nodes of the network are connected together their connections having specific ponderosities based on the transmitted information. Each node has many inputs, each with its ponderosity. The output is and input for other neurons presented sometimes as vectors or data matrixes. Connection ponderosities between neuron must not be known prior, they are determined with the aid of learning algorithm of the system. The ponderosity modifies the iteration so that input vector is closer as value to the preset, real vector for each input. Once taught neuron network can solve similar problems. Interpolation is made with fuzzy logic system achieving hybrid system.

These neural networks are used especially in solving technical problem, when data are not complete, the correlation between parameters are not linear, the decisions made by humans are based on intuition or the problems are quite complex and estimators' matrix is ill-defined.

ANN advantage consists in the fact that the network function without asking for detailed information about the system. Another major advantage of ANN is that it learns relatively easy the correlations between inputs and outputs and it even learns to simulate the relations between input and output parameters.

5. The analysis of expert systems

The analysis of expert systems - ES shows us that not the special module is connected with the knowledge of the domain. Knowledge implies both explicit knowledge and intrinsic (implicit) knowledge. Explicit knowledge are embodied in documentations, codes, standards, transferable or accessible procedures. Intrinsic knowledge implies both a professional culture and a constitutional one. They are found «hidden» inside man's mind, in its reasoning. These are harder to encode, communicate or free for access.
Accordingly, in order to approach diagnosis or analysis problems of the different Thermal Systems (TS) built artificial intelligence systems. The *comparison* between these three approach groups allows us the selection of the most appropriate work method.

Comparison elements	**Case-based reasoning (RBC)**	**Neural Network (NN)**	**Rule-based reasoning (RBR)**
Module of data building, their representation	Data regain for similar problems	Recognition of some valid models and standards	Rules type if-then
Module of data achievement	Old solved cases	Learning according to the learning algorithm. Input data ponderosity	According to human experience and to experts' ideas within domain
Expert's procedure in solving the problem	Extraction of similarity cases from database	Recognition of the correlation cases between input-output measures and it learns the network	Step-by-step, logically
Construction of the analysis system	Easy to build but it needs time	Black box. No need for detailed knowledge in the domain	Difficulties in knowledge acquisition (data, standards, codes etc.)
Data renewal	Handy	By learning in a trained manner	Handy
Their understanding	Hard	Acceptable	Easy

Table 1. Comparison elements.

The last researches bring light that the best approach is the accomplishment of a hybrid expert system where the modules can be built separately based on a proper inference engine.

6. Existent expert systems

6.1 The QuenchMiner

The ES was realized, several years ago, at the Center of excellence for heat treatments at Worcester Polytechnic Institute, USA. It was meant to help the specialists that make heat treatments. ES tries to give an answer to user's questions regarding the functional parameters in a heat treatment cycle, especially when material cools down. In figure 8 presents the structure of an expert system.

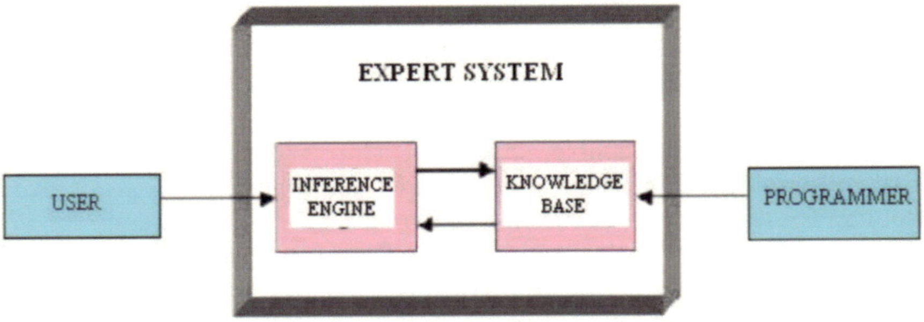

Fig. 8. Structure of the expert system (ES).

The knowledge base consists in basic rules and knowledge on the heat treatment (quenching) introduced by the expert in this domain. The database contains statements on quenching ways with details on the experimental conditions. The rules introduced into the database were achieved through "Data Mining" technique applied to the knowledge base. The data achieved from technical literature and reports regarding the experiences connected with materials quenching. The architecture of the expert system is shown in figure 9.

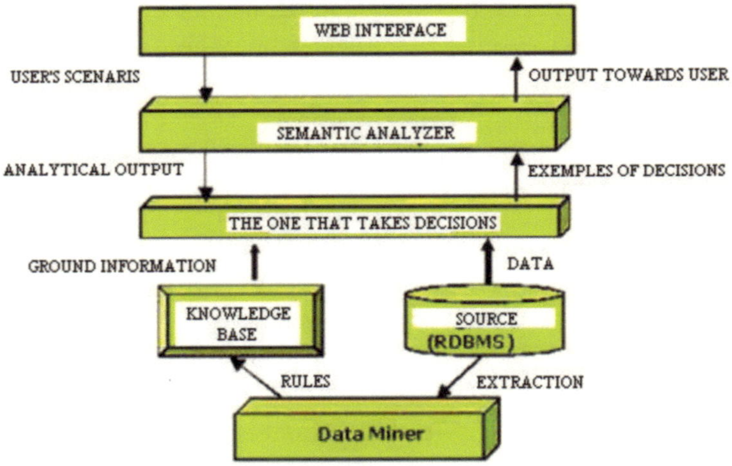

Fig. 9. Architecture of expert system ES.

The basic components are *knowledge base* and *inference engine* (decision engine). The decision engine uses as work technique the system based on rules and the examination technique *forward chaining*. The user introduces the data of the problem through a dialogue interface. The data are undertaken and processed into semantic analysis module and sent to inference Engine. This realizes a set of decisions by using the data stored into RDBMS module and the reasoning rules from knowledge base. Outputs from decision module reach again to the user by passing through semantic analysis module. Quench Miner helps the user to optimize the process of heat treatment. ES offers to the expert in heat treatment a technical support for his decisions.

Input parameters, which ES use, depend and select according to the problem that need to be analyzed. Quench Miner is focused on the analysis of the following problems from the process of heat treatment:

- Orientation of the material in coolant vertical or transversal and depends on material geometry.
- Cooling speed depends on viscosity of the coolant, its agitation speed the oxides layer from the surface of the material. It classifies in rapid, moderate or slow.
- Uniformity of cooling process such as uniform or non-uniform.
- Global coefficient of heat transfer depends on cooling speed, material density and specific heat and geometric factors. It classifies in high, average and low.
- Residual tensions in the material after heat treatment depend on material history and the entire cycle of heat treatment, the material supported. It classifies in negligible, moderate or high.
- Hardness of the material after treatment is influenced by cooling speed, carbon content and type of the coolant. It classifies in high, average and low.
- Deformation tendency of the material depends on cooling speed, nature of the coolant and residual stresses within material. It classifies in small, average and high.
- Cracking probability is influenced by the same parameters as deformation is.
- Input variables of the expert system.

List of the input variables is exhaustive, but between these, only those that influence the problem analyzed by the expert system are chosen.

- Coolant water, oil, polymer
- Temperature of the coolant high, average, low
- Agitation speed for coolant insufficient, moderate or excessive,
- Viscosity of the coolant big, average, small
- Agitation type that defines the way agitation realizes through pump, adjustment or compressor
- Circulation speed of the coolant
- Type of the coolant old or new
- Degradation of the polymer as coolant
- Material that must be treated, steel mark
- Material geometry
- Material surface and its section
- Material volume big, small
- Material density high, low
- Specific heat high, low
- Oxide layer from material surface,
- Material roughness rough or smooth
- Orientation of the material in the coolant
- Carbon content within material
- Grains structure of the material
- Plastic deformation of the material,

Output parameters for ES:

- Orientation of the material in the coolant
- Cooling speed,
- Uniformity of cooling process,
- Global heat transfer coefficient,
- Residual stresses in material,
- Hardness of the material,
- Cracking probability.

The user can select as output parameter one or more variables from those itemized above. We consider cooling speed as output parameter.

Input parameters:

- coolant: water
- temperature: high
- agitation speed: insufficient
- viscosity
- circulation speed of the coolant
- material
  - section: thin
  - volume:
  - oxide layer: thick
  - surface roughness: rough

We notice that the user must not complete all the lines. Certain fields are determined automate by inference engine ES processes input data and presents on the display the result of the analysis: rapid in our case.

Inference engine can also present intermediary reasoning based on rules from knowledge base such as:

- a coolant with small viscosity (water) implies a rapid cooling,
- an insufficient agitation implies a slower cooling
- the areas with thin walls implies a rapid cooling
- a thick oxide layer implies o slower cooling
- a rough surface implies a rapid cooling,
- high temperature of the coolant implies a slower cooling

Per total cooling is rapid.

The program is written using Java Expert System Shell, so-called JESS. Jess uses for program progress Forward Chaining examination technique. Inference rules apply directly to the knowledge base. Input data are stored in working memory. At every turn, the program gives a set of rules that satisfy the data from working memory. In order to "map" (fit) the rules with data from the database Jess uses RETE algorithm.

Rules apply or eliminate taking into account their specificity, the conflict between them and ponderosity.

Decisions that QuenchMiner expert system takes are actually estimations based on empiric relations experimentally ascertained and validated in practice. These are a support for the user in taking appropriate decisions.

Decisions taken into inference Engine base on the analysis of input data and output variables, ES identifies the dependences between variables based on cause-effect relations. The ponderosity of each input variable is determined by analyzing the impact or in output variable. In addition, it is analyzed influence tendency of each variable on cooling speed taking into account its ponderosity and compares between them these tendencies in order to model the final answer.

6.2 Expert system based on anterior cases RBC (Case-Based Reasoning)

Expert system based on anterior cases is, in fact, the process of solving new problems based on given solutions of some similar anterior problems. RBC lies on prototype theory explored in human cognitive sciences. RBC depends on the intuitive fact that new problems are often similar to those met anterior and their solutions will be similar to those given in the past. RBC does not offer concrete solutions, sure conclusions to the current problem.

(A. Aamodt and E. Plaza, 1994), proposed that case-based reasoning need to be described in four steps:

1. Recovery of the similar cases from the past. A case consists in a problem and its solution and the observations how it reached to this solution;
2. The use all over again of the solutions. It analyzes the connection between the anterior case and the current problem. It identifies the resemblances and differences between the two cases and adapts the solution to the current case;
3. Review of the solution. The new adapted solution tests and if necessary modifies;
4. Retain of the solution. The solution adapted to the new case is stored as a new case into memory.

Each task from those four steps divides in other tasks. Thus, to recover anterior cases we need to accomplish the following stages:

- *Cases identification, their search, initial match and selection of the most accurate case.*

To use all over again the solution we must realize the next steps such as solution copying, its matching and modification. The task regarding review of the solution implies its evaluation (by learning and simulation) and defects repair.

- *Retain of the solution implies its integration by its continuation, knowledge updating, the adequate index of the solution and the extraction of the main descriptors by justifying them for the found solution.*

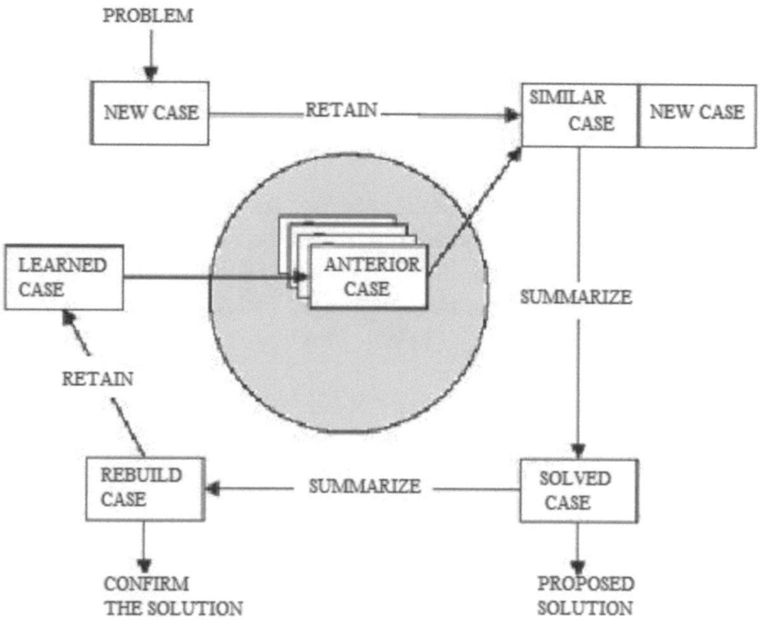

Fig. 10. Case-Based Reasoning general model.

Re-establish mechanism of the similar cases from the past is very important in method case. For this, the method of the closest neighbors is used. In this method considers that all the characteristics of the case are as much important, which practically does not confirm. Accordingly, it proposed to give different ponderosities for the most important characteristics based on the information they carry.

(Shin et al., 2000) proposed a hybrid method to regain knowledge made of CBR and neural networks technique. The system is adequate especially when the characteristics of the case are numerical expressed. A distance type normalized Euclidean measures the similarity of the characteristic features (Kwang and Sang, 2006). If X is the past case with the characteristics $x_1, x_2, ...x_n$ and takes part from class x_c and q the vector of the current problem with the characteristics q_f, then the difference between the two vectors defines through the relation

$$d(x,q)=\left(\left\|x_f-q_f\right\|^2\right) \tag{1}$$

by introducing value barriers, certain features can be considered similar between the two cases. If we introduce ponderosities for the characteristics of the case based on their importance then the distance between the two cases defines through the following relation

$$D(x,q)=\sqrt{}\Sigma wf2 \text{ x difference}(xf,\ qf)2 \tag{2}$$

where:

$$|x_f - q_f|, \text{ if f is characterized numeric}$$

$$difference(x_f, q_f)=\left|x_f-q_f\right|, \text{ if f has numerical value, or} \tag{3}$$

$$difference(x_f, q_f)=0, \text{ if f has symbolic value and } x_f = q_f, \text{ or} \tag{4}$$

$$difference(x_f, q_f)=1, \text{ for other cases} \tag{5}$$

If the characteristic features have symbolic or unsorted values that the featured that match can be numbered for the simple cases and it determines a similarity based on similar characteristics.

For the complex cases proposed a more complicated metric. Stanfill and Waltz proposed as measure "value difference metric" (VDM) that takes into account the similarity of characteristics value.

We consider two cases X and Y, which have N characteristic features x_i, respectively y_i. We suppose n – number of classes and f_i declared features and g characteristic class where c_l is a possible one. Under these conditions, VDM defines by the set of relations:

$$\begin{aligned}
&\Delta(X,Y)=\sum_{i=1}^{N}\delta(x_i,y_i)\\
&\delta(x_i,y_i)=d(x_i,y_i)w(x_i,y_i)\\
&d(x_i,y_i)=\sum_{l=1}^{n}\left|\frac{D(f_i=x_i \cap g=c_l)}{D(f_i=x_i)}-\frac{D(f_i=y_i \cap g=c_l)}{D(f_i=y_i)}\right|^k\\
&w(x_i,y_i)=\sqrt{\sum_{l=1}^{n}\left(\frac{D(f_i=x_i \cap g=c_l)}{D(f_i=x_i)}\right)^2}
\end{aligned} \tag{6}$$

D is the number of examples in a data set for learning that satisfies the requested condition.

$D(x_i, y_i)$ is a measure of similarity between the characteristics of X and Y.

$D(f_i = x_i \cap g = c_i) / D(f_i = x_i)$ represents the probability for a case with features x_i is classified in class c_l.

$w(x_i, y_i)$ represents the ponderosity with which x_i feature imposes the class.

An important characteristic of CBR is its correlation with learning process. This needs a set of techniques for extracting relevant knowledge from experience, to integrate the case into existent knowledge and to index the case to assimilate it with the similar cases. Learning can be:

- inductive,
- rapid,
- learning based on explanations through:
  - learning the most general rules;
  - learning of the rules more often used;
  - resignation of the unused rules so the learning system is not delayed.

6.3 Expert systems based on neural networks for the control of hardening control through induction of the material

The surface hardening of the material by induction heating followed by a heat treatment made of quenching and annealing is an old procedure often used in industry. The hardness prediction of the material after such a heat treatment is hard to achieve due to non-linear phenomena that take place and to their difficulty in simulation. More, the problem of process control proves to be very difficult. The use of artificial intelligence proves to be of good omen. At Southern-Illinois University, Technologies Department designed and realized an ES based on neural network for this purpose.

The furnace for induction heat treatment is made of a coil with a big diameter that makes a tunnel where the material for heat treatment passes through. The coil is supplied with high frequency currents. The material is transported through this tunnel with a certain speed given by an engine depending on the necessary time for heat treatment at a certain temperature.

Variables parameters:

- shifting speed of the material given by pulling speed of the engine,
- height of the trembler coil,
- temperature of the material at the furnace exit,
- time made by the material from furnace exit until it drops into a coolant for quenching.

All the parameters are expressed in distances.

Material hardness is determined by material speed in the furnace and temperature at furnace exit. The correlation between hardness and pulling speed of the engine and material temperature using a linear regression equation proved to be very weak. Correlation coefficient in R^2 is of 18.7%. In order to control the entire hardening process through induction, it was designed a neural network, which is capable to make predictions on hardness and functional parameters.

The system consists in two neural networks type "backpropagation" with a supervised learning module. Input parameters are pulling engine speed and material temperature.

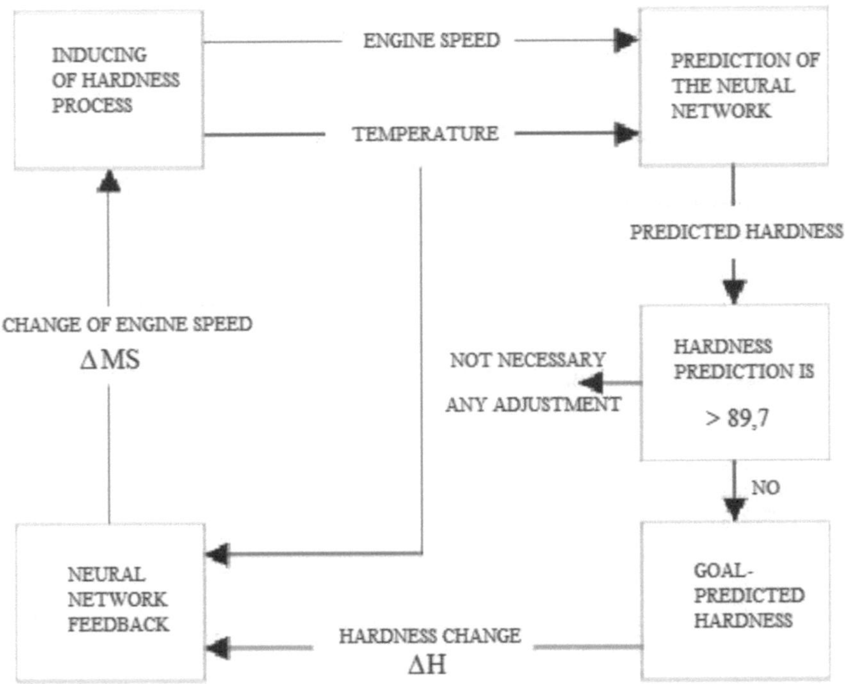

Fig. 11. Control system with an artificial neural network of the hardening process.

The first neural network was designed to predict on material hardness according to input parameters. The network consists in two input layers, three hidden layers and one output layer. For training, 30 set of data used and for tests 15 set of data used. The network was taught by admitting an error of 5% on the entire value range of the hardness. The value of the precise hardness in proportion to real hardness both at learning and at test is given in figures 12 and 13.

The sum of the square errors decreased considerably in relation to a linear regression anterior determined from 15.68 to 2.53.

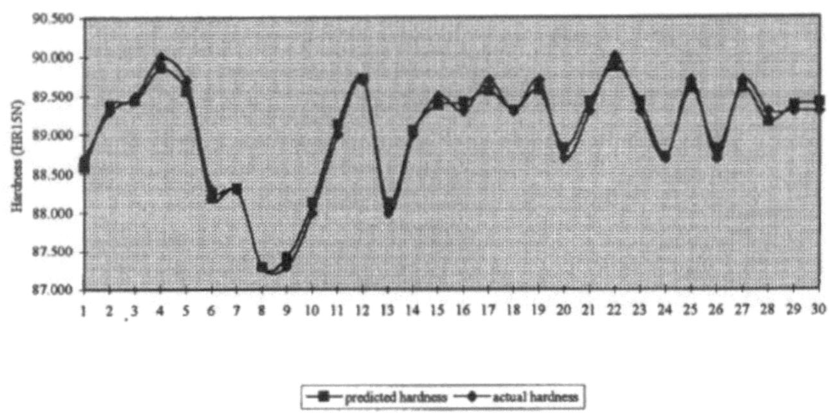

Fig. 12. Prediction of RN network for data used for learning: real hardness towards predicted hardness.

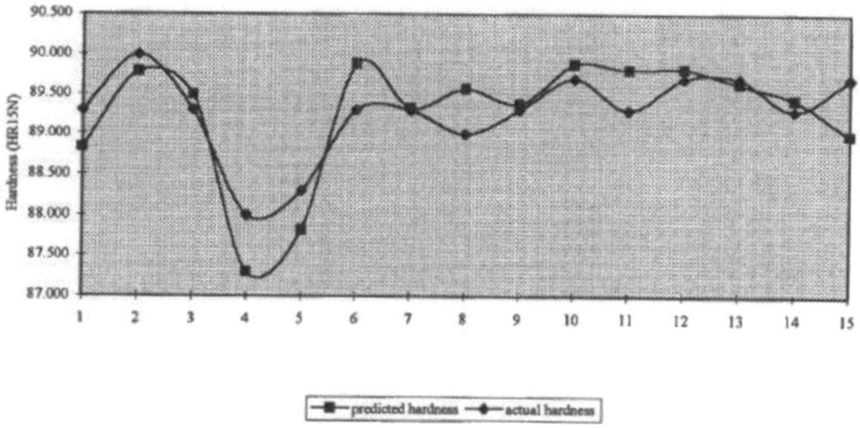

Fig. 13. Prediction of the network for test data: real hardness towards predicted hardness.

For the network that acts as feedback the same type of network adopted (backpropagation, supervised). The architecture is a little bit different meaning that the layer of intermediary neural has four layers. In a case the set of data for training is 14 and for tests 9 set of 3 data used. The network was taught with a tolerance of 5% on hardness range. The speed of pulling engine varies depending on the difference between predicted hardness and real hardness of the material. This difference is an input variable of the first layer of the network. The other input is made of material temperature.

7. Validity of expert system

The prediction of the neural network was tested with 32 set of real data. Each set contains two inputs speed of the engine and material temperature. The exit from the model is material hardness. In feedback neural network, input variables represent the difference between the value predicted by network and the real one and material temperature. Depending on this value, the pulling engine speed of the material through the furnace modifies so that the difference is smaller and the calculated value is closer to the real one. The compared results are given in table 2 and are graphically presented in figure 14.

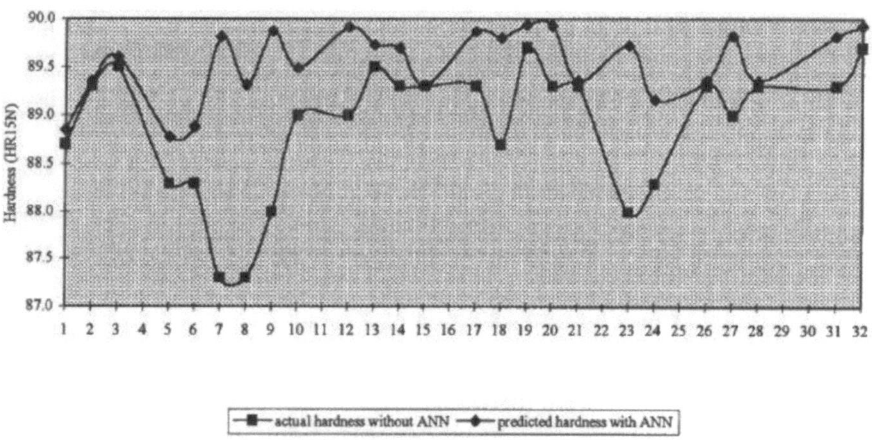

Fig. 14. Values of hardness without RNA in proportion to hardness values with RNA.

No.	Hardness without RNA (HR15N)	Hardness with RNA (HR15N)	Hardness modification (HR15N)
1	88.7	88.852	0.152
2	89.3	89.354	0.054
3	89.5	89.608	0.108
4	-	Adjusted	Necessary
5	88.3	88.780	0.480
6	88.3	88.890	0.590
7	87.3	89.817	2.517
8	87.3	89.314	2.014
9	88.0	89.871	1.871
10	89.0	89.495	0.495
11	-	Adjusted	Necessary
12	89.0	89.917	0.917
13	89.5	89.732	0.232
14	89.3	89.701	0.401
15	89.3	89.306	0.006
16	-	Adjusted	Necessary
17	89.3	89.865	0.565
18	88.7	89.807	1.107
19	88.7	89.941	0.241
20	89.3	89.933	0.633
21	89.3	89.354	0.054
22	-	Adjusted	Necessary
23	88.0	89.724	1.724
24	88.3	89.165	0.865
25	-	Adjusted	Necessary
26	89.3	89.366	0.066
27	89.0	89.821	0.821
28	89.3	89.354	0.054
29	-	Adjusted	Necessary
30	-	Adjusted	Necessary
31	89.3	89.825	0.525
32	89.7	89.929	0.229
inferior	88.8800	89.5488	
Standard deviation	0.6880	0.3587	

Table 2. Comparison between hardness without RNA and with RNA.

8. Conclusions and perspectives of expert systems

Even though, at the beginning, the followers of artificial intelligence promotion (AI) through expert systems hoped to develop some systems that would exceed through their performances the human experts, this desire did not fulfill, at least not now. This happened because knowledge acquisition within an ES is not a very simple process, as it may seem at a first glance. Why this process would be so complicated? Probably the easiest answer is that human expert gains, in time, not only knowledge but also *experience*. Knowledge itself allows the development of some reasoning based on rules (as in ES case). On another hand, *experience* allows the development of some *subliminal* reasoning (not accessible yet by computing programs), which in day-to-day life would translate by *instinct* or *inspiration*. Due to this, the majority of ES developed so far limited to relative tight domains that can be quantified in a rigorous and direct manner.

9. References

Aamodt, A., E.Plaza(1994),A I Com-Artficial intelligence Communications, IOS Press,vol 7:1,p39-59.

Alberg H., Simulation of Welding and Heat Treatment Modelling and Validation, Doctoral Thesis 2005:33 ISSN: 1402-1544, ISRN: LTU-DT - -05/33 -SE.

ASM Handbook - Heat Treatments, vol. IV, U.S.A., 1994.

Aylen Jonathan, Megabytes for metals: development of computer applications in the iron and steel industry, Ironmaking and Steelmaking, 2004, vol. 31, No.6.

Friedmann E.- Hiu, Jess the Rule Engine for the Java Platform, CA, USA 2003.

Han J. and M.Kamber: Data Mining:Concepts and Techniques, Morgan Kaufman Publisher, San Fransisco,Ca,USA,2001.

Hopgood Adrian A., The State of Artificial Intelligence, Advances in Computers, vol 65,p 1-75, 2005.

Kang J., Y. Rong, W. Wang, "Numerical simulation of heat transfer in loaded heat treatment furnaces", Journal of Physics, Vol. 4, France, No. 120, 2004, pp. 545-553.

Kolonder, Riesbeck and Schank,An introduction to case-based reasoning, Artificial Intelligence Review 6(1), pp. 3-34, 1992.

Kwang Hyuk Im, Sang Chan Park, Case-based reasoning and neural network expert system for personalization, Expert Systems with Applications 32(2006) 77-85.

Kwang Hyuk Im, Sang Chan Park, Case-based reasoning and neural network expert system for personalization, Expert Systems with Applications 32(2007) 77-85.

Lilantha Samaranayake, Distributed Control of Electric Drives via Ethernet, TRITA-ETS-2003-09, ISSN 1650{674xISRN KTH/EME/R 0305-SE}, Stockholm 2003.

Owhadi, J. Hedjazi, and P. Davami, Materials Science and Technology, 1998, 14, 245-250.

Romero Carlos E., Jiefeng Shan, Development of an artificial network based software for prediction of power plant canal water discharge temperature, Expert Systems with Applications 29(2005)835-838.

Saha Podder, A.S. Pandit, A. Murugaiyan, D. Bhattacharjee and R.K. Ray, Phase transformation behaviour in two C-Mn-Si based steels Ander different cooling rates, Ironmaking and Steelmaking, 2007, vol. 34, No.1.

Shin, C.K., Yun,U.T., Kim,H.K.&Park,S.C.(2000) A hibrid approach of neural network and memory-based learning to data mining, International Journal of IEEE Transactions on Neural Networks,11(3), 637-646.

Shin, C.K.,Yun,U.T., Kim,H.K.&Park,S.C.(2000) A hibrid approach of neural network and memory-based learning to data mining, International Journal of IEEE Transactions on Neural Networks,11(3), 637-646.

Shu-Hsien Liao, Expert System Methodologies and Applications-a decade review from 1995 to 2004,Expert Systems with Applications 28(2005),93-103.

Singh A., et al. Predicting microstructural evolution and yield strength of microalloyed hot rolled steel plate, Materials Science and technology, october 2004, vol. 20, 1317.

Topolov, E.V., Panferov, V.I., Câteva probleme de realizare a automatizării cuptoarelor industriale, Cernaia Metalurgiia, nr. 2, 1991, pp. 93-96.

Varde Aparna S., Mohammed Maniruzzaman, Elke A. Rundensteiner and Richard D. Sisson Jr., The Quench Miner Expert Syatem for Quenching and Distorsion Control, Worcester Polytechnic Institute(WPI),USA,2003.

Vizureanu, P., (2006) *Experimental Programming in Materials Science*, Mirea Publishing House, Moscow, 2006, 116 pg., ISBN 5-7339-0601-4.

Vizureanu, P., (2009) *Echipamente şi instalaţii de încălzire*, Editura PIM, Iaşi, 2009, 316pg., ISBN 978-606-520-349-5.

Vizureanu, P., Andreescu, A., Iftimie, N., Savin, A., Steigmann, R., Leiţoiu, S., Grimberg, R., (2007) Neuro-fuzzy expert systems for prediction of mechanical properties induced by thermal treatments, *Buletin I.P.Iaşi*, tom LIII (LVII), fasc. 2, secţia Ştiinţa şi Ingineria Materialelor, 2007, pg. 45-52.

Vizureanu, P., Ştefan, M., Baciu, C., Ioniţă, I., (2008) *Baze de date şi sisteme expert în selecţia şi proiectarea materialelor*, vol. II, Editura Tehnopress, Iaşi, 2008, 262 pg. (40 rânduri/pg.) ISBN 978-973-702-515-9.

Xu Xiaoli, Wu Guoxin and Shi Yongchao, Development of intelligent system of thermal analysis Instrument, Journal of Physics: Conference Series 13 (2005) 59–62.

Yescas M.A., Prediction of the Vickers Hardness in austempered ductil iron using neural networks, Int.J.Cast Metals Res. 2003,15, p513-521.

10

Interface Layers Detection in Oil Field Tanks: A Critical Review

Mahmoud Meribout[1], Ahmed Al Naamany[2] and Khamis Al Busaidi[3]
[1]*Petroleum Institute,*
[2]*Sultane Qaboos University,*
[3]*Petroleum Development Oman,*
[1]*United Arab Emirates*
[2,3]*Oman*

1. Introduction

An emulsion layer is a mixture of two or more liquids in which one of them - the dispersed phase, is present as droplets of microscopic size, distributed throughout the other, called continuous phase. The existence of such layer between oil and water is due to the crude properties, and contaminants such as asphaltenes and resins. A measurement system to determine the boundaries of this emulsion in a modern oil production field is necessary to extract the pure single phase liquids [1, 2, 3]. This would for instance reduce the usage of expensive two phase flow meters and avoid the installation of additional tank separators along the upstream oil pipeline. In addition, this would help collecting accurate daily oil production statistics from each oil station. One widely deployed solution consists to inject chemical substances to completely eliminate the emulsion layer and leave only a crisp oil-water interface which can then be detected relatively much more easier. However, this approach is costly, not environmental friendly, and leads to a significant increase of the retention time in the separator. This book chapter provides a survey on electronic-based-techniques which are capable to measure the high and low boundaries of the emulsion layer in real-time. It then describes in more details a new ultrasonic-based device along with the experimental results it could provide.

2. State of the art techniques for emulsion layer detection in oil tanks

In recent years various types of devices have been proposed and in some cases deployed in the oil field to measure the lower and upper positions of the emulsion layers. These devices require more challenging design considerations than the ones used for level measurement because of the inhomogeneity, opacity, and multitude of phases which usually exist inside the tank. In addition, inside the crude oil tanks, there is usually abundance of H2S substance which is a harmful gas which can cause a devastating blast in case of a small ignition of the electrical parts of the device. Thus, the zone assigned to the inside area of the crude oil tanks is classified as an extremely dangerous zone, namely Zone 0 area. This requires a careful design of the device by ensuring that the voltage, current, and capacitances do not exceed a certain limit. Recently, intensive research & development works have been performed on

the design of such devices. They can be usually classified as radioactive or non radioactive types, in addition of featuring one or many of the followings:
- The device is non intrusive and non invasive;
- The device can operate continuously and require a minimum of maintenance;
- The device is intrinsically safe and can operate in zone 0 areas; and
- The device is a clamp-on type and externally mounted.

2.1 Differential pressure-based device

One of the commonly used devices to measure the liquid-liquid interface inside crude oil tanks is the pressure sensor-based device. The pressure, P, at a given height, h, within a liquid of density, ρ, is given by [3, 4, 5]:

$$P = \rho g h \tag{1}$$

Figure 1 below shows the principle of measuring the interface level, h_1 within an uncovered tank containing water (density ρ_W) and oil (density ρ_O). A gauge differential pressure sensor for which one side is in direct contact with the bottom side of the tank, and the other side is in contact with the air provides the following gauge pressure, P_G:

$$P_G = (\rho_W g h_1) + (\rho_W g (H - h_1)) \tag{2}$$

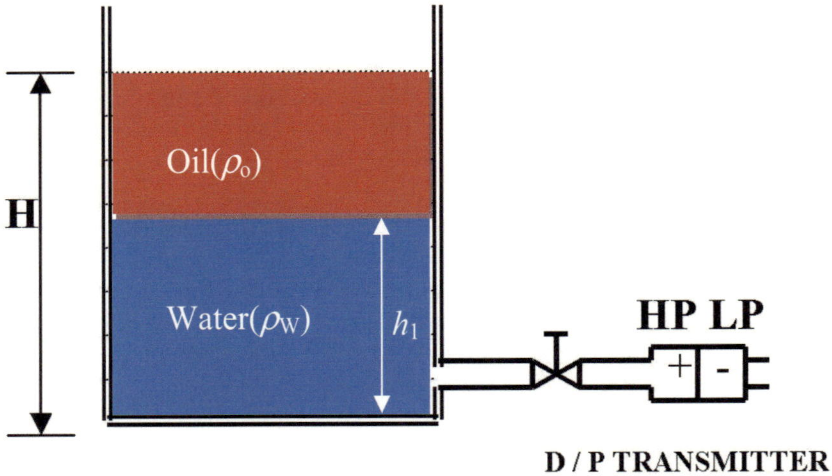

Fig. 1. Principle of interface level measurement using pressure sensors.

Where H is the height of the liquid. Hence, knowing H, ρ_W, and ρ_o one can determine the height of the interface, h_1. Note that the temperature compensation is usually required in these devices as the density of liquids varies with temperature. The main advantages of this technique are that the pressure sensors are cheap, not cumbersome, and can be easily installed in a tank. However it is suitable only when the interface separating the two liquids is crisp. In case a relatively thick layer containing mixed liquids separates the two liquids, the above design will not be any more applicable to determine the low and high positions of this layer. A possible design alternative with this kind of sensors would be to place an array of n pressure sensors along the vertical path of the tank which are separated by a constant distance, x (Figure 2). Hence, the lower and higher positions of the emulsion layer (h_1 and h_2 respectively in Figure 2) would correspond to the pressure sensors providing the following values:

$$P_1 = (\rho_W g h_1) \quad \text{and} \quad P_2 = (\rho_o g h_2) \tag{3}$$

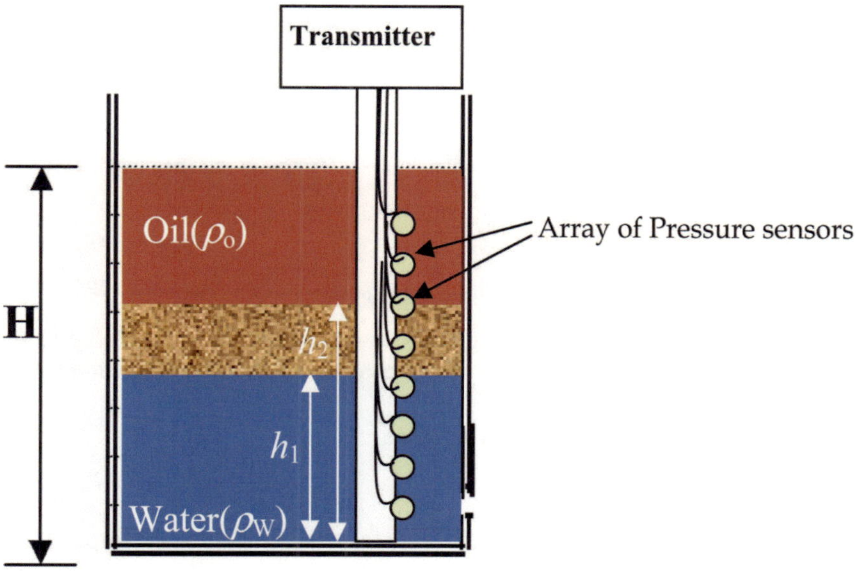

Fig. 2. Principle of emulsion layer measurement using pressure sensors.

Hence, for each height, h, the transmitter stores in its database the pressure values corresponding to water and oil respectively ($\rho_W gh$) and ($\rho_O gh$). It then proceeds to compare the actual pressure at height h, captured by the pressure sensor with these two stored values. The top height providing same ($\rho_W gh$) and lowest height providing same ($\rho_W gh$) corresponds to the lowest and highest interfaces respectively.

Note that in this case, the knowledge of the total height of the liquid (H in Figure 2) is not any more required. Providing one single sensor is possible if it is attached to an electro-mechanical system to provide precise motion of the sensor in vertical positions (Figure 3). This technique however is not recommended in oil industry as moving parts in contact with conductive materials are subject to fast corrosion which would affect then the precision of the associated devices.

The other problem with both designs (Figure 2 and Figure 3) is the extremely low sensitivity required for the pressure sensors. For instance, if a resolution of the device of x = 15 cm is sought, a sensor with a sensitivity of at least 0.210 psi would be required. Another not less important limitation of this device is its inability to deal with build-up problem which can be most likely be created on the sensor in case of crude oil. These are few reasons why pressure sensors-based devices have been used for level or crisp interface measurements, rather than emulsion layer measurement.

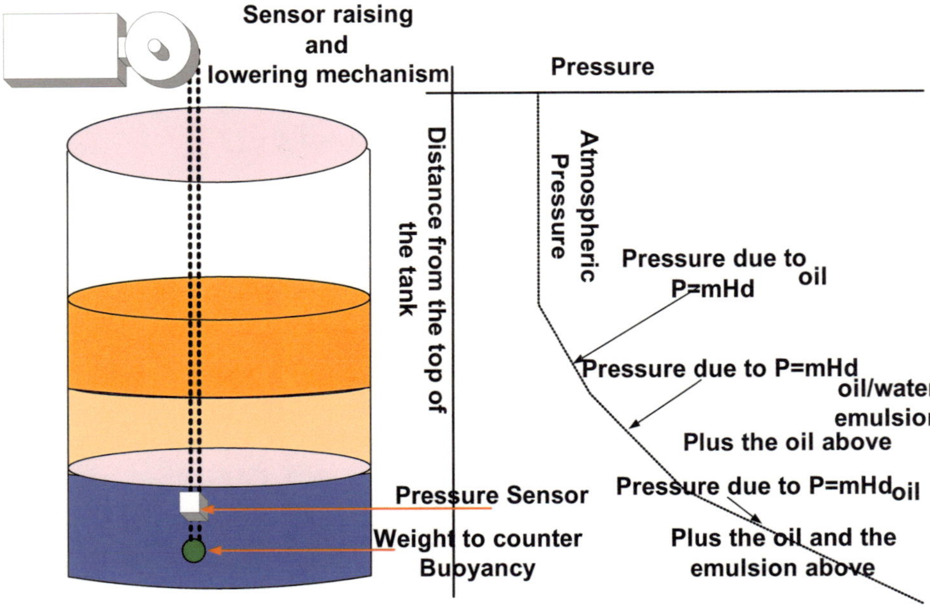

Fig. 3. Varying pressure as sensor level is changed.

2.2 Capacitive sensor-based device

Radio Frequency (RF) technology uses the electrical characteristics of a capacitor in several different configurations for interface measurement. Commonly referred to as RF capacitance, the method is suited for detecting the interface which might occur between or within liquids, slurries, or granular. Basically, when two conductive plates of area, *A*, are separated by a distance, d, the corresponding capacitance is proportional to the dielectric constant of the process enclosed within the plates, ε_r (Figure 4):

$$C = \varepsilon_0 . \varepsilon_r . A / d \quad (4)$$

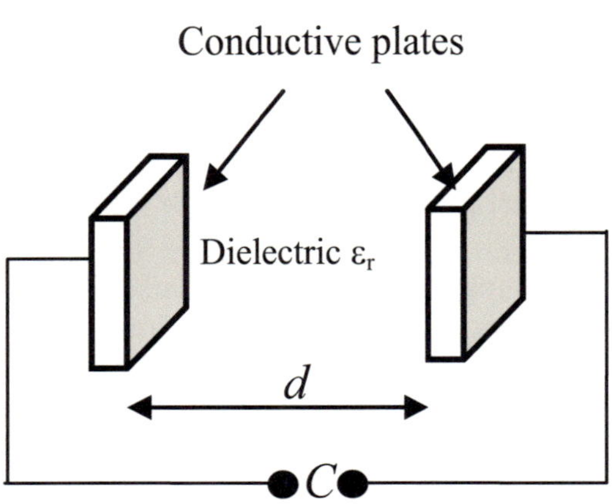

Fig. 4. Simple configuration of a capacitance.

In case of interface measurement, One plate can be the vessel wall, and the other one the measurement probe or electrode (Figure 5(a)). In another configuration, both plates are provided within the device (Figure 5(b)). For both configurations, the second plate (reference plate) should be connected electrically to the grounded metallic tank. Hence, in case of oil-water interface measurement, the capacitance gets short by water and thus the effective area of the plates change with the level of the water inside the tank. This leads to a linear trend between the height of the tank and the value of the capacitance.

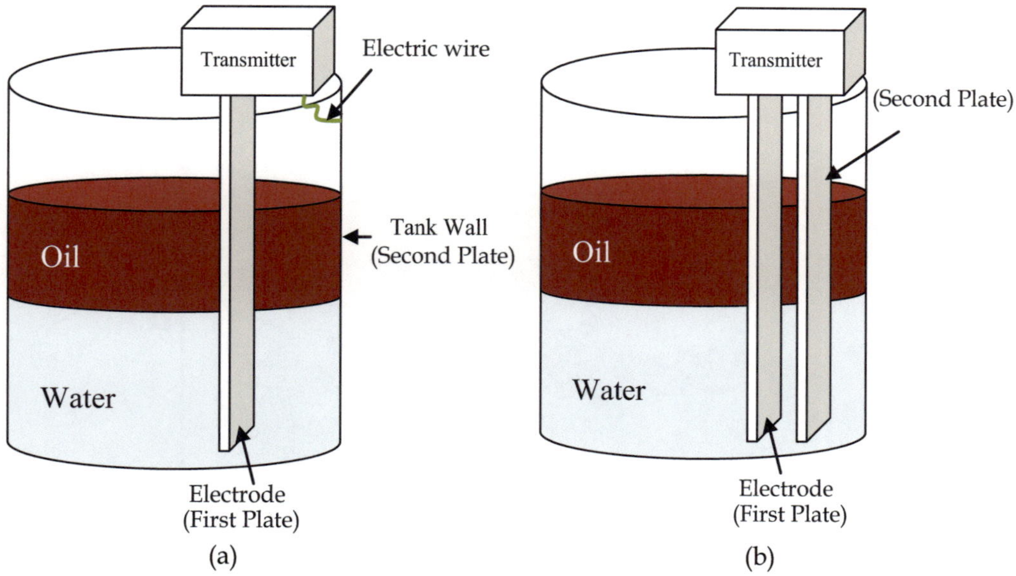

Fig. 5. Possible configurations of the capacitance probe for interface measurement (a) with one electrode only (b) with two electrodes.

The measurement of the emulsion layer using capacitance probe is possible by deploying a vertical array of capacitance sensors along the vertical axis of the tank. In this case, the transmitter measures the dielectric constant of the liquid existing between the plates to determine the water-cut (i.e. the fraction of water in the total volume of liquid) at that height. By doing same for all sensors of the array, a vertical profile of the liquid existing in the tank can be provided. The difficulty here however is that for water-cut values greater than 40%, the capacitances tend to lose their sensitivity preventing the transmitter to determine the profile corresponding to the lower half of the emulsion layer. Another difficulty of capacitance probes in general is their inability to deal with build-up substances that might be created at the surface of their sensors.

2.3 Radar or microwave-based device

Radar or microwave-based devices generate electromagnetic waves, typically in the microwave X-band (10 GHz) range, and then proceed by analyzing the received signal to determine the liquids interface levels in the tank. The microwave generator is usually placed on the top of the tank to beam microwaves downward and then receives one or several echo signals which might be generated by the liquids interfaces, as well as by the top level of the liquid and bottom area of the tank (Figure 6). The measurement of travel time for the signal (called the time of flight) of these echoes signals allow to determine the heights of these interfaces. For instance, in Figure 6, the height h of the oil-water interface is determined using the following equation:

$$h = \mathrm{H} - \left(0.5\left(t_1 / v_1 - t_2 / v_2\right)\right) \quad (5)$$

Where H is the distance between the transmitter and the ground (i.e. this corresponds to the height of the tank), t_1 and t_2, the transit time of the first and second echoes respectively, and v_1 and v_2 the speed of microwaves in the air and oil respectively.

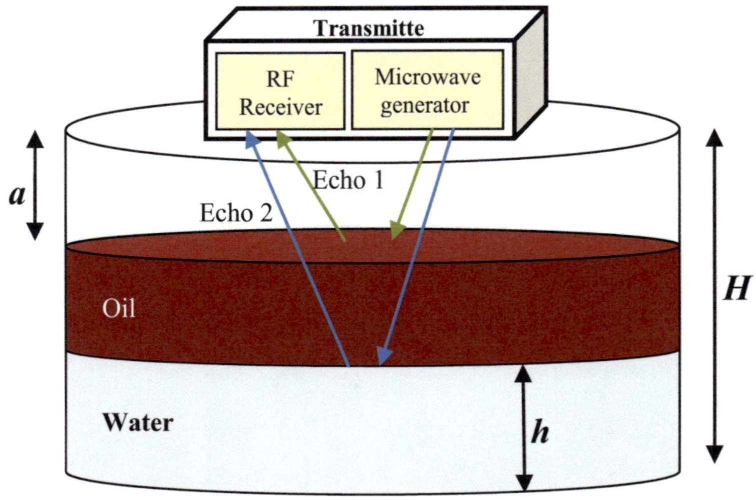

Fig. 6. Principle of radar-based device for interface level measurement

Note that in the above case, no echoes are reflected by the bottom wall of the tank since the water absorbs most of the microwave energy. For this same reason, the detection of the emulsion layer which might be created between oil and water using this type of device is difficult. However, one of the advantages of this technology is that the sensors are not intrusive and non invasive and hence no build-up substances are created on its sensing part. In addition, the device is not affected by possible changes of the environmental conditions (e.g. temperature and humidity) which facilitate its deployment in the field.

2.4 Radiation-based device

Recently, radiation-based instruments have been widely used in oil field, including for the measurement of interface levels in oil separators and tanks. Radioisotopes (such as Gamma sources) used for level measurement emit energy at a fairly constant rate and in a random fashion. Different radioactive isotopes are used, based on the penetrating power needed to "see" through the process vessel. The radiation from the source penetrates through the vessel wall and process fluid. In case of interface measurement, the radiation sensors are placed on a vertical array to measure the density profile across the height of the tanks. The Tracerco Density Profiler system (based on nuclear technology) [18, 19] is one the most famous devices using this technology (Figure 7). The instrument consists of a vertical array of a small, gamma ray emitting radioactive sources (Americium-241, the same radioisotope as is used in smoke detectors). The radiation is monitored by a vertical array of radiation detectors. The source and detector assemblies are secured in dip-pipes that project down into the separator. The radiation beam from each source is collimated so that only the radiation detector at the corresponding elevation detects it. The attenuation of the beam in the process material between the source and detector is related to the density of that material. Effectively, each source/detector pair functions as a density gauge. The outputs from the detectors give the density profile of the fluids inside the separator from which a precise measurement of the oil/water interface point can be obtained.

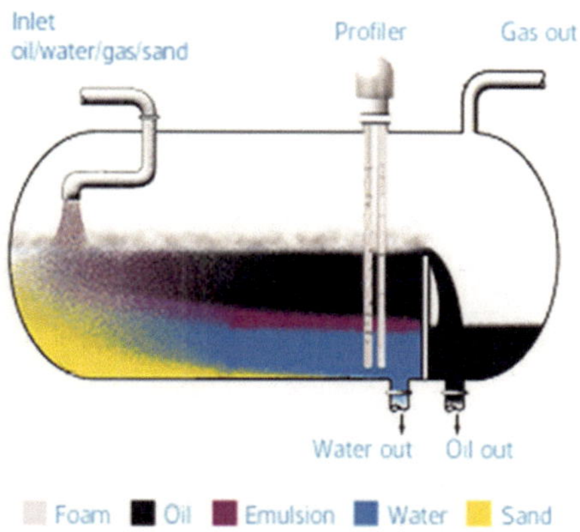

Fig. 7. The Nucleonic Tracerco's level measurement system ([18,19]).

The advantage of this technology is its ability to operate in harsh environments and to deal simultaneously with multitude of phases of different types (e.g. liquid and gas phases). In addition, it is extremely suitable for applications involving high temperatures and pressures or corrosive materials within the vessel [18.19]. However, there are a number of compensating factors that seem to prevent nuclear from becoming a truly universal technology. One factor is high cost which is estimated at 2-4 times that of other technologies. In addition, because of the safety risks that might occur in case of radiation lose, periodical inspections and approvals are vital.

2.5 Displacer-based device

Displacers or floats are some of the most commonly used interface measuring mechanisms for ages. They rely on the Archimedes principle which states that when a body is floated or immersed in a fluid, it loses weight equal to the weight of the liquid displaced [20][21]. Hence, when two liquids have densities ρ_1 and ρ_2 ($\rho_1 < \rho_2$), a floater with density ρ would float on the interface separating the two liquids if the following condition is satisfied:

$$\rho_1 < \rho < \rho_2 \qquad (6)$$

In case of emulsion layer measurement, a vertical array of several floats can be deployed in such a way that adjacent floats have densities which match the ones of liquids to be detected. For instance in Figure 8, the middle float would have a weight just larger than the oil and just lower than the highest level of emulsion to be measured.

These devices have the advantages to be simple, accurate and can be adapted to measure wide variations in fluid densities. However, once the sensor is set up and adjusted for specific density of the liquid, the fluids measured must maintain their density, which is not always the case in oil field tanks where the wide variation range of temperature leads to a change in the density of the liquid. Another possible source of errors in displacer/floats measurements is caused by sticky fluids such as heavy crude oil which can deposit on it and effectively change the displacement and causes a calibration shift.

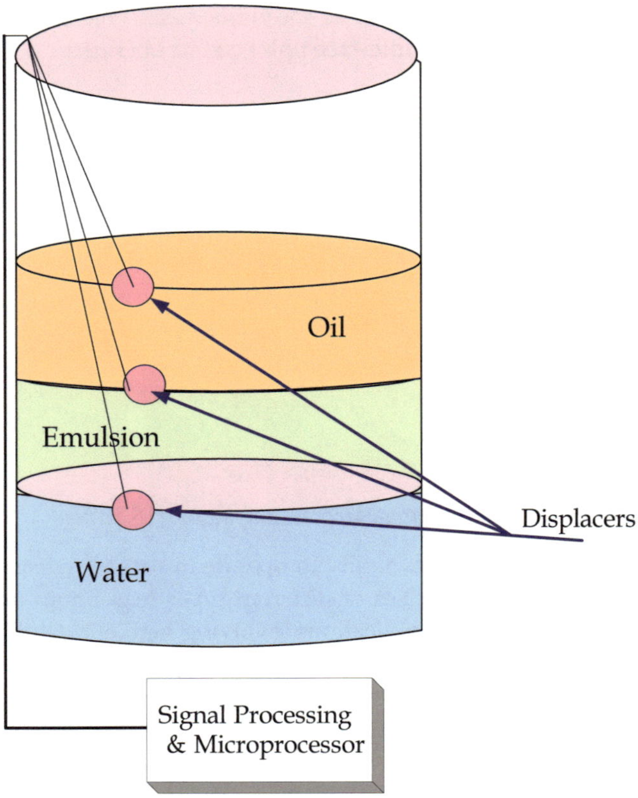

Fig. 8. Displacers floating at top of each liquid.

2.6 Vibrating switches-based device

Vibrating level switches detect the dampening that occurs when a vibrating probe submerged in the target fluid moves at a resonance frequency which can range from 85 to 400 Hz. This dampening is function of the density of the fluid surrounding it. Figure 9 shows the basic principle of the device. It comprises mainly a paddle, control and processing unit, a magnet, and reed switch. The control and processing unit uses a driver coil to induce a 85-400 Hz vibration in the paddle that is damped out when the paddle gets covered by a process material. Hence, the magnet which is screwed inside the paddle moves vertically up and down and the reed switch gets actuated whenever the magnet is located in front of the switch. By this way, the sensor can detect both rising and falling levels of the paddle whose speed depends on the process. Hence, by deploying a vertical array of these switches inside the oil tank, the liquid profile inside the tank can be obtained. These devices can detect liquid/liquid, liquid/vapor, and solid/vapor interfaces, and can also signal density or viscosity variations. In addition, they are able to operate at pressures reaching up to 3,000 psig and at temperatures ranging from -100 to 150°C (-150 to 300°F).

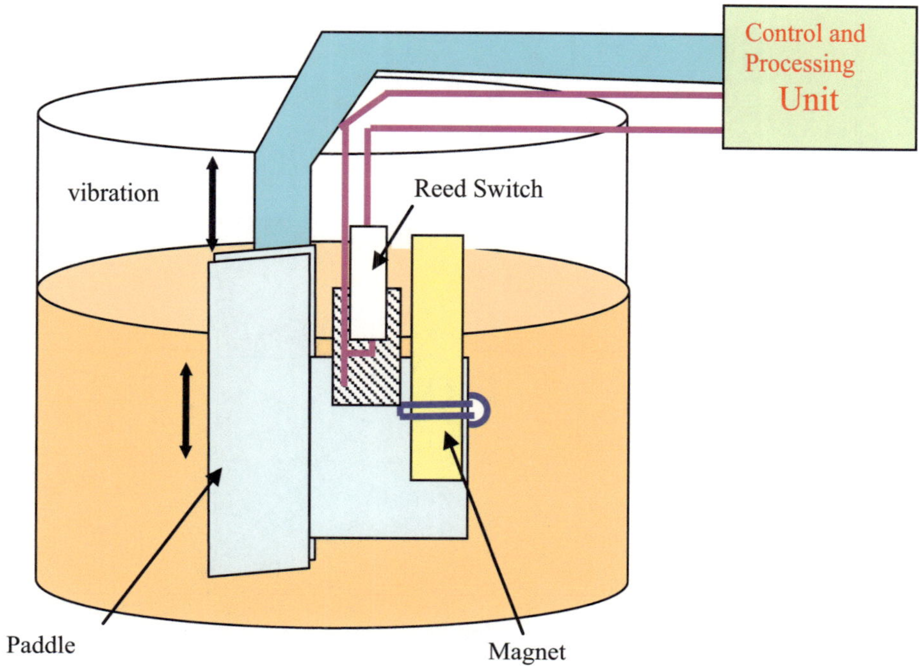

Fig. 9. Block diagram of the vibrating Switch for interface measurement

Also, the low operational frequency of these sensors makes the hardware-software design of the system easy and cheap. In addition, its fast response time, which is about 1 second, make real-time measurements possible. However, one major disadvantage of these sensors is the huge power required to drive the sensors up and down in the oil tank. Such motions may create some turbulences on the fluid which may induce some measurement errors. Another disadvantage of this device is the necessity to watch its sensing part immediately after each immersion in a sludge or slurry as they are extremely sensitive to material build-up or coating. In addition they are invasive and intrusive. These are few reasons why these sensors have been rarely deployed in the field.

2.7 Optical fiber-based device

In recent years, optical fiber sensors have been used in some oil field tanks as they have the capability to measure the pressure and temperature at different vertical positions of the tank and along one single optical fiber [3, 4, 5, 6, 7]. The basic concept is that the power propagating along the optical fiber is attenuated if part of its cladding is removed and if the external surrounding medium has a refractive index greater than that of the core. This is known as Fiber Brag Grating (Figure 10). Consequently the sensing element consists of a fiber that extends over the whole depth of the tank and whose cladding has been removed in equally spaced zones. Every time the liquid reaches or leaves one of these zones, the output power increases or decreases depending on the direction of the change of the liquid level. The liquid measurement is then carried by a discrete component analog signal conditioning circuit, which sums the up and down output power variations, each of which is counted separately. This prototype showed itself to have a good accuracy and an acceptable dynamic performance. The transducer resolution can be extremely low (less than 1 mm).

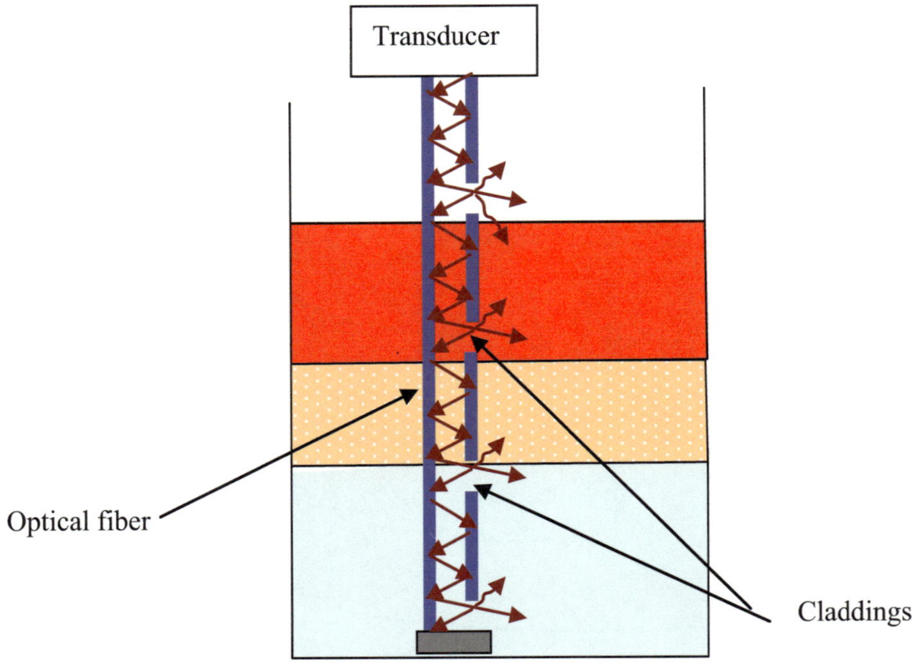

Fig. 10. Principle of multi-level measurements using optical fiber.

In practice, increasing the number of unclad zones per meter would decrease the output power changes when the liquid level nears the full-scale. Hence, if the resolution has to be improved, the sensitivity of the signal conditioning hardware must be increased, to allow useful output power variations to be distinguished from noise. One of the major advantages of this type of sensors is that the readings are not affected by the electrical interfaces that might be generated by the surrounding electrical cables or motors. In addition they are intrinsically safe and the signal cable can be deployed inside the tank without the need of any kind of certification. However, one of their main disadvantages is their incapacity to overcome the build-up problem.

3. An alternative: ultrasonic-based device

Detection of changes of composition in a medium with the aid of ultrasound waves has been disclosed in [9]. The probe comprises two ultrasonic sensors (one emitting and another receiving sensor) mounted into two vertical stands to detect the upper and lower levels of the emulsion layer inside a laboratory-scale tank of 1 meter height. Both sensors move up and down at the same horizontal level to provide information on the liquid within that level. However the system is not suitable to operate in relatively higher tanks (i.e. more than 3 meters tanks, which is the minimum height of storage or separation tanks in oil fields). One reason is that the electrical millivolt echo signal generated by the receiver ultrasound sensor can barely reach the electronics located at the top of the tank if their separating distance exceeds few meters. In addition, the system suffers from using relatively low ultrasonic frequencies (i.e. less than 180 kHz) which affects the accuracy of the measurement and prevents the device to detect relatively thin layers of sludge buildup commonly found at the surface of the sensors after few operating days.

In this book chapter, a new industrial prototype ultrasonic-based device, which overcomes the above drawbacks, is presented. It does not contain any moving part and has been demonstrated to effectively measure the emulsion levels, in addition to the amount of water-cut (i.e. percentage of water in oil) within the emulsion layer. The probe operates in a real oil field tank (e.g. a tank with a height equal to 4.35 m) by transmitting ultrasonic waves at its different heights in a time multiplexer manner. An embedded expert system algorithm is implemented in the transmitter situated at the top of the tank to find out if the fluid at the height of the ultrasound transducer which is being activated corresponds to oil, water, emulsion, or air. It uses as input features for the pattern recognition algorithm both the delay and number of echoes whose amplitude exceeds a predefined threshold. The determination of the water-cut within the emulsion layer is performed by an embedded feed forward neural network algorithm. Experimental results in various conditions of temperature showed a good accuracy for the detection of the emulsion layer and +/- 3 relative error for the computation of the water-cut within the emulsion layer.

3.1 Measurement principal and preliminary experimental setup

The measuring principle for measuring the position of the emulsion layer in the oil tank consists to use a one dimensional array of high frequency ultrasonic sensors (i.e. 3 MHz sensors have been used in this book). Each sensor of the array operates in transmit-receive mode to emit horizontally burst of ultrasonic waves through the medium (i.e. oil, water, emulsion, or foam) and then collects the received waves and convert them into electronic signals for further processing. This latter task is performed by the transmitter, which is fixed on the top of the tank, to measure the type of medium surrounding the actual sensor. By similarly driving all the sensors of the array, a vertical profile of the oil tank can be deduced. The usage of high frequency sensors, instead of low frequency is motivated by the fact that usually the crude oil leaves a thin layer of undesirable sludge buildup on the surfaces. Thus, a high resolution ultrasound imaging system is required to scale down to that small thickness. This book chapter treats this common practical problem, which, to our knowledge, has not been sufficiently tackled in the literature. Figure 11 shows the overall hardware bloc diagram of the system. The array of ultrasonic sensors are hold in cuboid boxes (two sensors per box) which are fixed to a vertical stainless steel bar though screws to occupy the complete height of the tank (i.e. 4.35 m). A second vertical stainless steel bar which is parallel to the first one by a separating distance of 5 cm is used as a reflector for the ultrasonic sensors. The usage of stainless steel material is motivated by the need to avoid the corrosion of the metallic bars which may lead to false measurements. One of the advantages of the proposed system is that it is modular, since adjacent sensors are connected to each other though a removable flexible stainless steel pipes which carry few electrical wires (i.e. for carrying power supply and sensor signals: See Section 3). In addition, the system is not invasive since the sensors are not in direct contact with the process liquid but protected with circular glass. Prior to a detailed design of the electronic system and its pattern recognition algorithm, a preliminary experimental setup was built to carry out the analog signals of each sensor of the array under various conditions of temperature, sensor depth, and flow rate of the mixed two phases liquid injected into the tank. The repetitiveness of the measurements and matching the collected database with theoretical concepts were sought out of this preliminary step of the design. In addition, the tightness of the sensor against any penetration of the liquid into the electronics had to be investigated for different depths. This is because the amount of acidity existing in the crude oil can easily attack the gaskets which protect the electronics, especially under high temperature and pressure. Following extensive experiments, it came out that the strongest epoxy can't sustain crude oil, whereas viton, which has been selected, could resist up to 5 bars pressure and 75 ^{0}C in contact with crude oil. The designed device is inserted inside a thermostat regulated and pressurized column of 4.7 meters height. This would allow testing the instrument at even deeper depth (e.g. up to 45 meters for some oil field separator tanks) since this latest, *h*, is proportional to the pressure, *p* (e.g. $h = \frac{p}{\rho g}$). Two pumps are used to inject either water or oil, from two outdoor storage oil and water tanks of 1 m^3 each respectively, towards the column creating an emulsion layer inside it. The liquid formed in the column may also be carried out into a separate storage tank under different flow rate, leading to a continuous testing with similar conditions than in the oil field. The operational cycle can be described in the following way: A pulse generator feeds each transmit transducer of the array under test with a sinusoidal burst of a predetermined number of periods through a connection network. This process continues for a predetermined number of times, where the acquisition is performed in a coherent fashion by a high bandwidth oscilloscope (i.e. 500 Msamples/sec) which was placed on the top of the tank (i.e. same connection points than the transmitter). The measured data were presented to the remote PC over the RS485 serial interface. Figure 12 shows the reflection signals generated by one of the ultrasonic sensors of the array and collected by the oscilloscope. Hence, several echo signals (more than seven in this case) could be observed. The first high-amplitude signal which follows the transmitted pulse however is not an echo signal but a reflection signal from the sensor's stainless-steel casing. Hence, a software delay of few µs is performed by the transmitter in order to discriminate this pulse from the real echoes. The removal of these latest is not required since it does not belong to the region of interest (i.e. before the actual echoes start to appear).

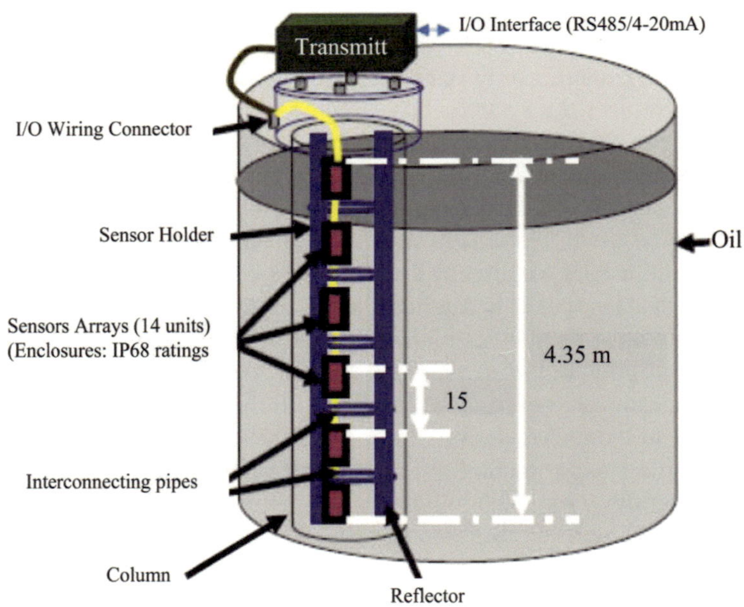

Fig. 11. Hardware overview

3.2 Feature extraction and pattern recognition algorithm

The discrimination between oil, water, and emulsion relies on a number of feature descriptors, some of them being meaningful and the rest being redundant, if not properly handled. The aim of this section is to highlight effects of some parameters on the ultrasound waves and how they can complement each other to achieve accurate results with low hardware complexity.

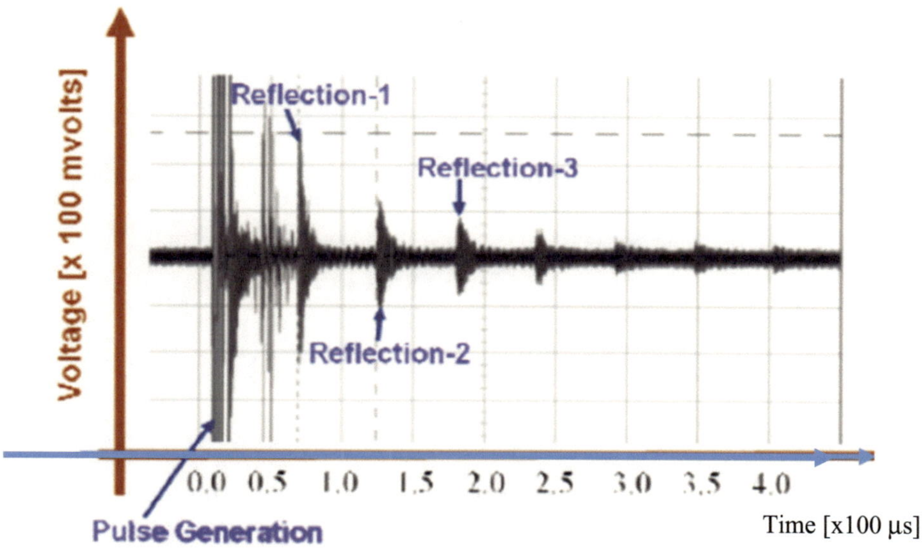

Fig. 12. Oscilloscope output displaying the echoes generated by one of the ultrasonic sensors

a. Effects of temperature and sensor depth in pure water and oil

As the experiments have to be carried out in outdoor where the temperature may vary within a relatively high range (from 20°C to 70°C), the effect of temperature on the ultrasound waves has been addressed. The speed of ultrasound waves (in [m/s.]) in water increases with temperature according to the equation [10]:

$$c(T) = a_1 + a_2T + a_3T^2 + a_4T^3 + a_5(S-35) + a_6Z + a_7Z^2 + a_8T(S-35) + a_9TZ^3 \ [ms^{-1}] \qquad (7)$$

Where T, S, and Z are temperature in degrees Celsius, salinity in parts per thousand and depth in meters, respectively. Where a_1 to a_9 are positive constants. However, in case of oil, the speed of the ultrasonic waves decreases with the increase of temperature [11]. Therefore, the detection of the emulsion layer in case of high temperature is easier since the delay tends to be larger. A mixture of oil and water would 3provide a speed between the speed of pure oil and speed of pure water. Consequently, knowing the actual temperature and salinity of the liquid, together with the speed of the ultrasonic waves in the liquid, it is possible to deduce the density of liquid using some well adopted pattern recognition algorithms. Figure 13 shows the effect of the temperature (from 20 to 85 °C) on the delay for one of the ultrasonic sensor of the array (i.e. sensor # 12). The delay here corresponds to the time it takes for echo to cross 100 mV for the first time. From Figure 13, it can be deduced that the delay can be used as one of the features for classification since it provides a clear discrimination between pure oil and pure water at a given temperature. However, as it will be highlighted in the next section, the computation of the water-cut may require the consideration of more additional parameters since various combinations of oil-water mixtures may lead to a same delay.

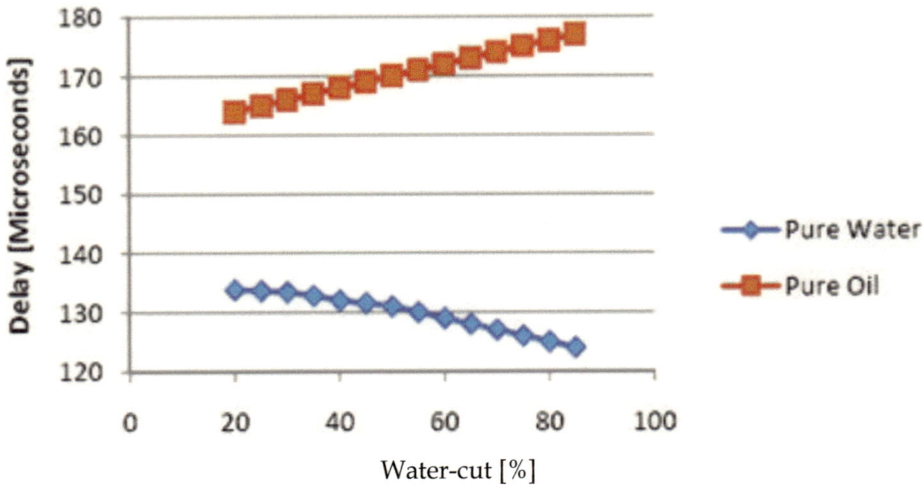

Fig. 13. Plot showing the effect of temperature on the delay of the ultrasonic wave for one of the sensor of the array [sensor # 12].

b. Effects of oil used

The type of oil used in our experiments is crude oil which is continuously injected into the oil tank creating a significant emulsion layer of undefined water-cut. The effect of the water-cut and the flow rate of the fluid carried out from the tank on the ultrasonic waves were sought out of this phase of experiments. As shown in Figure 14, in case of bubbles of oil (fluid2 in Figure 14) in water (fluid1 in Figure 14), the average delay of ultrasound waves (in seconds) are expected to vary according to the equation:

$$Delay = 2 \cdot \left[\frac{d1}{v(Fluid1)} + \frac{d2}{v(Fluid2)} \right] \tag{8}$$

Where d_1 and d_2 are the path lengths traversed by the ultrasonic wave in Fluid 1 and Fluid 2 respectively and v(Fluid1) and v(Fluid2) the sound speed in Fluid 1 and Fluid 2 respectively. In addition, the reflected wave, Pr in Figure 14, may be damped by the mixed fluid proportionally to its absorption coefficient, α, which has the following expression [12]:

$$\alpha = \frac{2\pi f \mu}{\rho c^3} \tag{9}$$

Where f is the frequency of the sound wave, μ the viscosity of the medium, ρ the density of the medium, and c the velocity of the sound in the medium.

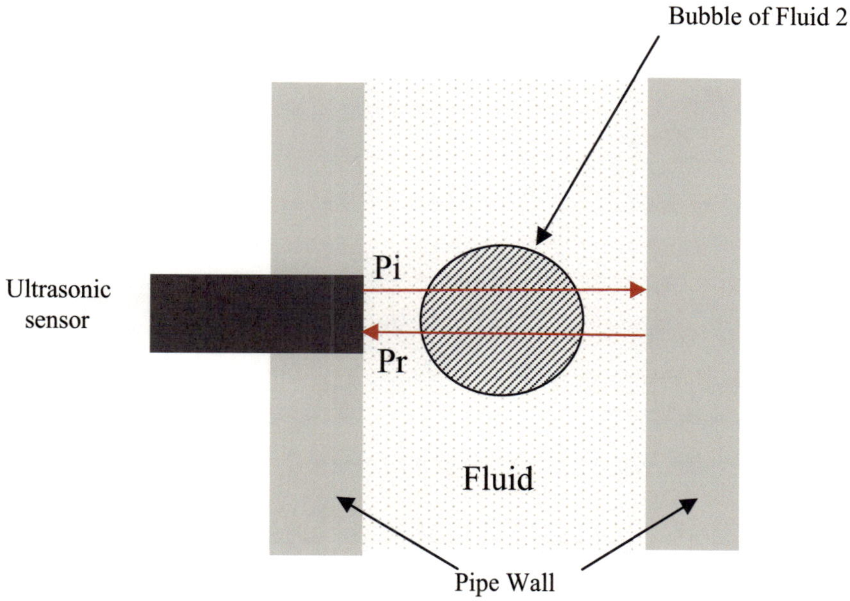

Fig. 14. Ultrasonic waves reflections with the presence of large bubbles.

Figure 15 shows the water-cut function of the delay for two sensors of the array (i.e. sensors #4 and 12) at 32°C. Hence, overall the delay follows a non linear increasing trend for both sensors. Similar trend was observed for the peak to peak voltage of the ultrasound wave. The usage of neural network technique for each sensor seems then to be a possible alternative for the pattern recognition algorithm to determine the water-cut surrounding the sensor. However, in some regions (points A and B in Figure 15), the delay is similar for two different values of water-cut. The reason is due to the output flow of the liquid inside the tank, which tends to move the ultrasonic wave in its direction, causing an extra delay. This is the reason why additional information regarding the flow velocity, v, of the liquid carried out from the column needs to be considered. This latest is function of the differential pressure, ΔP, between two sensors fixed along the array as follows [14]:

$$\Delta P = pgh + \frac{L \times f \times \rho \times v^2}{2d} \tag{10}$$

Where h is the distance separating the two pressure sensors, ρ the density of the liquid along the column, f is the friction factor (e.g. a Moody friction factor calculated using known roughness of an inner surface of the pipe), and d is the inner diameter of the pipe. The solution adopted in this book chapter consists then to add two pressure sensors in the array (i.e. in transducers 1 and 28 respectively), within which, the average density of the liquid is also estimated. Figure 16 shows the plot of the velocity function of the differential pressure for different fluid densities (ρ = 820, 910, and 950 kg.m^{-3}). Hence, overall the flow velocity follows the trend of equation 10. In practice, by using the pressure as additional input to treat the regions which are similar to A and B, a compensation of the delay function of the fluid velocity could be achieved.

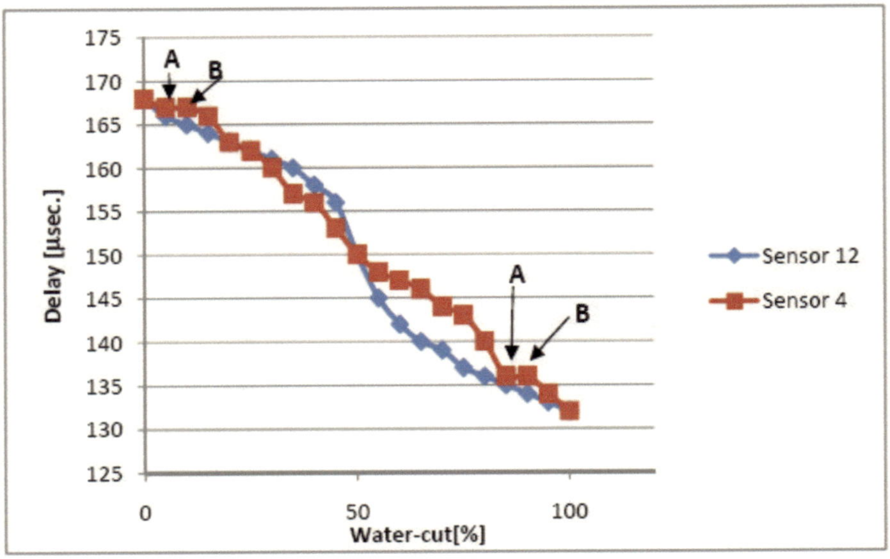

Fig. 15. Delay versus water-cut plot for two sensors of the array (Sensors 4 & 12)

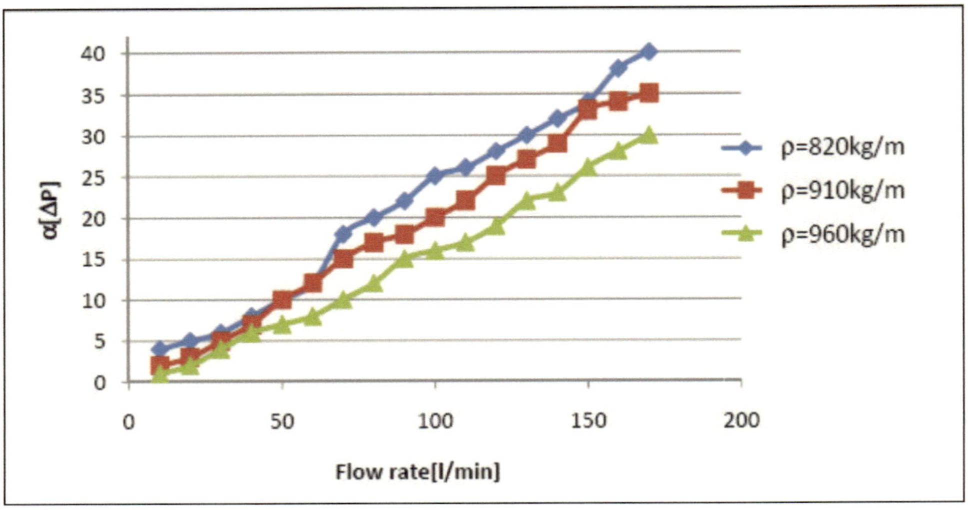

Fig. 16. Differential pressure versus flow rate for various liquid densities

c. Effects of liquid bubbles in the continuous phase

In addition to the liquid viscosity, the loose of energy of the transmitted ultrasonic wave may also be caused by the liquid bubbles which generate reflections according to the following equation [12]:

$$R = \frac{Z_2 - Z_1}{Z_2 + Z_1} \tag{11}$$

Where R is the ratio of reflected to the incident ultrasound waves' pressure, Z_1 the acoustic impedance of the liquid bubble, and Z_2 the acoustic impedance of the continuous phase. In

[13] the impedance and interaction processes for a wide range of materials of interest is provided. Hence, the level of decrease of the voltage amplitude of the received echo from the stainless steel reflector, and consequently the number of echoes, is function of the number of bubbles in the continuous phase. Consequently, as shown in Figure 17 (where the x-axis, "sensor level", corresponds to a given sensor numbered from bottom to top in the tank), the number of received echoes would provide an indication on the type of liquid surrounding the sensor (i.e. water, oil, or emulsion). In the Figure, sensor 9, 10, and 11 provided only 3 echoes, whereas sensors 12 to 16 provided more than 6 echoes. Sensors 1 to 8 could not provide any echo, since the corresponding liquid was foam.
Figure 18 shows the number of echoes, function of the water-cut. Overall, this number is higher for pure liquid than in case of emulsion. However, it does not provide information on the water cut. Accordingly, knowing the delay, peak to peak amplitude of the echo signals and their numbers, an estimation of the actual water-cut within the emulsion layer can be achieved.

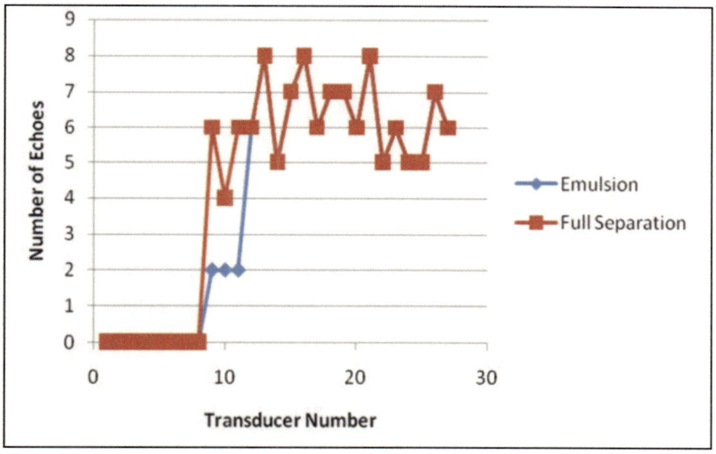

Fig. 17. Detecting the emulsion layer using the number of echoes.

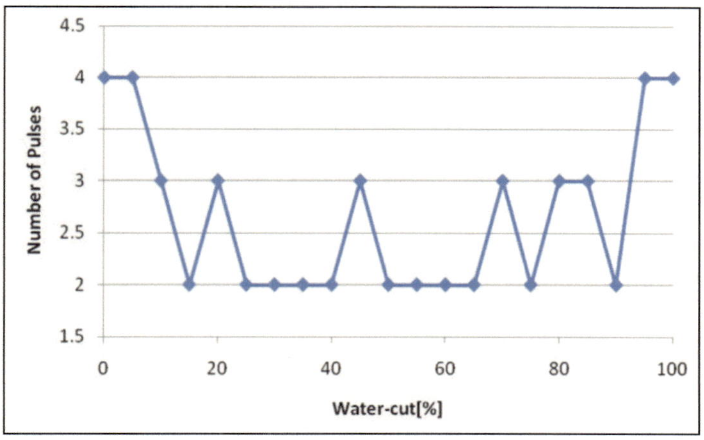

Fig. 18. Number of pulses versus water-cut.

d. Compensation of the sludge buildup

Besides the three aforementioned effects, the intrinsic properties of the crude oil may lead to the creation of a sludge buildup on the surfaces of the sensor and reflector (Figure 19), the thickness of which may vary from few mms to several cm. The challenge then is how to compensate for such layer during the measurements.

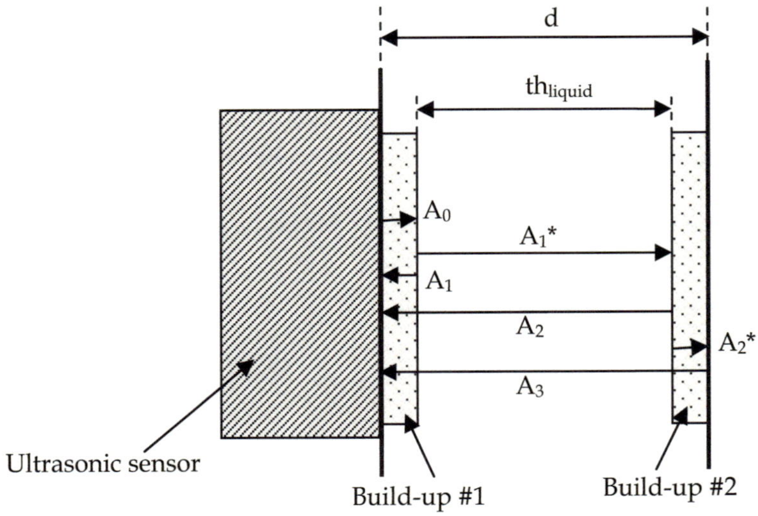

Fig. 19. Reflection of ultrasonic waves in the presence of sludge buildup.

From the above Figure, it is clear that when the liquid between the sensor and reflector is pure oil, the only reflection which may occur is the one caused by the reflector (i.e. A3 wave only in Figure 20(d)). A similar situation would occur in case no sludge buildup exists between the sensor and reflector. However, when the liquid is not pure oil, additional echoes may appear with the presence of the sludge buildup as shown in Figures 10(a) to (c). Hence three reflections might occur if both the surface of the sensor and the reflector have a sludge buildup on their surface (Figure 20(a)). On the other hand, in case the sludge buildup is formed exclusively on either the surface of the sensor or the reflector, then only two reflections are created (Figure 20(b) and (c)).

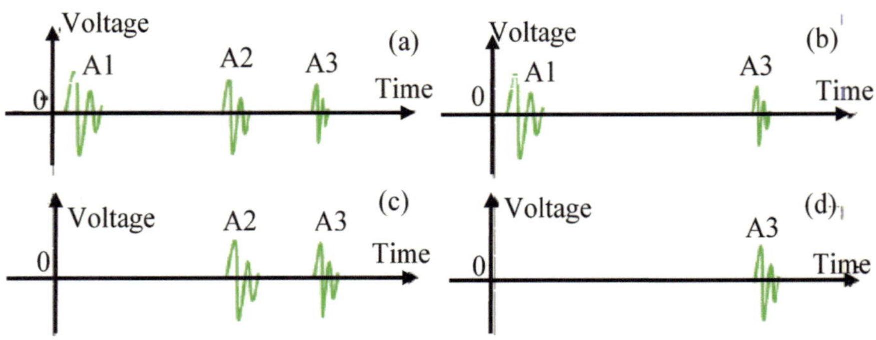

Fig. 20. Echoes waves due to sludge buildup when the phase between the sensor and reflector is not pure oil.

The goal here is to consider only echoes generated either by the stainless steel reflector or the surface of the sensor and mask out other echoes caused by the sludge build-up. Thus, the pattern recognition algorithm has to deal with a liquid of variable thickness, *th*liquid in Figure 19. One solution to compute this variable is to consider a time window of duration [0, *t*max], where *t*max is the maximal delay throughout the liquid (i.e. delay in case the path is 100% crude oil in this case) and then count the number of echoes, *N*echos, within this window. The value of *th*liquid could be then determined using one the following three equations:

$$th_{\text{liquid}} = \begin{cases} d - \dfrac{t[A_1] + t[A_3] - t[A_2]}{v_{oil}} & \text{for } N_{\text{echoes}} = 3 \\ d & \text{for } N_{\text{echoes}} = 1 \\ d - \dfrac{t[A_1]}{v_{oil}} \quad \text{OR} \quad d - \dfrac{t[A_3] + t[A_2]}{v_{oil}} & \text{for } N_{\text{echoes}} = 2 \end{cases} \tag{12}$$

Where *d* is the actual distance between the sensor and reflector (Figure 19) and *v*oil the speed of the ultrasonic wave in the crude oil. Hence, in case of two echoes, selecting one of the two possible values of *th*liquid would require to check the phase of the first echo received by the sensor. According to Equation 11, the phase corresponding to the transition sensor-sludge build-up-liquid-reflector is the inverse of the phase corresponding to the transition liquid-sludge build-up-reflector. Consequently, a proper exploration of the ultrasonic signals would overcome the errors of measurements introduced by the sludge built-up, which is impossible to achieve with other types of sensors such as the capacitance and conductance sensors. For a thickness, *th*liquid, the delay and peak to peak voltage to be considered for the ultrasonic waves can be scaled up for the pattern recognition algorithm to the following expressions:

$$Delay[d] = delay[th_{liquid}] \times \frac{th_{liquid}}{d}$$

and

$$Vp - p[d] = Vp - p[th_{liquid}] \times \frac{th_{liquid}}{d}$$

3.3 Pattern recognition algorithms

Following the above experimental setup, a pattern recognition algorithm has been designed and implemented (Figure 21). It is modular and consists of a loop of several sequential time domain processes which use as input patterns the echo signal's amplitude $a(t)$, delay $d(t)$, number of echoes, *N*echo(t), Temperature, $T(t)$, and differential pressure, $\Delta P(t)$. The estimation of the build-up thickness and the determination of the liquid flow-rate were already addressed in Section 2. The next two sections would present the algorithms to determine the type of liquid and compute the water-cut respectively.

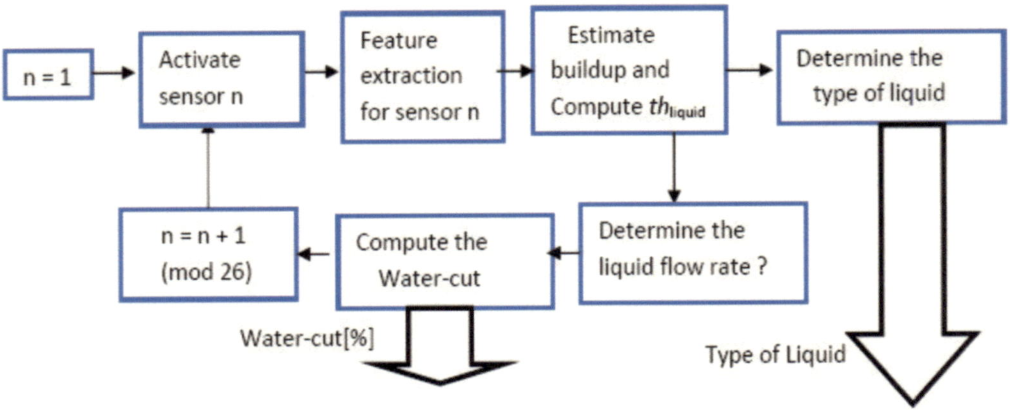

Fig. 21. Bloc diagram of the pattern recognition algorithm.

a. An expert system-based algorithm to determine the type of liquid

Figure 22 shows the flow chart of the algorithm. It consists of an expert system which uses the delay and number of echoes caused by the reflector as input parameters. The algorithm starts by activating the lowest sensor in the tank (i.e. n =1), from which it acquires the corresponding time delays and number of echoes. These two parameters are then processed by the expert system according to the elements of the database.

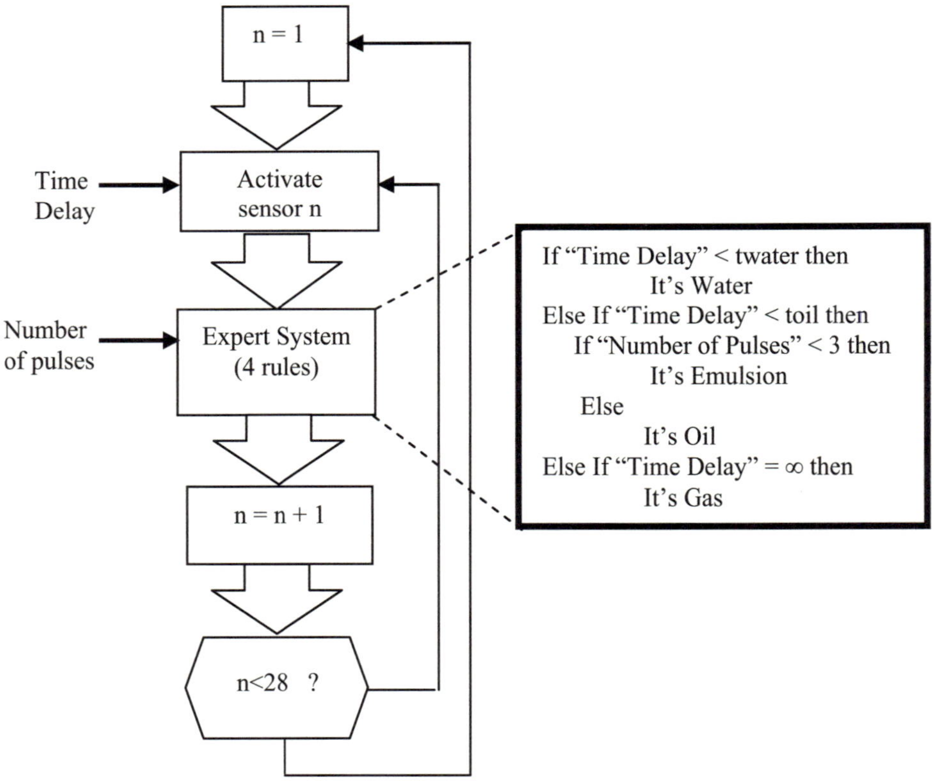

Fig. 22. Flow chart of the pattern recognition algorithm

Hence, for a time delay less than a threshold $t$water*(th_{liquid}/d) (where d is the distance between the sensor and reflector) the type of liquid being sensed by the actual sensor corresponds to water. Otherwise, in case the time delay is greater than oil*($t_{hliquid}/d$), then the liquid is either emulsion or oil depending on the number of pulses being collected (i.e. emulsion for less than 3 pulses, oil otherwise). Finally, in case no echo is detected, then the corresponding phase corresponds to foam or gas. Note that the thresholds, t_{water}*(th_{liquid}/d) and t_{oil}*(th_{liquid}/d) (e.g. according to Section 2.1(a) and Figure for an operation temperature ranging from 20 ^{0}C to 70 ^{0}C setting twater and toil to 140 µs and toil, = 150 µs, respectively is reasonable for thliquid = d) were selected in such a way that the classification is independent of the temperature. The same procedure is done for all sensors of the device to provide the water-cut profile of the column. This algorithm, which has been coded in assembly and implemented into the transmitter, has the advantage of being simple and does not require complicated hardware. However it is not capable to provide the water-cut value.

b. A neural network-based algorithm for water-cut computation

The second algorithm dedicated for water-cut computation is based on a feed forward neural network with backpropagation training. The motivation of using neural network is due to the fact that the elements of the database as shown in Figures 3, 5, and 6 are not linear and depend on several variables (i.e. temperature and flow rate). The topology that gave satisfactory results was: input layer of dimension 6, one hidden layer with 6 neurons and the output layer with **1** neuron for the water-cut value (Figure 23). This network demonstrated to be robust enough to determine the water-cut value within relatively low computation time. The first layer contains the six input variables (peak to peak voltage, delay, number of pulses within the time window [0, $t$max], phase of the ultrasonic wave, temperature, and ΔP). The training set had 94 exemplars, and also validation and test sets each with 47 exemplars, were employed. All sets were mutually exclusive, and contained exemplars spanning the considered water-cut range. The nodes in the hidden layer are connected to all nodes in adjacent layers. Each connection carries a weight, w_{ij}. Hence, the output of a node (j) in the hidden layer can be expressed as follows:

$$ui = g_j(\sum_{i=1}^{6} w_{ij} \times x_i) \tag{13}$$

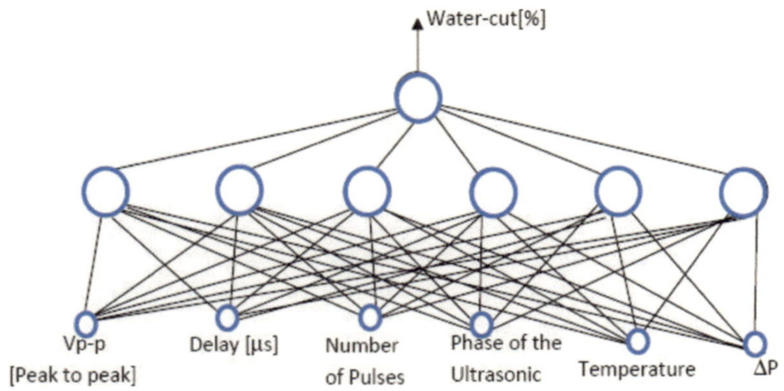

Fig. 23. Neural Network algorithm for water-cut determination

Where g_j is the activation function which is usually selected as non linear to enable the network to model to some extent some nonlinearities present in the problem. Following extensive experiments, the Logsig function was found to be the most appropriate in our case. Thus, for a particular input vector, the output vector of the network is determined by *feedforward* calculation. We progress sequentially through the network layers, from inputs to outputs, calculating the activation of each node using Eq. (7), until we calculate the activation of the output nodes.

3.4 Electronic design

The overall system is modular and consists of a 1-D array of tens of ultrasonic transducers which are connected to each other in a daisy chain manner via stainless-steel shielded wires and an embedded transmitter based on Reduced Instruction Set Computer (RISC) processor to perform control, data acquisition and real-time pattern recognition tasks. In addition it delivers the output results (i.e. low and high position of the emulsion layer) either as current loop 4-20 mA or RS-485 protocol to the remote control room. The temperature of the tanks which can reach up to 700C in summer season. Furthermore, and following the results obtained from the experimental setup, each transducer has been equipped with a temperature sensor. In addition, two pressure sensors were added to sensors 1 and 26 respectively.

3.4.1 Ultrasonic transducer

Each transducer comprises the sensor and its corresponding electronics (housed in stainless steel enclosures with IP-68 norm) and is provided with a periodical pulse repetition rate of approximately 10 Hz for the received echoes to die completely out before an excitation of 200 V peak to peak of the next burst cycle. Thus, the whole column which consists of 28 sensors can be scanned within 2.8 s. This is fast enough for oil field tanks, since they are filled with a maximal flow rate of 500 l/min (e.g. 22.8l/2.8 *sec,*), which corresponds to a negligible increase of the liquid height in the tank since the tank diameter usually exceeds 5 *m*. The returned echoes are pre-amplified and amplified with an accumulative gain of up to 30 *dB* using a variable gain amplifier which also provides pass-band filtering with a bandwidth of 3 MHz $\pm$ 200 KHz. The role of the filter is to reduce low frequency noises induced by the vibrations of the pipes which are connected to the tank. Thus, using this filter, the signal to Noise Ratio (SNR) of the signal in Figure 12 was improved from 9.4 dB to 16.4 dB which is high enough to perform pattern recognition tasks. The next step is then to emit similar echo signals to the transmitter for further processing. Figure 24 shows the electrical connections between the sensors and the transmitter. A set of only twelve (12) electrical wires (2 for DC power supply, 2 for signals and 8 for control) only connect adjacent enclosures in a daisy chain manner. Thus an analog switch is associated to each ultrasound sensor to enable/disable the high voltage (e.g. 200 *Volts*) pulse voltage generated by the transmitter based on the value carried out by the input address bus. The echo signal from the sensor is then amplified and carried out via a single shared wire to the transmitter. This design has the advantage to reduce the number of wires between the transducers to a constant value (12 wires), independently from the height of the tank or the target resolution. All the electronics parts were implemented in PCBs. In addition, the instrument is not invasive since the ultrasonic sensors are not directly in contact with the process fluid but protected with glass proving an EEx-m protection.

3.4.2 Transmitter

The transducers are sequentially enabled by the transmitter in a time multiplexed manner to sense the surrounding liquid. The corresponding analog echoes signal is then sent to the transmitter for digitalization at a sampling rate of 100 *Msamples/s* and for further processing. This latter task is handled by a RISC ARM-based processor which also transfers the final results (i.e. tank profile) to the remote control room.

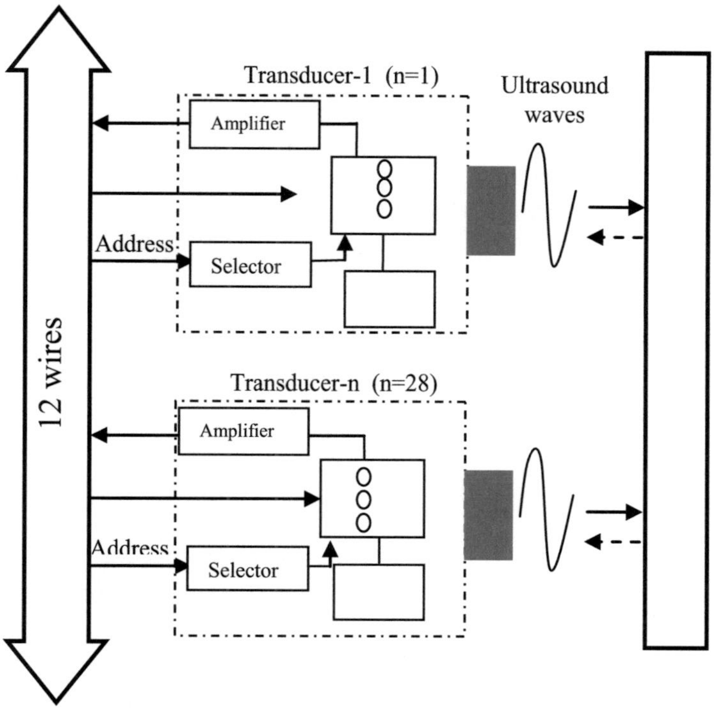

Fig. 24. Electronic design: Transducer-Transducer connections.

The transmitter also comprises a main processing unit that implements the pattern recognition algorithm and provides an Input/Output interface to/from the remote computer (RS485 or 4-20 mA standards which generates three levels corresponding to the bottom and top levels of the emulsion layer and the top level of the oil, as well as the tank profile), an amplifier module to amplify the signal to an acceptable level, and a pulser/selector circuit to activate each of the sensors in a time multiplexed manner with a short burst signal. The analog signal sent by the ultrasonic sensor is converted into digital by a high speed comparator for further processing.

4. Experimental results and discussions

The ultrasonic system has been immersed into the column and extensively assessed under different scenarios as follows: The oil tank and water tank continuously feed the column with various water-cut values by remotely adjusting the control valves placed after the oil pump and water pump respectively using a host computer. The fluid inside the tank is then simultaneously carried out into a storage tank, allowing a continuous supply of the mixed fluid into the column until both oil and water tanks become empty. Figure 25 shows the principle of the experiment. The assessment of the device is done by comparing the amount of water-cut measured at a specific height in the column (e.g. height corresponding to sensor #16) with the output of the water-cut meter which measures the amount of water in oil of the two phase outflow carried out from the column at the same height than sensor # 16. Figure 26 shows the results obtained from the two devices, where the "reference" signal is provided by the water-cut meter and "instrument" signal is provided by our acoustic system. It can be clearly observed the capability of our device to track fast water-cut variations, even within the critical range of 40- 60% which would not be possible with the capacitance or conductance probes. Note that in some situations, the water-cut meter indicates brief 0% water-cut, which is different from the output of the acoustic system. This might be due to the flow regime of the fluid crossing the water-cut meter where because the fluid is discharged from the column into the storage tank by gravity, no liquid is present at those time slots (which corresponds to 0% water-cut). Figure 27 shows another experiment covering higher water-cuts. Hence, it can be clearly observed the capability of the device to determine the profile of oil tanks for various values of water-cut. Overall, the averaged relative error for oil and water was always less than +/- 3%. It is defined respectively as:

$$Error(W)[\%] = \frac{Q_a(W) - Q_r(W)}{Q_r(W)} \times 100[\%] \quad and$$

$$Error(O)[\%] = \frac{Q_a(O) - Q_r(O)}{Q_r(O)} \times 100[\%]$$

Where $Q_r(W)$ and $Q_r(O)$ are the total quantities of water and oil respectively injected into the column and $Q_a(W)$ and $Q_a(O)$ the total amounts of water and oil respectively as computed by the instrument.

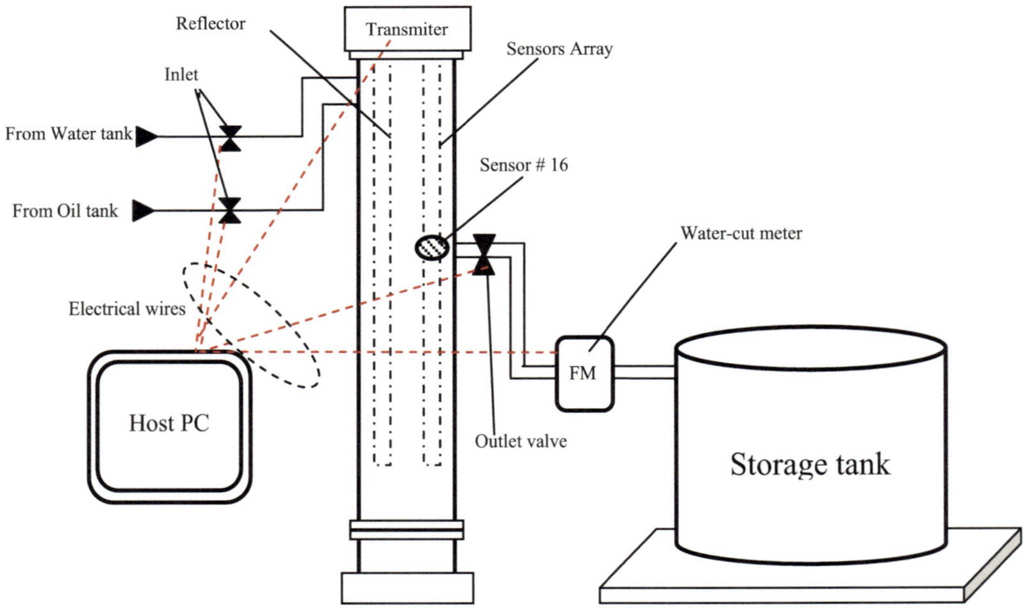

Fig. 25. Experimental setup to validate the accuracy of the device to measure the water-cut .

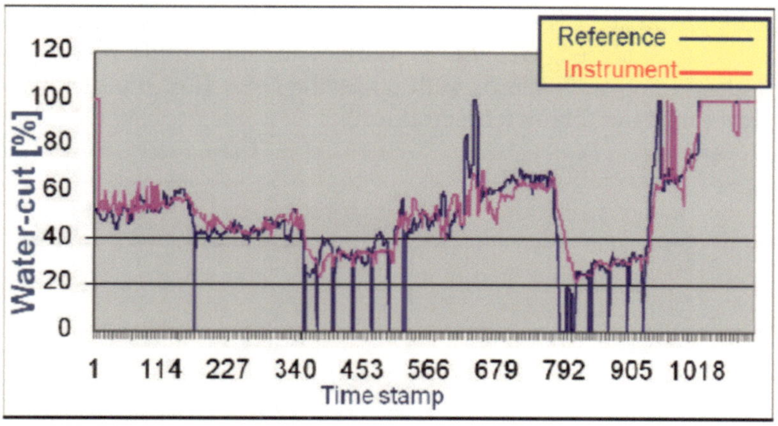

Fig. 26. Plot comparing the measured water-cut versus the reference.

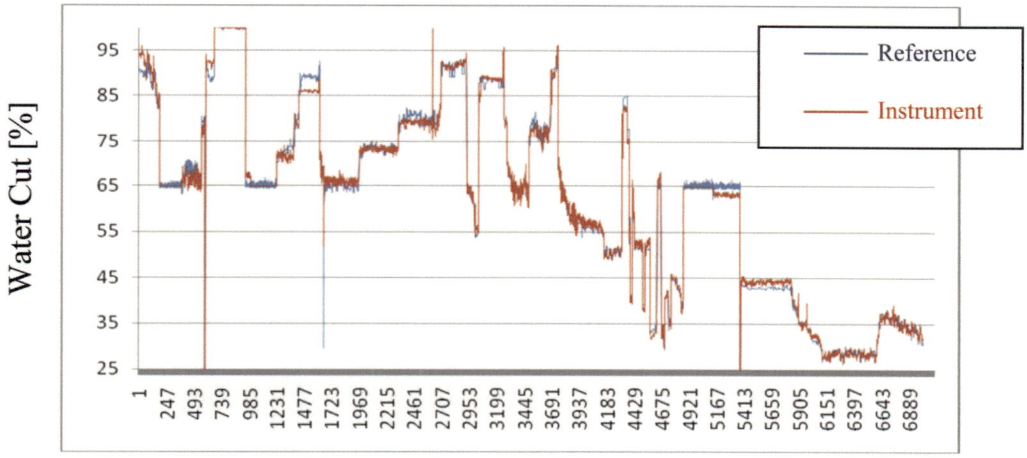

Fig. 27. Plot comparing the measured water-cut versus the reference for high water-cut.

Regarding the emulsion layer detection, Figures 18(a) and (b) shows the dynamic behavior of the emulsion for one of the sensors of the device (sensor #16) in case of water dominated (e.g. water fraction more than 90%) or oil dominated mixture (e.g. oil fraction more than 90%) respectively. It could be seen that in case of water dominant emulsion, the delay keeps decreasing since the bubbles of oil tend to disappear. However, in oil dominant emulsion, the delay keeps increasing since the bubbles of water tend to disappear.

Figure 29 shows the results of tracking the emulsion layer in the column. Initially, the column was filled with water (of height 285 cm) and oil (of height 75 cm). By filling the column with water (of height 30 cm), an emulsion layer has been created on the top of the column. As the water tends to move downward, the thickness of the emulsion layer tends to increases and reaches its maximum value at time t = 20 s. Next, pure oil starts to appear at the top of the tank and its thickness tends to increase until it reaches its maximal value at time = 78 s. Hence, the water thickness increases by 30 cm from its initial value. Figure 30 shows the graphical user interface in the computer of the control room showing a snapshot of the above experiment in which an emulsion layer was formed between the water and kerosene. The emulsion layer is represented by two windows: In window 1 the plot of the emulsion layer is represented, whereas in Window 3, the profile of the whole tank is represented by assigning each sensor with a specific color (e.g. Blue for water, pink for emulsion, yellow for gas, and brown for crude oil).

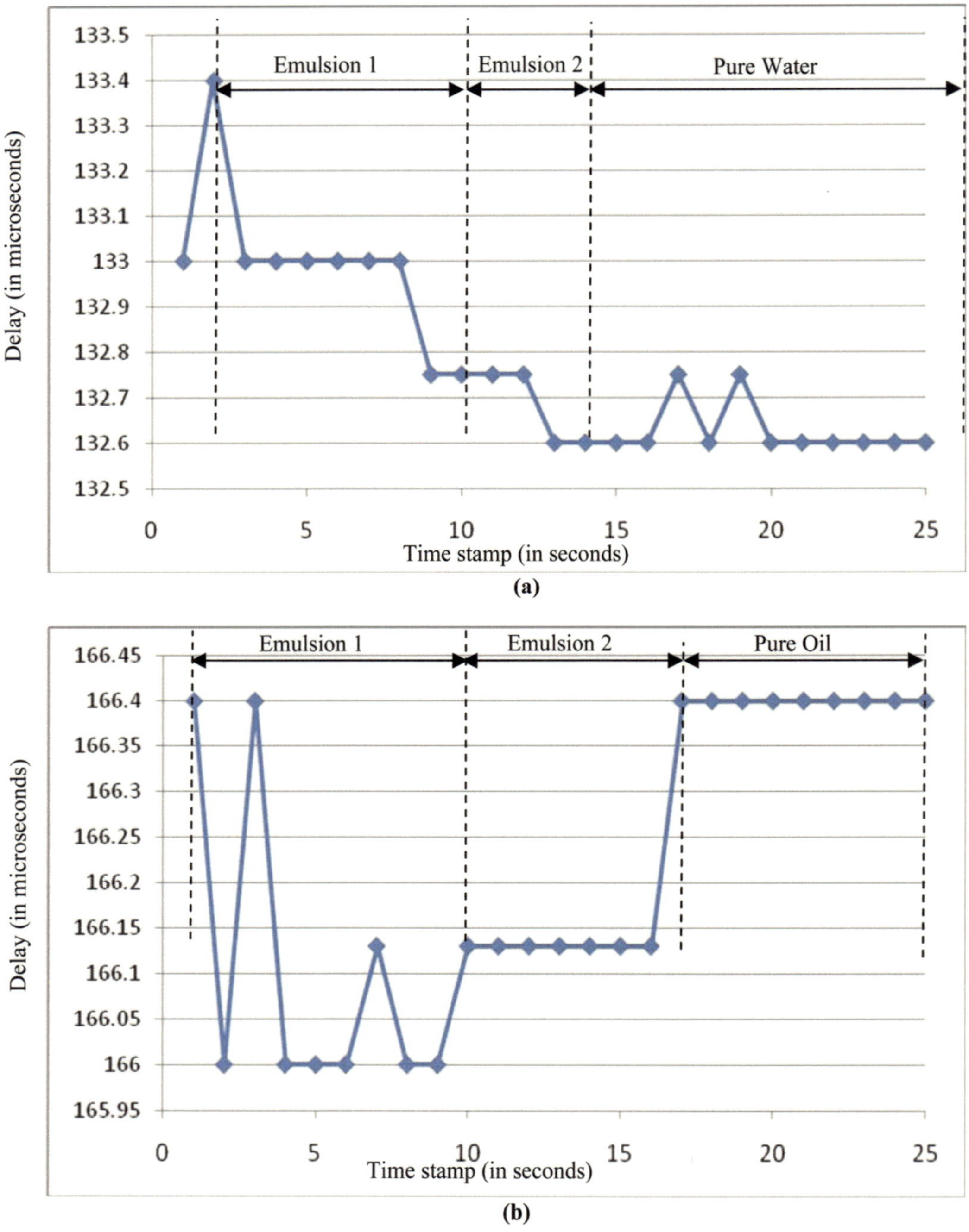

Fig. 28. Dynamic tracking of sensor 16 in water-dominant (a) and oil dominant (b) emulsion.

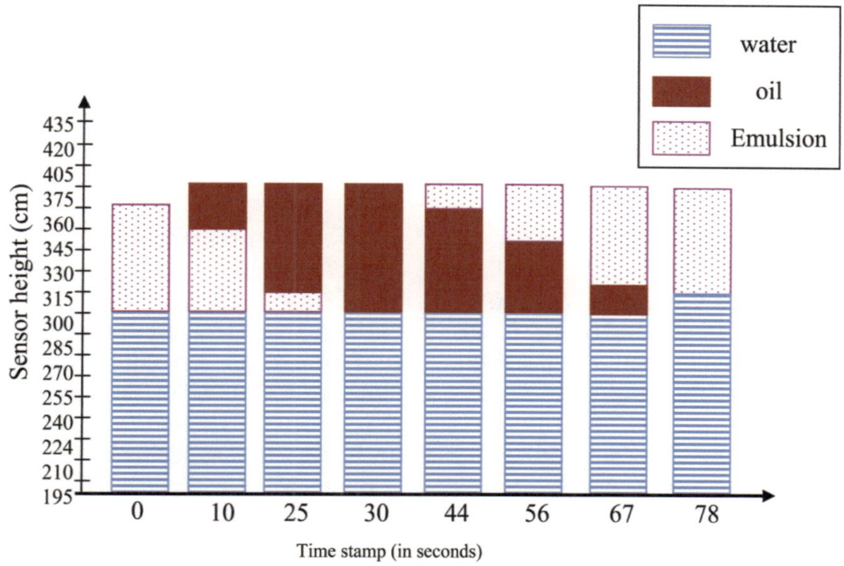

Fig. 29. Dynamic tracking of the emulsion layer.

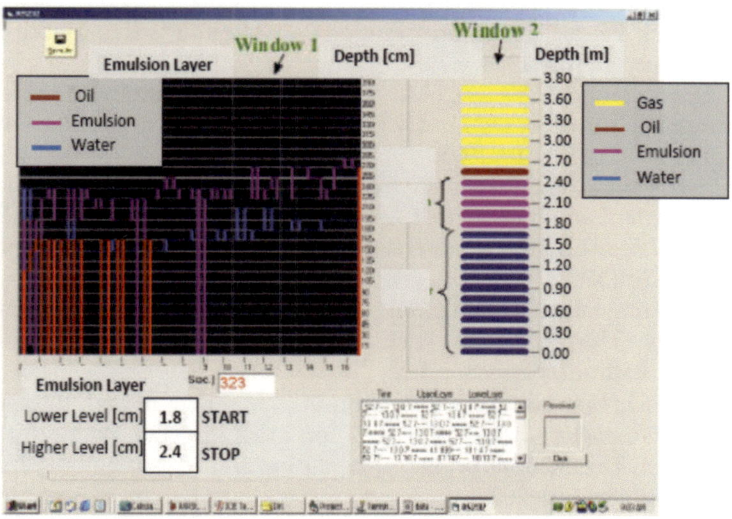

Fig. 30. Graphical user interface in the remote computer.

5. Conclusion

In this book chapter, a critical review on the most recent devices for emulsion layer detection was presented. At present, the radioactive-based device seems to be the most successfully commercially available devices from the accuracy point of view. However, because of the continuous danger it presents to the operator, oil companies are reluctant to use this technology in their field. This book chapter also presents an alternative safe solution which uses ultrasonic sensors. This device was designed, implemented and tested for real-time and accurate detection of the emulsion layer in a 4.35 m height tank. In addition, it was demonstrated that the instrument can provide the profile of the two phase liquid within a relative error of +/- 3%. The device is easy to maintain and install (no need to modify the oil tank) and is modular (i.e. Field Removable and Replaceable) and can deal with sludge buildup which may be caused by crude oil at the surface of the sensor and/or reflector.

6. References

[1] S.C. Bera, J.K. Ray, and S. Chattopadhyay, "A low-cost noncontact capacitance-type level transducer for a conducting liquid", IEEE Transactions on Instrumentation and Measurement, Volume 55, Issue 3, pp. 778 - 786, June 2006.

[2] W. Yin, A. Peyton, G. Zysko, and R. Denno "Simultaneous Non-contact Measurement of Water Level and Conductivity", in Proceedings of IEEE conference on Instrumentation and Measurement Technology (IMTC'2006), pp. 2144–2147, April 2006.

[3] Holler, G.; Thurner, T.; Zangl, H. and Brasseur, G; "A novel capacitance sensor principle applicable for spatially resolving downhole measurements", Proceedings IMTC/2002, Volume 2, pp. 1157 - 1160, Volume 2, May 2002.

[4] Weiss, M and Knochel, R, "A sub-millimeter accurate microwave multilevel gauging system for liquids in tanks", Microwave Theory and Techniques, IEEE Transactions on Volume 49, Issue 2, pp. 381 - 384 Digital Object Identifier 10.1109/22.903101, February 2001.

[5] R.Meador and H. Paap, "Emulsion Composition Monitor", U.S. Patent No. 4,458,524, date of Patent: 10 July 1984.

[6] Foden, P.R. Spencer, and R. Vassie, J.M.; "An instrument for-accurate sea level and wave measurement", Proceedings in OCEANS '98 Conference, pp. 405 - 408, Volume 1, 28 September-October 1st, 1998.

[7] Antonio Pietrosanto, and Antonio Scaglione "Microcontroller-Based Performance Enhancement of an Optical Fiber Level Transducer", from Giovanni Betta, *Associate Member, IEEE,* IEEE Transactions on Instrumentation and Measurement, Volume 47, No. 2, April 1998.

[8] Lee Robins, "On-line Diagnostics Techniques in the Oil, Gas, and Chemical Industry", in Proceedings Third Middle East Non-destructive Testing Conference, 27-30 November, Bahrain, Manama, 2005.

[9] Al-Naamany, A. M.; Meribout, M.; and Al Busaidi, K., "Design and Implementation of a New Nonradioactive-Based Machine for Detecting Oil-Water Interfaces in Oil Tanks", IEEE Transactions on Instrumentation and Measurement, Volume 56, Issue 5, pp. 1532 -1536, Oct. 2007.

[10] Mackenzie and Kenneth V.;"Discussion of sea-water sound-speed determinations". Journal of the Acoustical Society of America Volume 70, Issue 3, pp. 801-806, 1981.

[11] Urick R. J., "Sound propagation in the sea"; The Journal of the Acoustical Society of America, Volume 86, Issue 4, October 1989, pp. 1626.

[12] L. Kinsler, A. Frey, and A. Coppens, "Principal of Acoustics" John Wiley & sons, ISBN-13:9780471847892, 2000.

[13] L C Lynnworth, "Ultrasonic impedance matching from solids to gases", IEEE Transactions on Sonics and Ultrasonics, SU-12. (2). pp. 37-48, 1965.

[14] Lynnworth, L. C. and Magri, V., "Industrial Process Control Sensors and Systems", Ultrasonic Instruments and Devices: Reference for Modern Instrumentation, Techniques, and Technology, Volume 23 in the series Physical Acoustics, Academic Press, pp. 275-470, 1999.

11

Integrated Scheduled Waste Management System in Kuala Lumpur Using Expert System

Nassereldeen A. K, Mohammed Saedi and Nur Adibah Md Azman
Bioenvironmental Engineering Research Unit (BERU),
Department of Biotechnology Engineering, Faculty of Engineering,
International Islamic University Malaysia,
Malaysia

1. Introduction

Over the past decade, Malaysia has enjoyed tremendous growth in its economy and population, this resulted in an increase in the amount of waste scheduled generated. Furthermore, scheduled waste management has long been a problem area for local authorities in Kuala Lumpur. Continued illegal dumping by waste generators is being practiced at large scale due to lack of proper guidance and awareness. This paper reviewed discussed and suggested about service provided for scheduled waste management by an authority and international scenario of scheduled waste management. An expert system was developed to integrate scheduled waste management in Kuala Lumpur. The knowledge base was acquired through journals, books, magazines, annual report, experts, authorities and web sites. An object oriented expert system shell, Microsoft Visual Basic 2005 Express Edition was used as the building tools for the prototype development. The overall development of this project has been carried out in several phases which are problem identification, problem statement and literature review, identification of domain experts, prototype development, knowledge acquisition, knowledge representation and prototype development. Scheduled waste expert system is developed based on five types of scheduled waste management which are label requirements, packaging requirements, impact of scheduled wastes, recycling of scheduled wastes, and recommendations. Besides, it contains several sub modules by which the user can obtain a comprehensive background of the domain. The output is to support effective integrated scheduled waste management for KL and world-wide as well.

2. Scheduled wastes

Even though use of information technology plays a major role in application of technology nowadays, application of artificial intelligence (AI) is still in its infancy in Kuala Lumpur. During the last decade AI has grown to be a major of research in computer science. Varieties of AI-based application programs have been developed to address real life problems and have been successfully field-tested (L.C. Jayawardhanaa et al, 2003). As Kuala Lumpur still lacks proper systems of information assimilation, archival and delivery, AI tool can effectively be employed to solve for the management of scheduled waste.

Scheduled wastes are defined as wastes or combination of wastes that pose a significant present or potential hazard to human health or living organisms. This definition specifically excludes municipal solid waste and municipal sewage. Scheduled wastes are broadly classified into the categories of chemical wastes, biological wastes, explosives and radioactive wastes (Chapter 5 Waste Disposal). Scheduled waste management has long been a problem area for local authorities in Kuala Lumpur. Continued illegal dumping by waste generators is being practiced at large scale due to lack of proper guidance and awareness. In 2007, the Department of Environment Malaysia (DOE) was notified that 1 698.118 metric tones were generated. In addition, Kuala Lumpur has enjoyed tremendous growth in its economy. This has brought about a population growth along with a great influx of foreign workforce to cities. It resulted in an increase in the amount of waste generated. The main reason attributable to this deficiency is the lack of expertise in the scheduled waste management domain. The aim of this research is to address scheduled waste management in Kuala Lumpur by providing an expert system called Scheduled Waste Expert System (SWES). Currently, there are various facilities have been approved for management of scheduled wastes in Malaysia. These include 211 licensed waste transporters, 76 recovery facilities (non e-waste), 85 partial recovery e-waste facilities, 35 on-site incinerators, 3 clinical waste incinerators and 2 secured landfills (Department of Environment, Malaysia, 2008). For Kuala Lumpur, in 2007, there are 11 licensed waste transporters and 6 local off-sites recovery facilities (Laporan Tahunan Jabatan Alam Sekitar Wilayah Persekutuan, Kuala Lumpur 2002-2007). However, there are many of other potential sites which could be used as illegal dumped area. To guide the proper implementation of scheduled waste management, the need of expertise, in the form of human expert or a written program such as an expert system is crucial factor. In order to convey the expert knowledge to the operational level personnel, the most convenient and cost effective means is an expert system (Asanga Manamperi *et. al*, 2000).

3. International scenario of integration of scheduled waste management

Scheduled waste management has different meaning and classification according to the country. For example, most of the waste is classified under hazardous waste (HW) because of their physical characteristics that suitable with HW. HW can be classified on the basis of their hazardous nature which includes toxicity, flammability, explosively, corrosively and biological infectivity (Moustafa, 2001). According to Chinese law, solid waste is classified into three types: industrial solid waste (ISW), municipal solid waste (MSW) and hazardous waste (HW). According to the environmental statistics for the whole country in 2002, the quantity of ISW generated in China was 945 million tons, of which 50.4% was reused as source material or energy, 16.7% was disposed of simply, 30.2% was stored temporarily, and 2.7% was discharged directly into the environment. In recent years, the quantity of ISW generated in China has been increasing continually. Compared with 1989, the quantity of ISW generated in 2002 had increased by 66%. The categories of ISW are closely related to the industrial structure in China. (Qifei et. al, 2006).

The total volume of hazardous waste generated in Thailand in 2001 was 1.65 million tons, of which 1.29 million tons (78%) were generated by the nonindustrial (community) sector. As well as the industrial and nonindustrial sectors, a main source of hazardous waste generation is the transport of hazardous wastes from foreign countries into Thailand. More than 70% of the hazardous waste generated in Thailand is in the form of heavy metal sludge and solids. Other important groups of hazardous waste are oils, acid wastes, infectious wastes, solvents, and alkaline wastes. It has also been reported that petroleum refineries and the electroplating, textile, paper, and pharmaceutical industries are the primary producers of hazardous wastes in Thailand. Besides, for the nonindustrial hazardous waste is generated from everyday activities in nonindustrial or community sources, such as automotive repair shops, gas stations, hospitals, farm and households. Hazardous waste from community sources consist primarily of used oils, lead acid and dry-cell batteries, cleaning chemicals, pesticides, medical wastes, solvents, and fuels (Hiroaki et.al, 2003).

Amounts of wastes generated from industries in Dar es Salaam are estimated at 76 326 tonne per year (about 203.6 tonne per day or 58 kg per capita per year). The hazardous waste generation from industries in Dar es Salaam as estimated was a total of 46 340 tonne per year (about 127 tonne per day or 29 kg per capita per year). Assuming a negligible annual increase, the hazardous wastes production is about 40% of the total waste production in Dar es Salaam industries. The hazardous waste production levels in Dar es Salaam (Tanzania) can be estimated at 95 000 tonne per year or 3.8 kg per capita per year. The per capita waste generation rate is about 60% of that of Japan, 17% of Denmark and 3.8% of the Netherlands (Mato et. al, 1999).

In India, the HWs (Management and Handling) Rules, 1989, as amended in 2003 defined 36 industrial processes, which generate HW (HWM Rules, 2003). In order to encourage the effective implementation of the HW (M&H) Rules 1989 as amended in 2003. The key issues in India for HW management are the environmental health implications of uncontrolled waste generation, improper waste separation and storage prior to collection, multiple waste handling, the poor standards of disposal practices, and the non-availability of treatment/disposal facilities. The most influential issue is the scarcity of resources (skilled human as well as budgetary) in the country. The majority of the problems and challenges facing by India in managing HW are detailed.

4. Computer technique in waste management

There are many computer techniques in managing the waste worldwide. As an example, for Sri Lankan solid waste composting, BESTCOMP is used. BESTCOMP is one of the Expert System. BESTCOMP is short form from 'Born to guide for Solid waste COMPosting'. This system is based on several phases including problem identification, knowledge acquisition, knowledge representation, programming, testing and validation. It is composed of several basic components such as the user interface, knowledge base, inference mechanism and the database (L.C. Jayawardhanaa et. al, 2003).

Another Sri Lankan alternative is BESTFill for landfilling applications. An expert system was developed to assist proper implementation of landfill technology in Sri Lanka. This system contains several sub modules by which the user can obtain comprehensive background of the domain. The output is expected to support effective integrated solid waste management (Asanga et. Al, 2000).

Besides, for environmental site evaluation of waste management facilities, EUGENE model is used. This model is a sophisticated mixed integral linear programming model developed to help regional decision makers on long-term planning for solid waste management activities. The method used to embed waste management environmental parameters in the EUGENE model consists in building global impact index (GII) for all site or facility combinations (Vaillancourt et. al, 2002).

In addition, fuzzy goal programming approach is used for the optimal planning of metropolitan solid waste management systems. This system demonstrates how fuzzy, or imprecise, objectives of the decision maker can be quantified through the use of specific membership functions in various types of solid waste management alternatives (Ni-Bin et. al, 1997).
Another system that had been used was Analytic Network Process (ANP) and Decision Making Trial and Evolution Laboratory (DEMATEL) to evaluate the decision-making of municipal solid waste management in Metro Manila. ANP has a systematic approach to set priorities and trade-offs among goals and criteria, and also can measure all tangible and intangible criteria in the model while DEMATEL convert the relations between cause and effect of criteria into a visual structural model (Ming-Lang, 2008).

5. Methodology

Expert system (ES) has been chosen to organize part of the knowledge domain in scheduled waste management from all data collected to non-expert users (Nassereldeen, 1998). This knowledge should support them in term of label and packaging requirements, impact and recycling of scheduled wastes, recommendations, besides predicting the scheduled waste generated and population in Kuala Lumpur.

5.1 Visual Basic Expert System (VBES) development

Figure 1 below shows the flow diagram of this project, problem identification, problem statement, literature review and identifications of domain experts are done. For other phases

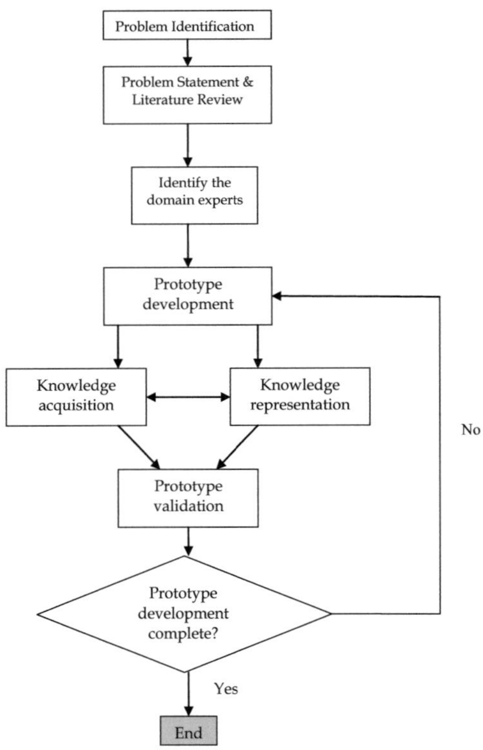

Fig. 1. Flow Diagram for Scheduled Waste Expert System

are elaborated below. Several entities in the integration of scheduled waste management system in KL. Five different entities of this process, each of which has many sub entity:

- Label Requirements
- Packaging Requirements
- Impact of scheduled waste
- Recycling of scheduled waste
- Recommendation

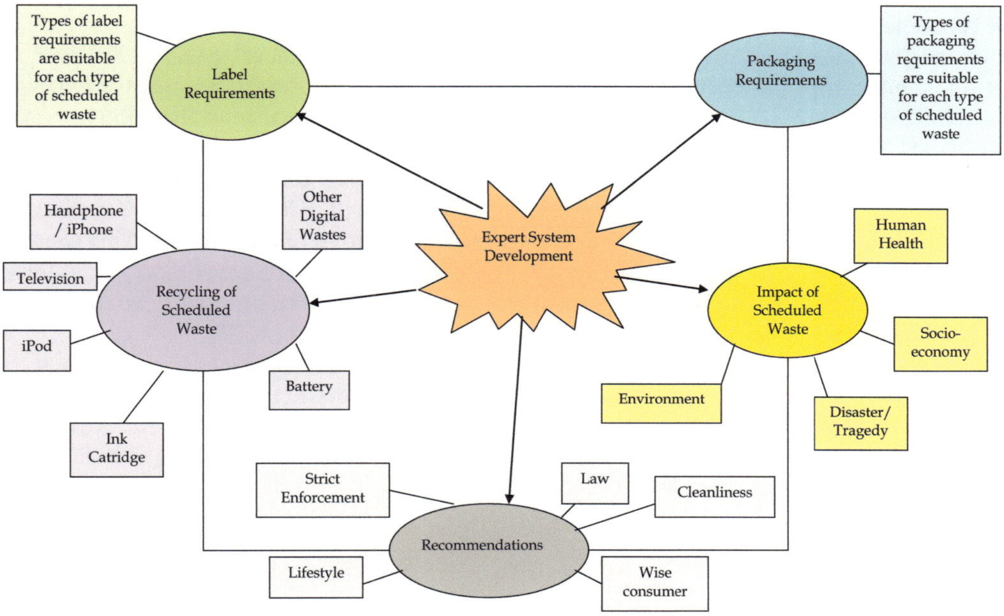

Fig. 2. Five Different Entities of Expert System Development

5.2 Building tool

For the development of Scheduled Waste Expert System (SWES), an expert system shell, Microsoft Visual Basic 2005 Express Edition, was preferred over conventional programming languages. This software was used because of its user friendly. In fact, many books that guide the author how to use this software are available in the library.

5.3 System requirements

- Operating System
  The user must have Windows 2003, XP, or 2000; Windows NT, 95, 98, or ME will not work.
- Available hard drive space
  The requirement varies with the edition and type of installation and whether other components such as Internet Explorer (IE) already are installed on the computer. The user should plan on the total installation taking between 2GB and 5GB (gigabytes). A large (at least 80GB) hard drive is relatively inexpensive and easy to install, so if remaining space on the existing hard drive is scarce, the user may wish to consider upgrading before installing Visual Basic 2005.
- Processor

According to Microsoft, a processor speed of 600 MHz (megahertz) is the minimum and 1 GHz (gigahertz) is recommended. Because upgrading a processor by replacing the motherboard is not so inexpensive or easy, another alternative is boosting your system RAM, discussed next if the user is on the borderline.

- RAM
  According to Microsoft, 128MB (megabytes) is the minimum, and 256MB is recommended.

5.4 Knowledge acquisition

Knowledge acquisition is the lengthiest process in building of an expert system. However, it is the single most important process of the knowledge engineer upon which quality of the expert system depends on. The central core of the knowledge base was acquired from the published text books, journals, magazines, experts, meeting authorities and pamphlet. This knowledge consists of well established facts, rules, theory and guidelines that had been practiced over many years. Annual Report of Department of Environment (DOE) related to statistics of scheduled waste generated have provided very valuable sources of information. This source of information provided a means to build a unique knowledge base for Scheduled Waste Expert System (SWES). All the sources are come from Department of Environment, Kuala Lumpur (DOE), Kuala Lumpur City Hall (DBKL), and Alam Flora Sdn. Bhd (AFSB).

Knowledge acquisition has now become relatively easy than two decades ago, due to the advancement of Internet facilities. Much valued information about management of scheduled waste of Kualiti Alam and Radicare, organization, companies, recycling procedure and so on, were acquired through the Internet. These were helpful in building the sub modules of the Scheduled Waste Expert System (SWES).

6. Results and discussion

6.1 User interface

Proper organization of the user interface is important since it is the part of the expert system that interacts with the user. The presence of a standard user interface framework not only simplifies development efforts, but also reduces user training and support requirements for users. In the SWES, the knowledge base was divided into five categories which are label requirements, packaging requirements, impact of scheduled wastes, recycling of scheduled wastes, and recommendations as shown in the Figure 3.

Fig. 3. Main User Interface of SWES

6.2 Rules for the ES

Through studying the annual report, magazine, journal, book and web sites, knowledge was translated into five sets of rules:

i. Label requirements
ii. Packaging requirements
iii. Impact of scheduled wastes
iv. Recycling of scheduled wastes
v. Recommendations

The major operations that can be done on the ES as in figure 4 are:

i. Clear, this command removes selected text in the text box
ii. Recommendation, Solution, Result & Comment, these commands give the best solution and comment about the selected case.
iii. Help, this command help the user how to use this system.
iv. Quit, this command prompts exit SWES.

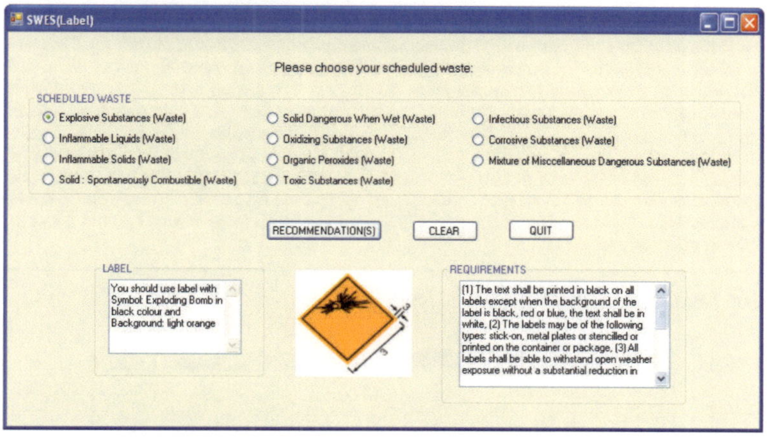

Fig. 4. The output after user click on any radio buttons

6.3 Rules for impact of Scheduled Wastes

The information is converted into ES rules in a simple language as in figure 5.

The rule will be in a form of radio button and the meaning of the rule is:

If the selection is RadioButton1, then Example SW 110 E-Waste <> (1) Toxic ingredients in E-Waste such as lead, beryllium, mercury, cadmium and bromibated flame retardants can pose both occupational and envitonmental health threats. (2) E-Waste that are lanfilled produce highly contaminated leachate which eventually pollutes the environment especially surface water and grounwater. (3) Acid and sludge obtained from melting computer chips if disposed into the ground will cause acidification of soil and subsequently contamination of groundwater. (4) Brominated flame retardant plastic or cadmium containing plastics are landilled, both polybrominated diphenyl ethers (PBDE) and cadmium may leach into the soil and groundwater. (5) Combustion of E-Waste will emit toxic fumes and gases that pollute the surrounding air. When E-Wastes are exposed to fire, metals and other chemical substances, extremely toxic dioxins and furans will be emitted. The toxic fall-out from open burning affects both the local environment and broader global air quality, depositing highly toxic byproducts in many places throughout the world. (6) If E-Wastes are discarded together with other household wastes, the toxic compnents will pose a threat to both health and the vital components of the ecosystem; if the selection is RadioButton2, then Example SW 311 Oil <> (1)

IF selection is RadioButton1
THEN Example SW 110 E-Waste <> (1) Toxic ingredients in E-Waste such as lead, beryllium, mercury, cadmium and bromibated flame retardants can pose both occupational and envitonmental health threats. (2) E-Waste that are lanfilled produce highly contaminated leachate which eventually pollutes the environment especially surface water and grounwater. (3) Acid and sludge obtained from melting computer chips if disposed into the ground will cause acidification of soil and subsequently contamination of groundwater. (4) Brominated flame retardant plastic or cadmium containing plastics are landilled, both polybrominated diphenyl ethers (PBDE) and cadmium may leach into the soil and groundwater. (5) Combustion of E-Waste will emit toxic fumes and gases that pollute the surrounding air. When E-Wastes are exposed to fire, metals and other chemical substances, extremely toxic dioxins and furans will be emitted. The toxic fall-out from open burning affects both the local environment and broader global air quality, depositing highly toxic byproducts in many places throughout the world. (6) If E-Wastes are discarded together with other household wastes, the toxic compnents will pose a threat to both health and the vital components of the ecosystem.

IF selection is RadioButton2
THEN Example SW 311 Oil <> (1) Oil that is illegall dumped can contaminate groundwater and nearby rivers, affect public health and financial implications. (2) The health impacts of direct and indirect exposure to oil include carcinogenic effects, reproductive system damage, respiratory effects, central nervous system effects and many more.

The rule in VB language;

```
If Me.RadioButton1.Checked Then
  Me.TextBox1.Text = ("Example SW 110 E-Waste <> (1) Toxic ingredients in E-Waste such as lead, beryllium, mercury, cadmium and bromibated flame retardants can pose both occupational and envitonmental health threats. (2) E-Waste that are lanfilled produce highly contaminated leachate which eventually pollutes the environment especially surface water and grounwater. (3) Acid and sludge obtained from melting computer chips if disposed into the ground will cause acidification of soil and subsequently contamination of groundwater. (4) Brominated flame retardant plastic or cadmium containing plastics are landilled, both polybrominated diphenyl ethers (PBDE) and cadmium may leach into the soil and groundwater. (5) Combustion of E-Waste will emit toxic fumes and gases that pollute the surrounding air. When E-Wastes are exposed to fire, metals and other chemical substances, extremely toxic dioxins and furans will be emitted. The toxic fall-out from open burning affects both the local environment and broader global air quality, depositing highly toxic byproducts in many places throughout the world. (6) If E-Wastes are discarded together with other household wastes, the toxic compnents will pose a threat to both health and the vital components of the ecosystem.")
```

Fig. 5. Rules for Impact of Scheduled Waste

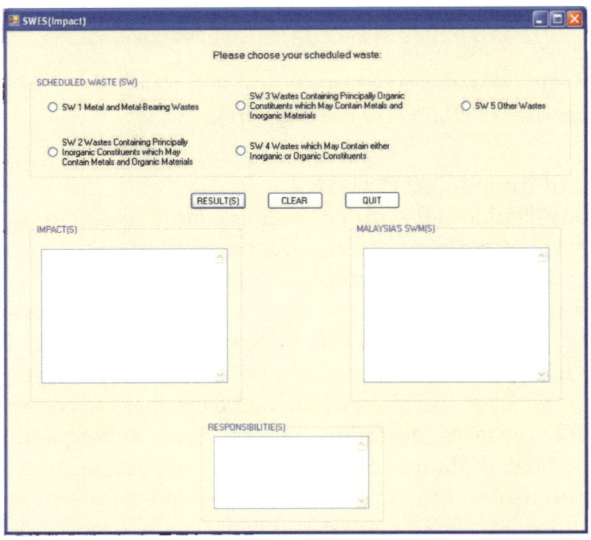

Fig. 6. Choices of Impact of Scheduled Waste

Oil that is illegall dumped can contaminate groundwater and nearby rivers, affect public health and financial implications. (2) The health impacts of direct and indirect exposure to oil include carcinogenic effects, reproductive system damage, respiratory effects, central nervous system effects and many more. The selection is continuously until RadioButton5.

Figure 6 shows the translation of the rule into impact of scheduled waste using VB while figure 7 shows the output after the user click on any radio buttons.

6.4 Scheduled Waste Expert System (SWES)

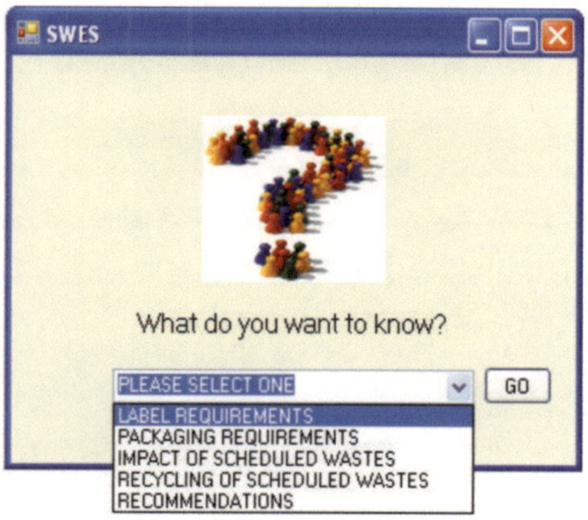

Fig. 7. Interface for Scheduled Waste Expert System

Once the user clicks on the SWES button at the main user interface, they will be five categories listed as in figure 7. Then, user can choose any categories and the system will give user the best solutions. The system will produce the answer through texts, graphs and pictures within a single form. Scheduled Waste Management module has been designed for the use of the novices to the field. It has been divided into premises and companies handling scheduled waste in Kuala Lumpur, labeling and packaging requirement, transportation, and process flow. For process flow, it divided into two which are Kualiti Alam's process flow and Radicare's process flow as in figure 8.

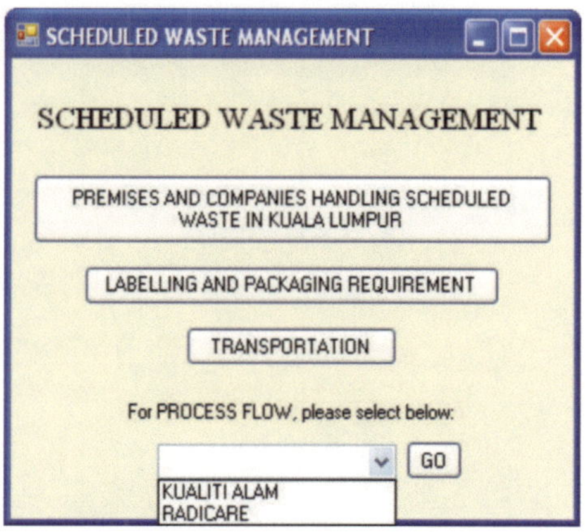

Fig. 8. Interface for Scheduled Waste Management Sub Module

6.5 System validation

In validating the scheduled waste expert system, it should be remembered that the purposes of the study are to develop on integrated scheduled waste management system in KL by using Visual Basic Expert System and to recommend a new approach for integration of scheduled waste management system in KL. Many expert system prototypes were tested and validated using case studies, the results of which were analyzed internally by the system developers themselves. Similarly in the case of the SWES, it was validated in two steps. As the first step, the system validation involved program debugging, error analysis as in the Figure 9 below, and output generation. After the code is corrected, no error occurs anymore as in the Figure 10. So, the program can be debugged.

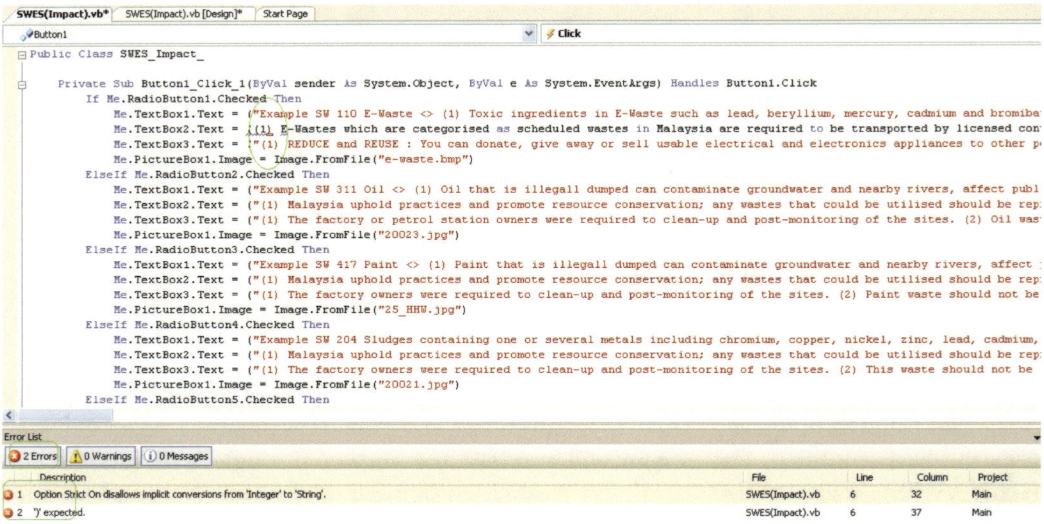

Fig. 9. Area in the circle shows error occurred during coding

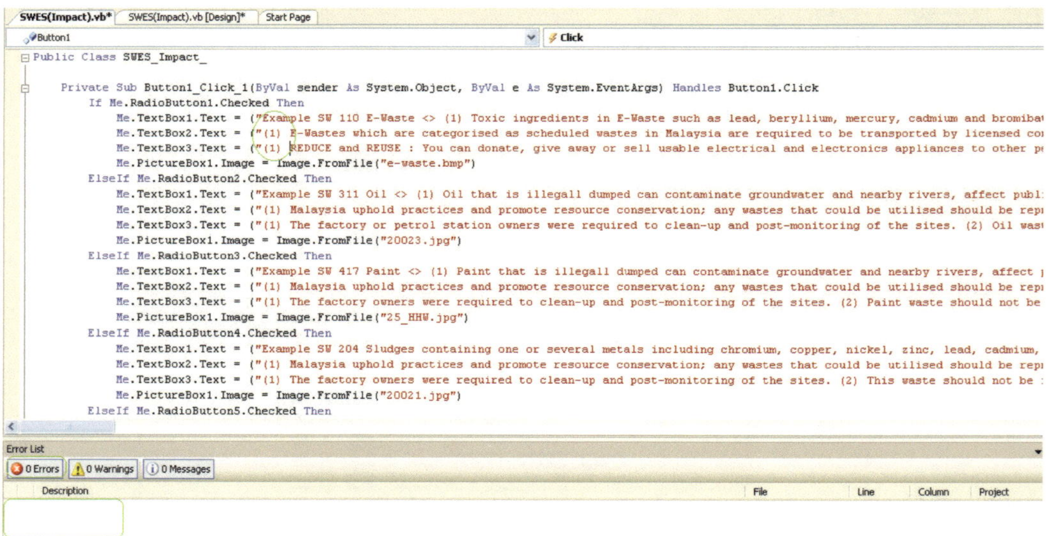

Fig. 10. Area in the circle shows no error occur after the code is corrected

Secondly, empirical data from DOE's data, journal and authority agents validated its performance. The objective was to evaluate the SWES's diagnostics capability by comparing its output with the data which were collected and documented during the knowledge acquisition phase. As an example, the output for estimation of scheduled waste generated and population in KL are validated with the statistics provided by the DOE and journal. According to DOE, scheduled waste generated is estimated increasing every year while according to the journal, population in KL will increase 4% every year. For label and packaging requirements and impact and recycling of scheduled waste are validated through the various sources such as magazines, DOE's annual report and web sites. For example, Figure 11 shows scheduled waste generated in 2002 is 1 560.420 tonne metric while Figure 11 shows scheduled waste generated in 2007 is 1 698.118 tonne metric. According to the DOE's statistics, the outputs show scheduled waste generated in 2002 and 2007 are same. So, the outputs are corrected and validated.

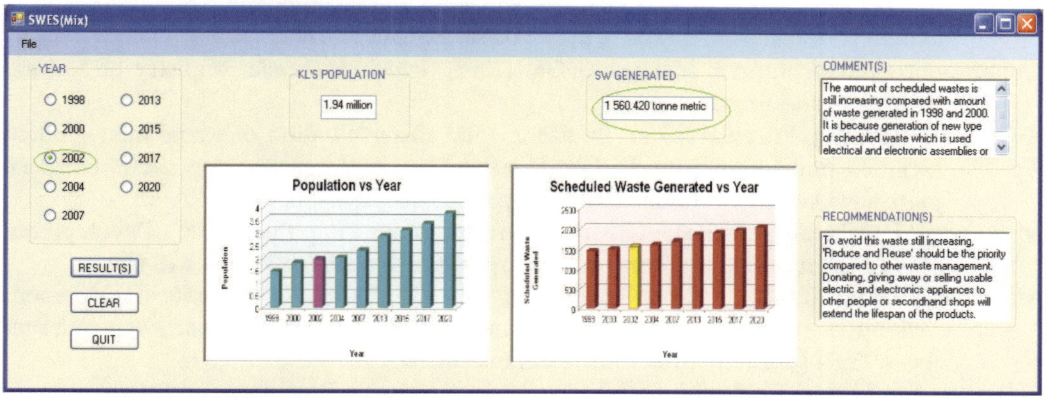

Fig. 11. Area in the circle shows scheduled waste generated in 2002 is 1 560.420 tonne metric

7. Conclusion

The purpose of the study includes understanding scheduled waste generated in Kuala Lumpur and service provided for scheduled waste management by the authority which is Department of Environment (DOE). In addition, scheduled waste management system in Kuala Lumpur will be developed by using Visual Basic Expert System (SWES). Finally, a new approach for integration of scheduled waste management system in Kuala Lumpur is recommended.

From the result obtained, the project can be considered as successful as the integrated program for scheduled waste management system had been developed. Scheduled waste expert system is developed based on five types of scheduled waste management which are label requirements, packaging requirements, impact of scheduled wastes, recycling of scheduled wastes, and recommendations. The knowledge base of this system is based on ruled-base expert system which is IF THEN rule and the acquisition knowledge that is gathered for this study is organized into this rules. The development of scheduled waste expert system consists of six main forms or interfaces which are photo gallery, scheduled waste management, literature, legislations, training tool, and scheduled waste expert system itself. It has been incorporated with several user interfaces in order to make the system user friendly as much as possible. SWES can also be used as a stand-alone learning tool in environmental studies and by others. Thus a system of much versatility has been developed.

This is use of tools of information technology to help in solve local problems in managing scheduled waste in an informative manner.

8. References

A. Moustafa; & Chaaban. (2001). Hazardous waste source reduction in materials and processing technologies. *Journal of Materials Processing Technology*. Vol 119 (2001), pp. 336-343, ISSN 0924-0136.

Chapter 5 Waste Disposal. Retrieved July 23, 2008, from http://www.ide.go.jp/English/Publish/Apec/pdf/97fe_015.pdfJayawardhanaa, L.C; A. Manipuraa; A. Alwisb; M. Ranasinghea; S. Pilapitiyac & Indrika A. (2003). BESTCOMP: expert system for sri lankan solid waste composting. *Expert System with Application*. Vol.24, (2003), pp. 281-286, ISSN 0957-4174.

Department of Environment, Malaysia DOE. (2008). *Impak*. Malaysia: Ministry of Natural Resources and Environment.

K. Vaillancourt. & J. Wauub. (2002). Environmental site evaluation of waste management facilities embedded into EUGENE model: A multicriteria approach. *European Journal of Operational Research*. Vol139, pp. 436-448, ISSN: 0377-2217.

M. Asanga; L.C. Jayawardhanaa; Ajith De Alwis & Sumith Pilapitiya. (2000). Development of An Expert System for Landfilling Applications in Sri Lanka. pp. 643-653.

Ming-Lang Tseng. (2008). Application of ANP and DEMATEL to evaluate the decision-making of municipal solid waste management in Metro Manila. *Environ Monit Asses*. ISSN (printed): 0167-6369. ISSN (electronic): 1573-2959.

Nassereldeen Ahmed Kabbashi. (1998). *An Expert System for Predicting Air Pollution due to Development*. (Master dissertation: Universiti Putra Malaysia).

Ni-Bin Chang & S. F. Wang. (1997). A fuzzy goal programming approach for the optimal planning of metropolitan solid waste management systems. *European Journal of Operational Research*. Vol99, pp. 303-321. ISSN: 0377-2217.

R.R.A.M. Mato & M.E. Kaseva. (1999). Critical review of industrial and medical waste practices in Dar es Salaam City. *Resources, Conservation and Recycling*. Vol25, pp. 271-287, ISSN 0921-3449.

Qifei Huang; Qi Wang; Lu Dong; Beidou Xi & Binyan Zhou. (2006). The current situation of solid waste management in china. *J Mater Cycles Waste Manag*. Vol.8, pp. 63-69. DOI 10.1007/s10163-005-0137-2.

12

Expert System Development for Acoustic Analysis in Concrete Harbor NDT

Mohammad Reza Hedayati[1], Ali Asghar Amidian[2] and S. Ataolah Sadr[3]
[1,2]University of Applied Science and Technology Faculty of Telecommunication,
[1]Information Technology Mechatronic Offshore (ITOM) &
[3]Port and Maritime Organization (PMO),
I. R. of Iran

1. Introduction

Port and Maritime Organization of Iran (PMO), in connection with a research project at Information Technology Mechatronic Offshore research and development cooperative society (ITMO), has added another dimension to its subsea inspection activities by introducing new methods of NDT and expert system for condition monitoring and assessment of concrete structures. ITOM provided a wide range of special and advanced techniques for most aspects of subsea and underwater. The repair of concrete structures under water presents many complex problems.

The harsh environmental conditions and specific problems associated with working underwater or in the splash zone area causes many differences. Proper evaluation of the present condition of the structure is the first essential step for designing long-term repairs. To be most effective, evaluation of the existing structure requires historical information on the structure and its environment, including any changes made to the structure over time, and the records of periodic on-site inspections or repairs.

Reduction of the human experts involvement in the diagnosis process has gradually taken place due to the recent developments in the modern Artificial Intelligence (AI) tools. AI is a research field between psychology, cognitive science and computer science with the overal goal to improve reasoning capabilities of computers. Artificial Neural Networks (ANNs), fuzzy and adaptive fuzzy systems, and expert systems are good candidates for the automation of the diagnostic procedures and e-maintenance application (Filippetti, et al., 1992 & Hedayati 2009). It is often necessary to test concrete structures after the concrete has hardened to determine whether the structure is suitable for its designed use. Ideally such testing should be done without damaging the concrete. The tests available for testing concrete range from the completely non-destructive, where there is no damage to the concrete, through those where the concrete surface is slightly damaged, to partially destructive tests, such as core tests and pullout and pull off tests, where the surface has to be repaired after the test.

The present work surveys the principles and a criterion of the diagnosis signal processing and introduces these achievements to an expert system technique. In this paper adoption of a new sensor is discussed and experimental results are presented for an expert system application, based on the concept of spectrum and cepstrum analysis of detected signals and the method of measuring defected parts of subsea concrete without disturbing their structures for a suspected part of the quay wall. A transducer using the principle of vibration sensors has been tried and considered to be suitable for measuring any probable damage due to irregular phenomena such as voids, mix separations and cracks on the suspected superficial portion of the subsea concrete structures. Such transducers are proposed to be the basis for condition monitoring of armored steel structure in the subsea concrete by analyzing the change of vibration sensed by related transducers of the testing probe.

It is a common observation that, when there were voids, mix separation or crack the reflected waves detected by the receiving sensor were different than those from the perfect areas. The results showed that the analysis of surface wave testing has the ability to detect changes in the constructed structures. The vibration signals which appear on the perfect part of structure, give a characteristic vibration signature. This signature provides a base line against which future measurements can be compared.

It is important to note that similar concrete structure in good condition will have similar vibration signature differing only in respect of their constructional and structural conditions tolerances.

2. Development of expert system

Knowledge built in to an expert system may originate from different sources. The prime source of knowledge for developing an expert system should be the domain expert. To design and develop knowledge based expert system, the specific knowledge domain or the subject domain must be acquired. The knowledge domain is to be organized so that the information can be structured in the computer program for effective use. In this respect, a knowledge engineer usually obtains knowledge through direct interaction with the expert. Fig.1 illustrates the process of data procurement for generating the knowledge base.

The domain of reinforced concrete diagnosis serves as a good example in the application area for:

1. Examining the different means currently used to store and transfer information,
2. The knowledge acquisition and knowledge engineering processes required for extracting that information and capturing it in a knowledge based expert system, and
3. Showing how the resulting knowledge based expert system provides an integrated framework for combining specifications, data, and models (Graham-Jones &Mellor 1995).

Fig. 1. Experts appropriate evaluations, assessment, data logging and generating the information for knowledge base in the Shid-Rajaee harbor

The scope of this research work is to integrate inspections and observations, specifications, standards of practice, and data related to quay-wall concrete structure diagnosis (QCD) and to make full use of the available information in the diagnosis process. Expert System (ES) focuses on integrating inspection of commonly encountered problems, specifications, standards of practice and data, both theoretical and empirical, into one cohesive tool. QCDES is a rule-based expert system which has been developed using the expert system shell. The main advantage of incorporating a modular design in QCDES is to have great flexibility in updating or adding modules in the future. The various modules of system development are represented graphically as follows:

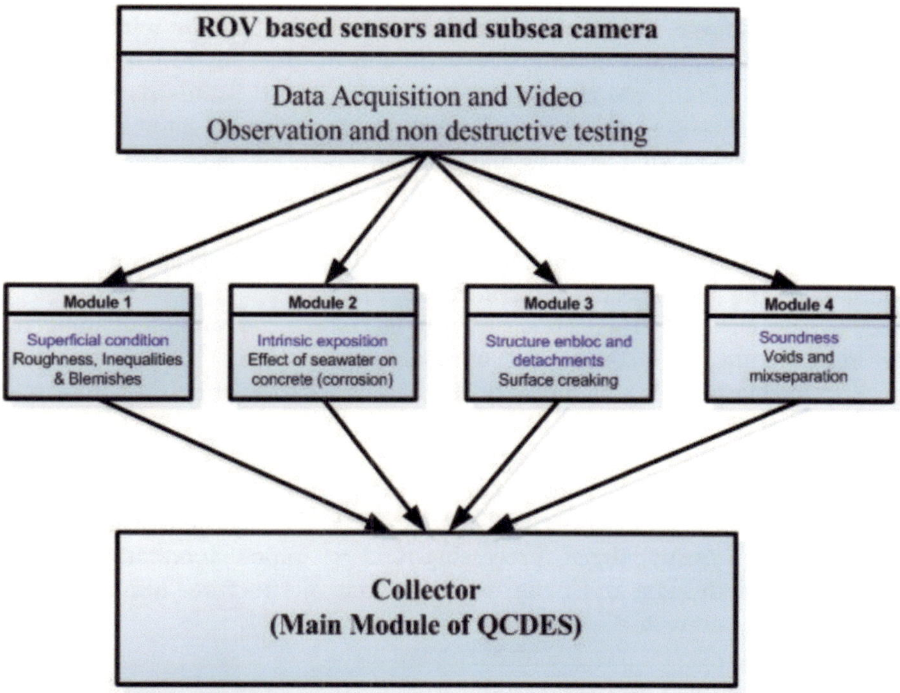

Fig. 2. The QCDES Modules

The development of QCDES has followed the development cycle as follows:

1. Identifying objectives and scope mixseparation
2. Knowledge acquisition (collecting data, reading literature and reports, discussions with domain experts, case studies, etc.)
3. Preliminary planning and choice of system
4. System design and development
5. Testing, validation and trials
6. Reviews and modifications
7. Implementation

3. Study of problem

Inspection of reinforced concrete structures in marine environment is important. The use of NDT techniques in combination with coring may enable one to detect the early onset of corrosion where appropriate steps may be taken to slow down the corrosion process. Such inspection procedures, however, are quite costly as they require experts to conduct the tests and interpret the results. To wait for the appearance of visible signs of corrosion in a structure such as rust stains and/or cracks before repair will be conducted is not cost effective. The presence of such visible signs is indicative of an advanced stage of corrosion which may require a thorough investigation of the entire structure in order to properly assess the type of repair or rehabilitation needed for the corroded structure.The use of prediction models, specifically, the time to initiate corrosion can provide useful information regarding the early onset of corrosion which allows one to appropriately schedule the required maintenance.

The subject of diagnosis of deterioration and other problems in reinforced concrete structures is indeed huge and enormously wide and of great interest to civil engineers. There are standards for the use of reinforced concrete (British Standards Institution, 1985 &1991). For the purposes of this research work specific domain knowledge relating to common symptoms of cracking, spalling and delamination is needed.

Vibration condition monitoring of harbor concrete structures makes use of vibration analysis for the following purposes:

1. Periodic routine vibration measurement to check their structural condition.
2. Trouble shooting for suspected constructional problems.
3. Check to ascertain that the concrete structure has returned to good operating condition after implementing the reconstruction or repair.
4. Check to enable planning of repair of the harbor concrete structures prior to harbor service shut- down.

Different defects cause the vibration signatures to change in different ways. A changed vibration signature provides a means to determine the source of problem as well as prior warning of the problem itself (Skala & Chobola 2005). This research work is limited to implementing the acoustic signal processing and condition monitoring of concrete structures in the splash zone and underwater portions of structures located in the lakes, rivers, oceans, or ground water.

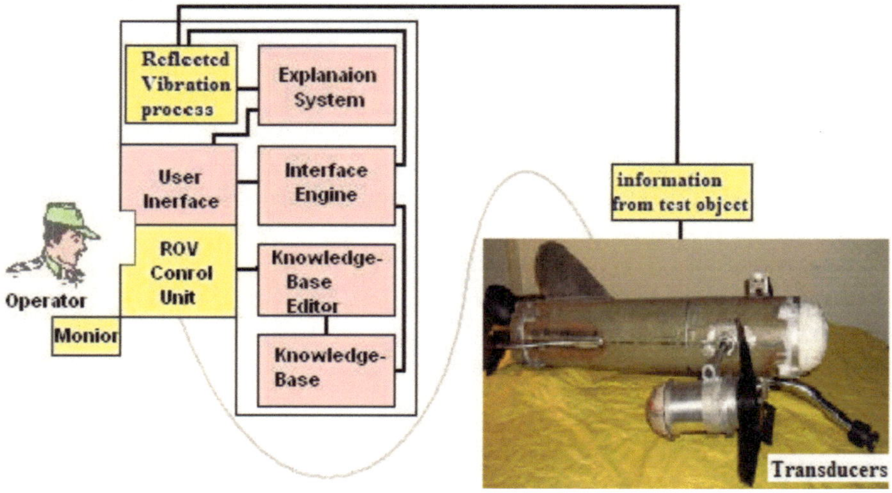

Fig. 3. The most important modules of proposed rule-based vibration signal diagnostic expert system

4. Deciding what action to take

Deciding on the appropriate action to take after a defect has been discovered depends on the potential hazard of the defect, the risk of continued structural deterioration, the technology available to repair the defect, the cost associated with the needed repair, and the intended remaining life of the structure. Following are the possible methods of concrete harbor inspection:

1. Visual inspection
2. Tactile inspection (Inspection by touch)
3. Underwater non destructive testing of concrete (signal processing)

5. Diving technology

Underwater work can be generally classified into one of three broad categories for accessing the work site:

1. Manned diving;
2. One-atmosphere armored suit
3. Manned submarine
4. Remotely operated vehicle (ROV).

The industry standards currently allow a diver using compressed air to work at 10 m for an unlimited period of time. If work is being performed at 20 m, however, the diver can only work for approximately 60 minutes over a 24-hour period without special precautions to prevent decompression sickness. The industry standard upper limit is 30 minutes of work time at 30m in seawater. If these limits are exceeded, precautions must be taken to decompress the diver.

Undoubtedly, the most dynamic growth in a particular underwater platform has been exhibited by Remotely Operated Vehicles (ROVs). ROVs look much like an unmanned version of a submarine. Fig.4 displays the application of the proposed model of ROV, especially equipped for NDT of quay wall in Shahid-Rajaee harbor. Thay are compact devices that are controlled by a remote crew. The operating crew and the vehicle communicate through an umbilical cord attached to the ROV. The crew operates the ROV with information provided by transponders attached to the frame of the ROV. Generally the pilot will maneuver the vehicle as closely as prudent to a point adjacent to the platform and over the work site. ROVs may be launched directly from the surface or from a submarine mother ship. Most ROVs are equipped with video and still photography devices. The vehicle is positioned by ballast tanks and thrusters mounted on the frame. Some ROVs are also equipped with robotic arms that are used to perform tasks that do not need a high degree of dexterity. Vehicles owned by industrial users range in depth capability from 200m to 2400 m; the average is 1300m. Structural investigations of underwater facilities are usually conducted as part of a routine preventive maintenance program, an initial construction inspection, a special examination prompted by an accident or catastrophic event, or a method for determining needed repairs. The purpose of the investigation usually influences the inspection procedures and testing equipment used. Underwater inspections are usually hampered by adverse conditions such as poor visibility, strong currents, cold water, marine growth, and debris build-up. Horizontal and vertical control for accurately locating the observation is difficult. A diving inspector must wear cumbersome life-support systems and equipment, which also hampers the inspection mission.

Fig. 4. The proposed ROV and incorporated diagnostic arm for inspection and NDT of a quay wall in Shahid-Rajaee harbor

Underwater inspections usually take much longer to accomplish than inspections of similar structures located above the water surface. This necessitates more planning by the inspecting team to optimize their efforts. Inspection criteria and definitions are usually established before the actual inspection, and the inspection team is briefed. The primary goal is to inspect the structural elements to detect any obvious damage. If a defect is observed, the inspector identifies the type and extent of the defect to determine how serious the problem may be. The inspector also determines the location of the defect so repair crews can return later to make the repair, or another inspection team can reinvestigate if necessary. Many divers who perform structural inspections do not have specific structural engineering training for this task. In this case, another person with the appropriate engineering background is normally employed to interpret the results of the inspection and make the appropriate evaluations. Moreover the diver using air as the breathing medium can expect some loss of judgement at 30m and a severe loss at depths over 45m owing to inert gas narcosis. Reportedly (Hughes 1972), the diver cannot always recognize the exact relationship of objects with the vertical and horizontal, and an error in judgement of up to 30 degrees may be expected.

6. Cleaning the NDT position

Every NDT device now in use requires that the surface of the structure be cleaned to bare concrete or metal in order to obtain accurate measurements. Depending on the environment, preparatory cleaning can be- and often is a more time consuming chore than the actual testing.

Concrete structures present a special cleaning problem where "clean" is, in fact, governed by how much fouling/corrosion material can be removed and not harm the parent material of structure. The cleaning chore involves removal of sensible organisms (barnacles, mussels, tube worms, algae anemones, etc.). The quantity of these organisms on a specific structure varies according to the environment, reproduction rates and other factors. Consequently, it is not possible to predict how many of a particular specie will be present. The depth of fouling organism growth also varies according to the specie. Generally, but not always, below 50-60m the population density decreases and the cleaning problem is considerably less.

Several techniques are used to remove marine growth on the quay wall structure. These include hydraulic grinders, brushes, scrapers, needle guns and high pressure water jets. In the present work the ROV based water jetting technique is employed for perfect surface cleaning of concrete and removal of marine growth. For NDT purposes of quay wall, the structure must be cleaned to at least bare concrete, any protrusions left on the surface can introduce an error into the results, and conversely, any abrasion causing removal of parent material of quay wall produces the same affect.

7. Underwater non-destructive testing of concrete

Among structures vulnerable to chloride attack include ports, bridges and other marine infrastructures. The economic importance played by these structures demands careful attention in the study of chloride ion penetration phenomena so as to minimize its damaging effects and extend the service life of these important structures. Studies of non-destructive testing (NDT) of concrete have shown that the following techniques and instruments are applicable to underwater work (Kornska et al 2003, Hedayati 2004). Six elementary types of underwater NDT and monitoring techniques are identified as: Visual, Magnetic, Sonic & Ultrasonic vibration and Radiography.

General surveys for condition monitoring of offshore concrete structures consist primarily of visual inspection and testing for:

1. Broken or bent members
2. Cracking and pitting
3. Corrosion
4. Marine fouling
5. Debris accumulation
6. Corrosion system effectiveness
7. Scouring at plateform base & Sedimentation wash

Since repair and rehabilitation of corroded reinforced concrete marine structures draw significant portion of the budget for infrastructures, the capability to accurately predict deterioration levels due to seawater attack, especially the time-to initiate corrosion, in reinforced concrete structures exposed to chloride-induced corrosion can translate to major economic savings and possible extension of service life of a member or a structure.

7.1 Visual inspection

The most obvious limitation to visual inspection is water clarity. For purposes of this discussion it will be assumed that water clarity is sufficient to allow viewing of at least 1m.The diver is capable of carrying out a survey by feel along in zero visibility, but it is difficult, if not impossible, to qualitatively assess the accuracy of this technique, particularly when the diver is wearing gloves and is uncertain of his location on the structure.

Visual inspections are carried out by divers, submersibles and ROV's. The ability of the human eye to detect cracks, bends, or concrete failure in quay wall structural members or any underwater structure varies considerably, depending upon which of these capabilities is used and the extent of marine fouling and corrosion which has taken place. If inspection place has not been cleaned visual observations can reveal the following:

1. Presence and nature of debris
2. Scope, depth and general nature of marine fouling
3. Collision or impact damage
4. Degradation (scouring) or aggradation (silting) at the sediment/water interface
5. Evidence of cracking (at time there is a color change in organisms immediately over a crack)

On a clean quay wall structure visual observations can reveal, in addition to the above:

1. Corrosion of reinforcements or prestressing tendons in concrete (by surface staining and spalling)
2. Hairline cracks
3. Sulphate attack in concrete (by crumbling)
4. Pitting (by surface relief)
5. Local corrosion (by color and relief)

In all of these instances the observations are surficial and dimensional values are approximations.

7.2 Magnetic reinforcing bar locator

A commercially available magnetic reinforcing bar locator (or pachometer) has been successfully modified for underwater use. The pachometer can be used to determine the location of reinforcing bars or any magnetic material in concrete structures, and either measure the depth of concrete cover or determine the size of the reinforcing bar if one or the other is known. The underwater version is designed for diver application, but it has been modified and used from an ROV.

A magnetic field is generated between two poles at either end of a hand-held probe shaped akin to a telephone receiver. A field is created. The meter measures any disturbance caused by magnetic material passing within the magnetic field generated by the probe. The magnitude of the disturbance is indicated on the instrument meter which may be calibrated to read directly in bar size and distance of the reinforcing bar from the probe. A clean surface is required for highest accuracy from the data acquisition system. The technique can be used as a measure of concrete erosion, or as a measure of reinforcement corrosion.

Techniques are available for approximating each variable if neither is known. Laboratory and field tests of the instrument demonstrated that the modification for underwater use had no effect on the output data.

7.3 Radar

Certain types of radar have been used to evaluate the condition of concrete up to 800 mm thick. Radar can detect delaminations, deteriorations, cracks, and voids. It can also detect and locate changes in material. Radar has been used successfully as an underwater inspection tool, and is being developed for possible future use. Radar with the antenna contained in a custom waterproof housing was used in 1994 in conjunction with pulse velocity testing to investigate the structural integrity in a concrete plug submerged 46 m in a water supply tunnel.

7.4 Ultrasonic testing

Ultra sonic NDT methods are employed underwater to detect and locate discontinuities or flaws and to measure thickness in steel, concrete and wooden structures and is capable of detecting internal material defects. (or any material which will transmit vibrational energy).
In the ultrasonic method an electric pulse is generated in the test instrument and transmitted to a transducer which converts the electronic pulse into mechanical vibrations. The vibrations are transmitted into the object being tested where they are scattered, attenuated, reflected or resonated. A portion of this energy returns to the transducer where it is reconverted to electonical energy and transmitted to the test instrument where it is amplified and displayed digitally. Interpretation of the data for defect presence, sizing, and significance must be conducted by highly skilled ultrasonic NDT technicians. The sound frequency emitted by the transducer for metals testing is high, generally in the range of 3.5 to 5 MHz.
Two different test techniques are used in ultrasonic NDT: Resonance techniques and pulse techniques. Resonance techniques are employed for measurement of test object thickness by measuring from one side only. Ultrasonic pulse techniques are used for flaw detection and may be classified as pulse echo wherein a single (transmit/receive) transducer is used, or through transmission wherein two transducers (one transmitter; one receiver) are employed. For Underwater testing ultrasonic pulse echo signal transducer and techniques are used exclusively.
As stated above, pulse velocity is determined by measuring the time of transmission of a pulse of energy through a known distance of concrete. In addition the measuring methods are divided in two ways: immersion and contact. In immersion testing the transducer is separated from the object but in contact testing the transducer is placed directly against the test object and mostly used in offshore inspection. Many factors affect the results, including aggregate content and reinforcing steel location. The results obtained are quantitative, but they are only relative in nature.
A special form of this technique is the pulse-echo method. The pulse-echo method has been used for the in-place determination of the length and condition of concrete piles.

7.4.1 Echo sounders

Another ultrasonic device, the echo sounders (specialty fathometers), can be useful for underwater rehabilitation work using termite concrete, both to delineate the void to be filled and to confirm the level of the tremie concrete placed. They are also effective in checking scour depth in a stream bed. They consist of a transducer that is suspended in the water, a sending/receiving device, and a recording chart or screen output that displays the water depth. High-frequency sound waves emitted from the transducer travel through the water until they strike the bottom and are reflected back to the transducer. The echo sounder measures the transit time of these waves and converts it to water depth shown on the display. When an echo sounder is used very close to the structure, however, erroneous returns may occur from the underwater structural elements.

7.4.2 Side-scan sonar

Side scan sonar images have been used to get detailed information about the seafloor (Fig.5). During the last three decades, advanced technologies lead to the increased use of digital collection with side scan instruments. A side-scan sonar system is similar to the standard bottom-looking echo sounder, except that the signal from the transducer is directed laterally, producing two sides looking beams. The system consists of a pair of transducers mounted in an underwater housing, or "fish," and a dual- channel recorder connected to the fish by a conductive cable. In the past several years, the side-scan technique has been used to map surfaces other than the ocean bottom. Successful trials have been conducted on the slopes of ice islands and breakwaters, and on vertical pier structures. Although the side-scan sonar technique permits a broad- scale view of the underwater structure, the broad beam and lack of resolution make it unsuitable for obtaining the kind of data required from local inspections of concrete structures.

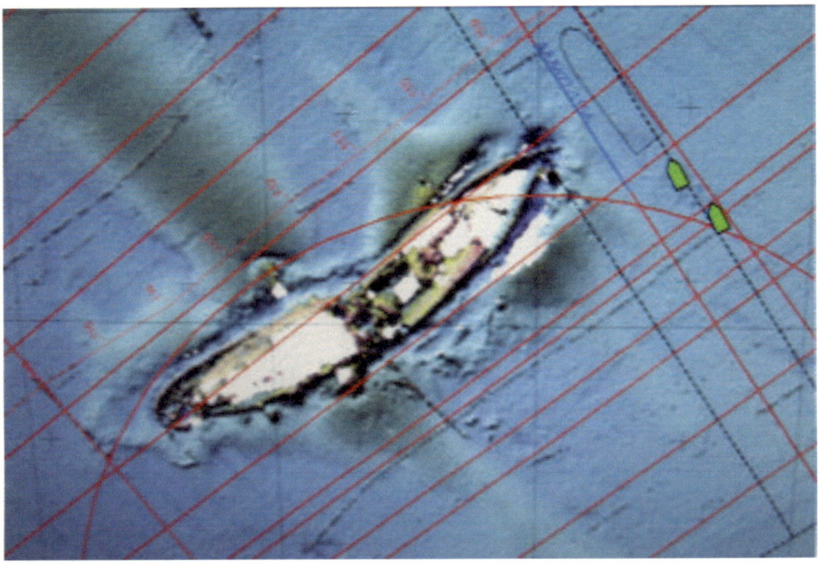

Fig. 5. Application of side-scan sonar in a salvage project and study of bottom protection by authors (Persian Gulf)

7.5 Underwater acoustic profilers

Because of known prior developmental work on an experimental acoustic system, acoustic profiling has been considered for mapping underwater structures. Erosion and down faulting of submerged structures have always been difficult to accurately map using standard acoustic (sonic) surveys because of limitations of the various systems. Sonic surveys, side-scan sonar, and other underwater mapping tools are designed primarily to see targets rising above the plane of the sea floor. Sampling and destructive testing also can be use when other methods are not possible. Produced by impacts on solid material as opposed to disbonded/delaminated material. Understanding the force-time function aids an inspector's abilities to sonically evaluate a material, as it takes less time for two elastic solids to separate subsequent to a collision. A similar analogy could be made by comparing the effect of walking on a sidewalk to walking in the mud. The sinking phenomenon that one experiences in the mud is similar to the extended time length of impact produced by a delaminated material. The "sinking" of the hammer or coin into the delaminated material results in a plastic deformation of the material, resulting in a duller or hollow sound.

The electronics industry has provided inspectors with equipment that is capable of detecting and recording the sonic wave signals that are produced by an impact. As a result, there are currently several commercially available products available for such signal acquisition. The most common devices for sonic data acquisition are the instrumented hammer and the smart hammer. The instrumented hammer was developed for the airline industry to be used in the detection of anomalies in airplane materials. It measures and records the force-time history and amplitude frequency of an impact via the use of an accelerometer embedded in the head of the hammer. The smart hammer was developed for the shipbuilding industry. This instrument measures and records the sonic response of an impact through a microphone. The microphone uses the sonic data, instead of the force data, to create an acoustic signal. Both impact-force data generators and impact-sound data generators have been proven to generate useful signals for non-destructive sonic testing. The information gained. Fig.6. illustrates the block diagram of proposed non destructive sonic testing system.

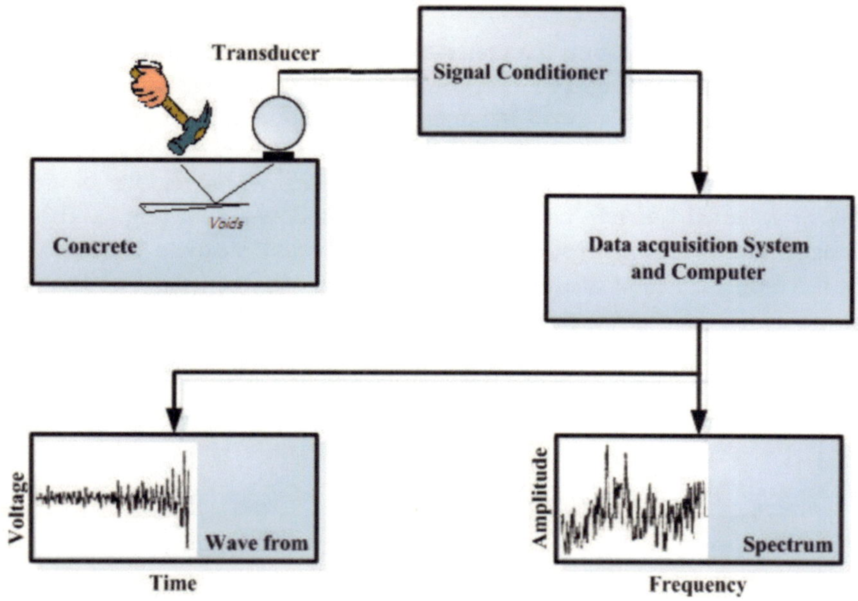

Fig. 6. Schematic diagram showing how impact-echo of proposed system works

7.5.1 Acoustic sounding

Acoustic sounding is used for surveying concrete structures to ascertain the presence of delaminations. Delaminations can be a result of poor concrete quality, debonding of overlays or applied composites, corrosion of reinforcement, freezing and thawing or global softening. The test procedures used for delineating delaminations through sounding include: coin tap, chain drag, hammer drag, and an electro-mechanical sounding device. The purpose of each test is to sonically detect deficiencies in the concrete. The American Society for Testing and Materials (ASTM) has created a standard, ASTM D 4580 – 86, which covers the evaluation of delaminations. The standard describes procedures for both automated and manual surveys of concrete. A major advantage to sonic testing is that it produces immediate results on near surface anomalies. The effectiveness of sonic testing relies heavily on the user's expertise in signal interpretation and consistency.

Soundings are taken by striking the concrete surface to locate areas of internal voids or delamination of the concrete cover. Although the results are only qualitative in nature, the method is rapid and economical and enables an expeditious determination of the overall condition. The inspector's ability to hear sound in water is reduced by waves, currents, and background noise. Soundings are the most elementary of NDT methods (Wu T et al 2000).

7.5.1.1 Impact hammer

A standard impact hammer (ASTM C 805), modified for underwater use, can be used for rapid surveys of concrete surface hardness. The underwater readings, however, are generally higher than comparable data obtained in dry conditions. These higher readings could be eliminated by further redesigning of the Schmidt hammer for underwater use. Data also can be normalized to eliminate the effect of higher underwater readings.

7.5.1.2 Coin-tap test

This important method of testing the concrete is one of the deepseated and most widely researched ways of sonic testing. The test procedure requires the inspector or operator to tap on the concrete sample with a small hammer, coin, or some other rigid object (impactor) while listening or recording the sound resulting from the impact. Areas of nondelaminated concrete will create a clear ringing sound upon impact while regions of delaminated, disbonded, or softened concrete will create a dull or hollow sound (Fig.7). This change in sonic characteristics is a direct result of a change in effective stiffness of the material. As a result, the force-time function of an impact and its resulting frequencies of an impact differ between areas of good and poor quality concrete (Cawley & Adams 1988)

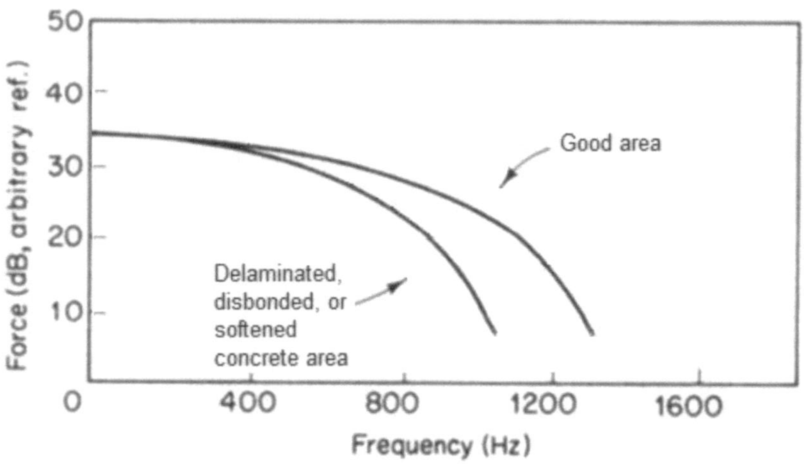

Fig. 7. Spectra of time histories for a typical tap test results

8. Spectru & cepstrum analysis

The vibration spectrum can be expressed on a linear frequency scale with constant bandwidth. This type of spectrum provides fine resolution at higher frequencies but a poor resolution at lower frequencies. Whereas a constant percentage bandwidth analyzer uses

logarithmic frequency scale and cover three decades with equal resolution. It is for this reason that the best analysis method for the comparison of spectra and fault detection is the use of constant percentage bandwidth with a logarithmic frequency scale (Farid Uddin 2003).
Cepstrum analysis is carried out to identify a series of harmonics or sidebands in the spectrum. Cepstrum may be considered to be the frequency analysis of frequency analysis. The power cepstrum is defined as:

$$C_p(\tau) = F^{-1}\{\log F_{xx}(f)\} \tag{1}$$

Where $f_x(t)$ is the time signal and its Fourier transform is

$$F_{xx}(f).$$

Fig. 8. shows a spectrum from a concrete structure in its deteriorated condition. It contains several harmonics. It is not possible to detect from this spectrum that there are two series of harmonics indicating two different phenomena.

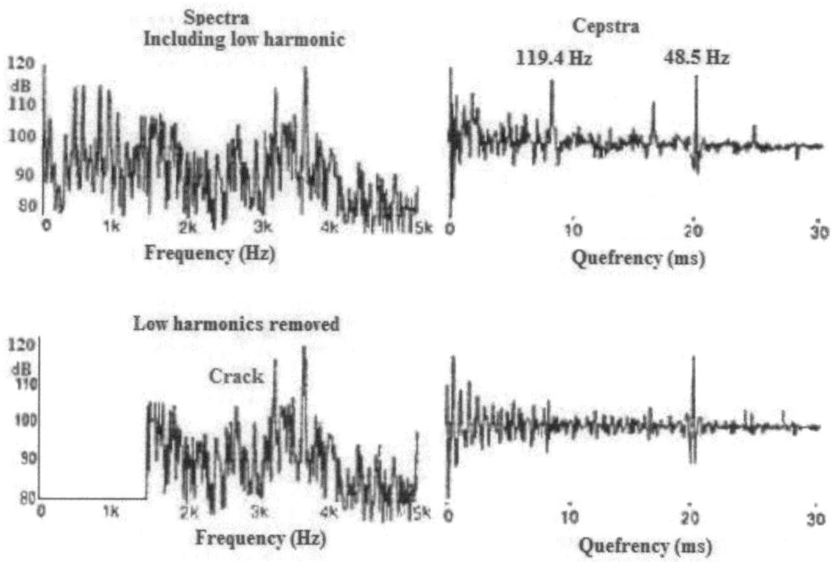

Fig. 8. The spectrum from a concrete structure in its deteriorated condition

Cepstrum of this spectrum is also give in the side. It may be seen that the cepstrum identifies these two families of harmonics (with a spacing of 48.5 Hz and 119.4 Hz respectively). Fig. 9 shows the edited spectrum such that frequencies below that of half of the impactor frequency are removed. The cepstrum of this spectrum is then calculated. The cepstrum does not show the 119.4 Hz component at all. It indicates that this component originates from the lower frequency range. The cepstrum does retain the 48.5 Hz component indicating its origin in the medium frequency range. It may thus be concluded that the impactor effect on the tested structure at 49.8 Hz may have an incipient fault while the recorded components at 119.4 Hz indicates delamination, voids or other fault.

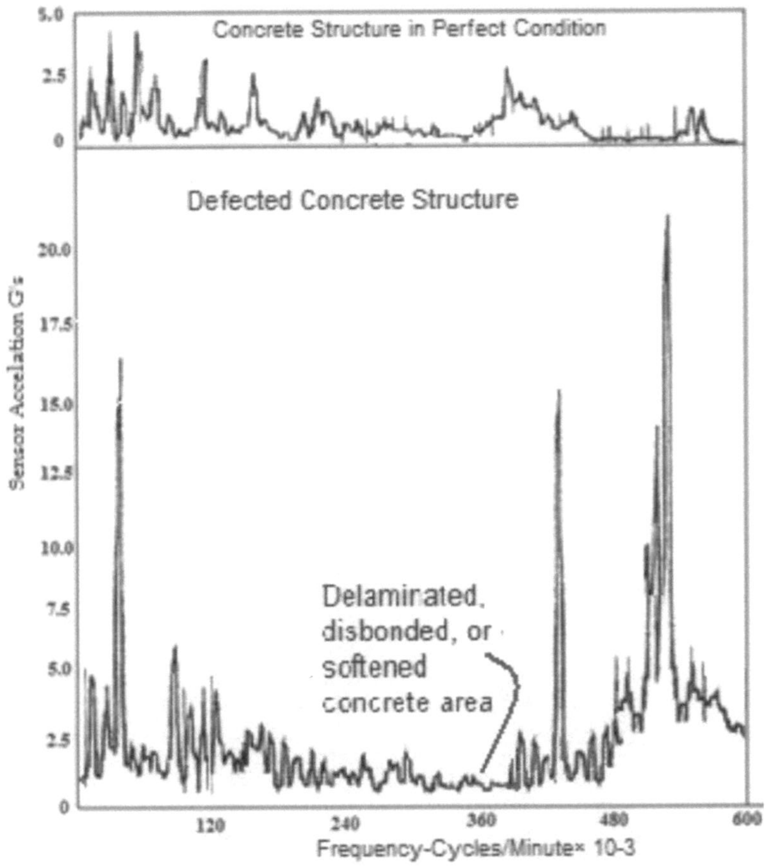

Fig. 9. Frequencies below that of half of the impactor frequency are removed.

In this research the Acousto - Vibration (AV) technology utilized to detect defects, such as voids and mix separations in the constructed pats.

9. Conclusion

The Reinforced Concrete Structure Diagnosis Expert System is implemented through this research work as a prototype rule based system using the Professional expert system shell. It is apparent that in the proposed method, the perfect undersea concrete structure should not produce vibration signals more than the normal value. This is never the case, for it is impossible to eliminate all asymmetries in the materials and geometry of the concrete and steel armor in the structure. It results from the measurements having been carried out that several predominant frequencies arise in the specimens under test.

To extract knowledge from the expert the knowledge engineer must become familiar with problem of vibration and acoustic analysis. The rule base system is goal driven using backward chaining strategy to test the collected structure vibration and acoustic properties information is true. The case specific data plus the above information with the help of explanation subsystem, allows the program to explain its reasoning to the user and will provide the expert system shell requirements. Significant difference can exist between the signals created by subsea concrete defects. The respective amplitudes of the mentioned signals may exceed each other in a different way in repeated measurements of the same specimen. This device serves as a base for development of expert system monitoring module. The change of reference signal with proposed expert system implies that something within the subsea concrete structure has altered and diagnosis is made.

By integrating the different modules, the proposed system has the power to provide diagnosis of problems in reinforced concrete harbor structures. This can assist civil engineering trainees, inspectorate staff, professional engineers as well as their top harbor management personnel regarding the likely problems so that early action can be taken.

The present work will be particularly of great assistance to new comers who are not familiar with the field and will facilitate them in gaining a better understanding of the causes of the problems and in making decisions about any necessary actions

10. References

British Standards Institution, (1985) "BS 8110: Part 1, Structural Use of Concrete", ,London.

British Standards Institution, (1991) "BS 5328: Parts 1 to 4, Specification of Concrete", London.

Cawley, P. and Adams, R.D. (1988) 'The Mechanics of the Coin-Tap Method of Non-Destructive Testing', J. Sound and Vibration, Vol 122, pp.299-316

Dym, Clive L. and Levitt, Raymond E.,(1991)"Knowledge Based Systems in Engineering",McGraw-Hill, New York, 1991, pp. 15& 404 ISBN. O-O7-018563-8.

Filippetti F., et al.(1992).Development of expert system knowledge base to on-line diagnosis of rotor electrical faults of induction motors. IEEE-Industry Applications Society Annual Meeting, Bologna, pp. 92-99

Farid Uddin A. K. M., Ohtsu M, Hossain K. M. A., and Lachemi M (2007).Simulation of reinforcement-corrosion-induced crack propagation in concrete by acoustic emission technique and boundary lement method analysis. Canadian J. of Civil Engineering, Oct , vol. 34, , no. 10, pp. 1197-1207

Graham-Jones, P. J., Mellor B. G. (1995) "Expert and knowledge-based systems in failure analysis" Engineering Failure Analysis, Volume 2, Issue 2, June, pp.137-149

Hughes, D.M. (1972) "Underwater inspection of offshore structructurs - method and results. Proc. Offshore Tech. Conf.,V.I, pp.541-546

Hedayati M. R. (2004).On-line condition monitoring of locomotives. Proceeding 7thRailway conf., Tehran, Iran. pp. 217-223

Hedayati M.R., (2009). Sub-sea fiber optic cable maintenance using a ROV-based flux leakage expert system. Journal of Artificial Life and Robotics 14(4):pp511-514

Korenska M, Chobola Z., Mikulková P., and Martinek J.(2003). On the application of impact-echo method to assess the quality of ceramic roofing tiles. IV. Conf. MATBUD, Krakow, pp. 239 - 244

Roddis, W. M. Kim, and Pasley, Gregory P., (1993) "Knowledge-Based Expert Systems in Concrete Materials: Uniting Specifications, Data, and Models," Presentation at the 1993 Fall Convention, American Concrete Institute

Skala J. and Chobola Z (2005), "Frequency Inspection as a Tool to Assess the Armature Corrosion. Workshop NDT 2005 Non- Destructive Testing at Engineering, Brno,pp. 159-161

WU, T. T. et al., (2000).On the Study of Elastic Wave Scattering and Rayleigh Wave Velocity Measurement of Concrete with Steel Bar. vol. 33, UK: NDT & E International, pp. 401-407

Part 3

Automation & Control

13

Conceptual Model Development for a Knowledge Base of PID Controllers Tuning in Open Loop

José Luis Calvo-Rolle[1], Ramón Ferreiro García[1], Antonio Couce Casanova[1], Héctor Quintián-Pardo[1] and Héctor Alaiz-Moreton[2]
[1]*University of Coruña*
[2]*University of León*
Spain

1. Introduction

In the area of control engineering work must be constant to obtain new methods of regulation, to alleviate the deficiencies in the already existing ones, or to find alternative improvements to the ones that were being used previously. This huge demand of control applications is due to the wide range of possibilities developed to this day.

Regardless of this increasing rhythm of discovery of different possibilities, it has been impossible at this moment to oust relatively popular techniques, as can be the 'traditional' PID control. Since the discovery of this type of regulators by Nicholas Minorsky (Mindell (2004) and Bennett (1984)) in 1922 to this day, many have been the works carried out about this controller. In this period of time there was an initial stage, in which the resolution of the problem was done analogically and in it the advances were not as notable as have been since the introduction of the computer, which permits to implement the known direct digital control structure Auslander et al. (1978), illustrated in figure 1.

Since then, the regulators have passed from being implemented in an analogous way to develop its algorithm control digitally, by signal digital processors. As well as carrying out the classic PID control in digital form, its development based on computer allows adding features to the regulator that with difficulty could have been obtained analogically.

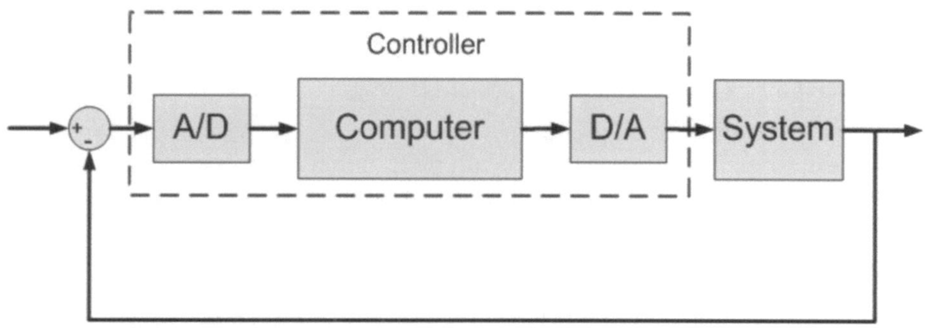

Fig. 1. Structure of direct digital control

It must be said there exist usual control techniques for the processes in any area, in which innovations have been introduced. But nevertheless, the vast majority of these techniques in their implementation employ PID traditional controllers, although in an improved way, increasing the percentage of use around 95% Astrom & Hagglund (2006). Its use is still very high due to various reasons like: robustness, reliability, relative simplicity, fault, etc.
The great problem of the PID control is the adjustment of the parameters that it incorporates. Above all in its topology Astrom & Hagglund (2006) Feng & Tan (1998), as a consequence of the investigations carried out in the area, the contributions made by specialists have been many, existing among them many methods to obtain the parameters that define this regulator, achieved through different ways, and working conditions pertaining to the plant being controlled. It must be highlighted that the methods developed to obtain the terms which in occasions are empiric if they are always directed to optimise defined specifications; the negative thing is that frequently when some are improved others get worse.
It is necessary to highlight that the empirical methods have been the first in to be discovered and normally they are the ones who are first learnt, in the training of technicians in this discipline. In this sense the parameters obtained in this manner through the application of formulas of different authors, are a starting point of adjustment of the regulator, being normally necessary to have to do fine adjustment.
Regardless of what has been said, in practice there is a big variety of regulators working in the industry with an adjustment far from what can be considered optimum Astrom & Hagglund (2006). This fact is originated among other reasons due to a lack of adjustment techniques by the users.
This fact creates the necessity to employ intelligent systems, due to the demand of a better performance and resolution of complex problems both for men as well as for the machines. Gradually the time restrictions imposed in the decision making are stronger and the knowledge has turned out to be an important strategic resource to help the people handling the information, with the complexity that this involves. In the industry world, intelligent systems are used in the optimization of processes and systems related with control, diagnosis and repair of problems. One of the techniques employed nowadays are knowledge based systems, which are one of the streams of artificial intelligence.
The development of knowledge based systems is very useful for certain knowledge domains, and also indispensable in others. Some of the more important advantages that the knowledge based systems offer are the following:

- Permanence: Unlike a human expert, a knowledge based system does not grow old, and so it does not suffer loss of faculties with the pass of time.
- Duplication: Once a knowledge based system is programmed we can duplicate countless times, which reduces the costs.
- Fast: A knowledge based system can obtain information from a data base and can make numeric calculations quicker than any human being.
- Low cost: Although the initial cost can be high, thanks to the duplication capacity the final cost is low.
- Dangerous environments: A knowledge based system can work in dangerous or harmful environments for the human being.
- Reliability: A knowledge based system is not affected by external conditions, a human being yes (tiredness, pressure, etc).

- Reasoning explanation: It helps justify the exits in the case of problematic or critical domain. This quality can be employed to train personnel not qualified in the area of the application.

Up to now the existing knowledge based systems for resolution of control systems have reduced features (Pang (1991) Wilson (2005) Zhou & Li (2005) Epshtein (2000) Pang et al. (1994) Pang (1993)), summarizing, in application of the method known as "Gain Schedulling" ?, which is based in programming the profits of the regulator with reference to the states variables of the process. For the cases in which the number of control capacities have increased, the knowledge based system, is applicable to specific problems. There is the possibility to implement knowledge based systems programming them in the devices, but without taking advantage of the existing specific tools of Knowledge Engineering Calvo-Rolle (2007) Calvo-Rolle & Corchado (n.d.).
In accordance with what has been said, the development of a PID conceptual model is described in this document to obtain the parameters of a regulator PID with the empirical adjustment method in an open loop; feasible in the great majority of cases in which such method is applicable. The model has been developed for six groups of different expressions (formulas) with highly satisfactory results, and of course expandable to more following the same methodology.
The present document is structured starting with a brief introduction topology PID regulator employed, along with the traditional technique of which the conceptual method is derived, an explanation of the method proposed that is divided in three parts: In the first part the tests done to representative systems are explained, in the second part how the rules have been obtained and in the third how the knowledge has been organised. It concludes with the validation of the proposed technique.

2. PID controller

There are multiple forms of representation of the PID regulator, but perhaps the most extended and studied one is the one given by equation 1.

$$u(t) = K\left[e(t) + \frac{1}{Ti}\int_0^t e(t)dt + Td\frac{de(t)}{dt}\right] \tag{1}$$

where u is the control variable and e is the error of control given by the $e = y_{SP} - y$ (difference between the specified reference by the entry and exit measured of the process). Therefore, the variable of control is the sum of three different terms: P which is proportional to the error, I which is proportional to the integral of the error and D which is proportional to the derivative of the error (expression 2). The parameters of the controller are: the gain proportional K, the integral time T_i and the derivative time T_d. If the function transfer of the controller is obtained and a representation of the complex variable is done, the form is the one illustrated in expression 2.

$$G_C(s) = \frac{U(s)}{E(s)} = K\left(1 + \frac{1}{T_i \cdot s} + T_d \cdot s\right) \tag{2}$$

There are several forms for the representation of a PID regulator, but for the implementation of the PID regulator used, defined in the previous formula and more commonly known as the Standard format Astrom & Hagglund (2006) Feng & Tan (1998), shown in the form of blocks in figure 2.

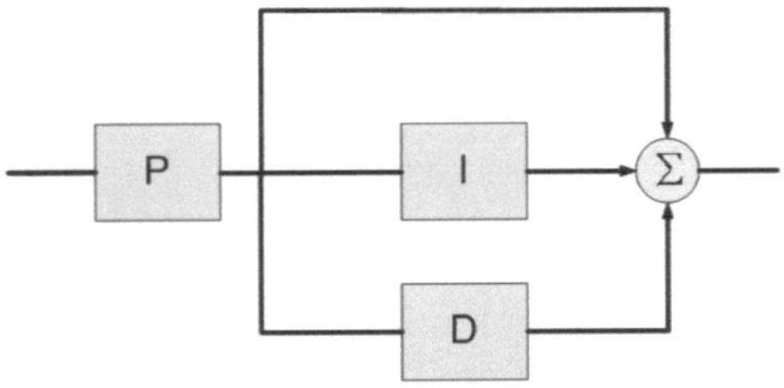

Fig. 2. PID regulator in standard topology

Infinite are the industrial processes whose normal function is not the adequate for certain applications. This problem, in many cases, is resolved through the employment of this regulator, with which defined specifications are obtained in the control of processes leading to optimum values for what was being done. The adjustment of this controller is carried out varying the proportional gain and the integral and derivative times.

3. Adjustment of the open loop of PID regulators

It is true that to this day there are analytical methodologies to obtain the parameters of a PID regulator, with the aim of obtaining an improved one or various specifications. From a chronological point of view, the empirical procedures were born before the obtaining of the parameters, and currently they are still used for various reasons like: the parameters are obtained in an empiric way, they are simple techniques, a given characteristic is optimized, good results are obtained in many cases, there is usually always a rule for the case that is trying to be controlled, etc.

3.1 Steps to obtain the parameters

The empiric techniques are based on the following steps:

1. Experimental establishment of certain characteristics of the response of the process that can be carried out with the plant working in open loop.
2. Application of formulas depending on the data previously obtained, to get the parameters of the regulator, with the aim that the function of the plant with the controller is within certain desired specifications.

3.2 Adjustment criteria

In the second stage the fact of situating the process within some desired specifications is stressed. From the point of view of the empiric adjustment it makes sense to talk about two types of principal specifications of the system in open loop, which are the ones stated hereafter:

1. Set point control: this specification indicates the capacity of the regulated system to achieve the changes made in the reference value.
2. Load disturbance: consists in the capacity of the system to attenuate possible noises or disturbances the charge/ load in a constant value of the reference value desired.

In figure 3 two examples can be observed of a system regulated by two PID controllers, adjusted to optimize both specifications previously mentioned. To the regulated systems a unit step is introduced, and after some time a disruption is provoked. As can be seen in the

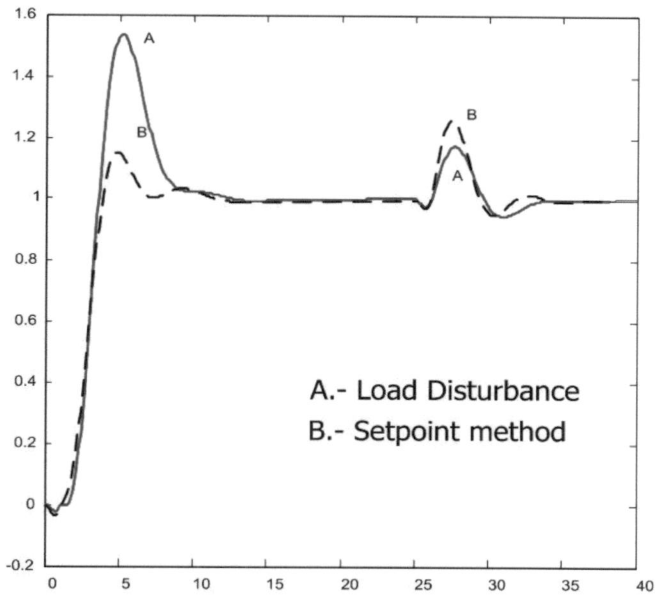

Fig. 3. Comparative between the Set point and Load disturbance response methods

curve identified as A corresponds to an adjusted regulator to improve the load disturbance criterion and, clearly the disturbance has less effect than in the set point response. With reference to curve B, the object was to regulate the system to improve set point control criterion, and it is done in a more effective way, because in the case of the initial step the temporary response is better than curve A, however it must be highlighted that in the disturbance the sensitivity is higher for curve B.
If various formulas are employed in the tuning, the one chosen will be the one with a more prudent response within the specification that is intended to achieve, and after that increasing or decreasing the influence of the parameters of the controller until the response requested is reached, avoiding to take the plant to a non desired functioning area.
After this, most different tuning criteria are discussed, making a classification according to experimental testing of the response features of the system carried out in open loop.

3.3 Measurements of the characteristics of the response of the process

Within the steps to follow mentioned earlier, to obtain the parameters of the PID regulator, of them, in which the purpose is to measure characteristics of the response of the process, can be done in different ways, by obtaining different results in some cases and very similar in others. These ways to obtain process characteristics are explained in the next sections called *MeasurementA* and *MeasurementB*.

3.3.1 Measurement A

The first method to get the parameters is based on the response of a system with a unit step input, similar to the one shown in figure 4.
This is the typical output of industrial processes with a unit step input, and that can be usually known as reaction curve. It gets near the response of a first order model with delay whose transfer function is the one shown in expression 3.

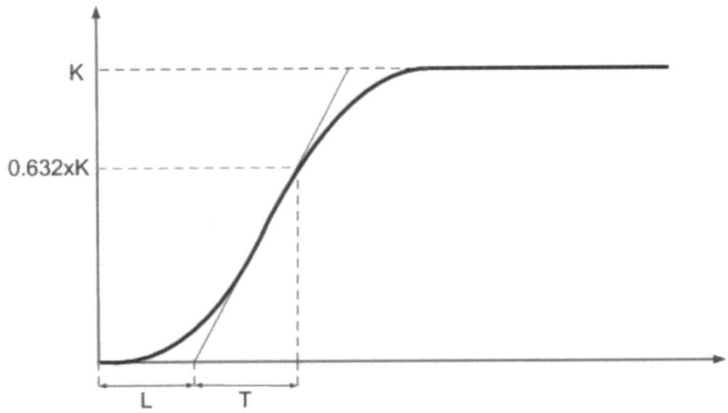

Fig. 4. Measurement A

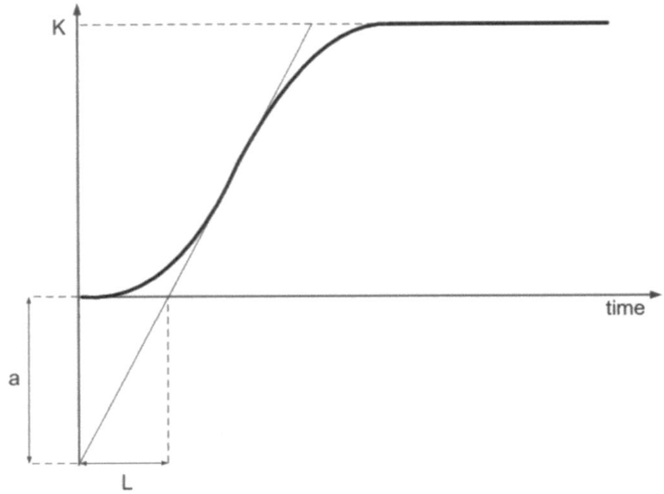

Fig. 5. Measurement B

$$G(s) = \frac{K}{1 + T \cdot s} e^{-s \cdot L} \tag{3}$$

The parameters L and T come from drawing a straight line in the point of maximum slope of the curve. L is found where the mentioned straight line cuts the axis of X and T comes from prolonging the straight line up to the cut with the corresponding horizontal to 63.2% of the value of the gain K of the system (steady state value with a unit step input), cutting point in which is situated the sum of the L and T in its X coordinate.

3.3.2 Measurement B

In this case, there is the same response than in the last case, what occurs is that the measurement is made for a different approximation. The graphic in which the measurement is made is shown in figure 5.

As it can be observed what is done in this case is prolong the line with the greater slope up to its cut with the Y axis, value which is defined as "a". And so a model with two parameters is obtained, with one transfer function represented by an integrator with a pure delay. In this case the system gets close to the transfer function according to the expression 4.

$$G(s) = \frac{a}{L \cdot s} e^{-s \cdot L} \tag{4}$$

3.4 Parameters calculation through application of formulas

Once the characteristics of the response of the process have been measured and it is acknowledged what specification wants to be optimized, the following is to apply formulas developed to fulfil the description sought, bearing in mind the scopes of application for which they were obtained. The application range for the case of empiric adjustment in an open loop comes defined usually by the existing relationship between the time delay L, and the time of increase T of the system with unit step input.

Different authors propose expressions, in function of the characteristics of the transient response measured, for the achievement of the parameters of the regulator. It must be highlighted that there are multiple expressions given, that work in an adequate form in certain cases for which they were developed. It is frequent also that the manufacturers of controllers deduce their own expressions that work satisfactory above all with the products that they manufacture and especially for those applications to which they are destined. Is must highlighted that there are no general equations that always work well, because of this it will be necessary to select the expressions that best adjust in each specific case to the control that is intended.

In this case study there are gathered those more known and usual ones Ziegler (1942) Kaya (1988) Chien (1952) that are employed in the achievement of the parameters of the PID regulators, even though the methodology followed can be used for any case. In table 1 the different expressions are used in the present study are shown, together with the scope of application in each case.

4. Design rules of PID regulators in open loop

In the first part of this section it is made a sweep at the different expressions of achievement of parameters of the PID regulator previously mentioned, in which the systems are controlled with this type of regulator, with the aim of obtaining some generic design rules, or in their case particular rules for certain types of systems.

Due to the general character of the rules it will be necessary to employ for them significant systems. In this aspect it has been opted to use a known source in this scope, which is the Benchmark of systems to control PID developed by Åström and Hagglund Astrom (2000). In this source a collection of systems is presented that: are usually employed in the testing of PID controllers, these systems are based in countless sources of importance and also the immense majority of the existing systems adapt to some of those included in this source.

4.1 Benchmark systems to which open loop empiric adjustment is not applicable

There are a set of systems included in the Benchmarking to which the empiric adjustment in open loop is not applicable. If for instance there is a system whose transfer function is the expression 5, which deals with a system of first order.

$$G(s) = \frac{1}{s+1} \tag{5}$$

Method	K_p	T_i	T_d	Application range
Ziegler-Nichols	$\frac{1.2}{a}$	$2 \cdot L$	$0.5 \cdot L$	$0.1 \leq \frac{L}{T} \leq 1$
Kaya-Scheib Set point regulation minimize IAE	$\frac{0.95}{K}\left(\frac{T}{L}\right)^{1.04432}$	$\frac{T}{0.9895+0.09539\frac{L}{T}}$	$0.50814 \cdot T\left(\frac{L}{T}\right)^{1.08433}$	$0 \leq \frac{L}{T} \leq 1$
Kaya-Scheib Set point regulation minimize ISE	$\frac{0.71959}{K}\left(\frac{T}{L}\right)^{1.03092}$	$\frac{T}{1.12666-0.18145\frac{L}{T}}$	$0.54568 \cdot T\left(\frac{L}{T}\right)^{0.86411}$	$0 \leq \frac{L}{T} \leq 1$
Kaya-Scheib Set point regulation minimize ITAE	$\frac{1.12762}{K}\left(\frac{T}{L}\right)^{0.80368}$	$\frac{T}{0.99783-0.02860\frac{L}{T}}$	$0.42844 \cdot T\left(\frac{L}{T}\right)^{1.0081}$	$0 \leq \frac{L}{T} \leq 1$
Chien, Hrones y Reswick load disturbances (0% overshoot)	$\frac{0.95}{a}$	$2.4 \cdot L$	$0.42 \cdot L$	$0.11 \leq \frac{L}{T} \leq 1$
Chien, Hrones y Reswick load disturbances (20% overshoot)	$\frac{1.2}{a}$	$2.0 \cdot L$	$0.42 \cdot L$	$0.11 \leq \frac{L}{T} \leq 1$
Chien, Hrones y Reswick Set point regulation (0% overshoot)	$\frac{0.6}{a}$	T	$0.5 \cdot L$	$0.11 \leq \frac{L}{T} \leq 1$
Chien, Hrones y Reswick (20% overshoot)	$\frac{0.95}{a}$	$1.4 \cdot T$	$0.47 \cdot L$	$0.11 \leq \frac{L}{T} \leq 1$

Table 1. Expressions of parameters of authors and scopes of application

Analyzing its output after introducing unit step, as can be seen in figure 6, the delay time L is inexistent. This leads to two consequences: the first is that it would be out of range for all the cases contemplated in the case study, and the second is that the parameters that would depend on L in the expressions is zero.

If there is a system with a transfer function as the one in the expression 6, which is an unstable system, when introducing a step type input, in no case it will not offer a limited exit and in consequence there is no L and T to introduce in different expressions.

$$G(s) = \frac{1}{s^2 - 1} \tag{6}$$

Another possibility within the contemplated functions in the Benchmark is the systems that possess an integral action like the one in expression 7

$$G(s) = \frac{1}{s^2 + s} \tag{7}$$

If a step input is introduced, the output has a form like the one indicated in figure 7. In it clearly it can be appreciated, that the output tends to infinite (saturation in real systems), and the time necessary raise time T cannot be obtained in the expressions to obtain the parameters, and therefore it is not applicable.

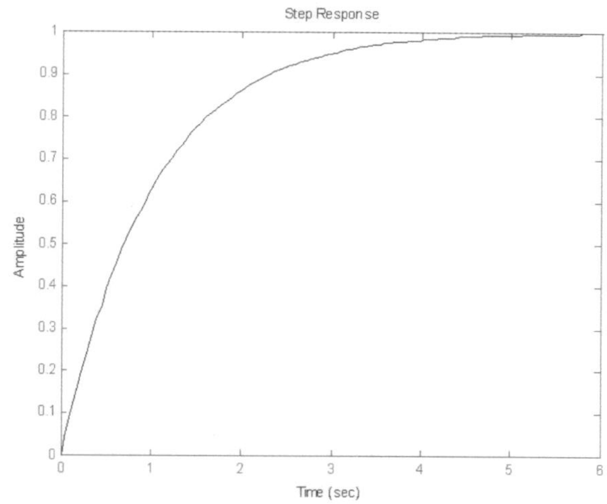

Fig. 6. First order system step response

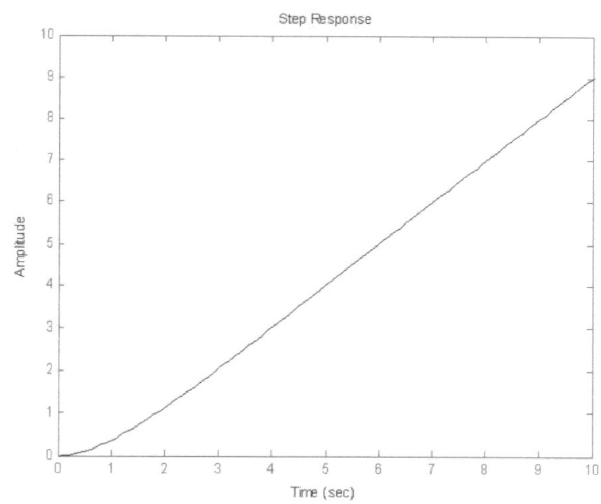

Fig. 7. System with integral action step response

4.2 Benchmark systems to which empiric adjustment in open loop is applicable

Apart from the types of systems that are found in some of the examples of the previous section, the rest can be regulated by a controller PID applying the empiric adjustment in open loop to obtain its parameters. If there is a transfer function like the one in expression 8, and an input step is introduced, the response value of the system is the one of figure 8, the so called reaction curve.

$$G(s) = \frac{1}{(s+1)^2} \tag{8}$$

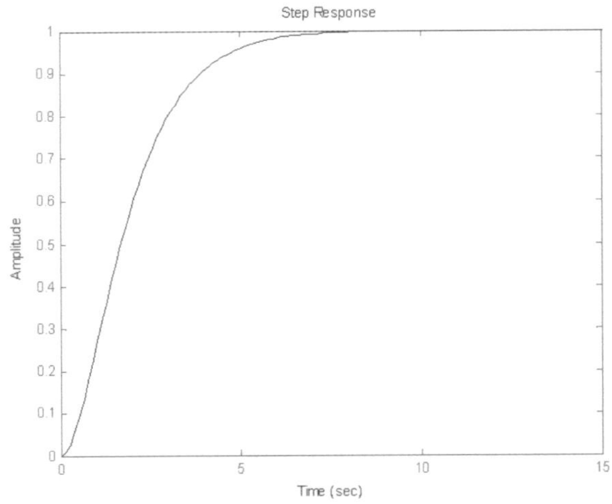

Fig. 8. Step response with typical reaction curve output

The features are set from the response of the process, in the graph of figure 8 obtaining in this case a value of $L = 0.2817$ and of $T = 2.7183$, what originates a relation $L/T = 0.1036$, that according to the application ranges, all the groups of expressions are viable except Chien, Hrones and Reswick expressions. Nevertheless analysis will be carried out in all the cases contemplated.

4.3 Analysis of the methods applied to obtain the rules

Having obtained the reaction curve and in consequence the characteristics of the response of the system, regulating it with the different expressions in the case study proceeds, extracting significant specifications like: response time, peak time, overshoot and settle time.
All the tests will be carried out on all the systems proposed Åström in Benchmark in which they are applicable, to check the results and be able to extract conclusions from which rules will be obtained. If system of the expression 8 is regulated, the results obtained are illustrated in figures 9 and 10.

5. PID controller conceptual modeling

The conceptual model of a domain consists in the strictest organization possible of knowledge from the perspective of the human brain. In this sense for the domain that is being dealt with in this case study, a general summarized model is proposed and shown in figure 11.
As can be observed it is divided in three blocks:

- Organization of the existing rules: In this block the aim is to organise the existing rules of the types of expressions, scopes of application range, change criteria in the load disturbance or follow up of the set point control criterion, etc.
- Organization of existing knowledge with new rules: This block is the meeting point between the other two, and it aims to organise the existing knowledge in an adequate way for which it will be necessary to create new rules.

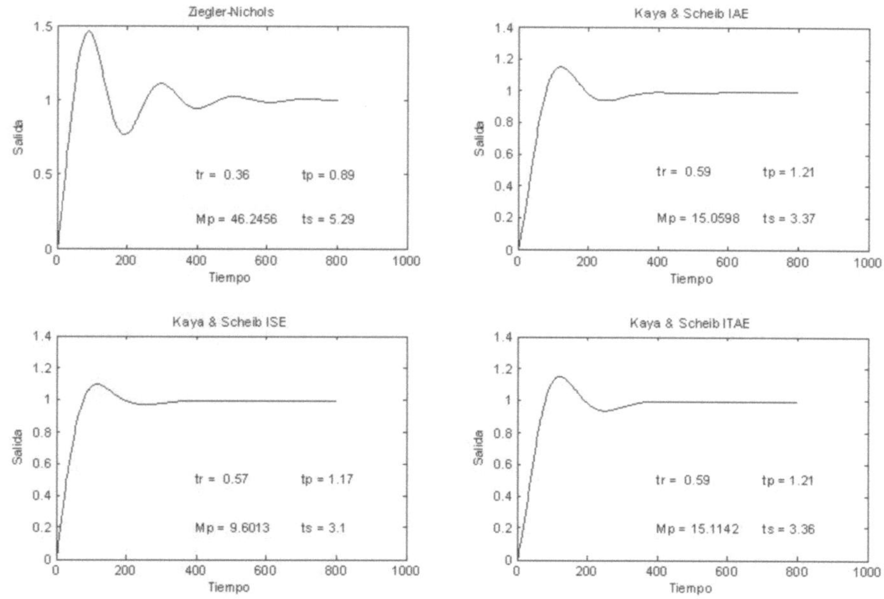

Fig. 9. Response of the system regulated by the expressions of Ziegler-Nichols and Kaya-Sheib for IAE, ISE and ITAE

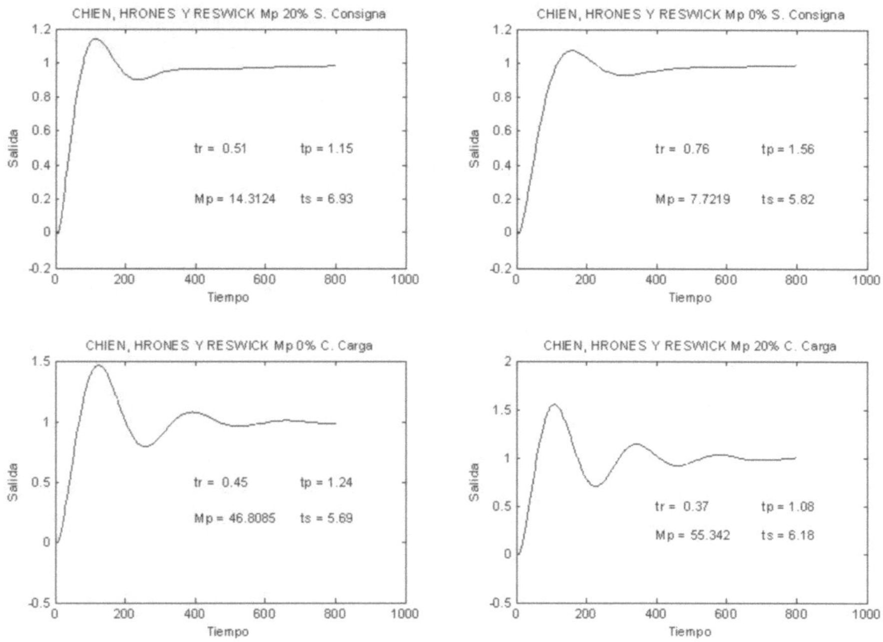

Fig. 10. Response of the system regulated by the expressions of Chien, Hrones and Reswick

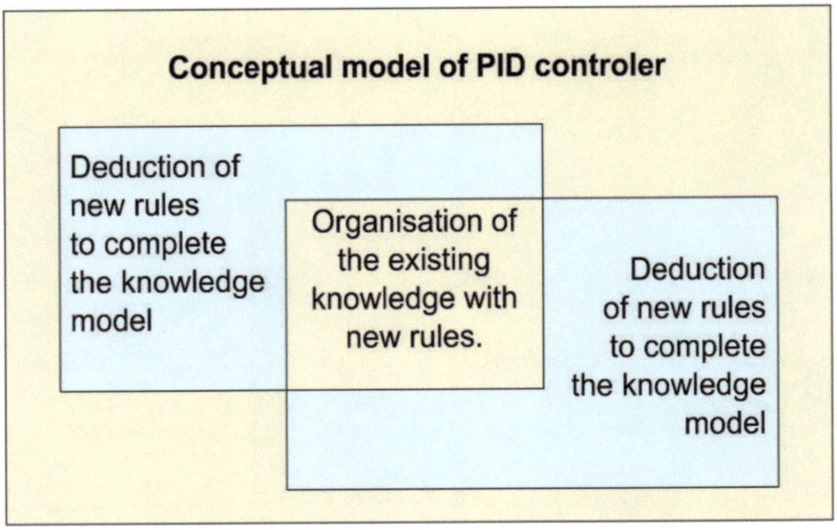

Fig. 11. General schema summarized from the conceptual model of empiric adjustment of PID regulators in open loop

- Deduction of new rules to complete the knowledge model: In this part it has been detected the necessity to deduce new rules to make a complete knowledge model, from the own system and the desired specifications, to the final derivation of the parameters of the controller in a reasoned way.

5.1 General diagram of knowledge in the open loop

In accordance with the steps deducted by the elaboration of the conceptual model, it is obtained a general diagram of the knowledge for the adjustment of PID controllers in open loop shown in figure 12.

Following the above a more detailed description of the knowledge schema is done, in different figures with their corresponding explanation. It starts with the corresponding part in the top right corner of the general diagram, detailed in figure 13.

In this part, the first thing to be done is to see if transfer function of the system is available. Following in both cases it is checked whether if it is a first order system with delay or if it were not the case it would not be possible to carry out the adjustment with this method. In the positive case if the transfer function is not available it concludes in the rules rg.2. If it is known the diagram of the left will be followed.

The corresponding part of the diagram of figure 14 is employed to discover if the system is a first order with delay one. For this, in first place it has to be checked if it stabilizes at a constant value with a unit step input and it is checked that there is no oscillation. If the previous is fulfilled, the next step is to check if there is a system with pure delay. With both affirmations it can be concluded that it is a system of this type, on the contrary it will not be.

After having checked that it is a first order with delay system, and also the transfer function is known, the characteristics of the response L and T are found, and it is checked if the relation L/T is found in the application range of the expression used in the case study (between 0 and 1) if it is not so, this method of design will not be applied. If the contrary applies, L/T is checked to see if it is bigger than 0.1 and if positive it can be applied to all the expressions contemplated. If it is inferior than 0.1 the question to ask the user is if he/she wishes to discard

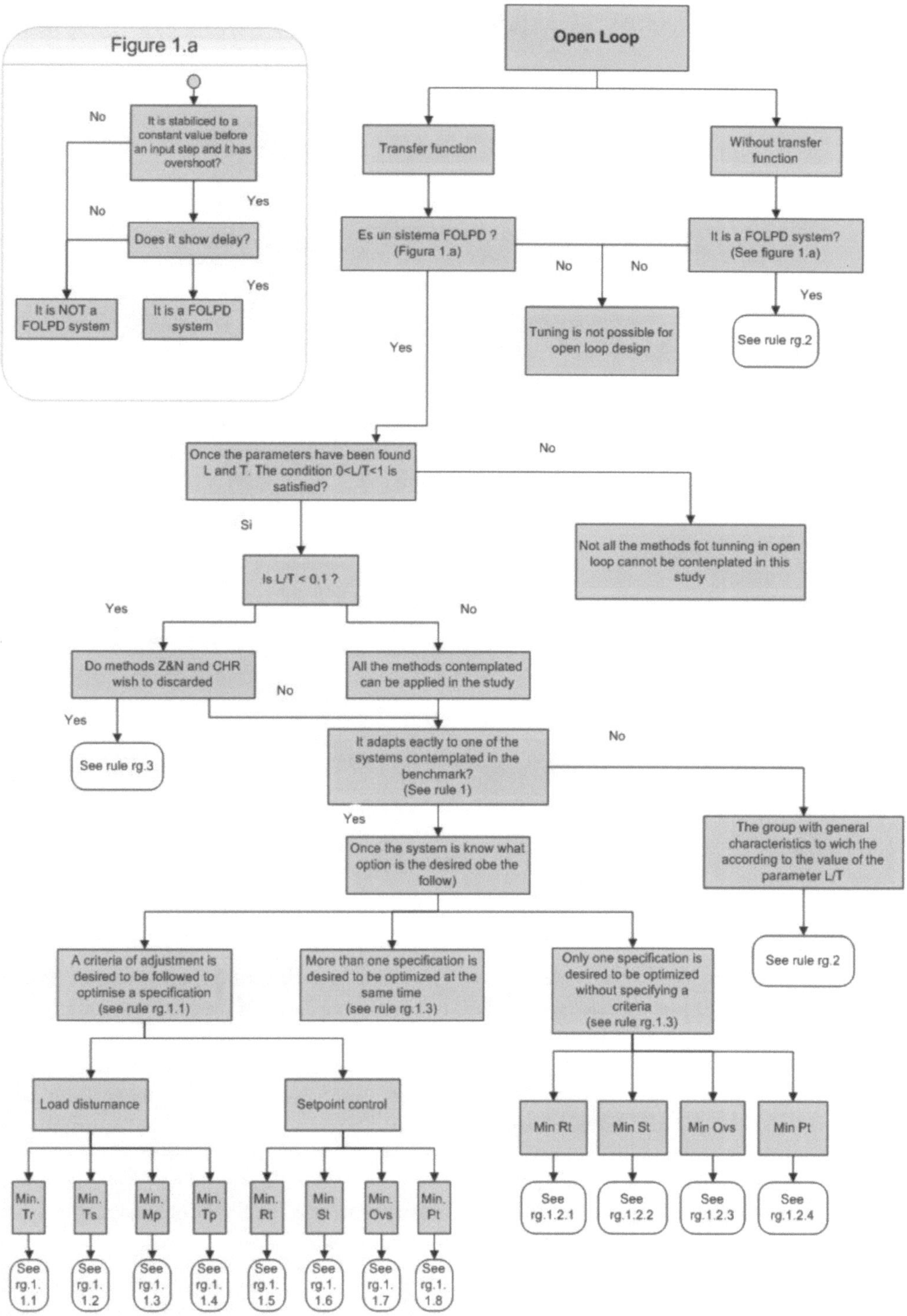

Fig. 12. General diagram of knowledge for open loop empirical tuning of PID controllers

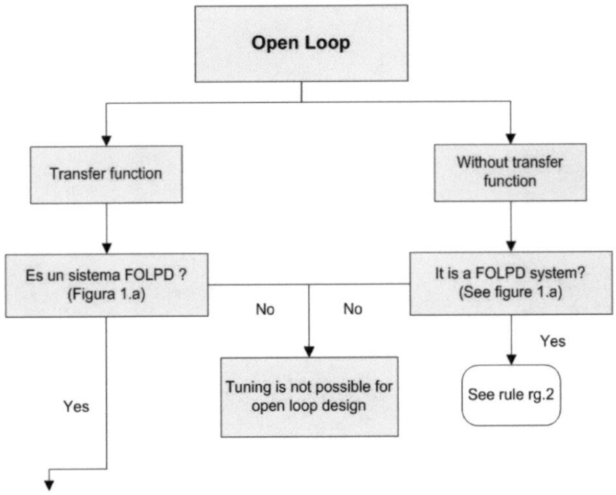

Fig. 13. Area 1 of the diagram

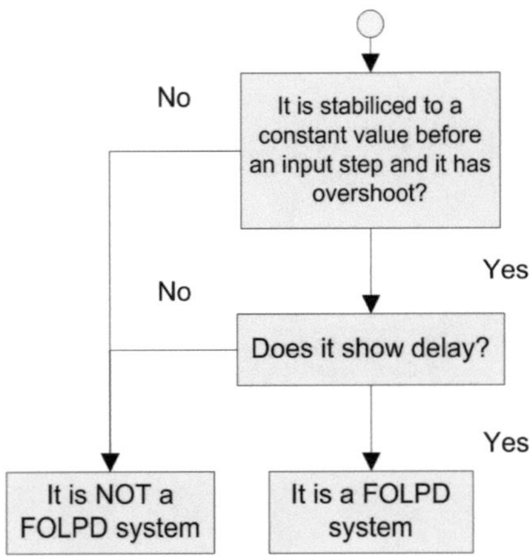

Fig. 14. Area 2 of the diagram

the expressions of Ziegler-Nichols and Chien, Hrones, Reswick for not being within its scope of application range. If they are not used it will apply rule *rg*.3 and if they are used all methods will be taken into account as if L/T were bigger than 0.1.

After the checks of the diagram of figure 15, the diagram of figure 16 folows, the first check is to see if it adapts to the transfer function of the system being regulate adapts to some of the related in the Benchmark. If it is not the case it will follow the diagram by the right-hand area and it determines a group with general characteristics to which the function of relation L/T belongs to, that will result with rule *rg*.2.

If the problem system adapts exactly to one of those mentioned in the Benchmark, the system is determined and it chooses one of the three following possibilities is chosen:

- Follow a criterion of adjustment (load disturbance or set point control) and also a certain specification will be optimized. And so for instance, if what wants to be done is regulate a system before changes in the load in which the objective is to optimize the response time then it will be necessary to follow rule *rg*.1.1.1.

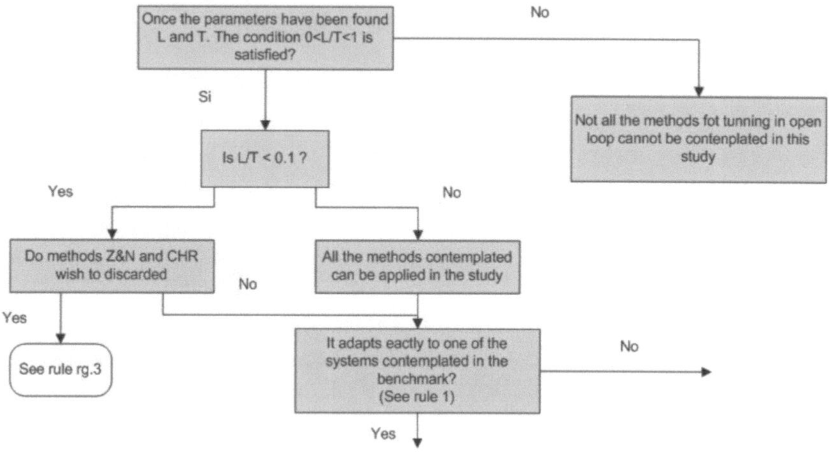

Fig. 15. Zone 3 of the diagram

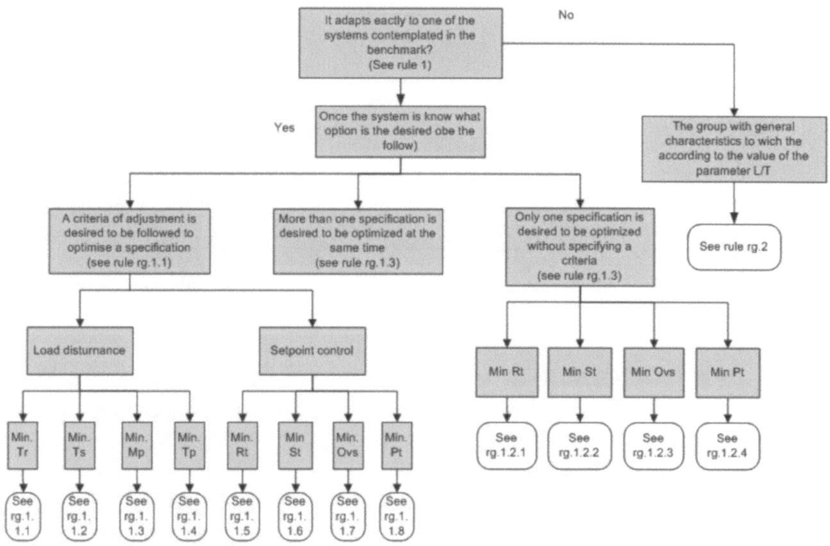

Fig. 16. Area 4 of the diagram

- If what is wanted is to optimize more than one specification simultaneously, rule *rg*.1.3 will be followed.
- If what is wanted is to optimize an independent specification of the criteria of adjustment. For instance, if what is wanted is to minimize the settling time whether it is for load disturbance or set point control criteria, rule *rg*.1.2.2 will be followed.

5.2 Deduction of rules to complete in knowledge model

As has been commented in the general summarized schema of knowledge, it is necessary to draw new rules to complete the knowledge model: In this part the need to do a model of complete knowledge model has been detected, from the system itself and the specifications

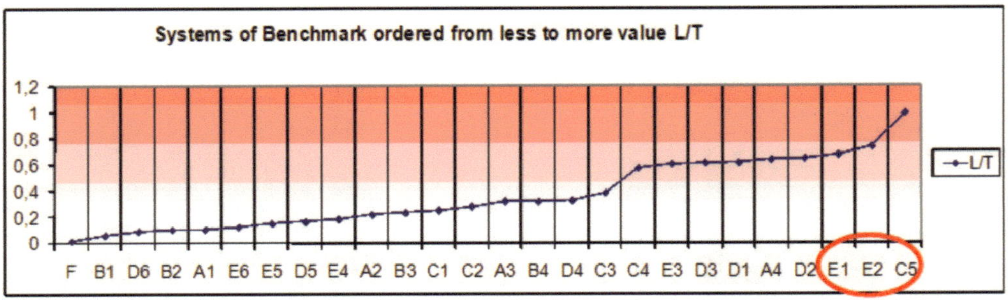

Fig. 17. Systems of Benchmark ordered from lower to higher L/T value.

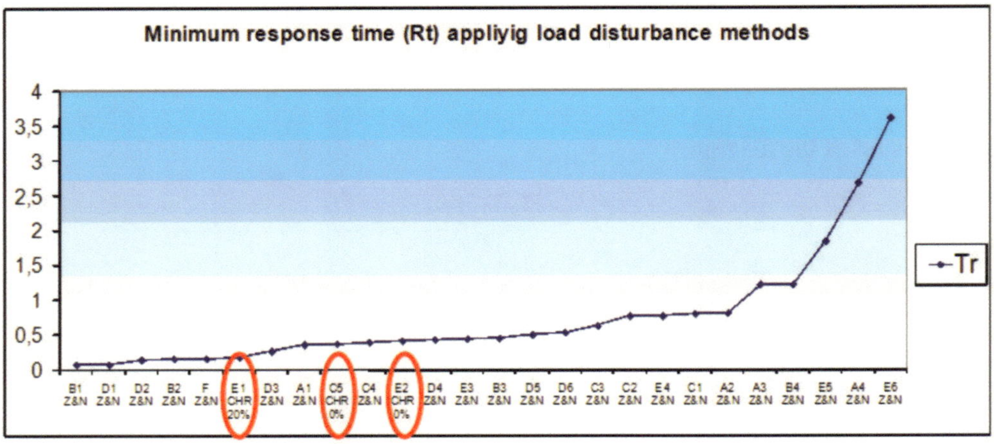

Fig. 18. Systems of Benchmark arranged from less to more value of response time for expressions with load disturbance criterion.

desired, up to the final obtaining of the parameters of the controller. In this sense two examples are shown in which the two possibilities of deduction of the rules are clarified.

5.2.1 Deduction of the rules RG1.1.1

It is pretended in this case to minimize the response time obtained, to regulate a system in which it is favoured the criteria of load disturbance. For this in the first place, the systems of the Benchmark are sorted lower to higher of the L/T relation, as is shown in figure 17.
Following we can see illustrated and sorted from lower to higher value of response time obtained for the expressions of changes in the load (figure 18), indicating in the graph also the expressions used in each case.
In the graph it is observed that in all cases except in three, the method of Ziegler-Nichols is employed. But contrasting the graphs 17 and 18, those systems have L/T relation similar and elevated, being all together in the end of the graph 17. And so, two rules can be established to regulate a system for load disturbance criterion, in which the time response is improved:

- If $L/T \geq 0.6763$ will apply CHR 0% overshoot load disurbance.
- If $L/T < 0.6763$ will apply Ziegler&Nichols.

Sistema	Minimo Tr	Minimo Ts	Minima Mp	Minimo Tp
F	0,16 (Z&N)	1,64 (Z&N)	47% (CHR 0% Mp)	0,44 (Z&N)
B1	0,08 (Z&N)	1,01 (CHR 0% Mp)	45% (CHR 0% Mp)	0,23 (Z&N)
D6	0,53 (Z&N)	5,19 (CHR 20% Mp)	45% (CHR 0% Mp)	2,07 (Z&N)
B2	0,16 (Z&N)	2,08 (Z&N)	47% (CHR 0% Mp)	0,44 (Z&N)
A1	0,36 (Z&N)	5,29 (Z&N)	46% (CHR 0% Mp)	0,89 (Z&N)
E6	3,6 (Z&N)	54,01 (CHR 0% Mp)	46% (CHR 0% Mp)	9,96 (Z&N)
E5	1,84 (Z&N)	29,27 (CHR 0% Mp)	47% (CHR 0% Mp)	5,53 (Z&N)
D5	0,5 (Z&N)	6,57 (CHR 0% Mp)	42% (CHR 0% Mp)	2,01 (Z&N)
E4	0,77 (Z&N)	11,51 (Z&N)	46% (CHR 0% Mp)	2,52 (Z&N)
A2	0,81 (Z&N)	12,87 (CHR 0% Mp)	45% (CHR 0% Mp)	2,14 (Z&N)
B3	0,45 (Z&N)	5,88 (CHR 0% Mp)	45% (CHR 0% Mp)	1,26 (Z&N)
C1	0,8 (Z&N)	12,81 (CHR 0% Mp)	45% (CHR 0% Mp)	2,28 (Z&N)
C2	0,77 (Z&N)	13,08 (CHR 0% Mp)	43% (CHR 0% Mp)	2,39 (Z&N)
A3	1,22 (Z&N)	21,15 (CHR 0% Mp)	41% (CHR 0% Mp)	3,4 (Z&N)
B4	1,22 (Z&N)	21,15 (CHR 0% Mp)	40% (CHR 0% Mp)	3,4 (Z&N)
D4	0,43 (Z&N)	7,76 (CHR 0% Mp)	39% (CHR 0% Mp)	1,87 (Z&N)
C3	0,63 (Z&N)	13,13 (CHR 0% Mp)	39% (CHR 0% Mp)	2,59 (Z&N)
C4	0,39 (Z&N)	16 (CHR 0% Mp)	40% (CHR 0% Mp)	2,72 (Z&N)
E3	0,44 (Z&N)	14,05 (CHR 0% Mp)	32% (CHR 0% Mp)	1,87 (Z&N)
D3	0,27 (Z&N)	11,77 (CHR 0% Mp)	37% (CHR 0% Mp)	1,59 (Z&N)
D1	0,08 (Z&N)	8,19 (CHR 0% Mp)	46% (CHR 0% Mp)	1,09 (Z&N)
A4	2,67 (Z&N)	68,87 (CHR 0% Mp)	24% (CHR 0% Mp)	8,86 (CHR 20% Mp)
D2	0,15 (Z&N)	10 (CHR 0% Mp)	44% (CHR 0% Mp)	1,33 (Z&N)
E1	0,18 (CHR 20% Mp)	10,17 (CHR 0% Mp)	51% (CHR 0% Mp)	1,53 (CHR 0% Mp)
E2	0,41 (CHR 0% Mp)	13,69 (CHR 0% Mp)	37% (CHR 0% Mp)	1,75 (CHR 0% Mp)
C5	0,37 (CHR 0% Mp)	90 (CHR 0% Mp)	102% (CHR 0% Mp)	3,11 (CHR 0% Mp)

Fig. 19. Groups rg.2.1. for changes in the load

The system E1 obtain its best response time using Chien, Hrones Reswick for overshoot of 20%, but when CHR of 0% is employed a very small error is obtained and so the rules are generalized.

5.2.2 Deduction of rules RG 2

This rule as can be observed in figures 13 and 16 is applied when the transfer function is not known, also in cases where it is known but does not adapt to any of the contemplated systems in the Benchmark. From it at the same time, a classification is going to be carried out, which will become three new rules.

- Rule rg.2.1- Groups with methods for load disturbance.
- Rule rg.2.2- Groups with methods set point control.
- Rule rg.2.3- Groups with methods for both criteria.

To create the groups with general characteristics, in a similar way than the previous case, the different systems are organised from less to more value with reference to L/T (figure 17). In this case, it is done in a table, because the purpose is to have generic groups in all the specifications. If for instance the case for rule rg 2.1 in which the systems are put together to follow the load disturbance criterion is shown, then refer to figure 19.
In the table the values of the specification in each case have been indicated, alongside the expressions for obtaining the parameters used to improve this specification. Next, a division

Comment	Number	Percent overall experiments
The expression indicated by the rule coincides with the one that has to actually be used.	24*cases*	66.6%
The expression indicated by the rule does not coincide with the one that has to actually be used, but the deviation is very small.	7*cases*	19.4%
The expressions indicated by the rule makes the system unstable	4*cases*	11.1%
The expressions indicated by the rule does not coincide with the one that has actually to be used so the deviation is considerable.	1*case*	2.7%

Table 2. Results of the validation

in groups is made in which the systems with groups of equal expressions are concentrated. Having this in mind, for instance systems $D3$, $D1$ and $A4$ with the condition that $0.6130 < L/T \leq 0.639$ ($D3$ to $A4$), and establish the following rules:

- To minimize the Response time, the method Ziegler&Nichols is applied.
- To minimize the Settle time, Chien, Hrones and Reswick 0% Mp.
- To optimize the Overshoot, Chien, Hrones y Reswick 0% Mp.
- To optimize the Peak time, Chien, Hrones and Reswick 20% Mp.

In spite of the systems D3 and D1 the best peak time result is obtained with ZN, if the rule for CHR of 20% a much smaller error is made than if the system A4 with ZN is regulated.

6. Validation

A validation of the conceptual model proposed is carried out. This will not be done on the cases in which the transfer function is known, and it is exactly adapted to one of the systems referred to in the Benchmark, but it will be carried out when the transfer function is not known or if it is known, and it does not adapt to any of the systems and also if both criteria are contemplated (load disturbance and set point control). The validation is done on 9 systems not contemplated in the Benchmark and it is checked for each one of the specifications that the model has Developer. There are a total of 36 checking cases, in which the results shown in table 2 are obtained.

Therefore it is considered that the model proposed has a satisfactory functioning, given that the general terms are the following:

- The scores are $31/36 = 86.1\%$
- The misses are $5/36 = 13.8\%$

7. Conclusions

The task of selection of the adjustment expression to be used has been resolved with the proposed technique in the present paper, thus through the follow up of the rules procedure the adjustment expressions can be selected for the case disposed of and also choose among them if more than one is applicable.
Having selected the expression or expressions to obtain the parameters, the calculation of these is carried out, following the procedure for the case that has been chosen previously in a structured way. And so the possible paths to be followed are resolved with rules, including those to reach a balance between specifications that do not improve in one same path.
When carrying out the conceptual modelling two relevant contributions have been obtained. First, clarity has been added in various stages of the adjustment of a PID. Second, some contradictions have been manifested between different expressions that have been resolved with it.
The procedure in real plants whose function transfer is different to the ones mentioned in the Benchmark, has been validated for the more restrictive cases of the deduced rules. The results obtained and presented in the corresponding section to validating satisfy the initial objectives when verifying the functioning of the rules in the plants used.

8. References

Astrom, K. & Hagglund, T. (2006). *PID controllers: Theory, Desing and Tuning*, Research Triangle Park, USA.

Astrom, K.J. Hagglund, T. (2000). Benchmark systems for pid control, *Preprints IFAC Workshop on Digital Control. Past, present and future of PID Control*, Elsevier Science and Technology, Terrasa, Spain, pp. 181 –182.

Auslander, D., Takahashi, Y. & Tomizuka, M. (1978). Direct digital process control: Practice and algorithms for microprocessor application, *Proceedings of the IEEE* 66(2): 199 – 208.

Bennett, S. (1984). Nicolas minorsky and the automatic steering of ships, *Control System Magazine* Vol. 4(No. 4): 10–15.
URL: *10.1109/MCS.1984.1104827*

Calvo-Rolle, J. & Corchado, E. (n.d.). A bio-inspired robust controller for a refinery plant process, *Logic Journal of IGPL* .
URL: *http://jigpal.oxfordjournals.org/content/early/2011/02/04/jigpal.jzr010.abstract*

Calvo-Rolle, J.L. Alonso-Alvarez, A. F.-G. R. (2007). Using knowledge engineering in a pid regulator in non linear process control, *Ingenieria Quimica* 32: 21 – 28.

Chien, K.L. Hrones, J. R. J. (1952). On the automatic control of generalised passive systems, *Transactions of ASME* 74: 175 – 185.

Epshtein, V. (2000). Hypertext knowledge base for the control theory, *Automation and Remote Control* 61(11): 1928–1933.

Feng, Y. & Tan, K. (1998). Pideasytm and automated generation of optimal pid controllers, *Third Asia-Pacific Conference on Control&Measurement*, Aviation Industry Press, Dunhuang, China, pp. 29–33.

Kaya, A. Scheib, T. (1988). Tuning of pid controllers of different structures, *Control Engineering* 7: 62 – 65.

Mindell, D. (2004). *Between human and machine: Feedback, Control, and Computing before Cybernetics*, Johns Hopkings Paperbacks edition, London.

Pang, G. (1991). An expert adaptive control scheme in an intelligent process control system, *Proceedings of the IEEE International Symposium on the intelligent Control*, IEEE Press, Arlington, Virginia, pp. 13–18.

Pang, G. (1993). Implementation of a knowledge-based controller for hybrid systems, *Decision and Control, 1993., Proceedings of the 32nd IEEE Conference on*, IEEE Press, San Antonio, TX , USA, pp. 2315 –2316 vol.3.

Pang, G., Bacakoglu, H., Ho, M., Hwu, Y., Robertson, B. & Shahrrava, B. (1994). A knowledge-based system for control system design using medal, *Computer-Aided Control System Design, 1994. Proceedings., IEEE/IFAC Joint Symposium on*, IEEE Press, Tucson, AZ , USA, pp. 187 –196.

Wilson, D. (2005). Towards intelligence in embedded pid controllers, *Proceedings of the Eight IASTED International Conference on Intelligent Systems and Control*, ACTA Press, Cambridge, USA, pp. 25–30.

Zhou, L. Li, X. H. T. & Li, H. (2005). Development of high-precision power supply based on expert self-tuning control, *ICMIT 2005: Control Systems and Robotics*, SPIE-The International Society for Optical Engineering, Wuhan, China, pp. 60421T.1–60421T.6.

Ziegler, J. Nichols, N. R. N. (1942). Optimum settings for automatic controllers, *Transactions of ASME* 64: 759 – 768.

14

Hybrid System for Ship-Aided Design Automation

Maria Meler-Kapcia
Gdansk University of Technology, Poland

1. Introduction

In carrying out the most important tasks of a shortage of ship design is the lack of formalized application methods, mathematical models and advanced computer support. Decisions and adopted solutions are often based on knowledge resulting from experience and intuition of designers. Use of information on previously executed projects of similar ships allow expert systems using the Case Based Reasoning method (CBR), which is a relatively new way of solving problems related to databases and knowledge bases.

This facilitates the efficient design of the ship as soon as possible [1]. A similar role has been neural networks, which can be taught on the basis of representative examples, and the results obtained from other sources (eg during the operation of the ship).

To achieve this purpose, a hybrid support system for ship design based on the methodology of CBR with some artificial intelligence tools such as expert system Exsys Developer along with fuzzy logic, relational Access database, and artificial neural network with backward propagation of errors. Hybrid systems forming a new class of artificial intelligence tools have to combine the capabilities of each of the tools used to solve specific problems. In the simplest case of the hybrid system is a combination of classical techniques of expert systems with neural networks [2], which was applied in developed computer-aided design system.

This system is intended to be ship-aided design automation, where most projects are using pre-built similar ships. The scope of the system, in addition to computer-aided design automation, were also aided design of ships at the initial stage, which determines the main parameters of the ship.

In order to find solutions to similar, previously used on ships developed its own algorithm for multiobjective optimization of weighted gains to search a database of similar ships [13]. The proposed algorithm was applied to computer-aided design ship's engine room automation, where the similarity may be of partial for example main propulsion (MP), power plants and individual installations, and the weighted sum of partial similarities is the similarity summary of the whole ship.

Using this algorithm, the selection is made of methods for calculating the similarity presented in the literature, adapted to the design of ships and their own methods, has not been used, based on the use of functions: rectangular, trapezoidal, triangular and Gaussian [13]. Using these methods, similarity analysis was conducted for the selection of ships, power and speed of main engine (ME). This analysis is intended comparison of selected methods and the selection of the best of them for computer-aided design automation engine room in the database application and expert system. Based on the results obtained are searched in a database similar ships, ie ships with the greatest similarity weighted summary. In the case of unsatisfactory results in the calculation of similarity, as a complementary, provided for a neural network learning algorithm. This algorithm is implemented in the system of Access and can be used for the selected database and its fields of any numeric type.

2. The structure and functions of computer-aided design ship's engine room automation

2.1 Searching for similar ships

System-aided design ship's engine room automation is an application that (improves) streamlines and facilitates greatly the design process automation monitoring and fitness of the ship. The application was developed using expert system Exsys [16] and is planned to work with the database management system Access [6] as a support system for ship design engine room automation, but can also be an independent operating tool, in a somewhat limited scale, only in the database Data Access (without the use of expert system), which lowers the cost of applications.

Searching for similar ships in the system can be realized in two ways:

- The selection of the ship by a similar expert system in conjunction with the application database and verifying the results obtained by a neural network
- looking like a ship through the database application with a possible revision of its design using neural network.

In both cases the results are verified by a neural network using back propagation algorithm. The neural network learned on the basis of design data stored in ships built in the database used to verify the project in case of setting it up on the basis of sub-projects from different ships (eg data on the drive from the ship BXXX, and power plants - BYYY). Structure aided design automation system is shown in Figure 1

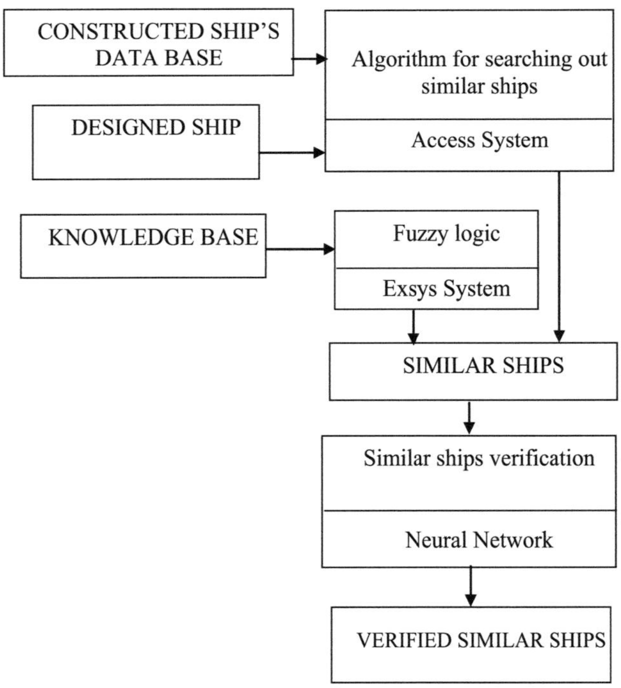

Fig. 1. Schematic design automation system for supporting the ship on the basis of similarity

A database contains data about objects and systems, devices and automation components from catalogs, or used on ships previously built. It can provide detailed information for designer about the elements of the automation systems used on ships constructed, as well as directory information on those systems and components.
Knowledge base system is the automation of selected elements of the project, which are implemented by the expert system based on the domain model (without the use of information on ships built). Based on the domain model can be made also an adaptation of the project, which takes place when the database was not found enough to like or ship found the ship has a relatively low similarity summary and the designer decides not to match an existing project for the design of self based on a knowledge base.

2.2 The hierarchical structure of automation

To achieve effective and transparent (formal) similar ships were searching the classification structure of engine room automation, which is multilayered and includes the following levels:

- the engine room
- systems
- objects
- control and measurement points.

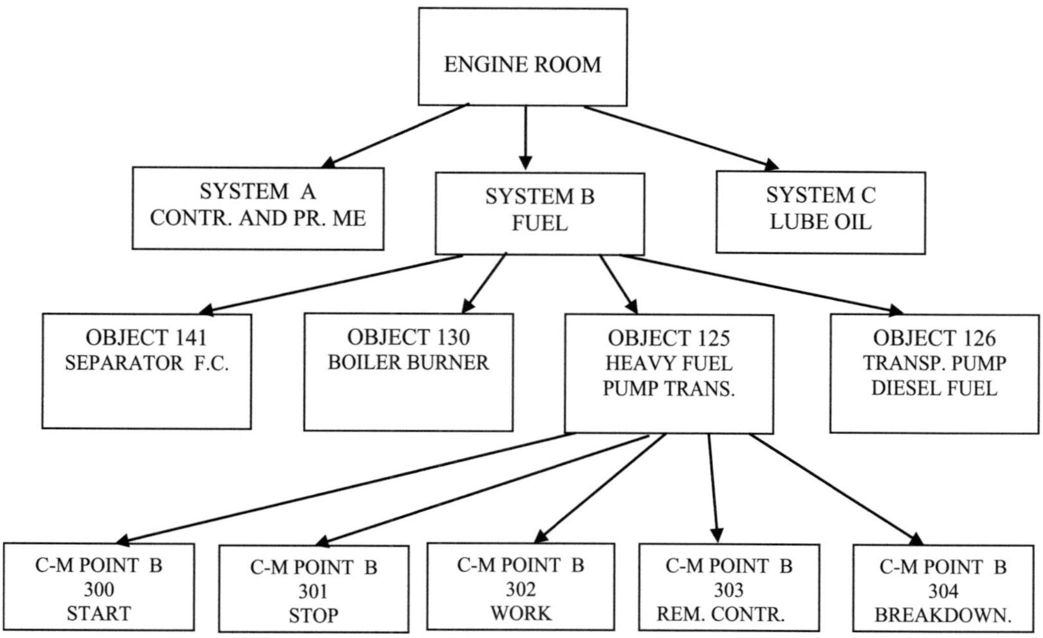

Fig. 2. The structure of design engine room automation on the example of fuel system

For the purposes of computer processing and editing of technical documentation automation adopted a single, numeric encoding systems and facilities installed in a power ships. However, automation components are encoded in accordance with international standards. It was assumed that the selection of automation objects is realized within the marine systems that, for most ships, are as follows:

- system control and protection ME,
- fuel system,
- lube oil system,
- fresh water system,
- a system of sea water,
- compressed air system,
- boilers and steam system,
- bilge system,
- power system,
- ballast system,
- other.

Different levels of this structure (for example, fuel system) are shown in Figure 2.

2.3 Algorithmization searches similar ships

To search for similar ships multiobjective optimization algorithm was used for the selection of automation based on a hierarchy of similarity: the whole engine room, her ships systems and objects designed (proposed) for the individual ships stored in the database. Tasks of this algorithm are as follows:

- Search for similarity between the structures of automation,
- Optimizing cost and scope of automation.

In the first stage of the algorithm is sought in the structure of the ship automation most similar like that described by the structure and number of elements present in the system automation (structure and number of objects, sensors, etc.). By comparing the structure of the automation of other ships built it to be classified in terms of fuzzy as: same, better or worse. Finding the best engine room automation structure is based on the provisions contained in the key project documents such as technical description and comparison of measurement equipment.

In the second stage of the algorithm, based on the existing structure, searches in the directories of the database systems and automation equipment, minimizing costs and maximizing capacity factor (range) of automation for these costs. At this stage, looking for a ship with a high density of automation possible with the relatively small cost - fuzzy optimization criterion.

Optimization method used here is based on a hierarchical optimization successively performed for all criteria.

- Arrange the criteria of importance (f_1) to least important (f_M)
- Find the optimal solution X^1 the primary criterion for f_1 and limitations
- Search for optimal solutions X^i, i = 2.3 ,..., M relative to the other criteria for the introduction of additional restrictions.

Keeping the cost calculation is done using two methods:

- using an estimate - in the initial stages of design based on the technical description and a base price of standard.
- using the exact - in the later stages of the design is based on information from a comparison of measurement and control equipment and bills of materials and details of offers and contracts for the purchase of equipment automation.

Accepted calculation method is based on an estimate of costs based on price information from the pre-built ships that are brought into the so-called. standard prices, ie price per unit for a ship with a standard contract for the equipment. A detailed list of the equipment along with the accepted price is the calculation of the cost of automation, which includes: an integrated alarm system / control / monitoring, maneuvering control panel desktop, remote control system ME, ME diagnostic system, generators, automation systems, pressure transducers, pressure switches, thermostats, level sensors, temperature sensors, etc. The criteria for the optimization algorithm includes:

- computing the minimum price
- the minimum delivery time
- maximum discount
- maximum warranty period
- the priority of the supplier or their lack of automation.

For determining the similarity of the ship used in the classical method of weighted profits. In this method, the coordinates of the vector of profits - the partial similarities are aggregated into a single function of income - a summary by the similarity transformation:

$$pg_{is} = \boldsymbol{ws} * \boldsymbol{ps_{is}}'$$
$$ps_{is} = sum((mo * m\, po_{is})')$$

where: pg_{is} - similar summary automation of the whole ship,
$\boldsymbol{ps_{is}}'$- Column vector of similarities of partial automation systems $[w_1 \ w_2 \ldots w_{ip} \ldots w_{lp}]$, $w_{ip} \in <0,1>$ and $\Sigma wg_{ip}[i]=1$,
mo - array of objects weighing individual systems
mpo_{is} - matrix of similarities of objects of individual systems
$_{is}$ - the ID of the ship,
* - the dot product.

The project built the ship automation can be adopted without any change or be subject to adaptation in accordance with the requirements of the designer of automation. Adaptation of the project built ship can be achieved in two ways:

- on the basis of other projects ships built,
- model domain - based.

Adaptation based on other ships built projects takes place when the partial similarity between the different systems of the ship similar (with the greatest similarity of the summary) are smaller than the similarities of the individual systems of other ships.

Adapting model domain - based [3] takes place when the database did not find enough like a ship or ship is found has a relatively low similarity summary and the designer decides not to match an existing project for the design of self. At each stage of development envisaged is the possibility of interference by the designer of automation.

3. Analysis of the similarity of the hierarchical automation engine room

3.1 Basics of calculating the similarity automation

The support system of the ship design automation similarity was related to characteristics of ships built in the engine room. It is assumed that the solutions for the automation are subject to certain features of the engine room in scheduled ship. Due to the large number of ships taken into account the characteristics of similarity is defined, broken down by certain groups of traits. The collection in question features (parameters) of the ships was divided into subsets with respect to the entire ship propulsion, power, and the following marine systems (installation): fuel, lube oil, fresh water, sea water, compressed air, boiler and steam system, bilge, in ballast, and others. The results of calculations of similarities in these subsets are defined as partial similarity. The study of similarity includes some parameters such as:

- general information: type of ship, load, number of refrigerated containers, the number of moving cars, the classification society, class automation
- main propulsion (MP): The number of main engines (ME), type ME, power ME, ME speed, the number of propellers, the type of propellers, the number of transmissions;
- power plant: the number of sets PG1 type, the type of PG1, power PG1, PG1 speed, number of sets PG2 type, the type of PG2, PG2 power, speed PG2, the number of shaft generators,
- the installation of fuel : the number of fuel valves, the number of fuel pumps, the number of centrifuges, the number of filters;
- bilge: number of valves, the number of bilge pumps.

To calculate the similarity of ships in the database application uses some functions of similarity (rectangular, trapezoidal, triangular, Gaussian, with a lower limit), and the expert system - fuzzy logic. The similarity of ships calculated in the database application is forwarded to the system Exsys in tabular form. Along with the similarities and partial summary of the database shall be the values of selected parameters on which the expert system calculates the fuzzy similarities and looks similar ships.
The system Exsys to the database are forwarded to the resulting maximum partial similarity with the corresponding identifiers of ships and ship's maximum aggregate similarity as the sum of the partial similarities. On this basis, the system searches the database of the ship as a ship like that.

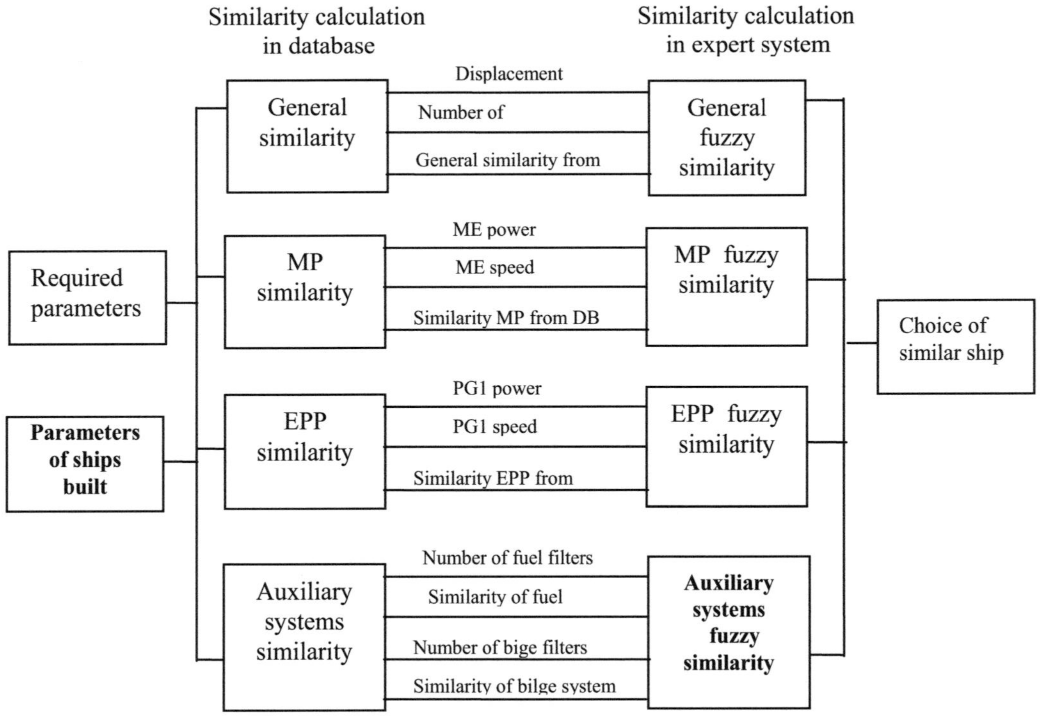

Fig. 3. Block diagram of a search for a similar ship in the database application and expert system

Example of searching for a similar ship is shown in Figure 3, where: MP - main propulsion, ME - the main engine, PG1 - generator of type 1, PG2 - generator of type 2.
The project on the basis of automation projects, other ships can be implemented:

- based on a draft of the ship similar or ship chosen project,
- by including the individual systems (objects) of ships built.

Maybe there is the adoption of the entire project before the ship was built (as a base project) or its adaptation projects on the basis of individual systems and (or) objects of other ships stored in the database.
Project base design can also be freely chosen by the designer of the ship built. In each scenario using the base project can then be modified several times based on systems built by other ships built in terms of both technical description and selection of equipment, such as by changing the design of systems (objects) that originate from other ships or may be supplemented and corrected by the addition of new and (or) removal of existing control and measurement points.
The search system or building automation built ship is carried out in two stages: the first stage of the search is looking for entries for the system (object) on all ships stored in the database, in the second stage, records are searched for the system (object) on the selected ship. The result of each stage is displayed on the screen, giving the designer the opportunity to review and compare the equipment of the system (object) to individual ships before the final choice.
Network activities of this process is shown in Figure 4.

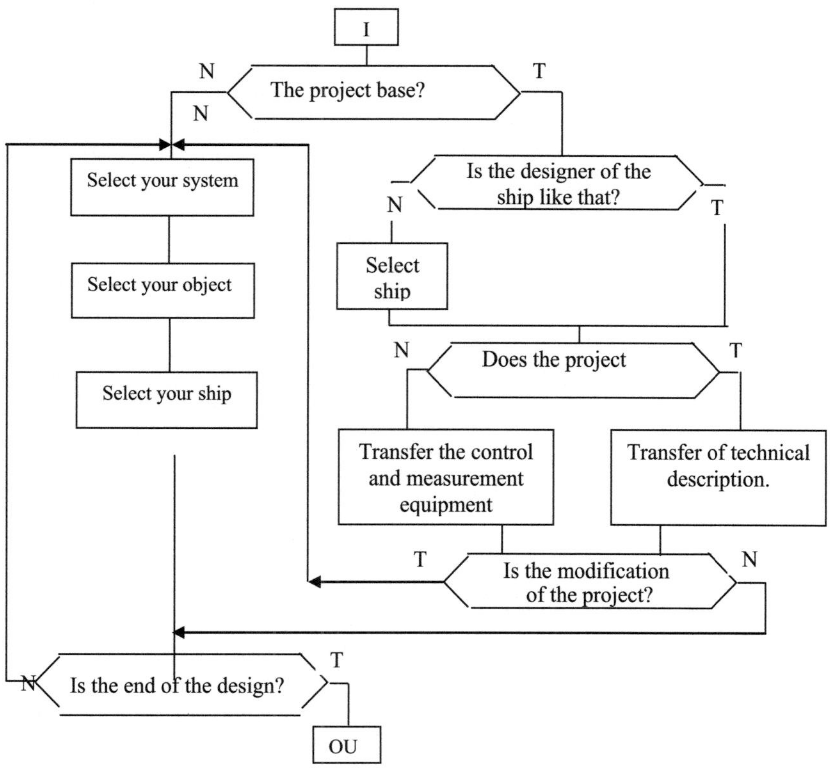

Fig. 4. A network activities of algorithm design engine room automation

3.2 Application of the similarity calculation functions of engine room automation

Functions of similarity is one of the most important element of case based reasoning method. Functions presented in the literature of this type (with a similar use) relate to the similarity collections without analyzing the similarity of the individual components. These functions do not provide such a large room for maneuver for the designer in search of similar ships, as proposed here functions of similarity. The fact that they may play a role similar to that of fuzzy logic improves their usability for two reasons:

- In database applications, ensure the implementation of fuzzy logic operators,
- It gives the possibility of waiving the application of expert system and reduce support automation for simplified variant (without the use of expert system).

The developed system of choice for calculating the similarity function depends on the design task, as well as the expectations of the designer. These functions provide greater flexibility in determining the ranges of values of the parameters input. Their selection should result from the need to include greater or lesser number of similar ships, for example for the similarity analysis of individual systems (installation). The designer may choose a specific function or function can be automatically applied at both the preliminary design, as well as in the selection process of automation.

The designer can specify the value of individual design parameters, as well as deviations and standard percentage points lower and upper, which are converted into real values and the limit of standard parameters. They may be of a symmetric, if their values are the same, or asymmetric, if different. Determining lower or higher ranges of parameters, such as in the design automation of the ship may be comfortable in a situation where the designer to adopt a tolerance for technical parameters is looking for solutions to the most profitable from an economic point of view, namely to the lowest price (with possible discounts and rebates) or shortest time of delivery.

The similarity of the resulting parameter is obtained as a weighted similarity of this parameter. The process of calculating the weighted similarities of each parameter is terminated after taking into account all the input parameters of the ship, and their weighted sum is a partial similarity of the MP. The sum of the similarities of partial similarity is the weighted aggregate of the whole ship, under which ships are searched on.

Based on sample data, the proposed board and the data contained in the database of ships built, as the ship is similar, the ship was named B500. The partial similarity of some ships from the database are contained in Table 1.

Ship	General sim	MP sim	EPP sim	INST sim	Weighted sum sim
B191	0,62	0,74	0,50	0,55	0,60
B222	0,15	0,33	**0,70**	**0,75**	0,48
B369	0,17	0,60	0,48	0,68	0,48
B500	**0,90**	**0,78**	0,55	0,73	**0,74**
B501	0,10	0,25	0,67	0,51	0,38
B683	0,13	0,56	0,68	0,50	0,47
B684	0,13	0,59	0,49	0,61	0,45

Table 1. The partial similarity of some ships

The partial similarity of the ship were calculated similar to the values of weights for each group of parameters, which was adopted by the arbitrary decisions of the designer on the basis of his experience (Table 2).

Kind of similarity	Weight of the parameter	Weighted value of the similarity
GENERAL SIM	0,1	0,09
MP SIM	0,4	0,312
EPP SIM	0,3	0,165
INST SIM	0,2	0,146

Table 2. Partial similarities of the similar ship

Partial similarity of the greatest value from a variety of ships (B500, B222) are shown in Table 3.

Kind of similarity	Ship	Weighted value of the similarity
GENERAL SIM	B500	0,09
MP SIM	B500	0,312
EPP SIM	B222	0,21
INST SIM	B222	0,15
SUM SIM	B500	0,76

Table 3. The biggest partial similarity

4. Application of selected methods for calculating the similarity

4.1 In the expert system and database application

Detailed analysis of selected methods for calculating the similarity between the ships was limited to the example of MP computer-aided design as an element of partial whole system, from which depends largely on ship engine room automation design.

The primary function of the system is developed to search a database of similar ships, which number may be quite varied and range from one up to several dozen ships. This is based on the applied similarity function, as well as the size and content of the database and assumed design parameters, such as ranges and thresholds of similarity functions. These parameters are determined by the designer before starting the search process similar ships. Next, data are required for the proposed ship. Then begins the process of calculating the similarity between the various parameters, including power and speed of the ME, then the similarity of the functions of the threshold. This process can be launched by the designer at any time and anywhere via the form shown in Figure 5.

MP partial similarity is calculated based on the similarity of number fields ME and non-numerical creating similar comprehensive MP. At this stage the table is created with the data of both source and calculated the similarities in the database application for Exsys (click for Exsys), on the basis of which similarities are calculated fuzzy.

In addition to calculating the similarity of ME in the database using the method of fuzzy logic in the expert Exsys system. This method was used to calculate the similarity between the parameters of the proposed board and the same parameters of individual ships built, as well as the similarity of other parameters of a numerical transferred from the database.

Application of fuzzy logic analysis of several examples (P1-P5) of design capacity and speed of the ME, and the results (weighted) for the calculation of similarity and prediction similar ships Exsys by the system shown in Table 4. In the case of a database of many ships of the same value of similarity in the table was placed first found a similar ship.

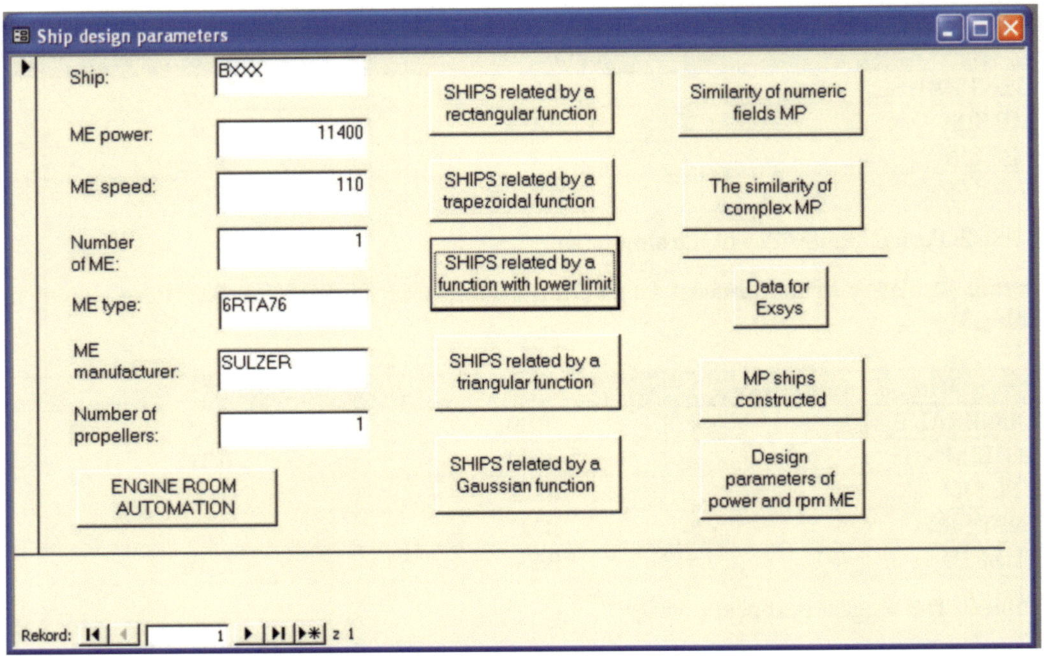

Fig. 5. Menu for calculating the similarity of ships on the example of the control system ME

Exemple	Designed power	Designed speed (rpm)	Number of similar ships	Values of maximal similarity	Similar ship power	Similar ship speed
P1	16200	107	3	0,6286	18160	110
P2	11400	110	20	0,6286	10800	118
P3	6600	150	1	0,8	6650	154
P4	11000	120	38	0,6286	13050	124
P5	17000	500	3	0,45	17400	530

Table 4. The results obtained in the similarity of MP Exsys system

Some examples have been found one (P3) or three (P1, P5) ships with a maximum similarity weighted summary, but sometimes also the number of ships with the same value of similarity is very high, eg in the P4 - 38, and P2 – 20.

For example, P2 analyzed the results concerning the maximum similarities ships Exsys calculated in the system using fuzzy logic, and calculated by using various functions in the database application using the sample (different) value deviations. Results for the three variants of border and standard deviations, respectively: [20.10] [40.20] [40.30] is shown in Table 5.

If the function of the lower bound and fuzzy logic in all three variants are the same values for the number of ships and the maximum value of similarity. For a rectangular function of deviations are negligible. For the triangular function is important to limit slippages value only because, by definition, the value of standard deviation is zero. For the Gaussian function increases in value and standard deviation limits search results more similar ships.

		Trapezoidal function		Gaussian function		Triangular function		Function with lower limit		Exsys Fuzzy logic	
ΔP_D i ΔP_G %	ΔO_D i ΔO_G %	Number of ships with maximal similarity	Value weighted similarity	Number of ships with maximal similarity	Value weighted similarity	Number of ships with maximal similarity	Value weighted similarity	Number of ships with maximal similarity	Value weighted similarity	Number of ships with maximal similarity	Value weighted similarity.
20	10	10	0,50	2	0,36	3	0,37	3	0,48	20	0,63
40	20	33	0,50	3	0,46	5	0,43				
40	30	54	0,50	6	0,48						

Table 5. The number of ships with the highest value of similarity according to particular functions in the database application and Exsys system

In the case of trapezoidal function with increasing values of deviation limits (lower and upper) and standard deviations of a growing number of ships, the most similar, with a maximum value of similarity is not changed, and for the analyzed case is 0.50. Keystone function in this respect is similar to fuzzy logic.

The number of ships of similar products using fuzzy logic is, in some cases very large, for example in Example P4 fuzzy logic method has been found up to 38 ships with a maximum value of similarity. Such a large number of similar ships is recognized in the membership function, which may involve some ranges of a large number of ships included in the database, while others will be limited to just one or several ships. Is dependent on the contents of a database - the types of ships in it are stored.

Mostly due to the use of fuzzy logic will be found to be a lot of ships with the highest value of similarity to the design ship. This method can therefore be applied to the initial classification of ships in the first stage of their search. Reduction of an excessive number of search ships may provide placement in a database or limit your search to the ships of the same type, for example, only the container [5].

4.2 In the neural network

The similarity of MP ships calculated in the application database and expert system can also be verified using the neural network with back-propagation of error, which was implemented in Visual Basic for Access, and can be used for any number of input and output parameters in the form fields database table [6]. In applications of neural networks is required to have numerous possible training set. Research results presented below are based on a set of hundreds of ships constructed. In studies that sought power dependencies, and then the engine speed from the main input parameters such as load capacity, length and width of the ship, its immersion and speed.

The calculations used a two-layer network with continuous unipolar activation function and the classical backward error propagation algorithm for weight change. The collection ships were divided into two subsets: learning and testing. To a set of testing randomly selected 25% of ships. All parameters of ships before the calculations were normalized to the range [0,1]. In this case, a computational cycle consisted of an introduction to the network input parameters of all the ships in succession from the training set. Completion of the network training followed when the mean square error in the cycle ec received less than the desired value. This error is related to the difference between the actual power of the ME and the power calculated by the network for the same ship.

The developed algorithm with the backward propagation of errors used for the selection of power and speed of the ME, is essential to select the database and table from which the field adopted as parameters for the network, resulting in a recall of relevant data for review.

After determining the number of cycles and the initial error value, as well as learning rates η_1 and correction η_2 is started learning network. The results obtained with the neural network are stored in a separate box "Calculate" the source table.

The values of all parameters of the network learning algorithm are introduced via the form shown in Figure 6.

In the process of network learning, consider the following problems:

1. selection of training set of sufficient size,

2. determination coefficients η_1 as the learning rate and η_2 as a correction factor weights,
3. definition of learning time.

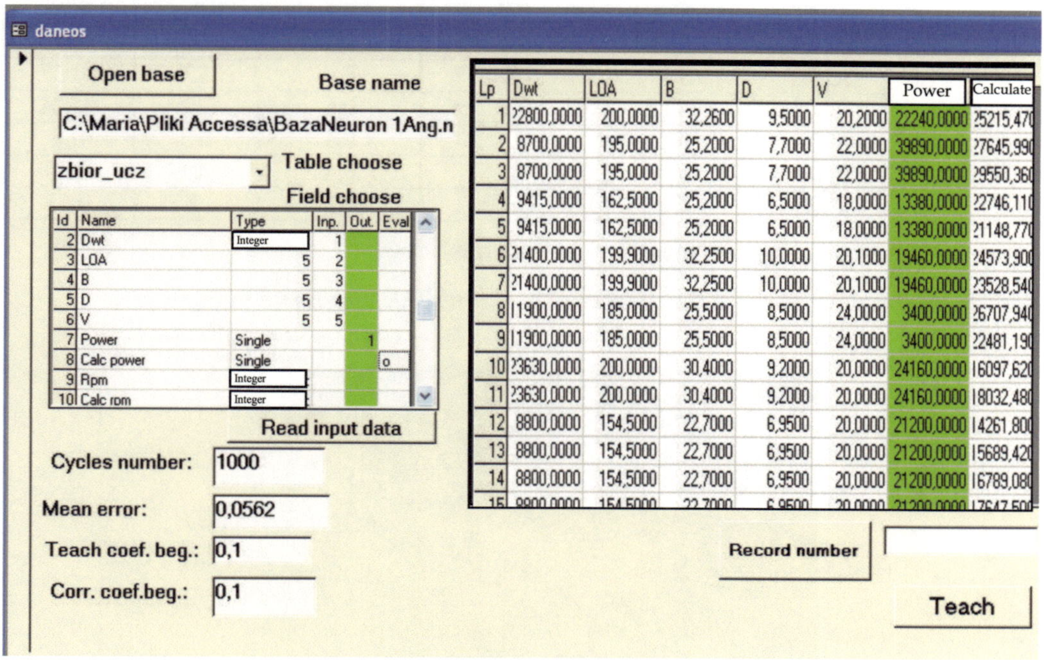

Fig. 6. Form to enter parameters of neural network

It is important to the skilful selection of learning rate η_1 [14], which has a huge impact on the stability and speed the process. η_2 coefficient is multiplied by a back propagated error and is responsible for the speed of learning. Too little value for this parameter makes the learning and convergence of networks is very slow, taking too much of its value the process of searching the optimal weight vector is divergent and the algorithm may become unstable [16]. η_2 coefficient is multiplied by the rate of change of weights in the previous step, "smoothing" too abrupt jumps connection weights. η_2 values should be selected on the basis of a compromise, so that further increases in weight accounted for a small portion of their current values (eg, several percent).

Selected examples of the use of neural network algorithm developed in the selection by the ME, based on size, load and speed of the ship shown in Table 6.

Research on selection of power ME on the basis of other design parameters, mainly the dimensions of the ship was carried out for example the number of cycles in the 100 - 30000, 50000 and even at the values of coefficients η_1 and η_2 equal 0.9 and 0.6 respectively and the values in the range 3 - 0.1 and 1 – 1.

In most cases, adopted the option of reducing the value of learning rates, which resulted in obtaining an average error within the limits: 0.034 - 0.06. In other cases, they applied the same values of coefficients, which contributed to the growth of average error, with a small number of cycles up to a value equal to 0.1. In one case, used to increase the value of coefficients, and the resulting average error does not differ from previous values.

Output parameters	Number of cycles	Number of input parameters	The values of coefficients		Learning time [min]	Average error
			η_1	η_2		
Power of ME	1000	5	0,9	0,6	1	0,06
	10000	5	0,9	0,6	7	0,04
	30000	5	0,9	0,6	13	0,037
	50000	5	0,9	0,6	20	0,034
	1000	5	0,1	0,1	0.5	0,1
	2000	5	1	0,1	1	0,05
	4000	5	0,1	0,1	2	0,05

Table 6. The results of neural network algorithm developed

Results of neural network for the number of cycles = 30000 are shown in Figure 7.

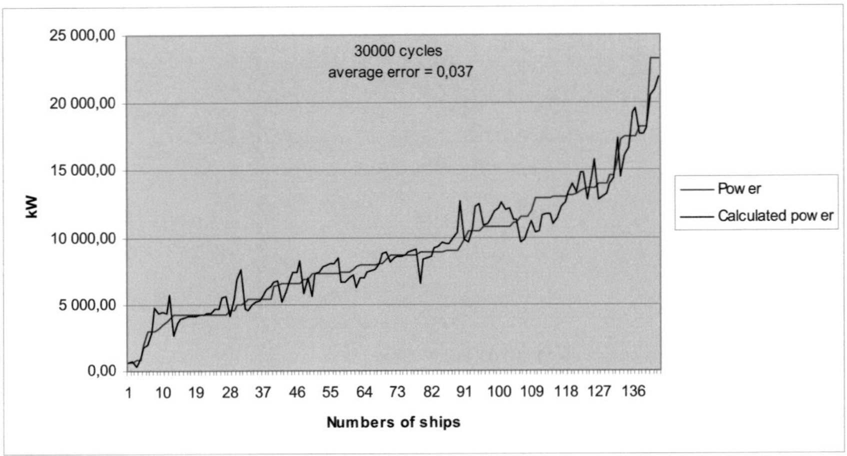

Fig. 7. Results of neural network for the number of cycles equal to 30,000

For comparison of these results was a test for the selection of neural network by ME, performed on a set of ships with a capacity of ME >13,000 kW and < 25,000 kW, as shown in Figure 8.

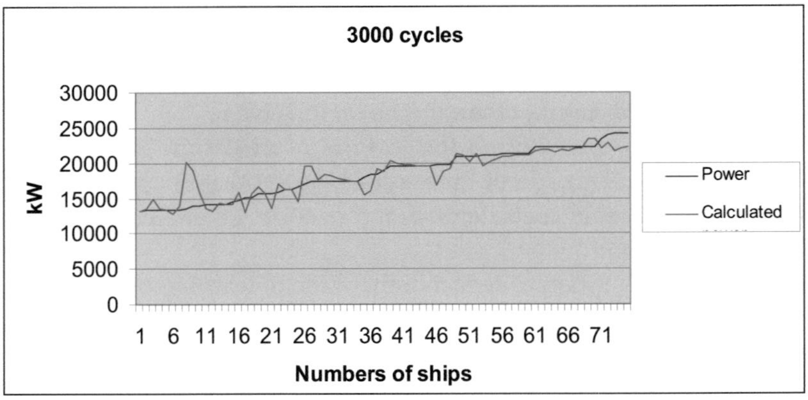

Fig. 8. The results of network training for a selected set of ships

The results of developed methods for calculating the similarity to support preliminary design of the ships used for the selection of main engine power, are summarized in Table 7. When searched the database under the ME value of ships for various functions for calculating the similarity is identical to the draft national (case 2, 3, 4, 6) - Tab. 7. results obtained with neural networks are worse. There is therefore no need to verification by the network, which is applicable in case you did not find enough similar vessels using the methods of calculating the similarity in the database application (cases 1 and 5) - Tab. 7. Then there is the process of verifying these results using neural network.

ME power design ship	ME Power of a similar ship				
	with the lower bound method	with the Gaussian function method	with the function of the trapezoidal method	with a triangular function	neural network
4350	4350	4350	4350	4350	2503
5500	5500	5500	5500	5500	5043
7400	7400	7400	7400	7400	7250
8043	4800	8048	8048	8048	6537
11100	13050	13050	12960	13050	11191
12000	10800	10800	10800	10800	11153
13050	13050	13050	12960	13050	12900
13700	13700	13700	13700	12960	13500

Table 7. Values of main engine power of ships like those obtained by using various functions

Comparison of sample results obtained on ships built in - the power values of the largest ships ME similarity in table 7 presents a chart (Figure 9).

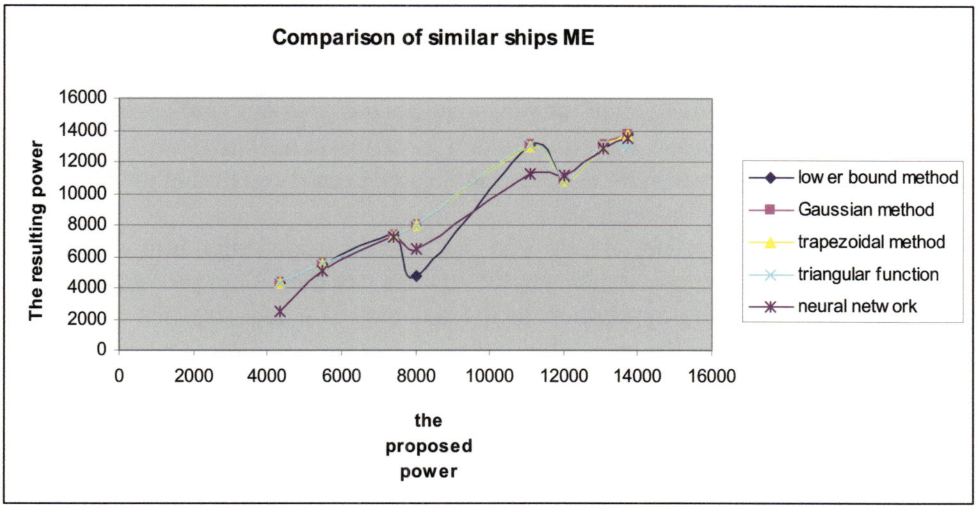

Fig. 9. Graphical comparison of ME under similar ships built according to different methods of calculating the similarity

From the presented examples show that various methods of calculation obtained similar values under the most similar ships are not always close to the power set of the proposed ship. This follows from the fact that similar ships are searched on the basis of similarities summary of all input parameters. An important role is played to determine the appropriate weight values of parameters, as well as test the limits of the ranges and their deviations. Similarity analysis was based on different types of ships built. We analyzed the results in the selection by the ME derived from the neural network. Differences similarities obtained using the various functions may be due the following reasons:

- highly diversified structure of the test set of ships in the database (different types, dimensions, purpose),
- too small a collection of ships in the database, which affects the results obtained with neural network.

5. Summary

The design engine room automation is often used similar design features of ships, since it constitutes the final design phase, in which there is a need to consider a wide range of information by the designer of automation in a relatively short time. Hence, the developed computer-aided design system, engine room automation was considered purposeful use of the CBR methodology, based on the similarity of the cases we present in detail the example of computer-aided design of the main propulsion.

Design automation system developed in the engine room can be implemented in various forms:

- Based on the partial similarities: general, main propulsion, power stations, selected installations (fuel and bilge) and the similarity of the entire ship as a weighted sum of partial similarities are searched in a database similar ships. Searching is done using the methods of calculating the similarity in the application database and fuzzy logic, which was used to calculate the similarity of the selected parameters of the ship, as well as partial similarities computed in the database.
- In the absence of similar arrangements in ships constructed for the possibility of self-design by a designer using the model elements of subject, which can serve both to adaptation and self-realization of the project by the designer of a similar ship.
- Multi-criteria optimization for the selection of automation based on a hierarchy of similarity: the whole power, its systems and objects, in case you find other similar ships, or arbitrary decision of the designer.

The developed hybrid system allows you to convert knowledge into formal rules, contributing to significant improvements in the efficiency of the design process engine room automation. Along with the application of the database is a tool to assist in the design process much automation in the most labor-intensive activities, it allows even the number of times (from several weeks to several days) to shorten the process of selecting the elements of automatic control and measurement points in the statement of apparatus, which has been confirmed by Experts in the practical implementation of this project document on the example chosen ship built. The application was created using Access database management system in collaboration with Exsys expert system, it also performs a complementary role for the expert system, providing the designer with the details and elements of the automation systems used on ships constructed, as well as directory information about these systems.

Usefulness and effectiveness of the search algorithm developed similar ships was confirmed in the developed computer-aided design system, engine room automation, which provides for the implementation of the multilevel structure of the automation.
Used, the system developed, the methodology for determining similarity of ships for the purpose of design provides a better measure of similarity, giving the designer a choice of similarity function according to the requirements and nature of the analyzed parameter. These features, functioning as a filter, help to increase flexibility in design automation, where often the technical parameters are accepted more or less tolerant because of the economic criteria of the project, as applied multi objective optimization algorithm, in case you find other similar ships on the basis of parameters general fitness, looking for a ship with a high density of automation possible with a relatively small cost of using a fuzzy criterion of optimization.

6. References

AAMODT A., PLAZA E.: Case-Based Reasoning, Foundation issues, methodological variations, and system approaches. Artificial Intelligence Communications, 1994, Vol, 7, No, 1, 39-59.

BOSE A., GINI M., RILEY D.: A case-based approach to planar linkage design, Artificial Intelligence in Engineering 1997, No 2, Vol 11.

BROUWER R.K.: A feed-forward network for input that is both categorical and quantitative, Neural Networks 2002, No 15.

CALLAHAN E.: MS Access 2002. Visual Basic, Microsoft Press, Warsaw 2000.

CLAUSEN H.B., LUTZEN M., FRIIS-HANSEN A., BJORNEBOE N.: Bayesian and neural networks for preliminary ship design, Marine Technology 2001, No, 4.

DOBSON R.: Programming MS Access 2000, Microsoft Press, Warszawa 2000.

DONGKON LEE, KYUNG - HO LEE. An approach to case-based system for conceptual ship design assistant, Expert Systems with Applications 16, 1999.

HEIAT A.: Comparison of artificial neural network and regression models for estimatingh software development effort, Information and software Technology, vol, 44, 2002, 911-922.

KORBICZ J., OBUCHOWICZ A., UCIŃSKI D.: Artificial Neural Network, Fundamentals and applications, Academic Publishing House, Warsaw 1994,

KOWALSKI Z., MELER-KAPCIA M., ZIELIŃSKI S., DREWKA M.: CBR methodology application in an expert system for aided design ship's engine room automation, Expert Systems with Applications 29, 2005, 256-263.

LEE D., LEE K., H.: An approach to case-based system for conceptual ship design assistant. Expert Systems with Applications,16 (1999).

MELER-KAPCIA M., ZIELIŃSKI S., KOWALSKI Z.: On application of some artificial intelligence methods in ship design. Polish Maritime Research 2005 no 1.

MELER-KAPCIA M. Algorithm for searching out similar ships within expert system of computer aided preliminary design of ship Power plant. Polish Maritime Research 2008 no 3.

RUTKOWSKA D., PILIŃSKI M., RUTKOWSKI L. Neural networks, genetic algorithms and fuzzy systems, WN-T, Warsaw 1999.

TADEUSIEWICZ R.: Neural networks. Academic Publishing House, Warsaw 1993,

USER MANUAL EXSYS Professional - Expert System Development Software, MULTILOGIC, May 1997.

ZAKARIAN V.L., KAISER M.J.: An embedded hybrid neural network and expert system in an computer- aided design system. Expert Systems with Applications, Vol 16, 1999.

15

An Expert System Structured in Paraconsistent Annotated Logic for Analysis and Monitoring of the Level of Sea Water Pollutants

João Inácio Da Silva Filho, Maurício C. Mário, Camilo D. Seabra Pereira, Ana Carolina Angari, Luis Fernando P. Ferrara, Odair Pitoli Jr. and Dorotéa Vilanova Garcia
Santa Cecília University, Group of Research in Applied Paraconsistent Logic, Brazil

1. Introduction

This chapter presents the development of a Expert System which was elaborated based on the Fundamentals of Paraconsistent Annotated Logic and aimed to help in the process of detection of physiological stress in organisms exposed to water pollution. The Paraconsistent Logic is a non-classical logic present as their main characteristics the acceptance of the contradiction in their structure. It is presented in this study the algorithms extracted from a type of Paraconsistent Logic nominated Paraconsistent Annotated Logic with annotation of two values PAL2v that are capable of simulating the applied methodology in Biology known as a neutral red retention assay. This method of biomarkers prepared with specific procedures has the goal of finding rates of exposure to marine pollution through the manipulation and study of cells from mussels. It was built a configuration of Paraconsistent Artificial Neural Network (PANN) composed of algorithms based on the principals of Paraconsistent Logic to compose the Expert System with the goal of simulating the biological method and help in the presentation of the cellular response. The process of analysis elaborated by the software consists of making a comparison with pre-established patterns through the Paraconsistent Network by biochemical/biological processes consolidated in the biology area and defined in the scope on the mussels cells' measures that presented determined behavior and biochemical reactions, as it is the biomarker of exposure and effect of marine pollution in the site of the samples collection. With this new approach of results, besides complete, they are presented as being more efficient by decreasing the points of uncertainty given by simple human observation. This way this work opens new fields for research of application of Artificial Intelligence techniques in the analysis and monitoring of the Marine Pollution.

2. The pollution problem

Used as man's source of food, raw material source and, afterwards, as a means of transportation, the oceans occupy practically 71% of the earth surface [NASCIMENTO et al 2002]. Nowadays, half of the world population is located in cities by the coast or in nearby regions. As a consequence of this, the marine environment, mainly coastal, ends up being affected by the debris of the human population, bringing up the difficult problem of marine pollution. In Brazil, there are two types of prior actions of pollution that reach more than 8 thousand kilometers of coast [NASCIMENTO et al 2002]. The first type is the marine and coast contamination from sewage and garbage, whose environmental and social consequences are felt instantly. Besides that, there is the sediment discharge in rivers coming from the deforestation and bad usage of the soil that also contributes to the increase of contamination in coastal areas. The second type involves the contamination from chemical polluents, mainly hydrocarbonates of petroleum and other persistent organic components and trace metals.

2.1 Polluents

It is known that the problem with pollution is associated to the characteristics of toxicity, persistency and bioaccumulation of substances linked to matters of social and economical costs [SOS TERRA VIDA 2005]. Among the groups of potentially damaging substances to the marine environment there are the ones classified as domestic sewage, petroleum and derivatives, trace metals, radioactive and organochloride materials. Among these, the domestic sewage is the biggest problem worldwide, being a volume of polluent material as well as related to concrete problems that cause public health damage. Relating to petroleum and derivatives, which are a basic energetic resource for our civilization, the pollution is a consequence of the huge volume transported and produced annually. They are stable and persistent and they cannot be degraded or destroyed by any biological or chemical process. The insertion of heavy metals in the oceans is mainly due to the industrial effluents in coastal areas. The radioactive materials, that are also a polluent source in the marine environment, are a consequence of decades of radioactive dejects that were settled or stocked in an inadequate way when produced by the nuclear industry. The organochlorides are very stable organic components, not much soluble in water, but very soluble or associate in lipids; therefore, they are easily bioaccumulated in organic structures. These components are widely disseminated in the ecosystems and their toxic effects may cause hepatic disturbance and affect the immunological and reproductive system of aquatic organisms.

2.2 The biomarkers for environmental diagnosis

The cell structures can be biochemically affected in the presence of sub lethal polluent concentrations, non stabilizing the internal balance of the cell [NICHOLSON, 2001]. These biological effects cause organic damage in species that act in a lasting and persistent way because the mechanisms of adaptation to the modified environment suffer from exhaustion and cannot stimulate the perfect functioning of the systems anymore, which leads the organic structures to death.

Through the usage of sensible biomarkers, a previous detection of stress in sub lethal levels in aquatic organic structures may help in the evaluation and environmental diagnosis before several changes reach the ecosystem. Some efficient and practical techniques that are already adapted to the local sensible organic structures are available for application in the monitoring of marine pollution.

3. Evaluation techniques for marine pollution

One of the biological procedures that employ biomarkers to assess marine pollution through de determination of physiological stress in by evaluating the integrity of lysosomal membrane is named Neutral Red Retention Assay [NICHOLSON, 2001]. This method consists in evaluating the environmental conditions and the bioavailability and effects of contaminants through the analysis of the biochemical and cellular answers of the local species before the animals suffer effects physiologically irreversible, reaching populations or even ecosystems. It can be verified that the toxicity of industrial effluents, the quality of the water and sediment in coastal ecosystems, the level of stress suffered by organic structures due to alterations in environmental conditions and the effect of substances or mixtures (synergism, addiction or antagonisms) having as variable the concentrations or time of exposure of these components.

3.1 Organism- test

The mussel used in the neutral red test for this procedure is the *Perna perna,* an organism of easy collection, with a bentonic habit that, for being sedentary and filter-feeding, it is potentially more subject to the action of toxic agents. Besides, these bivalves are tolerant for polluted environments; therefore, they accumulate in their tissues toxic substances that can be harmful to their own survival [KING, 2000].

The haemocytes of *Perna perna* showed the ability of discriminating impacted and non impacted areas through the integrity test of lysosomal membranes being able to be used as a quick and sensible biomarker in the detection of stress of beings as it is possible to have a correlation with chronic sub lethal effects.

3.2 Method of Neutral Red retention

The method used for analysis of time of retention of the neutral red dye [NICHOLSON, 2001] in haemocytes lysossome is described by Lowe [LOWE et al, 1995] as follows:

Using a hypodermic syringe of 2ml having 0,5ml of physiological solution, it is collected 0,5 ml of haemolymph of the posterior adductor muscle of the mussel. The content of the syringe is transferred to tubes of micro centrifuge of 2ml where it will be smoothly homogenized. 40 µl of this solution is put on a tube (haemolymph + physiological solution) over the surface of a slide treated previously with poly- L-lysine. These slides are incubated for 15 minutes in a dark and humid chamber. After the time of incubation, it is put over the slides 40 µl of solution of Neutral Red (NR). It is necessary 15 minutes more of incubation in the dark and humid chamber before starting the observations. In the first hour, the slides are examined every 15 minutes and in the second hour they are examined every 30 minutes. The final observation is performed after 180 minutes of exposure.

The NR retention time is obtained by the estimative of the proportion of cells showing liberation of dye for citosol and/or showing abnormalities in size, shape and color of lysosomes. At each time, the conditions are written down on a chart. It is important to point out that the slides must be observed on the microscope in the shortest time possible. This is to assure the consistency in the exam and because the neutral red is photosensitive. Once the lysosomes are responsible for the cellular digestion and gather a high concentration of contaminants, the destabilization of the lysosomal membrane in haemocytes exposed to expect environmental contaminants are affected faster by the toxin of the dye than healthy cells. Therefore, the necessary time to happen extravasations of Neutral Red dye for the citosol may reflect on the state of integrity on lysosomal membrane and this can be used as an indicator of exposure to conditions of environmental contamination [KING, 2000].

3.3 Presentation of results of the method of Neutral Red retention

The healthy haemocytes are bigger and present an irregular shape and once exposed to Neutral Red, the lysosomes can be seen as pink tinted small dots joined and the nucleus can be seen as a colorless sphere as the citosol [KING, 2000]. Stressed haemocytes tend to be spherical and smaller having bigger and darker lysosomes and citosol may be pink tinted because of the dye contained in the lysosomes. So, the criteria analyzed when observing the slides would be:

Criteria	Healthy Cells	Stressed Cells
Cells shapes	irregular	rounded
Cells sizes	large	smaller
Number of lysosomes	many	few
Size of lysosomes	small	Enlarged/ increased
Color of lysosomes	Pale red/ pink	Red or dark pink, orange, brown
Pseudopodes	Non visible	visible
Dye leak from cells	Non visible	visible

Table 1. Criteria evaluated

When more than 50% observed cells do not present sign of stress, it is used positive sign + in the table field according to the animal examined. When the cells present some sign of stress, the sign **+/-** can be used. The analysis finish when 50% of the cells or more show abnormal structure or dye leak for citosol and the negative sign - is used on the table [KING, 2000].

Organic Structures	Time(minute)					
	15	30	45	60	90	120
Control	+	+	+	+	+	+
Little stress	+	+	±	±	-	-
A lot of stress	±	-	-	-	-	-

Table 2. Table of results

4. Application of Paraconsistent Logics in the simulation of the technique of the method of neutral red retention

As shown on tables 1 and 2 in the method of neutral red retention, the procedure of identification of cells that present or not signals of stress is performed through systematic observations on the slides in an objective way and totally dependent on the Observer. This way of collecting data is subject to a high level of uncertainty to the biological method described. This way, it can be used techniques for the treatment of uncertainty with the goal of getting better results of efficiency of the method.

Recently, multiple theories and techniques of treatment of uncertain signs are being developed in Artificial Intelligence applying non-classic logics in the most varied areas [ABE, 1992] [DA COSTA et al, 1991]. The Paraconsistent Logic is a non-classic logic that has an important characteristic of presenting as a main advantage the capacity of treating appropriately contradictory information and, in some cases, there are significant advantages relating to the binary classic logic [DA SILVA FILHO et al, 2010]. In this work is used some

Algorithms extracted from Paraconsistent Annotated Logic that are interlinked in a Network of Paraconsistent Analysis [DA SILVA FILHO, 1999]. Thus, the Expert System uses the techniques of adequacy of these Networks to detect the level of pollution in the sea through the information obtained by the biological method that promotes the neutral red retention assay for the analysis of images in blood cells of mussels. There is a brief description of Paraconsistent Annotated Logic below and the algorithms that will be used in the Expert System.

4.1 Paraconsistent Annotated Logics

The Paraconsistent Annotated Logics are classes of Paraconsistent Logics that have a lattice associate and were introduced for the first time in programming logic by Subrahmanian [SUBRAHMANIAN, 1987]. The methods for treatment of uncertainty here presented use the fundamentals of an extension of Paraconsistent Annotated Logics named Paraconsistent Annotated Logic with annotations of two values (PAL2v) [DA SILVA FILHO, 1999] in which the principals are presented as follows.

4.2 The lattice associated to Paraconsistent Annotated Logic with annotation of two values

In Paraconsistent Annotated Logics PAL the proposed formulas come with annotations. Each annotation, belonging to a finite lattice τ, attributes values to its propositional corresponding formula [DA SILVA FILHO, 1999]. To obtain a bigger Power of representation about the annotations, or evidences, it is expressed the knowledge about a proposition, it is used a lattice formed by ordered pairs, such as:

$$\tau = \{(\mu, \lambda) \mid \mu, \lambda \in [0,1] \subset \Re\}.$$

In which case, it is fixed an operator $\sim: |\tau| \rightarrow |\tau|$ where; $\sim$ has the "meaning" of logic symbol of negation $\neg$ from the system that will be considered.
If *P* is a basic formula, the operator $\sim: |\tau| \rightarrow |\tau|$ is defined as:

$\sim [(\mu, \lambda)] = (\lambda, \mu)$ where, $\mu, \lambda \in [0, 1] \subset \Re$.

It is considered then:

(μ, λ): An annotation of *P*.

$P_{(\mu, \lambda)}$: *P* where the levels of favorable and unfavorable Evidence compose an Annotation that attributes a logical connotation to Proposition *P*.

This way the association of one annotation (μ, λ) to a proposition *P* means that the *Degree of Evidence* favorable in *P* is μ, while the unfavorable *Degree of Evidence*, or contrary, is λ.
Intuitively, in such lattice we have:

$P_{(\mu, \lambda)} = P_{(1, 0)}$: indicating 'existence of total favorable evidence and null unfavorable evidence', attributing a connotation of *Truth* to *P* proposition.

$P_{(\mu, \lambda)} = P_{(0, 1)}$: indicating 'existence of null favorable evidence and total unfavorable evidence', attributing a connotation of Falseness to *P* proposition.

$P_{(\mu, \lambda)} = P_{(1, 1)}$: indicating 'existence of total favorable evidence and total unfavorable evidence' attributing a connotation of Inconsistency to *P* proposition.

$P_{(\mu, \lambda)} = P_{(0, 0)}$: indicating 'existence of null favorable evidence and null unfavorable evidence', attributing a connotation of Indetermination to *P* proposition.

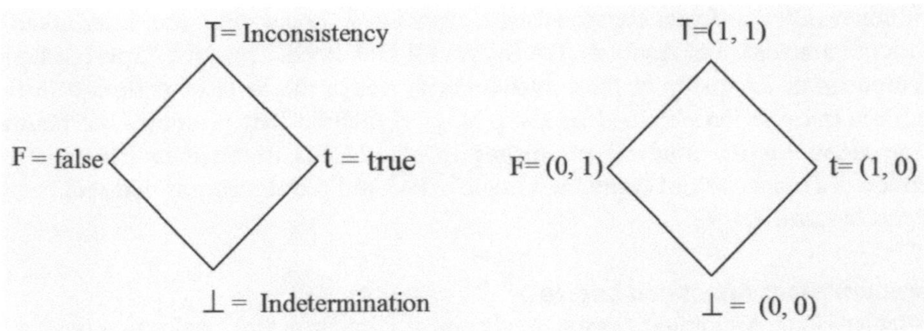

Fig. 1. Lattice associated to Paraconsistent Annotated Logics of annotation with two values PAL2v.

Through linear transformation in an unitary Square in a Cartesian Plan and the lattice represented by PAL2v we can reach the transformation [DA SILVA FILHO et al, 2010]:

$$T(x,y) = (x - y, x + y - 1) \tag{1}$$

Relating the components of the transformation *T*(x, y) according to the usual terminology of PAL2v, as:

$x = \mu$ favorable Evidence Degree

$y = \lambda$ unfavorable Evidence Degree

The first term obtained in the ordered pair of the equation of transformation (1) is:

$$x - y = \mu - \lambda$$

which we name Certainty Degree D_C. So, the degree of certainty is obtained by:

$$D_C = \mu - \lambda \tag{2}$$

And its values, that belong to the set $\Re$, vary in a closed interval +1 and -1 and are in the horizontal axle of the lattice, which is named "Axle of the Degrees of Certainty". When D_C result in +1 it means that the logic state resulting in the Paraconsistent analysis is True t, and when D_C result in -1 it means that the logic state result in the analysis is False F.

The second term obtained in the ordered pair of the equation of transformation that is:

$$x + y - 1 = \mu + \lambda - 1$$

which is named Contradiction Degree D_{ct}. So, the Degree of Contradiction is obtained by:

$$D_{ct} = \mu + \lambda - 1 \tag{3}$$

And its values, that belong to the set $\Re$, vary in the closed interval +1 e -1 and are in the vertical axle vertical of the lattice, which is named "Axle of the Degrees of Contradiction". When D_{ct} result in +1 means the logic state of analysis is the Inconsistent $\top$, and when D_{ct} result in -1 meaning that the logic state resulting in the analysis is Indeterminate $\bot$.

In practice the values of the Degrees of Evidence μ and λ they are obtained of sources of information of the physical world through Interval of Interest, or Universe of Discourse, with units of physical greatness of normalized values. As the Degrees of Evidence are independent, and whose values belong to the Set of the Real numbers, where they can vary in the interval between 0 and 1, then infinites logical states ε_τ are formed in the Lattice of LPA2v. The Paraconsistent Logical states are presented as:

$$\varepsilon_\tau = (D_C, D_{ct})$$

The result related to the Degree of Certainty D_C can be normalized becoming a Degree of Evidence that allows to be used as input for other LPA2v Algorithms. In that way, several propositions P1, P2,...can be analyzed through a a Network of Paraconsistent Analyses. The transformation of the Degree of Certainty in Degree of Evidence is made by the equation:

$$\mu_R = \frac{(\mu - \lambda) + 1}{2} \quad (4)$$

Were:

μ_R Resulting Evidence Degree
μ Favorable Evidence Degree
λ Unfavorable Evidence Degree

As example is considered the situation in that the measures made in the physical world present the following results:

$\mu = 0.89$ and $\lambda=0.28$

Then the Degrees of Certainty and of Contradiction they are calculated by the equations (2) and (3), respectively:

$D_C= 0.89-0.28 = 0.61$
$D_{ct}= 0.89+0.28 -1 = 0.17$

The Resulting Evidence Degree is calculated by the equation (4): $\mu_R=0.805$

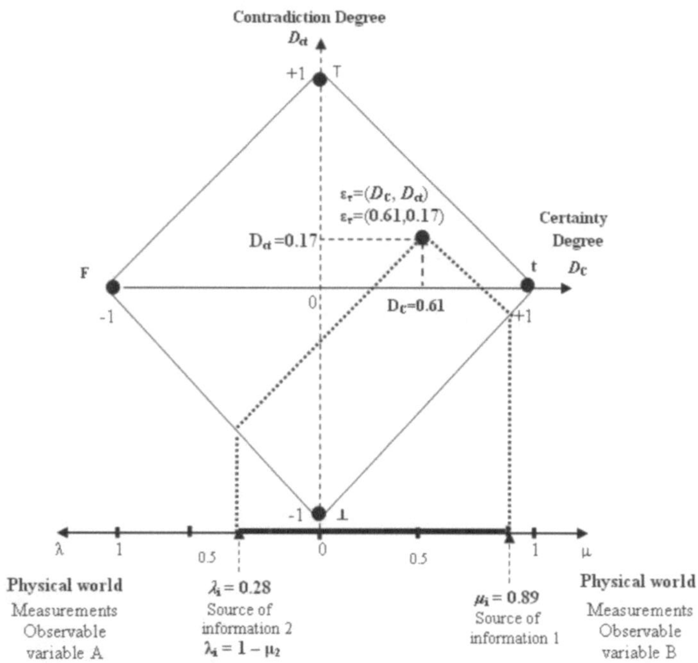

Fig. 2. Paraconsistent logical state ε_τ in the Lattice associated of the PAL2v.

In practice the value of the Degree it can return in the equation that established the Interval of Interest of the physical greatness for the decision making. The figure 2 shows a Paraconsistent logical state ε_τ that is constituted by the pair (D_C, D_{ct}) formed starting from the two degrees of evidence μ and λ given as example.

4.3 Artificial Paraconsistent neural cells

In the Paraconsistent analysis the main objective is to know the value, or degree of certainty, it can be assured that the proposition is False or True. So, it is considered as a result only the analysis of the value of certainty D_C. The value of degree of contradiction D_{ct} is an indicator that informs the measure of inconsistency about the information signals. If there is a low value of certainty or much inconsistency the result is undefined [DA SILVA FILHO et al, 2010]. In practice it is used values limits that help in the conclusions after the analysis of the proposition P. The Algorithm of the PAL2v Logic using values external limits is described to proceed.

4.3.1 Algorithm of the Paraconsistent Annotated Logic with annotation of two values

The Algorithm makes a paraconsistent analysis using only the equations obtained (2) e (3) of the lattice associated to PAL2v compared to the external limits:

*/ Input Variables */ μ, λ

The values for external limits:

V_{icc}, Limit value for inferior certainty, such as: $-1 \leq V_{icc} \leq 0$

V_{scc},, Limit value for superior certainty, such as: $0 \leq V_{scc} \leq 1$

V_{icct}, Limit value for inferior contradiction, such as: $-1 \leq V_{icct} \leq 0$

V_{scct},, Limit value for superior certainty, such as: $0 \leq V_{scct} \leq 1$

/Output Variables

Output Digital = S_1

Output Analogical = S_{2a}

Output Analogical = S_{2b}

*/Mathematics expressions */ as :

$D_C = \mu - \lambda$

$D_{ct} = \mu + \lambda - 1$

*/determination of the extreme logic states */

If $D_C \geq V_{scc}$ then $S_1 = t$

If $D_C \leq V_{icc}$ then $S_1 = F$

If $D_{ct} \geq V_{scct}$ then $S_1 = \top$

If $D_{ct} \leq V_{icct}$ then $S_1 = \bot$

Otherwise $S_1 = I$ Non definition

$D_{ct} = S_{2a}$ and $D_C = S_{2b}$

*/ End */

The values for externally adjusted control are limits that will serve as reference for analysis.

This LPA2v algorithm can be represented as a block that we name the Basic Paraconsistent Artificial Neural Cell- *b*PANC. The Paraconsistent Neural cells (PANCs) comprise the basic elements of the Artificial Neural Paraconsistent Networks [DA SILVA et al, 2010]. To compose it, it is used a basic Paraconsistent Artificial Cell a (*b*PANC).

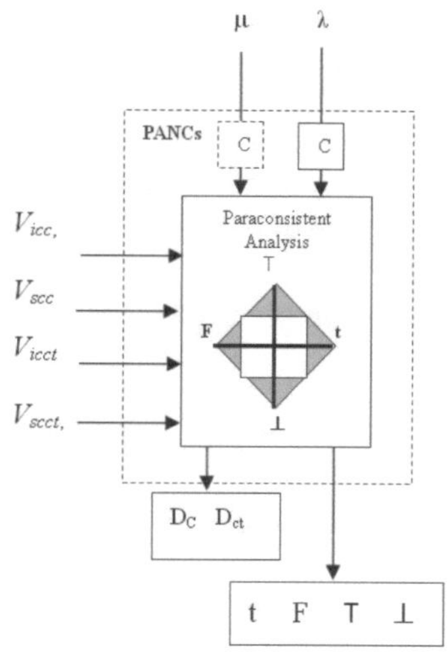

Fig. 3. The Basic Paraconsistent Artificial Neural Cell *b*PANC.

4.4 The learning Paraconsistent Neural Artificial cell for - *l*PANC

The cells for learning are used in Paraconsistent Neural Network as units of memory and pattern sensors in primary layers [DA SILVA FILHO, 2001]. For instance, an *l*PANC can be trained to learn a pattern using the method of Paraconsistent analysis applied through an LPA2v algorithm. In the process of learning where it is used as pattern the real values between 0 and 1 it is considered an equation to calculate the results of the successive values of degrees of belief $\mu_{r(k)}$ until it reaches value 1. So, for an initial value of degree $\mu_{r\,(k)}$, they obtain values $\mu_{r\,(k+1)}$ until the $\mu_{r\,(k+1)} = 1$.

Considering a process of learning of the pattern of True, therefore, the value of start 1, the equation for learning is:

$$\mu_{E(K+1)} = \frac{\left\{\mu_1 - (\mu_{E(K)C})l_F\right\} + 1}{2} \tag{4}$$

where:

$\mu_{E(k)C} = 1 - \mu_{E(k)}$ being l_F = learning Factor $0 \le l_F \le 1$

And for the process of learning of the pattern of Falseness, therefore, value of start 0, the equation is:

$$\mu_{E(K+1)} = \frac{\left\{\mu_{1C} - (\mu_{E(K)C})l_F\right\} + 1}{2} \tag{5}$$

where:

$\mu_{1c} = 1 - \mu_1$ being l_F = learning Factor $0 \le l_F \le 1$

For the two cases it is considered the cell that is completely trained when: $\mu_{E(k+1)} = 1$. The learning Factor l_F is a real value, equal or higher than 0, got arbitrarily through external adjustments. The higher the value of l_F higher is the learning process of the cell. If $l_F = 1$ we say that the cell has a natural capacity for learning. The natural capacity decreases as the l_F adjustment gets closer to 0.

4.4.1 Algorithm of the learning Paraconsistent Artificial Neural cell

The lPANC algorithm that makes the learning the pattern True is shown as follows:

1- Start: $\mu_{Er} = 1/2$ */ Output of the virgin cell */
2- Define: $l_F = C_1$ where $0 \leq C_1 \leq 1$ */ Insert the value as factor for learning */
3- Do: $\mu_2 = \mu_{Er}$ */ It connects the output of the cell in the input of the unfavorable evidence degree */
4- Do: $\mu_{2c} = 1 - \mu_2$ */ It applies the Complement Operator in the value of the input of the unfavorable evidence degree */
5- Do: $\mu_1 = 1$ */ it is applied the pattern of Truth */
6- Calculate the D_C value: $D_C = \mu_1 - \mu_{2C}$ */ It is calculated the degree of certainty*/
7- Do: $\mu_{er} = \frac{(D_C)C_1 + 1}{2}$ */the degree of evidence is found resulting the output through the equation (4) of Paraconsistent analysis */
8- If $\mu_{Er} \neq 1$ return to step 3
9- Stop.

The figure 4 shows the symbol of the *l*PANC and the characteristic curve of output for different values of learning Factor (l_F).

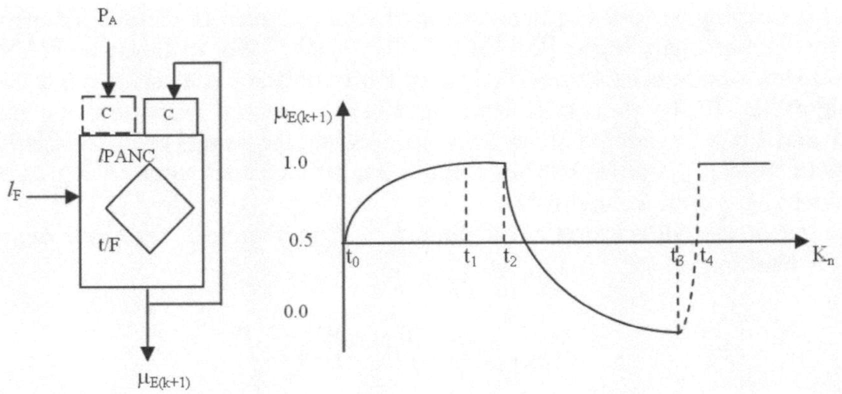

Fig. 4. Simplified symbol and the characteristic output graph of the Learning Paraconsistent Artificial Neural Cell (lPANC).

4.5 The Paraconsistent Artificial Neural Cell of Simple Logical Connection – $PANC_{SiLC}$

The Paraconsistent Artificial Neural Cell of Simple Logical Connection ($PANC_{SiLC}$) has the function of establishing logical connectives between representative signals of Degrees of Evidence. The main logical connection cells are those that do the operation of the maximization OR and of the minimization AND. For maximization, initially, a simple analysis is done through the equation of the Degree of Evidence, which will inform which of the two input signals is of higher value. With this information, the cell representative algorithm establishes the output signal. The utilized equation and the conditions that determine the output for a maximization process are exposed as follows.

Consider the input variables:

μ_{1A}, such that: $0 \leq \mu_{1A} \leq 1$, and μ_{1B}, such that: $0 \leq \mu_{1B} \leq 1$.

The Resultant Degree of Evidence is calculated by doing:

$\mu_{1A} = \mu_1$ and $\lambda_2 = 1 - \mu_{1B}$

$$\mu_E = \frac{(\mu_1 - \lambda_2) + 1}{2}$$

To determine the higher value input:

If: $\mu_E > 0.5 \rightarrow \mu_{1A} \geq \mu_{1B} \rightarrow$ The output is μ_{1A}

If: $\mu_E < 0.5 \rightarrow \mu_{1A} < \mu_{1B} \rightarrow$ The output is μ_{1B}

Figure 5 shows representative figure and the simplified symbol of $PANC_{SiLC}$, which does the maximization between the two Degrees of Evidence signals μ_{1A} and μ_{1B}.

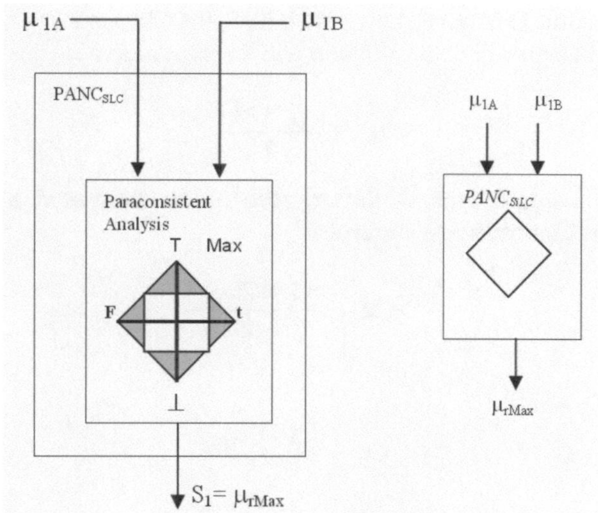

Fig. 5. Symbol of Paraconsistent Artificial Neural Cell of Simple Logical Connection ($PANC_{SiLC}$) in the maximization process (OR).

4.6 The Paraconsistent Artificial Neural cell of Equality Detection– $PANC_{ED}$

A Paraconsistent Artificial Neural Cell of Equality Detection ($PANC_{ED}$) consists of a Paraconsistent Artificial Neural Cell whose main function is to compare two values of Degrees of Evidence applied at the inputs and to generate a response relative to the equality in the closed interval between 0.0 and 1.0. Thus a $PANC_{ED}$ is a cell that supplies a Resultant Degree of Evidence that expresses an equality factor between two values applied at the inputs.

In a Paraconsistent Artificial Neural Network, the result of this comparison maybe utilized as recognition signal for a certain pattern one wishes to find or recognize in certain parts of the network. Therefore, the use of this cell is important in the function of pattern classification by PANNet.

To form the $PANC_{ED}$, the Normalized Degree of Contradiction will be calculated and its value will be compared to the Contradiction Tolerance Factor - Ctr_{TF}. This will define three output values, as follows:

- If the comparison done with the Contradiction Tolerance Factor Ctr_{TF} results in True, it means that the signals are considered equal. The signal at the output will be 1.0, indicating that the pattern was recognized.

- If the comparison done with the Contradiction Tolerance Factor Ctr_{TF} results in False, it means that the signals are considered unequal. The signal at the output will be 0.0, indicating that the pattern was not recognized.

Paraconsistent Artificial Neural Cell of Decision ($PANC_D$) has the main function of working as a decision node. Hence, the $PANC_{ED}$ may be described by means of an algorithm through the following equations from the fundamentals of PAL2v.

Consider the Degrees of Evidence applied at the inputs:
μ_{1A}, such that: $0 \le \mu_{1A} \le 1$ and μ_{1B}, such that: $0 \le \mu_{1B} \le 1$
The Unfavorable Degree of Evidence calculated by: $\lambda = 1 - \mu_{1B}$
The limit value:
Ctr_{TF} - Contradiction Tolerance Factor, such that: $0 \le Ctr_{TF} \le 1$
The Normalized Degree of Contradiction will be calculated by:

$$\mu_{ctr} = \frac{\mu_{1A} + \lambda}{2}$$

The limit values maximum and minimum recognition computed as the limit values, Superior and Inferior Contradiction Control:

$$Ctr_{CSV} = \frac{1 + Ctr_{TF}}{2}$$

and

$$Ctr_{CIV} = \frac{1 - Ctr_{TF}}{2}$$

The logical estate of output S_1 is obtained through comparisons done as follows:
If: $\mu_{ctr} = 0$ then: $S_1 = 1$ */Recognized Pattern*/
Else: $S_1 = 0$ */False*/

4.7 The Paraconsistent Artificial Neural cell of Decision– $PANC_D$

Paraconsistent Artificial Neural Cell of Decision ($PANC_D$) has the main function of working as a decision node in Paraconsistent Analysis Artificial Neural Networks. This cell receives input two signals. These are resulting signals from the analysis performed by other cells that compose the Network.

The output result will establish a conclusion of the analysis. Thus, a $PANC_D$ will only present one of the three values as result of the analysis:

a. Value 1, representing the conclusion "True"
b. Value 0, representing the conclusion "False"
c. Value 0.5, representing the conclusion "*Indefinition*".

The Decision Cell has one single external adjustment and it may be described by means of an algorithm. With the presented concepts, a mathematical model of a Paraconsistent Artificial Neural Cell of Decision is developed from the equations:

Consider input variables:
μ_1, such that: $0 \le \mu_1 \le 1$ and μ_2, such that: $0 \le \mu_2 \le 1$
Dec_{TF} - Decision Tolerance Factor such that: $0 \le Dec_{TF} \le 1$
The Unfavorable Degree of Evidence is obtained through

$$\lambda = 1 - \mu_2$$

The Resultant Degree of Evidence calculated by: $\mu_E = \frac{(\mu_1 - \lambda) + 1}{2}$

The *Falsehood* and *Truth* Limit Values: $T_{LV} = \frac{1 + Dec_{TF}}{2}$ and $F_{LV} = \frac{1 - Dec_{TF}}{2}$

Where: T_{LV} = *Truth Limit* Values

F_{LV} = *Falsehood Limit* Values

The logical states of output S_1 and S_2 are obtained through the comparisons carried out as follows:

If: $\mu_E \geq T_{LV}$ then: S1= 1 */True*/

If: $\mu_E \leq F_{LV}$ then: S1= 0 */False*/

Else: S1 = 0.5 */*Indefinition**/

With these observations, we will describe a Paraconsistent Artificial Neural Cell of Decision utilizing the input and output variables along with the adjustment signals.
The representation of a Paraconsistent Artificial Neural Cell of Decision ($PANC_D$) with its simplified symbol is in figure 6.

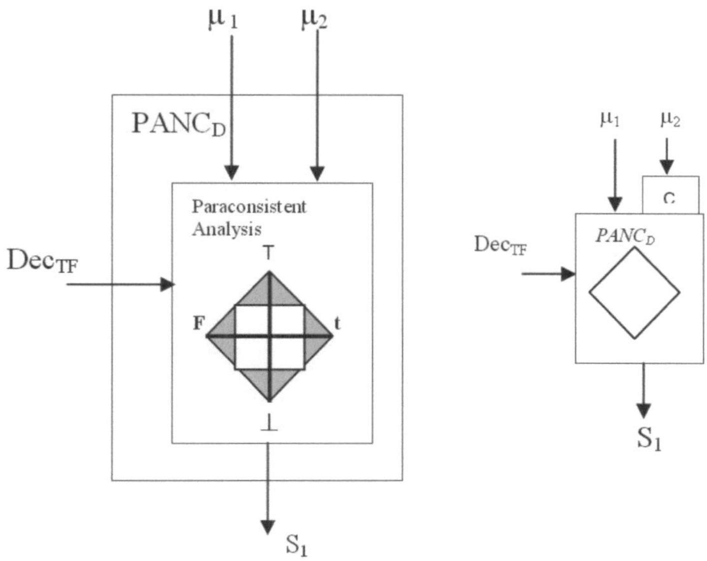

Fig. 6. Paraconsistent Artificial Neural Cell of Decision ($PANC_D$) with its simplified symbol

5. The expert system for analysis of marine pollution

The development of the application using Paraconsistent Artificial Neural network can be divided in parts to show the necessary steps for its achievement.

5.1 Description of the functions of the process for computer analysis for marine pollution

The computer program that composes the Expert System allows the following functions in the process of analysis:

5.a) The classification and identification of the patterns of cells of the bioindicator through the data obtained through analysis of images of the test of retention of the neutral red dye.
5.b) The analysis of the information through the Paraconsistent algorithm of the network simulating the test process of retention of the neutral red colorant.
5.c) Presentation of the Results through the Degrees of Evidence resulting according to the methodology of PAL2v.
The figures 7 and 8 show through diagrams the blocks of action of the Expert System in the treatment of the input signals:

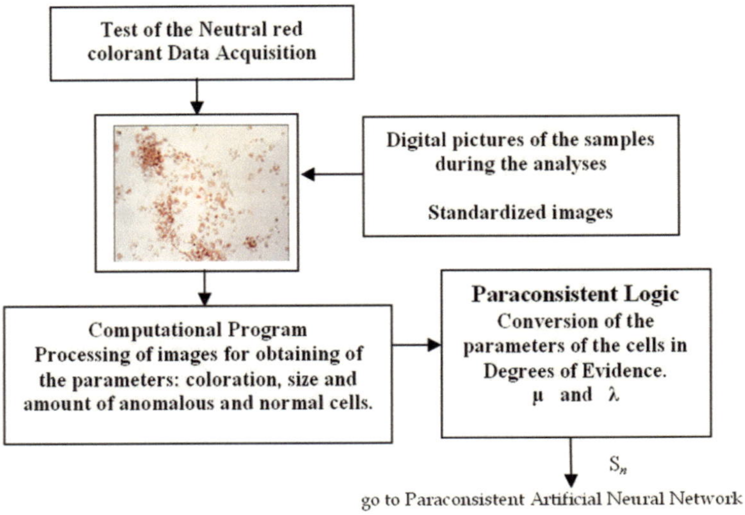

Fig. 7. Diagram of extraction of attributes from a slide of the test of the neutral red colorant of blood cells of mussels

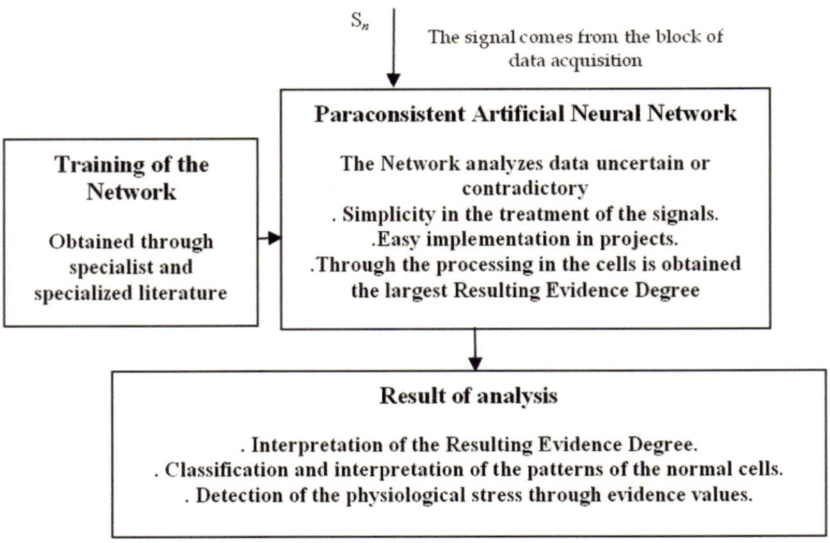

Fig. 8. Diagram in blocks of the Expert system with Paraconsistent Artificial Neural Networks applied to the method of obtaining the physiological stress cells.

5.2 Dada collection and separation in sets

The first steps of the process of development of the Paraconsistent Artificial Neural Network refer to the data collection related to the problem and its separation into a set of training and a set of tests. Following this there are the procedures of the parameters of the biological method for building the sets that were the same used in biology, such as, coloration and size of cells, time of reaction to the dye and quantity of stressed cells.

5.3 Detailed process for obtaining of the evidence degrees

The learning process links to a pattern of values of the Degrees of Evidence obtained starting from an analysis accomplished with mollusks from non polluted areas. The determination of the physiological stress will base on the amount and in the time of reaction of the cells in the presence of the Neutral Red Dye.

The pattern generates a vector that can be approximate to a straight line, without there are losses of information. As it was seen, the first observation of the analysis begins to the 15 minutes and it presents the minimum percentage of stressed cells. And the observation concludes when 50% of the cells of the sample present stress signs. Therefore, in order to normalize the evidence degree of pollution for counting of cells in relation to the time of analysis, it was obtained a straight line equation to make possible the analysis through the concepts of the Paraconsistent Annotated Logic. In that way, the equation can be elaborated with base in the example of the graph 1 (figure 9), obtained of the existent literature, where the time of 15 minutes is interpreted as evidence degree equal at one ($\mu = 1$), and the time of 180 minutes as evidence degree equal at zero ($\mu = 0$).

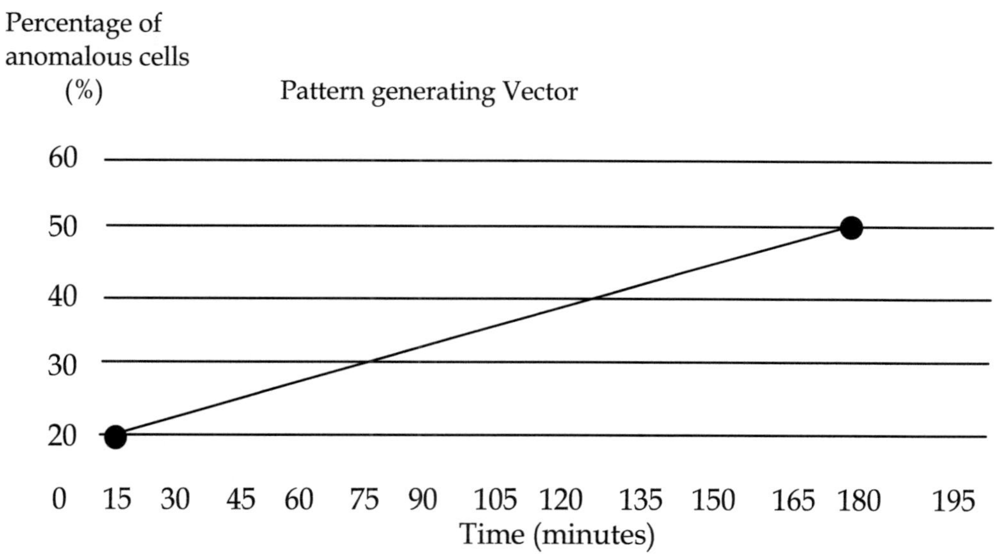

Fig. 9. Graph demonstrating example of a pattern of reference of an area no polluted.

This way, the mathematical equation that represents the pattern in function of the time of occurrence for 50% of stressed cells will have the form:

$$f(x) = ax + b \ .$$

$$\left| 1 = 15a + b \right. \qquad \text{beginning of the analysis}$$

$$\left| 0 = 180a + b \right. \qquad \text{end of the analysis}$$

Of the mathematical system, be obtained the values for:

$a = -1/165$ and $b = 180/165$ resulting in the function: $f(x) = \frac{-1}{165}x + \frac{180}{165}$

It is verified that this function will return the value of the evidence degree normalized in function of the final time of the test, and in relation to the pattern of an area no polluted.
The conversion in degree of evidence of the amount of cells for the analysis is also necessary. For that it is related to the degree of total evidence the total amount of cells and the percentage of cells stressed in the beginning (10%), and at the end of the test (50%).

$$\left| 1 = 0.5\text{x}Uda + b \right. \qquad \text{end of the analysis}$$

$$\left| 0 = 0.1\text{x}Uda + b \right. \qquad \text{beginning of the analysis}$$

With the resolution of the mathematical system, it is had: $a = (1/4)Ud$ and $b = -0.25$ and the equation in the following way: $f(x) = \frac{1}{0.4\text{x}Ud}x - 0.25$

Therefore, x represents the number of cells stressed in relation to the Universe of Discourse (*Ud*) of the cells analyzed during this analysis. With the due information, we will obtain the favorable evidence degree, one of the inputs of the Paraconsistent Neural network. After the processing of the information of the analyses with the obtaining of the evidence degrees, the data will go by a Lattice denominated of the Paraconsistent Classifier, which will accomplish a separation in groups, according to table 3 to proceed.

EVIDENCE DEGREE (μ)	GROUP
$0 \leq \mu \leq 0.25$	G_1
$0.26 \leq \mu \leq 0.50$	G_2
$0.51 \leq \mu \leq 0{,}75$	G_3
$0.76 \leq \mu \leq 1$	G_4

Table 3. Table of separation of groups in agreement with the evidence degree.

To adapt the values the degrees of evidences of each level they will be multiplied by a factor: m/n, where m = number of samples of the group and n = total number of samples. In other words, the group that to possess larger number of samples will present a degree of larger evidence.
Only after this process it is that the resulting evidence degrees of each group will be the input data for the Paraconsistent Artificial Neurall Cells. After a processing, the net will obtain as answer a degree of final evidence related at the standard time, which will demonstrate the correlation to the pollution level and a degree of contrary evidence. In a visual way the intersection of the Resulting Certainty Degree (Dc) and the Resulting Contradiction Degree (Dct) it will represent an area into Lattice and it will show the level of corresponding pollution.

5.4 Configuration of network

The definition of the network configuration was done in parts. First, it was defined the parameters of the algorithm of treatment and the way the calculation of the degrees of reaction of the samples through the mathematics were obtained by a pattern of reference. After that, it was done a classification and separation in groups using a Paraconsistent network with cells of detection of equality. These cells that make the network are the ones for decision, maximization, selection, passage and detection of equality cells. In the end of the analysis, the network makes a configuration capable of returning the resulting degree of evidence and a degree of result contradiction, which for the presentation of results will be related to the Unitary Square in the Cartesian Plan that defines regions obtained through levels of pollution.

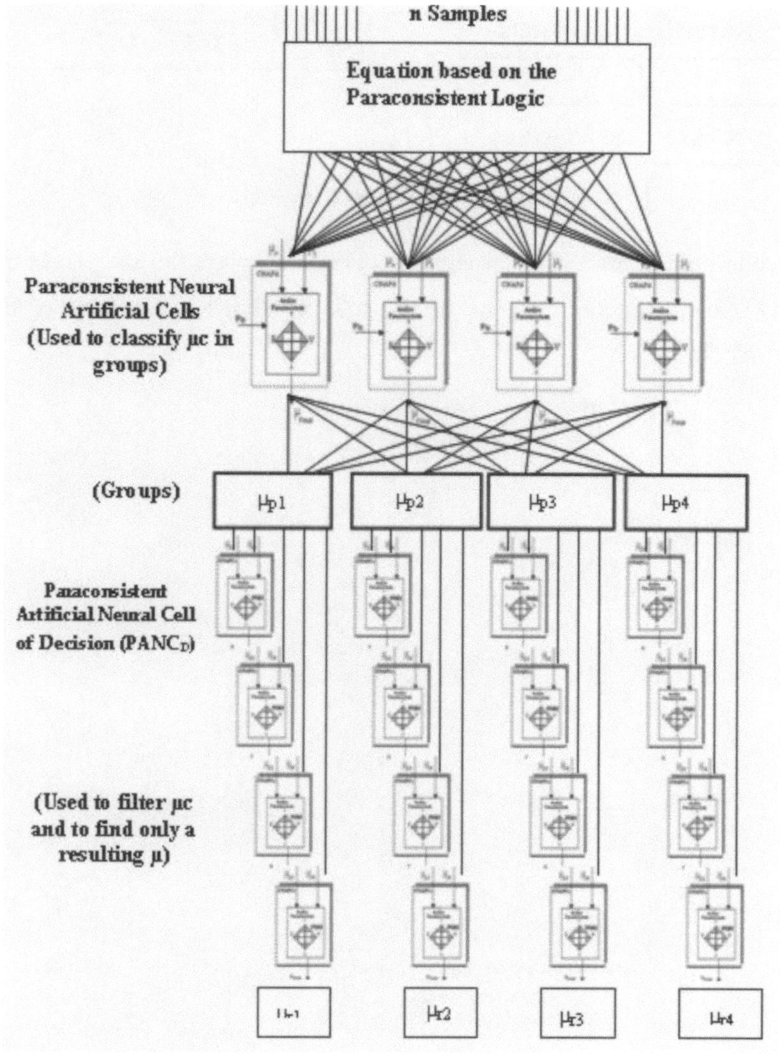

Fig. 10. The Paraconsistent network configuration.

The next figure 11 shows the flow chart with the main steps of the treatment of signals.

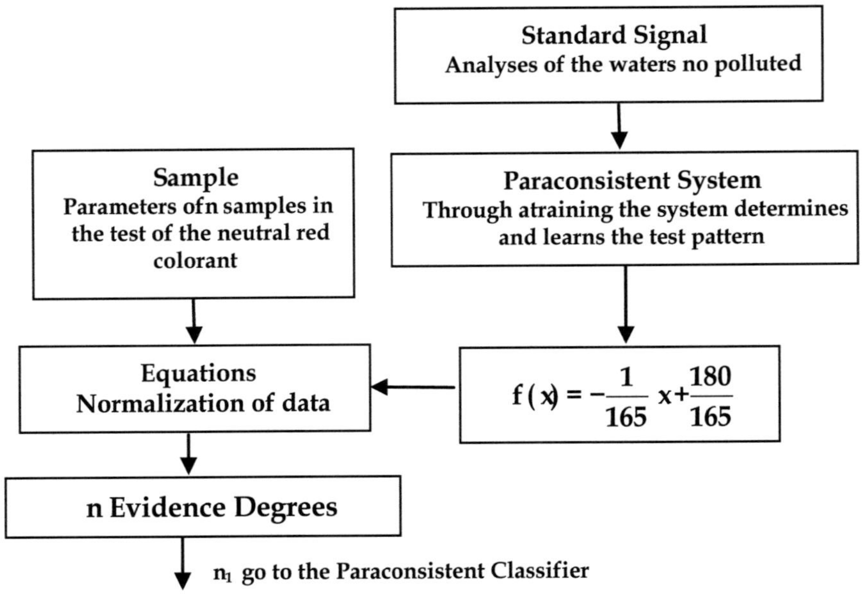

Fig. 11. Paraconsistent treatment of the signals collected through the analysis of the slides.

The figure 12 shows the configuration of the cells for that second stage of treatment of information signals.

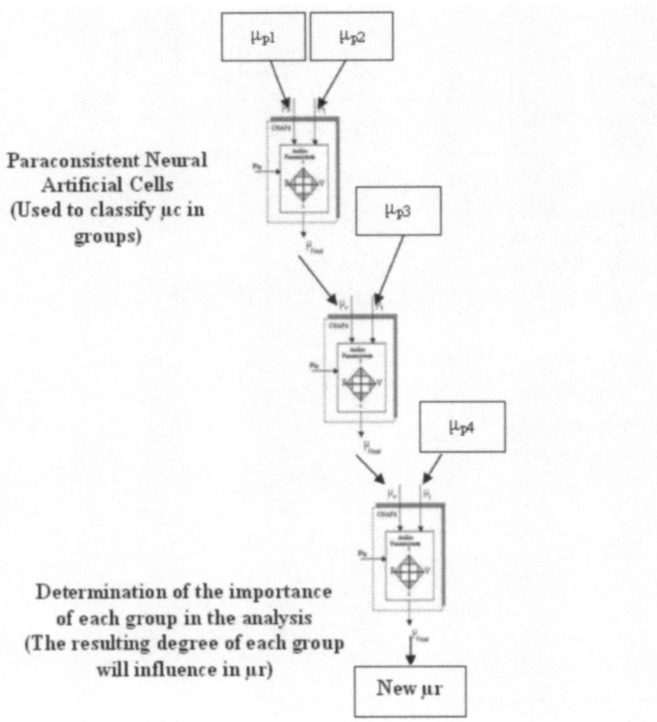

Fig. 12. Second Stage of the Paraconsistent Network - Treatment of the Contradictions.

The stage that concludes the analyses is composed of one more network of Paraconsistent Artificial neural Cells than it promotes the connection, classification through maximization processes. That whole finalization process is made making an analysis in the contradictions until that they are obtained the final values for the classification of the level of sea pollution. In the figure 13 is shown the diagram of blocks with the actions of that final stage of the Paraconsistent analyses that induce to the result that simulates the method for analysis of the time of retention of the Neutral Red Colorant through the Paraconsistent Annotated Logic.

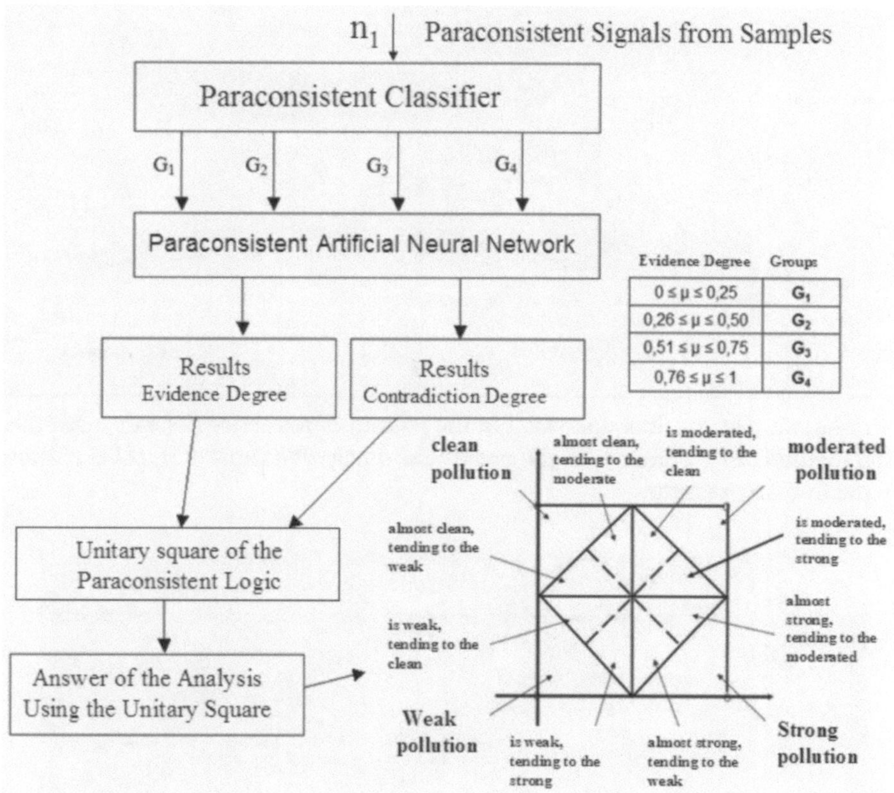

Fig. 13. Final Treatment and presentation of the results after classification and analysis of the Paraconsistent Signals.

5.4 Tests

During this stage, it was performed a set of test using a historical data base, which allowed determining the performance of the network. On the tests it was verified a good performance of the network obtaining a good indication for the system of decision of the Specialist System.

5.5 Results

After the analysis were performed and compared with the traditional method used in the biology process, we can observe that the final results are imminent. It was verified that the bigger differences between the two techniques are where the area is considered non polluted therefore, mussels were not exposed to pollution because the differences are

Neutral Red Assay: Results Table										
ÁREA LIMPA										
Date:	15/09/2001									
Sample:	ÁREA 6: CONTROLE									
Name:	CAMILO / DENIS									
Mussel	15	30	45	60	75	90	105	120	135	150	score
1	+	+-	+-	-							45
2	+	+-	-								30
3	+	+-	-								30
4	+	+-	+-	-							45
5	+	+	+-	+-	-						60
6	+	+-	-								30
7	+-	+-	-								30
8	+-	+-	+-	-							45
9	+	+	+-	-							45
10	+	+-	+-	+-	-						60
11	+-	-									15
12	+-	-									15
13	+	+-	-								30
14	+	+-	+-								45
15	+	+-	-								30
16	+	+-	-								30
17	+-	+-	+-	+-	-						60
18	+	-									15
19	+	+-	-								30
20	+	+-	-								30
FREQUÊNCIA	20 em 20	17 em 20	8 em 20	3 em 20					Tempo Referencia		36

Página 1

Fig. 14. Presentation of result of analysis 1 of the pattern of reference done through the traditional method. Pr = 38min with the positive and negative signs of the observations made by the human operator.

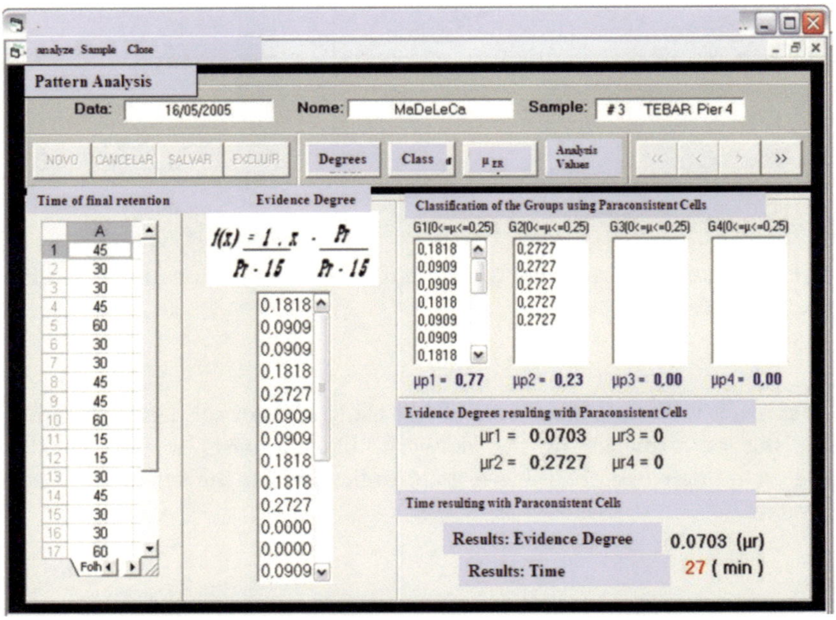

Fig. 15. Presentation of the result of analysis 1 of the pattern of reference done with the software elaborated with Paraconsistent Logic. Pr = 27min with the results in the form of Degrees of Evidence and classification of the tenor of sea pollution.

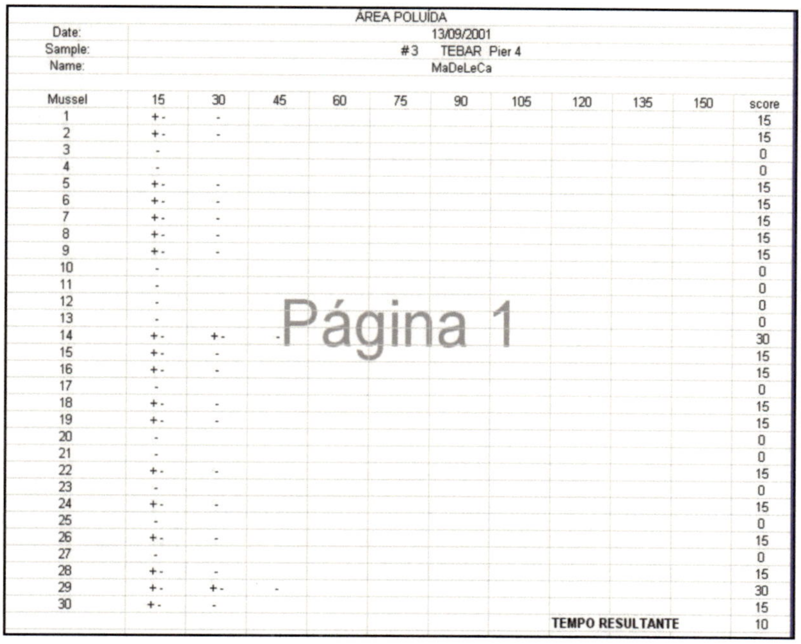

ÁREA POLUÍDA

Date: 13/09/2001
Sample: #3 TEBAR Pier 4
Name: MaDeLeCa

Mussel	15	30	45	60	75	90	105	120	135	150	score
1	+-	-									15
2	+-	-									15
3	-										0
4	-										0
5	+-	-									15
6	+-	-									15
7	+-	-									15
8	+-	-									15
9	+-	-									15
10	-										0
11	-										0
12	-										0
13	-										0
14	+-	+-	-								30
15	+-	-									15
16	+-	-									15
17	-										0
18	+-	-									15
19	+-	-									15
20	-										0
21	-										0
22	+-	-									15
23	-										0
24	+-	-									15
25	-										0
26	+-	-									15
27	-										0
28	+-	-									15
29	+-	+-	-								30
30	+-	-									15
								TEMPO RESULTANTE			10

Página 1

Fig. 16. Presentation of the result of analysis 2 of samples done through the traditional method. Tr = 10min with the positive and negative signs of the observations made by the human operator.

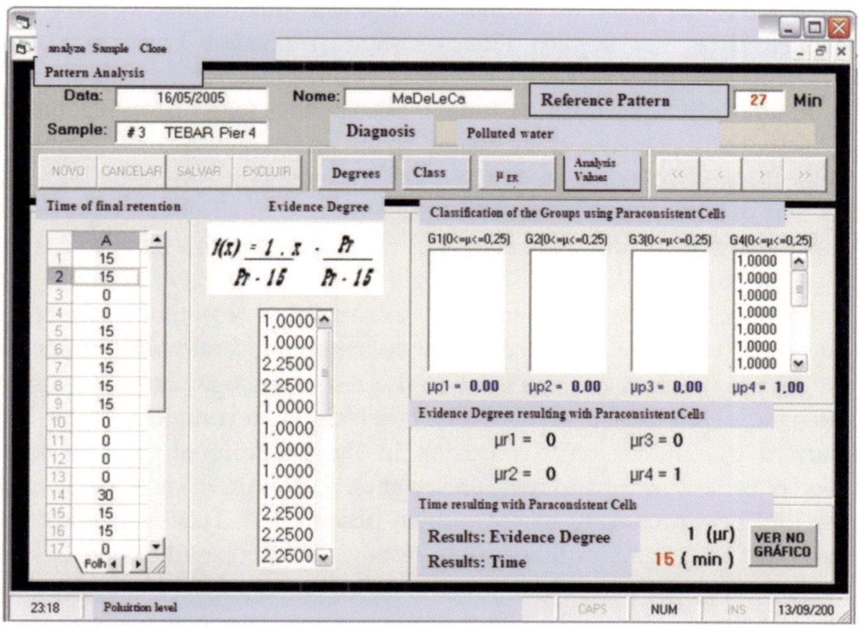

Fig. 17. Presentation of the results of analysis 2 of samples done through the software elaborated with Paraconsistent Logic. Tr= 15min with the results in the form of Degrees of Evidence and classification of the tenor of sea pollution.

outstanding in these conditions due to the pattern process that happens only with an arithmetic average of the analysis while the Paraconsistent Neural Artificial Network always takes into consideration the existing contradictions. Later studies are being performed for the comparison between the two methods of presentation, which can take to a better comparison of the amount. The following images show the ways of presenting the two methods, one done the traditional way and the other through the screen of data of the software of Paraconsistent Logic.
It is verified that the screens of the Software of the Paraconsistent Expert System brings the values of the Degrees of Evidence obtained and other necessary information for the decision making. To these values other relevant information are joined capable to aid in the decision making in a much more contusing way than the traditional system.

5.6 Integration

With the trained and evaluated network, this was integrated into an operational environment of the application. Aiming a more efficient solution, this system is easy to be used, as it has a convenient interface and an easy acquisition of the data through electronic charts and interfaces with units of processing of signals or patterned files.

6. Conclusion

The investigations about different applications of non-classic logic in the treatment of Uncertainties have originated Expert Systems that contribute in important areas of Artificial Intelligence. This chapter aimed to show a new approach to the analysis of exposure and effects of pollution in marine organisms connecting to the technique of Artificial Intelligence that applies Paraconsistent Annotated Logic to simulate the biological method that promotes the assay with neutral red. The biological method that uses a traditional technique through human observation when counting the cells and empirical calculations presents good results in its end. However, the counting of the stressed cells through observation of the human being is a source of high degree of uncertainty and obtaining results can be improved through specific computer programs that use non-classical logic for interpretation. It was checked in this work that the usage of a Expert System based in Paraconsistent Logic to get the levels of physiological stress associated with marine pollution simulating the method of retention of the Neutral Red dye was shown to be more efficient because it substitutes several points of uncertainty in the process that may affect the precision of the test. Although the first version of the Paraconsistent software used presented results which when compared to the traditional process showed that it has more precision in the counting of cells as well as the manipulation of contradictory and non consistent data through the neural net, minimizing the failures the most according to the human observation. This work also shows the importance of the investigations that search for new theories based in non-classical logic, such as the Paraconsistent Logic here presented that are capable of being applied in the usage of the technique of biomarkers. It is important that these new ways of approaching bring conditions to optimize the elaboration of a computer environment with the objective of using modern technological ways and this way getting results closer to the reality and more trustworthy.

7. Acknowledgment

Our gratefulness to the Eng. Alessadro da Silva Cavalcante for the aid in the implementation and tests of the Paraconsistent Algorithms in the Expert System.

8. References

ABE, J. M [1992] "Fundamentos da Lógica Anotada" (Foundations of Annotated Logics), in Portuguese, Ph D thesis, University of São Paulo, FFLCH/USP - São Paulo, 1992.

BISHOP, C.M. [1995] Neural Networks for Pattern Recognition. 1.ed. Oxford University Press, 1995.

BLAIR[1988] Blair H.A. and Subrahmanian, V.S. Paraconsistent Foundations for Logic Programming, Journal of Non-Classical Logic, 5,2, 45-43,1988

DA COSTA et al [1991] "Remarks on Annotated Logic" *Zeitschrift fur Mathematische Logik und Grundlagen der Mathematik*, Vol.37, 561-570, 1991.

DA SILVA FILHO et al [2010] Da Silva Filho, J. I., Lambert-Torres, G., Abe, J. M. *Uncertainty Treatment Using Paraconsistent Logic - Introducing Paraconsistent Artificial Neural Networks.* IOS Press, p.328 pp.. *Volume 211 Frontiers in Artificial Intelligence and Applications ISBN 978-1-60750-557-0 (print) ISBN 978-1-60750-558-7 (online) Library of Congress Control Number: 2010926677 doi: 10.3233/978-1-60750-558-7-i,* Amsterdam, Netherlands, 2010.

DA SILVA FILHO [1999] Da Silva Filho, J.I., Métodos de interpretação da Lógica Paraconsistente Anotada com anotação com dois valores LPA2v com construção de Algoritmo e implementação de Circuitos Eletrônicos, EPUSP, in Portuguese, Ph D thesis, São Paulo, 1999. 185 p.

DA SILVA FILHO et al[2006] Da Silva Filho, J.I., Rocco, A, Mario, M.C. Ferrara, L.F.P. *"Annotated Paraconsistent logic applied to an expert System Dedicated for supporting in an Electric Power Transmission Systems Re-Establishment"* IEEE Power Engineering Society - PSC 2006 Power System Conference and Exposition pp. 2212-2220, ISBN-1- 4244-0178-X - Atlanta USA - 2006.

FERRARA et al[2005] Ferrara, L.F.P., Yamanaka, K., Da Silva Filho. A system of recognition of characters based on Paraconsistent artificial neural network/. Advances in Logic Based Intelligent Systems. IOS Press. pp. 127-134, vol.132, 2005.

HALLIDAY [1973] halliday, J.S., The Characterization of Vector cardiograms for Pattern Recognition – Master Thesis, MIT, Cambridge, 1973.

LOWE et al [1995] Lowe, D. M. et al Contaminant – induced lysosomal membrane damage in blood cells of mussels Mytilus galloprovincialis from Venice lagoon: an in vitro study. Mar. Ecol. Prog. Ser., 1995. 196 p.

NASCIMENTO et al [2002] Nascimento,I.A, Métodos em Ecotoxologia Marinha Aplicações no Brasil, in portuguese, Editora: Artes Gráficas e Indústrias Ltda, 2002.262 p.

NICHOLSON [2001] Nicholson, S. Ecocytological and toxicological responses to cooper in *Perna viridis* (L.) (Bivalvia: Mytilidae) haemocyte lysosomal membranes, *Chemosphere*, 2001, 45 (4-5): 407 p.

HEBB [1949] Hebb, D. O. The Organization of Behavior, *Wiley*, New York, 1949.

SOS TERRA VIDA [2005] - Organização não governamental SOS Terra Vida. Poluição Marinha, 15 fev. 2005. in portuguese, available in: http://www.sosterravida.hpg.ig.com.br/poluicao.html. Access in 25 abr. 2008.

KING [2000] King, R, Rapid assessments of marine pollution - Biological techniques. Plymouth Environmental Research Center, University of Plymouth, UK, 2000. 37 p.

16

Expert System Based Network Testing

Vlatko Lipovac
University of Dubrovnik,
Croatia

1. Introduction

Networks today are not isolated entities as local-area networks (LAN) are often connected across campuses, cities, states, countries, or even continents by wide-area networks (WAN) that are just as diverse in their hardware interfaces and software protocols as LANs and may consist of multiple technologies including, too. Protocols are implemented in combinations of software, firmware, and hardware on each end of a connection. The state-of-the-art networking environment usually consists of several network operating systems and protocol stacks executing. A particular protocol stack from any manufacturer should inter-operate with the same kind of protocol stack from any other manufacturer because there are protocol standards that the manufacturers must follow. For example, the Microsoft Windows® TCP/IP stack should inter-operate with a Linux TCP/IP stack. Connections can be peer to peer, client to server, or the communications between the network components that create or facilitate connections such as routers, hubs, and bridges [1].

As converged IP networks become widespread, increasing network services demand more intelligent control over bandwidth usage and more efficient application development practices to be implemented, such as traffic shaping, quality-of-service (QoS) techniques etc. So, there is a growing need for efficient test tools and methodologies that deal with application performance degradation and faults. Network professionals need to quickly isolate and repair complex and often intermittent performance problems in their network and effectively hand over problems that are outside the network domain to the appropriate internal group or external vendor. Among the key technologies that are used for a variety of critical communication applications, we face a rapid growth of network managers' concerns, as sometimes they find their networks difficult to maintain due to high speed operation, emerging and escalating problems in real time and in a very complex environment such as: incorrect device configuration, poorly architectured networks, defective cabling or connections, hardware failures etc. On the other hand, some problems do not cause hard failures, but instead may degrade network performance and go undetected.

In particular, network management in such a diverse environment encompasses processes, methods and techniques designed to establish and maintain network integrity. In addition to its most important constituent - fault management, network management includes other activities as well, such as configuration management of overall system hardware and software components, whose parameters must be maintained and updated on regular basis.

On the other hand, performance management involves monitoring system hardware and software components' performance by various means. In addition, these tasks include monitoring network efficiency, too.

Finally, security management is gaining importance as both servers and fundamental network elements, such as bridges, routers, gateways and firewalls, need to be strictly administered in terms of authentication and authorization, network addresses delivery, as well as monitored for activities of a profile, other than expected.

Consequently, integrated network management is a continuum where multiple tools and technologies are needed for effective monitoring and control.

There are two fundamentally different approaches to network management: reactive and proactive. The reactive approach is the one most of us use most of time. In a purely reactive mode, the troubleshooter simply responds to each problem as it is reported by endeavouring to isolate the fault and restore service as quickly as possible. Without a doubt, there will always be some element of the reactive approach in the life of every network troubleshooter. Therefore, in the first phase - reactive management, IT department aims to increase network availability, where the required management features focus on determining where faults occur and instigating fast recovery.

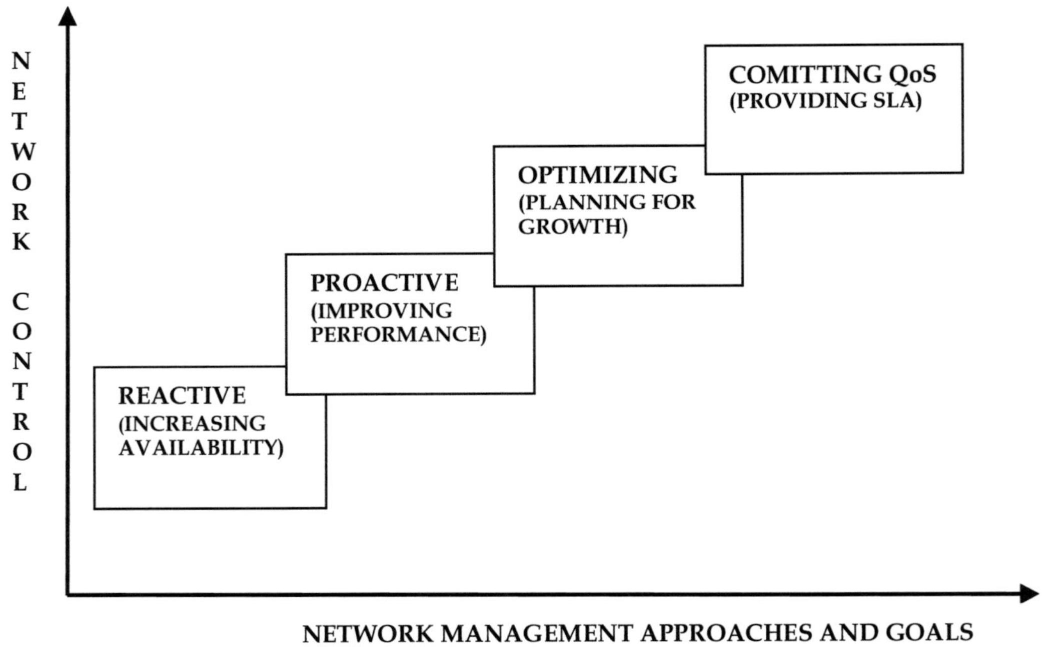

Fig. 1. Network management requirements escalation

The next phase towards increasing the network control, Fig. 1, is proactive management, which seeks to improve network performance. This requires the ability to monitor devices, systems and network traffic for performance problems, and to take control and appropriately respond to them before they affect network availability.

Optimization is the third phase that includes justifying changes to the network either to improve performance or maintain current performance, while adding new services. Trend analysis and network modeling are the key capabilities needed for optimization.

Finally, guaranteed service delivery phase involves gaining control of the criteria on which the IT organization is judged. Actually, modern network management should be primarily based on a service level agreement (SLA) that specifies precise quality characteristics for guaranteed services, stating the goals for service quality parameters that the network manager's critical responsibility is to achieve in terms of: average and minimum availability, average and maximum response time, as well as average throughput.

Nevertheless, in what follows, we will mostly be focusing troubleshooting. Analysts have determined that a single hour of network downtime for the major worldwide companies is valuated at multiple hundreds of thousands of dollars in lost revenue, and as much as about 5% of their market capitalization, while the average cost per hour of application outage across all industries, is approaching hundred thousand dollars, and is still rising. For industries such as financial services, the financial impact per hour can exceed several millions of dollars.

With this respect, the question that comes up here is whether the troubleshooting must be reactive?

Not necessarily, as the concept of *proactive troubleshooting* goes beyond the classic reactive approach, presuming that active monitoring and managing network health on an on-going basis should proceed even during the state of the network when it appears to be operating normally. By this way, the network manager is able to anticipate some problems before they occur, and is so better prepared to deal with those problems that cannot be anticipated.

Being proactive means being in control. Certainly, no one would argue against being in control. But exactly what does it take to be proactive? First of all, it takes investment of time it takes to actively monitor network health, to understand the data observed, to evaluate its significance and to store it away for future reference. Secondly, the right tools are needed, i.e. the test equipment that is capable of making the measurements necessary to thoroughly evaluate the network health. The test equipment should be able to accurately monitor network data, even during times of peak traffic load (in fact, especially then!), and intelligently and automatically analyze the acquired data.

1.1 Network management tools

There exists a wide range of appropriate test solutions for design, installation, deployment and operation of networks and services. Their scope stretches from portable troubleshooting test equipment to centralized network management platforms, where each tool plays a vital role by providing a window into a specific problem area, and is so designed for a specific purpose. However, no tool is the magic answer to all network fault management issues and does not everything a network manager typically needs to do.

Network management tools can be compared in many different dimensions. In Fig. 2, they are rated in terms of their strength in isolating and managing network faults, as well as in terms of breadth [2], [3]. With this respect, tools range from inexpensive handheld test sets aimed at physical level installation and maintenance, through built-in network diagnostic programs, portable protocol analyzers, distributed monitoring systems for multi-segment monitoring, and finally, to enterprise-wide network management systems. Many of the tools are complementary, but there is also quite a bit of overlap in capability.

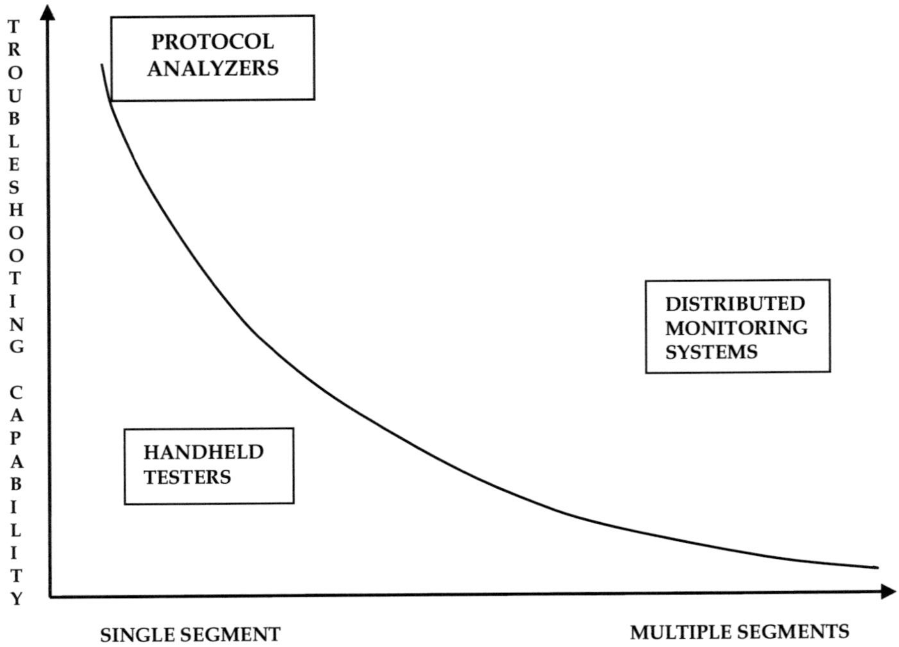

Fig. 2. Tools for fault isolation and analysis

Precise measurement of physical transmission characteristics is essential mostly for WAN testing, where tactical test instruments include interface testers and BER testers. Interface testers, also known as breakout boxes, display activity on individual signal lines, and are often used to perform quick checks on interface operating states at the first sign of trouble. They feature high-impedance inputs, so a signal under test is not affected by the testing activity and measurements can be made without interrupting network operation. In addition to simple go/no-go test panel indicator red and green LED lights, many interface testers have a built-in wiring block. This feature allows the operator to temporarily modify individual signal lines for test purposes.

Logic analyzers, oscilloscopes, or spectrum analyzers are sometimes required as well to make measurements that complement BER and interface testers and are helpful to determine the source of transmission problems. Other specialized line testing instruments, available for WAN troubleshooting, include optical time-domain reflectometers (OTDR) for fiber-optic links, and signal level meters for copper cables.

Protocol analyzers and handheld testers each view network traffic one segment at a time. Simple tools provide protocol decodes, packet filtering and basic network utilization, as well as error count statistics. More powerful tools include more extensive and higher level statistical measurements (keeping track of routing traffic, protocol distribution by TCP port number, etc...), and use expert systems technology to automatically point out problems on the particular network segment of interest.

On the other hand, distributed monitoring systems dramatically reduce mean-time-to-repair (MTTR) by eliminating unnecessary truck rolls for most network problems. These are designed to monitor multiple network segments simultaneously, using multiple data collectors – either software agents or even dedicated LAN or WAN hardware probes, generally semi-permanently installed on mission-critical or other high-valued LAN/WAN segments, to collect network performance data, typically following the format of the Remote

Monitoring (RMON) protocol [2], [3], which allows continuous monitoring of network traffic, enabling observation of decodes and keeping statistics on traffic that is present on the medium. The so acquired data are then communicated to a central network management analytical application, by means of in-band messages (including alarms when certain thresholds are exceeded), according to a certain protocol, mostly the Simple Network Management Protocol (SNMP), so that the software agents that reside on each of the managed nodes, allow the management console to see information specific to that node (e.g., the number of octets that have transited through a certain interface), or about a particular segment (e.g., utilization on a particular Ethernet bus segment), and control certain features of that device (e.g., administratively shutting down an interface).
For network troubleshooters, understanding how tool selection changes with the progress through troubleshooting process, is critical to being efficient and effective.
Strong correlation exists between a diagnostic tool being distributed or not, and whether the tool is used to *isolate* or to *analyze* network and system problems. In this sense, generally, strategic distributed monitoring tools are preferable for isolating faults, however, as compared to protocol analyzers, distributed monitoring systems (and handheld troubleshooting tools, too) typically provide only simple troubleshooting capability, while localized tactical tools - protocol analyzers usually come equipped with very detailed fault isolation capability, and are so preferable for investigating the problem cause in a local environment of interest [2], [3].

1.1.1 Protocol analysis

A simplified schematic diagram of data communications network is shown on Fig. 3, where traffic protocol data units (PDU) flow in between the user side (represented by the Data Terminal Equipment – DTE), and the network side (represented by the Data Communications Terminating Equipment - DCE). A protocol analyzer is considered as a device capable of passive monitoring of traffic and analyzing it either in real time, or in post-processing mode.

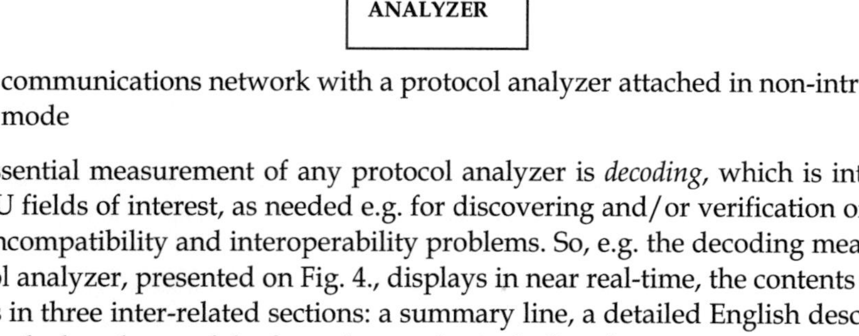

Fig. 3. Data communications network with a protocol analyzer attached in non-intrusive monitoring mode

The very essential measurement of any protocol analyzer is *decoding*, which is interpreting various PDU fields of interest, as needed e.g. for discovering and/or verification of network signalling incompatibility and interoperability problems. So, e.g. the decoding measurement of a protocol analyzer, presented on Fig. 4., displays in near real-time, the contents of frames and packets in three inter-related sections: a summary line, a detailed English description of each field, and a hex dump of the frame bytes, also including the precise timestamps of PDU (frame or packet) arrivals - crucial information that was used in the exemplar tests and analysis (characterizing congestion window) to follow in the next chapter [4].

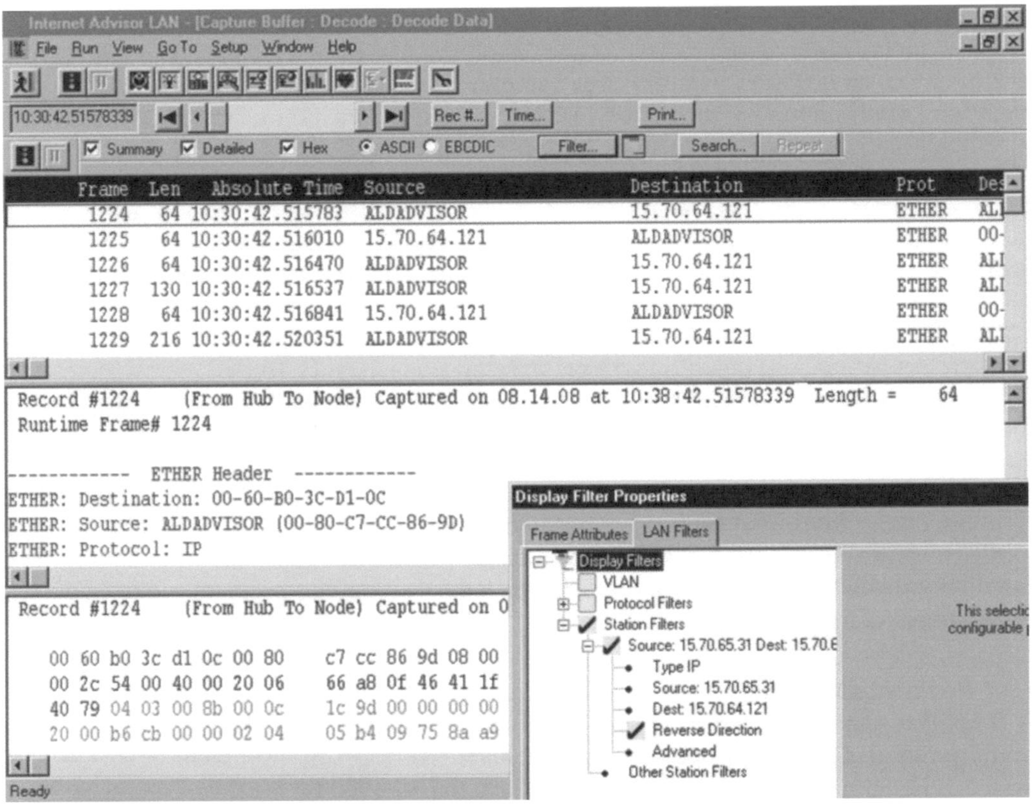

Fig. 4. Decoding of PDUs, with precise time stamping (100 ns resolution)

Specifically, the primary application of portable protocol analyzers is in-depth, detailed troubleshooting. But it would be wrong to automatically classify these powerful troubleshooting tools as appropriate only for top network protocols specialists, as state-of-the-art protocol analyzers provide powerful statistical measurements and expert systems capabilities which make these tools extremely easy to use, even for to less trained network staff.

In this sense, advanced state-of-the-art statistical analysis of traffic for a selected test station of interest often includes mutually correlated identification and characterisation of active nodes, their associated protocols and connected nodes, so providing an insight into the overall network activity of interest. So, for each active protocol stack and each active connection, line utilization and throughput (average, minimum or maximum), frame length and the number of bad frame-check-sequence (FCS) errors, will be indicated by these statistics measurements.

From the hardware platform point of view, there are several classes of portable protocol analyzers as well. However, the best type of analyzer to select depends on the size, complexity, and topology of the network involved.

Simple and inexpensive software-only applications run on standard network interface cards (NIC) and decode protocol frames, adding only rudimentary statistics measurements, while being capable of keeping up with network traffic only on low and moderately loaded networks. With limited data filtering or triggering, such products are moderately priced, and typically consume the host PC resources when running.

However, in high-speed networks, such as e.g. 1/10/100 Gbit/s LANs, higher-performance interface adapters and fast PC systems must be used in order to cope with high data volumes to be expected. Since standard NICs cannot accept all PDUs if their number exceeds a certain limit, some of them might be dropped (among them likely to be the ones most relevant for troubleshooting). In this sense, a very fast PC CPU is needed to be able to not only accept and process PDUs, but also ensure that filtering and triggering functions are performing in real time. On top of that, receive and transmit capture buffers must be deep enough, preferably with direct memory access (DMA), so to not share memory with other tasks of PC applications (among them the protocol analysis software). The NIC must have the option to switch off the local-only mode of operation (when, apart from the incoming PDUs bearing its own address, it would have seen only broadcasts), and so be able to forward all traffic it sees to the protocol analysis software.
On the other side, top high-performance protocol analyzers, Fig. 5, may also be built on a PC platform, but include special buffer memories, typically 256 Mbytes or more deep, which can be written to at very high speed, so insuring 100% data capture even under extreme traffic loads. The PDUs from such a dedicated capture buffer are processed by a RISC-based CPU, optimized for speed and accuracy, which feeds the information to protocol analysis application, running on the PC.

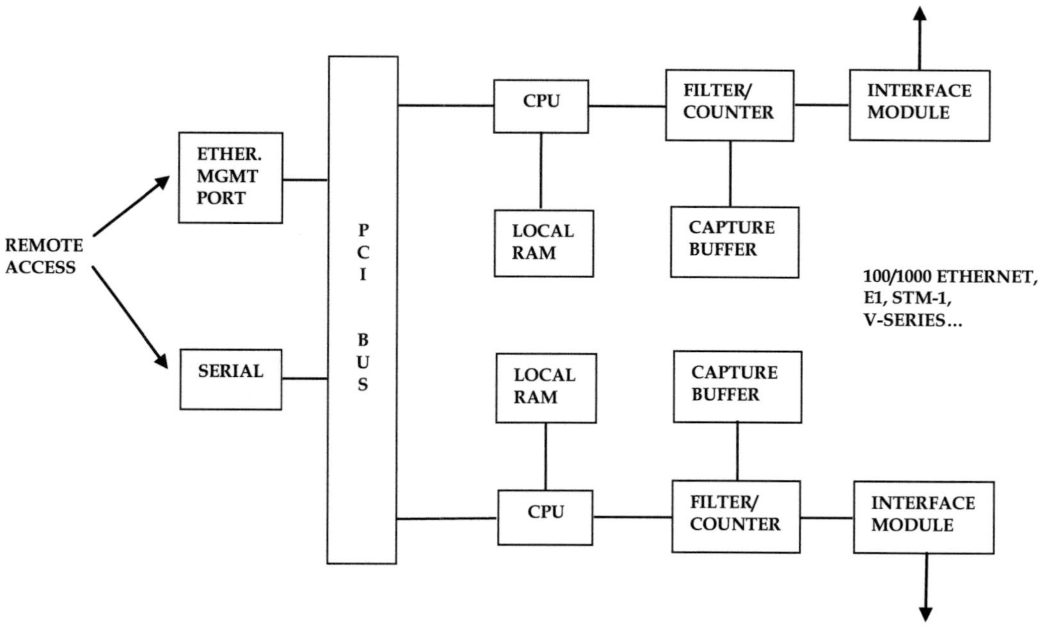

Fig. 5. Architecture of a dual-port HW protocol analyzer [4]

Such portable analyzers with dedicated hardware-based data acquisition, definitely provide much better capture performance than their software-based counterparts, as not only can they analyze and record all network traffic (time-stamped with great precision due to the high-resolution internal clock), but also generate network test traffic at wire speed (even in high-speed networks such as e.g. 10 Gb/s Ethernet). With such dedicated hardware, filtering can be accomplished in real time, regardless of filtering criteria (based on protocol, nodes and/or frame content) and instantaneous network utilization (whose peaks are most likely to coincide with eventual problems, and so are most needed to get captured and forwarded to the analysis). In addition, some real-time trigger actions (such as e.g. event-driven stops of data acquisition) can be associated to filtering. Furthermore, hardware-based protocol analyzers usually support simultaneous multi-port measurements and so enable performance testing on multiple LAN and WAN interfaces, e.g. on both sides of network components such as routers and bridges.

2. Expert network protocol analysis

As it was already mentioned, state-of-the-art high-end protocol analyzers often contain very powerful measurement sets providing much more information than just protocol decodes. This always includes statistical analysis of traffic, and, finally, the expert analysis, where the system compares network problems that occur to information in its knowledge database, and if any error scenario is found in the database that matches the discovered situation, the system suggests possible diagnoses and troubleshooting tips, so enabling automatic fault isolation [4].

This has become more and more necessary to adequately address the diversity of potential complex network problems that definitely deserve more comprehensive approach than just using traditional network troubleshooting, which is typically based on passive network measurements by means of a classic protocol analyzer, combined with a variety of ad hoc tests. Such methodology was satisfactory when network topologies were simple and faults resulted mostly from configuration or hardware and wiring failures, i.e. when the majority of network problems were in the physical layer of the protocol stack. Nowadays, with more intelligent network devices (e.g. integrated layer 2 switching and layer 3 routing), application/server load balancing (i.e. layer 4 - 7 switching and routing), more sophisticated security policies and devices, as well as QoS technologies, most network problems have crept up the stack. Consequently, unlike before, a rising percentage of network performance problems, faced by network managers, are attributed to higher OSI layers, namely 3, 4 through 7, rather than hard failures. These can include network software bugs, too many users trying to use the network at once and/or soak up the available network bandwidth, interoperability problems between protocol stacks because of different interpretations and implementations of standards, breached network security or software and hardware updates with unexpected results etc. Moreover, as deploying state-of-the-art complex, multi-services and multi-technology high-speed networks, including data, voice and streaming media applications, has become reality, delivering high-availability communication infrastructures for mission critical applications, and contracted QoS, as well as maintaining fast growing of sophisticated networks, imply that network downtime is not an affordable option at all. On top of that, dramatically rising network problems complexity also implies longer *Mean-Time–To-Repair* (MTTR), even without taking into account that quite often network managers rely on limited skill personnel.

Specifically, even a protocol analyzer that is equipped with the best data acquisition hardware and application-level decodes, as well as advanced statistical analysis (that identifies how busy is the network, who is connected to it and is using most network bandwidth, which protocols are the most active stations using, when they are using it, for what, and whether the network is reaching its capacity, etc.), in many instances, will not itself timely isolate complex problems on the network and diagnose who is causing them, if still the fault management process is mostly manual and so very time-consuming, requiring a great deal of expertise in many aspects of network technology.

This in turn means that, in order to keep up with the next-generation-network (NGN) challenges, troubleshooting methods have to change, as well to better address the rising need for more sophisticated test tools that will make the process more efficient by providing automated means for continuous higher-level identification of problems, with less human intervention, so making decisions on how to best manage the network, justified and so easier.
With this respect, state-of-the art protocol analysis often incorporates some sort of an expert system that offers a beneficial solution to these problems by continuous monitoring a network for performance degradation and faults in all 7 OSI layers, logging the results and then looking up its knowledge database, searching for eventual similarities with the currently identified network problems. Thus, the expert system capability of a protocol analyzer essentially not only takes advantage of but goes well beyond passive protocol following and statistical performance measurements, thus making fault diagnosis much more comprehensive. The intelligent protocol decodes automatically report on errors or deviations from the expected protocol, so reducing thousands of captured data frames to a short list of significant network events, and interpreting the significance of these events. This way, appropriately reported, such expert-analysis-isolated network abnormalities and inefficiencies significantly reduce the scope of potential causes of the problem (if not self-sufficiently pinpoint what it most likely might be), suggesting possible solutions that the network manager can consider to figure out what is wrong from the visible symptoms, so greatly speeding up the troubleshooting process. In other words, hand-in-hand with the proactive troubleshooting process is another methodology called *intelligent analysis*, which refers to the use of state-of-the-art data reduction tools available on today's test equipment, which facilitate rapid fault isolation, as a way to avoid network troubleshooting in (purely) reactive chaos.
Better yet, this way, network managers can even predict the possibility of network failures and take actions to avoid the conditions that may lead to problems.

2.1 Expert protocol analysis system basic components

A typical rule-based expert system consists of five components: knowledge base, inference engine, blackboard, user interface, and explanation facility, Fig. 6.

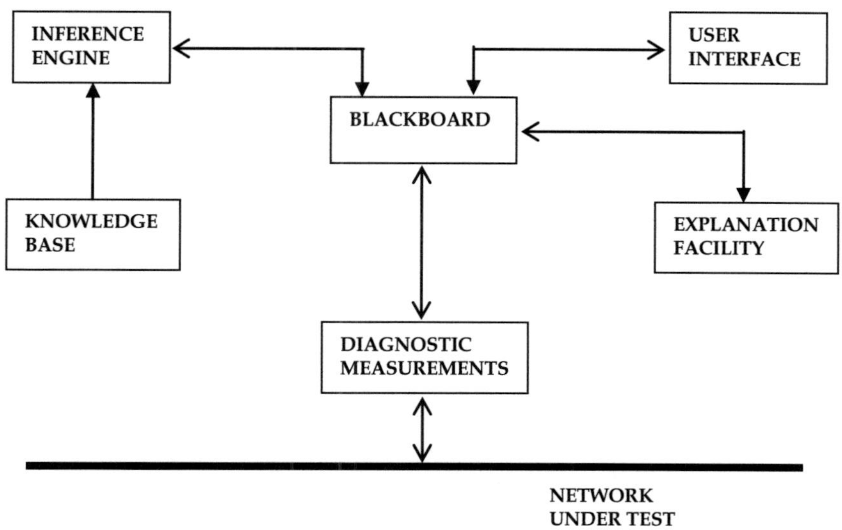

Fig. 6. Typical rule-based network expert system components

The knowledge base is a collection of data that contains the domain-specific knowledge about the problems being solved. The inference engine performs the reasoning function. It is the component of the inference engine that controls the expert system by selecting the rules from the knowledge base to access, execute and decide when a solution has been found. After performing measurements and observing the network for significant events, pending measurement results that satisfy the rules' preconditions are posted to the blackboard. The blackboard is a communication facility that serves as a clearinghouse for all information in the system, while the user interface allows the user to input information, control the reasoning process and display results. The explanation facility interprets the results by describing the conclusions that were drawn, explaining the reasoning process used, and suggesting corrective action.

An expert system used for network troubleshooting must have access to diagnostic functions to actively confirm the existence of faults and to gather information from other devices and network management systems on the network. It must generate alarms and log all pertinent information in a data base. Automated operation must be available so that human intervention is not required, and audit trails should be provided so that a network manager can later track problems.

An expert system must also be able to proactively obtain information about the state of the network to prove (or disprove) hypothesized problems. This is performed by the rules requesting information (via the inference engine) from the blackboard. The results of the measurements are posted to the blackboard to allow the inference engine to continue and eventually prove (or disprove) the hypothesized problem.

Often, real-time demands of troubleshooting a network exceed the performance capabilities of a conventional rule-based expert system. However, intelligent measurements can greatly improve the performance of a rule-based expert system. Measurements are considered to be intelligent if they actually interpret the information on the network, instead of simply reporting low level events such as frame arrivals. An example of an intelligent measurement would be one that monitors the network and provides a high-level commentary on significant network events and conversations between nodes by following the state of network transactions. It would indicate if a connection was established properly, ensure that the traffic level between nodes did not exceed a maximum limit, and identify new mappings between physical layer addresses and network addresses. The process of managing networks includes fault detection and isolation. Network faults refer to problems in areas such as physical media, traffic and routing, connection establishment, configuration and performance.

In what follows it will be briefly described how an expert system, embedded in a protocol analyzer, addresses the areas of fault detection and isolation, specifically in solving common faults in a complex network environment.

2.2 Network baselining and benchmarking

Understanding how the network under test operates is crucial in managing it proactively, so without it, a network manager will not have the information needed to make sound decisions concerning how his network is managed.

Does he have misconfigured servers and nodes that are sending extra data onto the network? Is the network overloaded? Is it time to upgrade hardware or software? Has that recent department relocation had an adverse affect on the network? How much growth has occurred on the network over the past year? Can it sustain that growth level for another year?

Two key processes need to be implemented to proactively manage the network: first, and most important, the network manager must *baseline* the network, so to get understanding who is using it and how it is being used. Essentially, a baseline is a set of statistical measurements made over a period of time, which characterizes network performance, Fig. 7. It is a snapshot of the characteristics of the network of interest.

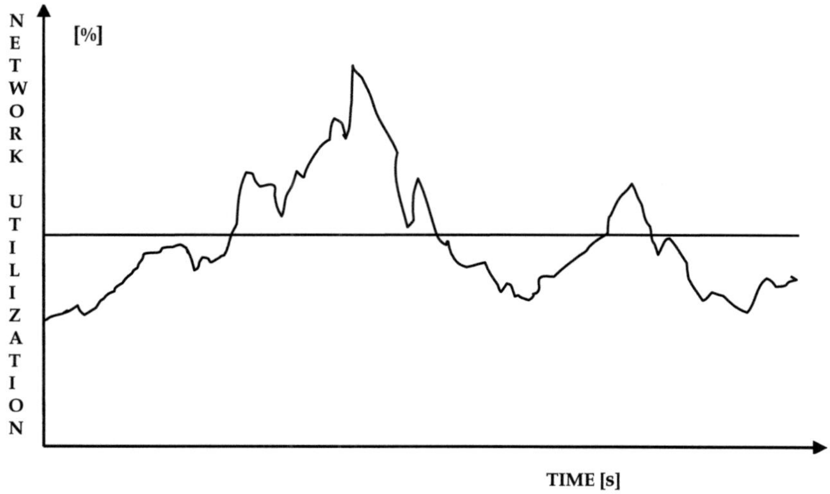

Fig. 7. An example of network baseline

Measurement results from recorded baselines describe normal operating conditions of the network, and so can provide points of reference - thresholds for future advanced statistical analysis and expert measurements, thus enabling discovery of eventual departures of multiple measurements results from their belonging thresholds, by reporting them as significant events (e.g. for TCP/IP or XoIP protocols), should anything go wrong sometime later. With properly set thresholds, e.g. such as the ones in Fig. 8, significant changes will be neither missed, nor unnecessarily interpreted as routine events.

Some of the so detected high-level ordered significant protocol events may indicate normal and desirable activity, while others might indicate the presence of potentially serious problems that should be present only in very rare instances. Following this classification are the "normal", "warning", and "alert" events, enabled in the configuration window of the above example, sorted by the order of their severity in indication that the identified problems could lead to network performance degradation or network failure [4].

By this way, baselining uncovers any network problems or inefficiencies so that they can be fixed before their major affect on users, which also enables better planning for growth. By looking at successive baselines, taken regularly over a long period of time, one will be able to observe trends and, based on them, plan for future, in terms of capacity growth and investments. Moreover, benchmarking applications and components before they are installed on the network provides the information needed to understand and predict their effect.

Thus, using the tactics of baselining to first understand the normal network operation and, when problems arise, perform another baseline and compare the results, problems can be quickly identified and/or inefficiencies in network operation exposed. This provides immediate opportunities for improving network performance by observing trends and recognizing changes, and so being able to anticipate and resolve problems before they become apparent to network users.

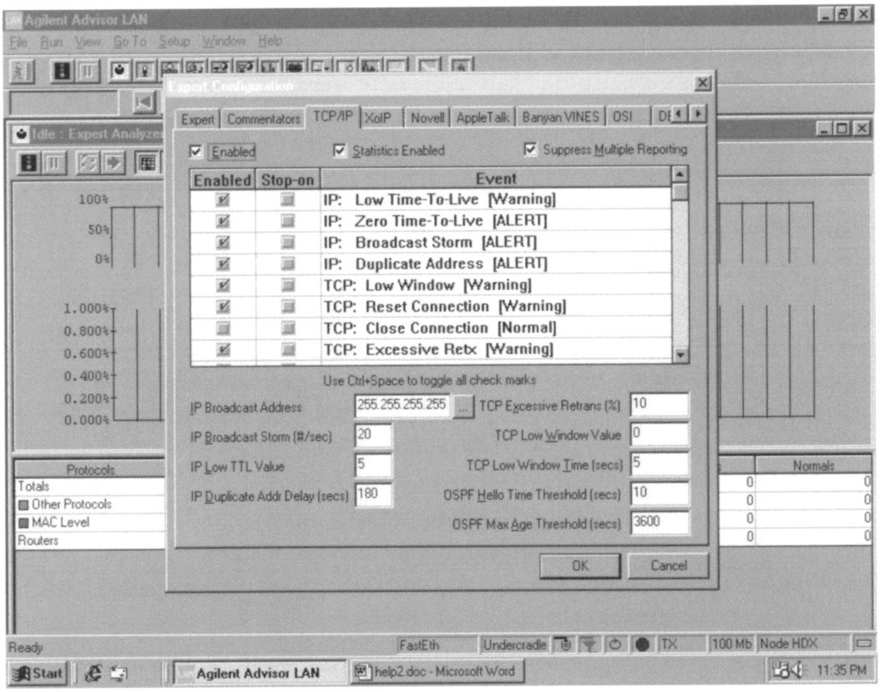

Fig. 8. Example of selected TCP/IP significant events for the related expert protocol analyzer measurements, and setup of baseline thresholds, to match particular network conditions

There are three main steps in performing a network baseline: collecting the data, creating the report and interpreting the results. First, the data must be collected either using a protocol analyzer, or a distributed network monitoring system agent, connected directly to the network segment of interest, such as the backbone and server ones, or the segments interconnecting separate networks (WAN interconnections first). The data should be collected for a fixed period of time, at similar time periods and at regular intervals, especially before and after large network adds, moves, or changes.

Before beginning the data collection process, one will first have to choose a sample period, which is the total period of time over which baseline measurements are made. The sample interval is the period of time over which each individual statistics is sampled and averaged, i.e. it is the amount of time between data points in the baseline data - the time resolution used to collect the data samples, Fig. 9.

As the sample interval gets larger, it will be less possible to resolve rapid changes in measured characteristics, as they will be averaged out. So, small sample intervals and small measurement periods should be used when fine resolution is required, which is usually appropriate for fault isolation or to obtain an instantaneous characterization of network health. On contrary, longer sample intervals and longer overall measurement periods are recommended when baselining for long-term trends, or gaining an overall picture of network health.

Typically, most appropriate sample intervals are e.g. 1 second samples for periods up to 2 hours, 1 minute samples for periods up to 24 hours, or 10 minutes to 1 hour samples, for periods of two or more days.

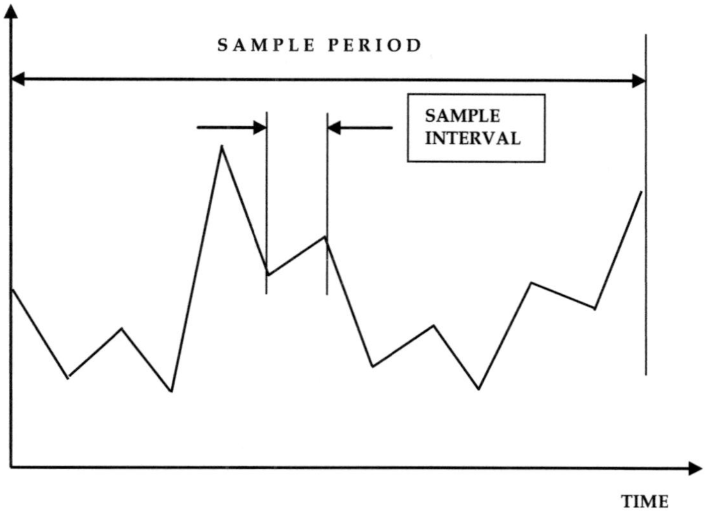

Fig. 9. Baseline sample interval and sample period

Both portable protocol analyzers and distributed monitoring systems provide the information necessary to baseline and benchmark the network, but, as it was already pointed out, each of them has its unique capabilities that can help troubleshoot problems or monitor network performance, respectively. Whatever devices are used as data collectors, enough data must be provided, with enough accuracy to provide the real insight into the network operational characteristics. Each network segment of interest should be baselined, as e.g. a computer-aided engineering (CAE) segment will have quite different characteristics than a segment running just business applications.

Collecting the data is important; however, if they are not presented in a clear and meaningful way, it will be very difficult to interpret them, as finally the network manager needs to look for abnormalities (such as e.g. high levels of network utilization, low average data packet size, high level of errored frames, or a file transfer protocol (FTP) with average data size of 100 bytes -indicating that the client or server could be configured incorrectly or overloaded etc.), trying to learn what is normal for his network over time, and comparing successive baselines to question any significant changes in traffic patterns or error levels. The baseline reports can also be used to set thresholds to be used as input to a rule-based automatic expert system that will review the baseline instead of a human network troubleshooter, and look for abnormal symptoms, to identify and question unusual traffic patterns for multiple protocol suites of interest. This will not only help in understanding how the network operates, but also to predict future changes in the network behaviour, before they actually occur (with potentially troublesome consequences).

2.3 Practical expert protocol analysis

The expert analysis must be executed on a truly multitasking machine, able to simultaneously and automatically run several measurements, comparing the measured values with their corresponding thresholds and so "feeding" the decision algorithm with input data. With such an arrangement in protocol analysis, PDUs are decoded nearly real-time, where the only reason for not fully real-time decoding is that other simultaneous processes can slow it down a bit. Intelligent expert system-based protocol decodes automatically follow each conversation, and report on errors or deviations from the expected protocol.

However, this usually comes integrated with a number of other powerful intelligent tools – mostly high-level protocol and node statistical analysis, which provide automatic node and protocol events discovery, and even complete network health audit. These intelligent analysis tools do much of the problem analysis work automatically, by separating the significant few events from thousands and millions of PDUs passing through the analyzer every second, where examining the details in individual PDUs for each protocol stack running only makes sense after real-time narrowing the focus (by the intelligent tools) just to significant events, such as connection resets, router misconfigurations, too slow file transfers, inefficient window sizes, and a number of other problems that might occur. Created this way, a short list of significant network events with their belonging interpretations and classifications, could suggest most likely network faults, so enabling quick high-level identifying network problems, i.e. the trade-in between the time to identify a problem, and the (so extended) time to solve it, thus greatly increasing the productivity by automating this process.

Most manufacturers call this capability an expert system or expert protocol commentator [2], [3], [4].

An illustrating example of a typical expert analysis top-level result is presented on Fig. 10, where too many retransmissions at TCP layer have been reported, slowing down the network.

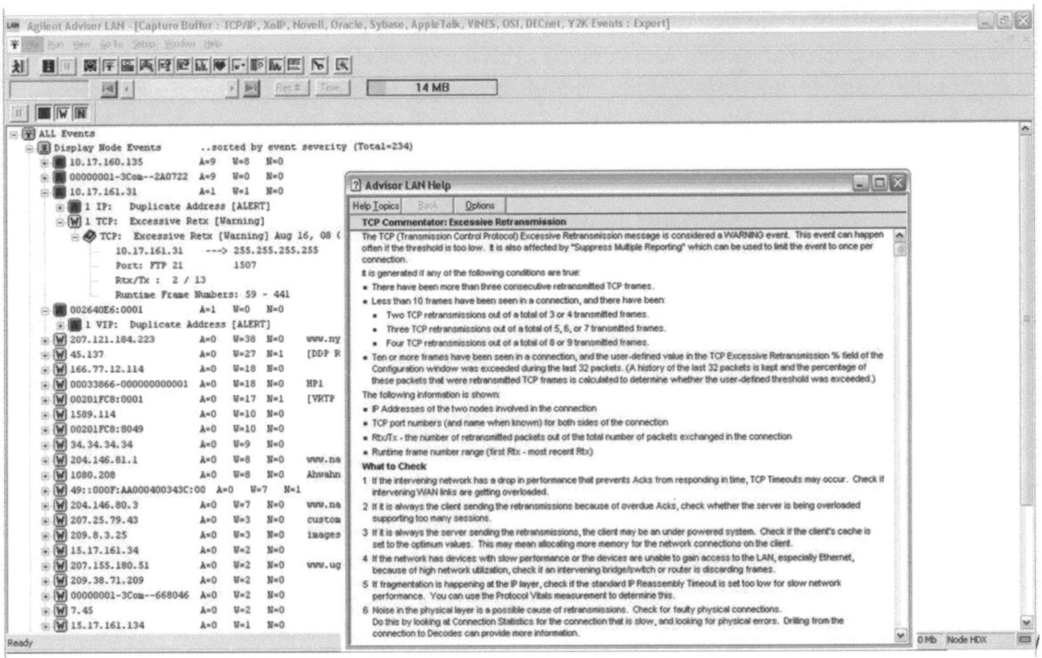

Fig. 10. An example of expert analysis based detection, isolation and classification of excessive TCP transmissions

As it can be seen from the display, the related event is classified as "warning", showing the node and connection information in one view, properly time-stamped, as well as possible causes (most likely noisy lines and/or inadequate IP *Time-To-Live* (TTL) setting). The alternative might be searching through decodes of thousands of captured frames to eventually figure it out. This hypothesis can be further investigated and verified through examining the frames with bad cyclic redundancy check (FCS), as well as through active out-of-service bit-error-ratio (BER) tests. (In general, some network faults just cannot be isolated without such stimulus/response testing. For example, observing Ethernet frames with the same IP address and different MAC addresses might indicate a duplicate IP address problem - but it might also be just a consequence of a complex router topology. However, ARPing the stations for their addresses will resolve the dilemma in seconds).

Other common examples of expert troubleshooter findings include e.g. router misconfigurations, slow file transfers, *inefficient window sizes* (that was used in congestion window analysis example to follow), TCP connection resets, protocol anomalies and mis-sequencing, inefficiently configured subnets (so enabling too much cross-subnet traffic and a router busier than it is necessary), utilization too high, too many broadcasts/multicasts or too much management traffic (both using considerable bandwidth), one or more computers transmitting errors, and many more.

On top of the advanced statistical analysis of active connections, stations and nodes involved, as well as expert classifications of significant events, often a sort of network "health" figure is estimated, based on the number of identified more or less severe events, whom the appropriate weighting factors are assigned to subtract the adequate amount (per each such identified event) from the value of 100%, as presented in Fig. 11, where from the top level display of the network health, more detailed investigations can be opened by drilling down into the related embedded expert or statistical analyses [4].

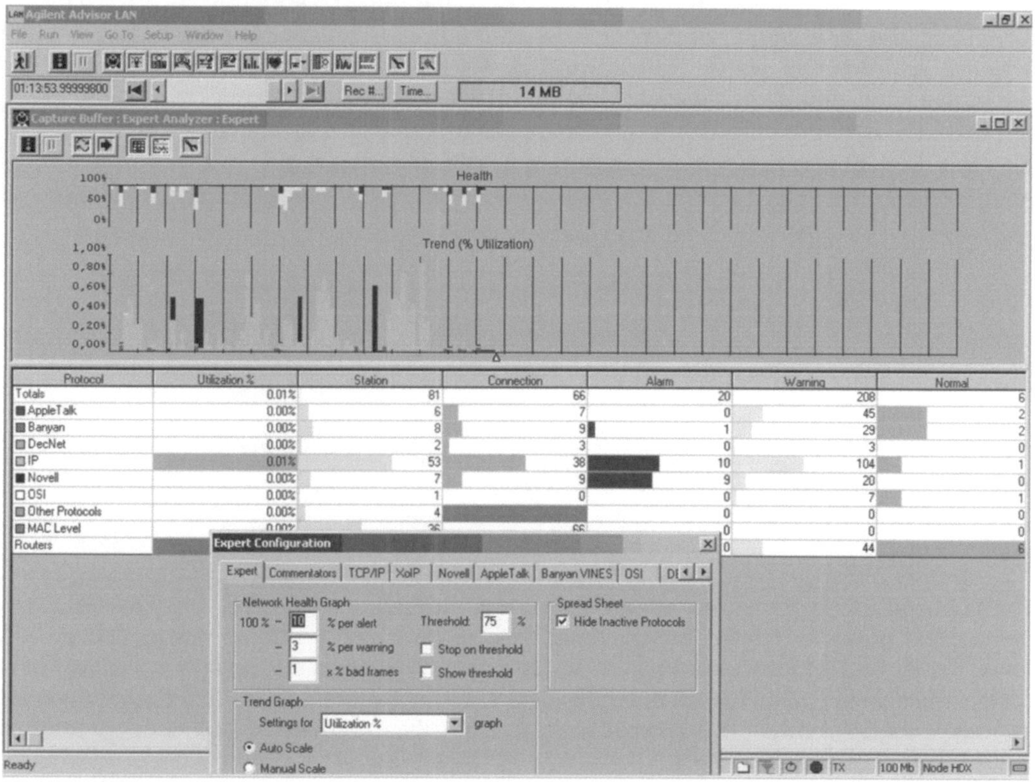

Fig. 11. Network health

3. An example of testing TCP traffic congestion by expert protocol analysis and statistical modelling

In what follows, an exemplar solution for expert-system-based distributed protocol analysis of TCP congestion window process in a major network with live transaction-intensive traffic (specifically, electronic financial transactions data transfer), during stationary time intervals, is presented [5], based on estimating actual congestion window size from measured data that mainly included decoding with precise time-stamps (100 ns resolution locally and 1 μs with GPS clock distribution), and expert-system findings, resulting from appropriate processing of network data, accordingly filtered prior to arriving to the hardware-based capture buffer.
In addition, a statistical analysis model is presented for evaluation whether the observed protocol data belonged to the specific (in this case, normal) cumulative distribution function, or whether two data sets exhibit the same statistical distribution - the condition-sine-qua-non for a stable interval with regard to TCP. Having identified such stationary intervals, the measured-data-based congestion window values were found to fit very well (with satisfactory statistical significance) to the truncated normal distribution. Finally, an appropriate model for estimation of relevant parameters of the congestion window distribution - its mean value and the variance, was developed and applied.
Transport Control Protocol (TCP) is a connection-oriented and so reliable protocol that much of Internet traffic uses at transport layer (the rest belongs to the connectionless User Datagram Protocol (UDP)). As a (sliding) window-based protocol, it controls sending rate at end-points, together with queuing mechanisms provided by routers [1].
It is the imperative to predict the performance of connections, so with this regard, the means for testing the congestion window process through experimental approach, is proposed here, as real Internet traffic was measured, the collected data processed (the so far elaborated way), and the additional statistical methods selected for case-specific analysis.

3.1 Flow control and managing congestion in TCP/IP networks

As it can be seen in Fig. 12, each TCP traffic PDU – segment is divided into the header and the data.

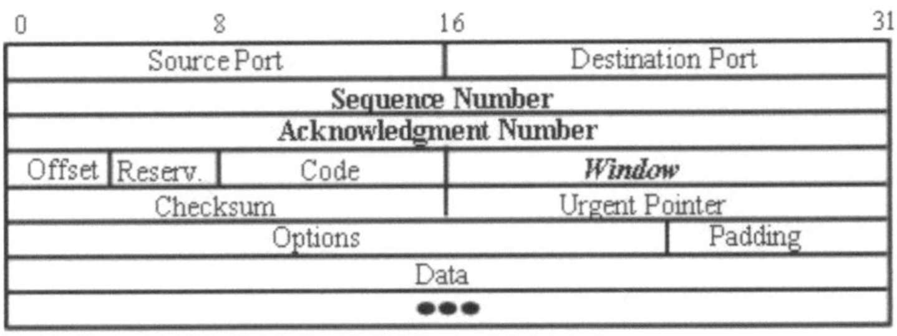

Fig. 12. TCP segment format

The TCP window is sometimes referred to as the "TCP sliding window" [1]. This field tells the receiver how many bytes the transmitting host can receive without acknowledgement. Thus, the sliding window size in TCP can be adjusted in real time, so it is a primary flow control mechanism, allowing more sender data to be "in flight", so that, this way, the sender gets ahead of the receiver (though not too far). Actually, the so advertised window informs sender of receiver's buffer space.
In original TCP design, this was the only protocol mechanism controlling sender's rate. However, this simple flow control mechanism keeps a (faster) sender from flooding with

traffic a (slower) receiver, while congestion control prevents a number of senders from overloading the *network*, adjusting to bandwidth variations, as well as sharing it among various data streams.

In real life, congestion is unavoidable; when two packets arrive at the same time, the node can only transmit one of them, and either buffer or drop the other. Specifically, if too many packets arrive within a short period of time, the buffer may eventually overflow, resulting with performance drop due to undelivered packets, packets consuming resources that are dropped somewhere else in the network downstream, spurious retransmissions of packets still "in flight" (leading to even more load)...

In mid-1980s, the Internet faced serious performance problems, until Jacobson/Karels devised TCP congestion control [1]. Generally, avoiding drops of too many packets and the so-called network congestion collapse, was based on: pre-arranging bandwidth allocations (with drawback of requiring negotiation before sending packets and potentially low utilization), differential pricing (i.e. not dropping packets for the best bidders), as well as dynamic adjusting of transmission rate that is increased when testing of congestion reflects its significant value, and is decreased otherwise (where drawbacks are: suboptimality and complex implementation) [8].

With this regard, the term "congestion window" denotes the maximum number of unacknowledged bytes that each source can have "in flight". This implies that, in other to conduct congestion control, each source must determine the available network capacity, so to know how many packets it can leave "in flight". Congestion-control equivalent of the receiver window principle should presume sending at the rate of the slowest component, in order to adapt the window by choosing its (maximal) size as the minimal out of the two values: the actual congestion window and the receiver window. So, upon detecting congestion, the congestion window must be (fast) decreased, as well as increased should no congestion was detected.

Detecting congestion by a TCP sender can be accomplished in a number of ways. For example, an indication can be if Internet Control Message Protocol (ICMP) *Source Quench* messages are detected on the network (either through protocol analyzer decoding, or expert analysis). However, this is not particularly reliable, because during times of overload, the signal itself could be dropped. Increased packet delays or losses can be another indicator, but also not so straightforward due to considerable non-congestive delay variations and losses (checksum errors) that can be expected in the network.

Anyway, no matter how congestion is detected, managing it must start from the fact that the consequences of over-sized window (packets dropped and retransmitted) are much worse than having an under-sized window (somewhat lower throughput). Therefore, upon success with last window of data, the TCP sender load should increase linearly, and decrease multiplicatively, upon packet loss [8]. This becomes a necessary condition for stable state of TCP [9], [10], [11].

Particular schemes for managing congestion window are out of scope of this paper and will therefore not be further explored here, as our experimental investigations and analysis focused just the estimation of statistical distribution of the stationary congestion window size.

The available test methods for studying communications networks range from mathematical modelling, through simulation (and/or emulation) to real-life measurements. We based this research on measuring the relevant parameters of test traffic by specialized hardware and analyzing the measurements' results by expert analysis and statistical modelling.

3.2 Architecture of the test system

A combined hybrid centralized (but) distributed expert analysis testing and troubleshooting solution, based on central server application, which controls and integrates expert protocol analysis, and distributed SNMP/RMON monitoring and analysis system, is the high-end solution in network management. Such an integrated solution consists of multiple expert protocol analyzers, RMON and other test agents, providing the means to solve complex problems, still spanning several network links and technologies and so enabling fastest progression from detection, identification and isolation of problems with availability, routing, QoS, etc., through network-wide view by RMON/MIB data, to resolution of problems by drilling-down into advanced statistics and expert analysis executed on a targeted protocol analyzer, where and when it comes out necessary (to troubleshoot).

The network under test consisted of LAN (Ethernet 100 Mbit/s to 1 Gbit/s) and WAN (Frame Relay) infrastructure of a major bank in/between their offices in three cities was used as a system under test. The network included dedicated workstations, residing at different locations around the network and exchanging test traffic, as well as of six distributed test system devices: hardware-based distributed protocol analyzers (DPA), from Agilent Technologies, aimed for protocol data acquisition and analysis. These were dispersed throughout various network segments of interest, either as network resident or temporarily installed for network performance testing. Their interwork was orchestrated by the central application server (running the Network Troubleshooting Center software of the same vendor), which controlled and integrated the distributed protocol data acquisition modules and their expert protocol analyses, and was accessible via two remote clients - consoles [5], Fig. 13.

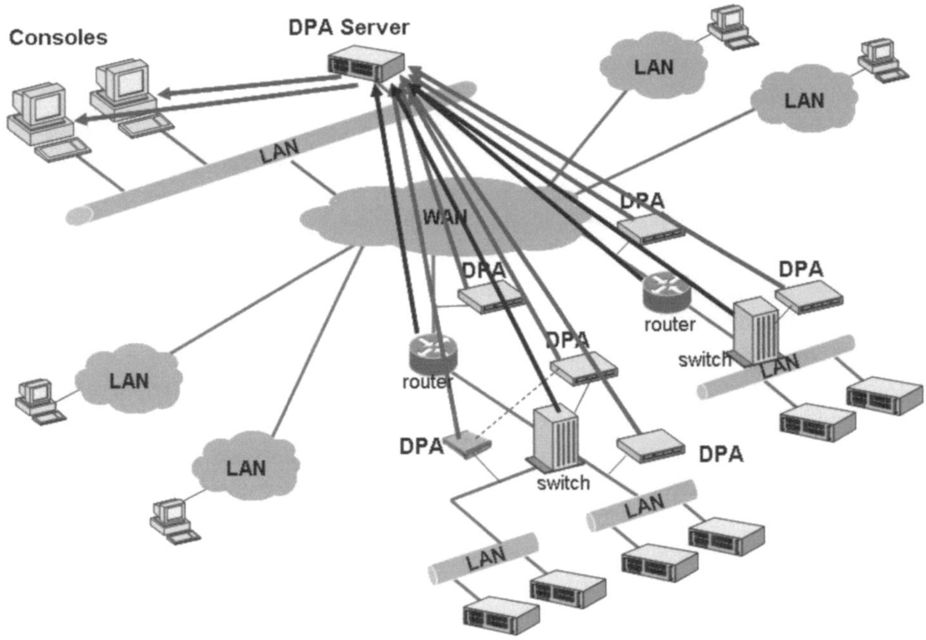

Fig. 13. Test scenario with distributed protocol analysis system spanning distant networks

By examining the precisely time-stamped TCP traffic PDUs - segments, using the tools of the non-intrusively attached DPAs, we were able to characterize the network, as well as its endpoints.

We performed many measurements throughout the day work time and in various environments: LAN - LAN and LAN-WAN-LAN. For each packet sent or received, DPAs registered its timestamp, sequence number and size. Multiple DPAs, with their 1Gb/s acquisition system, supporting real-time network data capture (to capture buffer memory) and filtering, were combined into time-synchronized multi-port tests, still using the same software features as with stand-alone protocol analyzer, such as e.g. decoding, statistical analysis and expert analysis [4]. Time synchronization among DPAs was achieved either via the "EtherSync" interfaces (where DPAs were daisy-chained, which allowed them to be synchronized to each other within ±100ns), or by means of the external GPS sources, providing the synchronization accuracy of ±1μs. (For the reference, the IETF's Network Time Protocol (NTP) could provide the synchronization accuracy of ±20ms or better, depending on the proximity of Network Time Servers (NTS)).

With this regard, the scenarios deployed included: multiple daisy-chained DPAs connected to a PC or a protocol analyzer either directly, or via a LAN, or multiple DPAs in a network with GPS, rather than NTP time synchronization.

The protocol analyzers used were equipped with both LAN and WAN interfaces, which provided physical connections and high-speed data acquisition hardware to get every frame on the network into any particular protocol analyzer. The packet slicing option was selected on capture buffer of the each interface, to enable the protocol analyzers to capture only the first part (e.g. fist 100 Bytes) of each packet, containing just the relevant header information, so that more packets for a given buffer size (of up to 256 Mbytes), could be stored. Mostly the *full buffer* option was used, where collecting data continued until the buffer was filled, when it was finally stopped.

The built-in capture filters were enabled, to control which frames were allowed to enter the capture buffer, and so to focus the analyzer (or just to save space in the capture buffer). As these filters are implemented in hardware, they were also used to trigger an action, such as halt or start collecting data on a matched frame, as well as either include or exclude matched frames from logging into the buffer, and later on to the hard disk of the analyzer's PC platform. Among a number of different available filter criteria, protocols (TCP, IP, etc.), specific fields (such as e.g. window size), frame attributes (such as erroneous or good frames etc.), and, in some instances, frame data bytes (the first 127 bytes) were used.

Associated to capture filters are statistics counters that provide counts of frames, packets and other events matching the selected filter criteria. These were set up and used for getting the precise statistics - histograms of the traffic events that were investigated.

With regard to specific measurements and data processing done, certainly the most rudimentary one was decoding from which the very essential information used for characterizing congestion window are precise timestamps of PDU arrivals, Fig. 4.

On top of data processing in each DPA, the appropriate postprocessing software (Agilent's Report Center) was used to accomplish multi-segment network baselining and benchmarking, with time correlation of data across the segments of interest. Using these multitasking measurement features enabled analyzing the raw data in different ways concurrently, such as e.g. to get correlated statistics between protocols, nodes (that use these protocols) and connections of each such end-station [4].

In order to estimate the sender's congestion window size from the collected data, it was necessary to identify (by filtering with appropriate criteria) the packets that have been sent from the sender, but have not yet arrived at the receiver, count them (by stats counters) and present as a function of time. The already presented features of the experimental system enabled fulfilling this task with great precision and accuracy. A simple application program - a counter - was used to add 1 to the actual congestion window size for each outgoing packet, at the time it was leaving the sender, and subtract 1 when/if that packet arrived at the receiver. With the exception of lost packets (that we can trace by various means, the easiest one by the expert analyzer, Fig. 10), which were excluded from the calculation, this accumulated sum well approximated the actual congestion window size almost in real time.

3.3 Statistical analysis model

In statistics, the Kolmogorov-Smirnov (K-S) test is used to find out if an empirical cdf of interest, based on finite samples, differs from a hypothesized continuous distribution function specified by the null hypothesis [12]. The very reason for wide use of the K-S test statistic is that it does not depend on the distribution function being tested, and also that it does not depend on adequate sample size (as e.g. the chi-square goodness-of-fit does). The higher the extent to which this test implies that the set up hypothesis has (or has not) been nullified - the significance level α (of the difference between the hypothesized values and the sample-based ones), obviously, the less likely it is that the investigated event could have been produced only by chance. So, in fact, the significance level is the probability that the null hypothesis could be wrongly rejected, when actually it should be accepted [12]. (Such a decision is commonly referred to as "false positive"). Among the popular levels of significance: 5%, 1% and 0.1%, in our model, we adopted the mid value.

The significance of a result is frequently expressed as its p-value, in such a way that smaller p-value reflects more significant result. So, when p-value, resulting from such a test, is smaller than the α-level, the null hypothesis is rejected and informally speaking, the results are classified as "statistically significant", where the lower significance level implies the stronger evidence.

3.3.1 Testing conformance to normal distribution

A sample Kolmogorov-Smirnov test [12] enables testing of a hypothesis that a certain distribution $F_{n\xi}(x)$ of a random variable ξ conforms to the given continuous cdf $F_{0\xi}(x)$.

$$H_0 : F_\xi(x) = P(\xi < x) = F_{0\xi}(x) \tag{1}$$

The empirical cdf $F_{n\xi}(x)$ is derived from the independent samples $(\xi_1, \xi_2, ..., \xi_n)$. The Kolmogorov-Smirnov statistics for a given $F_{0\xi}(x)$ is:

$$D_n = \sup_x \left| \hat{F}_{n\xi}(x) - F_{0\xi}(x) \right| \tag{2}$$

As it follows from the theorem of Glivenko-Cantelli [12], if the observed sample comes from the $F_{0\xi}(x)$ distribution, then D_n converges to 0. Furthermore, as $F_{0\xi}(x)$ is continuous, the rate of convergence of $\sqrt{n}D_n$ is determined by the Kolmogorov limit distribution theorem, stating:

$$\lim_{n\to\infty} \Pr(\sqrt{n}D_n < y) = K_\eta(y), \;\; 0 < y < \infty \tag{3}$$

where $K_\eta(y)$ is the Kolmogorov cdf (that does not depend on $F_{0\xi}(x)$, as pointed out above). Moreover, if the significance level of α is pre-assigned, then the tested null-hypothesis is to be rejected at the level α if:

$$\sqrt{n}D_n > y_\alpha \tag{4}$$

where the cut-off y_α is found by equalizing the Kolmogorov cdf $K_\eta(y)$ and 1-α:

$$\Pr(\sqrt{n}D_n \le y_\alpha) = K_\eta(y_\alpha) = 1-\alpha \;\Rightarrow\; y_\alpha = K^{-1}{}_\eta(1-\alpha) \tag{5}$$

Otherwise the null-hypothesis should be accepted at the significance level of α.
Actually, the significance is mostly tested by calculating the (*two-tail* [12]) p-value (which represents the probability of obtaining the test statistic values equal to or greater than the actual ones), by using the theoretical $K_\eta(y)$ cdf of the test statistic to find the area under the curve (for continuous variables) in the direction of the alternative (with respect to H_0) hypothesis, i.e. by means of a look-up table or integral calculus, while in the case of discrete variables, simply by summing the probabilities of events occurring in accordance with the alternative hypothesis at and beyond the observed test statistic value. So, if it comes out that:

$$p = 1 - K_\eta(\sqrt{n}D_n) < \alpha \tag{6}$$

then the null hypothesis is again to be rejected, at the presumed significance level α, otherwise (if the p-value is greater than the threshold α), the null hypothesis is not to be rejected and the tested difference is not statistically significant.

3.3.2 Identifying stationary intervals

While the main applications of the one-sample K-S test are testing goodness of fit with normal and uniform distributions, the two-sample K-S test is widely used for nonparametric comparing of two samples, since it is sensitive to differences in both location and shape of the empirical cdfs of two samples, so it is the most important theoretical tool for detecting change-points.
Let us now consider the test for the series $\xi_1, \xi_2, \ldots, \xi_m$ of the first sample, and $\eta_1, \eta_2, \ldots, \eta_n$ of the second, where the two series are independent. Furthermore, let $\hat{F}_{m\xi}(x)$ and $\hat{G}_{n\eta}(y)$ be the corresponding empirical cdfs. Then the K-S statistics is:

$$D_{m,n} = \sup_x \left| \hat{F}_{m\xi}(x) - \hat{G}_{n\eta}(y) \right| \tag{7}$$

The limit distribution theorem states that:

$$\lim_{m,n \to \infty} P\left(\sqrt{\frac{mn}{m+n}} D_{m,n} < z \right) = K_\zeta(z), \;\; 0 < z < \infty \tag{8}$$

where again $K_\zeta(z)$ is the Kolmogorov cdf.

3.3.3 Estimation of the (normal) distribution parameters

Let us consider a normally distributed random variable $\xi \in N(m, \sigma^2)$, where:

$$p_\xi(x) = \frac{1}{\sqrt{2\pi}\sigma} e^{-\frac{(x-m)^2}{2\sigma^2}} \tag{9}$$

Its cdf $\Phi_\xi(x)$ can be expressed as the standard normal cdf $\Phi(x)$ [12] of the ξ-related zero-mean normal random variable, normalized to its standard deviation σ:

$$\Phi_{\xi}(x)=\Pr(\xi\le x)=\int_{-\infty}^{x}\frac{1}{\sqrt{2\pi}\sigma}e^{-\frac{(u-m)^2}{2\sigma^2}}du=\Phi\left(\frac{x-m}{\sigma}\right)=\int_{-\infty}^{\frac{x-m}{\sigma}}\frac{1}{\sqrt{2\pi}\sigma}e^{-\frac{v^2}{2}}dv \qquad (10)$$

Normal cdf has no lower limit, however, since the congestion window can never be negative, here we must consider a truncated normal cdf. In practice, when the congestion window process gets in its stationary state, the lower limit is hardly 0. Therefore, for the reasons of generality, here we consider a truncated normal cdf with lower limit *l*, where $l\ge 0$.
Now we estimate the parameters *m*, *σ* and *l*, starting from:

$$\Pr(\xi>l)=1-\Phi\left(\frac{l-m}{\sigma}\right)=1-\int_{-\infty}^{\frac{l-m}{\sigma}}\frac{1}{\sqrt{2\pi}}e^{-\frac{v^2}{2}}dv=Q\left(\frac{l-m}{\sigma}\right) \qquad (11)$$

where: $Q\left(\frac{l-m}{\sigma}\right)$ is the Gaussian *tail* function [12].

The conditional expected value of *ξ*, just on the segment $(l, +\infty)$ is:

$$E(\xi/\xi>l)=\int_{l}^{+\infty}u\cdot\frac{1}{\sqrt{2\pi}\sigma\cdot Q\left(\frac{l-m}{\sigma}\right)}e^{-\frac{(u-m)^2}{2\sigma^2}}du \qquad (12)$$

By substituting: $\frac{u-m}{\sigma}=v,\ du=\sigma\cdot dv$ into (12.), we obtain:

$$\begin{aligned}E(\xi/\xi>l)&=\frac{1}{Q\left(\frac{l-m}{\sigma}\right)}\int_{\frac{l-m}{\sigma}}^{+\infty}(\sigma\cdot v+m)\frac{1}{\sqrt{2\pi}}e^{-\frac{v^2}{2}}dv=\\&=\frac{\sigma}{Q\left(\frac{l-m}{\sigma}\right)}\int_{\frac{l-m}{\sigma}}^{+\infty}v\frac{1}{\sqrt{2\pi}}e^{-\frac{v^2}{2}}dv+\frac{m}{Q\left(\frac{l-m}{\sigma}\right)}\int_{\frac{l-m}{\sigma}}^{+\infty}\frac{1}{\sqrt{2\pi}}e^{-\frac{v^2}{2}}dv=\\&=\frac{\sigma}{Q\left(\frac{l-m}{\sigma}\right)}\int_{\frac{l-m}{\sigma}}^{+\infty}v\frac{1}{\sqrt{2\pi}}e^{-\frac{v^2}{2}}dv+m=\\&=\frac{\sigma}{Q\left(\frac{l-m}{\sigma}\right)}\frac{1}{\sqrt{2\pi}}e^{-\frac{1}{2}\left(\frac{l-m}{\sigma}\right)^2}+m\end{aligned} \qquad (13)$$

Now, if we pre-assign a certain value *γ* to the above used tail function $Q(\cdot)$, then the corresponding argument (and so *m*) is determined by the inverse function $Q^{-1}(\gamma)$:

$$Q\left(\frac{l-m}{\sigma}\right)=\gamma\ \Rightarrow\ m=l-\sigma\cdot Q^{-1}(\gamma) \qquad (14)$$

so that (13.) can now be rewritten as:

$$m = E(\xi / \xi > l) - \frac{\sigma}{\gamma} \cdot \frac{1}{\sqrt{2\pi}} e^{-\frac{1}{2}\left[Q^{-1}(\gamma)\right]^2} \tag{15}$$

Substituting m from (14.) into (15.) results with the following formula for σ:

$$\sigma = \frac{l - E(\xi / \xi > l)}{Q^{-1}(\gamma) - \frac{1}{\sqrt{2\pi}\gamma} e^{-\frac{1}{2}\left[Q^{-1}(\gamma)\right]^2}} \tag{16}$$

Finally, substituting the above expression for σ into (14.), we obtain the expression for m:

$$m = \frac{\gamma \cdot Q^{-1}(\gamma) E(\xi / \xi > l) - l \frac{1}{\sqrt{2\pi}} e^{-\frac{1}{2}\left[Q^{-1}(\gamma)\right]^2}}{\gamma \cdot Q^{-1}(\gamma) - \frac{1}{\sqrt{2\pi}} e^{-\frac{1}{2}\left[Q^{-1}(\gamma)\right]^2}} \tag{17}$$

So it came out that, after developing formulas (16.) and (17.), we expressed the mean m and the variance σ^2 of the Gaussian random variable ξ, by the mean $E(\xi / \xi > l)$ of the truncated cdf, the truncation cut-off and the tabled inverse $Q^{-1}(\gamma)$ of the Gaussian tail function, for the assumed value γ. As these relations hold among the corresponding estimates, too, in order to estimate $\hat{m}$ and $\hat{\sigma}$, we need to first estimate $\hat{E}(\xi / \xi > l)$ and $\hat{\gamma}$ from the sample data:

$$\hat{E}(\xi / \xi > l) = \frac{\sum_{i=1}^{q} \xi_i N_i(\xi_i > l)}{\sum_{i=1}^{r} N_i(\xi_i > l)} \tag{18}$$

$$\hat{\gamma} = \frac{1}{n} \sum_{i=1}^{s} M_i(\xi_i \le l) \tag{19}$$

where N_i and M_i denote the number of occurrences (frequency) of particular samples being larger and smaller-or-equal than l, respectively, and $r,s \le n$.

So once we have estimated $\hat{E}(\xi / \xi > l)$ and $\hat{\gamma}$ by (18.) and (19.), we can then calculate the estimates $\hat{\sigma}$ and $\hat{m}$ by means of (16.) and (17.), which completes the estimate of the pdf (9.).

3.3.4 Results of the analysis

Initially, the network traffic was characterized with respect to packet delay variation and packet loss - that were, expectedly, considered as significant influencers on the congestion window. Accordingly, in many tests, for mutually very different network conditions and between various end-points, significant packet delay variation was noticed, Fig. 14.

However, the expected impact of the packet delay variation [7], [13] on packet loss (and so on congestion, i.e. to its window size), has not been noticed as significant, Fig. 15a, 15b.

Still, some sporadic bursts of packet losses were noticed, which can be explained as a consequence of grouping of the packets coming from various connections. Once the buffer of the router, using drop-tail queuing algorithm, gets in overflow state due to heavy incoming traffic, the most of or the whole burst might be dropped. This introduces correlation between consecutive packet losses, so that they, too (as packets themselves), occur in bursts. Consequently, the packet loss rate alone does not sufficiently characterize the error performance. (Essentially, "packet-burst-error-rate" would be needed, too, especially for applications sensitive to long bursts of losses [7], [9] [10], [13]).

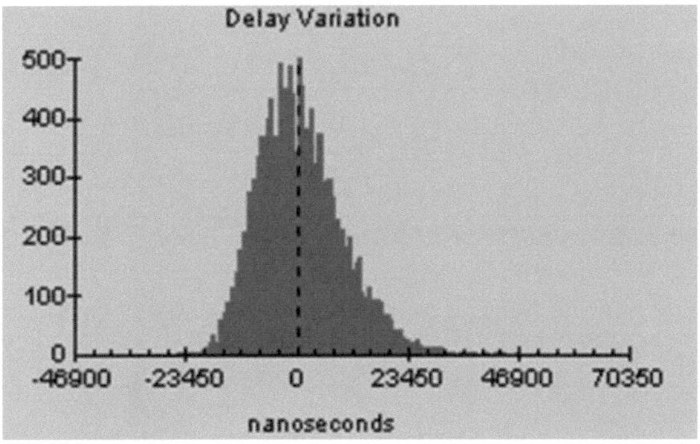

Fig. 14. Typical packet delay variation within a test LAN segment

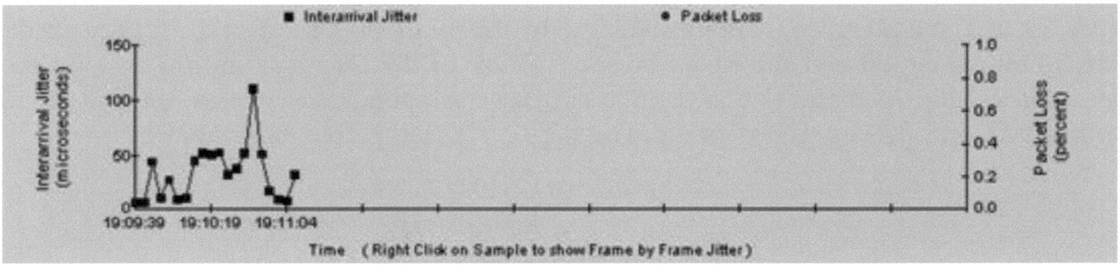

Fig. 15a. Typical time-diagram of correlated packet jitter and loss measurements

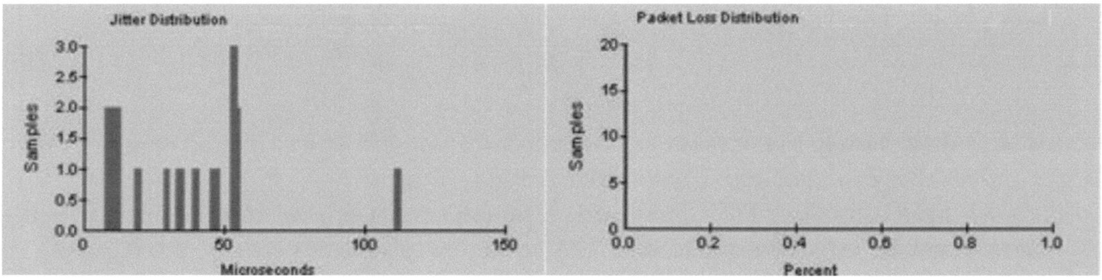

Fig. 15b. Typical histogram of correlated packet jitter and loss measurements

With this respect, one of our observations (coming out from the expert analysis tools we referenced in Section 2) was that, in some instances, congestion window values show strong correlation among various connections. Very likely, this was a consequence of the above mentioned bursty nature of packet losses, as each packet, dropped from a particular connection, likely causes the congestion window of that very connection to be simultaneously reduced [7], [8], [10].

In the conducted real-life analyses of the congestion process stationarity, the congestion window values that were calculated from the TCP PDU stream, captured by protocol analyzers, were considered as a sequence of quasi-stationary series with constant cdf that

changes only at frontiers between the successive intervals [12]. In order to identify these intervals by successive two-sample K-S tests (as explained above), the empirical cdfs within two neighbouring time windows of rising lengths were compared, sliding them along the data samples, to finally combine the two data samples into a single test series, once the distributions matched.
Typical results (where "typical" refers to traffic levels, network utilization and throughput for a particular network configuration) of our statistical analysis for 10000 samples of actual stationary congestion window sizes, sorted in classes with the resolution of 20, are presented in Table 1 and as histogram, on Fig. 16, visually indicating compliance with the (truncated) normal cdf, having the sample mean within the class of 110 to 130. Accordingly, as the TCP-stable intervals were identified, numerous one-sample K-S tests were conducted and obtained the p-values in the range from 0.414 to 0.489, which provided solid indication for accepting (with a=1%) the null-hypothesis that, during stationary intervals, the statistical distribution of congestion window was (truncated) normal.

$Pr(x_i\text{-}20 < x < x_i)$	278	310	624	928	2094	2452	1684	911	478	157	63	21
x_i	30	50	70	90	110	130	150	170	190	210	230	250

Table 1. Typical values of stationary congestion window size

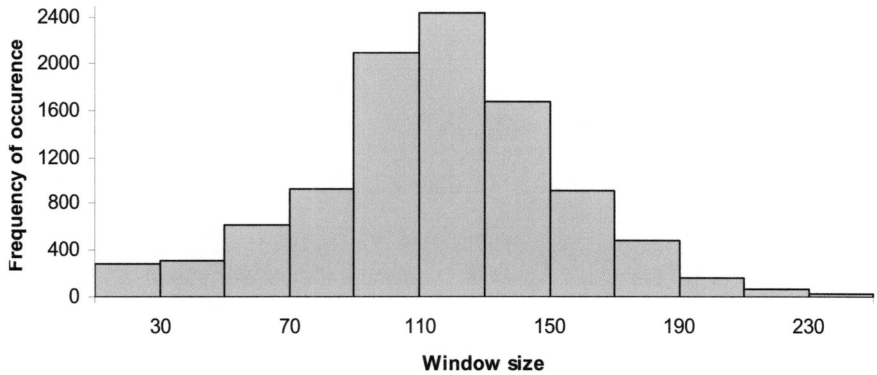

Fig. 16. Typical histogram of the congestion window

As per our model, the next step was to estimate typical values of the congestion window distribution parameters. So, firstly, by means of (19.), $\hat{\gamma}$ was estimated as one minus the sum of frequencies of all samples belonging to the lowest value class (so e.g., in the typical case, presented by Table 1 and Fig. 16, $\hat{\gamma}$=1-278/10000=0.9722 was taken, which determined the value $Q^{-1}(\gamma)$=-1.915 that was accordingly selected from the look-up table). Then the value of l=30 was chosen for the truncation cut-off and, from (18.), the mean $\hat{E}(\xi / \xi > l)$=117.83 of the truncated distribution was calculated, excluding the samples from the lowest class and their belonging frequencies, from this calculation.
Finally, based on (16.) and (17.), the estimates for the distribution mean and variance of the exemplar typical data presented above, were obtained as: $\hat{m}$=114.92 and $\hat{\sigma}$=44.35.

4. Conclusion

It has become widely accepted that network managers' understanding how tool selection changes with the progress through the management process, is critical to being efficient and effective. Among various state-of-the-art network management tools and solutions that have been briefly presented in this chapter, as ranging from simple media testers, through distributed systems, to protocol analyzers, specifically, expert analysis based troubleshooting was focused as a means to effectively isolate and analyze network and system problems. With this respect, an illustrating example of real-life testing of the TCP congestion window process is presented, where the tests were conducted on a major network with live traffic, by means of hardware and expert-system-based distributed protocol analysis and applying the appropriate additional model that was developed for statistical analysis of captured data.

Specifically, it was shown that the distribution of TCP congestion window size, during stationary intervals of the protocol behaviour that was identified prior to estimation of the cdf, can be considered as close to the normal one, whose parameters were estimated experimentally, following the theoretical model.

In some instances, it was found out that the congestion window values show strong correlation among various connections, as a consequence of intermittent bursty nature of packet losses.

The proposed test model can be extended to include the analysis of TCP performance in various communications networks, thus confirming that network troubleshooting which integrates capabilities of expert analysis and classical statistical protocol analysis tools, is the best choice whenever achievable and affordable.

5. References

[1] Comer, D. E., "Internetworking with TCP/IP, Volume 1; Principles, Protocols, and Architecture (Fifth Edition), Prentice Hall, NJ, 2005

[2] Burns, K., „TCP/IP Analysis and Troubleshooting Toolkit", Wiley Publishing Inc., Indianapolis, Indiana, 2003

[3] Oppenheimer, P. „Top-Down Network Design - Second Edition", Cisco Press, 2004

[4] Agilent Technologies, "Network Analyzer Technical Overview", 5988-4231EN, 2004

[5] Lipovac, V., Batos, V., Nemsic, B., "Testing TCP Traffic Congestion by Distributed Protocol Analysis and Statistical Modelling, Promet - Traffic and Transportation, vol. 21, issue 4, pp. 259-268, 2009

[6]Agilent Technologies, "Network Troubleshooting Center Technical Overview", 5988-8548EN, 2005

[7] A. Kumar,"Comparative Performance Analysis of Versions of TCP", *IEEE/ACM Transactions on Networking,* Aug. 1998

[8] M. Mathis, J. Semke, J. Mahdavi and T. J. Ott, "The Macroscopic Behavior of the TCP Congestion Avoidance Algorithm." Computer Communication Review, vol. 27, no. 3, July 1997

[9] K. Chen, Y. Xue, and K. Nahrstedt, "On setting TCP's Congestion Window Limit in Mobile ad hoc Networks", Proc. IEEE International Conf. on Communications, Anchorage, May 2003

[10] S. Floyd and K. Fall," Promoting the Use of End-to-End Congestion Control in the Internet", IEEE/ACM Trans. on Networking, vol. 7, issue 4, pp. 458 – 472, Aug. 1999

[11] H. Balakrishnan, H. Rahul, and S. Seshan, "An Integrated Congestion Management Architecture for Internet Hosts", Proc. ACM SIGCOMM, Sep. 1999

[12] M. Kendall, A. Stewart, "The Advanced Theory of Statistics", *Charles Griffin* London, 1966.

[13] T. Elteto, S. Molnar, "On the distribution of round-trip delays in TCP /IP networks", International Conference on Local Computer Network, 1999

17

An Expert System Based Approach for Diagnosis of Occurrences in Power Generating Units

Jacqueline G. Rolim and Miguel Moreto
Power Systems Group
Department of Electrical Engineering
Federal University of Santa Catarina, Florianópolis
Brazil

1. Introduction

Nowadays power generation utilities use complex information management system, as new monitoring and protection equipment are being installed or upgraded in power plants. Usually these devices can be configured and accessed remotely, thus, companies that own several stations can monitor their operation from a central office. This monitoring information is crucial in order to evaluate the power plant operation under normal and abnormal situations. Specially in abnormal cases, like fault disturbances and generator forced shutdown, the monitoring system data are used to evaluate the cause and origin of such disturbance.

As the data can be accessed remotely, in general the analysis is performed at a specific department of the utility. The engineers at this department spend, on a daily basis, a substantial amount of time collecting and analyzing the data recorded during the occurrences, some of them severe and others resulting from normal operation procedures. Example of a severe occurrence is the forced shutdown of a loaded generator due to a fault (short-circuit). Concerning normal occurrences, examples are the energization and de-enegization procedures and maintenance tests.

The main data used to analyze occurrences are disturbance records generated by Digital Fault Recorders (DFRs) and the sequence of events (SOE) generated by the supervisory control and data acquisition (SCADA) system. Usually this information is accessible through distinct systems, which complicates the analyst's work due to data spreading. The analyst's task is to verify the information generated at the power stations and to evaluate whether an important occurrence has occurred. In this case, it is also needed to identify the cause of the disturbance and to evaluate whether the generators protection systems operated as expected. Although this investigation is usually performed off line, it has become common in case of severe contingencies to contact the DFR specialist to ask for his advice before returning the generator to operation. Thus the importance to perform the analysis as quickly as possible (Moreto et al., 2009).

The excess of data that needs to be analyzed every day is a problem faced in most analysis centers. It is of fundamental importance to reduce the time spent in disturbance analysis as more and more data become available to the analyst as the power system grows and technology improves (Allen et al., 2005). In practice, engineers can't verify all the occurrences because of the number of records generated. It should be pointed out that a significant percentage of these disturbance records are generated during normal situations. This way, the development of a tool to help the analysts in their task is important and subject of several studies. Using such a tool, the severe occurrences can be analyzed in first place and an automated analysis result leading to a probable cause of the disturbance would greatly reduce the time spent by the analyst and improve the quality of the analysis. The remaining records corresponding to normal situations can be archived without human intervention.

To obtain a disturbance analysis result, specialized knowledge is necessary. Interpretation of the operative procedures of distinct power units, familiarity with the protection systems and their expected actions are just a few skills that the analyst should dominate. Thus, this task is suited for application of expert systems. The focus of this chapter is on the application of a set of expert systems to automated the DFR data analysis task using also the SOE.

The DFRs are devices that record sampled waveforms of voltage and current signals, besides the status of relays and other digital quantities related to the generator circuit. The DFR triggers and the data is recorded when a measured or calculated value exceeds a previously set trigger level or when the status of one or more digital inputs changes. Thus, when a disturbance is detected a register containing pre-disturbance and post-disturbance information is created in the DFR's memory, (McArthur et al., 2004).

Fig. 1 shows the typical quantities monitored by a DFR. The currents on the high voltage side of the step-up transformer ($I^{tf}_{A,B,C}$), the generator terminal voltage ($V_{A,B,C}$), the loading current ($I_{A,B,C}$), the neutral current/voltage (I_N, V_N) in addition to the field voltage and current (V_f, I_f) lead to a total of 13 analog quantities per generation unit that should be verified at each occurrence.

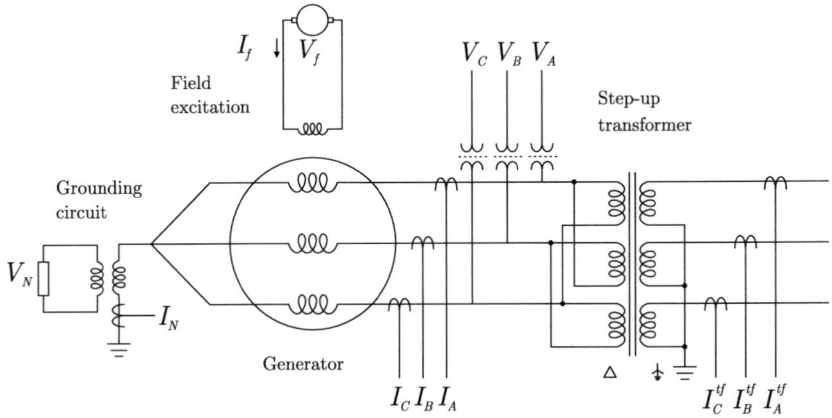

Fig. 1. Typical quantities monitored by DFRs in a power generation unit.

Several papers have been published in technical journals and conferences proposing and testing schemes to automate the disturbance analysis task. However, the majority are designed for fault diagnosis in transmission systems and for power quality studies, not considering the characteristics of generation systems.

Davidson et al. (Davidson et al., 2006) describe the application of a multi-agent system to the automatic fault diagnosis of a real transmission system. Some agents, based on expert systems and model based reasoning, collect and use information from the SCADA system and from DFRs.

Another paper (Luo & Kezunovic, 2005) proposed an expert system (ES) that makes use of data from DFRs and sequence of events of digital protection relays to analyze the disturbance and evaluate the protection performance. Expert systems are also employed in PQ studies as in Styvaktakis (Styvaktakis et al., 2002). In this paper the disturbance signal is segmented into stationary parts that are used to obtain the input data for the ES.

When applied to automated disturbance analysis of power systems, computational intelligence techniques are normally used in conjunction with techniques for feature extraction. The most common ones are the Fourier Transform (Chantler et al., 2000), Kalman Filters (Barros & Perez, 2006) and the Wavelet Transform (Gaing, 2004).

In this chapter we propose a scheme to automatically detect and classify disturbances in power stations. Two sources of information are used: disturbance records and sequence of events. The first objective of this scheme is to discriminate the DFR data that do not need further analysis from the ones resulting from serious disturbances. To do this the phasor type of disturbance record is used. The SOE is used in the scheme to complement the result obtained by the DFR data. Examples of incidents that do not require further analysis are: DFR data resulting from a voltage trigger during normal energization or de-energization of a generator; a protection trigger during maintenance tests of relays while the generator is off-line; or a trigger coming from another DFR without any evidence of fault on the monitored signals. The second objective is to classify the disturbance, using the waveform record, providing a diagnosis to help the analysts with their task.

The proposed methodology has been developed with collaboration from a power generation utility and a DFR manufacturer. The module which analyses the phasor record was validated using hundreds of DFR records generated during real occurrences in a power plant over a period of four months while the waveform record module was tested with simulated records and a real fault record.

Section 2 of this chapter presents a brief description of the sources of data used: Digital Fault Recorders and the SCADA system (responsible for generating the SOE). In Section 3 an overall view of the proposed scheme is shown. Sections 4 and 5 describe the two main modules proposed to diagnosing the disturbances that use phasor and waveform records. Some results and comments about the performance of the system are discussed in Section 6. Finally, some general conclusions are stated in Section 7.

2. Data sources

Currently most power utilities have communication networks that allow remote monitoring and control of the system. These networks make possible to access disturbance records and supervisory data in a centralized form. Next subsections will describe these data (disturbance records and sequence of events), which are used by the proposed scheme to automatically classify disturbances.

2.1 Digital fault recorders

Digital fault recorders are responsible for generating oscillographic data files. An oscillography can be viewed as a series of snapshots taken from a set of measurements (like generator terminal voltages and currents) over a certain period of time. Usually these records are stored in COMTRADE format (IEEE standard C37.111-1999)(IEE, 1999), when the DFR is triggered by one of the following situations:

- The magnitude of a monitored signal reaches a previously defined threshold level.

- The rate of change of a monitored signal exceeds its limit.
- The magnitude of a calculated quantity (active, reactive and apparent power, harmonic components, frequency, RMS values of voltage and currents, etc.) reaches the threshold level.
- The rate of change of a calculated quantity for instance, active power, exceeds its preset limit.
- The state of the DFR digital inputs change.

When the DFR triggers by some of the above situations, all digital and analog signals are stored in its memory, including the pre-fault, fault and post-fault intervals. Because the thresholds (also called triggers) are set at aiming to detect every fault, DFRs may also be triggered during normal situations. Examples of these situations are energization and de-energization of the machine and tests in protective relays while the generator is disconnected.

One of the main advantages of modern DFRs is their ability to synchronize their time stamp with the global position system (GPS) time base. Thus, in addition to synchronized waveforms, these devices are able to calculate and store a sequence of phasors of the electrical quantities before, during and after the disturbance. In general, one phasor is stored for each fundamental frequency cycle. Because of this lower sampling rate, a phasor record, also called "long duration record" may store several minutes of data, while the waveform record, called "short duration record" only records for a few seconds.

The approach described in this chapter uses the long duration record to pre-classify the disturbance and the waveform record to analyze the occurrences tagged as "important". The main reason for this choice of using firstly the phasor record is that in large generators the transient period of disturbance signals can be considerably long (dozens of seconds or even minutes). Short duration records usually do not cover the entire occurrence in these cases. This is particularly true in voltage signals, as in Fig. 2. The two signals depicted were recorded during the same disturbance, although they do not share the same time axis scale in this picture. The zero instant of Fig. 2(b) is located approximately at 175 seconds on Fig. 2(a).

As can be seen in Fig. 2(a), the transient lasts for approximately 20 seconds, several times longer than the duration of a typical waveform record (usually 4 to 6 seconds). This is clear in the waveform record shown in Fig. 2(b). In this case, using the waveform record, it is not possible to know whether the voltage will stabilize at a peak value of 0.5pu or decreases further to zero.

2.2 Supervisory system

The supervisory system is responsible, among other things, for registering the sequence of events in the utility's database. The SOE is a series of messages recorded every time the state of a digital input monitored by a Remote Terminal Unit (RTU) changes. The states monitored by RTUs are generally auxiliary contacts of protective devices, circuit breakers (CB) and switches. Typically, the following information is associated with each event stored in a SOE file:

- The time stamp and date of the event, usually with a degree of accuracy to within milliseconds and synchronized with GPS
- An indication of the substation or power plant where the event was recorded
- An indication of the circuit or equipment related to the event
- A unique tag associated with the digital input that originates the event

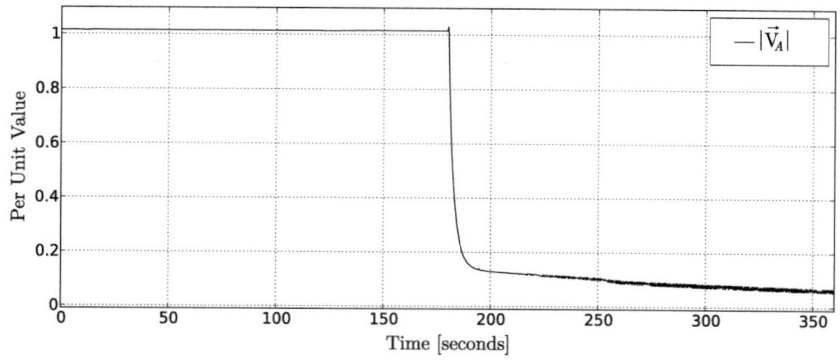

(a) Phasor record

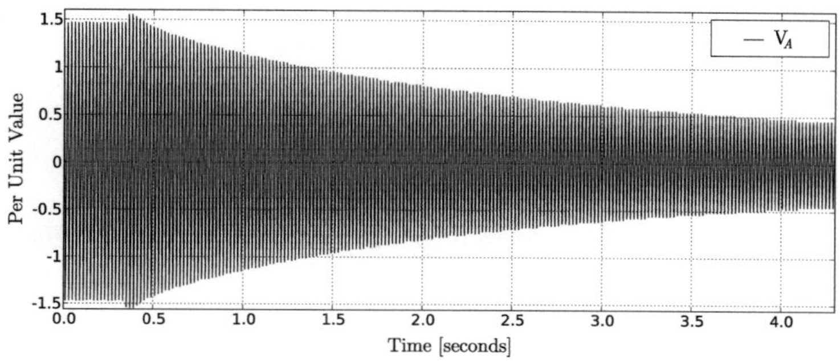

(b) Waveform record

Fig. 2. A disturbance in phasor and waveform record.

- A description of the event.

The listing bellow shows an example of three SOE messages.

```
 Time stamp  Stat. Date  Eq.           Description
19:13:58.088 UTCH Jun25 GT04 Reverse power relay 32G change to trip
19:13:58.104 UTCH Jun25 GT04 Generator lockout relay change to trip
19:13:58.137 UTCH Jun25 GT04 Main GT04 circuit breaker change to open
```

3. The proposed scheme

In the proposed scheme the first data to be processed is the phasor data recorded by the DFR. This first module is detailed in (Moreto & Rolim, 2011). It is composed of an expert system reasoning over the characteristics of the symmetrical components calculated using phasor records divided into pre- and post-disturbance segments. Regardless of the DFR analysis conclusion, the SOE from SCADA system is analyzed by a second expert system. Finally the results of both analysis (DFR and SOE) are correlated in order to achieve the final conclusion. The phasor record analysis can be interpreted as a filter where the serious disturbances (like those resulting from short-circuits) are separated from the other situations, thus, fulfilling the first objective of this work. These serious cases are then submitted to the second step of the proposed scheme where the waveform record is used because of its higher sampling rate. The goal is to detect if a short-circuit occurred and where (in the generator terminals or in the nearby power grid) and classify it according to its type like phase-to-graund fault, phase-phase fault and so on. This step is derived from the second objective stated at the introduction. The overall structure of the proposed scheme is depicted by Figure 3.

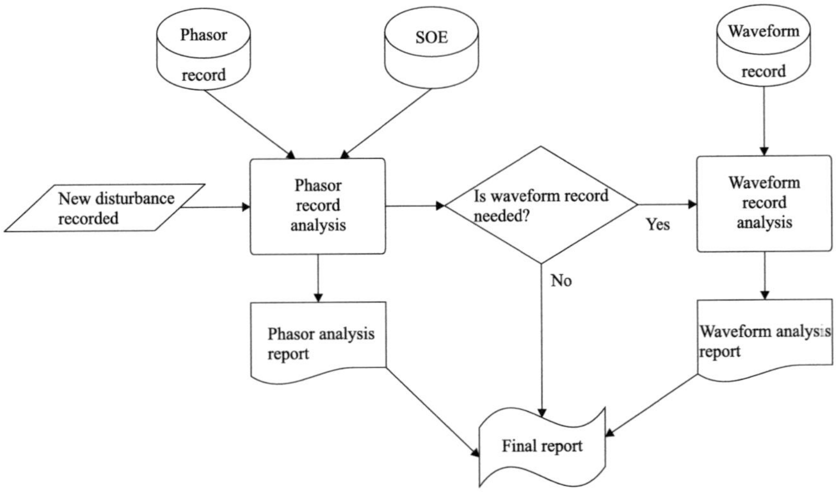

Fig. 3. Structure of the proposed scheme.

The phasor record analysis and waveform record analysis are described in the next sections.

4. Phasor record analysis

The phasor analysis is started when a new disturbance record is available at the analysis center. The phasor record along with the SOE are then analyzed by the proposed scheme. The disturbance record and SOE data are read from the DFR and SCADA databases available at the utilite's office. Only the SOE recorded during the disturbance record time lapse is used. Fig. 4 shows the structure of the proposed scheme. The disturbance record is firstly preprocessed and segmented into pre- and post-disturbance parts. For each of these parts the mean values are calculated composing the feature set used by the decision making expert system.

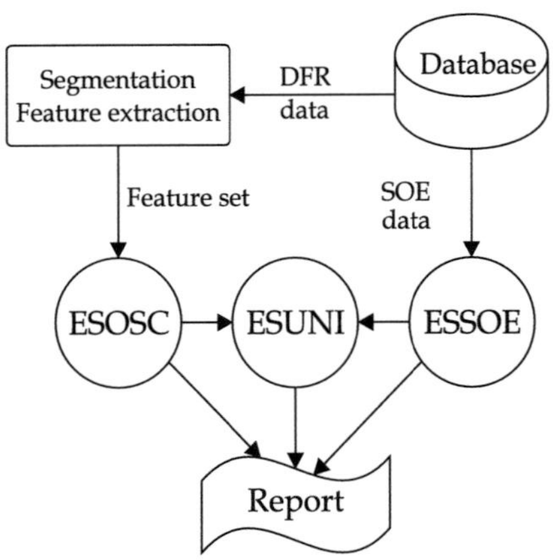

Fig. 4. Structure of the proposed phasor analysis scheme.

The decision making process is made by three expert systems: ESOSC uses the features calculated from the disturbance record to achieve a result concerning the DFR data; ESSOE uses the sequence of events to obtain a complementary result and ESUNI correlates the results

from both expert systems. All the messages and conclusions achieved during the decision making process are included in the phasor record analysis report.
The following subsections give an overview of the functional blocks of Fig. 4. A detailed description of each block can be found in (Moreto & Rolim, 2011).

4.1 Segmentation and feature extraction

The segmentation and feature extraction process is represented by the block diagram in Fig. 5 where indexes ABC and 012 denote the three electrical phases and three symmetrical components (zero, positive and negative) respectively. The operator $(|.|)$ is the absolute value and $(\vec{.})$ represents a vector quantity.

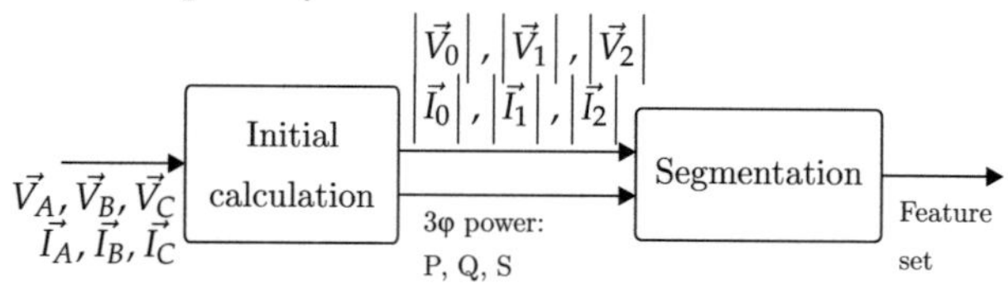

Fig. 5. Segmentation and feature extraction.

The recorded quantities are initially normalized to *per unit* (pu) values followed by the calculation of the symmetrical components (Grainger & Stevenson, 1994) and complex power. The segmentation process is applied to these calculated quantities in order perform a feature extraction in each segment. The signals are split into parts before and after the transient.
In (Moreto & Rolim, 2008), the authors propose a detection index that is suitable to segment phasor records that contain slower disturbances as observed in large power generators. This index is calculated using Equation 1.

$$di(n) = \sigma_\Delta(n) = \frac{1}{\Delta - 1} \sum_{i=n}^{n+\Delta} (|\vec{y}(i)| - \mu_\Delta)^2 \tag{1}$$

Where n is the sample index, $|\vec{y}(i)|$ is the absolute value of the considered phasor quantity at sample i, Δ is the window width, σ_Δ is the standard deviation calculated over this window and μ_Δ is the mean value of the data window. In this chapter, the chosen Δ was 480 samples (8 seconds).
When $di(n)$ exceeds a certain threshold δ, point n belongs to a disturbance segment. Consequently the first point where $di(n) > \delta$ indicates the beginning of a disturbance interval which ends after the last point where $di(n) > \delta$.
Fig. 6 presents an example of the segmentation process. The magnitude of the voltage phasor record is segmented according to the gray bar. The calculated detection index is also shown in the picture.
The mean value of the samples before and after the detected disturbance interval are stored in the ESOSC facts data base.

4.2 ESOSC: Expert system for oscillographic analysis

This expert system is responsible for analyzing the data provided by the segmentation procedure. Based on the pre- and post-disturbance data, ESOSC can classify the long term oscillographic record in several categories.
ESOSC is represented by the diagram in Fig. 7. It is composed of 19 rules that will be described in the following paragraphs.

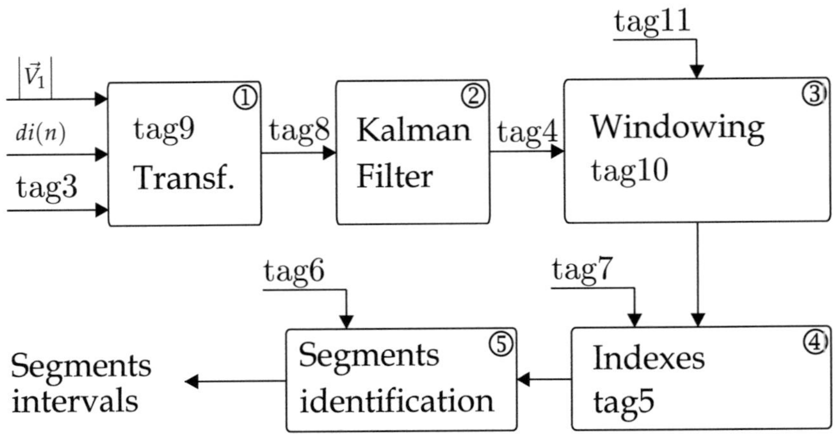

Fig. 6. Example of data segmentation and proposed detection index.

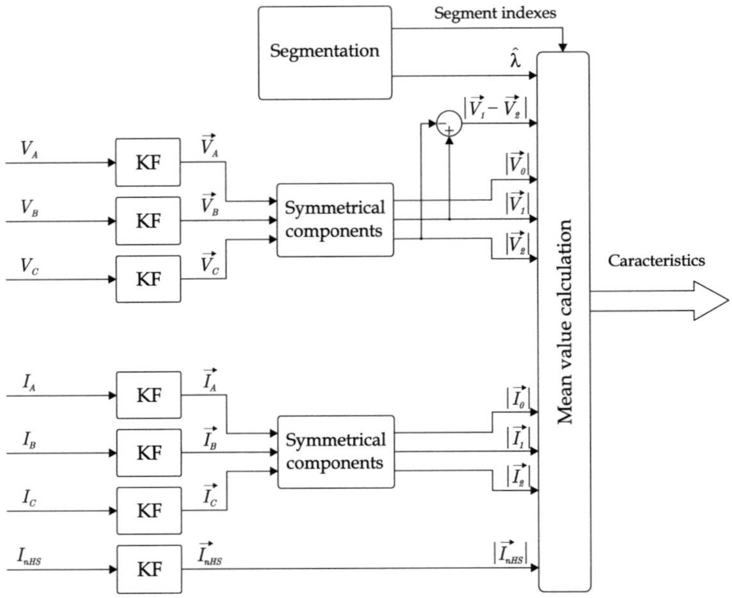

Fig. 7. ESOSC representation.

The ESOSC implementation is based on the CLIPS expert system shell with the facts being created using CLIPS' template objects. Each input fact contains three slots:

- Name: String with the processed quantity, such as I_0, I_1, I_2, V_0, V_1, V_2 or P.
- PreValue: Mean value of the named quantity calculated over the pre-disturbance segment.
- PostValue: Mean value of the named quantity calculated over the post-disturbance segment.

The ESOSC knowledge base is composed of two sets of rules. The set called *Characteristics identification rules* uses the input facts as premises. According to the pre-disturbance and post-disturbance values of each quantity, these rules create a new type of fact called *Characteristic fact* which stores information about the characteristic identified in each quantity.

Table 1 shows the premises of each characteristics identification rule and the type *characteristic fact* obtained (conclusion of the rule).
Each row of Table 1 corresponds to a rule. Some of these rules have a third premise about the difference between the pre- and post-disturbance values of the quantity being evaluated.

Rule conclusion	*Pre* [*pu*]	*Post* [*pu*]	Additional premise
Step-up from 0	< 0.05	> 0.05	
Step-down to 0	> 0.05	< 0.05	
Step-up	> 0.05	> 0.05	$(Post - Pre) \geq 0.1pu$
Step-down	> 0.05	> 0.05	$(Pre - Post) \geq 0.1pu$
No variation			$\text{abs}(Pre - Post) \leq 0.1pu$

Table 1. ESOSC: Premises and conclusions of characteristics identification rules

Depending on the values of the pre- and post-disturbance segments of a quantity one of the rules in Table 1 is fired and a new *characteristic fact* is created. These facts are composed by the following information slots:

- Name: String with the processed quantity, such as *I0, I1, I2, V0, V1, V2* or *P*.
- Type: A string indicating the characteristic type. The values can be: Step-up from 0, Step-down to 0, Step-up, Step-down and No variation.
- Value: The value associated with each characteristic. Normally the difference between the pre and post-segments mean values. In the case of the *No variation* rule, this value is the post-disturbance mean value.

Another set of rules was created to reason about the *Charateristic facts*. These rules correlate the characteristics identified in different quantities for example, between positive sequence voltages and currents. They also provide a conclusion about the disturbance generating a *Result fact*. Table 2 shows the premises of each rule of this set which is called *Characteristic relation rules*. The logical operators used to associate multiple premises are also indicated.
The rules in Table 2 conclude about the occurrence based on the disturbance record. In some cases the oscillographic record is not enough to obtain a definitive conclusion (Moreto & Rolim, 2011) and the SOE can be used to complement the result. The SOE analysis is performed by the Expert System for SOE analysis (ESSOE).

4.3 ESSOE: Expert system for SOE analysis

ESSOE has two objectives: the first is to complement the ESOSC analysis (when it is inconclusive) and the second is to provide an independent analysis, which is confronted with the ESOSC.
Prior to the execution of the ESSOE, the sequence of events recorded during the oscillography time lapse is selected. This selection is then classified and stored in a structured way as shown in Fig. 8.
The events which refer to the generation unit under analysis are picked up from the SCADA database and classified according to the four classes of Fig. 8:

- Protection Relays: The tripping events of protective relays are in this class. For each event the data read are time stamp of the event (date and hour with millisecond precision), state of the event (operated or normal), a code indicating the function of the relay according to the ANSI classification and a description of the event. Usually, when the protection device returns to its normal state another event is generated.

Rule	Quantity	Characteristic type	Characteristic value
Energization	and{ V^+	Step-up from 0	$> 0.9pu$
	or{ I^+	Step-up from 0	
	I^+	No variation	$< 0.05pu$
De-energization	and{ V^+	Step-down to 0 or step-down	$> 0.8pu$
	or{ I^+	No variation	$< 0.05pu$
	P	No variation	$< 0.1pu$
Isolated unit	and{ V^+	No variation	$> 0.9pu$
	I^+	No variation	$< 0.05pu$
Synchronism	and{ V^+	No variation	$> 0.9pu$
	I^+	Step-up from 0	
Normal operation	and{ V^+	No variation	$> 0.9pu$
	I^+	No variation	$> 0.05pu$
Out of service	V^+	No variation	$< 0.05pu$
Forced shutdown	and{ V^+	Step-down to 0	
	I^+	Step-down to 0	
	P	Step-down to 0	
Load increment	and{ V^+	No variation	$> 0.9pu$
	or{ I^+	Step-up	
	P	Step-up	
Load decrement	and{ V^+	No variation	$> 0.9pu$
	or{ I^+	Step-down	
	P	Step-down	

Table 2. ESOSC: Premises and conclusions of characteristics relation rules

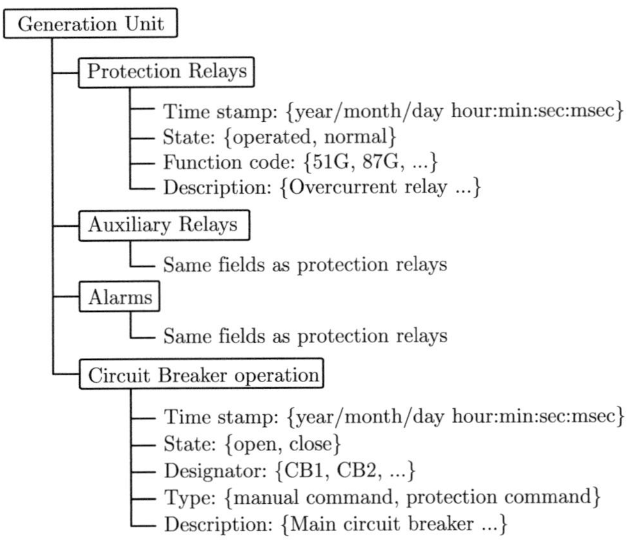

Fig. 8. Structure of sequence of events data.

- Auxiliary Relays: This class is used to represent the auxiliary relays, such as lockout relay (86), circuit breaker opening relay (94) and any other auxiliary device. The information fields are the same as the protection relays class.
- Alarms: All the events that are only informative (they do not represent any protective action) are grouped in this class.

- Circuit Breaker operation: This represents the events of opening and closing Circuit Breakers (CB).

Among these classes each event is classified according to its function for instance, overcurrent relay (ANSI 51), lockout relay (ANSI 86), main circuit breaker, manual opening of the circuit breaker and several other functions. The classification of the events is carried out performing a previous configuration of the system where the user informs the associations of SCADA monitored events with the classes.
Fig. 9 shows a representation of the sequence of event analysis that is based on the ESSOE whose input facts are the classified events and their status read from SOE database.

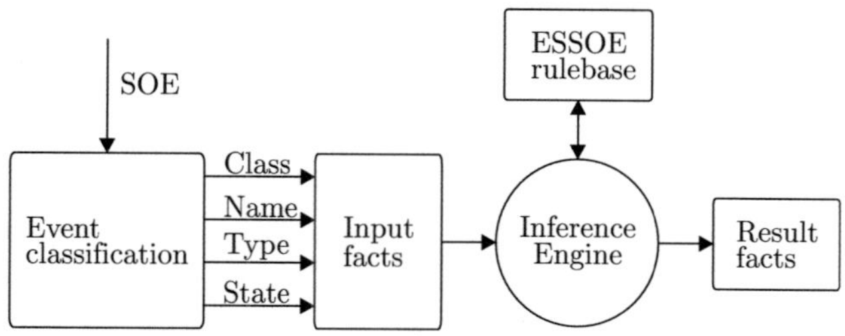

Fig. 9. ESSOE representation.

The knowledge base is formed by a set of rules obtained from the protection scheme of every generation unit with the collaboration of protection specialists. It is necessary to know which protective devices trip the circuit breakers, which ones are the auxiliary relays and their actions, the energization and de-energization procedures of the unit and other relevant characteristics or procedures associated with each generation unit. From these studies it is possible to write several rules. The ESSOE has 8 rules for the following situations: *de-energization*, *reverse power de-energization*, *isolated unit de-energization*, *protection testing* (maintenance), *generator lockout*, *synchronization* of unit, *forced shutdown* and the *no events*. (Moreto & Rolim, 2011).
The SOE analysis and oscillographic analysis should be correlated in order to obtain a final conclusion about the occurrence (Moreto & Rolim, 2011). This is the objective of the Expert System for generation Unit analysis (ESUNI).

4.4 ESUNI: Expert System for Unit analysis

The ESUNI is responsible for correlating the results from oscillograph (ESOSC) and sequence of events (ESSOE) analysis providing a diagnosis about the generation unit. It consists of an expert system with a set of simple rules that compares each result. These rules, listed in Table 3, represent a set of possible final results from the phasor record and sequence of events analyses (Moreto & Rolim, 2011).
A "no result" is obtained when none of the Table 3 rules is satisfied. The most common causes of "no result" conclusion are:

- Failures in the data collection system, such as missing events in the SOE
- Synchronization failure between the oscillographic records and the SOE
- Spurious events in SOE due to noise at RTU inputs
- Wrong connections of current or voltage transformers with the DFR

When the conclusion is "no result" or "fault", a subsequent analysis is needed, using the waveform record in order to detect and classify possible faults.

ESUNI conclusion	ESOSC	ESSOE
Normal operation	Normal operation	No events
	Load increment	No events
	Load decrement	No events
Out of service	Out of service	No events
Reverse power de-energization	De-energization	De-energization with 32G
Normal de-energization	De-energization	De-energization
Energization	Energization	Generator lock-out
	Energization	Synchronism
Protection system tests	Out of service	Protection testing
Isolated unit operation	Isolated unit	No events
Synchronism	Synchronism	Synchronism
	Isolated unit	Synchronism
	Normal operation	Synchronism
Fault or forced shutdown	Forced shutdown	Forced shutdown

Table 3. ESUNI rule set.

5. Waveform record analysis

The structure of the waveform record analysis scheme is composed by the following processing blocks that are executed in sequence (Fig. 10): Data acquisition; data segmentation; data feature extraction; and decision making (expert system based).

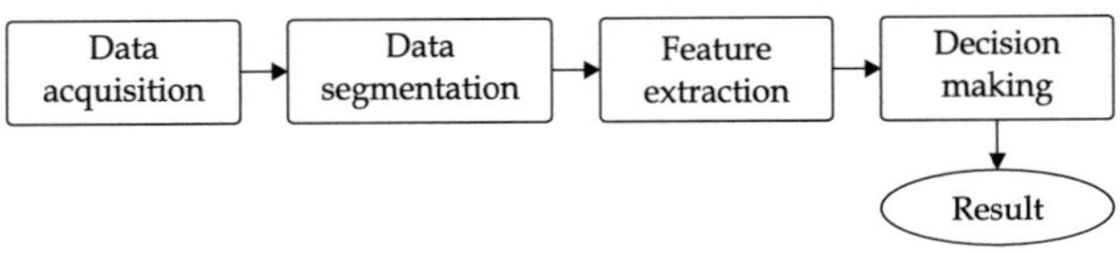

Fig. 10. Processing blocks of the waveform analysis scheme.

Data acquisition is the process of reading and interpreting the data stored in DFR records. These data are the sampled waveforms of voltages and currents acquired at the generator terminals. The segmentation block is responsible for detecting transients in the acquired data, resulting in a set of pre-fault, fault and post-fault segments. An Extended Complex Kalman Filter (ECKF) is used for this purpose (Nishiyama, 1997). For each detected segment a feature extraction is performed and those features will be used as inputs to the decision making process. Parameters of the signal estimated by the ECKF and also by linear Kalman Filters (KF) are used to calculate the input features of the expert system.
The occurrence analysis based on the DFR waveform records is also performed by an expert system. The input facts are the calculated features and the output fact is the type of disturbance. Development of the rule set was made based on several simulations of a power generating unit bay composed a hydraulic turbine, a synchronous machine, a speed regulator, a voltage regulator and a step-up transformer. In the simulated system this unit is connected to an slack bus which represents a bulk power system.
The processing blocks of Fig. 10 will be discussed in detail in the following subsections.

5.1 Data segmentation

Segmentation consists of splitting a disturbance record that is not stationary into a series of segments that can be considered stationary (Bollen & Gu, 2006). Through a segmentation process, traditional tools like Fourier analysis can be applied to each segment without the errors that would occur when such tools are employed in non-stationary signals. An example of segmentation is shown in Fig. 11.

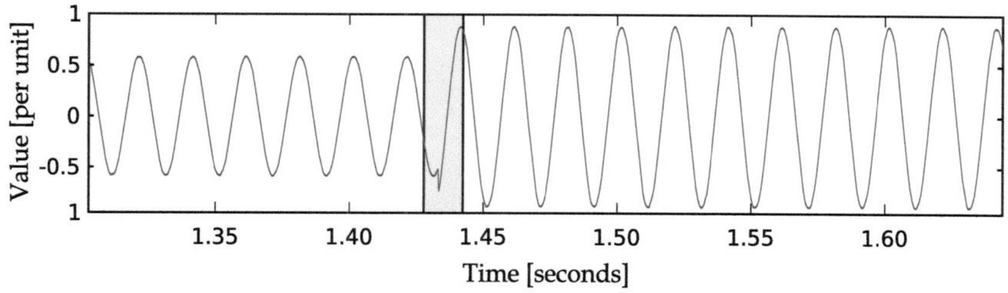

Fig. 11. Exemple of waveform record segmentation.

Several signal processing tools can be employed in the segmentation process. The most common ones are the Short Time Fourier Transform (STFT) (Gu & Bollen, 2000), the Wavelet Transform (Silva et al., 2006; Ukil & Zivanovic, 2007) and adaptive filters like Kalman Filters (Bollen & Gu, 2006; Styvaktakis et al., 2002). The segmentation schemes proposed in the literature are not appropriate for power generation units, because they have not been designed for segmenting slow transients like the example of Fig. 2(b). To overcome this limitation a new segmentation scheme is proposed in this chapter. This scheme is based on an extended complex Kalman filter (ECKF). Before the explanation of the signal model used and the segmentation algorithm, a brief introdution to Kalman filters is presented.

5.1.1 Kalman filters

The Kalman filter (KF) is a recursive and efficient estimation process that minimizes the mean square error of a signal model based on measured values. The process uses a observation variable obtained from the measurements (DFR data) to estimate the state variables. In its basic formulation, the relation between the states and the measurements and the relation between the actual states and previous ones are assumed to be linear. This implies that the model to be estimated can be written as state variables where all Matrix elements are constants (Bollen & Gu, 2006):

State equations: $$\mathbf{x}_{k+1} = \Phi_k \mathbf{x}_k + \mathbf{w}_k \quad (2)$$

Observation equations: $$y_k = H_k \mathbf{x}_k + \mathbf{v}_k \quad (3)$$

where $\mathbf{x}_k$ is the state vector at instant k; Φ_k is the state transition matrix that provides the relation between instants k and $k+1$ and H_k is the observation matrix that relates the states with the measurements y_k. $\mathbf{w}_k$ and $\mathbf{v}_k$ are vectors representing the noise of the model and the measurements respectively. It is assumed that both are white noise, non correlated, with zero mean and covariance matrix $Q_k = E\left\{\mathbf{w}_k \mathbf{w}_k^T\right\}$ and $R_k = E\left\{\mathbf{v}_k \mathbf{v}_k^T\right\}$ where E is the expected value operation.

The recursive calculation of the Kalman filter starts from an initial estimation of the state vector $\hat{\mathbf{x}}_0$ and the error covariance matrix $\hat{P}_0$. With these values the Kalman gain K_k is calculated for sample k:

$$K_k = \hat{P}_{k-1} H_k^{*T} \left[H_k \hat{P}_{k-1} H_k^{*T} + R \right]^{-1} \quad (4)$$

where the operations denoted by * e ^{T} are the complex conjugate and transposition, respectively. R is the covariance of the measurement noise, assumed constant and acts as a speed adjustment parameter of the filter.

With the updated gain, the covariance matrix is also updated,

$$\hat{P}_k = \hat{P}_{k-1} \left(I - K_k H_k \right) \tag{5}$$

as well for state vector, using the new measurement y_k to correct it:

$$\hat{\mathbf{x}}_k = \hat{\mathbf{x}}_{k-1} + K_k \left(y_k - H_k \hat{\mathbf{x}}_{k-1} \right) \tag{6}$$

The term between parenthesis in Equation 6 is called innovation or residual. I is the identity matrix.

Finally a projection of the states and covariance matrix is calculated:

$$\mathbf{x}_{k+1} = \Phi_k \mathbf{x}_k \tag{7}$$

$$\hat{P}_{k+1} = \Phi_k \hat{P}_k \Phi_k^{*T} \tag{8}$$

With the projected values, the k index is incremented and a new iteration begins with the application of Equation 4. The process continues until $k = N$, where N is the total number of samples.

If the relations of the state equations and observation equations are non-linear, the extended Kalman filter (EKF) is more adequate. In EKF the matrix operations of Equations 2 and 3 are replaced by nonlinear functions:

$$\mathbf{x}_{k+1} = \phi_k \left(\mathbf{x}_k \right) + \mathbf{w}_k \tag{9}$$

$$y_k = \mathbf{h}_k \left(\mathbf{x}_k \right) + \mathbf{v}_k \tag{10}$$

To apply the EKF, the non-linear model (Equations 9) and the output equation (Equation 10) are linearized using the first term of the Taylor series. As a result, Equations 4, 5, 6 and 8 become (Girgis & Hwang, 1984):

$$\Phi_k = \left. \frac{\partial \phi_k \left(\mathbf{x}_k \right)}{\partial \mathbf{x}_k} \right|_{\mathbf{x}_k = \hat{\mathbf{x}}_k} \tag{11}$$

$$H_k = \left. \frac{\partial \mathbf{h}_k \left(\mathbf{x}_k \right)}{\partial \mathbf{x}_k} \right|_{\mathbf{x}_k = \hat{\mathbf{x}}_{k-1}} \tag{12}$$

5.1.2 Signal model

In this chapter the parameters of the signal model are estimated by a extended Kalman filter. The proposed model, expressed in Equations 13 to 15 is a complex sinusoid with a damping coefficient:

$$y_k = z_k + v_k \tag{13}$$

where:

$$z_k = e^{\lambda t_k} A_1 e^{j(\omega_1 t_k + \varphi_i)} \tag{14}$$

$$\omega_1 = 2\pi f_1, \qquad t_k = k\Delta t \tag{15}$$

The term A_1 represents the sinusoid magnitude, φ_i the phase angle and f_1 the system's fundamental frequency (usually 50Hz or 60Hz). The exponential damping coefficient is given by λ, and Δt is the sampling period.

This model can be written in state variable form (Nishiyama, 1997):

$$\begin{bmatrix} x_{k+1}(1) \\ x_{k+1}(2) \end{bmatrix} = \begin{bmatrix} 1 & 0 \\ 0 & x_k(1) \end{bmatrix} \begin{bmatrix} x_k(1) \\ x_k(2) \end{bmatrix} \tag{16}$$

$$y_k = \begin{bmatrix} 0 & 1 \end{bmatrix} \begin{bmatrix} x_k(1) \\ x_k(2) \end{bmatrix} + v_k \tag{17}$$

where:

$$x_k(1) = e^{\lambda\Delta t + j\omega_1\Delta t} \tag{18}$$

$$x_k(2) = A_1 e^{\lambda k\Delta t + j(\omega_1 k\Delta t + \varphi_1)} = z_k \tag{19}$$

As the model is non-linear, the equations of the EKF have to be used. It should be pointed out that the measured signals are complex quantities, obtained from the three phase components using the $\alpha\beta$ transform as in (Dash et al., 1999; Hase, 2007).
With the estimated states it is possible to estimate of the fundamental frequency ($\hat{f}_{1k}$), exponential damping coefficient ($\hat{\lambda}_k$), fundamental component magnitude ($\hat{A}_{1k}$) and phase angle ($\hat{\varphi}_{1k}$) using the following relations:

$$\hat{f}_{1k} = \frac{\omega_{1k}}{2\pi} = \frac{1}{2\pi\Delta t}\text{Imag}\left(\ln\left(\hat{x}_k(1)\right)\right) \tag{20}$$

$$\hat{\lambda}_k = \frac{1}{\Delta t}\text{Real}\left(\ln\left(\hat{x}_k(1)\right)\right) \tag{21}$$

$$\hat{A}_{1k} = |\hat{x}_k(2)| \tag{22}$$

$$\hat{\varphi}_{1k} = \text{Imag}\left(\frac{\hat{x}_k(2)}{|\hat{x}_k(2)|\,\hat{x}_k(1)^k}\right) \tag{23}$$

5.1.3 Segmentation algorithm

The overall scheme of the proposed segmentation algorithm is shown in Fig. 12.

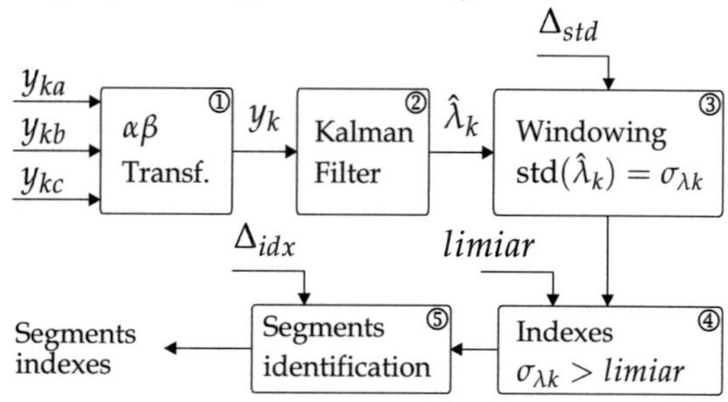

Fig. 12. Proposed segmentation scheme.

Each block in Fig. 12 is described in the following paragraphs:

5.1.3.1 ① Complex signal calculation

The measured complex signal y_k is obtained from the three phase measurements contained in the disturbance record (y_{ka}, y_{kb} and y_{kc}) using the $\alpha\beta$ transform (Hase, 2007) of Equations 24 and 25.

$$\begin{bmatrix} y_{k\alpha} \\ y_{k\beta} \end{bmatrix} = \sqrt{\frac{2}{3}} \begin{bmatrix} 1 & -\frac{1}{2} & -\frac{1}{2} \\ 0 & \frac{\sqrt{3}}{2} & -\frac{\sqrt{3}}{2} \end{bmatrix} \begin{bmatrix} y_{ka} \\ y_{kb} \\ y_{kc} \end{bmatrix} \quad (24)$$

$$y_k = y_{k\alpha} + j y_{k\beta} \quad (25)$$

5.1.3.2 ②Kalman filter calculation

The extended complex Kalman filter is applied to y_k and the parameter $\hat{\lambda}_k$ is estimated. This signal is used to segment the disturbance record.

5.1.3.3 ③Detection index calculation

The signal $\hat{\lambda}_k$ is submitted to a windowing procedure where at each window of length Δ_{std} the standard deviation is calculated. The result of the sliding windows calculations is the detection index $\sigma_{\lambda k}$, similar to the detection index applied for the phasor record segmentation.

5.1.3.4 ④Threshold comparison

A new segment is identified as the period when the detection index exceeds a given threshold. Thus, the threshold detection gives the beginning and the ending of the segments.

5.1.3.5 ⑤Segments identification

The segments identified at the previous step are analyzed in such a way that those considered close enough are grouped in a single segment. The parameter Δ_{idx} correspond to the minimum time interval between two consecutive segments. The time instants of the beginning and ending of each segment are used to calculate the features that will be used by the expert system.

5.2 Feature extraction

The process of feature extraction is based on the fundamental frequency phasors of each monitored quantity, obtained through a set of linear Kalman filters. The signal model used is the number 1 of (Kennedy et al., 2003). From these calculated phasor parameters, the symmetrical components are calculated. Finally, a mean value of each symmetrical component magnitude is calculated in each segment. This process is depicted in Fig. 13.
The inputs are the voltages (V_A, V_B and V_C) and currents (I_A, I_B and I_C) at the terminals of the generator and the neutral current at the high side of the unit's step-up transformer (I_{nHS}). These quantities are usually monitored by the DFRs at power stations.

5.3 Decision making

An expert system is the core of the waveform analysis. This tool is suitable to this application, due to its ability to represent the knowledge applied by the specialist to solve the problem. The facts knowledge base of this expert system is composed of facts containing the calculated quantities stated in the previous subsection for each segment identified. The fields that compose these facts are described in Table 4.
The fields "Disturb." and "Classific." are used during the reasoning process to store the results of the analysis. That is, their content shows the classification of each disturbance segment.
By defining the facts structure, the rule base can be described. These rules can be grouped in sets to facilitate the explanation process, but they coexist simultaneously at the expert system knowledge base. The defined sets are:

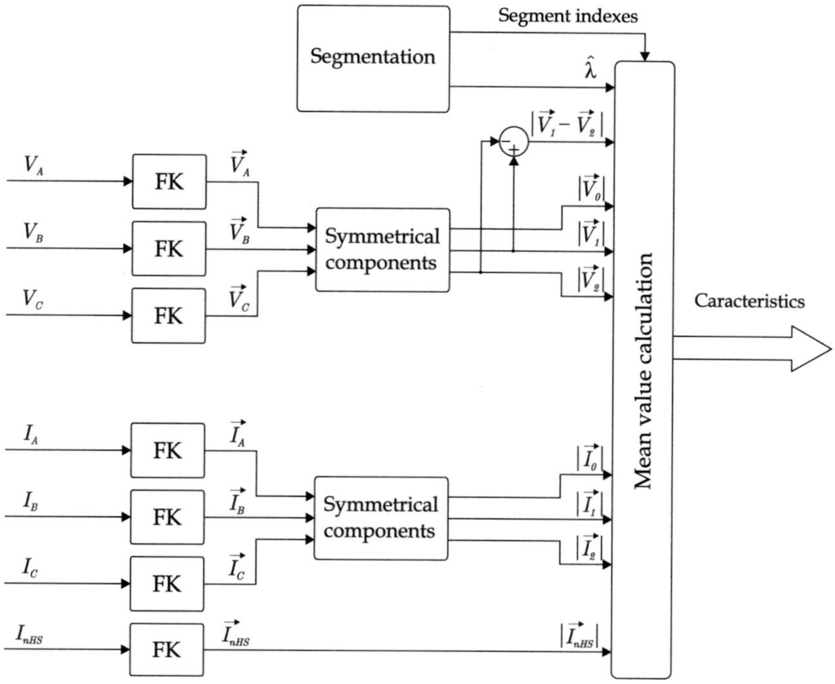

Fig. 13. Feature extraction process.

Field or slot	Description
Num	Number of the segments
V0m	Mean value of the zero sequence voltage modulus
V1m	Mean value of the positive sequence voltage modulus
V2m	Mean value of the negative sequence voltage modulus
I0m	Mean value of the zero sequence current modulus
I1m	Mean value of the positive sequence current modulus
I2m	Mean value of the negative sequence current modulus
InATm	Mean value of the high side neutral current modulus
CexpVm	Mean value of the damping coeficient $\hat{\lambda}_k$
ModV12m	Mean value of $\vec{V}1 - \vec{V}2$ modulus
Disturb.	Type of identified disturbance
Classific.	Classification of the disturbance

Table 4. Fact contents of the waveform analysis expert system.

- Fault detection rules.
- Classification of normal situations rules.
- Fault classification rules.

Each rule set is described below.

5.3.1 Fault detection rules

The objective of this set of rules is to determine if a segment shows characteristics of a short circuit (balanced or unbalanced) or represents a normal operative situation. These rules are

mainly based on the values of negative sequence voltages and currents, which indicate an imbalance between the three phases.
The conclusion of the rules is the fulfillment of the field "Disturb." with a corresponding code. When rule-based expert systems are build in CLIPS platform, this modification is equivalent to the redefinition of the fact in the knowledge base.
Table 5 summarizes de fault detection rules. The symbol $\Leftarrow$ is used to denote a field modification within in the fact. The premises column shows the thresholds used to detect each type of disturbance and also the logical operators "and" and "or".

Rule conclusion	Action	Premises
Normal operation	Disturb.$\Leftarrow$"normal"	V2m $< 0.1pu$ and I2m $< 0.07pu$ and I1m $< 1.1pu$
Unbalanced fault	Disturb.$\Leftarrow$"unbalanced"	V2m $> 0.1pu$ or I2m $> 0.07pu$
Balanced fault	Disturb.$\Leftarrow$"balanced"	V2m $< 0.1pu$ or I2m $< 0.07pu$ and I1m $> 1.1pu$

Table 5. Premises of fault detection rules.

5.3.2 Classification of normal situation rules

These rules are responsible for classifying the segment were "normal" operative situation have been detected in, for instance: de-energization, normal operation, generator unloaded, generator shutdown and so on. The rules for classifying normal situations are presented in Table 6.

Rule conclusion	Action	Premises
Normal operation with load	Classifi.$\Leftarrow$"normal load"	V1m $> 0.9pu$ and I1m $> 0.05pu$ and Disturb. = "normal"
Normal operation without load	Classifi.$\Leftarrow$"normal no load"	V1m $> 0.9pu$ and I1m $< 0.05pu$ and Disturb. = "normal"
Shutdown	Classifi.$\Leftarrow$"shutdown"	V1m $< 0.1pu$ and I1m $< 0.05pu$ and Disturb. = "normal"
De-energization	Classifi.$\Leftarrow$"De-energization"	$0.1 <$V1m$< 0.9pu$ and I1m $< 0.05pu$ and CexpVm < -0.2 and Disturb. = "normal"

Table 6. Premises and actions of the rules to classify normal situations.

In this rule set, the premises are based on the positive sequence values, but they will not fire if an acceptable imbalance or overload situation is detected as a *Disturb. = "normal"* condition is needed. The classified operative conditions are: normal operation with load (nominal voltage and current), normal operation without load (nominal voltage and no current), generator shutdown (no voltages and currents) and de-enegization (voltage at intermediate levels with exponential decrease and no current).

5.3.3 Fault classification rules

These rules a used to classify those cases when an imbalance condition is detected. Their premised are based on the relations between the symmetrical components values obtained by short circuit analysis theory (Grainger & Stevenson, 1994). These relations are stated below for two phase faults.

$$\vec{I1} \approx -\vec{I2} \tag{26}$$

$$\vec{V1} \approx \vec{V2} \tag{27}$$

$$\vec{V0} \approx \vec{I0} \approx 0 \tag{28}$$

Concerning two phase to ground faults, the relations are the following:

$$\vec{I1} \approx -\vec{I2} - \vec{I0} \tag{29}$$

$$\vec{V1} \approx \vec{V2} \approx \vec{V0} \tag{30}$$

And for single phase to ground:

$$\vec{I1} \approx \vec{I2} \approx \vec{I0} \tag{31}$$

$$\vec{V1} \approx \vec{V2} + \vec{V0} \Rightarrow -\vec{V1} + \vec{V2} + \vec{V0} \approx 0 \tag{32}$$

The relations mentioned are valid in the faulted point of the system. If a fault occurs in the nearby system (like in the power plant substation), they will be influenced by the distance to the fault and by the connections of the power transformer. Most of the step-up transformers employed in generation units have Δ-Y configuration. This way, a single phase to ground fault at the transformer high voltage side is "seen" as a two phase fault at the generator terminals. In order to discriminate ground faults and phase faults at the transformer high voltage side the neutral current I_{nHS} is used. The presence of this current indicates a ground fault in the high voltage side. Table 7 shows the set of rules used to classify the disturbances.

The classification of each segment, along with the messages generated by each rule, are stored sequentially (using the same order of the segments) in the waveform analysis report. In the event of a fault, the analysis conclusion is its classification otherwise it is the normal operation classification. The expert engineer can then check the report where all the information needed is condensed, which result in less time spent and an improvement of the quality of the analysis.

6. Results

The approach explained in the previous section, has been tested using real data from a coal fired thermal power plant in Brazil. This power plant has four 24 MVA turbogenerators. The DFR monitors the terminal voltages and load currents from the four turbogenerators (G1 to G4).

The scheme is implemented as a standalone application written in *python* language. The expert systems have been implemented in CLIPS and interfaced with the routines in python. Some results of phasor and waveform record automatic analyses are presented in the following subsections.

Rule conclusion	Action	Premises
Double phase fault at terminal	Classifi.⇐"fault dP term"	V0 $<$ 0.05pu and ModV12 $<$ 0.2pu and Disturb. = "unbalanced"
Double phase to ground at terminal	Classifi.⇐"fault dPg term"	V0 $>$ 0.05pu and ModV12 $<$ 0.2pu and Disturb. = "unbalanced"
Single phase to ground at terminal	Classifi.⇐"fault Pg term"	V0 $>$ 0.05pu and -0.1 <(-V1+V2+V0)< 0.1pu and Disturb. = "unbalanced"
Ground foult at high side	Classifi.⇐"ground fault high"	V0 $<$ 0.05pu and InHS $>$ 0.2pu and Disturb. = "unbalanced"
Double phase fault at high side	Classifi.⇐"dP high side"	V0 $<$ 0.05pu and InHS $<$ 0.2pu and ModV12 $>$ 0.2pu and Disturb. = "unbalanced"

Table 7. Premises and actions of fault classification rules.

6.1 Phasor record analysis

An oscillograph database corresponding to four months of registered occurrences was used to test the proposed phasor analysis scheme. The results for the four generation units are stated in Table 8. This table shows the conclusions achieved by the proposed methodology.

Specialist's diagnosis	Correct result	No result	Total
Normal operation	170	0	170
Normal operation: load increase	3	0	3
Normal operation: load decrease	7	0	7
Out of service	129	0	129
Reverse power de-energization	11	6	17
Normal de-energization	1	4	5
Energization	2	4	6
Isolated unit	3	1	4
Synchronism	1	1	2
Fault	1	1	2
Totals:	328	17	345

Table 8. Phasor record results (Moreto & Rolim, 2011).

The classification shown in the first column of Table 8 was provided by the specialist responsible for the task. The results summarized in this table show that the diagnosis provided by the automatic tool were correct in more than 95% of the cases. They also show that the majority of the occurrences came from oscillographies recorded during normal situations or when the generators were out of service. Therefore, for most cases, the manual analysis by a specialist is not necessary. With the proposed scheme the engineer should only check the fault cases and the cases where there is no result from the automated analysis module. As a result, less time is spent in selecting, downloading and opening oscilographic records and SOE data, and engineer may focus his attention on the important cases.

It is important to point out that the automatic system never presented a wrong diagnosis and the number of cases that should be verified by the specialists or the waveform analysis module was reduced from 345 to 17.

6.2 Waveform record analysis

The development and testing of the proposed waveform analysis scheme was made using simulated cases. This is motivated by the fact that the number of fault occurrences in power generation units are much smaller in comparison with normal situation records. Thus, there are not enough cases involving all the fault types in order to fully validate the scheme with real data. In order to overcome this problem, a simulated model is employed. This model consists of a hydroelectric generation unit with the corresponding voltage and speed controllers connected through a Δ-Y step-up transformer to a slack bus which represents the bulk power system. The model used is the *Power turbine* demonstration system distributed along with the *SimPowerSystems* blockset of the Matlab/Simulink© program.
In order to show the performance of the methodology with real data, a case study of a short circuit is also presented.

6.2.1 Simulation results

In order not to extend excessively the length of this text with tables and figures of each fault type, the simulation results are presented in a descriptive form. Several simulations were carried out with the variation of different parameters for each fault type: single phase to ground, two phase to ground, two phase and three phase. The faults were applied at the generator terminals and at the high voltage side of the transformer. A discussion of the results is presented in the following items:

- Fault resistance variation: the four fault types were simulated considering fault resistances of 0.01Ω, 0.1Ω, 0.5Ω, 1Ω and 5Ω. The scheme classifies correctly the fault segments with resistance 0.01Ω and 0.1Ω. In the cases with resistance higher than 0.5Ω the scheme is able to correctly detect the fault, but the classification is compromised due to the small increase in currents (around 1.5 pu for the worst case) during the fault. Although the classification was not obtained, the fault was correctly detected in all cases, which is enough to signal the analyst that that record should be manually verified. For faults at the high voltage side, the fault resistance limit that compromises the classification is 1Ω due to the same reason.
- Variation of the involved phases: The scheme makes no distinction of which phase is involved with the fault (phases A, B, C, AB, BC or AC). In other words, the results do not change with the variation of these fault characteristics.
- Incidence angle: For the cases with fault resistance of 0.01Ω the incidence angle was varied in ±5 milliseconds that correspond to approximately 1/3 of a fundamental frequency cycle of 60 Hz. No influence of this parameter was observed in the results.

6.2.2 Case study

This case study uses data from a real occurrence where a failure of a surge arrester on phase B resulted in a solid (fault resistance near zero) single phase to ground fault at the high voltage side of the step-up transformer.
Figs. 14(a) and 14(b) show the estimated magnitudes of voltages and currents during the segmentation process. As can be seen, there is an expressive overcurrent and a significant voltage drop until the fault is extinguished.
The symmetrical components of voltages and currents are presented in Fig. 15. The gray bar represents the fault segment identified by the segmentation process. The calculated characteristics (described by Table 4) obtained in each of the 3 segments can be seen in Table 9. When the characteristics are applied to the expert system, the rule activations stated bellow is obtained:

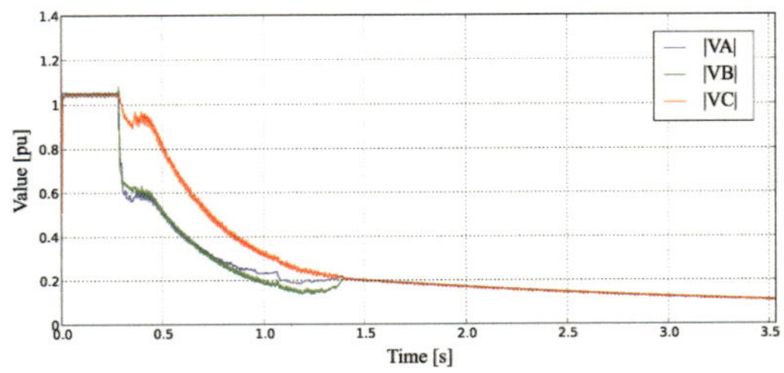

(a) Phase voltages

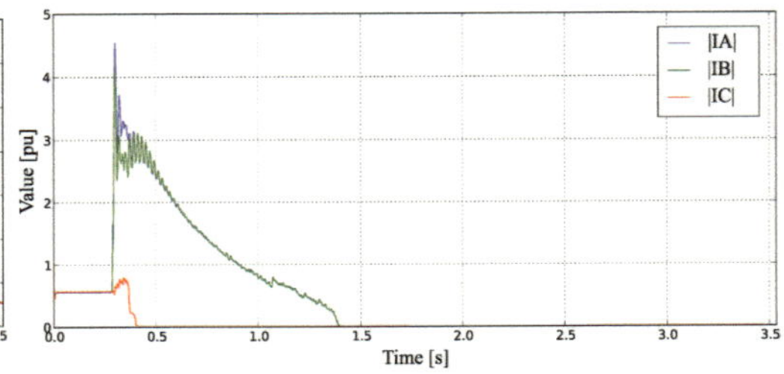

(b) Phase currents

Fig. 14. Fundamental frequency estimated magnitudes of phase quantities during the occurrence.

⇒Segment 0: Fault detection rule - normal operation
⇒Segment 0: Normal situation classification - Normal operation with load
⇒Segment 1: Fault detection rule - unbalanced fault
⇒Segment 1: Fault classification rule - **Ground fault at high voltage side**
⇒Segment 2: Fault detection rule - normal operation
⇒Segment 2: Normal situation classification - De-energization

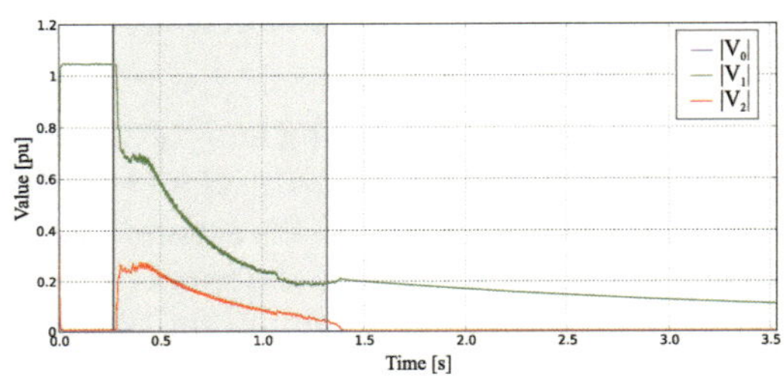

(a) Sequence voltages

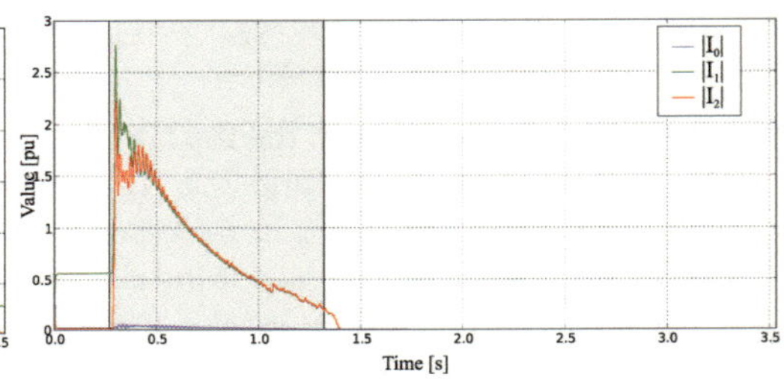

(b) Sequence currents

Fig. 15. Fundamental frequency estimated magnitudes of the symmetrical components during the occurrence.

	Mean value in the segments:		
Feature	0	1	2
V0m	0.011	0.001	0.001
V1m	1.038	0.392	0.151
V2m	0.011	0.137	0.003
I0m	0.025	0.020	0.002
I1m	0.559	0.870	0.006
I2m	0.013	0.837	0.006
InHSm	0.020	0.629	0.001
CexpVm	0.041	-1.709	-0.249
ModV12m	1.035	0.469	0.150

Table 9. Feature extraction result.

The waveform analysis scheme has correctly classified the disturbance, identifying the situation in each segment. During the first segment (0) the generator is under normal operation with nominal voltage and approximately 0.6 pu of load. During the fault period (segment 1) the characteristics indicate a high voltage side ground fault. After the fault end (segment 2) the generator voltage continues to reduce exponentially, characterizing a de-energization process.

7. Conclusions

This chapter described a scheme that combines signal processing routines with expert systems for diagnosing occurrences of power generation units. The approach consist in a two level methodology. The first level is responsible for a pre-classification, using the digital fault recorder phasor records and sequence of events. The analyses are executed independently. So, if one source of information fails, the conclusion will be *no result*, starting the second level that provides a classification of the occurrence using the waveform record. In case of an abnormal operation, the engineer has to manually verify the data.

The results attested that the proposed scheme can significantly help the analysts by providing a classification of each occurrence. The system was able to identify common situations when the oscillographic data may be automatically archived with a high percentage of success. Therefore the engineers may focus their attention on the most important cases, such as, faults or forced shutdowns. For these cases the waveform record analysis is performed in order to determine whether the record corresponds to a fault case and to provide a fault classification. The knowledge base of the expert systems have been built based on extensive studies about the generator protection philosophy and operational procedures of the power plant. The knowledge base of the expert system responsible for analyzing the sequence of events should be reevaluated for each power plant, as their protection schemes and monitored events can be different. The expert system for phasor record analysis does not need to be changed from one power plant to another.

The waveform analysis scheme was developed using a simulation model. Several simulation parameters were changed and the proposed methodology was able to detect the fault in all cases. The case study with real data showed that the scheme is suitable to be used in practice in order to facilitate the task performed by the engineer at the analysis center.

This chapter also presented a new segmentation procedure for waveform records based on the exponential damping coefficient, suitable for being applied to data from power generation systems that shows slow transients, like the de-energization case.

8. References

Allen, D., Apostolov, A. & Kreiss, D. (2005). Automated analysis of power system events, *IEEE Power and Energy Magazine* 3(5): 48–55.

Barros, J. & Perez, E. (2006). Automatic detection and analysis of voltage events in power systems, *IEEE Transactions on Instrumentation and Measurement* 55(5): 1487–1493.

Bollen, M. H. J. & Gu, I. (2006). *Signal Processing of Power Quality Disturbances*, IEEE Press Series on Power Engineering, 1 edn, Wiley-IEEE Press.

Chantler, M., Pogliano, P., Aldea, A., Tornielli, G., Wyatt, T. & Jolley, A. (2000). The use of fault-recorder data for diagnosing timing and other related faults in electricity transmission networks, *IEEE Transactions on Power Systems* 15(4): 1388–1393.

Dash, P., Pradhan, A. & Panda, G. (1999). Frequency estimation of distorted power system signals using extended complex kalman filter, *IEEE Transactions on Power Delivery* 14(3): 761–766.

Davidson, E., McArthur, S., McDonald, J., Cumming, T. & Watt, I. (2006). Applying multi-agent system technology in practice: automated management and analysis of scada and digital fault recorder data, *IEEE Transactions on Power Systems* 21(2): 559–567.

Gaing, Z.-L. (2004). Wavelet-based neural network for power disturbance recognition and classification, *IEEE Transactions on Power Delivery* 19(4): 1560–1568.

Girgis, A. & Hwang, T. (1984). Optimal estimation of voltage phasors and frequency deviation using linear and non-linear kalman filtering: Theory and limitations, *IEEE Transactions on Power Apparatus and Systems* PAS-103(10): 2943–2951.

Grainger, J. J. & Stevenson, W. D. (1994). *Power System Analysis*, McGraw-Hill, Inc., New York, USA.

Gu, Y. & Bollen, M. (2000). Time-frequency and time-scale domain analysis of voltage disturbances, *IEEE Transactions on Power Delivery* 15(4): 1279–1284.

Hase, Y. (2007). *Handbook of power system engineering*, 1 edn, John Wiley & Sons Ltd.

IEE (1999). *IEEE Standard Common Format for Transient Data Exchange (COMTRADE) for Power Systems.*

Kennedy, K., Lightbody, G. & Yacamini, R. (2003). Power system harmonic analysis using the kalman filter, *Power Engineering Society General Meeting, 2003, IEEE*, Vol. 2, pp. –757 Vol. 2.

Luo, X. & Kezunovic, M. (2005). Fault analysis based on integration of digital relay and dfr data, *IEEE Power Engineering Society General Meeting*, Vol. 1, IEEE PES, San Francisco, CA, USA, pp. 746–751.

McArthur, S. D. J., Davidson, E. M., Hossack, J. A. & McDonald, J. R. (2004). Automating power system fault diagnosis through multi-agent system technology, *37th International Conference on System Sciences*, IEEE Computer Society, Big Island, Hawaii.

Moreto, M. & Rolim, J. G. (2008). Automated analysis of digital fault recorder data in power generating plants, *International Journal of Innovations in Energy Systems and Power* 3(2): 1–6.

Moreto, M. & Rolim, J. G. (2011). Using phasor data records and sequence of events to automate the classification of disturbances of power generating units, *Electric Power Systems Research* In Press, Corrected Proof: –.

Moreto, M., Rolim, J. G. & Varela, F. S. (2009). Automating the diagnosis of occurrences in power plants using data from dfr and sequence of events: an expert system based methodology, *15th Int. Conf. intell. Syst. Appl. to Power Syst.*, IEEE, Curitiba, Brazil, pp. 1–6.

Nishiyama, K. (1997). A nonlinear filter for estimating a sinusoidal signal and its parameters in white noise: on the case of a single sinusoid, *IEEE Transactions on Signal Processing* 45(4): 970–981.

Silva, K. M., Souza, B. A. & Brito, N. S. D. (2006). Fault detection and classification in transmission lines bases on wavelet transform and ann, *IEEE Transactions on Power Delivery* 21(4): 2058–2063.

Styvaktakis, E., Bollen, M. H. J. & Gu, I. Y. H. (2002). Expert system for classification and analysis of power system events, *IEEE Transactions on Power Delivery* 17(2): 423–428.

Ukil, A. & Zivanovic, R. (2007). Application of abrupt change detection in power systems disturbance analysis and relay performance monitoring, *IEEE Transactions on Power Delivery* 22(1): 59–66.

18

Fuzzy Based Flow Management of Real-Time Traffic for Quality of Service in WLANs

Tapio Frantti and Mikko Majanen
VTT Technical Research Centre of Finland
Finland

1. Introduction

Designing heterogeneous bandwidth limited communication systems that support a wide variety of applications, including file transfer, web browsing, interactive games, audio and video calls, and emerging real-time virtual world and social media applications is a challenging task because there is a shortage of resources to satisfy all traffic demands and diverse quality of service (QoS) requirements. For example, the current Internet architecture supports only best-effort service class which is not enough especially for delay sensitive real-time multimedia applications. Therefore, to improve QoS for specified traffic in the Internet, the end nodes (hosts) should make a bandwidth reservation through all the intermediate nodes, like access points and routers, by using some sort of resource reservation. For the QoS guarantee, the IETF has worked on the resource reservation protocol (RSVP) that can be used to hard resource reservation: an endpoint uses RSVP to request a simplex flow through the network with specified QoS bounds and the intermediate nodes, like routers, along the path either agree to honor the request or deny it. It is a transport layer protocol designed to reserve resources across a network. RSVP operates over an internet protocol versions 4 or 6 (IPv4 or IPv6) and provides receiver-initiated setup of resource reservations for multicast or unicast data flows. The drawback of the RSVP is that all the routers along the path must agree the resource reservation for QoS guarantee. However, no any QoS system can satisfy all users' demands if the network traffic exceeds network capacity. Another disadvantage is that the reserved virtual links do not necessarily use the network capacity optimally. Therefore, we focus here to the cognitive flow management of delay sensitive constant bit rate real-time traffics, such as voice over internet protocols (VoIP), video calls, and interactive games, to improve QoS in Wireless Local Area Networks (WLANs).

The Internet has two independent flow problems. Internet protocols need end-to-end *flow control* and a mechanism for intermediate nodes, like routers and access points, to control the amount of traffic known as the *congestion prevention and control* mechanism. *Flow control* is closely related to the point-to-point traffic between a sender and a receiver. It guarantees that a fast sender cannot continually send datagrams faster than a receiver can absorb them. *Congestion* is a condition of severe delay caused by an overload of datagrams at intermediate nodes. Usually congestion arises for two different reasons: a high-speed computer may be able to generate traffic faster than a network can transfer it or many computers send datagrams simultaneously through a single router, even though no single computer causes the problem. Hence, the congestion control can be considered more as a global issue whereas flow control is more a local, point to point, issue with some direct feedback from the receiver to the sender.

The term *cognition* refers to the processing of information, applying knowledge, and changing preferences. In the communication networks, cognition can be used to improve the performance of resource management, quality of service, security, control algorithms, or many other network goals. Here we define *cognitive flow management* as a cognitive process that can perceive current network conditions, and then plan, decide, and act on those conditions for improved quality of service.

In our earlier publications (Frantti & Majanen, 2010; Frantti et al., 2010) we presented and compared PID (Proportional, Integral, Derivative) and fuzzy control systems, which adjust packet size of UDP (User Datagram Protocol) based uni- or bidirectional traffic flow on WLANs according to prevailing channel conditions. They aimed to optimize packet sizes of real-time traffic flows for the prevailing connection for higher end-to-end throughput by fulfilling the overall application dependent delay requirement. In this chapter, the *aim of the flow management system is to adjust appropriate packet size and transmission interval of the source node's constant bit rate traffic flows for prevailing network conditions to achieve application dependent quality of service requirements*. Hence, the research question can be stated here as follows: *"How to manage constant bit rate real-time traffic flows so that application dependent quality of service requirements are achieved with the optimal network capacity?"*. Although the main goal of this work is related to the quality of service of WLAN systems and the simulations and results were performed for the IEEE 802.11*b* system, the approach and the techniques are not limited to these systems, but are easily applicable to other packet switched networks as well.

The organization of the rest of the chapter is as follows. Section 2 presents a literature review of the weak resource reservation and quality of service in communication networks. It also presents a review of the packet size optimization in wireless networks. Section 3 briefly summarizes the structure and channel access of the WLANs. Section 4 introduces the principles of service classification whereas Section 5 gives an introduction to weak resource reservation, like congestion prevention and control, flow control and denying and/or degrading services and reduction of channel access competition by admission control. In Sections 7 and 8 are briefly summarized the basic principles of the developed PID and fuzzy system based controllers. Section 9 depicts the developed simulation model and simulation scenarios. Section 10 comprises achieved results with the controllers. Finally, conclusions are presented in Section 11 .

2. Literature review

2.1 Hard resource reservation

For the QoS guarantee, the IETF has worked on the transport layer protocol called resource reservation protocol (RSVP) that can be used to hard resource reservation across a network. Integrated Services is often associated with RSVP. The Integrated Services architecture divides the flows to different service classes (e.g. guaranteed service class for intolerant applications that require that a packet never arrives late), and then RSVP is used for reserving the needed resources for each service class.

2.2 Weak resource reservation: packet scheduling and queueing methods

Weak resource allocation schemes without actual reserved virtual links closely includes packet scheduling schemes and queueing methods (Kleinrock, 1975). The queueing algorithm can be thought of as allocating bandwidth to packets on the intermediate nodes. The most popular queueing algorithm is First-In-First-Out (FIFO), which determines the service order of packets based on their arrival order. In Priority Queueing (PQ), traffic classes with the highest priority are forwarded with the least delay (Huitema, 2000; Nagle, 1987; Sanjay & Hassan, 2002). In Class Based Queueing (CBQ) traffic classes are forwarded with equal share (Floyd & Jacobson, 1995), *e.g.*, Round Robin (RR) algorithms process packets in turn with equal share and achieve very high accuracy and fairness in the output bandwidth sharing but cannot provide tight delay guarantees (Nagle, 1985). In Fair Queueing (FQ) techniques, like the Weighted Fair Queueing (WFQ), are assigned a weight to each output queue (Demers et al., 1989). However, scheduling and queueing methods provide a rather weak form of resource reservation and cannot guarantee QoS, because weights are only indirectly related to the bandwidth the flow receives. The another problem of these methods and their modifications is that they are quite static in their operations. The latest development of scheduling methods is directing to the dynamic adaptation of scheduling parameters which gives better overall performance. There exists some related articles such as (Crawford & Marshall, 2001; Horng et al., 2001; Sayenko et al., 2006; 2003) devoted to the adaptive WFQ. In Horng et al. (2001) the developed adaptive approach to WFQ is a variation of fair queue algorithm with dynamic priority scheduling. An adaptive approach to WFQ that uses a concept of revenue to adapt weights is presented in Sayenko et al. (2003). This adaptive WFQ algorithm is later extended in (Sayenko et al., 2006) to an comparison and analysis of several adaptive scheduling algorithms: Revenue-based adaptive WFQ (RA-WFQ), revenue-based adaptive Weighted Round Robin (RA-WRR) and revenue-based adaptive Deficit Round Robin (RA-DRR). In Crawford & Marshall (2001) a new fast packet scheduling algorithm called Dynamic Weighted Fair Queuing (DWFQ) is created. We have considered in our previous publication fuzzy expert systems for adaptive weighted fair queueing and service classification (Frantti & Jutila, 2009).

2.3 QoS in wireless networks

Wireless network protocols are designed based on a layered approach, where each layer in the protocol stack is designed and operated independently. The interfaces between layers are rather static. There are many studies that examine QoS provisioning in wireless networks with a layered perspective, concentrating only on one layer at the time, *e.g.* on power control or modulation/rate adaptation on the physical layer, scheduling or channel access on the MAC layer, admission control or routing on the network layer, rate or congestion control on the transport layer, or video and image coding schemes on the application layer. Perkins & Hughes (2002) includes a survey of QoS support for wireless mobile ad hoc networks including QoS routing protocols, resource reservation schemes, and QoS aware MAC layers. QoS aware MAC layers for wireless ad hoc networks are also reviewed in Kumar et al. (2006). However, strict layered design is not optimal for wireless multihop networks because of their dynamic nature. In wireless networks the layers should cooperate more closely to jointly optimize the overall performance, especially in case of real-time applications with high bandwidth and/or stringent delay requirements. Many studies, *e.g.* (Goldsmith & Wicker, 2002; Huusko et al., 2007; Lamy-Bergot et al., 2010; Qu et al., 2005; Setton et al., 2005), on wireless networks show that a cross-layer design can significantly improve the system performance. A cross-layer approach seeks to enhance the performance of a system by breaking the independence of the layers by jointly designing multiple protocol layers. Zhang & Zhang (2008) surveys multiple possibilities for cross-layer interactions in wireless multihop networks.

Fuzzy set theory has also been used for enhancing the QoS in wireless networks. For example, authors in (Khoukhi & Cherkaoui, 2008) present a fuzzy decision support system for wireless ad hoc network. They use fuzzy set theory for best-effort traffic regulation, and propose schemes for real-time traffic regulation, and admission control. Chan et al. (2001) apply fuzzy set theory to employ decision criteria such as user preferences, link quality, cost, or quality of service (QoS) for handover decision scheme.

2.4 Packet size optimization for connection quality

Korhonen & Wang (2005) have studied the effect of packet size on loss rate and delay in IEEE 802.11 based WLAN. The analysis shows that there is a straightforward connection between bit error characteristics and observed delay characteristics. This information can be useful in adjusting application level framing under different network conditions. For example, an intelligent streaming application could optimize end-to-end delay and wireless resource utilization by analyzing the delay pattern for packets with different lengths. In general, it is shown throughout the literature that the performance of wireless networking is sensitive to the packet size, and that significant performance improvements are obtained if a "good" packet size is used. For example, authors in (Bakshi et al., 1997) show this for TCP traffic over wireless network. Chee & David (1989), Lettieri & Srivastava (1998), and Chien et al. (1999) do study of the relationship between frame length and throughput, but they do not propose any exact method to dynamically control the frame length. Packet size optimization has been studied also in several other perspectives, like energy efficiency in (Sankarasubramaniam et al., 2003) and security in (Younis et al., 2009), but these solutions are statistical in nature, meaning that the packet size is optimized beforehand. Work done in (Smadi & Szabados, 2006) is somehow related to our work, but even in this article the focus is different, error recovery in communication rather than optimal packet size in the first place. PLFC (Sheu et al., 2000) is the most similar to our approach presented in this chapter. PLFC is a fuzzy packet length controller for improving the performance of WLAN under the interference of microwave oven. The input parameters for the fuzzy controller are the packet length and the packet error rate. It is shown that PLFC improves the throughput of UDP traffic compared to using fixed length packets.

In the most recent of our publications (Frantti & Majanen, 2010; Frantti et al., 2010) we presented and compared PID and fuzzy control systems, which adjust packet size of UDP based uni- or bidirectional traffic on WLANs according to prevailing channel conditions. In other words, (Frantti & Majanen, 2010; Frantti et al., 2010) considered flow control for a fixed delay requirements. The delay can be defined as the time taken by a packet to traverse the network. Here the aim of the flow management system is to achieve quality of service requirements of the real-time applications with the optimal network capacity. Hence, the control system adjusts appropriate packet size and transmission interval of the source node's real-time traffic flows for the maximum number of such real-time connections as VoIP calls, video calls, and interactive games.

3. Wireless local area network

The market for wireless communications has grown rapidly since the introduction of the 802.11*b*, *g*, and *a* WLAN standards offering performance almost comparable to the Ethernet. The 802.11*b*, *g*, and *a* standards specify the lowest (physical) layer of the OSI reference model and a lower part (MAC) of the next higher layer (data link layer). The standards specify also the use of the 802.2 link layer control protocol, which is the upper portion of the data link layer.

The IEEE 802.11*b* wireless local area networks use the 2.4 GHz ISM (Industrial, Science and Medical) license-free frequency band, which is divided into 11 usable channels. Any particular network can use only less than half of these in operation, but all network hardware is built to be able to listen to and transmit on any of the channels. The sender and receiver must be on the same channel to communicate with each other.

The IEEE 802.11*b* network can be set to work in an Independent Basic Service Set (IBSS), in a Basic Service Set (BSS) or in an extended service set (ESS) mode. The IBSS is an ad hoc group of independent wireless nodes which communicate on a peer-to-peer basis. A standard refers to a topology with a single access point as a BSS. The arrangement with multiple access points is called an ESS (B. Bing, 2002). In ESS nodes transmit data to the nearest access point, which delivers it either to another node in the coverage area or to some other node(s) on the Internet. In WLANs nodes can transmit only when a communication channel is unoccupied. The channel access is regulated by media access control (MAC) protocols, which are typically contention-based protocols. The IEEE 802.11*b* MAC supports two modes of operation: the Point Coordination Function (PCF) and the Distributed Coordination Function (DCF). The PCF provides contention free access, while the DCF uses the carrier sense multiple access with collision avoidance (CSMA/CA) mechanism for contention based access. Here we consider only DCF mode, because PCF mode is not commonly used and it is not a part of, *e.g.*, the Wi-Fi Alliance's interoperability standard (Leung et al., 2002; Li & Ni, 2005).

In contention-based MACs, the transmission bursts intervals for nodes are irregular (transmission jitter) and vary according to the type of transmitted traffic and the number of nodes competing or reserving the channel. The packet interval is also dependent on the packet length. Therefore, the packet transmission interval and the channel access time are decreased, when the packet size is reduced. This increases channel reservation competition and may lead to the network congestion and decreased throughput of the network. On the other hand, when the packet payload is increased, the number of packets sent from the source node is reduced and the packet interval becomes longer. Then the channel is free for a longer period of time between packets, which reduces the channel reservation competition and increases the probability of getting a free channel. However, when the packet size increases the bit errors caused by the channel increase the probability of a packet error, which increases packet loss and decreases throughput. The channel access time depends on also the type of traffic exchange. For example, in connection-oriented communication also acknowledgement (ACK) frames have to compete the channel access time in reverse direction, which decreases network node's channel access time in forward direction, too.

The IEEE 802.11*e* defines a set of QoS enhancements for WLAN applications. It was included in the 802.11-2007 standard together with amendments *a, b, d, g, h, i,* and *j* in July 2007. Instead of PCF and HCF, 802.11*e* defines HCF Controlled Channel Access (HCCA) and Enhanced Distributed Channel Access (EDCA). Both HCCA and EDCA defines Traffic Categories (TC), which can be used for separating voice, video, best effort, and background traffic from each other.

In EDCA, shorter contention window (CW) and arbitration inter-frame spacing (AIFS) are used for higher priority traffic packets. As a result, higher priority packets are sent a little bit earlier on average than lower priority packets during contention periods. EDCA has also contention-free periods called Transmit Opportunity (TXOP). A TXOP is a bounded time interval during which a station can send as many frames as possible as long as the duration of the transmissions does not extend beyond the maximum duration of the TXOP. For voice and video traffic, the maximum duration of the TXOP is greater than for other type of traffic. Wi-Fi Multimedia (WMM) certified APs must be enabled for EDCA and TXOP.

HCCA works pretty similar to PCF. However, in contrast to PCF, in which the interval between two beacon frames is divided into two periods of CFP and CP, the HCCA allows AP to initiate CFP almost anytime to send or receive a frame to or from a station in contention-free manner. During a contention-free periods the AP controls the access to the medium. During the contention periods, all stations function in EDCA. In addition to Traffic Classes (TC), HCCA defines also Traffic Streams (TS), which allows a sort of per-session service instead of per-station queuing. AP can coordinate these streams in any fashion it chooses. This makes HCCA perhaps the most complex coordination function, but on the other hand, HCCA allows the QoS to be configured with great precision. For example, QoS-enabled stations may request some specific QoS parameters (data rate, jitter, etc.), which should allow advanced applications like VoIP and video streaming to work more effectively. HCCA support is not mandatory in WMM certified APs.

4. Service classification

4.1 QoS parameters

The term QoS itself refers to statistical performance guarantees that a network can make. Typical QoS parameters can be categorized to cost, format, performance, synchronization and user classes. Cost parameters include costs of connection and data transfer. Compression, frame rate, and resolution are format parameters. Bit rate and delays are typical performance parameter whereas skews in multimedia transmission is an example of synchronization parameters. User parameters are, for example, subjective voice and quality of image. It is up to transport layer to examine the parameters, and determine whether it can provide the required service. The typical transport layer QoS parameters are: connection establishment delay and failure probability, throughput, transit delay, residual error ratio, protection, priority and resilience (Tanebaum, 1996).

4.2 Service categories

Due to rich space of application requirements, a richer service model than best-effort service is needed to meet the need of applications. This leads to to a service model with more than just the best-effort class, each class available to meet the needs of some set of applications. There are two broad categories developed to provide a range of qualities of service: *fine-grained* and *coarse-grained* approaches. Fine-grained approaches provide QoS to individual applications or flows whereas coarse-grained approaches provide QoS to large classes of data or aggregared traffic.

Integrated Services, which is a QoS arhitecture developed in the IETF (Internet Engineering Task Force) and often associated with RSVP (Resource Reservation Protocol) is an example of the fine-grained approches. The Integrated Services architecture allocates resources to individual flows. The IETF IntServ working group developed specifications of a number of service classes, such as guaranteed service and controlled load, designed to meet the needs of some of the application types. It also defined how to use RSVP to make reservations using these service classes. Guaranteed service class is designed for intolerant applications, which require that a packet never arrive late. The network should guarantee that the maximum packet delay has some specified value. Controlled load service class is aimed to meet the needs of tolerant, adaptive applications. Tolerant applications run quite well on networks that are not heavily loaded. The aim of the controlled load service is to emulate a lightly loaded network for those applications that request the service, even though the network as a whole may in fact be heavily loaded. The trick to this is to use a queuing mechanism, such as weighted fair queuing to isolate the controlled load traffic from the other traffic (Peterson & Davie, 2007).

In the coarse-grained category lies, for example, perhaps the most widely used QoS mechanism *Differentiated Services*. The Differentiated Services allocates resources to a small

number of traffic classes. Many proposed Differentiated Services approaches simply divide traffic into two classes. The purpose is to add the service model in small increments in order to avoid difficulties that network operators already experience just trying to keep a best-effor internet running smoothly (Peterson & Davie, 2007).
In this work the aim of the flow management system is to achieve quality of service requirements of the real-time applications for the maximum number of such real-time connections as VoIP calls, video calls, and interactive games.

5. Weak resource reservation

In this chapter the resource allocation schemes without actual reserved virtual links is referred as a weak resource allocation. It closely includes packet scheduling schemes and queueing methods, congestion control and prevention, admission control and flow control.

5.1 Scheduling and queueing

One main tool for implementing network QoS are the intelligent scheduling and queueing algorithms. Queueing algorithms participate in congestion control and prevention and for allocating resources. In congestion prevention, routers monitor the output lines and allocate resources for different applications efficiently. Powerful resource allocation to individual traffic flows is closely in conjuntion with choosing the right kind of packet scheduler. If there is a situation that network resources cannot serve all flows, queues will start to build up in routers. A packet scheduler is in important role in dequeueing the packets and keeping track of the network resources. In datagram-based Internet all the resources are shared on a per-packet basis compared to the traditional circuit-switched telephone system where all flows are completely isolated from each other. If there is a shortage of resources to satisfy all traffic demands, bandwidth must be shared fairly to all competing flows.
Queueing disciplines can be classified into work-conserving and non-work-conserving (Wang, 2001). Work-conserving discipline always schedules packets when there are packets waiting for service in the queue. Most of the well-known schedulers are work-conserving. However, non-work-conserving algorithms are also competent because they are proposed to reduce jitter and buffer size in the network while they only schedule packets that are considered to be eligible.
The most popular queueing algorithm is the First-In-First-Out (FIFO) which determines the service order of packets strictly based on their arrival order. In Priority Queueing (PQ) (Nagle, 1987), traffic classes with the highest priority are forwarded with the least delay. The drawback of PQ algorithms is that packets with lower priority can suffer from unfair service treatment. Round Robin (RR) algorithms (Nagle, 1985) and its extensively used versions Weighted Round Robin (WRR) (Hahne, 1986) and Deficit Round Robin (DRR) (Shreedhar & Varghese, 1995) process packets in turn with equal share. RR scheduling techniques cannot achieve very good accuracy and fairness when sharing the output bandwidth. Another drawback is that RR algorithms are not able to provide tight delay guarantees. These problems were defeated with Fair Queueing (FQ) techniques (Demers et al., 1989) of which the Weighted Fair Queueing (WFQ) is no doubt the most popular and studied one. Several commercial router and switch vendors are implementing WFQ in their products.

5.2 Congestion prevention and control

For the Internet congestion and resource control has been a research challenge for a long time. Congestion occurs when the aggregate demand for a resource exceeds the available capacity of the resource, *i.e.*, congestion conditions occur when a network cannot handle all the traffic that is offered. An increase of the offered load does not necessarily imply an increase of throughput but it may even happen in congestion condition that the throughput is reduced as the offered load increases which may due to, *e.g.*, the aggressive retransmission techniques used by some network protocols to compensate packet loss. Resulting effects include long delays, wasted resources due to lost or dropped packets, or even possible congestion collapse, in which all communications in the entire network ceases. Therefore, it is evident that certain mechanisms is required to maintain good network performance and to prevent the network from being congested.

For the congestion handling there are two main approaches, namely *congestion control* and *congestion prevention*. Congestion control is a reactive method and comes into play after the network is overloaded. Congestion control involves the design mechanisms to limit the demand-capacity mismatch and dynamically control traffic sources when such a mismatch occurs. Especially for real-time traffic, it is important to understand how congestion arises and find efficient ways to keep the network operating within its capacity. The basic design issues of the congestion control are what to feedback to sources and how to react to the feedback. However, endpoints, *i.e.*, the source and destination do not usually have the details of congestion point(s) and reason(s). Intermediate nodes, on the other hand, can use network layer techniques like ICMP (Internet Control Message Protocol, one part of the Internet protocol family) to inform hosts that congestion has occured.

The most widely used congestion control mechanisms are *drop-tail, active queue management, DECbit mechanism, random early detection* and it's numerous variants, *explicit congestion notification*, and *partial buffer sharing*. *Drop-tail* works on first-in-first-out queue, which drops incoming packets when the queue becomes full. *Active queue management* detects congestion and acknowledges the sources about it before queue gets overflow. *DECbit mechanism* is based on the congestion notification bit in the packet header. It provides feedback to the sources for flow control. In *random early detection* incoming packets are dropped probabilistically before the queue becomes full. *Explicit congestion notification* extends random early detection in a way that instead of dropping a packet it marks it when the average queue size lies between specific threshold values. *Partial buffer sharing* scheme controls the allocation of buffer to various traffic classes with the delay constraints to meet diverse QoS demands. Interested reader finds more information about the congestion control mechanisms, for example, from (Ahmad et al., 2009).

Congestion prevention is a proactive approach and it acts before the network is overloaded, *i.e.*, it plays a major role before the network faces congestion. Congestion prevention aims to reduce congestion by designing good protocols and it takes proactive actions without relying on the network status. Congestion prevention covers different policies at the transport, network, and data link layer such as retransmission, acknowledgement, flow control, admission control, and routing algorithm. The end systems typically negotiate with the network and after that systems act independently. The end-systems get no information from the network about the current traffic and network status. However, in wireline networks intermediate nodes, such as routers, can monitor their output lines' load. Hence, whenever the utilisation of a line approaches a specified threshold level, the router transmits *choke* datagrams to the sources in order to give warning signals to them. The source nodes or hosts are required to reduce transmission rate to the specified destination by n percentage. Another paradigm that has been suggested for use in congestion prevention is *weighted fair queuing*, where a router selects datagrams from multiple queues in a round robin way to the idle output line. The router weights more bandwidth to some services than others. In packet switched networks it is also possible to allow new virtual circuits by routing traffic via a different, uncongested, route. Another alternative solution is to negotiate an agreement between the hosts and network during the connection set up by specifying the volume and the shape of the traffic as well as quality of service requirements.

If congestion does not disappear with the preventive actions, routers can throw away datagrams they cannot handle (*load shedding*). They can do it either randomly or in a rational way, for example, when dropping a file transfer, a newer one is more rational than an older one due to acknowledgement and retransmission procedures. On the contrary, in real-time data transfer newer ones are more valuable than older ones. In congestion prevention it is also suggested to use media access layer solutions, like decreasing excessive overhead, retransmissions and auto-rate fallback.

5.3 Admission control

In wireless networks, admission control and resource reservation mechanisms are commonly proposed for congestion prevention. In admission control, after congestion threat has been signalled, no more connections are allowed to be set up until the congestion has gone away. Admission control is crude but simple and robust to implement, and has been used in telephone systems for decades.

5.4 Flow control

Problems of congestion control, like congestion collapse, are largely related to the flow control of TCP (Transmission Control Protocol). TCP adjusts a source node's transmission rate according to the rejected number of datagrams (TCP considers it as a congestion measure) in the network. During the flow control of TCP session, a sender transmits W (W=size of the transmission window) datagrams per time unit and starts to wait for acknowledgements from the receiver. The receiver sends an acknowledgement signal for each datagram, which it has received. If all the datagrams are received, the source increases the size of the window (additive increment), while if a datagram is dropped the size of W is halved (multiplicative decrement). This is also called a *sliding-window* scheme. The drawback of it is that the transmission rate is decreased only after the detection of datagrams losses, which causes a time delay (due to round trip time, RTT) and results in buffer overflows in routers and further losses of datagrams. Hence, it is obvious that the flow control of TCP with the sliding window scheme is not sufficient for flow and congestion control in terms of the network performance and overall quality of service.

On the other side, real-time flows with stringent delay requirements make use of UDP (User Datagram Protocol), which lacks the mechanism to regulate the amount of data being transmitted. UDP does not return acknowledgements and cannot signal congestion to the sender. The inability of UDP flows to regulate transmission rate at the transport layer makes them especially vulnerable to congestion. Therefore, for the UDP sessions, applications have to provide some form of flow control on their own.

6. Congestion and flow control in WLANs

In access networks, like WLANs, congestion occurs when the load on the network is temporarily greater than the resources. Congestion typically causes packet loss due to collisions, which arises when several nodes try to send at the same time, *i.e.*, try to do channel reservation at the same time with CSMA/CA MAC, decreasing significantly transmission rate and increasing dramatically delay.

In WLANs delay and throughput are very much dependent on the packet size, packet transmission interval, and the node connection density. Therefore, in a congested state one

can either decrease load by denying and/or degrading services or reduce channel access competition by access control and/or packet size and transmission interval control.
Congestion can be identified via monitoring, *e.g.*, the *percentage share of discarded datagrams, average queue lengths*, and the *percentage share of datagrams that are timed out and retransmitted* on access points, and monitoring the *average value* and *variance of a datagram's delay* on destination nodes. A natural step after monitoring and identification is to transfer information from the congested places (destination nodes, access points) to places where control actions can be performed (source nodes, access points). However, the nodes do not know whether the cause of the packet loss is due to congestion or low signal to noise ratio.
Here we use an embedded fuzzy expert system on the destination nodes to keep WLAN network operating within its capacity. In our system the destination node monitors congestion by measuring *average one-way delay error* and the *change of one-way delay error* (error = delay - target value) as congestion information, defines packet size decrement/increment according to them, and delivers packet size information to the source node.

7. Proportional-integral-derivative controller

A proportional-integral-derivative (PID) control is a widely used feedback control mechanism. A PID controller calculates an error value as the difference between a measured process variable and a desired setpoint and attempts to minimize the error by adjusting the process control inputs. The *proportional* value determines the controller's reaction to the current error, the *integral* value determines the reaction based on the sum of recent errors, and the *derivative* value defines the reaction to the rate at which the error has been changing. The weighted sum of these three actions is used to adjust the process, such as the packet payload size of the transmitter, via a control element.
In the developed PID controller, one-way delay error (E_d = proportional value = delay - target value), sum of the recent errors (I_d = integral value), and the change of error (ΔE_d = derivative value) are used as the input values. The output value of the controller is the change of the packet payload size. The new packet payload size is the change of the packet payload size + earlier packet size. The developed controller can be presented in the equation form as follows:

$$P_i(t) = K_p \times E_d(t) + K_i \times \int_{-3}^{0} E_d(t)\,dt + K_d \times \frac{\Delta E_d(t)}{dt}, \tag{1}$$

where P_i is the change of the packet payload size, K_p (=0.75) is a proportional amplifier, K_i (=0.20) is an integration amplifier, K_d (=0.1) is a derivation amplifier, and t is time.
The controller is located at the user terminal. The controller was designed to update the transmission packet size on the source in order to reach an application dependent target end-to-end delay with the maximum throughput in the prevailing channel conditions. For example in VoIP calls (Andrews et al., 2007) and in action games (Balakrishnan & Sadasivan, 2007), it is preferred that the absolute one-way delay should remain below 100 ms. Maximum throughput instead of the fixed minimum required throughput is needed for example for the video conversations with scalable video coding. Video conversations have a strict end-to-end delay requirement but flexible throughput requirement. Therefore, with the same delay but higher throughput it is possible to use better video coding for higher quality of videos.

8. Fuzzy flow controller

Fuzzy set theory was originally presented by L. Zadeh in his seminal paper "Fuzzy Sets" in *Information and Control 1965* (Zadeh, 1965). Fuzzy logic was developed later from fuzzy set theory primary to reason with uncertain and vague information and secondary to represent knowledge in operationally powerful form. In the fuzzy set theory the name *fuzzy sets* are used to distinguish them from the *crisp sets* of the conventional set theory. The characteristic function of a crisp set C, $\mu_C(u)$, assigns a discrete value (usually either 0 or 1) to each element u in the universal set U, *i.e.*, it discriminates members and non-members of the crisp set (then for each element u of U, either $u \in C$ or $u \notin C$). The characteristic function can be generalized in fuzzy set theory so that the values assigned to the elements u of the universal set U fall within a prespesified range (usually to the unit interval [0, 1]) indicating the membership grade of these elements in the fuzzy set F. Then it is not necessary that either $u \in F$ or $u \notin F$. The generalized function is called *membership function* and the set defined with the aid of it is a *fuzzy set*, respectively. The membership function assigns to each $u \in U$ a value from the unit interval [0, 1] instead of dual value set {0,1}.

A fuzzy control was originally developed to include a human operator's or system engineer's expertise, which does not lend itself to being easily expressed in PID -parameters or differential equations but rather in situation/action rules. In this study a fuzzy expert system based controller was developed to handle the problems of large overshoot, large steady state error and long-rise time that are evident in the classical systems (Chang & May, 1996). Li & Lau (1989) have shown that the fuzzy proportional-integral controller is less sensitive to large parametric changes in the process and is comparable in performance to the conventional PI controller for small parametric changes. In the fuzzy control system the input and output variables are represented in linguistic form after fuzzyfication of physical values into linguistic form. In this application the input variables are the *average one-way delay error* and the *change of one-way delay error*, the output value is the *packet size increment*. This is so called *two-input, single output control strategy*. For the accurate one-way delay measurement, the clocks of the network nodes were synchronized by beacon signals broadcasted every 100 ms from the access point.

The major components of an expert system are the knowledge base and inference engine. The knowledge base contains the expert-level information necessary to solve domain specific problems, *i.e.*, the knowledge bases are domain specific and nontrasferable. The information is generally presented in the rule form, although, *e.g.*, semantic nets and belief networks are also used. The inference engine interacts both with the knowledge base and a system memory, which includes the facts about the current problem. Pattern matching occurs between the rules in the knowledge base and the recorded facts in the working memory to select the relevant rules applicable (Leondes, 1998).

In fuzzy expert system based control applications, a rule base includes a control policy, which is usually presented with linguistic conditional statements, *i.e.*, if-then rules. Here we present the rule base in the matrix form and the reasoning is done by linguistic equations, see Juuso (1992) and Frantti & Mahonen (2001). Linguistic equations provide a method for developing and tuning adaptive expert systems without rule-based programming. The main advantages of the linguistic equations are the compact size of rule base and computational efficiency. Linguistic equations are also effective in presentation and solving massive rule bases which easily lead to maintenance and testing problems. In the inference engine, the control strategy produces the linguistic control output, which is transformed back into the physical domain in order to find the crisp control output value for the packet size increment. In fuzzy set theory reasoning can be done either using *composition based* or *individual based inference*. In the former all rules are combined into an explicit relation and then fired with fuzzy input whereas in the latter rules are individually fired with crisp input and then combined into one overall fuzzy set. Here we used individual based inference with Mamdani's implication. The main reason for the choice was its easier implementation (the results are equivalent for both methods when Mamdani's implication is used). Interested reader finds more information about fuzzy controllers, for example, from (Driankov et al., 1994).

8.1 Fuzzy expert system

In the developed fuzzy expert system (FES) based controller, the fuzzy proportional, integral, and derivative parts (FPID) are included to improve the controller's performance. The structure of the developed fuzzy controller for the packet size definition is presented in Figure 1. The fuzzy controller monitors incoming traffic, defines the change of packet size for the source node, and transmits a packet size control command to the source node by acknowledgements. The actual fuzzy system, which is located at the user terminal, has three modules: a fuzzyfication module, a reasoning module and a defuzzyfication module.

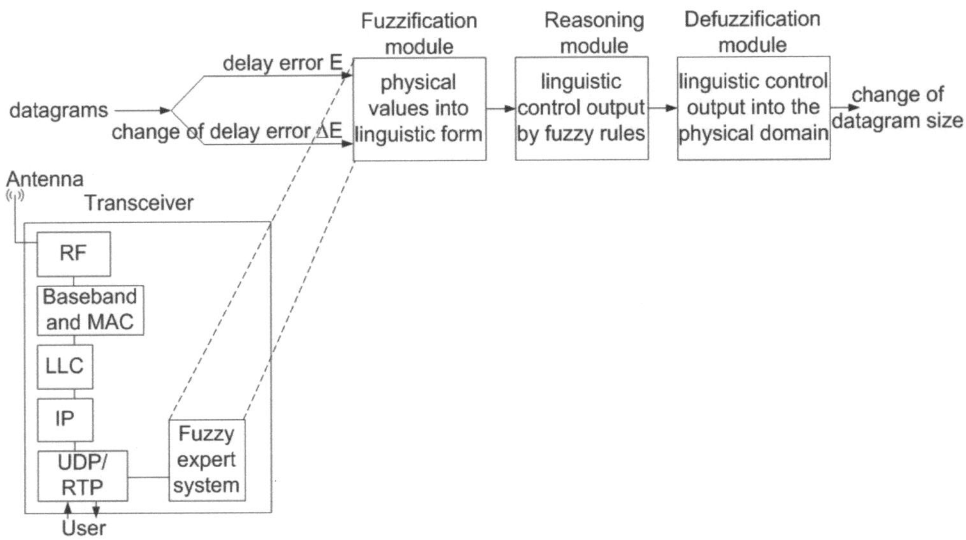

Fig. 1. Fuzzy model for packet size control.

The one-way delay error (E_d) and the change of it (change of the delay error, ΔE_d) are used as the input values for the fuzzy reasoning model. Input variables are represented in linguistic form after fuzzyfication in the fuzzyfication module. Fuzzyfication procedure is illustrated in Figures 2 and 3. In Figure 2, the delay error E_d is -24.92 ms, which is *negative big* at the grade of 0.48 and *negative small* at the grade of 0.52. The change of delay ΔE_d is 6.46 ms, which from one's part is *zero* at the grade of 0.77 and from other part is *positive small* at the grade of 0.23, see Figure 3.

In this application, a linguistic model of a system was described by linguistic relations. The linguistic relations form a rule base (25 rules, see Figure 5) that can be converted into numerical equations. Suppose, as an example, that X_{ij}, *i=1,2; j = 1,..., m* (*j* is uneven number), is a linguistic level (*e.g.,negative big, negative small, zero, positive small, and positive big*) for a variable X_i. The linguistic levels are replaced by integers $\frac{-(j-1)}{2}, ..., -2, -1, 0, 1, 2, ..., \frac{(j-1)}{2}$. The direction of the interaction between fuzzy sets is presented by coefficients $A_{ij}=\{-1, 0, 1\}$, *i=1,2; j = 1,..., m*. This means that the directions of the changes in the output variable decrease or increase depending on the directions of the changes in the input variables (Juuso, 1993). Thus a compact equation for the output Z_{ij} is:

$$\sum_{j=1}^{m}\sum_{i=1}^{2} A_{ij}X_{ij} = Z_{i,j}. \qquad (2)$$

The mapping of linguistic relations to linguistic equations for this application is described in Figure 5. For example, we can read from Figure 5 that *IF* E_d *IS negative small AND* ΔE_d *IS zero THEN the change of packet size IS positive small.* In linguistic equations this can be presented as $\lceil \frac{(-1*-1+-1*0)}{2} \rceil = 1$. A more detail reasoning example is given in Section 8.2.

The most important properties for a set of rules are *completeness, consistency, continuity* and *interaction*. *Completeness* of rules means that all kinds of combinations of input variables results in an appropriate output value. The rule base is *consistent* if it does not contain any contradiction[1]. It can be formulated as in (Driankov et al., 1994): A set of rules is inconsistent if there are at least two rules with the same rule-antecedent and different rule-consequent. *Continuity* means that neighboring rules have no output fuzzy sets with an empty intersection. Definitions of neighboring rules are given for example in (Driankov et al., 1994) as follows: two rules are neighbors, if their cells are neighbors in matrix representation of a rule base. An *interaction* of a set of rules is defined many ways in the literature. Driankov et al. (1994) state that a set of fuzzy rules interacts if composition based inference does not equal individual based inference.

In the defuzzyfication module the control strategy produces the linguistic control output, which is transformed back into the physical domain to find the crisp output value for the change of packet size. In the defuzzyfication phase the center of area method (CoA) was used. The defuzzyfication procedure is illustrated in Figure 4. From Figure 4 it can be seen that the change of packet size is *positive small* at the grade of 0.52 and *positive big* at the grade of 0.48. The crisp output value is the center of the area, *i.e.*, the new packet size is 43 bits bigger than the earlier value.

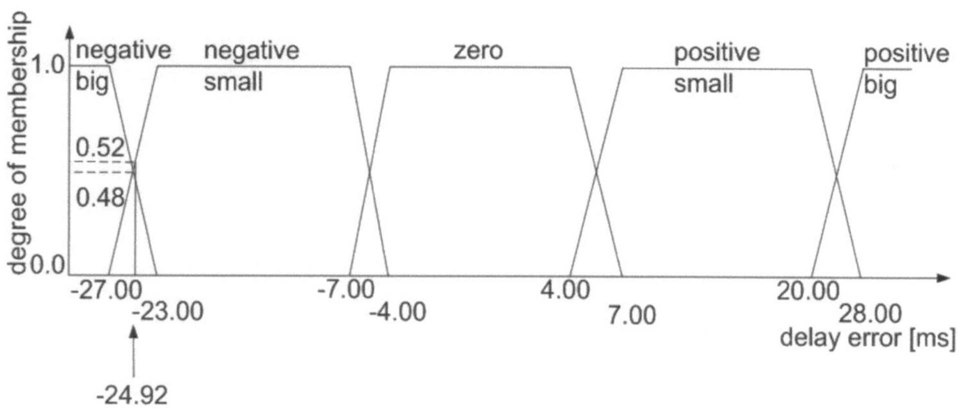

Fig. 2. Fuzzy membership functions for the E_d.

8.2 Reasoning example

The developed fuzzy expert system was designed to update the transmission packet size in order to reach a target end-to-end delay with the maximum throughput in the prevailing channel conditions. Consider as an example, that the E_d is -24.92 ms, which is after

[1] In the literature it is also defined like continuity below.

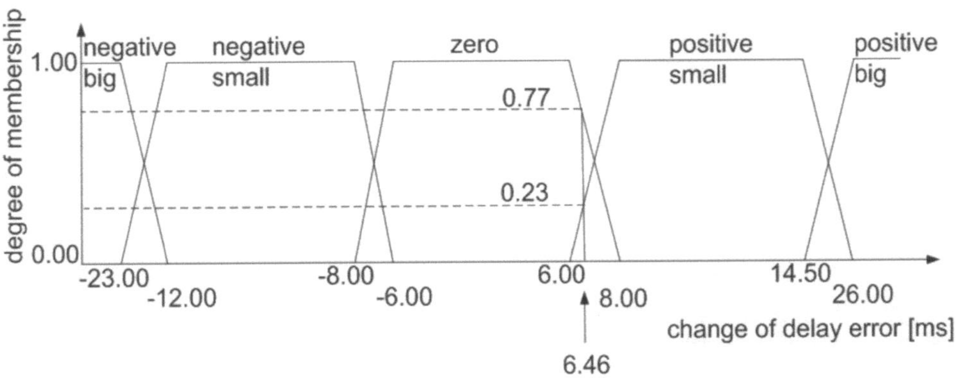

Fig. 3. Fuzzy membership functions for the ΔE_d.

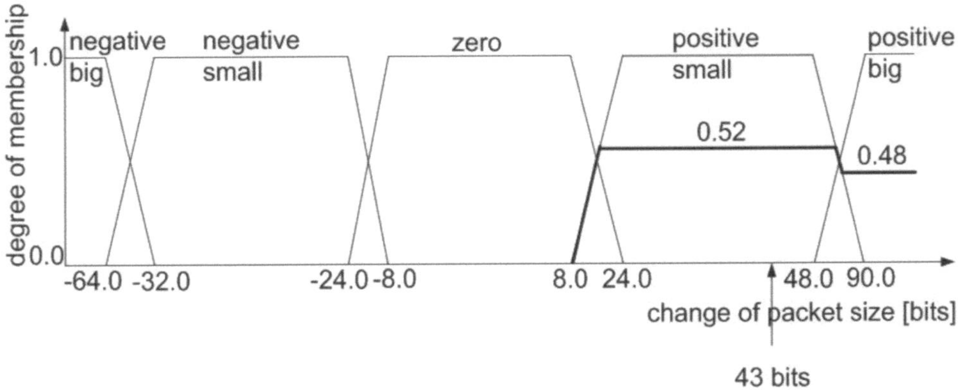

Fig. 4. Fuzzy membership functions for the change of packet size.

fuzzyfication in linguistic form *negative big* at the grade of membership 0.48 and *negative small* at the grade of membership 0.52 (see Figure 2). Suppose that the ΔE_d is 6.46 ms, which is after fuzzyfication in linguistic form *zero* at the grade of membership 0.77 and *positive small* at the grade of membership 0.23 (see Figure 3). Now we can read from Figures 2, 3 and 5 that

IF E_d IS NB at the grade 0.48 AND ΔE_d IS ZE at the grade 0.77 THEN the change of packet size IS PB at the grade 0.48

IF E_d IS NB at the grade 0.48 AND ΔE_d IS PS at the grade 0.23 THEN the change of packet size IS PB at the grade 0.23

IF E_d IS NS at the grade 0.52 AND ΔE_d IS ZE at the grade 0.77 THEN the change of packet size IS PS at the grade 0.52

IF E_d IS NS at the grade 0.52 AND ΔE_d IS PS at the grade 0.23 THEN the change of packet size IS PS at the grade 0.23

In linguistic equations this can be presented as follows:

$\lceil \frac{(-2*-2+-1*0)}{2} \rceil = 2$ at the grade min(0.48,0.77)

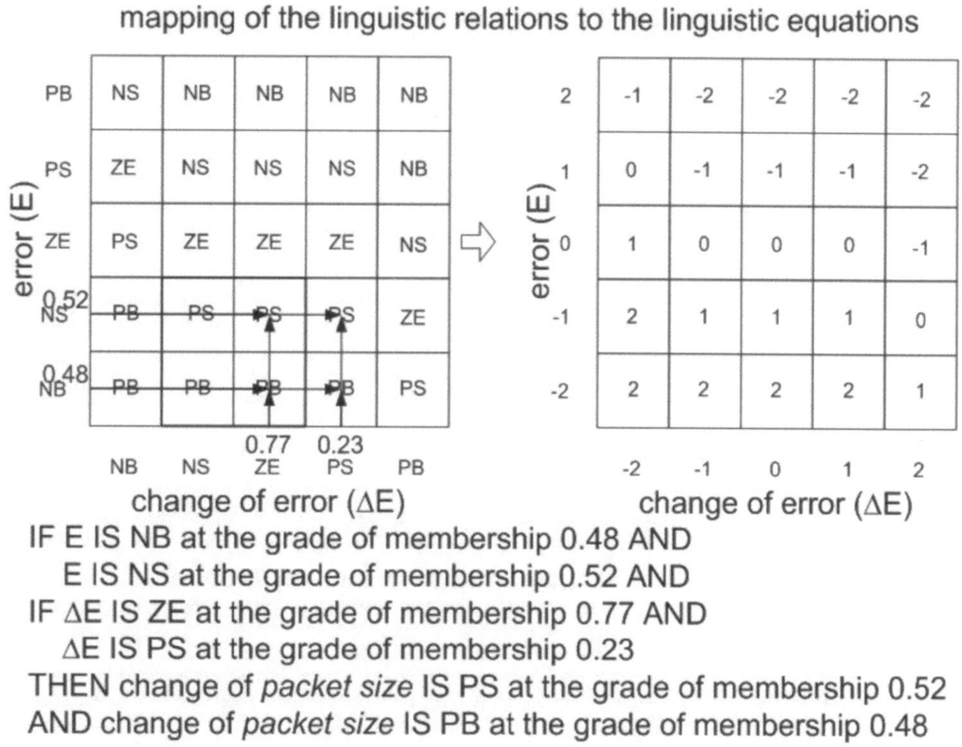

Fig. 5. Fuzzy rule base and mapping of the linguistic relations to the linguistic equations.

$$\lceil\frac{(-2*-2+-1*1)}{2}\rceil = 2 \text{ at the grade min(0.48,0.23)}$$

$$\lceil\frac{(-2*-1+-1*0)}{2}\rceil = 1 \text{ at the grade min(0.52,0.77)}$$

$$\lceil\frac{(-2*-1+-1*1)}{2}\rceil = 1 \text{ at the grade min(0.52,0.23)}$$

where $\lceil\rceil$ returns the next highest integer value by rounding up the value if necessary. Using individual based inference with Mamdani's implication the weight value is *positive big* at the grade of membership 0.48 (max(0.48,0.23)) and *positive small* at the grade of membership 0.52 (max(0.52,0.23)). Therefore, the crisp output value is 43 bits (see Figure 4), which is used in the user equipment to update a new packet size to be 43 bits bigger than earlier. The rule base does not allow the packet size decrease below 256 bits or increase over 11520 bits but keeps the packet size between [256, 11520] bits.

8.3 Adaptation

In order to adapt to application dependent delay requirements, the developed fuzzy expert system needs as an input an application dependent target (maximum acceptable) delay value. It then controls real-time traffic flow(s) by optimizing packet sizes for the target delay on the prevailing channel conditions. In addition, to keep membership functions and inference logic independent from the absolute dependency of delay value and packet size, the expert system use relative input values (*delay error* and the *change of delay error*). The expert system also defines the increment of the packet size as an output value instead of the absolute packet size.

With absolute input variable, like *delay*, the membership functions should be redefined for all the possible target delay values.

8.4 Computational complexity

Flow control by the definition of the packet size on the mobile nodes increases node's computational complexity. The implementation decision of the fuzzy control method is a trade-off between complexity, required computational time, required RAM (Random Access Memory) and program memory and achieved advantages of the algorithm. The fuzzy feedback control also lightly increases communicational load by transmitting application level acknowledgements after every 200 received packets. However, for the UDP sessions, applications have to anyway provide some form of flow control on their own. Fuzzyfication phase requires at the most two $\times$ nine comparisons, two $\times$ two addition and two $\times$ one multiplications. In the comparisons crisp input values are compared to the parts of the membership functions, which cover the dynamic ranges of the input variables, see Figure 2. After the comparisons, when the fired fuzzy label(s) are identified, the degree of membership is defined by multiplying the interval of corner point and crisp value by the angle of the line. Multiplication is not needed if the crisp point sets to the top area, *i.e.*, the degree of membership is 1.0. Reasoning process for linguistic equations requires in the worst case eight multiplications, four additions, four divisions, and six min/max comparisons. In the defuzzyfication phase, it is required at most two $\times$ two additions and two $\times$ five multiplications for the definition of horizontal component of the center of area. All in all, the developed control method increases at most 56 computations for fuzzy packet size definition. According to Koomey (2010) it can be estimated that one operation requires 1.2-1.8 nJ and thus 56 operations requires about 84 nJ, if the value 1.5 nJ/operation is used. The estimated energy consumption per transmitted packet is then $\frac{84}{200}$ nJ = 0.42 nJ, which is less than or equal to $\frac{1}{3}$ of the energy consumption one elementary operation requires.

Parameter	Value
Simulation time	200 s
Wireless hosts	6-10
Protocols	IP/UDP/RTP
MAC	CSMA/CA
MAC data rate	11 Mbit/s
carrier frequency	2.4 GHz
transmitter power	2.0 mW
thermal noise	-110 dBm
sensitivity	-85 dBm
snirThreshold	4 dB
Simulation area	600 x 400 m
VoIP data rate	64 kbit/s
Video Phone data rate	384 kbit/s
Interactive game data rate	40 kbit/s

Table 1. Parameters for the simulations.

9. Network simulations

The simulation studies were done with OMNeT++ 4.0 simulator (http://www.omnetpp.org) with the INETMANET framework. The simulation model consisted of 6-10 wireless hosts in an infrastructure, *i.e.* basic service set (BSS), mode and one IEEE 802.11*b* WLAN access point. The nodes were close to each other (max. distance between any two nodes was about 12.7 m). The distance from a host to the access point (AP) varied between 14.1 and 26.9 m. The nodes were not moving and it was assumed that the nodes were synchronized using, *e.g.*, access point's beacon message. The most important simulation parameters are shown in Table 1.
In *Scenario 1*, the performance of VoIP traffic was studied. The VoIP traffic data rate was 64 kbit/s. The used fixed packet size was 400 bits, *i.e.*, the packet interval was 6.25 ms. The VoIP calls were made in pairs, *i.e.*, host0 and host1 formed one pair, host2 and host3 another pair, and so on. All hosts measured the delay for the packets, used the developed packet size optimization algorithms to calculate the optimum packet size for 25 ms target delay (for protocol, queueing and propagation) and reported it to its pair after every 200 packets by sending an UDP acknowledgement message. Then the pair adjusted its packet size. Also the packet interval was adjusted in order to keep the data rate constant.
Scenario 2 included in addition to VoIP traffic also other real-time applications. Video phone application had 384 kbit/s data rate with 7680 bits packet size and 20 ms packet interval. Interactive game had 40 kbit/s data rate with 400 bits packet size and 10 ms packet interval. Also these applications were used in pairs, too. All hosts measured the delay for the packets, used the developed packet size optimization algorithms to calculate the optimum packet size for 25 ms target delay, and reported it back to its peer after every 200 packets by an UDP acknowledgement message.

10. Results

10.1 Delay and throughut

The developed flow controllers were designed for interactive real-time application such as VoIP calls, video calls, and interactive games to reach an application dependent target end-to-end delay and to maximize the number of real-time connections in an access point's coverage area. Therefore, the conducted simulation scenarios measured delay and throughput when the packet payload size was fixed, adjusted by the developed PID controller, and adjusted by the developed fuzzy controller.
The delay and throughput evaluations were performed as a function of packet size and varying number of connections. The results in our earlier publication (Frantti & Majanen, 2010) showed that there is an optimal packet size with respect to the overall delay and packet loss rate, which depends on the number and type of real-time connections. In practise, the amount of background traffic changes as a function of time and it is not possible to manually choose optimal fixed packet sizes for the current background traffic level. Therefore, we ended to use the value of 400 bits because as an average it seems to give the best results.
The overall delay in VoIP and video calls contains delays in the MAC layer, the link layer, the TCP/IP protocol stack, propagation delay in the radio channel, queueing delays in intermediate nodes, speech and video coding delays, jitter buffer delay, and the lookahead delay of codec. The size of the jitter buffer was varied from 70 ms to 110 ms depending on the packet payload sizes. For longer packets, the jitter buffer was shorter than for shorter packets due to the longer delay caused by speech coding for longer packets in order to keep the overall delay for all the packets below 150 ms. According to (Andrews et al., 2007), absolute delay should not exceed 150 ms for good voice communication quality and it is preferred

VoIP traffic	Delay			Throughput		
	OF [ms]	FC [ms]	PID [ms]	OF [Kbit/s]	FC [Kbit/s]	PID [Kbit/s]
Host one	27.6	2.1	1.0	30.5	64.8	64.2
Host two	28.0	2.0	4.9	29.3	63.2	62.6
Host three	27.7	2.0	6.1	32.2	64.0	63.4
Host four	28.2	2.1	5.6	29.6	64.0	63.4
Host five	28.0	1.9	5.7	29.5	63.9	63.3
Host six	27.7	1.9	5.6	30.5	64.1	63.5

Table 2. Delay and throughputs in *Scenario 1* when the fixed packet size of 400 bits, fuzzy controller (FC) and PID controller (PID) were used. Protocol, queueing and propagation delay limit was 25 ms. Throughput limit 64 Kbit/s. VoIP traffic. Six interactive calls.

VoIP traffic	Delay			Throughput		
	OF [ms]	FC [ms]	PID [ms]	OF [Kbit/s]	FC [Kbit/s]	PID [Kbit/s]
Host one	64.0	3.8	17.7	8.8	63.8	57.9
Host two	62.2	5.6	17.4	9.0	62.3	56.5
Host three	73.8	5.6	22.8	12.7	63.0	57.4
Host four	67.4	5.8	20.2	11.7	63.0	57.2
Host five	95.4	3.8	25.4	13.2	62.8	57.3
Host six	86.5	4.0	19.9	13.5	63.2	57.7
Host seven	123.0	5.4	31.4	11.1	63.2	57.3
Host eight	113.9	5.8	30.1	12.3	62.8	57.3

Table 3. Delay and throughputs in *Scenario 1* when the fixed packet size of 400 bits, fuzzy controller (FC) and PID controller (PID) were used. Protocol, queueing and propagation delay limit was 25 ms. Throughput limit 64 Kbit/s. VoIP traffic. Eight interactive calls.

that the absolute delay should remain below 100 ms for VoIP calls. Therefore, the delay from the jitter buffer and speech coding was designed to be a constant 125 ms, which consist of 70-110 ms delay of jitter buffer, 10-50 ms delay of audio samples coding and 5 ms lookahead delay of speech coding algorithm. Due to constant 125 ms delay, the protocol, queueing and propagation delay should remain below 25 ms to fulfil 150 ms delay limit.

Table 2 presents delay (protocol + queueing + propagation delays) and throughput for the fixed packet size of 400 bits, for the fuzzy controlled flows, and for the PID controlled flows with three connection pairs, *i.e.*, six hosts. The average delays were 27.9 ms for the fized packet size, 2.0 ms for the fuzzy controlled flows, and 4.8 ms for the PID controlled flows. The average throughputs were 30.3 Kbit/s for the fized packet size, 64.0 Kbit/s for the fuzzy controlled flows, and 63.4 Kbit/s for the PID controlled flows.

Table 3 presents delay (protocol + queueing + propagation delays) and throughput for the fixed packet size of 400 bits, for the fuzzy controlled flows, and for the PID controlled flows with four connection pairs. The average delays were 85.8 ms for the fized packet size, 5.0 ms for the fuzzy controlled flows, and 23.1 ms for the PID controlled flows. The average throughputs were 11.5 Kbit/s for the fized packet size, 63.0 Kbit/s for the fuzzy controlled flows, and 57.3 Kbit/s for the PID controlled flows.

VoIP traffic	Delay			Throughput		
	OF [ms]	FC [ms]	PID [ms]	OF [Kbit/s]	FC [Kbit/s]	PID [Kbit/s]
Host one	77.1	8.6	0.9	8.1	59.5	15.8
Host two	75.3	11.1	1.2	6.3	55.8	15.1
Host three	114.7	17.2	9.4	7.3	56.5	14.9
Host four	98.8	15.9	67.8	7.8	56.4	15.4
Host five	139.9	9.2	0.9	8.3	56.7	18.1
Host six	116.8	9.3	85.6	10.0	56.8	16.1
Host seven	160.7	23.1	104.5	8.8	57.1	18.3
Host eight	151.2	21.7	103.8	8.4	56.7	17.5
Host nine	182.1	24.8	133.4	7.0	55.8	12.6
Host ten	150.5	10.5	107.8	9.1	58.0	16.7

Table 4. Delay and throughputs in *Scenario 1* when the fixed packet size of 400 bits, fuzzy controller (FC) and PID controller (PID) were used. Protocol, queueing and propagation delay limit was 25 ms. Throughput limit 64 Kbit/s. VoIP traffic. Ten interactive calls.

Table 4 presents delay (protocol + queueing + propagation delays) and throughput for the fixed packet size of 400 bits, for the fuzzy controlled flows, and for the PID controlled flows with five connection pairs. The average delays were 126.7 ms for the fized packet size, 15.1 ms for the fuzzy controlled flows, and 61.5 ms for the PID controlled flows. The average throughputs were 8.1 Kbit/s for the fized packet size, 56.9 Kbit/s for the fuzzy controlled flows, and 16.1 Kbit/s for the PID controlled flows.
Table 5 presents delay (protocol + queueing + propagation delays) and throughput in *Scenario 2* for the fixed packet size of 400 bits, for the fuzzy controlled flows, and for the PID controlled flows with VoIP (throughput requirement 64 Kbit/s) call, video call (throughput requirement 384 Kbit/s) and interactive game (throughput requirement 40 Kbit/s) connection pairs. With the developed fuzzy and PID controllers delay and throughput limits are perfectly achieved. The applications work relatively well also with the fixed 400 bits packet size except of a bit lower throughput than required for video call and interactive game. Therefore, it can be stated from the results that controllers are not necessarily required with the very low network load if an optimal fixed packet size is known. However, in practise, the amount of background traffic changes as a function of time and it is not possible to manually choose optimal fixed packet sizes for the current connection, which further enhances the need of the control even for the low network load.
Table 6 presents delay (protocol + queueing + propagation delays) and throughput in *Scenario 2* for the fixed packet size of 400 bits, for the fuzzy controlled flows, and for the PID controlled flows with two VoIP (throughput requirement 64 Kbit/s) calls, two video calls (throughput requirement 384 Kbit/s) and one interactive game (throughput requirement 40 Kbit/s) connection pairs. It can be seen that the developed controllers can fulfil the delay time requirement. The fuzzy controller responds satisfactorily to the throughput requirements even if the throughput is a bit too low for video calls and interactive game connection.
Table 7 presents delay and thropughput of two pairs of VoIP calls, video calls, and interactive games. It can be seen that only the fuzzy controller manage to keep delay within the requirement. The throughput is a bit lower than required for perfect connection but still very near the perfect level.

Connection types	Delay			Throughput		
	OF [ms]	FC [ms]	PID [ms]	OF [Kbit/s]	FC [Kbit/s]	PID [Kbit/s]
VoIP connection	12.4	2.6	1.0	62.3	63.6	64.0
Video call	12.9	4.4	3.4	375.4	384.0	384.0
Interactive game	12.1	2.5	2.6	38.8	40.0	40.0

Table 5. Delay and throughputs in *Scenario* 2 when the fixed packet size of 400 bits, fuzzy controller (FC) and PID controller (PID) were used. Protocol, queueing and propagation delay limit was 25 ms. Throughput limits were 64 Kbit/s for VoIP call, 384 Kbit/s for video call, and 40 Kbit/s for interactive game. One VoIP call, one video call, and one interactive game connection.

Connection types	Delay			Throughput		
	OF [ms]	FC [ms]	PID [ms]	OF [Kbit/s]	FC [Kbit/s]	PID [Kbit/s]
VoIP connection 1	100.6	10.2	30.4	9.7	61.8	53.7
VoIP connection 2	127.9	13.0	34.5	9.6	61.9	52.8
Video call 1	82.2	9.2	14.3	79.3	371.8	325.1
Video call 2	87.4	10.2	15.4	79.2	371.5	324.1
Interactive game 1	141.5	10.3	31.4	7.9	38.7	33.7

Table 6. Delay and throughputs in *Scenario* 2 when the fixed packet size of 400 bits, fuzzy controller (FC) and PID controller (PID) were used. Protocol, queueing and propagation delay limit was 25 ms. Throughput limits were 64 Kbit/s for VoIP call, 384 Kbit/s for video call, and 40 Kbit/s for interactive game. Two VoIP call, two video call, and one interactive game connection.

The aim of the developed fuzzy flow management system is to adjusts appropriate packet size and transmission interval of the source node's constant bit rate real-time traffic flows for prevailing network conditions to achieve application dependent quality of service requirements with the optimal network capacity. From the results (see Tables 2 - 7) it can be seen that with the increasing load, the delay increases and throughput degrades smoothly towards QoS limits when the fuzzy controller was used. Hence, in order to guarantee the quality of service of the different applications, an admission control is required either to accept or to deny new connections depending on the prevailing network conditions. In our case the access point, with the fuzzy controller in network nodes, allows new prioritized real-time connections when the required overall capacity of them remains below 900 Kbit/s. For the PID controller, the capacity limit should be around the 480 Kbit/s.

10.2 Response times

Table 8 presents throughput and corresponding averaged packet sizes of real-time traffic with different amount of background traffic for 100 ms target delay. The optimum packet size value

Connection types	Delay			Throughput		
	OF [ms]	FC [ms]	PID [ms]	OF [Kbit/s]	FC [Kbit/s]	PID [Kbit/s]
VoIP connection 1	120.4	18.0	112.2	7.4	59.1	7.6
VoIP connection 2	144.2	14.7	127.6	7.8	60.1	7.4
Video call 1	87.0	14.8	90.5	63.6	354.0	61.1
Video call 2	92.9	15.4	82.7	72.7	357.1	75.8
Interactive game 1	173.0	16.2	161.0	6.9	37.4	5.9
Interactive game 2	236.0	12.7	175.9	4.8	37.5	5.9

Table 7. Delay and throughputs in *Scenario 2* when the fixed packet size of 400 bits, fuzzy controller (FC) and PID controller (PID) were used. Protocol, queueing and propagation delay limit was 25 ms. Throughput limits were 64 Kbit/s for VoIP call, 384 Kbit/s for video call, and 40 Kbit/s for interactive game. Two VoIP call, two video call, and two interactive game connection.

Background traffic	Average packet size			Throughput		
	OF [bits]	FES [bits]	PID [bits]	OF [Kbit/s]	FES [Kbit/s]	PID [Kbit/s]
(0.010,0.100)	10900	10552	10538	1518	2149	2130
(0.010,0.090)	9750	9366	9324	1285	1907	1874
(0.010,0.085)	8800	8897	8455	1180	1804	1763
(0.010,0.080)	8200	8276	7876	1051	1686	1593
(0.010,0.075)	7100	7103	7034	900	1457	1429
(0.010,0.070)	6200	6207	5793	715	1255	1175

Table 8. Throughputs and corresponding averaged packet sizes with different amount of background traffic. Delay limit 100 ms. Initial packet size was 256 bits. One-directional traffic. OF = Optimized fixed.

depends on the amount of traffic on the network. It was defined separately for all background traffic levels in each scenarios by measuring and depicting delay as a function of packet size by a large set of simulation runs. Therefore, it is an optimal value for the observed unchanged circumstances. For the results shown in Table 8, the transmitting host had an application that sent a packet to another host every 1 ms starting with the packet size of 256 bits. Receiving host measured the delay for the packets, used the developed packet size optimization algorithms to calculate the optimum packet size for 100 ms target delay, and reported it to the transmitting host after every 200 packets by sending an acknowledgement message. The surrounding nodes transmit packets at random intervals i, where $i \in [0.010\,s, 0.070\,s]$ - $i \in [0.010\,s, 0.100\,s]$. The conducted simulations measured also rise and settling times of the controllers with the different level of the background traffic. For example, Figures 6 - 7 *a* and *b* present throughput as a function of time in, when the packet size was adjusted by the FES and PID controllers

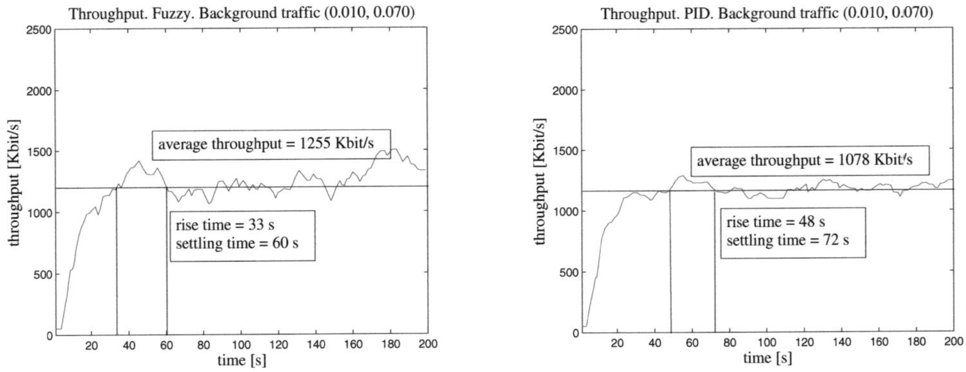

(a) (b)

Fig. 6. Throughput as a function of time when the packet size was adjusted by a.) the FES and b.) the PID controller and the surrounding nodes transmit packets at random intervals i, where $i \in [0.010\,s, 0.070\,s]$.

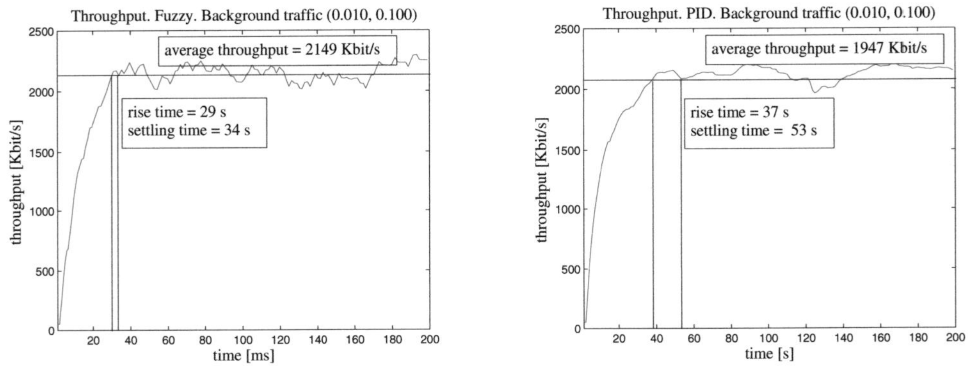

(a) (b)

Fig. 7. Throughput as a function of time when the packet size was adjusted by a.) the FES and b.) the PID controller and the surrounding nodes transmit packets at random intervals i, where $i \in [0.010\,s, 0.100\,s]$.

and the target delay was 100 ms. The packet transmission interval of surrounding nodes was varied in Figures 6 - 7 from $i \in [0.010\,s, 0.070\,s]$ to $i \in [0.010\,s, 0.100\,s]$.

Table 9 presents rise and settling times of the controllers with 100 ms target delay when the packet transmission interval of surrounding nodes is varied from $i \in [0.010\,s, 0.070\,s]$ to $i \in [0.010\,s, 0.100\,s]$. The average (averaged over the different amount of disturbing background traffic of surrounding nodes) rise and settling times were 41.5 s and 53.2 s for the FES based controller, and 58.5 s and 78.3 s for the PID controller. The developed controllers manage to set packet payload size values to the prevailing optimum level very fast and accurately. However, the rise and settling times of the FES are about 29 % and 32 % lower than for the PID, *i.e.*, it can be stated that the FES controller adapts faster and adjust better to traffic load changes, which is an important feature especially in congestion situation.

Background traffic	Rise time		Settling time	
	FES [s]	PID [s]	FES [s]	PID [s]
(0.01,0.100)	29	37	34	53
(0.01,0.090)	47	88	58	123
(0.01,0.085)	42	62	60	71
(0.01,0.080)	38	53	44	72
(0.01,0.075)	60	63	63	79
(0.01,0.070)	33	48	60	72

Table 9. Rise and settling times of controllers with different amount of background traffic. Initial packet size was 256 bits. Delay limit was 100 ms.

11. Conclusion

This chapter considered an embedded fuzzy control system for cognitive flow management of delay sensitive real-time traffic to improve quality of service (QoS). The management system adjusts transceivers' traffic flow(s) for prevailing network conditions to achieve application dependent delay and throughput quality of service requirements with the optimal network capacity. The fuzzy flow management system was compared to conventional PID control system. The controllers were located at user terminals. The models were validated by simulating voice over IP (VoIP) calls, video phone conversations, and interactive games in OMNeT++ network simulator.

The results showed that the developed controller manages to set packet payload size values to the prevailing optimum level very fast and accurately and they also managed to keep average delay below the target value. For the VoIP conversations, the fuzzy flow management controller doubles the amount of quality controlled connections compared to fixed 400 bits packet payload size calls and PID controlled calls. Therefore, we can state that the developed model enables WLANs to increase the number of concurrent users and improve quality of the real-time connections. The fuzzy control system also adapt to various application level requirements, like an application dependent delay limit, with low computational complexity.

12. Acknowledgement

This work was supported by TEKES (Finnish Funding Agency for Technology and Innovation) as part of the Future Internet programme of TIVIT (Finnish Strategic Centre for Science, Technology and Innovation in the field of ICT).

13. References

Ahmad, S., Mustafa, A., Ahmad, H., Bano, A. & Hosam, A. (2009). Comparative Study of Congestion Control Techniques in High Speed Networks, *(IJSIS) International Journal of Computer Science and Information Security* 6(2): 222–231.

Andrews, J., Ghosh, A. & Muhamed, R. (2007). *Fundamentals of WiMAX - Understanding Broadband Wireless Networking*, first edn, Prentice Hall, United States.

B. Bing (2002). *Wireless Local Area Networks: The New Wireless Revolution*, 1st edition edn, John Wiley & Sons, Inc., New York.

Bakshi, B., Krishna, P., Vaidya, N. & Pradhan, D. (1997). Improving Performance of TCP over Wireless Networks, *ICDCS '97: Proceedings of the 17th International Conference on Distributed Computing Systems (ICDCS '97)*, IEEE Computer Society, Washington, DC, USA, pp. 365–373.

Balakrishnan, M. & Sadasivan, M. (2007). Mobile Interactive Game Interworking in IMS, *White Paper. http://www.infosys.com/offerings/engineering-services/product-engineering/white -papers/Documents/mobile-gaming-paper.pdf* .

Chan, P. M. L., Sheriff, R. E., Hu, Y. F., Conforto, P. & Tocci, C. (2001). Mobility management incorporating fuzzy logic for a heterogeneous IP environment, *IEEE Communications Magazine* 39(12): 42–51.

Chang, P. & May, B. W. (1996). Adaptive Fuzzy Power Control for CDMA Mobile Radio Systems, *IEEE Transactions on Vehicular Technology* 45(2): 225–236.

Chee, K. & David, J. (1989). Packet Data Transmission Over Mobile Radio Channels, *IEEE Trans. on Vehicular Technology* 38: 95–101.

Chien, C., Srivastava, M. B., Jain, R., Lettieri, P., Aggarwal, V. & Sternowski, R. (1999). Adaptive Radio for Multimedia Wireless Links, *IEEE Journal on Selected Area in Communications* 17: 793–813.

Crawford, L. & Marshall, A. (2001). A dynamic and fast packet scheduling algorithm for open and programmable networks, *The Seventeenth UK Teletraffic Theory Symposium*, Dublin, Ireland.

Demers, A., Keshav, S. & Shenker, S. (1989). Analysis and simulation of a fair queueing algorithm, *SIGCOMM '89: Symposium proceedings on Communications architectures & protocols*, ACM, New York, NY, USA, pp. 1–12.

Driankov, D., Hellendoorn, H. & Reinfark, M. (1994). *An Introduction to Fuzzy Control*, 2nd edition edn, Springer-Verlag, New York.

Floyd, S. & Jacobson, V. (1995). Link-sharing and resource management models for packet networks, *IEEE/ACM Trans. Netw.* 3(4): 365–386.

Frantti, T. & Jutila, M. (2009). Embedded Fuzzy Expert System for Adaptive Weighted Fair Queueing, *Expert Systems with Applications, Elsevier Science* Vol. 36, No. 8: 11390–11397.

Frantti, T. & Mahonen, P. (2001). Fuzzy Logic Based Forecasting Model, *Engineering Applications of Artificial Intelligence* 14(2): 189–201.

Frantti, T. & Majanen, M. (2010). *Internet Traffic Shaping in WLANs by Packet Size Control*, first edn, Nova Science Publishers, Inc., NY.

Frantti, T., Majanen, M. & Sukuvaara, T. (2010). Delay Based Packet Size Control in Wireless Local Area Networks, *ICUFN 2010 The Second International Conference on Ubiquitous and Future Networks, June 16-18, 2010, Jeju Island, Korea. Invited paper.*, Jeju Island, Korea.

Goldsmith, A. & Wicker, S. B. (2002). Design challenges for energy-constrained ad hoc wireless networks, *IEEE Wireless Commun. Mag.* 9(4): 8–27.

Hahne, E. (1986). *Round robin scheduling for fair flow control in data communication networks*, Ph.d. dissertation lids-th-1631, Lab. Inform. Decision Syst., MIT, Cambridge, MA.

Horng, M. F., Lee, W. T., Lee, K. R. & Kuo, Y. H. (2001). An adaptive approach to weighted fair queue with QoS enhanced on IP, *IEEE Region 10 International Conference on Electrical and Electronic Technology*, Vol. 1, pp. 181–186.

Huitema, C. (2000). *Routing in the Internet (2nd ed.)*, Prentice Hall PTR, Upper Saddle River, NJ, USA.

Huusko, J., Vehkapera, J., Amon, P., Lamy-Bergot, C., Panza, G., Peltola, J. & Martini, M. (2007). Cross-layer architecture for scalable video transmission in wireless network, *Signal Processing: Image Communication* 22(3): 317–330.

Juuso, E. (1992). Linguistic Equations Framework for Adaptive Expert Systems, *in* J. Stephenson (ed.), *Modelling and Simulation 1992, Proceedings of the 1992 European Simulation Multiconference*, pp. 99–103.

Juuso, E. K. (1993). Linguistic Simulation in Production Control, *in* R. Pooley & R. Zobel (eds), *UKSS'93 Conference of the United Kingdom Simulation Society*, Keswick, UK, pp. 34–38.

Khoukhi, L. & Cherkaoui, S. (2008). Experimenting with Fuzzy Logic for QoS Management in Mobile Ad Hoc Networks, *IJCSNS International Journal of Computer Science and Network Security* 8(8): 372–386.

Kleinrock, L. (1975). *Queuing Systems*, first edition edn, John Wiley & Sons, New York.

Koomey, J. G. (2010). Outperforming Moore's Law, *IEEE Spectrum* March 2010: 68.

Korhonen, J. & Wang, Y. (2005). Effect of Packet Size on Loss Rate and Delay in Wireless Links, *Proceedings of the 2005 IEEE Conference on Wireless Communications and Networking, vol. 3.*, IEEE Communications Society, New Orleans, LA USA, pp. 1608–1613.

Kumar, S., Raghavan, V. S. & Deng, J. (2006). Medium access control protocols for ad-hoc wireless networks: A survey, *Ad-Hoc Netw. J.* 4(3): 326–358.

Lamy-Bergot, C., Fracchia, R., Mazzotti, M., Moretti, S., Piri, E., Sutinen, T., Zuo, J., Vehkapera, J., Feher, G., Jeney, G., Panza, G. & Amon, P. (2010). Optimisation of multimedia over wireless IP links via X-layer design: an end-to-end transmission chain simulator, *Multimedia Tools and Applications* .

Leondes, C. T. (ed.) (1998). *Fuzzy Logic and Expert Systems Applications*, 6 edn, Academic Press, San Diego, California, USA.

Lettieri, P. & Srivastava, M. B. (1998). Adaptive Frame Length Control for Improve Wireless Link Range and Energy Efficiency, *Proceeding of the IEEE INFOCOM'98*, IEEE communications Society, San Francisco, USA, pp. 564–571.

Leung, K. K., McNair, B., Cimini, L. & Winters, J. H. (2002). Outdoor IEEE 802.11 Cellular Networks: MAC Protocol Design and Performance, *Proc. of the IEEE International Conference on Communications 2002 (ICC 2002), Vol. 1*, pp. 595–599.

Li, T. & Ni, Q. (2005). Performance Analysis of the IEEE 802.11e Block ACK Scheme in a Noisy Channel, *Proc. IEEE BroadNets05*, pp. 551–557.

Li, Y. F. & Lau, F. (1989). Development of Fuzzy Algorithm for Servo Systems, *IEEE Control Systems Magazine* 9(3): 65–72.

Nagle, J. (1985). On packet switches with infinite storage, *RFC 970*, Internet Engineering Task Force.

Nagle, J. (1987). On packet switches with infinite storage, *Communications, IEEE Transactions on [legacy, pre - 1988]* 35(4): 435–438.

Perkins, D. D. & Hughes, H. D. (2002). A survey on QOS support for mobile ad hoc networks, *Wireless Commun. Mobile Comput.* 2: 503–513.

Peterson, L. L. & Davie, B. S. (2007). *Computer networks: a systems approach*, 4th edition edn, Morgan Kaufmann Publishers Inc., San Francisco, CA, USA.

Qu, Q., Pei, Y. & Modestino, J. W. (2005). Cross-layer QoS control for video communications over wireless ad hoc networks, *EURASIP J. Wireless Commun. Network* 5: 743–756.

Sanjay, K. & Hassan, M. (2002). *Engineering Internet Qos*, Artech House, Inc., Norwood, MA, USA.

Sankarasubramaniam, Y., Akyildiz, I. & McLaughlin, S. (2003). Energy Efficiency Based Packet Size Optimization in Wireless Sensor Networks, *Proceedings of the First*

IEEE International Workshop on Sensor Network Protocols and Applications, 2003., IEEE Communications Society, Anchorage, Alaska, USA, pp. 1–8.

Sayenko, A., Hämäläinen, T., Joutsensalo, J. & Kannisto, L. (2006). Comparison and analysis of the revenue-based adaptive queuing models, *Comput. Netw.* 50(8): 1040–1058.

Sayenko, A., Hämäläinen, T., Joutsensalo, J. & Siltanen, J. (2003). An adaptive approach to wfq with the revenue criterion, *ISCC '03: Proceedings of the Eighth IEEE International Symposium on Computers and Communications*, IEEE Computer Society, Washington, DC, USA, p. 181.

Setton, E., Yoo, T., Zhu, X., Goldsmith, A. & Girod, B. (2005). Cross-layer design of ad hoc networks for real-time video streaming, *IEEE Wireless Commun. Mag.* 12(4): 59–65.

Sheu, S.-T., Lee, Y.-H., Chen, M.-H., Yu, Y.-C. & Huang, Y.-C. (2000). PLFC: The Packet Length Fuzzy Controller to Improve the Performance of WLAN Under the Interference of Microwave Oven, *Global Telecommunications Conference, 2000. GLOBECOM '00. IEEE. Volume: 3*, IEEE Communications Society, San Francisco, USA, pp. 1427–1431.

Shreedhar, M. & Varghese, G. (1995). Efficient Fair Queueing Using Deficit Round Robin, *SIGCOMM*, pp. 231–242.

Smadi, M. & Szabados, B. (2006). Error-recovery Service for the IEEE 802.11b Protocol, *IEEE Transactions on Instrumentation and Measurement* 55: 1377–1382.

Tanebaum, A. (1996). *Computer Networks*, 3rd edn, Prentice Hall, New Jersey, USA.

Wang, Z. (2001). *Internet QoS: Architectures and Mechanisms for Quality of Service*, Morgan Kaufmann Publishers Inc., San Francisco, CA, USA.

Younis, M., Farrag, O. & D'Amico, W. (2009). Packet Size Pptimization for Increased Throughput in Multi-Level Security Wireless Networks, *Military Communications Conference, 2009. MILCOM 2009.*, IEEE Communications Society, Boston, USA, pp. 1–7.

Zadeh, L. (1965). Fuzzy Sets, *Information and Control* 8: 338 – 353.

Zhang, Q. & Zhang, Y.-Q. (2008). Cross-layer design for qos support in multihop wireless networks, *Proc. of the IEEE, Vol. 96, No. 1.*

19

Expert System for Automatic Analysis of Results of Network Simulation

Joze Mohorko[1], Sasa Klampfer[2], Matjaz Fras[2] and Zarko Cucej[1]
[1]*University of Maribor, Faculty of Electrical Engineering and Computer Science,*
[2]*Margento R&D d.o.o.,*
Slovenia

1. Introduction

The simulation of communication networks is an important task in the process of network planning and optimization processes. Such methodologies assure a higher probability for networks to operate successfully under different critical conditions, which are difficult or unpractical to be tested in the real networks. Typical applications of such simulations are the simulation of military tactical radio networks. The manual analyses of network simulation results, is a very time-consuming task and requires expert knowledge to correctly interpret such results. This is a good motivation to develop the system for automatic analysis with expert knowledge, which will ease the process of mission planning and training. For such needs, we have developed the simulation methodology and tools, supported by the expert system, which are going to be presented in detail within this chapter.

During this chapter, we will briefly introduce expert systems (further ES), Command and Control Information Systems used in NATO and known solutions to simulate such systems.

The ES is defined as an intelligent computer program with a certain level of expert knowledge, which using procedures to solve exactly specified problems. All definitions for expert systems, in many books, are quite similar, and they describe the way such system includes a rigid range of expert (specialized) knowledge or research domain. Within this area, it is capable of creating intelligent decisions. This is some kind of imitation, where a system tries to capture behavior of skills. Using the acquired knowledge; a system can analyze input/output information, solve problems, and utilize utensil decisions within the problem domain. From this point of view, these systems cannot solve all kinds of problems, but they can solve well-known and deduced problems. It is stated in one of the references that expert systems are based on knowledge (Hart, 1998, pg. 7), respectively on an information handler base. Classification by Sauter places an expert system on the right side of the straight line, where we can find systems, which handle information. Expert systems are closely related to artificial intelligence methods. As a rule, they share quality and quantity information, probability theory, fuzzy set theory, and a number of arithmetic and logic rules, based on heuristic expectations.

Output decisions, from the ES, are usually good, but it is unnecessary for them to be optimal. We can use these systems throughout a wide spectrum of human creativity, such as interpretations, announcements, diagnostics, shapes recognition, planning, debugging, repairing, control, etc.

In 2001, the Multilateral Interoperability Programme was established in order to advocate successful and harmonized operational functions for international peace keeping forces. The aim of the Multilateral Interoperability Programme (MIP) is to achieve international interoperability of Command and Control Information Systems (C2IS) at all military levels, in order to support multinational, combined and joint operations and the advancement of digitization within the international area. C2IS (TIS PINK is Slovenian acronym) is designed to control: operations, logistics, and the communication information stored in the C2IEDM (Command and Control Information Exchange Data Model) data bases. In Slovenian case, the Sitaware program packet is the graphic user interface of C2IS system. Replications of data between C2IEDM data bases, regarding individual military units, are managed by the IRIS replication mechanism (IRM) service. Both systems were developed by the Danish company, Systematic.

Simulations with modeling and analyzing of tactical communication system characteristics, has become one of the main network development tools, which enable evaluation prior deployment in the real world. Such methodologies assure a higher success probability for tactically critical operations on military fields. Various simulation systems exist for military tactical networks. NETWARS is a well known program, developed by the US Department of Defense. It is based on the OPNET Modeler simulation technology. OPNET Modeler is one of the most powerful simulation tools for communication networks, devices and protocols as well as their planning, analysis, and optimization.

Our research has been focused on a national project with aims that are directed towards the increase of efficiency, when using Slovenian C2IS information technology. This entailed research into the interdependence between the C2IS information and communication systems as well as the development of simulation methodologies and tools that enable C2 (Command and Control) optimization of communication systems. These tools and methodologies are briefly described in the second section and the main problem of manual analysis of simulation results is introduced as well. This analysis became time-consuming in many cases and very difficult in areas, where thousands of data must be simultaneously analyzed. The primary concept of this paper is located in the third section, where the known expert system theory is briefly introduced. Our definition of tactical network quality measures, and the architecture of our expert system implementation for the automatic analysis of tactical network performance simulations is introduced in the continuation. Section 4 contains an example of the use of our developed expert system. The chapter ends with conclusions.

2. Structure of expert systems

In this section, we will describe three main parts of expert systems: knowledge base, reasoning mechanism, and user interface (UI), which is very important as well. Also included is a definition of Fuzzy sets, as part of an expert system reasoning mechanisms, used in our solution.

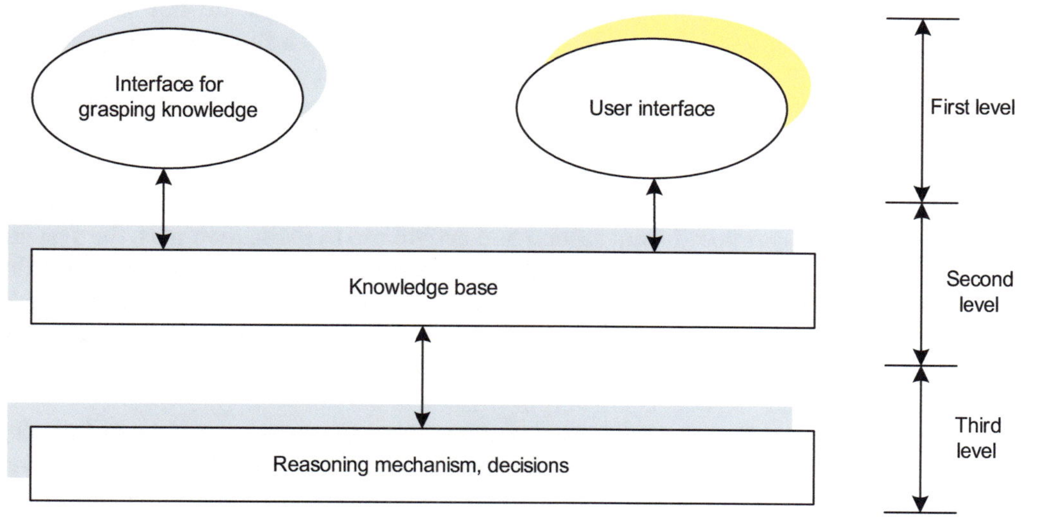

Fig. 1. Basic elements of an expert system.

2.1 Knowledge base

Knowledge base is used to store knowledge. Two different kinds of knowledge produce a knowledge base:

- Declaration knowledge describes objects (facts and rules), which are treated by the expert system, and where the relation between such objects exists.
- Procedural knowledge contains information about the previously mentioned objects. This information helps us to find the point, where certain conclusions and final solutions can be obtained.

Knowledge base quality is one of the most important factors in this case. Base quality is a function concerned with base dimensions and knowledge quality. A wide-spread base with high expert knowledge leads to a high-performance expert system. Knowledge must be stored in the base in the right format, because an expert system must understand it, that it can create correct decisions derived from such knowledge. Different methods or formalisms are used for knowledge presentation. From this point of view, its declaration must be hierarchically-settled, heterogeneous, and must have a flexible notation structure. Notation structure flexibility is needed for the later incorporation of new cognitions and also to change records. Hierarchy is needed for vertical connections between superior and inferior types of objects in the knowledge base. The formalisms or methods for knowledge presentation include symbolic presentations, which can be split into four groups:

- production rules,
- logic presentation,
- semantic networks and
- frames.

The most useful is the method that is based on production rules. Logical relations between objects in the problem areas are described by rules of type *if – then*. Generalize therefore, if *A* then *B*, or if condition *P* is fulfilled, then conclusion *S* should be valid with trust factor *G*. An example of logical relation is: if the quantity of atmospheric precipitations is high and still raining, then with huge probability, we can affirm that people do not suffer from dryness. The left-side of rule *A* represents conditions, respectively a situation where the rule is usable; however, the right-side (*B*) defines consequence, decision, or rule action. Each side can contain more elements, which are mutually connected to logic operators, such are: *AND*, *OR*, *NOT* (not very often). We can explain the means of the production rule in the following manner: *A* is valid if we can obtain *B* from *A*, and then we can also consume that *B* is valid. This is the principle for deriving facts, respectively inferences, from active production rules. Inference is a process, composed from section and activation. In the section part, the system finds out whose rules are convenient and within a convenient rule set, choose a proper rule for activation. After a successful activation, a procedure must be executed and a proper fact must be obtained. Such obtained facts are then inserted into the knowledge base. All communication directions go through the facts in the knowledge base, because rules cannot activate other rules.

The production rule consists of a rule and a pattern. The pattern represents part of a rule, which is used for further comparisons with facts in the data collection. This rule is used for executions, where we obtain newly derived facts again. When executing inferences as a forward process, the pattern must be on the left-side of the rule and the rule on the right-side. Using the opposite inference process, everything is inverse to this. Each rule is part of the whole knowledge and independent from other rules. The rule addition procedure is relatively simple because records, with production rules, allow system transparency when answering questions, such as *how* and *why*. A huge drawback to these systems is looping complexity; repetition of the mass rules set, and blurred probability during rule execution. Knowledge can also be presented using mathematical logic, with first order predicate computation, etc. Predicate computation has advantages in fast algorithms to prove sentences, which are based on resolution axiom. In this way we can, in the simplest way, define relations and the structuring of data. Furthermore, as in the case of production rules, this method is also not ideal for our needs, because it does not have enough mechanisms for the 'soft' knowledge modeling.

The beginning of the frame theory is described in (Siler & Buckley, 2007) detail and the semantic networks are described in (Van Emden & Kowalski, 2003, Liebowitz, 2004, and Krishnamoorthy & Rajeev, 1996).

2.2 Reasoning mechanism

Reasoning mechanism is the main part of an expert system. It controls the operation of the whole ES. The mechanism must actively use the knowledge base to deal with data, coming into the system, and for the derivation of suitable facts.

The mechanism is composed of inquiring and reasoning processes, which help in the solution search process. The most useful is reasoning method, especially in cases, when we want to derive new facts from given knowledge, through the use of production rules and forward or backward reasoning mechanisms.

Forward-decision process uses an inductive procedure, where, the algorithm tries to find the proper one, from known sets of facts, which leads to the required aim. Induction is a form of reasoning that makes generalizations based on individual instances. A satisfactory solution must be compared with the production rules pattern on the left-side of the rule. If the left-side is equal to the fact on the right-side, the agreement rule must be activated. The activated rule adds a new fact into the operational memory, which is derived from the core, respectively from the right-side of the rule. Derived facts now have equal rights, as in the reasoning process (Siler & Buckley, 2007, Krishnamoorthy & Rajeev, 1996). A backward-decision uses deductive execution. Deduction is a form of reasoning that proceeds from general principles or premises and derives the particular information. The main goal of backward-decision is oriented towards rejecting or confirming the truth of the goal-hypotheses. Hypothesis can be, for example "water level is high". Firstly, the mechanism checks if it is possible to confirm the goal-hypothesis using a fact in the operational memory, otherwise it looks for a rule, which can confirm the hypothesis (Siler & Buckley, 2007, Krishnamoorthy & Rajeev, 1996). Usually, systems with backward-decisions are more efficient in comparison to forward-decision systems, because they reduce search space, and quickly find a proper solution. Such systems can be used, when in advance-defined trivial goals exists.

2.3 User interface

The expert system user interface takes care for a comfortable communication between the system and (unskillful) users. It provides an insight view into the problem solving process, carried out by inference. The user interface translates the information given by the user, in a form suitable for computer manipulation, decisions and interpretations made by the system and present them to the user in an intelligible written textual or graphical form. User interface usually allows interaction with the environment and other systems, as external databases are, for example. The most commonly used expert system user interfaces are in the form of: questions and answers, menus, hypertext, natural language, graphical interfaces, etc. The user interface is one of the most critical elements in the whole expert system, because a bad user interface can lead to limited or ineffective use. Furthermore, user interface design is generally more demanding than the standard computer applications, since the information, that are exchanged between the user and the system, are generally more complex. Data processing in such a system is more demanding as well.

2.4 Fuzzy sets

Fuzzy sets are a generalization of regular crisp sets (Krishnamoorthy & Rajeev, 1996). Meanwhile, the appurtenance function of a crisp set has a stock value {0, 1} (a specific element belongs or does not belong to this set); the appurtenance function of a fuzzy set (μ_A) has a stock value within the interval [0, 1]. We can reason, that a specific element in fuzzy set is contained by appurtenance, which is $\in [0, 1]$.
For example, data of received power from the OPNET simulation graph is observed. For a received-power, set *A={x; data in x is acceptable}* is defined. Such set contains all acceptable data. If we look at this set as on an ordinary set, we can specify data, which fully belongs to it or even does not fully belong to it (two possibilities). A problem appears about the 'acceptability' definition. In regular sets, passages between appurtenance and non-appurtenance are sharp (discrete). Passages between appurtenance and non-appurtenance in fuzzy sets are soft, slow and continuous.

3. Modeling and simulations of tactical networks

In this section the OPNET modeler tool is briefly presented, to the level, needed to understand our simulation methodologies and tools developed around it.

The research project, mentioned in the introduction, incorporates the following working packages, which will be introduced in the continuation:

- development of methodologies for OPNET simulation of hierarchical wireless tactical networks using IRIS Replication Mechanism (IRM) and
- development of the TPGEN helper application, that enable user-friendly entry and editing of tactical network parameters (radio parameters, IRM contract parameters, parameters for statistical description of tactical data sources), to the OPNET simulation data model.

3.1 OPNET Modeler

The developed tactical network simulation system is based on the OPNET simulation tools, similar as in NETWARS and INCOT case. We used OPNET Modeler Wireless Suite for Defense, which supports high fidelity protocols and equipment models within a scalable simulation environment, which is capable of simulating wireless and also wired networks. It supports scalable wireless simulations, incorporating terrain influences in path-loss calculations using different propagations models, mobility, and 3D visualization. The OPNET Modeler is an object oriented communication simulation tool, with a hierarchical modeling environment, which uses graphical user interfaces (editors) - network, node and process editors. The *network editor* enables a graphical description of network topology, while a *node editor* is used to describe communication devices, protocols, and connections between them, using layers of the ISO/OSI model. The *process editor* is an upgrade of C language, and uses a powerful finite state machine (FSM) approach to represent different communication algorithms and protocols. The OPNET Modeler is used for modeling and simulation of communication networks and, at the same time, it enables the construction and study of communication infrastructure, individual devices, protocols and applications (OPNET, 2007).

3.2 An OPNET model of IRIS replication mechanism

The aim of the project, described in previous sections, is focused towards optimization of tactical communication networks, where units operate under the various conditions. In order to archive this, we need flexible tools that enable the modeling and simulation of communication systems. We chose the OPNET Modeler, which already has a reference in tactical network simulations through NETWARS and INCOT solutions. In regard to modeling the C2IS system for simulation; we were faced with two tasks:

- modeling a tactical radio network and
- modeling the traffic created by the C2IEDM model for information exchange (IRM in our case).

We choose the station model for modeling the tactical radio network, by considering the following:

- The model has to support mobility (possibility to input the trajectory of movement).
- Field influences on a radio wave-spread. OPNET offers a variety of different models for a radio wave-spread, such as the Longley-Rice (Longley & Rice, 1968) and TIREM models (TIREM/SEM Handbook, 1994). TIREM is the best choice for non-urban areas (Chrysanthou, Breakall, Labowski, Bilen, & J., 2007).
- Possibility of setting radio parameters, such as channel frequency, transmitting power, receiver's sensitivity, physical characteristics (frequency jumping)

- Possibility of antenna modeling.

For modeling traffic, as created by IRM, the station simulation model has to enable the following:

- stochastic traffic modeling,
- communication using broadcast IP protocol,
- communication using peer-to-peer IP protocol and
- support for communication protocols used in tactical radio networks.

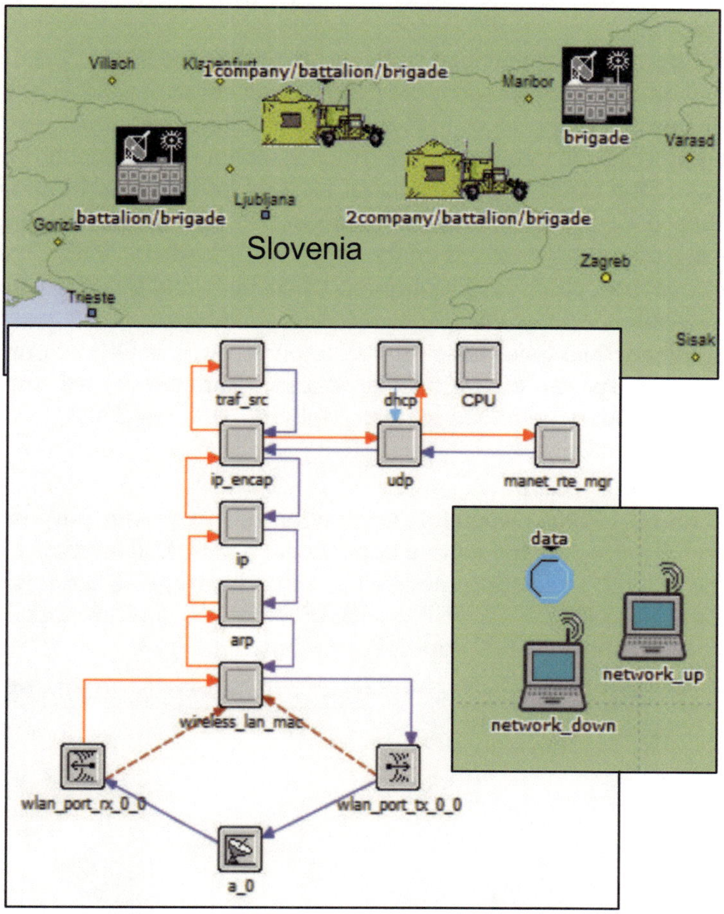

Fig. 2. Above -tactical network example, below right - unit modeled as a mobile subnet with two MANET stations, and dedicated data structure used as a database for storing TPGen parameters, below left - MANET station structure with additional antenna model.

Both modeling tasks are highly correlated, thus they could not approach independently. Considering the above demands, we choose a MANET (Mobile Ad hoc Network) generic station for the OPNET model, which is the best option for both tasks. The topology of the tactical network (shown above in Fig. 2), in the OPNET simulation's tool, is built-up by a specially developed library of tactical units. Each tactical unit (shown below right, in Fig. 2) is modeled by an OPNET subnet, which consists of two MANET stations and an additional process node, used to store additional attributes that are needed to describe a tactical

network. All parameters of the tactical network and tactical units (radio parameters, data sources, IRM contract) are defined by the developed TPGen application. One station is intended for communication with superior units, others for communication with lower units within the tactical network hierarchy. The MANET stations used in these models needed some modification for our purposes; therefore, an antenna was added (below left in Fig.2) in the first phase. This modification gives us an opportunity to choose different predefined antennas or create a new one, by using the OPNET tool, called the Antenna Pattern Editor. In our simulations, we used an isotropic antenna pattern with a uniform transmission gain in all spatial directions.
For traffic modeling, a method that uses traffic generators of the MANET stations have been developed, based on data sources statistical descriptions, regarding IRM contracts. We have developed mathematical mapping of IRM contracts, defined by contract matrices, and data sources, defined by vector of data sources in order to obtain the traffic matrix. This matrix is needed to configure the MANET traffic generators used in TPGen application, as described in (Mohorko, Fras, & Cucej, 2007). The data sources used during this mapping are obtained through network traffic analysis based on the captured (Wireshark, 2008, Chakravarti, 1967) traffic of the test network when IRM replication mechanism and SitaWare are used. During this analysis, we estimate the statistical parameters of network traffic processes, such as packet size and inter-arrival times for each traffic source, such as GPS sensor, manual entry of data, etc. For purposes of estimating statistic parameters we used our traffic defragmentation method, as described in (Fras, Mohorko, & Cucej, 2008).

3.3 TPGen application

Developed TPGen (TIS PINK Generator) application has two main purposes. First out of two is a user-friendly entering and editing of parameters of tactical networks, which have an influence on the OPNET simulation model. The second purpose is automatic mapping of simulation parameters into the OPNET model, according to the developed mathematical model. The user interface of TPGEN application is shown in Fig. 3.

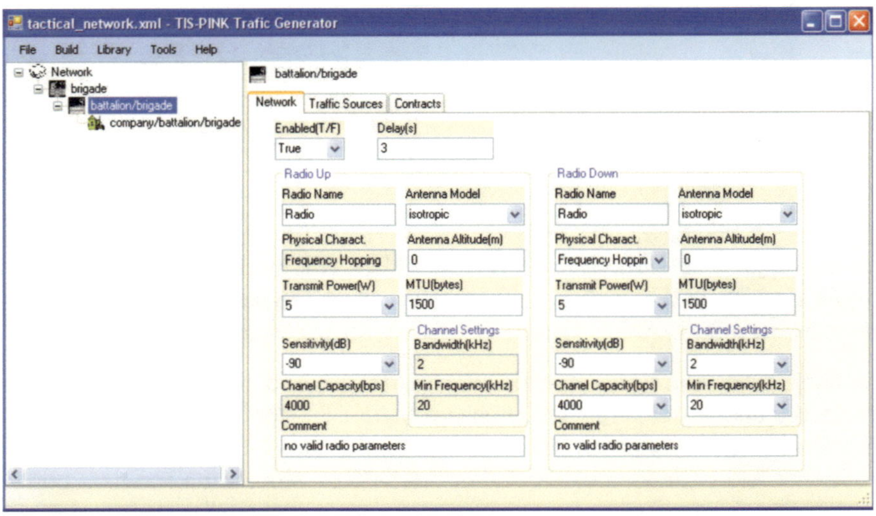

Fig. 3. TPGen application, where tree-view is visible in the left panel and *network editor* on the right panel.

Data exchange, between OPNET Modeler and application TPGen, is performed by XML formatted OPNET model data files. The basic components of the TPGen application user interface are: hierarchical tactical network tree-view visualization, network editor (sensitivity, transmitted power, channel capacity, etc.), traffic source's editor (statistical descriptions of traffic sources) and IRM contract editor (to define which data sources will be mediated between tactical nodes and which type of communication protocol will be used). TPGen editor also incorporates libraries of: military units, stations, data sources and contracts, and they considerably ease the work of tactical network planners. Application TPGen also ensures an automatic entry of certain parameters into MANET station models, which are invisible to the user, but are required for OPNET simulation (IP address, destination IP address, BSS identifier, etc.). TPGen application usage, when we simulate tactical networks, is schematically presented by the use-case diagram in Fig. 4.

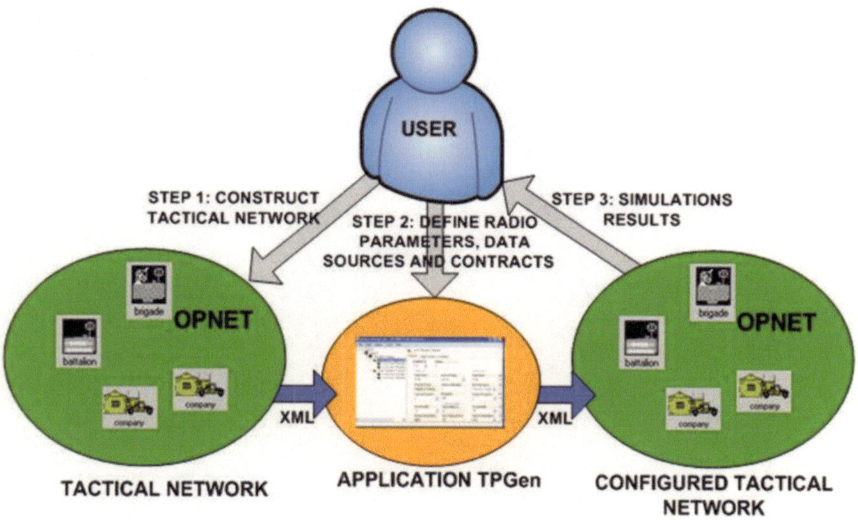

Fig. 4. Use-case diagram of tactical network simulations.

The whole modeling procedure consists of the following four basic steps:

1. In the first step, user must compose a hierarchical tactical network, by placing icons from the libraries of military tactical units on a virtual terrain-map of the OPNET *project editor* (see upper part in Fig. 2). Then a simulation scenario must be exported as a XML model file for use in TPGen application (step 1 in Fig. 5).
2. User then imports the XML model file into TPGen application. For each tactical unit, radio parameters must be defined, and data sources and IRM contracts as well. All entered parameters are stored in prepared data structure inside the OPNET models, as shown in the lower right corner of Fig. 2. Users then export modified XML model file from the TPGen application.
3. In this step, user must import configured XML model file of tactical network back into OPNET Modeler. Trajectories of movement can be defined for individual units. A user can then choose statistics that he/she wants to observe after the simulation, simulation parameters defined, and after the simulation and analyze results are run(step 3 in Fig. 4).
4. For new scenarios, it is necessary to repeat steps 2 and 3 on Fig. 4.

4. Expert system for analyzing performances of tactical network

This is the main part of the chapter in which we describe our expert system solution for automatic analysis of network performance.
There are many reasons why we decide to build such an expert system:

- Network simulation results (output vectors), obtained by OPNET modeler simulation, are represented graphically in a form, which is not user friendly, in order to identify whether results satisfy our expectations or not (Fig. 5).
- Some of the tactical network parameters are not measurable directly by a single simulation statistic. It is necessary to develop expert algorithms that perform complex analysis over many simulation statistics simultaneously, in order to evaluate parameters, such as radio visibility, message competition rate, etc.)
- During OPNET Modeler simulation, statistics are not included in regards to geographical positions of individual tactical units, which can also be mobile. This information is crucial within the tactical network optimization process. For this reason, we implement functionality into the expert system that enables linking between expert system results and the positions of tactical units, with the use of the developed tactical player tool (Globacnik, Mohorko, & Cucej, 2008).

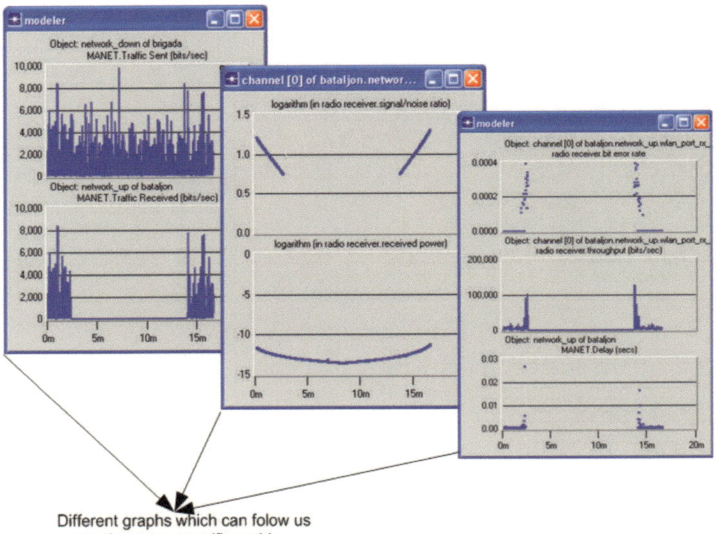

Fig. 5. Obtain graphical simulation results from OPNET.

Our expert system, shown in Fig. 6, uses two input data sets. The first is the XML file which contains information about tactical network topology and settings. The second input data set is the OPNET Modeler simulation output vector file with data records of the chosen statistics. From both files, a hierarchical data structure is then built, which is used as unified input data for our analysis system. An expert system algorithm performs data operations on this data structure and stores results into the same structure. The report generator produces two report files. The first is for detailed analysis using Tactical player, and the second one is user readable, which contains information about network performance and directions for network improvements.

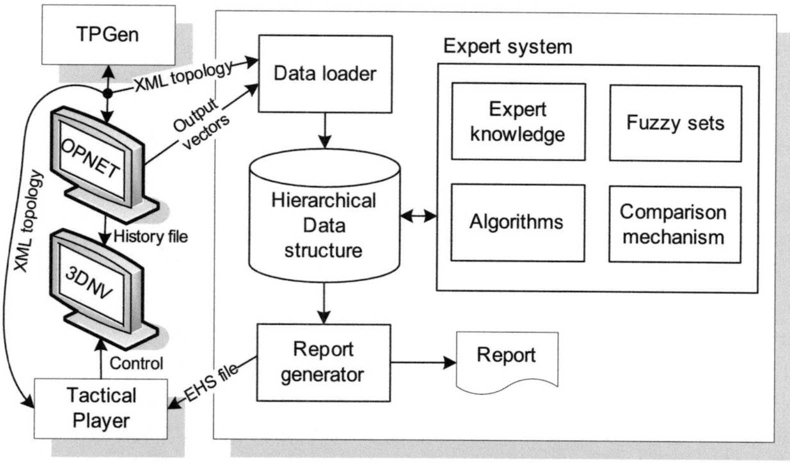

Fig. 6. A block diagram of expert system, and correlation with other developed modules.

4.1 Tactical network evaluation algorithms

Transmitter bandwidth utilization analysis, using the fuzzy-set theory: Traffic between tactical radio network participants is determined by the so-called IRM contracts, which define who communicates with whom, and which data sources they should use for this. The intensity of data sources is defined by a statistical description of transaction size and transaction packets inter-arrival time. Contract can be of a broadcast type, which means that traffic can be received by all participants of the subnet, or peer-to-peer type, where communication is performed between pairs of participants. Bandwidth utilization is an important network parameter, and it is a good indicator of bandwidth overloading, which can lead to extreme delays or data loss, caused by timeouts. Near to 90% of long term utilizations are alarming situations. In such cases, the intensity of data sources must be decreased or network topology must be redesigned. Utilization is a parameter that can be easyly measured, because it is a generic OPNET Modeler statistic. In our expert system, for this statistic, we have defined alarming conditions by using fuzzy logic methods.

Traffic delay analysis: Traffic delay is also one of the generic OPNET Modeler statistics. This parameter is a good indicator for Quality of Services (QoS) in tactical networks, which is very important for applications such as Voice over IP (VoIP). Analysis of delays is treated in a similar way as in the utilization case.

Message completion rate is a very important evaluation parameter of tactical networks. It is the ratio between the number of received and transmitted messages. This parameter is very difficult to estimate from generic OPNET Modeler statistics, particularly for complex tactical networks. Tactical radio units simultaneously receive traffic from many sources. Graphical simulation results are cumulative, and there is not any information about source addresses for particular received packets. This is the reason, why we decided to modify the OPNET tactical unit model on the C programming language level, in order to perform additional logging of all received and transmitted traffic, with information about time-stamp, transaction packet size, destination, and source IP address. Using expert analysis algorithms, we search and count the number of transmitted messages that are also received on another side. In such way, the new statistic is build-up. Such created statistics are not originally presented in OPNET Modeler tool. Different factors, such as terrain agitation, vegetation, transmitter power, the receiver sensitivity, interferences, etc., have an influence on the message completion rate. In broadcast type of transmissions, such an estimation of message completion rate is credible. In the peer-to peer case, it is expected that this is an estimation of lower boundary, because the application level protocols that are not implemented by OPNET simulation, increase this level in the really tactical networks, through the use of retransmission mechanisms.

Radio visibility analysis: Radio visibility is a parameter, which tells us whether if radio transmitters and receivers can communicate. It depends on transmitter power, receiver sensibility, the distances between them, terrain influences, etc. In contrast to the previous described analyses, we developed a special OPNET modeler simulation scenario, where for each military unit; we allocate a precisely defined time slot during which the transmitter transmits short packets (pings). All time slots of units from the same subnet form periodically-repeated sequences. Expert analysis algorithm check, if the packets have been received within the expected time-slots or not. Those areas where packets are not received do not have radio visibility. An attentive reader will ask oneself why it is necessary to design a new simulation scenario, and why the packet must be as short as possible? The reason for the new scenario with uniquely defined time slots is, that in the cases of simultaneously active multiple receivers and transmitters, impossible to detect the appurtenance of points on a graph, using statistics such as received power, signal to noise ratio, bit error rate, etc. This is because each of these points can be caused by multiple transmitters. Minimal packets must be selected using reason that inducts minimal influence on transmitter delays. Received power can also be reused, but only the statistic which is chosen on each receiver. In this case, fuzzy set membership function is used, obtained from experimental measurements.

During the analysis procedure, each parameter is compared with a predefined membership function, as is defined in Fig. 7. A similar approach is used in the case of delay and estimation of utilization values, where a similar membership functions are in use, which determines appurtenance of observed parameter to the fuzzy set. The following appurtenance functions can be used: Gaussian, triangle, trapezium, sigmoid, etc. Our case uses half of the left side trapezium function. In regards to Fig. 7, values which are under 80% of appurtenance to the fuzzy set are marked as critical values, where radio communication falls down, meanwhile values between 80% and 95% appurtenance are conditionally acceptable, 96% to 99% acceptable, and values equal to 100% fully acceptable. A description also worth for the delay and utilization values classification, but there are different ranges declared for the appurtenance function.

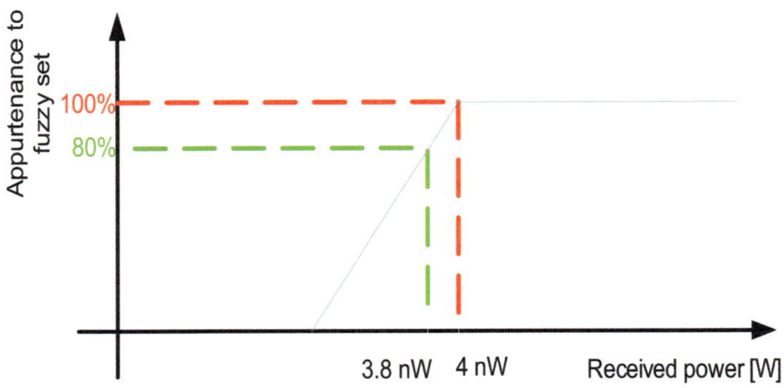

Fig. 7. Definition of fuzzy set membership function example, for received power.

4.2 Expert system design

Expert system user interface, as is shown in Fig. 8, enables users to choose any interesting OPNET Modeler simulation statistic from the analyzed output vector. User can also observe the additional results which are obtained during the expert analysis process, described in the previous section. When the analysis of desirable parameters is chosen, then the procedure of expert analysis begins.

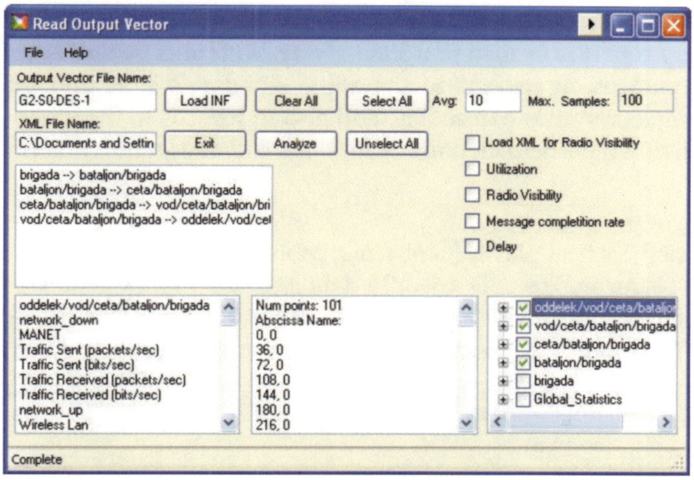

Fig. 8. Expert system user interface.

The expert system creates two output files. The first is user readable in a report form and the second is the so-called expert history system (EHS) file intended for the Tactical player. The EHS file is comma-delimited formatted textual file. Each record (message) in this file has information about time-stamp, statistic name, value, error condition, and comments about possible problems. Such messages are then displayed in our developed Tactical Player software, for each time-stamp and for each unit; position of units is also synchronously visualized over a virtual terrain in 3DNV player, as shown in Fig. 12. Messages are displayed in the form of subtitles. Another type of expert system output file is the user readable report file. This file contains tabular and textual descriptions as a result of expert system analyses for the specific observed tactical network. This is a description about the percentage of radio visibility between tactical node pairs; message competition rates, etc., throughout the whole tactical mission. The user report consists of three parts: global, node and summary reports (Fig. 9).

Global report | Node reports | Sumarize report

Node	Statistic	Value	Comment
Global	MANET Delay	0.00604	
Global	Common Utilization	0.65541	
Global	Avarage Transmitters Utilization	0.16901	Avarage in [%]
Global	Avarage Receivers Utilization	1.14182	Avarage in [%]
Global	MANET UP avg. Delay	0.0083	
Global	MANET DOWN avg. Delay	0.0083	
Global	Wireless LAN UP avg. Delay	0.00557	
Global	Wireless LAN DOWN avg. Delay	0.003	
Global	Message Completion Rate	97.77077	Completion Rate [%]
Global	received power (W)	-56.71	dB
Global	bit error rate	0	BER

Fig. 9. Global report for a person who plans the tactical mission.

- The global report (Fig. 9) contains data about the entire tactical network. Means that presented average global parameters are displayed as a global delay, global transmitters/receivers utilization, global delay on transmitters/receivers, global average radio visibility loss, global average percentage completion rate, etc. These parameters are in correlation with the entire network, observed as one unit.
- The node report contains all average information about each individual participating unit/node within the communication process.
- The summary report is formed in a similar way, with information about radio visibility loss in percentages, in regards to the entire simulation time and information about message completion rates percentage, and also in regards to the entire simulation time for each individual participation unit within the communication process.

4.3 Tactical player

We have developed Tactical player (Globacnik, Mohorko, & Cucej, 2008) to visualize the ES results. Tactical player makes user friendly data examination, by emphasizing those data, which are marked as problematic by the ES, in order to control 3D visualizations of tactic radio units, etc. The input of Tactical player is the output file of expert system EHS.

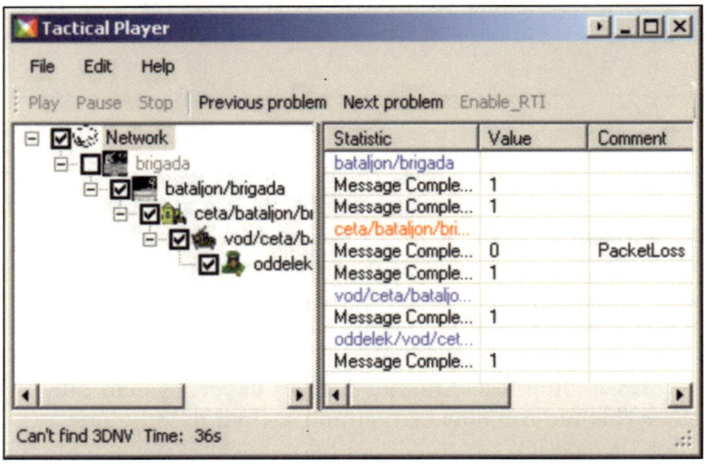

Fig. 10. Developed Tactical player, and players' user interface (main window).

Fig. 10 shows the main window of the developed Tactical player. This Tactical player is divided into two parts. Located in the left window is a topological tree-structure of participating units in the communication process. This part is similar to the TPGen application. The right window shows data and messages from the expert system. Located in the toolbar, on the top of the window, are the controls for the OPNET history player, and above those are menus. The status bar at the bottom of the program lets us know about the presence of a History player and about the recognized history player time, which is necessary for time synchronization. The program supports two working modes; so called "online" and "offline". In an "online" mode, the program works in conjunction with the 3DNV history player, as it is shown in Fig. 11 and Fig. 12.

Inside the OPNET, 3DNV history player runs a recorded simulation history. Time synchronization between the Tactical player and the 3DNV history player is performed with the help of a time code OCR recognition. In this mode, we can also use 3D presentation with

MAK Stealth 3DNV, where we can see realistic movements of military units over a virtual terrain, and their simulation data. A simple example of 3D visualization is given in Fig. 12, where we can see one of the units (in this case a helicopter), and the data of node statistics around it. The second mode is the so-called "offline" mode, where we do not use any external program. In this mode, it is only possible to directly jump to a desired time and move over the EHS data, which are marked as problematic by the expert system.

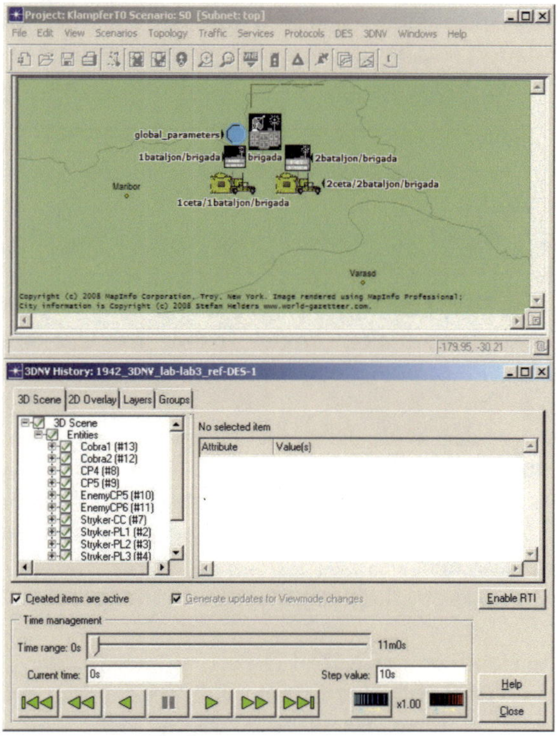

Fig. 11. OPNET Modeler (above) and History player (below).

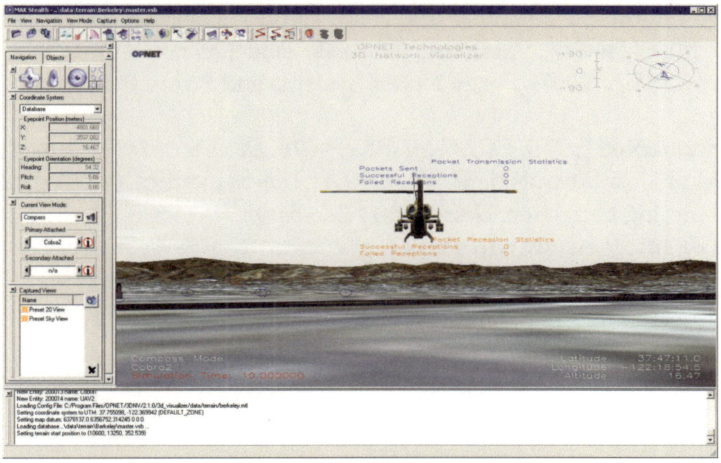

Fig. 12. 3DNV visualization with MAK Stealth application.

5. Conclusion

Manual performance evaluation of tactical communication networks, using OPNET Modeler simulation results, is a very time-consuming task, which also needs a high degree of expert operational knowledge. The developed expert system, with the help of a knowledge base, will automate this process and suggest steps for solving the communication problems of tactical networks. Developed expert system for tactical network evaluation is, in combination with Tactical player, a solution, which offers a deeper understanding of simulation results for a specific planned tactical mission. This leads to a development of better and more reliable tactical networks, which play a critical role in military operations.

6. References

Chakravarti, L. R. (1967). Handbook of Methods of Applied Statistics, Volume 1. *Wiley and Sons*, 392-394.

Chrysanthou, C., Breakall, J. K., Labowski, K. L., Bilen, S. G., & J., G. W. (2007). A Simplified Analytical Urban Propagation Model (UPM) for Use in CJSMPT. *Proceedings MILCOM 2007 - IEEE Military Communications Conference, Orlando, FL*.

Fras, M., Mohorko, J., & Cucej, Z. (2008). Packet size process modeling of measured self-similar network traffic with defragmentation method. *Proceedings of IWSSIP2008 Conference, Bratislava, Slovakia*.

Globacnik, G., Mohorko, J., & Cucej, Z. (2008). Result visualization in tactical network simulation. *International Conference on Software, Telecommunications and Computer Networks (SoftCOM), Split*.

Krishnamoorthy, C. S., & Rajeev, S. (1996). Artificial Intelligence and Expert Systems for Engineers.

Liebowitz, J. (2004). The Handbook of Aplied Expert Systems.

Longley, A. G., & Rice, P. (1968). Prediction of Tropospheric radio transmission over irregular terrain. *A Computer methods, ESSA Tech. Rep. ERL 79-ITS 67, U.S. Government Printing Office, Washington DC*.

Mohorko, J., Fras, M., & Cucej, Z. (2007). Modeling of IRIS Replication Mechanism in a Tactical Communication network, using OPNET. *Computer Networks, Elsevier*.

OPNET. (2007). http://www.opnet.com/products/modeler/home.html. *Web page*.

Siler, W., & Buckley, J. J. (2007). Fuzzy Expert Systems and Fuzzy Reasoning. *Book - Willey & Sons*.

TIREM/SEM Handbook. (1994). ECAC-HDBK-93-076. *Department of Defense*.

Van Emden, M. H., & Kowalski, R. A. (2003). The Semantics of Predicate Logic as a Programming Language. *University of Edinburgh*.

Wireshark. (2008). http://www.wireshark.org/.